What Might Have Been: The Social Psychology of Counterfactual Thinking

Edited by

Neal J. Roese
Northwestern University

and

James M. Olson
University of Western Ontario

LEA LAWRENCE ERLBAUM ASSOCIATES, PUBLISHERS
1995   Mahwah, New Jersey

Lawrence Erlbaum Associates, Inc., Publishers
10 Industrial Avenue
Mahwah, New Jersey 07430

Cover design by Kate Dusza

Library of Congress Cataloging-in-Publication Data

What might have been : the social psychology of counterfactual
    thinking/edited by Neal J. Roese, James Olson.
        p.   cm.
    Includes bibliographical references and index.
    ISBN 0-8058-1613-5 (alk. paper). — ISBN 0-8058-1614-3 (pbk. :
alk. paper)
    1. Thought and thinking. I. Roese, Neal J. II. Olson, James M.
BF441.W46 1995
153.4—dc20   95-8025
                                                       CIP

Books published by Lawrence Erlbaum Associates are printed on acid-free paper,
and their bindings are chosen for strength and durability.

Printed in the United States of America
10 9 8 7 6 5 4 3 2

Contents

Preface   vii

1   Counterfactual Thinking: A Critical Overview   1
Neal J. Roese and James M. Olson

2   Counterfactual Constraints   57
Eric P. Seelau, Sheila M. Seelau, Gary L. Wells,
and Paul D. Windschitl

3   Individual Differences in Counterfactual Thinking   81
Margaret Kasimatis and Gary L. Wells

4   Comparison Processes in Counterfactual Thought   103
David Dunning and Scott F. Madey

5   Living in Neither the Best Nor Worst of All Possible
Worlds: Antecedents and Consequences of
Upward and Downward Counterfactual Thinking   133
Matthew N. McMullen, Keith D. Markman,
and Igor Gavanski

6   Functions of Counterfactual Thinking   169
Neal J. Roese and James M. Olson

7   Dysfunctional Implications of Counterfactual Thinking:
    When Alternatives to Reality Fail Us   199
    Steven J. Sherman and Allen R. McConnell

8   Through a Glass Darkly: Worldviews,
    Counterfactual Thought, and Emotion   233
    Janet Landman

9   Some Counterfactual Determinants of Satisfaction
    and Regret   259
    Thomas Gilovich and Victoria Husted Medvec

10 With an Eye Toward the Future: The Impact
    of Counterfactual Thinking on Affect, Attitudes,
    and Behavior   283
    *Faith Gleicher, David S. Boninger, Alan Strathman,
    David Armor, John Hetts, and Mina Ahn*

11 Counterfactual Thought, Regret, and Superstition:
    How to Avoid Kicking Yourself   305
    Dale T. Miller and Brian R. Taylor

12 Counterfactual and Contrastive Reasoning
    in Explanations for Performance:
    Implications for Gender Bias   333
    Ann L. McGill and Jill G. Klein

13 Counterfactual Thinking and Coping
    With Traumatic Life Events   353
    Christopher G. Davis and Darrin R. Lehman

14 Varieties of Counterfactual Thinking   375
    Daniel Kahneman

Author Index   397

Subject Index   407

Preface

> There are ever so many ways that a world might be; and one of these many ways is the way that this world is.
>
> —David Lewis (1986, p. 2)

Within a few short years, research on counterfactual thinking has mushroomed, establishing itself as one of the signature domains within social psychology. This sudden popularity is easily understood. Counterfactual thinking is something familiar to nearly everyone. Even if they have not previously heard the term *counterfactual*, people instantly recognize it, once it has been defined for them, as something with which they are intimately acquainted. Few indeed have never regretted some action or yearned to have avoided some circumstance. But it is the childlike wonder with which we gaze on "what might have been," into realms of possible, alternative worlds, which truly underlies the excitement of counterfactual research. What if Kennedy had survived his assassin's bullets into a second term in the White House? What if the Nazis had triumphed over the Western democracies in the Second World War? What if your parents had never met? There is something at once obsessively compelling and oddly unsettling about confronting the unrealities that might well have been. In intermixing fantasy and free-form creativity with the tangible truths of our lives, such subjunctive suppositions have the potential to inform, enrich, emote, and even entertain us. As Douglas Hofstadter wrote, "Think how immeasurably poorer our mental lives would be if we didn't have this creative capacity for slipping out of the midst of reality into soft 'what ifs'!" (p. 643).

The traditionally identified starting point in the history of social-cognitive research on counterfactual thinking was a brief yet provocative book chapter written by Danny Kahneman and Amos Tversky in 1982. In this first milestone, they identified many of the directions counterfactual theorists have taken their work over the ensuing years, touching on such issues as determinants of counterfactual thoughts, their connection to perceptions of causality, and their emotional consequences. The compelling metaphor of the mental "simulation," of setting initial conditions then "running" a scenario through to possible outcomes as may be done with computer-based models, was born here. The next milestone was the publication of the multifaceted norm theory in 1986. There, Danny Kahneman and Dale Miller described the mechanisms of exemplar-based online construction of comparison standards. Now regarded as one of the most influential theoretical statements to have emerged in the 1980s, its impact has extended not only to counterfactual research but also to work on categorization, stereotypes, and impression formation. There has not yet been a third, single theoretical milestone that continues the progression initiated by these two influential papers. Rather, there has been a striking proliferation of empirical research projects citing and directly inspired by Kahneman and Tversky (1982) and Kahneman and Miller (1986). Extending into numerous theoretical and applied veins, counterfactual research is rapidly becoming one of the most dynamic and exciting theoretical approaches in social-cognitive psychology.

This volume is an attempt to capture some of this excitement. Sufficient progress has been made in the understanding of counterfactual thinking that a "critical mass," of sorts, has been reached. The time seemed ideal for bringing together into a single volume the most recent thoughts and the most cutting-edge research of active counterfactual theorists. Our hope is to create that third milestone: a single source for current theory in which past achievements are refined and new directions charted. Although theorists from a variety of conceptual backgrounds, both within and without psychology, have speculated on the nature of counterfactuals, this volume focuses on the efforts of experimental social psychologists. As such, the chapters included here reflect the dominant theoretical concerns of social psychology, such as an emphasis on 1) construal and interpretation rather than on the objective truth value of counterfactual propositions, on 2) the roles of motivation and processing goals in determining counterfactual effects, and on 3) the wide-ranging impact of situational influences on counterfactual thought processes. Although this volume might be said to have grown directly out of the symposium *Counterfactual Research: Current Issues and Recent Research*, chaired by us and held at the 1993 convention of the American Psychological Association in Toronto, we must confess that the two projects evolved in tandem. The list of contributors to this volume was taking shape even as Tom Gilovich, Faith Gleicher, Keith Markman, Neal Roese, and Jim Sherman were making their presentations at that symposium. By the summer of 1994, final drafts of the chapters had all been received.

This volume's overarching emphasis on current theory is illustrated in the lead chapter by Roese and Olson. Our goal in this chapter is to provide a comprehensive and critical overview of counterfactual research as it has been conducted by social psychologists. We trace threads of counterfactual ideas through philosophical, cognitive psychological, and developmental psychological work, then examine in detail the conclusions derived from the social psychological approach. We attempt to impose order on various and often disparate findings with a two-stage motivational model of counterfactual generation, a model we hope will eventually inform and clarify future research endeavors. In chapter 2, E. Seelau, S. Seelau, Wells, and Windschitl examine some of the basic rules that constrain counterfactual generation. If pressed, people can imagine virtually anything, yet their spontaneous thoughts of "what if" and "if only" tend to be remarkably disciplined, constrained to a much more finite set of possibilities. E. Seelau et al. discuss three main classes of constraints: those based on basic laws of the workings of the universe, those based on availability of information in memory, and those based on higher-order goals and purposes. Not only are some counterfactual possibilities more frequently generated than others across individuals, but, as illustrated in chapter 3, some counterfactuals are more commonly considered than others by certain kinds of individuals. In this chapter, Kasimatis and Wells review work on individual differences in counterfactual thinking, exploring interpersonal variation not only in terms of mere quantity but also in terms of qualitative differences in such thought processes. In chapter 4, Dunning and Madey examine mechanisms of comparative reasoning. These authors contend that the pairwise contrast between a factual and counterfactual event is crucially influenced by framing. For example, which of the two comparison targets is made the focus of assessment can substantially influence judgments.

The next three chapters reflect an ongoing concern with the global consequences of counterfactual thinking. McMullen, Markman, and Gavanski (chapter 5) examine some of the benefits of counterfactual thinking, using evidence from a cunning set of "gambling" experiments. Feelings of control and empowerment are just one of several consequences they discuss. Roese and Olson continue this approach in chapter 6. Here we describe the results of several experiments that document how specific content-based subtypes of counterfactual thoughts may be beneficial to the individual both emotionally and in terms of future preparativeness. In sharp contrast to this functionalist approach, Sherman and McConnell (chapter 7) examine how counterfactual thinking may be dysfunctional. Covering wide tracts of social psychological terrain, these authors pull together numerous diverse findings to identify specific biases and other deleterious consequences that may emerge from counterfactual thought processes.

Affect becomes a major focus in the next block of chapters. Landman (chapter 8) discusses some of the different ways in which people's world-views may be manifested in their counterfactual thoughts and in their subsequent emotional experiences. In chapter 9, Gilovich and Medvec explore a curious paradox: Although the results of some laboratory research indicate that people regret their actions more than their inactions, common wisdom as well as some provocative survey findings indicate the opposite; that is, when looking back on their lives, people most regret what they did not do. These authors include the reader on their empirical quest to solve this fascinating mystery. In chapter 10, Gleicher, Boninger, Strathman, Armor, Hetts, and Ahn discuss some of the effects of counterfactual thinking on people's current emotions, ongoing attitudes, and future actions. Sorrow over what might have been may sometimes, as these authors show, be tempered by hope over what may yet be. These authors also present evidence indicating that counterfactuals may, under the right circumstances, be effective tools for persuasion. Chapter 11 addresses the question of why so many students believe that they should never change an answer on a multiple-choice exam and that their first answer is invariably the correct one. Miller and Taylor show how such beliefs may emerge from the normal mechanisms of counterfactual thinking. Specifically, they show how the prospect of future regret may bias current decisions and how counterfactuals may bias baserate judgments to create superstitious beliefs.

In the next two chapters, the authors carry the predominantly theoretical focus of counterfactual research to more applied, real-world concerns. In chapter 12, McGill and Klein examine two forms of reasoning, counterfactual and contrastive, demonstrating how interactions between such forms of reasoning may give rise to gender bias and other prejudiced evaluations. In chapter 13, Davis and Lehman describe some of their work with victims of traumatic life events, documenting the important role of counterfactual thoughts in coping. Finally, in the closing chapter, Kahneman takes stock of where we counterfactual researchers have come from, where we are, and where we are headed.

The passion and energy contained in these chapters lead us to conclude that even if we had not put this book together, someone else most surely would have.

We extend our thanks to Judith Amsel, Ray O'Connell, Patrick Con-
nolly, Amy Pierce, Marcy Pruiksma, and the staff at Lawrence Erlbaum
Associates, and to Vuk Vuksanović and the graphic arts staff at Q-Design.
We would also like to thank our families, Karen plus the dachshunds
Willy and Nina, and Mary, Rebecca, and Sara, for their support during
our work on this project. Without them, its construction would have been
far more arduous and its completion far less rewarding.

Neal Roese
Jim Olson
September 1994

If we didn't have birthdays, you wouldn't be you.
If you'd never been born, well then what would you do?
If you'd never been born, well then what would you be?
You *might* be a fish! Or a toad in a tree!
You might be a doorknob! Or three baked potatoes!
You might be a bag full of hard green tomatoes.
Or worse than all that . . . You might be a WASN'T!
A Wasn't has no fun at all. No, he doesn't.
A Wasn't just isn't. He just isn't present.
But you . . . You are YOU! And, now isn't that pleasant.

—Dr. Seuss (1959)

1

Counterfactual Thinking: A Critical Overview

Neal J. Roese
Northwestern University

James M. Olson
University of Western Ontario

> *If matters had fallen out differently, she wondered, might she not have met some other man? She tried to picture to herself the things that might have been—that different life, that unknown husband. He might have been handsome, intelligent, distinguished, attractive. . . .*
> —Flaubert (1857/1950, p. 57)

Tales of human suffering are replete with examples of thoughts of what might have been, of what could have occurred if only a few subtle details had been different. The tormented mistress of Flaubert's novel, *Madame Bovary*, bored with her provincial life, dreams of a better one and a better husband. The ability to imagine alternative, or *counterfactual*, versions of actual occurrences appears to be a pervasive, perhaps even essential, feature of our mental lives (e.g., Hofstadter, 1979, 1985).

The term *counterfactual* means, literally, contrary to the facts. Some focal factual outcome typically forms the point of departure for the counterfactual supposition (e.g., Madame Bovary's angst). Then, one may alter (or *mutate*) some factual antecedent (e.g., her marriage) and assess the consequences of that alteration. Thus, counterfactuals are frequently conditional statements and, as such, embrace both an antecedent (e.g., "If Madame Bovary had married a better man") and a consequent ("she would have been happier"). For present purposes, we restrict our use of the term counterfactual to alternative versions of past or present outcomes, although we are aware that others have also used the term to describe future possibilities (e.g., Hoch, 1985; M. Johnson & Sherman,

1

1990). Thus, in the present analysis, an essential feature of a counterfactual conditional is the falsity of its antecedent, in that it specifies a prior event that did not occur (Goodman, 1947). The consequent may or may not be false; if it is, the mutation of the antecedent *undoes* the factual outcome.[1]

Experimental social psychologists have attempted to identify empirically the precursors, underlying processes, and consequences of counterfactual thinking in research programs dating back almost 20 years. Yet, fascination with counterfactual suppositions, with "possible worlds," dates back considerably further, at least as far back as the writings of classical Greek philosophers. Our purpose in this chapter is to introduce readers to the topic of counterfactual thinking as social psychologists have conceptualized it.

We frame this discussion by first considering the rich intellectual tradition dedicated to understanding the nature of counterfactual conditionals. We then review the theoretical basis of counterfactual research, examining the mechanisms underlying counterfactual reasoning. We then discuss factors that influence the generation of such thoughts and the consequences of considering them. These determinants are conceptualized in terms of outcome-based motivational factors and antecedent-based factors that may differentially influence the mere generation and the semantic content of counterfactual thoughts. Further, we note that the consequences of counterfactual generation derive from either of two distinct mechanisms: contrast effects and causal inferences. By referring explicitly to these two mechanisms in our survey of the consequences of counterfactual thinking, we provide a more rigorous conceptual integration of previously insular findings. To conclude, we discuss some conceptual issues of concern in interpreting the extant literature and in moving toward future research.

COUNTERFACTUAL THINKING: HISTORICAL ROOTS

Philosophical Perspectives

The consideration of what might have been and what may yet be has long fascinated philosophers. Plato and Aristotle examined in their writings the epistemological status of subjunctive suppositions and unseen yet tangible ideal forms. These ideas were embraced more vigorously by

---

[1]Goodman (1983) used the term *semifactual* for cases in which the consequent remains true. These propositions, focusing on the same outcome having come about by alternative means, are frequently prefaced by "even if" rather than "if only" (e.g., "Even if Madame Bovary had married the dashing Rodolphe, she would still have grown discontented").

the German philosopher, Leibniz, in the seventeenth century. Leibniz argued that an alternative reality (or "world") is *possible* to the extent that it contradicts no formal laws of logic. Thus, there could well be an infinite number of possible worlds. Leibniz's interest in possible worlds was largely theological: In formalizing proofs for the existence of God, he argued that God must have contemplated all possible worlds before creating this one, and that this one represents the best of all possible worlds (see Rescher, 1969 for a historical review).

Discussions of possible worlds met with considerable skepticism until the 20th century, when the study of modalities (i.e., nonexistent possibilities) achieved greater respect following its more rigorous elucidation via newly developed systems of symbolic logic (see Kvart, 1986; Loux, 1979; Reichenbach, 1976). Controversially, Lewis (1973b, 1986) argued that possible worlds exist to the same extent as this one: "Our actual world is only one world among others. We call it alone actual not because it differs in kind from all the rest but because it is the world we inhabit" (1973b, p. 85).[2] However, more moderate voices echoed the axioms of cognitive psychology in affirming Aristotle's dictum that actuality is prior to possibility (Rescher, 1979). That is, any conception of possible worlds must be fabricated from a cognitive substrate derived from tangible experience: "Unrealized possibility ultimately roots in the mind-correlative capabilities of the real" (Rescher, 1975, p. 217).

Modern philosophical treatment of the modal nature of reality assumes some consideration of *all* possible worlds. Within this field, the study of counterfactuals occupies a more tightly circumscribed domain. Loux (1979) explained, "When I say that if the Blue Jays were to win the pennant, Toronto would go wild, I am not saying that in every possible world where the Blue Jays win the pennant, Toronto goes wild; for there obviously are possible worlds where the Blue Jays win the pennant and few, if any, of the citizens of Toronto find the event very interesting" (p. 33). Rather, a counterfactual typically posits one possible world that is imaginally very close to the real world, containing only a very few (or just one) features that differentiate it from this world.

Specific discourse aimed at counterfactuals per se has generated fascinating controversies, frequently focusing on the truth value of counterfactual statements (e.g., Chisholm, 1946; Goodman, 1947, 1983; Nute, 1980). As noted in our introduction, all counterfactuals are necessarily false, insofar as their antecedents refer to some state of affairs that was not so. Evaluation of the veracity of counterfactual propositions cannot,

---

[2]Interestingly, a similar view is echoed by some physicists, who derive assertions of the multiplicity of worlds from the tenets of quantum mechanical theory (e.g., Deutsch & Lockwood, 1994).

therefore, proceed simply via rules of logic; additional, inherently psychological principles of reasoning must be posited. For example, Rescher (1964) suggested that counterfactual propositions will be accepted as true to the extent that they are predicated on alterations to episodic specifics as opposed to negations of general laws. Thus, for example, counterfactuals involving deletions of someone's behavior last Tuesday will be viewed as more "truthful" than deletions of the earth's gravity. In general, the question of what constitutes true, or natural, counterfactuals (e.g., "If I had a million bucks, I could buy a new house") as opposed to more absurd statements (e.g., "If I *were* a million bucks, I'd be green") continues to generate controversy (e.g., Lewis, 1973a; Nute, 1980), as too does the problem of inferring the causal contingency between a counterfactual antecedent and consequent (e.g., To what extent does having a million bucks lead to buying houses?). As we discuss later, these same problems have stimulated and informed psychological theories of counterfactuals (e.g., Kahneman & Miller, 1986; Wells & Gavanski, 1989).

Psychological Perspectives

Interest among psychologists in counterfactuals is, of course, a much more recent development. Within the field of cognitive psychology, researchers have examined counterfactuals from the perspective of explicating basic processes of learning and memory. For example, Fillenbaum (1974) discovered that memory for counterfactual statements (e.g., "If he had caught the plane, he would have arrived on time") was slightly more accurate than for semantically similar causal statements (e.g., "He did not arrive on time because he did not catch the plane"), suggesting at the very least that people are adept at cognitive manipulations of counterfactual information. Although causal information is easily abstracted from counterfactual conditionals, people are well able to encode counterfactual information in memory as semantically complex conditional propositions, rather than first reducing it to simpler, basic propositions (Carpenter, 1973). Regarding the content of counterfactual thoughts, Revlis and colleagues provided experimental confirmation for Rescher's (1964) conjecture that people prefer belief-contravening propositions that involve alterations to particulars rather than universals (Revlis & Hayes, 1972; Revlis, Lipkin, & Hayes, 1971). In this way, counterfactuals maintain consistency with general laws of the world, with changes occurring mainly to narrowly episodic elements (see also Braine & O'Brian, 1991).

A notable controversy within the cognitive literature focused on counterfactual generation as a test of the Sapir–Whorf hypothesis, that is, of whether language critically constrains cognitive perceptions and representations of the world. Bloom (1981) provided evidence that expression and comprehension of counterfactual statements was substantially weaker among Chinese speakers than among American English speakers. Bloom pointed to the absence in Chinese of any syntactical or lexical equivalent of the English-language subjunctive ("if–then") form as the linguistic cause of this cultural difference. Bloom (1981, 1984) argued, therefore, that it was the availability of subjunctive linguistic structures that permitted the cognitive manipulation of might-have-been scenarios. Au (1983, 1984), however, noted that Bloom's materials may have been idiomatically biased and that Chinese speakers could reason counterfactually with little difficulty if this bias were removed (see also Liu, 1985). The current consensus seems to be that language and culture influence the content of counterfactuals and also their application in specific situations but that "most people with an adequate level of education possess the skills of hypothetical reasoning and the ability to think in a counterfactual fashion" (Markus & Kitayama, 1991, p. 234; see also Lardière, 1992; Vorster & Schuring, 1989).

Relatedly, the work of Sternberg and Gastel suggested that the ability to reason counterfactually and to deal, more generally, with imaginal possibilities, is an important component of intelligence (Sternberg & Gastel, 1989a, 1989b). Developmental researchers have examined the age of onset of logically valid counterfactual reasoning, linking it to Piaget's fourth and final stage of cognitive development, the formal operations stage (Markovits & Vachon, 1989; Wing & Scholnick, 1986). Thus, most people are able to reach logically valid conclusions through counterfactual reasoning by the time they reach their teen years, although the ability to fabricate fictional scenarios in the context of imaginative play occurs much earlier, at around the age of 4 or 5 years.

Social Psychological Perspectives

Social psychologists seek generally to examine the global cognitive functioning of the individual within a broader, social context. The three characteristics of social psychology identified by Ross and Nisbett (1991) effectively illuminate what distinguishes sociopsychological approaches to counterfactual thinking from the approaches discussed previously. First, social psychology is predicated on situationism, such that external antecedents in social situations are viewed as prime determinants of the generation and content of counterfactual thoughts. Thus, qualitative descriptions of focal outcomes were among the first causal factors to be linked empirically by social psychologists to counterfactual thinking. Second, a focus on construal emphasizes the unique importance of individual interpretation of social situations. Thus, unlike their philosophical counterparts, social psychologists tend to ignore the objective truth value of counterfactual propositions in favor of examining their perceived plausibility and meaningfulness to the individual. Third, the goals and motivational states of individuals as they operate within a larger social system are also taken by social psychologists to be crucial determinants of counterfactual thinking. Thus, for example, aversive outcomes and thwarted plans have been shown to affect counterfactual thinking. With the social psychological approach, a high premium is also placed on the global psychological consequences of counterfactual thinking. Attributions of blame and responsibility, self-inference, emotions, coping, and adjustment are examples certifying the breadth of counterfactual effects identified by social psychologists.

In summary, the social psychological approach is perhaps the broadest and most general of the psychological approaches to counterfactual thinking, embracing the totality of an individual's feelings, perceptions, motivations, and goals within the larger context of social interaction. In the sections that follow, we examine the theories of counterfactual thinking and their supporting research explicated by social psychologists. First, we examine basic mechanisms integral to the formation of counterfactual thoughts. Next, we discuss the factors influencing counterfactual generation in terms of the determinants of their availability and semantic content. Then, we examine some of the psychological and behavioral consequences of engaging in counterfactual thought. Last, we consider directions for future research.

BASIC PROCESSES

Two theoretical questions form the heart of theory aimed at elucidating the processes underlying counterfactual thinking: What triggers counterfactual generation and, once triggered, what constrains the content of such thoughts? Norm theory has been the guiding theoretical formulation for the bulk of social psychological research on counterfactual thinking. In the next section, we first examine the process of counterfactual generation according to norm theory. We then examine the motivational underpinnings of counterfactual generation, noting how a motivational model may complement the perspective offered by norm theory. Finally, we turn to the relation between counterfactuals and causal inference.

Norm Theory

The aim of norm theory is the description of the psychology of surprise, that is, of the judgmental processes that occur in response to specific experiences and that result in post hoc inferences of surprisingness. Like other social judgment theories, norm theory focuses on the pairwise comparison between an experiential outcome and some cognitive anchor. The direction and magnitude of the discrepancy between the outcome and the anchor determine various cognitive and affective reactions. For example, a student's receiving a D on an essay when her or his standard is a B evokes negative affect (e.g., disappointment). Previous social judgment theories postulated global a priori standards, ones derived from past experience. For example, Helson's (1964) conception of adaptation level focused on the average level of outcomes to which the individual had become accustomed. Thibaut and Kelley's (1959) comparison level was similarly defined in terms of the average of all relevant outcomes known to the individual, weighted by their salience, but desire and deservingness also played a role in its definition.

The innovation of norm theory over these previous formulations was the assertion that judgmental standards, or *norms*, may be constructed online, after and in direct response to specific outcomes. Of course, the cognitive substrate out of which norms are constructed is extant cognitions (i.e., beliefs and expectancies derived from past experience). The particular character of each norm is a combination of a priori beliefs reconstructed uniquely in light of a specific outcome. Thus, unlike the global anchors specified by previous social judgment theories, norms are specific and vary as a function of the specific timbre of their evoking outcomes (McGill, 1993).

According to norm theory, outcomes differentially evoke an aggregate of relevant exemplars, which together constitute the outcome's norm. The norm may be an imagistic representation of the outcome itself (e.g., imagery of receiving a B on an essay, derived from exemplars of previous, similar circumstances). To the extent that an outcome evokes a norm that is similar to the outcome, the outcome is termed *normal*. *Abnormal outcomes* are those that evoke norms that differ from the factual outcome and, hence, are counterfactual in nature (i.e., alternative outcomes). Kahneman and Miller (1986) used the term *mutability* to describe whether antecedents (and hence the aggregate norm) are mainly similar or dissimilar to the outcome.

Mutability refers to the relative ease with which elements of reality can be cognitively altered to construct a counterfactual statement. When a norm is evoked, aspects of the outcome that are immutable (difficult to alter imaginatively) are retained in the evoked norm, whereas mutable aspects are altered. Thus, whether the norm is similar or dissimilar (counterfactual) to the outcome depends on the presence of mutable antecedent elements occurring prior to the outcome. Greater perceived mutability of antecedents leads to more available counterfactual representations.

For the average person, some things are very mutable (e.g., effort), whereas other things seem relatively immutable (e.g., gravity). Of course, with some effort it is possible to mutate imaginatively virtually any event or characteristic, but the utility of the mutability construct derives from the observation that there are regularities to the ease with which factual elements are mutated and that, as Hofstadter (1985) argued, there are natural "fault lines of the mind" (p. 239) along which reality is cognitively dissected. Many factors potentially influence mutability; for example, exceptional elements may be more mutable than typical elements. Thus, a counterfactual would be constructed by effecting some change to the mutable element (i.e., an exceptional antecedent). The various factors theorized to influence antecedent mutability are considered in a later section of this chapter.

The basic mechanism by which counterfactuals are constructed is the conversion of mutable (e.g., exceptional or unusual) antecedents back into their normal (or default) values. The general result is that counterfactuals recapitulate expectancies. When John learns that he has failed a midterm examination following a particularly pernicious night of drinking, norm theory would predict John's thoughts to be that he would have passed had he drunk in greater moderation. Drinking in moderation and passing the exam represent John's default expectancies for exam situations. This general process of normalization contributes to the realism and hence, perhaps, to the ultimate usefulness of counterfactual thoughts (Kahneman & Tversky, 1982b). Absurd counterfactuals tend not to arise spontaneously; rather, feasibility limits their deviation from reality (Folger, 1984; S. Taylor & Schneider, 1989).

In summary, outcomes evoke norms, and whether these norms approximate or diverge from outcomes depends on the mutability of antecedent elements. When mutable antecedents precede the outcome, the outcome will appear abnormal, and counterfactual alternatives will be more available. In the absence of mutable antecedents, counterfactual alternatives will be less available, and the outcome will appear normal, perhaps even inevitable (cf. Fischhoff, 1982).

Motivational Considerations

Norm theory describes the cognitive processes underlying reactions to specific events without reference to motivational determinants. That is, affect, intentions, and goals play no role in its predictions. But consider the counterfactuals that may spontaneously occur to Sam and Susan. Both witness from a street corner a speeding car hit a small boy. Sam has never seen the boy before; Susan is the boy's mother. Clearly, the propensity to cognitively undo the outcome would be driven to a far more powerful and ferocious extent in Susan than in Sam. The differences in the quantity and vigor of counterfactual thinking in these two individuals reflect motivational differences.

We use the term *motivation* here in its most basic, generic sense: the impulsion to avoid aversive stimuli and to approach gratifying stimuli (McClelland, Atkinson, Clark, & Lowell, 1953; Tolman, 1932). For our purposes, we assume that these behaviors are mediated by affect (McClelland et al., 1953), which we conceptualize as reflecting a simple survival mechanism common to higher level, ambulatory organisms. Negative affect (e.g., pain) motivates avoidance behavior, whereas positive affect (pleasure) motivates approach behavior. Counterfactual generation can be conceptualized in terms of these simple dynamics. If outcomes that elicit negative affect motivate avoidance behavior, one result may be metaphorically similar attempts to avoid the outcome cognitively (i.e., to mentally avoid, or undo, it in one's own head). This foundational impulsion to undo painful past events is aptly depicted in Fig. 1.1.

In an effort to clarify our review of the counterfactual literature, we distinguish between two stages of counterfactual construction: counterfactual availability and semantic content (cf. Gleicher et al., 1990; Miller, Turnbull, & McFarland, 1990). By counterfactual availability, we mean the mere consideration that a factual outcome might not have occurred. In contrast, the semantic content of a counterfactual specifies the means by which some alternative outcome might have been brought about (i.e., the imaginative alteration of a mutable, factual antecedent that might have led to another outcome). The first stage reflects the presence of a vehicle, so to speak, whereas the second represents the occupants of that vehicle. Two classes of factors may affect these two stages of generation. First, motivational variables (e.g., outcome valence, involvement) can influence either availability or content. These factors are outcome based, in that their conceptual basis reflects descriptions of the target outcome (e.g., whether that outcome is positive or negative, involving or unin-

For Better or For Worse® by Lynn Johnston

FIG. 1.1. The motivational basis of counterfactual thinking: Undoing an aversive past event. *FOR BETTER OR FOR WORSE* (1993), by Lynn Johnston Prod., Inc. Reprinted with permission of UNIVERSAL PRESS SYNDICATE. All rights reserved.

volving). Second, mutability variables (e.g., exceptionality, salience) can also influence either availability or content, but these are antecedent based, in that they reflect descriptions of the antecedents leading to the target outcome (e.g., whether the antecedent is exceptional or typical, salient or nonsalient). The conceptual relation of these elements is depicted in Figure 1.2 with bolder arrows signifying links that are described in detail in this review. An example may clarify these distinctions. Recall the example of John in the previous section, who failed an exam after a night of unusually heavy drinking. According to norm theory, the most available counterfactual that might occur to John is "If only I hadn't drunk so much, I would have passed." The antecedent element of unusually heavy drinking is mutable by virtue of its exceptionality; the counterfactual is then constructed by returning this exceptional element to its default value (e.g., no drinking), with the consequence that the outcome would have been avoided.[3] Of course, both the factual antecedent as well as the outcome were exceptional (unexpected) in this case; the counterfactual returns both of these to their default values. According to our two-stage description, the initial impetus for counterfactual generation is the negativity or unexpectedness of the outcome itself (failing). This motivates John to consider the avoidance of that outcome (Stage 1). Thus, outcome-based motivational factors constitute the engine driving counterfactual thinking. Then, the presence of an exceptional antecedent is embraced as one means by which the outcome could have been avoided (Stage 2). Variables reflecting the mutability of antecedents therefore predict the semantic content (or specific timbre) of the resulting counterfactual.

In a later section, we review evidence for the operation of four outcome-based motivational factors (expectancy, outcome valence, involvement, and closeness). These factors are discussed primarily in terms of their impact on availability (Link 2 in Figure 1.2); however, they can also influence the semantic content of counterfactual thoughts (Link 1 in Figure 1.2). For example, outcome valence or involvement might predict the strategic generation of counterfactuals targeting specific issues or actions. Such patterns are described by functional models of counterfactual thinking and are discussed in two chapters of the present volume (see McMullen, Markman, & Gavanski, chapter 5; Roese & Olson, chapter 6). Because such interpretations of Link 1 are discussed in detail elsewhere, we focus primarily on Link 2. In another section, we review evidence describing the operation of five antecedent-based mutability factors (exceptionality, actions versus inactions, controllability, stability,

---

[3]Exceptional here means unexpected. We use *exceptionality* to describe antecedent-based effects (thereby maintaining consistency with previous publications), but use *expectancy* to describe outcome-based effects. Readers should keep in mind that both terms denote essentially the same thing.

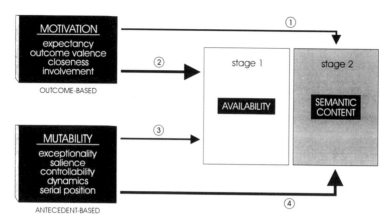

FIG. 1.2. A two-stage model of counterfactual generation.

serial position). These are discussed mainly in terms of their influence on content (Link 4 in Figure 1.2), although we believe that these variables might also affect availability (Link 3). This relation is asserted by norm theory, but to our knowledge, it has not been specifically documented by research. Moreover, the conceptual basis underlying predictions for this link are unclear. Thus, our discussion rests mainly on demonstrations that antecedent-based factors influence the semantic content of counterfactual thoughts. (E. Seelau, S. Seelau, Wells, and Windschitl further discuss constraints on counterfactual generation in chapter 2.)

Counterfactuals and Causality

All counterfactual conditionals are causal assertions (cf. Kahneman & Varey, 1990; Mackie, 1974; White, 1990). Causal assertions may almost always be expressed as conditional propositions. However, not all conditionals are causal: Some conditionals assert simple correlations or rules (e.g., The proposition, "If today is Thursday, then tomorrow is Friday," does not mean that Thursday causes the next day to be Friday). But counterfactuals, by virtue of the falsity of their antecedents, represent one class of conditional propositions that are always causal. The reason for this is that with its assertion of a false antecedent, the counterfactual sets up an inherent relation to a factual state of affairs. That is, a counterfactual always refers to some true conditional relation of events or features (e.g., thinking "If only I were taller, then I'd be happier," is inherently linked to one's actual height and actual happiness). This reference of the counterfactual conditional to a specific, relevant factual conditional creates the essential requirements for Mill's (1872) method of difference, which is, of course, the principal technique by which scientists infer causation.

Just as causal conclusions can be derived from the true experiment, in which two parallel factual occurrences are contrasted, so too can they be derived from the pairwise contrast between a factual and a counterfactual occurrence. To the extent that the two occurrences (terminating in divergent outcomes) differ only in the presence of a particular antecedent, this antecedent can be inferred to be causal (Mackie, 1974; Nute, 1980; Swain, 1978; White, 1990). Thus, running a counterfactual simulation in one's head amounts to a proxy experiment (cf. Einhorn & Hogarth, 1986; Hilton & Slugoski, 1986; Lipe, 1991). It is instructive to note that in fields of inquiry in which true experiments cannot be implemented (e.g., history, law), counterfactual test cases are accepted methods of inferring causation (e.g., Fearon, 1991; Hart & Honoré, 1959; Tetlock & Belkin, 1994).

The assertion that all counterfactuals contain causal implications does not mean that counterfactuals are *necessary* for a causal inference to take place. Not all causal inferences are necessarily mediated by counterfactual reasoning: Causal schemata (Kelley, 1972b) and current processing goals (Sanbonmatsu, Akimoto, & Biggs, 1993) can influence causal inferences independently of any mediating counterfactual comparisons. Moreover, blame assignment can be influenced by numerous factors in addition to counterfactual simulations (Davis & Lehman, chapter 13; N'gbala & Branscombe, in press). Rather, all that can be said is that a counterfactual supposition provides sufficient information to draw a causal conclusion. Thus, previous attributional research may or may not have implications for the study of counterfactuals, but the study of counterfactuals always has the potential to inform attributional theory.

Wells and Gavanski (1989) performed the initial empirical demonstration that counterfactual assessments influence judgments of causality. In order for an antecedent to be judged as causal, it must be mutable and it must undo the outcome. Because manipulations of mutability can be confounded with factors already known to influence causality, these authors manipulated whether or not the deletion of a salient antecedent action undid an outcome. Participants read about a woman who, because of a rare digestive disease, suffered a fatal reaction to the alcohol contained in her lunch, which was chosen by her companion. In one condition, her lunch companion chose between two dishes both made with wine. In the other condition, only the chosen dish contained wine. Mentally, altering the lunch choice in the first condition does not undo the outcome (e.g., "Even if he had chosen the other lunch, she still would have become sick"); it does indeed undo the outcome in the second condition ("If only he had ordered the other dish, she wouldn't have become sick"). As expected, participants cited the companion's choice of dishes as more causally significant in bringing about the woman's death in the second than in the first condition. Thus, whether or not a specific antecedent counterfactually undoes an outcome influences perceptions of that antecedent's causal impact. Recent theoretical work has centered on the "effect to be explained" as a focal component of causal inference. That is, perceivers do not wish merely to explain an outcome per se but rather the divergence between an outcome and some default alternative (Hilton, 1990; Hilton & Slugoski, 1986; McGill, 1989, 1991; Miller, B. Taylor, & Buck, 1991). This perspective assumes that outcomes are perceived against a causal background of expected or default counterfactual representations (Hart & Honoré, 1959; Mackie, 1974). The deviation between a factual outcome and its default defines the effect to be explained. To be perceived as causal, an antecedent must also be a deviation from some default, inasmuch as it was present for the focal outcome but typically does not occur (i.e., is absent in the default version). Thus, causality is ascribed to antecedents that deviate from default expectancies (a conclusion central to norm theory). One implication of this approach is that perceptions of cause may change as one alters the causal background (and hence defines different default conditions).[4]

McGill (1989), for example, showed that different causal backgrounds may explain the actor–observer effect (the tendency to attribute one's own behavior externally but others' behavior internally). Requesting a perceiver to explain his or her own actions spontaneously elicits an intrapersonal background (e.g., "Why did I behave this way today but not on other occasions?"), whereas explaining someone else's behavior elicits an interpersonal background (e.g., "Why did this person, as opposed to others, behave this way?"). Consequently, perceivers typically emphasize situational factors to account for the intrapersonal variation salient in examinations of their own behavior but emphasize dispositional factors to account for the interpersonal variation made salient by someone else's behavior. McGill was able to eliminate this actor–observer effect by explicitly specifying the contrast to be explained. More generally, implicit rules of conversation and explicit causal questions may suggest appropriate causal backgrounds (Hilton, 1990; McGill, 1990a, 1990b; McGill & Klein, 1993; Slugoski, Lalljee, Lamb, & Ginsburg, 1993).

Miller et al. (1991) noted that deviation from a category prototype also constitutes an effect to be explained. In their research on "gender gaps,"

---

[4]The effect-to-be explained perspective describes causal attributions for unexpected outcomes, but, of course, perceivers may also seek to explain expected or typical outcomes (e.g., J. Johnson, Boyd, & Magnani, 1994; Lalljee & Abelson, 1983). Although the factors triggering causal explanation per se may differ for these two cases, the consideration of a counterfactual contrast yields similarly informative causal information in both cases.

these authors showed that for some domains (e.g., the average American voter), men are the default gender. When men and women diverge in their voting behavior, that is, exhibit a gender gap (e.g., compared to women, men showed a stronger preference for Bush over Dukakis in the 1988 American presidential election), explanations typically focus on the deviation from the default (e.g., What is it about women that makes them dislike Bush?) rather than on the default itself (e.g., Why do men like Bush?). In domains for which women are the prototype (e.g., teaching), explanations for gender gaps focused on the behavior of men. Thus, the effect to be explained can be thought of as a deviation from default expectancies or a deviation from category prototypicality. Cause is ascribed to whatever accounts for the deviation.

Ambitious attempts to reinterpret traditional attributional theories have been based on the reasoning described above. Hilton (1990) noted that Jones and Davis' (1965) analysis of noncommon effects derives from the same logic as the effect-to-be-explained perspective. In a related vein, Hilton and Slugoski (1986) theorized that consensus, distinctiveness, and consistency (Kelley, 1967) define the critical contrast case, or causal background, against which a target outcome is compared. For instance, low-consensus information (e.g., few others do it) casts the target individual into focus as an abnormal condition that deviates from the default (the behavior of others); hence an internal attribution is warranted. Similarly, low-consistency information (e.g., the outcome rarely occurs) highlights the current circumstances as an abnormal condition that deviates from default circumstances; hence an external attribution is warranted. Hilton and Slugoski (1986) and Lipe (1991) showed that the dominant attributional frameworks advanced by social psychologists (e.g., Jones & Davis, 1965; Kelley, 1967) can be explained by the unifying notion that information salient to the perceiver cues one or another causal background, which takes the form of a counterfactual contrast case. Importantly, causal backgrounds (i.e., counterfactuals) derive from individuals' extant expectancies (either implicitly or explicitly held) for the target situation.

The foregoing research is based on the assumption that causal reasoning begins by the person's identifying a focal outcome, comparing it to a counterfactual outcome, then seizing on an antecedent that accounts for the discrepancy (cf. Lalljee & Abelson, 1983). That antecedent is then perceived to be the primary "cause." Such outcome-contrastive processing (termed *backward causal inference* by Einhorn & Hogarth, 1986, and *contrastive reasoning* by McGill & Klein, 1993) emphasizes the precursors to a focal outcome. That is, processing focuses on the outcome, then compares it to a counterfactual variation of the outcome, and asks, Sherlock Holmes style, what prior condition might account for the discrepancy between the two outcomes. But counterfactuals may also mediate causal inference by a somewhat different process. Reasoning may begin with the person's focusing first on a target antecedent, with the goal of speculating about its causal potency (i.e., what consequences it might engender). Such antecedent-contrastive processing (termed *forward causal inference* by Einhorn & Hogarth, 1986, and *counterfactual reasoning* by McGill and Klein, 1993),[5] begins with some antecedent and its known outcome, which is then contrasted to a counterfactual case with that antecedent removed.[6] The extent to which the counterfactual outcome deviates from the factual outcome determines the causal potency of the target antecedent. McGill and Klein (1993; see also chapter 12) showed that individuals react to requests to explain an outcome with outcome contrasts but evaluate potential causal antecedents with antecedent contrasts. The counterfactual literature, including the two-stage model described in this review, focuses on the evocation of counterfactual processing that is outcome-contrastive. Although untested, we assume that most spontaneously evoked counterfactual thoughts are outcome-contrastive and that antecedent-contrastive processing is the result of a more deliberate, effortful process that targets a specific causal question.

In research by Dunning and Parpal (1989), the frame of a causal question was found to influence inferences of causal potency regarding a specific antecedent. These authors found that people who focused on the *increased* benefits of a chosen action ascribed greater causal potency to that action than those who focused on the *reduced* benefits associated with forgoing the action. These authors suggested that the effect is in part due to the relatively greater weight that perceivers give to facilitative than to inhibitory factors (Hansen & Hall, 1985), a bias perhaps restricted to success outcomes (Bouts, Spears, & van der Pligt, 1992). Also, greater contrast between a factual and a counterfactual outcome is perceived when the former rather than the latter is made the subject of comparison (see also McGill, 1990b). Dunning and Madey discuss these ideas further in chapter 4.

Counterfactuals are thus intimately related to causal inference. A counterfactual conditional always contains causal implications, though there may be great variation in the salience or applicability of those implications. In a later section, we point to the role such causal implications may play in the various consequences that follow from counterfactual thinking.

---

[5]McGill and Klein (1993) used the terms *contrastive reasoning* versus *counterfactual reasoning* even though, as they pointed out, both are essentially counterfactual inferences. That is, both feature a contrast between a factual and a counterfactual occurrence.

[6]Of course, people may not only simulate the consequences of a factual antecedent's removal (a *subtractive counterfactual*) but may also simulate the consequences of adding a new antecedent that was not present in reality (an *additive counterfactual*). Both are equally informative of causal potency (Roese & Olson, 1993b).

Conclusion

The dominant theoretical perspective guiding counterfactual research has been Kahneman and Miller's (1986) norm theory. This perspective asserts that counterfactuals are constructed online in response to specific evoking outcomes and that the content of counterfactuals tends to recapitulate the expectancy for that outcome. Certain elements of reality are more mutable than others; it is these that tend to be altered in the construction of a counterfactual representation. We also suggested that an account of the motivational influences on counterfactual thinking may complement the ideas set forth in norm theory. According to this view, an important, perhaps primary, engine driving the evocation of counterfactuals is the motivation to undo unwanted or unexpected outcomes. Once counterfactual generation has been triggered in this way, other, antecedent-based factors (described by norm theory) may constrain the content of the resulting counterfactual representations. In the next two sections, we review evidence describing the factors that affect counterfactual generation. This review is organized around the partition of counterfactual generation into two stages. First, we examine outcome-based factors mainly in terms of their impact on availability, but note as well their role in constraining content. Second, we describe antecedent-based factors, principally in terms of their influence on the semantic content of counterfactual thoughts.

OUTCOME-BASED DETERMINANTS
OF COUNTERFACTUAL GENERATION

Norm theory posits that the relative availability of counterfactual thoughts per se is a function of the mutability of antecedent situational characteristics. That is, the extent to which some feature of an evocative outcome would slip, or mutate, into a more expected value, would determine whether a counterfactual representation would come to mind. This representation would embrace all the immutable characteristics of the factual outcome, differing only in a very few mutable characteristics. If none of the features is mutable, then counterfactual representations would be relatively less forthcoming, and the outcome would be viewed as inevitable (cf. Fischhoff, 1982). As we noted previously, this mechanism does not take into account the motivational factors inherent in reactions to valued or aversive outcomes. That is, people may be impelled to undo an aversive outcome even in the absence of mutable antecedent features.

In this section, we build on the previous attempt by Miller et al. (1990) to elucidate factors influencing mere availability of counterfactual thoughts. By separating availability from semantic content, we are suggesting a two-stage model in which certain motivational, outcome-based factors trigger the initial undoing of the outcome, following which, other factors constrain the semantic content of the resultant counterfactual thoughts (cf. Gleicher et al., 1990). The variables described here are discussed mainly in terms of their role in triggering counterfactual availability. They may also, however, influence the content of those counterfactuals: People may generate counterfactuals, the semantic content of which reflects their strategic reaction to certain outcomes. Recent functionalist depictions of counterfactual thinking have identified just such strategic patterns (Markman, Gavanski, Sherman, & McMullen, 1993; Roese, 1994). For example, people may react to failure by generating counterfactuals that focus specifically on the actions of others (e.g., "If Karen had done her fair share, we wouldn't be in this mess"). Such self-serving counterfactuals may serve the function of affective enhancement, in that they attribute blame externally (Roese & Olson, 1993a). The strategic generation of counterfactuals in response to various current needs that are situationally induced is the topic of two subsequent chapters (5 and 6); hence we do not examine this perspective in detail here.

As we noted previously, there is significant overlap between counterfactual and attributional thinking. This overlap suggests that many of the factors identified as triggers of attributional thinking can also trigger counterfactual thinking. This theoretical parallel serves as a useful heuristic in this discussion. Thus, some of the factors discussed also figure prominently in theoretical articulations of the causal antecedents of mere attributional processing (e.g., Hastie, 1984; Weiner, 1986).

Expectancy

From an evolutionary perspective (e.g., Dennett, 1991), expectancies represent one of the most basic functions of the brains of ambulatory organisms, permitting effective navigation through unknown and potentially stormy environmental waters (Olson, Roese, & Zanna, in press). According to various expectancy-value theories, the link between stimulus–response contingencies and subsequent behavior is mediated by cognitive processing (Bolles, 1972; Tolman, 1932). Whether automatic or explicit, such cognitive processing embraces general attempts to make sense out of the environment, to form causal theories explaining specific outcomes, and to generate expectancies for future outcomes based on these theories. Expectancies are therefore output from cognitive activity designed to permit effective mastery over the environment (Weiner, 1986).

Understanding why something occurred is clearly beneficial: "The attributor is not simply . . . a seeker after knowledge; his latent goal in attaining knowledge is that of effective management of himself and his environment" (Kelley, 1972a, p. 22). Without such predictive management skill, people "could neither avoid nor prevent, but would be at the mercy of seemingly fickle events in the environment" (Heider, 1958, p. 257). Expectancies that are disconfirmed signal to the organism that the environment was not understood, not "mastered." Thus, enhanced processing following disconfirmed expectancies in order to regain mastery has obvious survival value (Berlyne, 1960).

Consistent with this reasoning, a range of experimental evidence suggests that disconfirmed expectancies trigger, in general, more effortful cognitive activity (Stern, Marrs, Millar, & Cole, 1984), and more specifically, more vigorous attributional thinking (Hastie, 1984; Kanazawa, 1992; Pyszczynski & Greenberg, 1981; Weiner, 1985). Given the previously argued overlap between attributional and counterfactual thinking, disconfirmed expectancies should have a similar generative impact on the latter as well as on the former (Gavanski & Wells, 1989).

The role of disconfirmed expectancies is central to Kahneman and Miller's (1986) norm theory. According to these authors, outcomes that are expectancy inconsistent (i.e., abnormal) recruit representations that are counterfactual and that are expectancy congruent (i.e., normal). However, norm theory did not draw a clear distinction between the content of counterfactual thoughts (mutability) as opposed to their mere generation (availability). For example, in a typical study in support of norm theory, researchers would compare the counterfactual thoughts generated by participants in response to a negative outcome (e.g., a fatal automobile accident) that was preceded by either an exceptional or a routine action (e.g., the driver might have taken either a rarely or a frequently travelled route home). The content of such counterfactuals typically embraces mutations of antecedent actions that are exceptional rather than routine. We argue, however, that such counterfactuals are triggered *in the first place* by the unexpectedness (or negativity) of the automobile accident itself; manipulations of antecedent exceptionality within a scenario in which the motorist *drives home safely* would likely be moot, as the motivational impulsion to create an alternative would be absent. Norm theory's specification of exceptionality (or expectancy disconfirmation) as a determinant of counterfactual content is treated in more detail later. Of concern here is not whether counterfactuals tend to recapitulate expectancies but whether disconfirmed expectancies trigger the mere availability of counterfactual thoughts.

Increased counterfactual thinking following disconfirmed expectancies has not been directly demonstrated, however. A paradigm employing a measure of spontaneous counterfactual generation would be required, but such techniques have so far been rarely reported in this literature (but see Markman et al., 1993; Roese & Olson, 1995, for exceptions). Nevertheless, given the theoretical justification and empirical support from related literatures, disconfirmed expectancies represent likely determinants of counterfactual availability.

Outcome Valence

"Just as a stream flows smoothly on as long as it encounters no obstruction, so the nature of man and animal is such that we never really notice or become conscious of what is agreeable to our will. On the other hand, all that . . . is unpleasant and painful impresses itself upon us instantly, directly, and with great clarity" (Schopenhauer, 1851/1970, p. 41). A wealth of evidence now attests to this phenomenological asymmetry of reactions to positive versus negative outcomes (S. Taylor, 1991). Compared to positive outcomes, negative outcomes recruit more active, effortful, and directed cognitions. The evolutionary and adaptive significance of this tendency is clear: Negative outcomes are acute, signifying a problematic state of affairs that must be rectified instantly. Hence, across many species, internal systems igniting "fight or flight" responses are highly reactive to negative stimuli, producing rapid physiological and behavioral changes. In contrast to this acute avoidance mechanism, acquisition of gratifying stimuli is chronic, occupying the bulk of the organism's time against a backdrop of essentially neutral outcomes. As with disconfirmed expectancies, negative outcomes signal to the organism that the environment was not mastered. Thus, enhanced processing following negative outcomes that permits the avoidance of future negative outcomes has obvious survival value (Berlyne, 1960).

A recent review by S. Taylor (1991) highlighted a range of evidence demonstrating the asymmetrical cognitive consequences of negative versus positive outcomes. Negative outcomes (mediated by negative affect) produce a narrowing of attentional focus (Fiedler, 1988), quicker decision making (Isen & Means, 1983), more complex and systematic information processing (Schwarz, 1990), and more intense attributional thinking (Bohner, Bless, Schwarz, & Strack, 1988; Hastie, 1984; Weiner, 1985, 1986; but see Kanazawa, 1992, for an exception).

Consistent with this reasoning is the suggestion by several theorists that counterfactual thinking is more likely to follow negative outcomes than positive outcomes (e.g., Gavanski & Wells, 1989; Gleicher et al., 1990; Boninger, Gleicher, & Strathman, 1994; J. Johnson, 1986; Kahneman & Miller, 1986; Landman, 1987). The available evidence is somewhat indirect, however. In a study by Landman (1987), for example, participants decided which of two actors depicted in a scenario would feel worse. One protagonist acted overtly, whereas the other considered an action but then decided against it. Actions have been theorized to be more mutable than failures to act (see the next section); given the principle of emotional amplification (discussed later), affective reactions should be more extreme if the outcome follows an action than if it follows an inaction. Results of Landman's (1987) study supported this notion: In the case of a negative outcome, participants attributed greater regret to the protagonist who acted than to the protagonist who failed to act. However, perceived elation following a positive outcome was relatively unaffected by this manipulation, suggesting that counterfactual thoughts mediated affective reactions to the negative but not reactions to the positive outcome.

Using similar logic, Gleicher et al. (1990) manipulated outcome valence and the salience of counterfactual alternatives in a scenario that again depicted the actions versus inactions of two protagonists. In a replication of Landman's (1987) findings, participants in the negative-outcome condition attributed greater regret to the protagonist who acted than to the one who failed to act. This effect was strong regardless of how salient the relevant alternative was. In contrast, the action–inaction effect was weaker following a positive outcome but highly sensitive to the salience manipulation. When the counterfactual alternative was made salient to participants, the action–inaction effect was heightened nearly to the level observed in the negative-outcome condition. These findings suggest that people base affective judgments on counterfactuals spontaneously following negative outcomes but only when prompted following positive outcomes. The failure to link these findings to a directly measured counterfactual mediator, however, remains troublesome.

This is especially so in light of several failures to replicate the outcome-valence effect. For example, Roese and Olson (1993a) manipulated outcome valence in two scenario studies and found that participants recorded counterfactual alternatives to both positive and negative outcomes with similar frequency (see also Roese & Olson, 1993b, 1995, for similar null findings). The null results of these studies may be explained rather simply in terms of the nonspontaneous nature of the counterfactual solicitations. Perhaps asking people directly obscures naturally occurring propensities to react with greater or fewer spontaneous counterfactual thoughts. This criticism cannot be applied, however, to the Markman et al. (1993) research, based as it was on spontaneous counterfactual thoughts vocalized onto a tape recording. Here, again, no differences in the frequency of spontaneously recorded counterfactual thoughts emerged as a function of outcome valence. These authors noted one possible explanation: The uniform unexpectedness of both positive and negative outcomes might have so powerfully stimulated counterfactual generation that further variation as a function of outcome valence might have been unlikely.

Given the weight of conceptual and indirect empirical support, however, it remains likely that negative outcomes do enhance counterfactual availability. One possible resolution to this inconsistency reflects the motivational basis of counterfactual thinking. Because negative outcomes are aversive, people should be motivated to avoid them, if not directly, then imaginatively by mentally undoing the outcome. Positive outcomes should motivate no such avoidance. Perhaps the outcome valence effect will be observed only to the extent that the outcomes in question are involving and have a tangible impact on the individual. Thus, future researchers may demonstrate the effect in situations with more powerful motivating factors and with more profound implications for the self (cf. Davis & Lehman, chapter 13; Davis, Lehman, Wortman, Silver, & Thompson, 1995).[7]

Outcome valence may also influence the content of counterfactual thoughts. Functional perspectives have provided the most compelling evidence of such a relation: These posit the strategic generation of counterfactuals of specific content in reaction to various situational demands (Markman et al., 1993; McMullen et al., chapter 5; Roese, 1994; Roese & Olson, chapter 6). People may generate counterfactuals to improve themselves in the future (a preparative function) or to enhance their current affect (an affective function). In documenting such strategic uses, researchers have focused on at least three categorization schemes to describe the content of counterfactuals so generated. First, counterfactuals may be *upward* (describing alternatives that are better than the actual outcome) or *downward* (describing alternatives that are worse than actuality). Upward counterfactuals may be more useful than downward counterfactuals in illuminating paths by which success might be achieved in the future. Consistent with a functional perspective, Markman et al.'s (1993) results showed that upward counterfactuals were generated more frequently following failure than following success outcomes, suggesting that individuals conceived such thoughts when they were most needed. Second, counterfactuals that are *additive* (describing the addition of a new ante-

---

[7]Although the role of disconfirmed expectancies and negative outcomes have been described separately here, the natural correlation between the two must be emphasized. That is, people tend to expect positive outcomes (McGill, 1989; Weinstein, 1980). Thus, negative outcomes are frequently unexpected. Kanazawa (1992) found that the effect of disconfirmed expectancies completely accounted for any impact of negative outcomes on spontaneous attributional thinking. In contrast, Bohner et al. (1988) found that the intensity of attributional thinking varied as a function of outcome valence but not prior subjective probability. For our purposes, we retain the conceptual separation of these two factors but emphasize that both may be based on the same survival-based control mechanism. Specifically, both may trigger negative affect, which may be the central mediator that accounts for the effects of both (cf. Dennett, 1991; McClelland et al., 1953; Olson et al., in press; Tolman, 1932).

cedent) as opposed to *subtractive* (describing the removal of a factual antecedent) may be more useful as well. At least to the extent that multiple responses were possible, the specification of an addition is more informatively specific than a subtractive counterfactual. Also consistent with a functional perspective, Roese and Olson (1993b) demonstrated that additive counterfactuals were generated more frequently following failure than following success outcomes. Third, counterfactuals may be *internal* (focusing on the actions of oneself) or *external* (focusing on the actions of others). Roese and Olson (1993a) showed that individuals with high self-esteem tended to generate external counterfactuals following failure (thereby blaming others) but internal counterfactuals following success (thereby taking credit). Such a self-serving pattern may have obvious affective benefits (see McFarland & Ross, 1982; S. Taylor & Brown, 1988). Thus, outcome valence has been shown in several cases to influence the semantic content of counterfactual thoughts.

Closeness

One of the more fascinating yet least understood variables that potentially influences counterfactual availability is the perceived closeness of an outcome to a more desired, alternative outcome. Kahneman and Miller (1986) pointed to antecedent mutability as the chief mediator of perceptions of closeness, but beyond this factor, basic perceptions of nearness to an outcome, analogous to both spatial and temporal proximity, may influence counterfactual generation. A runner who loses a race by a hair may have thoughts of almost winning to a much greater extent than a runner who loses by 10 feet. The oft-repeated scenario involving Mr. Crane and Mr. Tees (from Kahneman & Tversky, 1982b) is also based on this effect: Mr. Tees is perceived to be much more disappointed with having missed his plane by 5 minutes than is Mr. Crane, who missed his by half an hour.

   This reasoning suggests the fundamentally analog nature of counterfactual representations. There appears to be some dimension of closeness along which achieved outcomes are compared to desired outcomes (cf. Thibaut & Kelley, 1959, for a discussion of comparison levels, and Lewin, Dembo, Festinger, & Sears, 1944, for a discussion of level of aspiration). An outcome that approximates (but does not reach) a goal is more likely to create the feeling that "it almost happened" than outcomes that come nowhere near a goal. Of course, the same pattern obtains for dreaded outcomes: A narrowly avoided debacle would similarly inspire counterfactually derived feelings of relief that "it didn't happen" (cf. J. Johnson, 1986; Kahneman & Varey, 1990) to a greater extent than a disaster easily averted. It may be that closeness is the principal factor triggering the spontaneous generation of downward counterfactuals (alternatives that are worse than the focal outcome). The previously described factors (expectancy, outcome valence) are argued to influence mainly upward counterfactuals, which focus on expected or desired outcomes. We argue that the relative frequency of generation of downward counterfactuals do occur spontaneously but only as a function of closeness, that is, when a worse outcome clearly almost happened.

The analog representation of goal proximity is a concept developed in some detail by Kurt Lewin (e.g., 1936, 1951) in his discussions of topological psychology. Indeed, his elegant "force field" diagrams were an attempt to quantify the psychological (but not necessarily physical) distance separating the individual from desired goal-states. Later, Heider (1958) further discussed this dimension of closeness, noting that it must embrace temporal as well as spatial analogs. These early theorists emphasized the relation between perceived nearness to a goal and frustration at not attaining it, a relation mediated by imaginings of the positive affect engendered by goal attainment.

Meyers–Levy and Maheswaran (1992) presented direct evidence that perceived closeness influences counterfactual availability. In two experiments, participants read persuasive appeals depicting negative events (e.g., a house fire) that could have been avoided had some recommended action taken place. For example, in the second experiment, the target actor could have avoided the loss of prized personal possessions had he purchased insurance. When the avoidance of the outcome was temporally close (e.g., fire ravages the home of the target actor who forgot to send in an insurance policy only 3 days earlier) rather than temporally distant (e.g., the fire and forgotten policy are separated by 6 months), thoughts were more likely to be spontaneously recorded in a free thought-listing task.

Miller et al. (1990) speculated on the process underlying this effect. These authors suggested that counterfactual closeness is a function of the intuitive, implicit mental models of the world and its operation that people carry around in their heads. These models may give rise to what have been labeled *implicit expectancies* (Olson et al., in press), which describe rules-of-thumb for the workings of reality. The relative ease with which the parameters of a mental model may be revised determines the availability of counterfactual representations. If, for example, the change to a parameter is small or falls within some critical range of smallness, then a counterfactual should be more available. If the change is too large to be plausible, counterfactual alternatives to the outcome are less easily generated. To return to poor Crane and Tees, the alteration in time for Mr. Tees is small enough that the prospect of it being made up (e.g., by driving faster to the airport) falls within the range of intuitive plausibility. Thus, it is easier to imagine Mr. Tees boarding his plane in time. In contrast, the magnitude of change necessary to reduce Mr. Crane's 30 crucial minutes to zero is inconsistent with mental models of freeway traffic and airline delays. Thus, people find it more difficult to imagine how Mr. Crane could have made it onto his flight (cf. Miller & McFarland, 1986).

Changes to parameters need not be based on plausible causal factors to evoke counterfactual thoughts. For example, Turnbull (1981) found that people who failed to win a lottery prize were more disappointed when their lottery tickets held numbers countably close to the winning numbers. Although completely irrelevant to the prospect of winning, a number that is one digit away from a number on a winning lottery ticket apparently generates perceptions of counterfactual closeness that are similar to those of narrowly losing a race or missing a plane (cf. Heider, 1958).[8] Clearly, closeness may be variously conceived in numerical, spatial, or temporal terms.

Kahneman and Varey (1990) examined closeness in a somewhat different light. They suggested the concept of the *close counterfactual*, defined in terms of three essential components. First, close counterfactuals are not phrased as conditional propositions but simply as alternative outcomes. Second, they reflect alternatives that are objectively close (in terms of a priori probabilities) to having become actuality, as opposed to those that are subjective and unverifiable. For example, if Sally buys 90% of the raffle tickets printed by her neighborhood school and still loses, a close counterfactual is that she almost won with a preoutcome probability of .90. Third and perhaps most important, close counterfactuals derive also from the perception of a *propensity* toward an unrealized outcome. Propensities, in this sense, refer to the dynamic, preoutcome, actional cues that suggest an increasing trend toward the occurrence of a target outcome. Consider a day at the races. Two horses, X and Y, are both given identical odds to win before the race begins. Horse X falls quickly behind, then makes rapid advances toward the leader, while horse Y maintains a steady third-place position. In the end, both fail to show, but the perception that horse X nearly won seems far more irresistible than the perception that horse Y nearly won. But note that the preoutcome likelihoods of winning were identical for both horses: According to Kahneman and Varey, it is the dynamic, perhaps accelerating, movement toward a win that triggers the counterfactual that X almost won (see also Hsee, Salovey, & Abelson, 1994). The feeling that "we were *going to win* but blew it only in the last few seconds" is an especially poignant one

---

[8]Hofstadter (1979) begins his discussion of counterfactuals by describing a friend whose uncle "was almost the president of the U.S." (p. 641): During World War II he was skipper of the PT 108. Hofstadter is quick to remind his younger readers that John F. Kennedy had been skipper of the PT 109.

for gamblers and sports fans, attesting to the important impact of close counterfactuals on emotional reactions. This section has documented some of the widely variegated approaches to the concept of counterfactual closeness. From the early writings of Lewin and Heider to more contemporary work, closeness suggests the most obvious initial approach to conceptualizing counterfactual availability, yet a unified description of this mechanism remains elusive. We look forward to future research on this construct that may clarify its operation as well as offer an integration with the other factors described here.

Involvement

People are involved in an outcome if it has the potential to affect them personally in some way. To the extent that individuals feel personally involved in an outcome, they tend to direct greater cognitive activity toward processing information relevant to that outcome. This pattern has been thoroughly examined in the context of attitude research, in which involvement in, or perceived personal relevance or importance of, some issue increases effortful processing of persuasive messages (Eagly & Chaiken, 1993). As well, evidence suggests that attributional thinking about an outcome is more intense when the individual is personally involved in the outcome (Berscheid, Graziano, Monson, & Dermer, 1976; Harkness, DeBono, & Borgida, 1985).

The previously described research by Meyers-Levy and Maheswaran (1992) indicated that counterfactual availability is also heightened by involvement. Participants read persuasive appeals and learned that their appraisal would have either a large (high involvement) or small (low involvement) impact on a subsequent policy decision. Although this manipulation did not reflect personal involvement in the outcome per se, it was expected that participants would be motivated to invest greater effort when their judgments had greater consequences for others. The appeals described negative events that could have been avoided had some recommended action taken place. In both studies, participants recorded more counterfactual statements (in spontaneous thought-listing tasks) referencing the target action under high than low involvement conditions. Involvement may not only exert a main effect on counterfactual availability but also very likely moderates the influence of the other variables discussed in this section, such as outcome valence (Macrae & Milne, 1992). Thus, for example, negative outcomes may trigger increased counterfactual processing relative to positive outcomes, but this effect may be especially strong to the extent that the outcome is involving.

Involvement may also shape the semantic content of counterfactual thoughts. Evidence for this relation comes from two studies. The first was an examination of defensive counterfactual judgments (Roese, Black, & Olson, 1994). Participants read scenarios depicting an automobile accident in which the perpetrator was either high or low in similarity to them (a manipulation of involvement that reflects personal threat). In the high-similarity condition, participants were more likely to undo the outcome by mutating aspects of the situation rather than by mutating the actions by the perpetrator. This defensive pattern of causal judgment, in which blame was deflected from the perpetrator only when participants felt similar to him or her (and hence were threatened by the prospect that they themselves might be blamed in similar circumstances), underscores the importance of motivational factors in dictating the content of counterfactual thoughts.

Macrae and Milne (1992) also provided evidence for the involvement–content link. Participants read scenarios depicting a young woman who became ill after eating out. The preceding circumstances were described as exceptional or routine. Some participants were encouraged to empathize with the young woman (i.e., to identify with her by imagining the scenario from her perspective), whereas others were asked to adopt the restaurant owner's perspective. The tendency for sympathy for the victim to be enhanced by exceptional as opposed to routine antecedents (affective consequences of counterfactual thinking are discussed later) was amplified by the "victim set" and reduced by the "perpetrator set," relative to a control condition. Thus, involvement with the victim of an accident moderated the negative impact of thoughts that the accident might have been avoided.

These three research efforts provide preliminary evidence for the role of involvement in counterfactual thinking. Additional research is needed, however, to document more directly the moderating impact of involvement with respect to outcome valence. Specifically, it remains to be shown that counterfactual alternatives to negative outcomes will be generated with greater vigor when individuals are personally connected to rather than mere observers of those outcomes. Such a demonstration would demand paradigms more ecologically valid than the simple scenario studies described here.

Conclusion

Described in this section were four outcome-based factors that may affect counterfactual generation: expectancy, outcome valence, closeness, and involvement. We focused largely on the role these factors may play in the availability of counterfactual thoughts, although these factors may also constrain content. These factors are inherently motivational in nature, and negative affect plays an important mediating role in all of them.

Thus, disconfirmed expectancies and negative outcomes may independently elicit negative affect (McClelland et al., 1953; Olson et al., in press), as would the perceived closeness to a desired yet unobtained goal. Further, involvement may moderate the extremity of negative affect generated by these three factors. It may be that the root influence on counterfactual availability is affect, which many have posited to be a central, survival-oriented control mechanism within higher ambulatory organisms. Empirical evidence directly confirming the role of these four factors in triggering availability is still scant, however; thus many of the conclusions reached here remain speculative. Nevertheless, the conceptual relation between counterfactual and attributional thinking suggests that general principles derived from study of the latter may be applied fairly confidently to the former.

ANTECEDENT-BASED DETERMINANTS
OF COUNTERFACTUAL GENERATION

The assessment of factors affecting the mutability of antecedents has been one of the most active areas of counterfactual research, derived in large part from the theoretical formulations presented by Kahneman and Tversky (1982b) and Kahneman and Miller (1986). The factors considered here were tabulated and considered in some detail by these authors. Our purpose is to update previous accounts by considering recent evidence and contrasting interpretations of the mechanisms underlying mutability effects.

The distinction between availability and content is an important one for our analysis. Norm theory specifies the causal impact of mutability (and hence content) on availability, such that manipulations of those factors described in this section influence the availability of counterfactual thoughts (Link 3 in Figure 1.2). Although we agree with this proposition, we also note the utility of conceptually separating availability and content in terms of the respective factors influencing them. In the present section, we examine antecedent-based factors, those that center conceptually on the antecedent events leading to the focal outcome. The bulk of this discussion focuses on the effect these factors have on the content of counterfactual thoughts. Although we do not deny that antecedent-based factors may also affect availability, the paucity of evidence supporting this relation limits our discussion of it.

After several years of research focusing primarily on antecedent-based factors, quite a few conceptually distinct variables have been articulated, framed in terms of the construct of mutability. We attempt to streamline this list into a smaller subset of factors that can, at a more basic level, account for the findings to date.

Exceptional Versus Routine Antecedents

A central assertion of norm theory is the tendency to mutate exceptional antecedent elements into more routine, default elements. Thus, an outcome is more likely to be undone through the alteration of an exceptional rather than a routine aspect of the situation preceding that outcome (Kahneman & Miller, 1986). The classic empirical demonstration was based on a scenario depicting a fatal automobile accident (Kahneman & Tversky, 1982b). The car of the victim, Mr. Jones, who is on his way home from work, is hit by a car driven by an intoxicated driver. The exceptionality of antecedents was manipulated on a between-participants basis: Some participants read that Mr. Jones left work unusually early but drove home via his usual route. Other participants learned that he departed at his usual time but took an unusual route home. When asked to consider how the accident could have been avoided, participants tended to mutate the exception rather than the norm. Thus, when departure time was exceptional (i.e., unusual), participants noted that Mr. Jones would still be alive if he had left work later; when the route taken was exceptional, they observed that Mr. Jones should have adhered to his usual route. Several studies have replicated and extended this effect (e.g., Buck & Miller, 1994; Lundberg & Frost, 1992; Wells, B. Taylor, & Turtle, 1987).

Kahneman and Miller (1986) interpreted the effect as reflecting a fundamental tendency to create counterfactual simulations that instantiate normality or typicality. Counterfactuals, constrained by reality and feasibility, tend to move in a direction that brings simulated occurrences closer to implicit, default expectancies of how the world works (i.e., counterfactuals recapitulate expectancies). Gavanski and Wells (1989), however, offered an alternative view. These authors suggested that returning exceptional antecedents to their default status may not be a general principle but, rather, may be limited to cases in which the outcome is also exceptional (as was the case in previous demonstrations, e.g., an automobile accident). They proposed instead that counterfactual judgments may operate according to a correspondence heuristic (cf. Einhorn & Hogarth, 1986; see also Bouts et al., 1992), in which exceptional outcomes are presumed to follow from exceptional antecedents and normal outcomes are presumed to follow from normal outcomes. Gavanski and Wells showed that perceivers tend to undo exceptional outcomes by altering exceptional antecedents to make them more normal (e.g., a straight-"A" student might react to a failed exam by focusing on unusual preexam behaviors, such as heavy drinking, that she should have avoided), but perceivers undo normal outcomes by altering both normal and exceptional antecedents toward greater exceptionality (e.g., a mediocre student might react to yet another failure by thinking he should have studied harder and bought extra study materials).

The causal implications of these counterfactuals are the key to understanding the logic of this demonstration. In the former case, the student
assumes that an exceptional cause resulted in her exceptional outcome (i.e.,
heavy drinking caused failure). In the latter case, the student assumes that
a more normal cause resulted in his normal outcome (i.e., lack of effort
caused failure).

The generality of the exceptionality effect was cast in further doubt by
Davis et al. (1995), who assessed counterfactual generation following
traumatic life experiences, such as the death of a loved one. Although
counterfactual thinking appeared to be a common reaction to sudden
loss, it did not vary systematically as a function of the exceptionality of
preoutcome actions. Rather, people tended to focus on mundane, everyday behaviors that they themselves should or should not have performed.
This finding is also at odds with the interpretation of Gavanski and Wells
(1989), who would make the same prediction as did Kahneman and
Tversky (1982b) for outcomes that are extremely unexpected and negative.

The motivational perspective of this chapter suggests a reconciliation
of these three views. It should be pointed out that, *by definition*, exceptional
events are rare. Yet, counterfactual thinking seems to be common, often
triggered by the motivational factors we have cited. Therefore, the
majority of counterfactual thoughts generated on an everyday basis must
necessarily involve mutations of relatively mundane antecedents, and it
was these that were primarily sampled in the Davis et al. (1995) research.
However, even if these antecedents were relatively routine, Kahneman
and Miller (1986) were essentially correct in noting that resultant
counterfactuals very rarely alter actuality in the direction of greater
exceptionality. Instead, mundane antecedents may be replaced by other
mundane antecedents. Yet, given the awareness of an exceptional
antecedent, we believe that individuals will seize upon it first for
counterfactual processing. Overall, the available evidence converges on
the conclusion that expectancies play a central role in mutability.

Actions Versus Inactions

Kahneman and Tversky (1982a) suggested that actions are more mutable
than failures to act. That is, it is easier to generate counterfactuals based
on the deletion of a factual action than it is to imagine an action that was
not in fact performed (see also Kahneman & Miller, 1986; Miller et al.,
1990). The mechanism underlying this effect was linked to the expectancies (norms) of typical social situations, in which actions are perceived
to be abnormal (and thus more mutable), whereas inaction is more typical
(Kahneman & Miller, 1986; Landman, 1987).

Unlike evidence documenting the role of exceptionality in antecedent
mutability, the initial demonstrations of action–inaction effects were

based entirely on within-subject assessments of affect, with counterfactual thoughts presumed to be the principal mediator. The previously described experiments by Gleicher et al. (1990) and Landman (1987) are examples. Participants were presented simultaneously with similar outcomes experienced by two protagonists, one of whom performed an outcome-relevant act and one who considered doing so but decided against it. Participants attributed more extreme affect to the protagonist whose outcome followed from overt actions than from inactions (see also Epstein, Lipson, Holstein, & Huh, 1992). Note, however, that because counterfactual thoughts were not recorded, it is uncertain whether or not they mediated this effect. Gleicher et al. (1990) included a counterfactual-salience manipulation that produced effects that were consistent, however, with a counterfactual mediator: When participants were informed directly of a counterfactual alternative, the action–inaction effect was enhanced (but, as predicted, only in the positive outcome condition).

The general conclusion that actions are more mutable than inactions was challenged by the findings of Davis et al. (1995). Despite the frequency of counterfactual thoughts following sudden loss, these thoughts did not vary systematically as a function of preoutcome actions versus inactions. Roese and Olson (1993a, 1993b) similarly failed to detect a propensity to mutate actions over inactions, but approached the problem from a slightly different theoretical vantage point. Examining the implicit, intuitive expectancies with which individuals enter social situations, previous evidence does not support the notion that actions are more abnormal than inactions, at least not as a general rule. However, expectancies for action versus inaction may vary as a function of outcome valence, particularly in achievement situations. For most, success is intended and expected (McGill, 1989; Weinstein, 1980); hence, success may typically be seen as a result of deliberate, facilitative actions (cf. Hansen & Hall, 1985). Failure, however, is unwanted and unexpected; people, therefore, tend to see it as resulting from a failure to act appropriately. Further, people in Western cultures generally value internally driven actions (Jellison & Green, 1981) and seem to subscribe to a principle of personal control, whereby positive action is appropriate and normative. Also, people often overestimate the degree to which outcomes can be controlled (Langer, 1975). These various factors may generate the perception that success and failure result from the presence or absence, respectively, of appropriate, planned acts. These expectancies were demonstrated directly by Roese and Olson (1993b) in a pilot survey.

This reasoning suggests a divergence in the undoing of success and failure. Specifically, undoing success should involve the removal of a successful, appropriate, antecedent action (i.e., a subtractive counterfactual, such as, "If she hadn't studied, she would have failed"). Undoing failure, on the other hand, should involve the addition of a new antecedent action that would have enhanced the chances of success (i.e., an additive counterfactual, such as, "If he had bought the study guide, he would have passed"). The results of three scenario studies support this reasoning (Roese & Olson, 1993a, 1993b). In all three, outcome valence was manipulated on a between-participants basis, with the number of additive versus subtractive counterfactuals recorded by participants serving as the dependent measure. No preference for deleting over adding actions was observed, but outcome valence moderated the relative generation of additive and subtractive counterfactuals as predicted. In other studies, participants were shown to mentally simulate actions versus inactions on request with equivalent alacrity (Anderson & Godfrey, 1987; Roese, 1994), thereby adding converging, though indirect, evidence that suggests the equivalent ease of mutating actions and inactions.

These findings obligate a reinterpretation of the action–inaction effect. Given the available evidence, Landman's (1987) suggestion that the basic element of salience accounts for action–inaction effects remains the most plausible interpretation. Perhaps the most striking aspect of the within-subject demonstrations (Epstein et al., 1992; Kahneman & Tversky, 1982a; Gleicher et al., 1990; Landman, 1987) is the isolation of a single causal antecedent in the test scenarios, as opposed to the field of multiple antecedents used by Roese and Olson (1993a, 1993b). When an action is isolated and contrasted to an isolated missed opportunity to act, that action is more salient than an action among many (Fazio, Sherman, & Herr, 1982), thus leading to its greater mutability. Indeed, results of previous research have clearly shown that cause is more often attributed to antecedents of greater salience (S. Taylor & Fiske, 1978). A basic tendency to mutate salient antecedent elements likely underlies the action–inaction effect (cf. Landman, 1993) and, as we have already noted, expectancies for action versus inaction within different situations may also powerfully determine mutability. We conclude that the factor of action–inaction has no special relevance to mutability, but that the evidence to date may be described more parsimoniously by the factors of salience and expectancy. This issue is discussed further by Davis and Lehman (chapter 13), by Gilovich and Medvec (chapter 9), and by Kahneman (chapter 14).

Controllable Versus Uncontrollable Antecedents

Controllable antecedents tend to be more mutable than uncontrollable antecedents. That is, people tend to make alterations to preoutcome elements that can be directly controlled, altered, or manipulated (cf. Miller et al., 1990). Girotto, Legrenzi, and Rizzo (1991) presented participants with a scenario in which the protagonist's drive home is delayed by several occurrences. Participants tended to mutate aspects of the scenario under the protagonist's direct control (e.g., stopping for beer on the way home) rather than aspects not under his control (e.g., waiting for a flock of sheep to cross the road). In two of three studies reported, however, controllability was confounded with internality; thus, given the relation between counterfactual and attributional thinking, the finding might simply have been a restatement of the fundamental attribution error (Ross, 1977). Importantly, however, the third study demonstrated the effect even when all antecedents were internally derived. N'gbala and Branscombe's (in press) Experiment 2 provides further confirmation of the effect. In a more ecologically valid test of the controllability hypothesis, Markman, Gavanski, Sherman, and McMullen (1995) charted counterfactuals generated by participants as they played a computerized game of chance. Participants again showed a marked tendency to mutate whatever aspect of the game they perceived themselves to control. McMullen et al. discuss the role of perceived control in greater detail in chapter 5.

The basis for this effect is consistent with the survival value of control and mastery previously described. We have argued that one of the basic purposes counterfactual thinking may serve is to attain mastery over the environment by avoiding the recurrence of negative outcomes while navigating toward positive outcomes. It is simply more functional, then, for counterfactuals to focus on controllable aspects, as such aspects may be subsequently manipulated for the individual's betterment. But note also that people *expect*, perhaps to an often unrealistic degree, to exert control over their lives (Langer, 1975). The factor of controllability may therefore also be related to the basic factor of expectancy.

Dynamic Versus Static Antecedents

Several counterfactual demonstrations are consistent with the proposition that dynamic aspects of reality are more mutable than are static aspects. That is, antecedent elements that fluctuate or vary at an observable rate are more likely to be varied mentally than are unchanging elements. This general tendency is also deducible from Kelley's (1967) model of attributional thinking. Factors that are dynamic are more likely to be seen as covarying with an outcome and, hence, may be seen as more causal, relative to unchanging factors. The dynamic-versus-static factor perhaps comes closest to the spirit of the definition of mutability. Factors that change in the external world are more easily altered in mental representations, again referencing the analog nature of counterfactual simulations. Thus, unstable factors such as effort should be more mutable than stable factors such as ability (cf. Girotto et al., 1991).

This idea was evident in a scenario involving a weightlifter who deviated in both body weight and performance from experimentally established norms. When asked how they would counterfactually alter the scenario to make it more normal, participants were more likely to alter the protagonist's performance than to alter his body weight (Kahneman & Miller, 1986).[9]

Kahneman and Varey's (1990) discussion of close counterfactuals provides an analogous description based on *dispositions* and *propensities*. They defined a disposition in terms of the background probabilities of attaining some outcome, whereas a propensity is a dynamic tendency or acceleration toward that outcome. *Disposition neglect* refers to the greater weight given to dynamic changes as opposed to background assumptions in retrospective judgments. That is, after an outcome is known, people prefer to mutate dynamic propensities (e.g., actions) rather than static dispositions (e.g., traits). These authors presented an illustrative case of two among several runners, one "who is in contention and is known to have a strong finish . . . and one who has been catching up with the leader" (p. 1105). Both runners lose by the same distance: "The first did not show a strong finish and the second never quite caught up" (p. 1105). The counterfactual that the second runner almost won seems more compelling than the counterfactual that the first almost won, even though both were separated by same physical distance from the winner. The means by which the first could have won were static (ability to achieve a strong finish), whereas those for the second runner were dynamic (catching up during the race). Thus, the greater mutability of the dynamic over the static factor triggers the perception that the second runner almost won.

The distinction between dynamic and static antecedents yields several novel predictions as well. Ignorance of the natural variation inherent in some element may restrict its mutability and, therefore, its identification as a causal factor. In this vein, McGill (1989) offered the example that citizens living under "historically corrupt political rule tend to characterize the abuse and torture of fellow citizens as the result of agitation on the part of the victim rather than the product of a political system gone awry" (p. 198). Thus, a failure to appreciate the possible variability of governmental behavior means that less blame is attributed to it. In a similar vein, new elements may be more mutable than elements in existence for longer periods of time. Thus, in public policy discussions, changes to laws or procedures may tend to focus on alterations to recent rather than older enactments. Consider the recent conflict in the Balkans, where blame tends to focus on the highly mutable actions of NATO, the UN, and the US (newer and arguably more dynamic institutions) rather than on the entrenched ethnic hatred among Catholic Croatians, Muslim Bosnians, and Orthodox Serbs, hatred that may be traced back at least 5 centuries.

---

[9]This demonstration was originally intended to establish the differential mutability of causes versus effects. We believe that the differential mutability of dynamic versus static antecedents more completely accounts for the observed pattern of responses.

Very likely, it is salience that may be the root of any dynamic versus static effects. Processes that are in motion may simply draw more attention than processes at rest, in the same way that actions may be more salient than inactions. The factor of dynamic-versus-static antecedents has not been examined systematically, yet its basic character echoes through the research reviewed here. Those conducting future research on this factor and related ideas should do so with the awareness that salience may play a role in its effects.

Serial Position

Very frequently outcomes are the result of multiple occurrences comprising a serial chain. A recurring theme in both counterfactual and attributional research is whether serial position influences judgments of causality. Attributional research has shown that people perceive those events occurring early in a serial chain to exert greater causal impact (e.g., Brickman, Ryan, & Wortman, 1975). Similarly, Wells et al. (1987) found that in constructing counterfactual versions of a scenario, early events were more mutable than later events.

The primacy effect of antecedent mutability seems to be restricted to cases in which the chain represents a causal sequence (i.e., the initial event triggers the second, which triggers the third, etc.). In such cases, the latter events may appear more constrained and, hence, less mutable than the initial event. In contrast, Miller and Gunasegaram (1990) showed that later events are more mutable in chains consisting of independent events. Thus, early events that are not explicitly linked in a causal fashion to later ones tend be presupposed, or taken as immutable parts of the causal background. Again, this effect may derive from the greater salience of recent events than of earlier events.

Antecedent order effects on mutability are likely weaker than the effects of the other factors cited in this discussion. In order for such effects to be detected, some degree of equivalency of occurrences within the sequence apparently must exist. When occurrences differ along some of the other dimensions affecting mutability, these differences erase any order effects. Thus, controllable antecedents are more mutable than uncontrollable antecedents, and exceptional antecedents are more mutable than normal antecedents (Girotto et al., 1991), regardless of their respective positions within serial chains (cf. Vinokur & Ajzen, 1982).

Conclusion

We have described five antecedent-based factors in this section. Antecedents elements that are exceptional, salient, controllable, dynamic, or recent tend to be more mutable than their counterparts, that is, to be seized on more readily in the construction of a counterfactual version of an outcome. These factors thereby constrain the semantic content of counterfactual thoughts and as well may influence counterfactual availability. Additionally, antecedents perceived to be more mutable are also those typically ascribed greater weight in causal judgments. The available evidence does not consistently support the previous assertion that actions are more mutable than inactions; rather, this effect disappears under various conditions and may be explained more parsimoniously by reference to expectancy and salience.

In reviewing these factors, it is important to stress that mutability is not so much a variable (at least not one that can yet be measured) as it is a post hoc description. As we have argued here, elements of the world that are perceived to change are also more easily changed in people's minds. Elements that are typical, static, or expected are less easily changed mentally, by virtue of their unchanging nature in the real world. From this light, the analog nature of counterfactual representations appears to be a defining feature of their operation.

CONSEQUENCES OF COUNTERFACTUAL THINKING

An understanding of the psychological and behavioral consequences of engaging in counterfactual thinking underscores the pragmatic relevance of charting such thought processes. Such consequences range across affective responses, social judgments, self-inferences, expectancies, and behaviors. Varied as these consequences may seem, they are all rooted in two main mechanisms: contrast effects and causal inferences. The nature of contrast effects was previously described in the context of norm theory; some effects described in the following discussion derive from a contrast between some factual outcome and a salient alternative (e.g., the affect-mediated victim compensation described by Miller & McFarland, 1986). The close relation between counterfactual and causal thinking has already been noted; other effects that we describe flow from counterfactually mediated enhancement of causal attribution to some target (e.g., the hopefulness effects described by Boninger et al., 1994).

A basic difference between these two effects is in the link between the antecedent and the outcome contained in the counterfactual proposition. For causal inferences, the relation between the antecedent and the outcome is crucial: Both must be salient for causal effects to occur. In the case of contrast effects, only the alternative outcome must be salient for these effects to occur. Thus, close counterfactuals (i.e., those that specify an alternative outcome but no antecedent) may be implicated in contrast effect findings but not in causal findings.

The discussions that follow are organized into two main groups. First, we examine research describing the affective consequences of counterfactual thinking. Second, we describe examinations of the cognitive (i.e., judgmental) consequences of counterfactual thinking. A very natural third section would focus on the behavioral consequences of such thought processes, but there are currently too few experimental demonstrations to warrant such a separate discussion. (The contents of this volume suggest that this state of affairs is changing; see Gleicher et al., chapter 10; Miller & Taylor, chapter 11; Roese and Olson, chapter 6.)

Affect

Counterfactual thoughts may influence affective experiences via both contrast and causal-inference effects. A major feature of Kahneman and Miller's (1986) norm theory is its principle of emotional amplification, that is, that "the affective response to an event is enhanced if its causes are abnormal" (p. 145). The principle is reducible in large part to a contrast effect (Schwarz & Bless, 1992; Sherif & Hovland, 1961) cued by the salience of a counterfactual anchor. Stated more simply, a given outcome will be judged to be worse if a more desirable comparison anchor is salient, better if a less desirable anchor is salient (Dermer, Cohen, Jacobsen, & Anderson, 1979). To the extent that factors influencing mutability in turn make a counterfactual anchor more salient, the contrast effect is enhanced.

As a simple demonstration of this affective contrast effect, Roese (1994, Experiments 1 and 2) had participants record details of an unpleasant life event, then induced them to consider alternatives that were better (upward counterfactuals) or worse (downward counterfactuals) than the actual event. Those induced to generate upward counterfactuals subsequently reported more negative affect than those who generated downward counterfactuals. Similarly, Markman et al. (1993) showed that situational factors (e.g., a negative outcome) that evoked upward as opposed to downward counterfactuals heightened feelings of dissatisfaction. The relation between direction of counterfactual comparison and affect remained significant even after the influence of those situational factors was controlled statistically (see also Bulman & Wortman, 1977; Davis et al., 1995; Folger, Rosenfield, & Robinson, 1983). This counterfactual contrast effect is, of course, mechanistically identical to contrast effects involving salient positive or negative social-comparison targets (Brickman & Bulman, 1977; Strack, Schwarz, Chassein, Kern, & Wagner, 1990; S. Taylor, Buunk, & Aspinwall, 1990) or recollections of long past positive or negative life events (Strack, Schwarz, & Gschneidinger, 1985). In all these cases, an anchor made temporarily salient to participants created shifts in perceptions of current affect.

Less obvious effects occur when antecedent mutability is manipulated. Recall that more mutable antecedents may make counterfactuals more available, thereby creating indirectly a more salient comparison anchor. For example, the presence of exceptional (as opposed to routine) and actional (as opposed to inactional) antecedents causes more negative affective reactions to unfortunate outcomes (Gleicher et al., 1990; Kahneman & Miller, 1986; Miller & Turnbull, 1990; Landman, 1987). Thus, manipulations of mutability create more salient upward comparison anchors, thereby rendering the factual outcome more negative by contrast. More extreme emotional reactions are the result (Kahneman & Tversky, 1982b).

Beyond the generality of the contrast effect, Kahneman and Miller (1986) noted that certain emotions are specifically predicated on counterfactual inferences. These *counterfactual emotions*, such as disappointment, regret, and relief, could not occur without a prior counterfactual inference. It is difficult to experience regret per se without first noting that things might have turned out better. Landman (1993), in her extensive and insightful examination of the experience of regret, distinguished it from other types of negative affect in part by its connection to counterfactuals (see also Landman, chapter 8). Some experimental evidence supports the notion that counterfactuals play a more central role in such emotions than in other affective experiences (Boninger et al., 1994; Lecci, Okun, & Karoly, 1994). Moreover, counterfactual emotions themselves may be differentiated on the basis of the types of antecedents that are mutated. For example, Niedenthal, Tangney, and Gavanski (1994) showed that the experience of shame is predicated on counterfactual inferences that undo characterological aspects of the self (e.g., "If only I were stronger, things would've turned out better"), whereas guilt relies on counterfactual inferences that undo one's behavior (e.g., "If only I had been honest, things would've turned out better"). Temporal perspective may often interact with counterfactual thinking in determining the extent of regret. Gilovich and his colleagues (Gilovich & Medvec, 1994, chapter 9, in press; Gilovich, Medvec, & Chen, 1995) showed that people regret their actions to a greater extent in the short term, but more often regret their failures to act when looking back over longer periods of time.

Through his self-discrepancy theory, Higgins (1987) attempted to identify further the counterfactual precursors to specific emotional experiences. Dejection, as a particular subclass of negative affect, follows from the contrast between one's current life situation and an idealized, hoped-for state of affairs (e.g., "I should be able to afford a house by now"), made salient by various experimental techniques (e.g., Higgins, Klein, & Strauman, 1985). Fear and anxiety, on the other hand, may follow from the contrast between one's present situation and beliefs about what one ought to have accomplished (typically based on the expectations of others, such as one's parents).

We argued previously that downward counterfactuals tend to occur spontaneously only to the extent that a negative outcome *almost* occurred. Thus, a perception of closeness to a possible outcome triggers spontaneous downward thoughts, whereas upward counterfactuals may be spontaneously elicited not only by the perceived closeness but also by the unexpectedness or negativity of the outcomes. We noted also that counterfactuals may be generated strategically (i.e., effortfully). For example, dysphoric individuals may intentionally consider downward possibilities in order to make themselves feel better. Some preliminary evidence suggests that this pattern may occur when the outcome in question is perceived to be uncontrollable; hence, the misfortune cannot be remedied through deliberate action (Roese & Olson, 1995; see also Wills, 1981).

The research reviewed here supports the contention that emotional amplification rests on contrast effects (Miller & McFarland, 1986, discussed later; Roese, 1994); but counterfactually-mediated causal inference can also play an important role in affective experience. Consider the case of generating an upward counterfactual: A contrast effect would produce more negative affect, but the realization that a better outcome *might have occurred* may inspire hopefulness and other positive feelings. This latter effect would clearly rest on the causal inference that some action could have produced success in the past and, hence, may be employed in the future to bring about similar success. Such effects were demonstrated directly by Boninger et al. (1994; see also Gleicher et al., chapter 10). Individuals who were led to realize that an action might have produced success in the past and could well produce success in the future reported more positive affect. These effects occurred only when mutating a target action *undid* a prior negative outcome, thus linking the effect clearly to causal inference. Moreover, these effects were particularly evident in individuals dispositionally more likely to focus on future outcomes. Emotional amplification by causal inference need not proceed in a direction opposite to a contrast effect, as in the previous example. The realization that an aversive incident might have been avoided can heighten distress (e.g., "I could have *done* something!") rather than mitigate it if future possibilities are not salient to the individual.

Judgments of Victimization

Reactions to victimization are social judgments that may be potentially mediated by affect, a pattern permitting further exploration of the contrast effect and causal inference mechanisms described previously. In the case of the former, thinking that a victim's misfortune could easily have been avoided, thus providing a salient upward comparison anchor, may render the tragedy more poignant, causing the perceiver to feel greater sympathy for the victim, relative to judgments without so salient an anchor.

This logic received its initial test by Miller and McFarland (1986). Participants read of a man who was assaulted while visiting a convenience store. The man was described as visiting (a) the store he most commonly frequented, (b) another, rarely visited store for "a change of pace," or (c) the rarely visited store because the preferred store was closed for renovations. As suggested by norm theory, going to a rarely visited store (i.e., an abnormal condition) should be a more mutable antecedent than visiting a preferred store (i.e., a normal condition); hence counterfactuals should be more available in the former condition. Participants indeed recommended greater compensation for the victim in the former than in the latter condition. Compensation did not differ, however, as a function of whether the abnormal condition was internally or externally derived (conditions b vs. c), thus supporting the interpretation that it was a contrast effect rather than a causal attribution that accounted for the emotional amplification effect. Miller and McFarland, therefore, interpreted their results in terms of heightened sympathy evoked by more salient perceptions that the tragedy could have been avoided. The findings from a second study described by these authors supported this conclusion, with a replication based on a manipulation of perceived closeness to a possible outcome: The absence of a clear causal antecedent in this particular study made a causal inference mechanism interpretation particularly implausible. Macrae (1992; Macrae, Milne, & Griffiths, 1993) replicated the victim-compensation effect and further showed that people were more punitive in their judgments of perpetrators under exceptional rather than under normal circumstances.

Counterfactual effects involving causal inference have also been implicated in judgments of victimization (Branscombe, Crosby, & Weir, 1993; Branscombe & Weir, 1992; Burris & Branscombe, 1993). If the victim's actions are perceived to be abnormal (and hence more mutable) in terms of stereotype incongruency, the victim's actions may be seen as having played a greater causal role in bringing about the incident. For example, rape victims who offered a high degree of resistance (thereby disconfirming a stereotype-based expectancy of female submissiveness) were blamed more for their misfortune than those offering more moderate (and expected) resistance (Branscombe & Weir, 1992). That a counterfactually based causal inference mediated the effect of stereotype incongruity on judgments of blame was not shown directly, but the conclusions drawn by Branscombe and her colleagues are consistent with the effect-to-be-explained perspective described in our discussion of counterfactuals and causality. Stereotype incongruity is, essentially, low-consensus information (Kelley, 1967), which draws attention to an interpersonal causal background (Hilton & Slugoski, 1986). This causal background consists of more "normal," stereotypical others who presumably are not rape victims. Causality would then be ascribed to the factor that accounts for the discrepancy between the target outcome and the causal background—in this case, the personality and behavior of the target individual. Perceptions of perpetrators of negative incidents may be similarly biased by stereotype-incongruency information (Branscombe et al., 1993).

Further research is needed, however, to confirm the mechanism of counterfactual mediation. That a rape victim is judged more punitively to the extent that she actively resists her attacker is at odds with predictions resulting from more traditional attributional perspectives. Working from Kelley's (1967, 1972a) perspective, for example, weak or moderate resistance by the victim could be interpreted as a factor that facilitates rape, thus leading to the discounting of the rapist as a causal factor. In contrast, strong resistance should presumably impede the attacker; thus, if the attack nevertheless takes place, the rapist's role is augmented and may, therefore, be seen as more causally important. From this perspective, the greater the resistance offered, the less the victim should be blamed. Any evidence that the victim went out of her way to avoid her victimizing experience should therefore reduce the blame ascribed to her, not increase it. Nevertheless, Branscombe and Weir's (1992) data cannot be accounted for by this mechanism, whereas they are well explained by their norm theory account. An important theoretical issue emerging from this work is the relation between norm theory, with its focus on the deviation of outcomes from normative expectancies, and Kelleyesque attributional models, with their specification of the interplay of parallel facilitative and inhibitory causal inputs.

Suspicion

Consider a chocolate-chip-cookie-loving child permitted to have just one cookie before dinner. You know that the cookie jar contains only one chocolate chip cookie and nine oatmeal cookies. The child has been instructed to close his eyes and eat whichever cookie he grabs. The child then appears with his coveted chocolate chip cookie, proclaiming that he indeed closed his eyes and just happened to select the object of his desire. Would you be at all suspicious?

Such was the starting point for a program of research described by Miller, Turnbull, and McFarland (1989) through which they attempted to link counterfactual thinking to the phenomenology of suspicion. Unlike previous assertions that the ease of constructing an outcome alternative influences judgment, these authors suggested that the ease of mentally replicating *that same* outcome may also influence judgment. Outcomes that can be replicated in many ways are judged to be likelier than outcomes that cannot be mentally replicated. In a test of this proposition, participants were presented with either of two versions of the previously described cookie scenario. In one, the child selects the one chocolate chip from a bowl also containing 19 oatmeal cookies. In the other, the child also retrieves the chocolate chip, but the bowl initially contained 10 chocolate chip and 190 oatmeal cookies. Although the objective likelihood of selecting a chocolate chip cookie is identical in both conditions, Miller et al. expected greater suspicion when the number of ways of imagining the outcome's occurrence by chance was few than many (no other way vs. 9 other ways). As predicted, participants in the 1–20 condition were more suspicious of the child than those in the 10–200 condition.

An essential feature of Miller et al.'s (1989) theorizing was that differences in suspicion would emerge as a function of postoutcome processing rather than preoutcome expectancies. Control conditions, in which participants learned of the same proportions of cookies but did not learn what the child got, rated the likelihood of drawing a chocolate chip cookie identically in both conditions. Miller et al. concluded that although participants entered their respective conditions with identical expectancies based on the available probabilities, differences in suspicion emerged as a function of post hoc mental simulation of the outcome.

Kirkpatrick and Epstein (1992) offered a different interpretation of these findings, one drawn from their distinction between experiential (based on perhaps inaccurate rules of thumb) and rational (based on logical inferences) thought processes. These authors argued that the Miller et al. (1989) suspicion effects reflected neither mental simulation of replicated outcomes nor any specific postoutcome processing. Instead, they noted that people tend spontaneously to make experiential judgments based on common experience but are able to make rational judgments when requested to do so. Thus, participants who were more suspicious in the 1–20 condition were simply more likely to base their judgment on the experiential heuristic that a "1-in-any-large-number" probability typically carries the colloquial meaning of "extremely unlikely." In contrast, when asked to rate probability or likelihood, participants are able to bypass this heuristic, process more rationally, and respond more accurately.

Results of several studies have supported this reasoning, the most compelling of which involved participants who blindly drew beans from bowls with the prospect of winning real money. Participants would win $4 if they drew a red bean, nothing if they drew a white bean. One bowl contained 1 red and 9 white beans, the other 10 red and 90 white. Participants were much more likely to choose to draw from the 10–90 bowl than from the 1–9 bowl. Thus, when presented with an engaging situation, participants behaved exactly as Miller et al. would have predicted, but on a *preoutcome* basis, thus precluding postoutcome simulation as a mediator of the effect. Noteworthy, however, is that Miller et al. (1989) theorized that mental simulation and not postoutcome processing per se was what mediated suspicion. Kirkpatrick and Epstein (1992) did not provide evidence that directly demonstrated some other form of heuristic thinking instead of simulation as the crucial mediator. Nevertheless, their reinterpretation of findings previously ascribed to mental simulation constitutes a dangerous signal to counterfactual researchers. Direct evidence for a counterfactual mediator has been lacking in previous experimental efforts, a deficiency necessitating more compelling procedural improvements that can withstand challenges from other theoretical perspectives.

Self-Inference

Perceptions of the self represent one of the most pervasive theoretical concerns of social psychology, highlighting their central role in human existence. The contribution entailed by a counterfactual approach is a more basic, mechanistic one. As we noted in the previous sections, contrast effects cued by a salient, counterfactual anchor may be an important mechanism underlying affective experience. Linked to such affect are self-evaluations, the valence and magnitude of which vary with the nature of the counterfactual. Upward counterfactuals may trigger negative self-evaluations, with the magnitude of the discrepancy between factual and counterfactual states varying directly with the extremity of those evaluations (Davis et al., 1995; Higgins et al., 1985; Markman et al., 1993). Similarly, downward counterfactuals may elicit more positive self-evaluations that also vary with the magnitude of the factual–counterfactual discrepancy.

Counterfactual effects on self-inference may also be rooted in causal inference. A wide range of attributional research has already documented the impact of causal inference on self-evaluations (e.g., Olson & Zanna, 1990; Weiner, 1986). Roese and Olson (1993a) examined the relation between counterfactually based causal inference and the self. In two experiments, participants imagined their reactions to scenarios ending in either success or failure. Participants with high self-esteem undid success by mutating their own actions but undid failure by mutating the actions of another actor, thereby assuming credit for success but blaming others for failure (a self-serving bias). Participants with low self-esteem exhibited the reverse pattern (a self-denigrating bias). On the one hand, the findings may reflect basic motivational differences based on self-esteem: Individuals with high self-esteem are perhaps more likely to actively protect and enhance their self-image than are those with low self-esteem (Taylor &

Brown, 1988). On the other hand, these findings also echo norm theory in that self-esteem differences may entail expectancy differences, which in turn determine the content of counterfactual thoughts. Those with high self-esteem may expect success to follow from their own actions; they may, therefore, undo success by deleting their own actions. In contrast, individuals with low self-esteem expect failure and, therefore, undo failure by mutating their own actions. In either case, counterfactual inferences may influence and reinforce self-inferences, in that both those with high self-esteem and those with low self-esteem may differentially make causal judgments consistent with their respective self-images. Kasimatis and Wells (chapter 3) discuss in detail the role of self-conceptions and other individual differences in counterfactual thinking.

Expectancies

We previously noted the important relation between expectancies and counterfactuals. The disconfirmation of expectancies, either implicitly or explicitly held, increases the availability of counterfactual representations. Although counterfactuals are constructed online in response to focal outcomes, the basic substrate out of which they are generated is a priori beliefs and expectancies regarding that outcome. Counterfactuals are constructed by converting deviations back into their default expectancies, such that counterfactuals recapitulate expectancies. Informed by the postulates of norm theory, research has amply demonstrated the crucial causal linkage of expectancies to counterfactuals (Kahneman & Miller, 1986; Kahneman & Tversky, 1982b; McGill, 1993; Olson et al., in press; Wells et al., 1987).

The reverse causal relation may also be true. Because counterfactual propositions are causal propositions, they may imply appropriate future actions. For examnple, if Jake's father comes to believe that Jake would have passed an exam had Jake bought a study guide, Jake's father is highlighting the causal potency of owning a study guide. This belief suggests an expectancy for future actions. Jake's father may recommend to his son that he buy the study guide, with the expectancy that by his making use of it, Jake will improve his performance on an upcoming exam. Thus, there is an intriguing reciprocal relation between expectancies and counterfactuals. Expectancies can influence counterfactuals, and these same counterfactuals may, in turn, influence subsequent, but more specific, expectancies (Boninger et al., 1994; M. Johnson & Sherman, 1990; Olson et al., in press; Sherman, 1991). Miller and Taylor (chapter 11) discuss further the influence of counterfactuals on expectancies and how this relation may give rise to a variety of superstitious beliefs.

Roese (1994, Experiment 2) demonstrated directly the impact of counterfactuals on expectancies within the context of achievement behavior.

Participants recalled a recent exam on which they had performed poorly, then were induced to generate upward counterfactuals (how they might have performed better), downward counterfactuals (how they might have performed worse), or no counterfactuals at all. Those who generated upward counterfactuals (focusing on specific actions that might have improved their performance) subsequently gave higher intention ratings (collected in the context of a separate portion of the experiment) to perform success-facilitating behaviors for future exams, relative to the two other conditions. Certain subtypes of counterfactual thoughts (namely, upward counterfactuals) may thus lead to heightened intentions to perform relevant behaviors in the future, an effect based on a causal-inference mechanism. Roese (1994, Experiment 3) showed that these intentions are linked to behavior as well. Participants induced to generate upward as opposed to downward counterfactuals later performed better on an anagram-solving task, at least in part because they had followed through on counterfactual-related intentions. This experiment is one of the few demonstrations of counterfactual effects on actual behavior but is conceptually consistent with similar demonstrations of expectancy-based mental simulations (e.g., Sherman, Skov, Hervitz, & Stock, 1981; Taylor & Pham, in press).

Conclusion

The various consequences that may follow from counterfactual thinking reviewed in this section are organized broadly into affective and judgmental effects. These consequences may be described in terms of two distinct mechanisms: contrast effects and causal inferences. By referring explicitly to these two mechanisms in our survey of the consequences of counterfactual thinking, we hoped to integrate some previously insular findings. In the final section, we examine several issues that emerge from the counterfactual literature and point to appropriate directions for future research.

RESOLUTION

Our aim in this chapter was to review research aimed at elucidating the antecedents, processes, and consequences of counterfactual thinking. Much of this research has been informed by Kahneman and Miller's (1986) norm theory, which asserts that counterfactuals are constructed online in response to specific evoking outcomes and that the content of counterfactuals tends to recapitulate the expectancies for the target outcome. Certain elements of reality are more mutable, or mentally changeable, than others; it is these that people tend to alter in constructing a counterfactual representation. We organized our review around two stages of construction: The initial generation of counterfactual thoughts per se (availability) and the alterations to actuality within the counterfactual representation (semantic content). According to this view, the primary engine driving the evocation of counterfactuals is the motivation to undo unwanted or unexpected outcomes (outcome-based factors). Once counterfactual generation has been motivated, the factors posited in norm theory to underlie mutability (antecedent-based factors) may, in combination with some outcome-based factors, then constrain the content of resulting counterfactual representations. We have interpreted the extant counterfactual literature in light of this two-stage partition, but clearly, further work is required to document fully some of the assertions we have made. In addition, a variety of conceptual issues and potential pitfalls emerge from scrutiny of the extant literature. It is to these that we finally turn.

One question to which we have already alluded is the extent to which counterfactual processing represents a cognitive shortcut versus a more effortful mode of thinking. As originally conceived, the relative ease of constructing an alternative is a heuristic employed in a variety of judgments (Kahneman & Tversky, 1982b). In subsequent attempts to unify attributional models under a counterfactual umbrella (e.g., Hilton & Slugoski, 1986; Lipe, 1991), researchers conceived of such thought processes as a more effortful, systematic form of thinking. The available evidence points to an affirmation of both descriptions. Certainly, ease of imagery-based construction mediates many social judgments. Further, the motivational perspective that we have developed here suggests that counterfactuals are evoked automatically by certain motivating circumstances. Nevertheless, counterfactual reasoning may also be directed toward problems in effortful attempts at troubleshooting. In general, the diversity of counterfactual effects reviewed here, embracing both heuristic and systematic modes of thought, underscores their pervasive psychological importance.

Several authors have criticized the counterfactual literature for its reliance on simple, uninvolving scenario studies. We agree with the recommendation by Davis et al. (1995) and Markman et al. (1993, 1995) that future counterfactual research may proceed more profitably by using more realistic, mundane, yet personally involving social situations. As Markman et al. (1995) pointed out, the scenario paradigms dominating previous research may be so uninvolving as to preclude meaningful conclusions regarding affect and motivation. We adopt a somewhat more cautious stance, however. Although we agree that scenario studies are not without their drawbacks, their heuristic value for initial theory as-

46   ROESE AND OLSON

sessment and extension is undeniable. Thus, scenario studies should
perhaps not be used as publishable end points for research programs,
but as starting points. Their results may then be combined with findings
based on other paradigms, providing a much needed methodological
convergence on relevant theoretical conclusions. Perhaps a more important methodological issue with clear conceptual implications is the lack
of behavioral measures in this literature. With very few exceptions, counterfactual research has been based on simple paper-and-pencil ratings.
But also with few exceptions, however, theory has been predicated on
the expectation that counterfactuals involve important behavioral consequences. As well, everyday behavior provides a continuous stream of
information theorized to influence counterfactual representations. By in-
corporating real behavior into counterfactual research methodologies, the
field can not only generate a more compelling empirical base but also
tap into a rich source of fresh insight. The work presented in this volume
represents a clear move in this direction.

   Perhaps the most pervasive challenge to future counterfactual research
is the persistent lack of direct evidence that supports the mediating role
of counterfactuals in various social judgments. Typically, a manipulation
of mutability is followed by some affective or judgmental measure, with
a particular counterfactual thought assumed to mediate the observed
effects (e.g., Branscombe & Weir, 1992; Landman, 1987; Macrae, 1992;
Miller & McFarland, 1986; Miller et al., 1989). Although such demonstrations may be consistent with counterfactual theory, they do not rule out
competing perspectives with similar predictions but based on different
mechanisms (e.g., Epstein et al., 1992; Kirkpatrick & Epstein, 1992). The
present situation parallels that of dissonance theory in the late 1960s:
With self-perception theory challenging its presumed theoretical basis by
making parallel but mechanistically divergent predictions, researchers in
the 1970s and early 1980s were forced toward subtler experimental procedures that could provide more exact specification of the mechanism of
dissonance reduction (Cooper & Fazio, 1984; Croyle & Cooper, 1983;
Zanna & Cooper, 1976). We believe similar directions are in order for
counterfactual research. Although we agree with most of the conclusions
derived from the research presently reviewed, we fear challenges from
noncounterfactual perspectives that are difficult to refute in the absence
of more compelling mechanistic evidence. Therefore, we encourage counterfactual researchers to develop subtler and more sophisticated paradigms to provide more compelling documentation of the role of counterfactual thought processes in social judgment.

   Counterfactual thinking is an essential feature of consciousness. Few
indeed have never pondered a lost opportunity nor regretted a foolish
utterance. And as Steiner (1975) pointed out, it is from counterfactual

articulations of better possible pasts that individuals may realize more desirable futures. Indeed, counterfactual thought processes may be one of the central components of the human experience. Recent neurological findings indicate that among the deficits that accrue from damage to the prefrontal cortex (such as global deficits in personality, memory, and insight) is an inability to generate counterfactual thoughts (Knight & Grabowecky, 1995). Echoing the theme of functionality that pervades much of this volume, these authors noted that "without such [mental] simulations, it is difficult [for individuals with prefrontal cortex damage] to avoid making the same mistakes over and over again" (p. 1359). Counterfactual thoughts represent an empirically definable and measurable feature of individuals' mental lives; research examining these thoughts may therefore be uniquely poised to shed new light on the very essence of human consciousness. Given the implications of research on counterfactual thinking for numerous domains of psychology, we anticipate eagerly the many insights that may be gleaned from future work by social psychologists in this rapidly expanding field.

ACKNOWLEDGMENTS

This chapter was written while the first author was supported by a postdoctoral fellowship and while the second author was supported by a research grant, both from the Social Sciences and Humanities Research Council of Canada. We are grateful to Nyla Branscombe, Faith Gleicher, Karen Grabowski, Dale Miller, and Jeff Sherman for their valuable comments on previous drafts of this chapter. Principal writing of this chapter took place while the first author was a postdoctoral fellow at the University of California at Santa Barbara. The ideas expressed here benefited greatly from comments by the faculty and graduate student participants of a counterfactual thinking discussion group that met at UCSB during the 1993–94 academic year.

REFERENCES

Anderson, C. A., & Godfrey, S. S. (1987). Thoughts about actions: The effect of specificity and availability of imagined behavioral scripts on expectations about oneself and others. *Social Cognition, 5,* 238–258.

Au, T. K. (1983). Chinese and English counterfactuals: The Sapir–Whorf hypothesis revisited. *Cognition, 15,* 155–187.

Au, T. K. (1984). Counterfactuals: In reply to Alfred Bloom. *Cognition, 17,* 288–302.

Berlyne, D. E. (1960). *Conflict, arousal, and curiosity.* New York: McGraw–Hill.

Berscheid, E., Graziano, W., Monson, T., & Dermer, M. (1976). Outcome dependency: Attention, attribution, and attraction. *Journal of Personality and Social Psychology, 34,* 978–989.

Bloom, A. H. (1981). *The linguistic shaping of thought: A study in the impact of language on thinking in China and the West.* Hillsdale, NJ: Lawrence Erlbaum Associates.

Bloom, A. H. (1984). Caution—the words you use may affect what you say: A response to Terry Kit-Fong Au's "Chinese and English counterfactuals: The Sapir–Whorf hypothesis revisited." *Cognition, 17,* 275–287.

Bohner, G., Bless, H., Schwarz, N., & Strack, F. (1988). What triggers causal attributions? The impact of valence and subjective probability. *European Journal of Social Psychology, 18,* 335–345.

Bolles, R. C. (1972). Reinforcement, expectancy, and learning. *Psychological Review, 79,* 394–409.

Boninger, D. S., Gleicher, F., & Strathman, A. (1994). Counterfactual thinking: From what might have been to what may be. *Journal of Personality and Social Psychology, 67,* 297–307.

Bouts, P., Spears, R., & van der Pligt, J. (1992). Counterfactual processing and the correspondence between events and outcomes: Normality versus value. *European Journal of Social Psychology, 22,* 387–396.

Braine, M. D., & O'Brian, D. P. (1991). A theory of if: A lexical entry, reasoning program, and pragmatic principles. *Psychological Review, 98,* 182–203.

Branscombe, N. R., Crosby, P., & Weir, J. A. (1993). Social inferences concerning male and female homeowners who use a gun to shoot an intruder. *Aggressive Behavior, 19,* 113–124.

Branscombe, N. R., & Weir, J. A. (1992). Resistance as stereotype-inconsistency: Consequences for judgments of rape victims. *Journal of Social and Clinical Psychology, 11,* 80–102.

Brickman, P., & Bulman, R. J. (1977). Pleasure and pain in social comparison. In J. M. Suls & R. L. Miller (Eds.), *Social comparison processes: Theoretical and empirical perspectives* (pp. 149–186). Washington, DC: Hemisphere.

Brickman, P., Ryan, K., & Wortman, C. B. (1975). Causal chains: Attribution of responsibility as a function of immediate and prior causes. *Journal of Personality and Social Psychology, 32,* 1060–1067.

Buck, M. L., & Miller, D. T. (1994). Reactions to incongruous negative life events. *Social Justice Research, 7,* 29–46.

Bulman, R. J., & Wortman, C. B. (1977). Attribution of blame and coping in the "real world": Severe accident victims react to their lot. *Journal of Personality and Social Psychology, 35,* 351–363.

Burris, C. T., & Branscombe, N. R. (1993). Racism, counterfactual thinking, and judgment severity. *Journal of Applied Social Psychology, 23,* 980–995.

Carpenter, P. A. (1973). Extracting information from counterfactual clauses. *Journal of Verbal Learning and Verbal Behavior, 12,* 512–521.

Chisholm, R. M. (1946). The contrary-to-fact conditional. *Mind, 55,* 289–307.

Cooper, J., & Fazio, R. H. (1984). A new look at dissonance theory. In L. Berkowitz (Ed.), *Advances in experimental social psychology* (Vol. 17, pp. 229–266). New York: Academic Press.

Croyle, R., & Cooper, J. (1983). Dissonance arousal: Physiological evidence. *Journal of Personality and Social Psychology, 45,* 782–791.

Davis, C. G., Lehman, D. R., Wortman, C. B., Silver, R. C., & Thompson, S. C. (1995). The undoing of traumatic life events. *Personality and Social Psychology Bulletin, 21,* 109–124.

Dennett, D. C. (1991). *Consciousness explained.* Boston: Little, Brown.

Dermer, M., Cohen, S. J., Jacobsen, E., & Anderson, E. A. (1979). Evaluative judgments of aspects of life as a function of vicarious exposure to hedonic extremes. *Journal of Personality and Social Psychology, 37,* 247–260.

Deutsch, D., & Lockwood, M. (1994). The quantum physics of time travel. *Scientific American, 270*(3), 68–74.

Dunning, D., & Parpal, M. (1989). Mental addition and subtraction in counterfactual reasoning: On assessing the impact of actions and life events. *Journal of Personality and Social Psychology, 57,* 5–15.

Eagly, A. H., & Chaiken, S. (1993). *The psychology of attitudes.* Fort Worth, TX: Harcourt, Brace, Jovanovich.

Einhorn, H. J., & Hogarth, R. M. (1986). Judging probable cause. *Psychological Bulletin, 99,* 3–19.

Epstein, S., Lipson, A., Holstein, C., & Huh, E. (1992). Irrational reactions to negative outcomes: Evidence for two conceptual systems. *Journal of Personality and Social Psychology, 62,* 328–339.

Fazio, R. H., Sherman, S. J., & Herr, P. M. (1982). The feature-positive effect in the self-perception process: Does not doing matter as much as doing? *Journal of Personality and Social Psychology, 42,* 404–411.

Fearon, J. D. (1991). Counterfactuals and hypothesis testing in political science. *World Politics, 43,* 169–195.

Fiedler, K. (1988). Emotional mood, cognitive style, and behavior regulation. In K. Fiedler & J. Forgas (Eds.), *Affect, cognition, and social behavior* (pp. 100–119). Toronto: Hogrefe International.

Fillenbaum, S. (1974). Information amplified: Memory for counterfactual conditionals. *Journal of Experimental Psychology, 102,* 44–49.

Fischhoff, B. (1982). For those condemned to study the past: Heuristics and biases in hindsight. In D. Kahneman, P. Slovic, & A. Tversky, (Eds.), *Judgment under uncertainty: Heuristics and biases* (pp. 335–351). New York: Cambridge University Press.

Flaubert, G. (1950). *Madame Bovary* (A. Russell, Trans.). London: Penguin. (Original work published 1857)

Folger, R. (1984). Perceived injustice, referent cognitions, and the concept of comparison level. *Representative Research in Social Psychology, 14,* 88–108.

Folger, R., Rosenfield, D., & Robinson, T. (1983). Relative deprivation and procedural justifications. *Journal of Personality and Social Psychology, 45,* 268–273.

Gavanski, I., & Wells, G. L. (1989). Counterfactual processing of normal and exceptional events. *Journal of Experimental Social Psychology, 25,* 314–325.

Gilovich, T., & Medvec, V. H. (1994). The temporal pattern to the experience of regret. *Journal of Personality and Social Psychology, 67,* 357–365.

Gilovich, T., & Medvec, V. H. (in press). The experience of regret: What, when, and why? *Psychological Review.*

Gilovich, T., Medvec, V. H., & Chen, S. (1995). Commission, omission, and dissonance reduction: Coping with the "Monty Hall" problem. *Personality and Social Psychology Bulletin, 21,* 182–190.

Girotto, V., Legrenzi, P., Rizzo, A. (1991). Event controllability in counterfactual thinking. *Acta Psychologica, 78,* 111–133.

Gleicher, F., Kost, K. A., Baker, S. M., Strathman, A. J., Richman, S. A., & Sherman, S. J. (1990). The role of counterfactual thinking in judgments of affect. *Personality and Social Psychology Bulletin, 16,* 284–295.

Goodman, N. (1947). The problem of counterfactual conditionals. *Journal of Philosophy, 44,* 113–128.

Goodman, N. (1983). *Fact, fiction, and forecast* (4th ed.). Cambridge, MA: Harvard University Press.

Hansen, R. D., & Hall, C. A. (1985). Discounting and augmenting facilitative and inhibitory forces: The winner takes almost all. *Journal of Personality and Social Psychology, 49,* 1482–1493.

Harkness, A. R., DeBono, K. G., & Borgida, E. (1985). Personal involvement and strategies for making contingency judgments: A stake in the dating game makes a difference. *Journal of Personality and Social Psychology, 49*, 22–32.

Hart, H. L., & Honoré, A. M. (1959). *Causation and the law.* Oxford, England: Clarendon.

Hastie, R. (1984). Causes and effects of causal attributions. *Journal of Personality and Social Psychology, 46*, 44–56.

Heider, F. (1958). *The psychology of interpersonal relations.* New York: Wiley.

Helson, H. (1964). *Adaptation-level theory.* New York: Harper & Row.

Higgins, E. T. (1987). Self-discrepancy: A theory relating self and affect. *Psychological Review, 94*, 319–340.

Higgins, E. T., Klein, R., & Strauman, T. (1985). Self-concept discrepancy theory: A psychological model for distinguishing among different aspects of depression and anxiety. *Social Cognition, 3*, 51–76.

Hilton, D. J. (1990). Conversational processes and causal explanations. *Psychological Bulletin, 107*, 65–81.

Hilton, D. J., & Slugoski, B. R. (1986). Knowledge-based causal attribution: The abnormal conditions focus model. *Psychological Review, 93*, 136–153.

Hoch, S. J. (1985). Counterfactual reasoning and accuracy in predicting personal events. *Journal of Experimental Psychology: Learning, Memory, and Cognition, 11*, 719–731.

Hofstadter, D. R. (1979). *Gödel, Escher, Bach: An eternal golden braid.* New York: Vintage Books.

Hofstadter, D. R. (1985). *Metamagical themas: Questing for the essence of mind and pattern.* New York: Basic Books.

Hsee, H. K., Salovey, P., Abelson, R. P. (1994). The quasi-acceleration relation: Satisfaction as a function of the change of velocity over time. *Journal of Experimental Social Psychology, 30*, 96–111.

Isen, A. M., & Means, B. (1983). The influence of positive affect on decision-making strategy. *Social Cognition, 2*, 18–31.

Jellison, J. M., & Green, J. (1981). A self-presentation approach to the fundamental attribution error: The norm of internality. *Journal of Personality and Social Psychology, 40*, 643–649.

Johnson, J. T. (1986). The knowledge of what might have been: Affective and attributional consequences of near outcomes. *Personality and Social Psychology Bulletin, 12*, 51–62.

Johnson, J. T., Boyd, K. R., & Magnani, P. S. (1994). Causal reasoning in the attribution of rare and common events. *Journal of Personality and Social Psychology, 66*, 229–242.

Johnson, M. K., & Sherman, S. J. (1990). Constructing and reconstructing the past and the future in the present. In E. T. Higgins & R. M. Sorrentino (Eds.), *Handbook of motivation and cognition: Foundations of social behavior* (Vol. 2, pp. 482–526). New York: Guilford.

Jones, E. E., & Davis, K. E. (1965). From acts to dispositions: The attribution process in person perception. In L. Berkowitz (Ed.), *Advances in experimental social psychology* (Vol. 2, pp. 219–216). New York: Academic Press.

Kahneman, D., & Miller, D. T. (1986). Norm theory: Comparing reality to its alternatives. *Psychological Review, 93*, 136–153.

Kahneman, D., & Tversky, A. (1982a). The psychology of preferences. *Scientific American, 246*(1), 160–173.

Kahneman, D., & Tversky, A. (1982b). The simulation heuristic. In D. Kahneman, P. Slovic, & A. Tversky, (Eds.), *Judgment under uncertainty: Heuristics and biases* (pp. 201–208). New York: Cambridge University Press.

Kahneman, D., & Varey, C. A. (1990). Propensities and counterfactuals: The loser that almost won. *Journal of Personality and Social Psychology, 59*, 1101–1110.

Kanazawa, S. (1992). Outcome or expectancy? Antecedent of spontaneous causal attribution. *Personality and Social Psychology Bulletin, 18*, 659–668.

Kelley, H. H. (1967). Attribution in social psychology. In D. Levine (Ed.), *Nebraska symposium on motivation* (Vol. 15, pp. 192–240). Lincoln: University of Nebraska Press.

Kelley, H. H. (1972a). Attribution in social interaction. In E. E. Jones, D. E. Kanouse, H. H. Kelley, R. E. Nisbett, S. Valins, & B. Weiner (Eds.), *Attribution: Perceiving the causes of behavior* (pp. 1–26). Morristown, NJ: General Learning Press.

Kelley, H. H. (1972b). Causal schemata and the attribution process. In E. E. Jones, D. E. Kanouse, H. H. Kelley, R. E. Nisbett, S. Valins, & B. Weiner (Eds.), *Attribution: Perceiving the causes of behavior* (pp. 151–174). Morristown, NJ: General Learning Press.

Kirkpatrick, L. A., & Epstein, S. (1992). Cognitive-experiential self-theory and subjective probability: Further evidence for two conceptual systems. *Journal of Personality and Social Psychology, 63*, 534–544.

Knight, R. T., & Grabowecky, M. (1995). Escape from linear time: Prefontal cortex and conscious experience. In M. S. Gazzaniga (Ed.), *The cognitive neurosciences* (pp. 1357–1371). Cambridge, MA: MIT Press.

Kvart, I. (1986). *A theory of counterfactuals.* Indianapolis, IN: Hackett.

Lalljee, M., & Abelson, R. P. (1983). The organization of explanations. In M. Hewstone (Ed.), *Attribution theory: Social and functional extensions* (pp. 65–80). Oxford, England: Blackwell.

Landman, J. (1987). Regret and elation following action and inaction: Affective responses to positive versus negative outcomes. *Personality and Social Psychology Bulletin, 13*, 524–536.

Landman, J. (1993). *Regret: The persistence of the possible.* New York: Oxford University Press.

Langer, E. J. (1975). The illusion of control. *Journal of Personality and Social Psychology, 32*, 311–328.

Lardière, D. (1992). On the linguistic shaping of thought: Another response to Alfred Bloom. *Language in Society, 21*, 231–251.

Lecci, L., Okun, M. A., & Karoly, P. (1994). Life regrets and current goals as predictors of psychological adjustment. *Journal of Personality and Social Psychology, 66*, 731–741.

Lewin, K. (1936). *Principles of topological psychology.* New York: McGraw–Hill.

Lewin, K. (1951). *Field theory in social science: Selected theoretical papers.* New York: Harper & Row.

Lewin, K., Dembo, T., Festinger, L., & Sears, P. S. (1944). Level of aspiration. In J. M. Hunt (Ed.), *Personality and the behavior disorders* (pp. 333–378). New York: Roland Press.

Lewis, D. (1973a). Causation. *Journal of Philosophy, 70*, 556–567.

Lewis, D. (1973b). *Counterfactuals.* Cambridge, MA: Harvard University Press.

Lewis, D. (1986). *On the plurality of worlds.* New York: Basil Blackwell.

Lipe, M. G. (1991). Counterfactual reasoning as a framework for attribution theories. *Psychological Bulletin, 109*, 456–471.

Liu, L. G. (1985). Reasoning counterfactually in Chinese: Are there any obstacles? *Cognition, 21*, 239–270.

Loux, M. J. (1979). Introduction: Modality and metaphysics. In M. J. Loux (Ed.), *The possible and the actual: Readings in the metaphysics of modality* (pp. 15–64). Ithaca, NY: Cornell University Press.

Lundberg, C. G., & Frost, D. E. (1992). Counterfactuals in financial decision making. *Acta Psychologica, 79*, 227–244.

Mackie, J. L. (1974). *Cement of the universe: A study of causation.* London: Oxford University Press.

Macrae, C. N. (1992). A tale of two curries: Counterfactual thinking and accident-related judgments. *Personality and Social Psychology Bulletin, 18*, 84–87.

Macrae, C. N., & Milne, A. B. (1992). A curry for your thoughts: Empathic effects on counterfactual thinking. *Personality and Social Psychology Bulletin, 18*, 625–630.

Macrae, C. N., Milne, A. B., & Griffiths, R. J. (1993). Counterfactual thinking and the perception of criminal behaviour. *British Journal of Psychology, 84*, 221–226.

Markman, K. D., Gavanski, I., Sherman, S. J., & McMullen, M. N. (1993). The mental simulation of better and worse possible worlds. *Journal of Experimental Social Psychology, 29*, 87–109.

Markman, K. D., Gavanski, I., Sherman, S. J., & McMullen, M. N. (1995). The impact of perceived control on the imagination of better and worse possible worlds. *Personality and Social Psychology Bulletin, 21*, 588–595.

Markovits, H., & Vachon, R. (1989). Reasoning with contrary-to-fact propositions. *Journal of Experimental Child Psychology, 47*, 398–412.

Markus, H. R., & Kitayama, S. (1991). Culture and the self: Implications for cognition, emotion, and motivation. *Psychological Bulletin, 98*, 224–253.

McClelland, D. C., Atkinson, J. W., Clark, R. A., & Lowell, E. L. (1953). *The achievement motive*. New York: Appleton–Century–Crofts.

McFarland, C., & Ross, M. (1982). Impact of causal attributions on affective reactions to success and failure. *Journal of Personality and Social Psychology, 43*, 937–946.

McGill, A. L. (1989). Context effects in judgments of causation. *Journal of Personality and Social Psychology, 57*, 189–200.

McGill, A. L. (1990a). Conjunctive explanations: The effect of comparison of the target episode to a contrasting background instance. *Social Cognition, 8*, 362–382.

McGill, A. L. (1990b). The effect of direction of comparison on the selection of causal explanations. *Journal of Experimental Social Psychology, 26*, 93–107.

McGill, A. L. (1991). The influence of the causal background on the selection of causal explanations. *British Journal of Social Psychology, 30*, 79–87.

McGill, A. L. (1993). Selection of a causal background: Role of expectation versus feature mutability. *Journal of Personality and Social Psychology, 64*, 701–707.

McGill, A. L., & Klein, J. G. (1993). Contrastive and counterfactual thinking in causal judgment. *Journal of Personality and Social Psychology, 64*, 897–905.

Meyers–Levy, J., & Maheswaran, D. (1992). When timing matters: The influence of temporal distance on consumers' affective and persuasive responses. *Journal of Consumer Research, 19*, 424–433.

Mill, J. S. (1872). *A system of logic, racionative and inductive* (8th ed.). London: Longmans, Green, & Reader. (Original work published 1843)

Miller, D. T., & Gunasegaram, S. (1990). Temporal order and the perceived mutability of events: Implications for blame assignment. *Journal of Personality and Social Psychology, 59*, 1111–1118.

Miller, D. T., & McFarland, C. (1986). Counterfactual thinking and victim compensation: A test of norm theory. *Personality and Social Psychology Bulletin, 12*, 513–519.

Miller, D. T., Taylor, B., & Buck, M. L. (1991). Gender gaps: Who needs to be explained? *Journal of Personality and Social Psychology, 61*, 5–12.

Miller, D. T., & Turnbull, W. (1990). The counterfactual fallacy: Confusing what might have been with what ought to have been. *Social Justice Research, 4*, 1–19.

Miller, D. T., Turnbull, W., & McFarland, C. (1989). When a coincidence is suspicious: The role of mental simulation. *Journal of Personality and Social Psychology, 57*, 581–589.

Miller, D. T., Turnbull, W., & McFarland, C. (1990). Counterfactual thinking and social perception: Thinking about what might have been. In M. P. Zanna (Ed.), *Advances in experimental social psychology* (Vol. 23, pp. 305–331). New York: Academic Press.

N'gbala, A., & Branscombe, N. R. (1995). Mental simulation and causal attribution: When simulating an event does not affect fault assignment. *Journal of Experimental Social Psychology, 31*, 139–162.

Niedenthal, P. M., Tangney, J. P., & Gavanski, I. (1994). "If only I weren't" versus "If only I hadn't": Distinguishing shame and guilt in counterfactual thinking. *Journal of Personality and Social Psychology, 67*, 585–595.

Nute, D. (1980). *Topics in conditional logic*. Dordrecht, Holland: D. Reidel.

Olson, J. M., Roese, N. J., & Zanna, M. P. (in press). Expectancies. In E. T. Higgins & A. W. Kruglanski (Eds.), *Social psychology: Handbook of basic principles*. New York: Guilford.

Olson, J. M., & Zanna, M. P. (Eds.). (1990). *Self-inference processes: The Ontario symposium* (Vol. 6). Hillsdale, NJ: Lawrence Erlbaum Associates.

Pyszczynski, T. A., & Greenberg, J. (1981). Role of disconfirmed expectancies in the instigation of attributional processing. *Journal of Personality and Social Psychology, 40*, 31–38.

Reichenbach, H. (1976). *Laws, modalities, and counterfactuals*. Los Angeles: University of California Press.

Rescher, N. (1964). *Hypothetical reasoning*. Amsterdam: North–Holland.

Rescher, N. (1969). *Essays in philosophical analysis*. Pittsburgh, PA: University of Pittsburgh Press.

Rescher, N. (1975). *A theory of possibility*. Oxford, England: Basil Blackwell.

Rescher, N. (1979). The ontology of the possible. In M. J. Loux (Ed.), *The possible and the actual: Readings in the metaphysics of modality* (pp. 166–189). Ithaca, NY: Cornell University Press.

Revlis, R., & Hayes, J. R. (1972). The primacy of generalities in hypothetical reasoning. *Cognitive Psychology, 3*, 268–290.

Revlis, R., Lipkin, S. G., & Hayes, J. R. (1971). The importance of universal quantifiers in a hypothetical reasoning task. *Journal of Verbal Learning and Verbal Behavior, 10*, 86–91.

Roese, N. J. (1994). The functional basis of counterfactual thinking. *Journal of Personality and Social Psychology, 66*, 805–818.

Roese, N. J., Black, M., & Olson, J. M. (1994). *Perceived similarity and defensive counterfactual thinking: Evidence for motivational determinants of counterfactual content*. Unpublished manuscript.

Roese, N. J., & Olson, J. M. (1993a). Self-esteem and counterfactual thinking. *Journal of Personality and Social Psychology, 65*, 199–206.

Roese, N. J., & Olson, J. M. (1993b). The structure of counterfactual thought. *Personality and Social Psychology Bulletin, 19*, 312–319.

Roese, N. J., & Olson, J. M. (1995). Outcome controllability and counterfactual thinking. *Personality and Social Psychology Bulletin, 21*, 620–628.

Ross, L. (1977). The intuitive psychologist and his shortcomings: Distortions in the attribution process. In L. Berkowitz (Ed.), *Advances in experimental social psychology* (Vol. 10, pp. 174–221). New York: Academic Press.

Ross, L., & Nisbett, R. E. (1991). *The person and the situation: Perspectives of social psychology*. New York: McGraw–Hill.

Sanbonmatsu, D. M., Akimoto, S. A., & Biggs, A. (1993). Overestimating causality: Attributing effects of confirmatory processing. *Journal of Personality and Social Psychology, 65*, 892–903.

Schopenhauer, A. (1970). *Essays and aphorisms* (R. J. Hollingdale, Trans.). London: Penguin. (Original work published 1851)

Schwarz, N. (1990). Feelings as information: Informational and motivational functions of affective states. In E. T. Higgins & R. M. Sorrentino (Eds.), *Handbook of motivation and cognition: Foundations of social behavior* (Vol. 2, pp. 527–561). New York: Guilford.

Schwarz, N., & Bless, H. (1992). Constructing reality and its alternatives: An inclusion/exclusion model of assimilation and contrast effects in social judgment. In L. L. Martin & A. Tesser (Eds.), *The construction of social judgment* (pp. 217–245). Hillsdale, NJ: Lawrence Erlbaum Associates.

Sherif, M., & Hovland, C. I. (1961). *Social judgment: Assimilation and contrast effects in communication and attitude change*. New Haven, CT: Yale University Press.

Sherman, S. J. (1991). Thought systems for the past as well as for the future. In R. S. Wyer, Jr. & T. K. Srull (Eds.), *Advances in social cognition, Vol. 4: The content, structure, and operation of thought systems* (pp. 173–195). Hillsdale, NJ: Lawrence Erlbaum Associates.

Sherman, S. J., Skov, R. B., Hervitz, E. F., & Stock, C. B. (1981). The effects of explaining hypothetical future events: From possibility to probability to actuality and beyond. *Journal of Experimental Social Psychology, 17,* 142–158.

Slugoski, B. R., Lalljee, M., Lamb, R., & Ginsburg, G. P. (1993). Attribution in conversational context: Effect of mutual knowledge on explanation-giving. *European Journal of Social Psychology, 23,* 219–238.

Steiner, G. (1975). *After Babel: Aspects of language and translation.* New York: Oxford University Press.

Stern, L. D., Marrs, S., Millar, M. G., & Cole, E. (1984). Processing time and the recall of inconsistent and consistent behaviors of individuals and groups. *Journal of Personality and Social Psychology, 47,* 253–262.

Sternberg, R. J., & Gastel, J. (1989a). Coping with novelty in human intelligence: An empirical investigation. *Intelligence, 13,* 187–197.

Sternberg, R. J., & Gastel, J. (1989b). If dancers ate their shoes: Inductive reasoning with factual and counterfactual premises. *Memory and Cognition, 17,* 1–10.

Strack, F., Schwarz, N., Chassein, B., Kern, D., & Wagner, D. (1990). Salience of comparison standards and the activation of social norms: Consequences for judgments of happiness and their communication. *British Journal of Social Psychology, 29,* 303–314.

Strack, F., Schwarz, N., & Gschneidinger, E. (1985). Happiness and reminiscing: The role of time perspective, affect, and mode of thinking. *Journal of Personality and Social Psychology, 49,* 1460–1469.

Swain, M. (1978). A counterfactual analysis of event causation. *Philosophical Studies, 34,* 1–19.

Taylor, S. E. (1991). Asymmetrical effects of positive and negative events: The mobilization–minimization hypothesis. *Psychological Bulletin, 110,* 67–85.

Taylor, S. E., & Brown, J. D. (1988). Illusion and well-being: A social psychological perspective on mental health. *Psychological Bulletin, 103,* 193–210.

Taylor, S. E., Buunk, B. P., & Aspinwall, L. G. (1990). Social comparison, stress, and coping. *Personality and Social Psychology Bulletin, 16,* 74–89.

Taylor, S. E., & Fiske, S. T. (1978). Salience, attention, and attribution: Top of the head phenomena. In L. Berkowitz (Ed.), *Advances in experimental social psychology* (Vol. 11, pp. 249–288). New York: Academic Press.

Taylor, S. E., & Pham, L. B. (in press). Mental simulation, motivation, and action. In P. M. Gollwitzer & J. A. Bargh (Eds.), *Action science: Linking cognition and motivation to behavior.* New York: Guilford.

Taylor, S. E., & Schneider, S. K. (1989). Coping and the simulation of events. *Social Cognition, 7,* 174–194.

Tetlock, P. E., & Belkin, A. (1994). *Counterfactual thought experiments in world politics: Logical, methodological, and psychological perspectives.* Unpublished manuscript.

Thibaut, J. H., & Kelley, H. H. (1959). *The social psychology of groups.* New York: Wiley.

Tolman, E. C. (1932). *Purposive behavior in animals and men.* New York: Appleton–Century–Crofts.

Turnbull, W. (1981). Naive conceptions of free will and the deterministic paradox. *Canadian Journal of Behavioural Science, 13,* 1–13.

Vinokur, A., & Ajzen, I. (1982). Relative importance of prior and immediate causes: A causal primacy effect. *Journal of Personality and Social Psychology, 42,* 820–829.

Vorster, J., & Schuring, G. (1989). Language and thought: Developmental perspectives on counterfactual conditionals. *South African Journal of Psychology, 19,* 34–38.

Weiner, B. (1985). "Spontaneous" causal thinking. *Psychological Bulletin, 97*, 74–84.

Weiner, B. (1986). *An attributional theory of motivation and emotion.* New York: Springer–Verlag.

Weinstein, N. D. (1980). Unrealistic optimism about future life events. *Journal of Personality and Social Psychology, 39*, 806–820.

Wells, G. L., & Gavanski, I. (1989). Mental simulation of causality. *Journal of Personality and Social Psychology, 56*, 161–169.

Wells, G. L., Taylor, B. R., & Turtle, J. W. (1987). The undoing of scenarios. *Journal of Personality and Social Psychology, 53*, 421–430.

White, P. A. (1990). Ideas about causation in philosophy and psychology. *Psychological Bulletin, 108*, 3–18.

Wills, T. A. (1981). Downward comparison principles in social psychology. *Psychological Bulletin, 90*, 245–271.

Wing, C. S., & Scholnick, E. K. (1986). Understanding the language of reasoning: Cognitive, linguistic, and developmental influences. *Journal of Psycholinguistic Research, 15*, 383–401.

Zanna, M. P., & Cooper, J. (1976). Dissonance and the attribution process. In J. H. Harvey, W. J. Ickes, & R. F. Kidd (Eds.), *New directions in attribution research* (Vol. 1, pp. 199–217). Hillsdale, NJ: Lawrence Erlbaum Associates.

2

Counterfactual Constraints

Eric P. Seelau
Sheila M. Seelau
Gary L. Wells
Paul D. Windschitl
Iowa State University

There is a delightful, creative short story written by Roger Zelazny (1981) in which time reverses for a man who then manages to change a critical event and undo his wife's untimely death.

> He blew smoke through the cigarette and it grew longer. The clock told him it was 10:33 going on 10:32. . . . He turned the pages from left to right, his eyes retracing their path back along the line. (p. 417)

Zelazny captures the reader's fascination and elicits occasional surprise at what time reversal would be like:

> He raised the telephone, said "good-bye," untold Murray that he would not be coming to work again tomorrow, listened a moment, recradled the phone and looked at it as it rang. . . . He backed his way to the funeral parlor, parked it, and climbed into the limousine. They backed all the way to the graveyard. . . . The casket was taken back to the hearse and returned to the funeral parlor. . . . The tears ran up his cheeks. (pp. 420–421)

Time reversal takes the man back to a heated argument that prompted his wife's stormy exit from their house on the evening of her death. Transported in time, the man is able to alter a critical event: Rather than stubbornly refusing to give in, he apologizes to his wife. By changing his response, the man effectively prevents his wife's tragic death.

In recent years, social and cognitive psychologists have taken interest in people's ability to mentally simulate changes to antecedent events in order to undo factual outcomes. This process of mental simulation has been called *counterfactual thinking*, imagining how a factual outcome could have been otherwise, given different circumstances (Kahneman & Tversky, 1982). Following an outcome, especially an unexpected or emotionally impactful one, people sometimes engage in a search for the causes of the outcome. This tendency is true of both dramatic outcomes that almost occurred and those that almost did not occur. By engaging in counterfactual thinking, people are able to alter preceding events in their minds and to consider alternatives to the outcome that occurred.

In Zelazny's (1981) "Divine Madness," the man learns that the events preceding his wife's death can actually be altered. His motive for changing the course of events is quite clear: to undo his wife's death. Given that people in the real world cannot alter the flow of past events, it is somewhat less clear why they engage in counterfactual thinking. One function of counterfactual thought is to help people understand why something happened. Understanding the causal role of preceding events may help people to avoid similar negative outcomes or to replicate positive outcomes in the future (e.g., Wells, Taylor, & Turtle, 1987). Understanding, prediction, and control are only a few of the reasons one may engage in counterfactual thinking. In this chapter, we discuss how various reasons for considering alternatives can affect both the process of counterfactual thinking and the outcome of that process.

Theory and research on counterfactual thinking have generally taken two directions. One line of research has been directed primarily at the question of how or whether counterfactual thoughts affect other types of judgments. The assumption is that, although people cannot alter reality as could the character in Zelazny's story, counterfactual thinking can have a profound effect on how they interpret and react to reality. To test this assumption, a number of researchers have utilized scenarios in which the antecedent events leading to a dramatic outcome are varied or in which the outcome itself is varied (Gleicher et al., 1990; Johnson, 1986; Landman, 1987; Weiner et al., 1994; Wells & Gavanski, 1989). Participants in these studies were asked to make various judgments about the characters in a scenario, including assessments of blame, causality, personality characteristics, and affective reactions. Although the participants were not always asked to consider alternatives to reality, that is, to engage in counterfactual thinking, their judgments generally appeared to be affected by the consideration of "what might have been." For example, Landman (1987) described an *actor effect*, by which respondents assumed a stronger affective reaction for people who undertook actions preceding a dramatic outcome than for those who failed to act but experienced the same outcome. Specifically, actors were assumed to feel more regret for a negative outcome and more elation for a positive outcome than were nonactors. For instance, respondents judged that a man who changed employers and was subsequently laid off from work would feel more regret than a man who merely considered changing employers before being laid off. Similarly, respondents judged the elation felt by a person who attained a positive outcome following an action to be greater than the elation felt by a person who attained the same positive outcome following inaction.

Understanding why the judgments concerning actors and nonactors differ is difficult, unless it can be assumed that people were entertaining counterfactual scenarios. Apparently the process of counterfactual thinking can affect both people's perceptions and judgments about an outcome, even if such thinking cannot change the outcome itself.

A second line of research and theory has been directed at the processes governing counterfactual thought. Researchers have relied heavily on Kahneman and Miller's (1986) norm theory to explain the types of antecedent events that are likely to be mentally mutated in the process of undoing factual outcomes. According to norm theory, an event that has easily imaginable alternatives is more likely to be mentally mutated than an event without such alternatives. Researchers have invoked norm theory to explain the differential mutability of exceptional versus normal events, actions versus inactions, and foreground versus background events (Kahneman & Tversky, 1982; Landman, 1987; Wells et al., 1987).

The ease of imagining alternatives to an event can surely affect the likelihood of a person's mentally mutating that event. However, it is not necessarily an event with many easily imaginable alternatives that is the most likely to be altered in the process of undoing an outcome. For example, simply drawing a person's attention to an antecedent event may increase the likelihood of its being mentally mutated. In this chapter, we discuss various characteristics of antecedent events that influence the likelihood of their being mentally mutated. We also outline and explore new ideas about the basic processes that govern the generation, selection, and expression of counterfactual thoughts.

THE CONCEPT OF COUNTERFACTUAL CONSTRAINTS

Our framework rests on the assumption that, although any factual outcome can be mentally undone by alterations to innumerable prior events or conditions, there are psychological "rules" that constrain people's considerations of which events or conditions to mentally mutate. We use the term *counterfactual constraints* to refer to these rules. A constraint is a mechanism that precludes entire sets of events from consideration for mutation, even though the counterfactual alteration of these events would undo the outcome. In other words, there are certain types of antecedents that people are not likely to mutate, although changing them would change the outcome. Our understanding of the process of counterfactual thinking invokes a model in which entire classes of mutations either are never considered or are rapidly eliminated from consideration. Counterfactual constraints serve the purpose of restricting all possible alternatives to a practical subset.

We propose that there are three general categories of constraints that govern counterfactual generation and selection: natural-law constraints, availability constraints, and purpose constraints.

Three Categories of Constraints

Counterfactual thinking could be considered a type of fantasy and, as such, would not be constrained by the laws of nature. Fantasy can allow people to defy the laws of gravity, to reverse aging processes, to create matter, and so on. We argue that counterfactual thinking, unlike free-form fantasy, is strongly constrained by people's knowledge of the laws that govern the world around them. Hence, our first category, composed of *natural-law* constraints, encompasses people's understanding of natural laws.[1]

Concepts such as gravity, the direction of time, and the speed of light are generally considered to be constants in the universe and are therefore left unchanged in most of the alternative representations that people construct. It is the unchanging nature of universal laws that discourages their counterfactual mutation. Because the downward pull of gravity on an airplane is the same whether the plane crashes or safely reaches its destination, it is not surprising that no one undoes a plane crash by saying, "If only the plane had fallen up." People are more likely to focus on such contributing causal factors as human or mechanical error in their counterfactual mutations. We argue that it is people's implicit knowledge of the constant effects of basic laws of science and nature, such as gravity, that constrains the counterfactuals they generate.

This is not to say that natural laws cannot be mentally mutated, for it is possible for people to consider worlds in which these constants do not exist. Science fiction writers are masters at exploring possible effects of natural-law suspension, creating for the reader other worlds that, al-

---

[1]By natural laws, we do not necessarily mean the actual laws of nature as understood in formal sciences; rather, we mean people's perceptions or understanding of them. For example, when people's intuitions about physics are at odds with the actual laws of motion (e.g., McCloskey, 1983), it is their intuitions that constrain the counterfactuals they generate.

though operating by a different set of rules, seem believable. Our point is that, when confronted with unexpected outcomes in their everyday lives, it is unlikely that people will consider mutating universal constants.

Most research on counterfactual thinking to date has focused on variables that are regulated by our second category, *availability* constraints. For instance, the relative mutability of salient versus nonsalient events (Gleicher et al., 1990), exceptional versus normal events (e.g., Gavanski & Wells, 1989; Kahneman & Tversky, 1982), actions versus inactions (e.g., Landman, 1987), and commissions versus omissions (Baron, 1992) can be understood as operating through availability (Tversky and Kahneman, 1973). That is, the likelihood of a person's mentally mutating salient events, exceptions, and actions is a function of the ease with which these events come or are brought to mind, relative to other events. Compared to normal events, for example, exceptional events are more salient, and are thereby more available and more likely to be mentally mutated.

The norm theory conception of availability (Kahneman & Miller, 1986) focuses on the relative ease of one's imagining, not the events themselves, but alternatives to the events in a series. According to norm theory, events that have easily imaginable alternatives are more likely to be mentally mutated than events for which no such alternatives exist. That is, if it is difficult for one to imagine alternatives to an event, that event will not be mentally mutated. Rather, one will mutate an event for which alternatives are easily brought to mind. Thus, according to norm theory, it is the availability of alternatives to an event that determines the likelihood that the event will be mentally mutated.

We argue that the ease of imagining alternatives to an event is only one determinant of its availability for mental mutation. Our conception of availability focuses on the relative ease with which certain events in a series come to a person's mind. An antecedent event is available because of the properties of the event itself, rather than because of the properties of possible alternatives to that event. In their discussion of the availability heuristic, Tversky and Kahneman (1974) pointed out that familiarity, salience, recency, and imaginability all affect the retrievability of instances from memory. Thus, an event for which there are numerous imaginable alternatives will not necessarily be more available for mental mutation than other events in a series. For example, some events may be more available than others because they occurred more recently. We argue that the events that are likely to be mutated are those that are highly available to the mental simulator, whether as a function of salience, recency, familiarity, imaginability, or some related property.

Although there are many possible events that a person may change in order to undo an outcome, we argue that the set of events that constitute acceptable candidates for counterfactual mutation can also be constrained by a person's purpose or motive for engaging in counterfactual thought. Our third category, composed of *purpose* constraints, encompasses people's reasons for considering alternative outcomes to factual events. Sometimes a person engages in counterfactual thinking about an outcome in order to determine causality, whereas at other times a person may be trying to assess fault. The intent with which one engages in counterfactual thought can constrain both the alternatives that are generated and the thoughts that are publicly expressed. For example, a person who is trying to determine who was at fault for an accident will consider how the accident might have been avoided, that is, will imagine ways in which things could have turned out better. Counterfactual thoughts in which the outcome might have turned out worse might not even be generated because those alternatives do not help determine who or what was at fault. On the other hand, although a person trying to console someone might imagine ways in which things could have been better and ways in which things could have been worse, counterfactuals in which things could have been better are constrained from public expression. Thus, although both types of counterfactuals might be generated, only those consistent with a person's purpose will be overtly expressed.

We believe that the three types of constraints are qualitatively distinct in the way that they vary along two dimensions: the *automaticity* of the process and the *lucidity* of counterfactuals that violate the constraint. Automaticity refers to the classic distinction drawn in memory theory between controlled and automatic processing (Shiffrin & Schneider, 1977). An automatic search is an efficient, unconscious process that rapidly produces consistent responses to familiar stimuli. On the other hand, controlled processes are slower and less efficient because they demand conscious effort. However, controlled searches are also much more flexible than are automatic searches because they can be easily influenced or altered by conscious considerations. We propose that natural-law and availability constraints restrict mutable events to a contextually relevant subset through a relatively automatic process. In contrast, purpose constraints invoke a more controlled, deliberate process.

Limitations of the human information-processing system preclude the contemplation of the infinite possibilities that may undo an outcome. In almost all cases, the imagining of deviations from natural laws does not produce psychologically satisfying counterfactual thoughts. For example, one's considering the effect of gravity on a suicide jumper's leap from a high-rise building does not provide an adequate explanation for his or her death. Natural-law constraints operate automatically to prevent valuable cognitive resources from being expended on such unproductive diversions, allowing the mental simulator to focus on alternatives that will more effectively further the goals of counterfactual thinking.

Similarly, availability constraints provide a starting point for productive counterfactual thinking, serving to focus people's attention on promising junctures (i.e., possible turning points). Faced with an infinite number of possible events that can be mutated in innumerable ways, people will automatically restrict counterfactual thoughts to events that stand out for some reason. In many cases, people engage in counterfactual thinking in a search for the cause of a particular outcome. Often, the mental mutating of the most available (e.g., salient) event in a sequence will provide a suitable explanation for the outcome's occurrence. Although a person's focusing on salient antecedents will not always lead to an acceptable understanding of the situation, the use of availability is usually an efficient way of narrowing the likely causes of an outcome. The initial selection of a few, highly available antecedent events saves the mental simulator from conducting a more taxing mental search immediately following every outcome.

Purpose constraints function through a more conscious, deliberate form of processing than do the other two types of constraints. Controlled processing allows people to interpret and evaluate counterfactuals to assess whether they meet their needs. The counterfactual thoughts that result from natural-law and availability constraints are not always appropriate or useful in a particular context. The mental simulator is free at all times to override these automatic constraints in order to imagine possibilities that are unlikely to arise without conscious attention. It is often the person's intention or purpose for engaging in counterfactual thought that determines which mutations are the most beneficial. Thus, purpose constraints may guide the search for and selection of useful counterfactuals. Purpose also affects which counterfactuals are overtly expressed. There are times when the thoughts resulting from mental simulation are not appropriate to the situation, and the person may choose not to express those counterfactuals, as is the case with any other thoughts.

The three categories of constraints also vary in the degree to which violations of the constraints would be considered lucid. Lucid counterfactuals are those that seem plausible, rational, and appropriate given the context in which they are generated or expressed. Nonlucid counterfactuals are those that seem implausible, irrational, or inappropriate in light of that context. Furthermore, lucidity entails coherence as well as plausibility. For a counterfactual to be lucid, the overt expression of an internal musing must be understandable and interpretable by a listener. Nonlucid counterfactual statements are incomprehensible at best and, more often, are apt to seem preposterous or absurd.

A mental mutation that violates an availability constraint can still be a lucid thought. For example, people who are asked to imagine how a mugging could have been avoided may be more likely to mutate an exceptional event (such as a man's leaving the office later than usual) than a normal event (the man's walking home by his usual route). However, mutating the normal event can still produce a lucid counterfactual (the man's walking home by a different route than usual).

In contrast, a mutation that violates a natural-law constraint is not likely to be lucid. When reading about a tragedy in which an entire village was suddenly buried in snow, a person would find it pointless to imagine the avalanche crashing up instead of down the mountain. The earth's gravity and the laws of motion are constant, predictable forces and are therefore present in most of the alternative realities that people are likely to consider. The imagining of alternative worlds in which these laws do not operate serves no practical purpose, and overtly expressing such ideas would seem irrational. For example, if a person tries to explain away an accidental drowning by saying, "If only we could breathe under water, this kind of thing would never happen," a listener will likely dismiss the statement as nonsensical and unenlightening. A serious consideration of the speaker's suggestion results in the realization that if humans could breathe under water, the concept of drowning would lose its meaning altogether. It is this type of logical inconsistency and irrelevance that makes violations of natural-law constraints nonlucid.

Violations of purpose constraints can also produce nonlucid counterfactuals. If one's purpose is to provide counseling for the victim's families, finding fault with the villagers for living at the foot of a mountain would be improper. In the context of offering consolation, the expression of such counterfactual thoughts as, "If only they hadn't decided to settle in the valley," would not be lucid. To a member of the family expecting words of consolation, the statement would seem inappropriate, if not absurd (see Davis & Lehman, chapter 13).

In the following sections, we elaborate on the three categories of counterfactual constraints and the dimensions along which they vary. Table 2.1 is a useful referent for this discussion.

Natural-Law Constraints

We argue that the primary, or initial, constraint operating on the generation of counterfactual thoughts is the knowledge of natural laws held by the mental simulator. Our conception of natural law encompasses various laws of science, such as those that govern motion, time, causality, physics, mathematics, and biology. These are laws that people are unlikely to mentally mutate. Participants in our studies (e.g., Gavanski & Wells, 1989; Seelau, Rydell, & Wells, 1993; Wells & Gavanski, 1989; Wells et al., 1987) rarely produced counterfactuals that violated the laws of nature, and such mutations seem to almost never occur in normal discourse. It is true that

TABLE 2.1
Three Categories of Counterfactual Constraints:
Dimensions and Examples

Category of Constraint	Automaticity Dimension	Lucidity Dimension	Examples
Natural Law	Automatic	Violations not lucid	Laws of physics Laws of motion Laws of time Laws of biology Laws of causality Laws of mathematics
Availability	Automatic	Violations lucid	Knowledge Normality Near misses Action Order of events
Purpose	Controlled	Violations not lucid	Causality Control Blame Consolation

people sometimes contemplate matters without overtly expressing their thoughts. However, we think that the absence of violations of natural-law constraints in people's overt statements coincides with an absence of conscious consideration of such mutations. We do not deny the capacity of people to engage in fantasies in which objects fall up instead of down, effects precede causes, time is frozen, and so on, but we believe that such mutations are not part of the normal process of counterfactual thinking.

Natural-law constraints develop as people learn about the functioning of the world around them. These constraints change over time as people age and gain experience. A child might imagine that water can flow uphill or that the sun can set in the east, but as the child ages, he or she will learn that such things are not possible and will focus on alternatives that do not conflict with natural laws. Thus, as people become more familiar with the laws that govern their reality, they will consider fewer impossibilities in their search for valid counterfactuals.

Lucidity of Violations. Although mutations that violate the laws of nature can undo an outcome, they are not lucid. If people do not mutate the presence of gravity in order to undo the death of a suicide jumper, it is not because such a mutation would fail to undo the outcome. Rather, mutating the effect of gravity falls outside of the domain of events that are normally considered possible in the world. Violations to the laws that govern motion, time, causality, mathematics, and biology may seem equally implausible. Thus, we believe that counterfactual thoughts are restricted to those that are plausible given the natural laws operating in the world. Nonlucid mutations do not make sense to the mental simulator or to anyone else who shares the same knowledge of the laws of nature.

Automaticity of the Process. The elimination of counterfactuals through natural-law constraints is an automatic process. Although an infinite number of mutable junctures exist in any chain of events, the knowledge that an individual has accumulated about natural laws precludes the consideration of alternatives that could not possibly occur. For example, the understanding that the forward passage of time is immutable makes it both unnecessary and unproductive for a person to imagine the possible effect of time reversal on every outcome.

Natural-law constraints can be violated with conscious effort. It is possible for people to mentally mutate the laws of nature in order to assess the consequences of their suspension. In certain contexts, it is even reasonable for them to express alternatives that fall outside the realm of normal possibility. For instance, a teacher can vividly demonstrate the effects of the earth's gravitational pull by asking the students to imagine what would happen if the law were suspended. Such a request, which might seem unusual or pointless under any other circumstances, is perfectly reasonable in the context of scientific instruction.

Availability Constraints

Most of the research and theory on counterfactual thinking has been directed at the question of which antecedent events people mutate in order to change an outcome. We argue that many of the observed regularities have involved some aspect of mental availability. We use the availability concept broadly to refer to the propensity for an event to come to a person's mind (Tversky & Kahneman, 1973).[2]

In a sequence of events leading to a dramatic outcome, various characteristics make a subset of these events highly available. Among the variables that affect the selection of mutable events through the process of availability are the perceiver's knowledge of the factual events, whether the events were normal or exceptional, whether the events were acts of

---

[2]Different terminology is used in chapter 1 and in this chapter to denote essentially the same concepts. Roese and Olson (chapter 1) use the term *mutability* to refer to antecedent-based factors that can influence semantic aspects (as opposed to the mere frequency) of counterfactual generation (e.g., exceptionality, salience, order of events, etc.). In this chapter, these same factors fall under the rubric of *availability*. Roese and Olson use the term availability in a slightly different sense: to describe the mere generation versus the absence of counterfactuals as conscious thoughts.

omission or commission, whether the events appeared in the foreground or in the background, and the extent to which the outcome was almost different (i.e., a "near miss"). Variables that fall in the availability category tend to be conceptually and operationally correlated. For example, actions are more salient, evoke greater attention, and tend to appear more in the foreground than do inactions. Near misses also tend to be salient and to elicit attention. Both actions and near misses are likely to be reported in a description of how an outcome occurred and thereby become part of the reader's factual knowledge. We argue that the conceptual overlap between the variables in this category is a function of their similarity along a dimension of availability. Near misses, actions, foreground events, and events of which the perceiver has knowledge all are more available than their counterparts, a characteristic that increases the likelihood that these types of events will be mutated.

Knowledge of the Factual Events. One of the central variables constraining a perceiver's set of available counterfactuals is his or her limited knowledge of the facts of an event sequence. Researchers have noted that people seldom mutate events or actions that have not been made explicit. When presented with Kahneman and Tversky's (1982) auto accident scenario, participants typically did not mutate unmentioned events that would have caused the victim to arrive at the intersection earlier, even though any number of such events might have prevented the accident's occurrence. For example, participants might have suggested that the driver would have arrived at the intersection earlier "If only he hadn't been forced to wait for the train to pass," even though no train was ever mentioned in the scenario. Rather than creating such junctures, however, participants preferred to mutate events that were made explicit in the scenarios.

Wells et al. (1987) similarly noted that their respondents tended not to mutate enabling conditions or characters' actions that were not noted in the scenarios. However, the mutation task itself may demand no imagination of unmentioned possibilities. For example, Wells and his colleagues asked respondents to "list six ways in which the events in the story could be changed so that the outcome of the story would be different" (p. 423). Even when the instructions are less pointed (e.g., "List six things that could have been different to have changed the outcome"; Gavanski & Wells, 1989, p. 319), people seem to assume that all noteworthy antecedents have been made explicit in the scenario and therefore do not engage in the mental simulation of unmentioned antecedents. This is not to say that people never create junctures in order to change causal sequences. People sometimes infer the existence of certain facts and mutate an unmentioned event or action, but such mutations are rare.

Normality. People are more likely to mutate events that are perceived to be exceptional rather than events that are perceived to be normal (Kahneman & Tversky, 1982; Wells et al., 1987). Kahneman and Tversky (1982), in their seminal article on counterfactual thinking, reported that people who read the story of a man who was killed in an automobile accident were more likely to mutate an exceptional event (e.g., the man's leaving work earlier than usual) than a normal event (e.g., the man's taking his usual route home).

According to norm theory (Kahneman & Miller, 1986), the availability of alternatives to an exceptional event is greater than the availability of alternatives to a normal event; this greater availability increases the likelihood of the exceptional event's being mutated. We argue that exceptional events are more likely to be mutated than are normal events because events that are infrequent or unusual tend to be more salient than routine or familiar events. Therefore, the greater likelihood of a person's mutating an exceptional event is not a function of the availability of alternatives to that event, but rather a function of the availability of the event itself.

Near Misses. The thought that something "almost happened" is a rich, underresearched concept (see Kahneman & Varey, 1990, for a provocative theoretical and empirical treatment of the concept). A basketball game lost by a point or a lottery ticket one number away from the winning one are examples of outcomes that inspire counterfactual thoughts. When something almost happens, or almost did not happen, people often consider what could have been different to have changed the outcome. Thus, outcomes that almost happened elicit the counterfactual thought process.

Although near misses play an important role as counterfactual-eliciting outcomes, they can also be very salient antecedent events that led to an outcome. Consider a football game that was lost by 2 points. A common reaction might be that the losing team could have won if they had made a successful field goal at some point during the game. Imagine further that the field-goal kicker made two attempts, the first of which fell short by 15 yards, and the second of which bounced off the goal post. The second attempt could certainly qualify as a near miss and would likely be the most available of the two attempted field goals. When such dramatic events occur, people's mental simulations tend to be constrained to considerations of how mutations to the near miss might have altered the outcomes (Johnson, 1986). Although a successful completion of either of the field goals during the football game would have changed the final score, it is the "off-the-post" second attempt that is the more salient and therefore the one more available for mutation.

Order of Events. Miller and Gunasegaram (1990) presented participants with a written scenario describing a coin-flip game. Two people
flipped coins of equal value, and the outcomes were kept hidden from
view. The players were told that if both coins landed with the same side
up (i.e., two heads or two tails), both people would win $1000. If the
coins landed with different sides up (i.e., one head and one tail), neither
player would win anything. The coin outcomes were revealed sequen-
tially: The first coin showed a head; the second coin showed a tail. This
game produces a very strong sense that the revelation of the second
person's coin is the only significant event. When asked which event was
easier to undo, 89% of the participants indicated that it was easier to
imagine the second coin being different, rather than the first. This example
illustrates that the order of events matters a great deal in the mental
simulator's selection of a mutation, even though the events have equal
value in determining an outcome.

Like most order effects reported in the psychological literature, some
conditions produce primacy and some produce recency effects. Results
of counterfactual thinking studies have indicated that people are more
likely to mutate earlier than later events in a series (primacy effect) when
there is a causal relation between the events, such that the later events
are the direct result of earlier events (Johnson, Ogawa, Delforge, & Early,
1989; Wells et al., 1987). The mutating of later events in a series (recency
effect) may be more likely to occur when the antecedents are independent,
that is, when there is no causal relation between the events (Kahneman
& Miller, 1986; Miller & Gunasegaram, 1990).

We suspect that the relationship between event order and the likelihood
of an event being mutated is much more complex than research to date
suggests. Perhaps the causal nature of the event series (i.e., whether or not
there is a causal relationship between events) is a critical variable in
determining whether primacy and recency effects occur, but that question
has not been examined closely. At present, we can suggest only that some
events are more available than others to the mental simulator and that there
are other circumstances that determine whether a primacy or a recency
effect occurs. The order of events can affect the likelihood that antecedents
will be mutated, but the selection of events is still a function of the
availability of the events. Our point here is that mutations to some events
are constrained by the enhanced availability of a particular event in a
sequence, even when each event is equally capable of undoing the outcome.

Action–Inaction. Results of numerous studies have shown that actions are more mutable than inactions and influence other judgments
more than do inactions (e.g., Gleicher et al., 1990; Landman, 1987). For

example, Landman (1987) found that people anticipated greater regret for actions that led to an undesirable outcome than for inactions that led to the same outcome. People also anticipated enhanced positive affect when a positive outcome was the result of action rather than of inaction. This pattern is related to the observation that people hold others more at fault for commissions than for equally harmful omissions (e.g., Baron, 1992; Spranca, Minsk, & Baron, 1991). Participants who read about a person who committed an act that led directly to a negative outcome awarded more compensation to the victim than did participants who read about a person who omitted an act that would have prevented the negative outcome (Spranca et al., 1991).

As we stated previously, the variables that operate according to the availability heuristic overlap conceptually. Actions may be more likely to be mutated than inactions in part because people consider actions to be exceptions and inactions to be norms or because they perceive actions as foreground and inactions as background. Each of the variables in this category has qualities that enhance its availability (see Roese & Olson, chapter 1, for further discussion of this factor).

Lucidity of Violations. Variables in the availability-constraint category restrict possible mutations to a subset of all events via the ease or difficulty with which those events come to a person's mind. Unlike natural-law constraints, violations to availability constraints do not result in nonlucid counterfactuals. Although it may not immediately occur to a person to change a norm, to mutate an inaction, or to mentally manipulate the middle event in a sequence, doing any of these will still produce lucid counterfactual thoughts. For example, consider a woman who buys an evening paper from the same newsstand on her way home from work every night. On one particular night, however, she stops to buy a paper at a newsstand two blocks before the stand she normally goes to, and a purse-snatcher steals her handbag while she is waiting for her change. The most available juncture in this case is likely to be the exceptional event: the woman's choice of newsstands that evening. Thus, mutations are likely to be constrained to that event (e.g., "If only she had stopped at her usual newsstand"). However, violating the availability constraint by mutating a normal event, such as the woman's habit of stopping to buy a newspaper at all, still results in a lucid counterfactual (e.g., "If only she hadn't stopped to buy a newspaper that night").

Automaticity of the Process. Availability constraints operate automatically to restrict a large set of mutable possibilities to those events that are most salient to the mental simulator. Thus, the availability of exceptions, actions, and recent events makes people more likely to mutate those types of events than other types. However, anything that enhances the availability of the norm, the inaction, or the middle event in a sequence should also increase the likelihood that it will be mutated.

If a person is unable to engage in conscious processing (for example, if distracted or under a cognitive load), the counterfactual thoughts generated will be mutations to the most available events. Of course, people can imagine alternatives to less available events if they engage in a more controlled form of processing. When people have a particular purpose for considering alternatives to reality, they are especially likely to engage in controlled processing that allows them to override the automatic natural-law and availability constraints.

Purpose Constraints

In most of the research studies directed at the mutability of different types of events, people are simply asked to list changes to prior events that would undo a particular outcome. We presume, however, that in real life people typically engage in a counterfactual assessment with some particular purpose in mind. Among these purposes may be the assigning of blame, the consoling of a victim, the gaining of a sense of controllability, or the understanding of how or why an outcome occurred. It seems likely that the selection of counterfactuals is, in part, governed by a person's purpose for engaging in counterfactual thinking.

Consider the example of a boy who loses a leg because of an automobile accident. The most available mutation may be one that undoes the accident altogether (e.g., "If only he had stayed home that night"). However, a friend who wishes to console the victim's mother may reject such "if only" statements in favor of more comforting statements along the lines of "It could have been worse." The goal of consolation is the reduction of negative affect; therefore, suggestions to a mother of ways in which her child could have avoided the accident would be inconsistent with that goal. Thus, a person's reason for generating counterfactuals may serve to eliminate entire sets of alternatives that, in general, would undo the outcome but that, in a particular context, are inappropriate or counter to that purpose (see also Davis & Lehman, chapter 13). We discuss a number of reasons for which people engage in a counterfactual thinking process and how these different purposes serve as counterfactual constraints in the production and expression of alternatives.

Assessing Causality. One of the primary reasons for a person's thinking about a dramatic or surprising outcome is to gain an understanding of how or why it occurred. There are innumerable events that, when mentally mutated, will result in the undoing of an outcome, but not all of these events can be considered causal. N'gbala & Branscombe (1995) demonstrated that although events that are necessary precursors to an outcome will be mutated, only those that are sufficient to have produced the outcome will be considered causal. In other words, antecedents that enable an outcome to occur but are not sufficient in themselves to have determined the outcome will not be considered causal. Only antecedents that are sufficient to have produced the outcome are considered the causal determinants of an outcome. For example, after learning the reason that the space shuttle *Challenger* exploded, many people might have thought, "If only the O-rings had been properly tested." This counterfactual thought provides an adequate explanation for the disaster because the defective O-rings were sufficient under the launch conditions to cause the shuttle's explosion. The counterfactual thought "If only it had rained that day" might also have occurred because clear skies were necessary for the launch. Few people, however, would have suggested that the sunshine caused the *Challenger* disaster. The imagining of alterations to the weather conditions does not provide a satisfying causal explanation for the explosion because, even though clear weather is necessary for a launch, clear weather is not sufficient to cause an explosion. There were undoubtedly many conditions necessary for the shuttle's lift-off that day, including clear weather conditions, yet the mutating of these conditions does not provide a psychologically satisfying explanation for the disaster.

Controlling Future Outcomes. Another reason that a person might engage in counterfactual thinking is to control future occurrences. Through the mutation of critical events, the mental simulator can determine which conditions to create to repeat a positive outcome and which circumstances to avoid to circumvent another negative outcome. People who wish to improve their future performance tend to generate *upward counterfactuals*, imaginings of how things might have been better, in an effort to bring about those events in the future (Markman, Gavanski, Sherman, & McMullen, 1993; Roese, 1994). When the purpose is the control of future events, counterfactuals are likely to be constrained to a set of necessary and controllable conditions. In other words, mutations are restricted to events not only that are necessary for the outcome to occur but also that the mental simulator will be able to influence in the future. For example, if a person whose car was hit by an intoxicated driver wishes to avoid similar accidents, the counterfactual "If only I had been looking in my rear view mirror" is reasonable because it focuses on an action that the victim can control in the future. On the other hand, the counterfactual "If only the drunk driver had fallen asleep in the parking lot" is not reasonable, even though it would also have undone the accident. Imagining changes to the intoxicated driver's behavior does not serve the victim's purpose for engaging in counterfactual thinking because it will not help the victim to avoid similar future incidents. Although mutations to events that are beyond a mental simulator's control (such as the intoxicated driver's action) may be useful in the context of the person's trying to determine causality, they are not helpful in the context of her or his trying to control future occurrences. If a person's goal is to control future events, counterfactual thinking may be particularly beneficial for a situation that is likely to be repeated and for which the circumstances that led to the outcome can be manipulated by the individual (see also McMullen, Markman, & Gavanski, chapter 5).

Assigning Blame. In reaction to Kahneman and Tversky's (1982) auto accident scenario, respondents frequently mutated the mildly unusual behavior of Mr. Jones that led to his death and relatively rarely mutated the other driver's behavior. However, the scenario clearly stated that the other driver was speeding and that he violated a red light signal. Surely, mutations to Mr. Jones' time of leaving work or route would not be dominant if the participants' purpose were to assign blame. Similarly, it is quite reasonable to assume that a jury charged with assessing damages or setting remunerative sanctions would restrict the focus of their deliberations to those actions that could be considered blameworthy.

Blameworthy actions are restricted to those over which the actor had control and that were directly linked to a foreseeable outcome (see Shaver, 1992). Consider a woman who is attacked when passing through an alley at night. Perhaps she could have foreseen such an incident, but she had no real control over what her attacker did in the alley. Therefore, the counterfactual "If only she hadn't been in the alley" in the context of assigning blame is inappropriate, even though many people probably do generate it. Consider the postal worker who shot his fellow employees after he was fired from his job. Is the worker's supervisor to blame for the incident because he fired the man? Certainly the supervisor had control over whether or not to fire the man, but he could not have foreseen what the employee would do when he was fired. Also, as is true of the woman in the alley, the supervisor could not control the perpetrator's actions. Thus, when a person's purpose is to assign blame, relevant counterfactuals are those he or she perceives to involve both foresight and controllability (see also McGill & Klein, chapter 12).

Consoling Others. When a person's goal is to console others, it is advantageous to lead others to focus on ways in which the situation could have been worse. For example, when a person says to the mother of a boy who lost his leg because of an auto accident, "He was very fortunate," we recognize that such a statement would be absurd unless both the speaker and listener shared an unspoken counterfactual thought (e.g., that the child might have been killed). Therefore, when one's purpose is consolation, the types of counterfactuals that are typically eliminated from consideration are those that would have made the outcome better (i.e., *upward counterfactuals*).

Counterfactuals in which the outcome could have been worse (i.e., *downward counterfactuals*) not only help console others in need but also may help people to console themselves as well. Roese (1994) found that people who generated downward counterfactuals when thinking about negative outcomes felt better than those who generated upward counterfactuals.

When a person's intent is to console another person, counterfactuals that might have made the outcome better may come to mind; in accordance with the intended goal, however, the person publicly expresses only downward counterfactuals, which reflect ways in which the outcome could have been worse. Imagine trying to console the mother of the young accident victim by saying, "If only you had bought a car with airbags." If one's purpose is to find fault for the severity of the boy's injuries, there would be no constraints against counterfactuals of this type. However, when consolation is the primary goal, counterfactuals overtly expressed by the speaker are constrained to those that are consistent with that purpose. The public expression of alternatives that violate the consolation purpose tends to yield socially inappropriate statements (see also Davis & Lehman, chapter 13).

Lucidity of Violations. The purpose that a person has for engaging in counterfactual thinking does not always limit the counterfactuals that the person entertains. One's purpose for counterfactual thinking does, however, provide a context that restricts the set of alternatives that seem reasonable or appropriate for the person to express. Recall our discussion of lucidity in the context of violations to natural-law constraints. Although violations to that category are also not lucid, the concept of lucidity takes on a slightly different meaning in reference to purpose constraints. When we propose that the counterfactuals that violate purpose constraints are not lucid, we mean that those counterfactuals would not be considered sound because they are inconsistent with the mental simulator's purpose. It does not make sense for a person who is trying to console the relatives of an accident victim to express a counterfactual such as "If only he hadn't gone through that yellow light." Nor does it make sense for a person who is trying to determine who is to blame for the accident to state, "At least you didn't lose both your legs." Given the purpose that each of these individuals has for considering alternatives to factual events, the expression of statements that are counter to their respective purposes is not rational, clearheaded, or appropriate.

Automaticity of the Process. Unlike the natural-law and availability constraints, which operate through automatic processes, purpose constraints are part of a relatively deliberate, controlled process. This controlled processing allows a person to determine which events are useful to mutate and which counterfactuals are appropriate to express in order to fulfill a particular purpose. In order for people to determine which counterfactuals are beneficial in reaching their respective goals, they must engage in some conscious thought processes. Having conscious control over the decision of which events to mutate allows people to override the automatic constraint processes that would otherwise guide their counterfactual thinking. Without a controllable component, counterfactual thinking would be a relatively predictable and extremely limited process, rather than a flexible and exceedingly practical cognitive tool.

CONCLUSION

Among the three categories of counterfactual constraints, the natural-law constraint category may be the least psychologically interesting because of its face validity and because it does not lend itself readily to novel predictions or experimental manipulations. We do, however, consider the constraints in this category to be extremely influential in the counterfactual thinking process due to their ability to eliminate large sets of possible mutations without conscious effort on the part of the mental simulator.

Availability constraints also operate automatically (i.e., unconsciously) to restrict mutable events to the most available subset. People naturally attend to salient events, and available events tend to be mutated to the exclusion of other events in a series. Exceptions, near misses, and actions are highly available to the perceiver, and as a result, are more likely to be mutated than their less salient counterparts. Researchers of counterfactual thinking have generally focused on variables that fall in the availability-constraints category.

Largely ignored has been the purpose or reason for a person's engaging in counterfactual thought, our third category of constraint. Purpose almost certainly affects which events are mutated and definitely affects which counterfactuals are publicly expressed. Researchers must recognize the implications that this variable has for studies in which counterfactual thoughts are elicited. For example, studies in which participants are asked to undo an outcome by completing an "If only . . ." stem may leave participants unclear as to why they are being asked to consider alternatives. There may be cases in which a state of uncertainty or ambiguity is acceptable, or even intended. In such cases, the researcher must be careful not to imply a particular purpose, because the implied purpose will probably change the counterfactuals that people will express. On the other hand, if it is desirable for participants to respond with a particular purpose in mind, the researcher must be careful to make that purpose explicit in the instructions. Left to their own devices, people may adopt purposes of their own, which may or may not coincide with those of the researcher. In either event, adoption of a purpose will affect the mental mutations that people generate and report.

Purpose constraints may help explain apparent differences between the counterfactuals that people express in laboratory experiments and those they express in reaction to actual traumatic events in their lives. Davis, Lehman, Wortman, Silver, and Thompson (1995) found that people who had lost a child or spouse in an automobile accident tended not to mutate exceptions rather than norms and that they tended to mutate inactions rather than actions. We suspect that the typical laboratory experiment, in which participants are merely asked to imagine how the outcome could have been otherwise, is relatively devoid of counterfactual purpose constraints. The absence of such constraints promotes automatic processing based merely on availability. Real-life traumatic events, on the other hand, are more likely to be associated with a person's purpose for engaging in counterfactual thinking (e.g., to assign blame or to assess causality), a purpose which produces a deeper analysis that can override automatic processes.

At times, purpose constraints may be a function of the role that the mental simulator plays in a given situation. For example, an attorney defending a man accused of rape might mutate behaviors of the rape victim (e.g., her acceptance of a ride home from a stranger) in an attempt to shift the blame away from the defendant. On the other hand, the prosecuting attorney, in an attempt to prove the defendant's guilt, would likely focus on the defendant's actions (e.g., the defendant's forcing his way into the victim's home). Furthermore, a law-enforcement official might generate a completely different set of counterfactuals in an effort to prevent the recurrence of such a crime (e.g., "If only we had increased our neighborhood patrols"). Thus, people's roles can partially determine their purposes for engaging in counterfactual thinking, the events they mutate, and the counterfactuals that they express.

In addition, a person's role may affect the availability of mutable events. Consider the possible thoughts of people mulling over an armed robbery of a convenience store. The clerk involved may find the robber's gun to be quite salient and entertain counterfactuals such as "At least he didn't fire his gun." The store owner may find herself entertaining an unpleasant counterfactual because she was one day late in the installation of a new security system. Finally, a police officer, viewing the tape from the store's surveillance camera, may think, "If only the robber had looked up long enough for us to get a good view of his face." The role a person plays in a given situation affects his or her knowledge, focus of attention, and so on, all of which in turn affect the mental availability of events and possibilities and the resultant counterfactuals that are considered. To a lesser extent, a person's role may determine how natural-law constraints affect his or her counterfactual thinking. A person with sophisticated knowledge in an area of expertise (e.g., physics) probably has a very different conception of which events are reasonable to mutate than does a person with less knowledge or experience.

Examples such as these led us to reject postulating a strict hierarchy of constraints on counterfactual thinking. At first glance, it may appear that there is a natural order of constraints: Natural-law constraints are automatically triggered and restrict an infinite set of possible mutations to a relevant subset from which the most available events are most likely to be mutated. Purpose constraints further restrict the selection of counterfactual thoughts that are overtly expressed. Clearly, however, a person's purpose or role can affect the availability of events and, thus, which events are subsequently mutated. Such exceptions may call a general hierarchical structure into question. At the very least, they suggest that the constraints on counterfactual generation and selection may not operate unidirectionally.

The concept of counterfactual constraints provides a useful framework for the evaluation of past research in the area of counterfactual thinking and contributes some new ideas that are worthy of empirical investigation. There is clearly room for elaboration of the dimensions that distinguish the categories, for the inclusion of novel categories, and for the inclusion of more variables within the categories. In addition, an exploration of the distinctions between the processes and the outcomes of counterfactual thinking would be beneficial. Purpose constraints are especially interesting in this regard, because they affect both the generation of counterfactuals and the expression of counterfactual thoughts to others.

REFERENCES

Baron, J. (1992). The effect of normative beliefs on anticipated emotions. *Journal of Personality and Social Psychology, 63*, 320–330.

Davis, C. G., Lehman, D. R., Wortman, C. B., Silver, R. C., & Thompson, S. C. (1995). The undoing of traumatic life events. *Personality and Social Psychology Bulletin, 21*, 109–124.

Gavanski, I., & Wells, G. L. (1989). Counterfactual processing of normal and exceptional events. *Journal of Experimental Social Psychology, 25*, 314–325.

Gleicher, F., Kost, K. A., Baker, S. M., Strathman, A. J., Richman, S. A., & Sherman, S. J. (1990). The role of counterfactual thinking on judgments of affect. *Personality and Social Psychology Bulletin, 16*, 284–295.

Johnson, J. T. (1986). The knowledge of what might have been: Affective and attributional consequences of near outcomes. *Personality and Social Psychology Bulletin, 12*, 51–62.

Johnson, J. T., Ogawa, K. H., Delforge, A., & Early, D. (1989). Causal primacy and comparative fault: The effect of position in a causal chain in judgments of legal responsibility. *Personality and Social Psychology Bulletin, 15*, 161–174.

Kahneman, D., & Miller, D. T. (1986). Norm theory: Comparing reality to its alternatives. *Psychological Review, 93*, 136–153.

Kahneman, D., & Tversky, A. (1982). The simulation heuristic. In D. Kahneman, P. Slovic, & A. Tversky (Eds.), *Judgments under uncertainty: Heuristics and biases* (pp. 201–208). New York: Cambridge University Press.

Kahneman, D., & Varey, C. A. (1990). Propensities and counterfactuals: The loser that almost won. *Journal of Personality and Social Psychology, 59*, 1101–1110.

Landman, J. (1987). Regret and elation following action and inaction: Affective responses to positive versus negative outcomes. *Personality and Social Psychology Bulletin, 13*, 524–536.

Markman, K. D., Gavanski, I., Sherman, S. J., & McMullen, M. N. (1993). The mental simulation of better and worse possible worlds. *Journal of Experimental Social Psychology, 29*, 87–109.

McCloskey, M. (1983). Intuitive physics. *Scientific American, 248*(4), 122–130.

Miller, D. T., & Gunasegaram, S. (1990). Temporal order and the perceived mutability of events: Implications for blame assignment. *Journal of Personality and Social Psychology, 59*, 1111–1118.

N'gbala, A., & Branscombe, N. R. (1995). Mental simulation and causal attribution: When simulating an event does not affect fault assignment. *Journal of Experimental Social Psychology, 31*, 139–162.

Roese, N. J. (1994). The functional basis of counterfactual thinking. *Journal of Personality and Social Psychology, 66*, 805–818.

Seelau, E. P., Rydell, S. M., & Wells, G. L. (1993, June). *Counterfactual processing can lead to increased rape victim blame.* Poster session presented at the Fifth Annual Convention of the American Psychological Society, Chicago, IL.

Shaver, K. (1992). Blame avoidance: Toward an attribution intervention program. In L. Montada, S. H. Filipp, & M. Lerner (Eds.), *Life crises and experiences of loss in adulthood* (pp. 163–178). Hillsdale, NJ: Lawrence Erlbaum Associates.

Shiffrin, R. M., & Schneider, W. (1977). Controlled and automatic human information processing: II. Perceptual learning, automatic attending, and a general theory. *Psychological Review, 84*, 127–190.

Spranca, M., Minsk, E., & Baron, J. (1991). Omission and commission in judgment and choice. *Journal of Experimental Social Psychology, 27*, 76–105.

Tversky, A., & Kahneman, D. (1973). Availability: A heuristic for judging frequency and probability. *Cognitive Psychology, 5*, 207–232.

Tversky, A., & Kahneman, D. (1974). Judgment under uncertainty: Heuristics and biases. *Science, 185*, 1124–1131.

Weiner, R. L., Gaborit, M., Pritchard, C. C., McDonough, E. M., Staebler, C. R., Wiley, D. C., & Habert, K. S. (1994). Counterfactual thinking in mock juror assessments of negligence: A preliminary investigation. *Behavioral Sciences and the Law, 12*, 89–102.

Wells, G. L., & Gavanski, I. (1989). Mental simulation of causality. *Journal of Personality and Social Psychology, 56*, 161–169.

Wells, G. L., Taylor, B. R., & Turtle, J. W. (1987). The undoing of scenarios. *Journal of Personality and Social Psychology, 53*, 421–430.
Zelazny, R. (1981). Divine madness. In T. Carr & M. H. Greenberg (Eds.), *A treasury of modern fantasy* (pp. 417–423). New York: Avon.

3

Individual Differences in Counterfactual Thinking

Margaret Kasimatis
Hope College

Gary L. Wells
Iowa State University

Kelly (1970) suggested that an individual's mental construction of a situation guides his or her thoughts, feelings, and behaviors in that situation. However, findings from recent research have suggested that people not only construct current situations but also *reconstruct* past events. One way people might reconstruct past events is to engage in counterfactual thinking, which is a form of mental simulation in which a person imagines how some factual outcome might easily have turned out differently (Kahneman & Tversky, 1982). For example, people might think "If only Ted Kennedy had not tried to drive Mary Jo Kopechne home that night, he might be President today."

Counterfactual processing has been found to be a common response to negative events. For example, Davis, Lehman, Wortman, Silver, and Thompson (1995) found that 48% of their respondents spontaneously reported undoing in their minds about a motor vehicle accident in which they lost a child or spouse something that would change the outcome of the event. Similarly, Landman and Manis (1992) found that over half of their respondents reported that they would do something differently in their life if they had it to do over again.

Although counterfactual thinking appears to be a common response to dramatic events, research findings suggest that counterfactual thinking is more likely to occur under some circumstances than under others. Most of the factors that appear to influence when counterfactual thinking occurs are related to the mutability of events, which refers to how easily a person can imagine an event differently to undo an outcome (Wells & Gavanski, 1989). Various aspects of the context or situation influence the perceived mutability of an event. For example, researchers have found that people are more likely to undo exceptional events than normal ones (Kahneman & Miller, 1986); that people are more likely to undo actions than inactions (Landman, 1987); and that earlier rather than later events in a sequence are more likely to be undone when events form a causal chain (Miller & Gunasegaram, 1990; Wells, B. R. Taylor, & Turtle, 1987). When events are independent, however, later events are more mutable than earlier ones (Miller & Gunasegaram, 1990). It has also been suggested that amount and type of counterfactual thinking are determined by purpose, that is, what the individual is trying to accomplish in that situation (E. Seelau, S. Seelau, Wells, & Windschitl, chapter 2 of this volume).

One such purpose for a person's engaging in counterfactual thinking might be to make various social judgments. For example, people use the mutability of an event to make attributions of causality (Wells & Gavanski, 1989). Further, Miller and McFarland (1986) found that when mock jurors could easily imagine a positive alternative to a negative event, they felt more sympathy for the victim and consequently awarded him or her greater compensation.

Additional research results suggest that counterfactual thinking serves specific functions which can be roughly categorized as either problem focused or emotion focused (Lazarus & Folkman, 1984). In terms of the emotion focused functions of mental simulations, researchers have suggested that certain types of counterfactuals can cause one to feel better about the outcome of a situation or can serve to regulate emotional states (Roese, 1994; S. Taylor & Schneider, 1989). Counterfactuals also may help one to reestablish self-esteem after a negative event (S. Taylor & Schneider, 1989). In terms of problem focused functions, mental simulations can make an event seem more real (S. Taylor & Schneider, 1989) and may help a person determine the viability of a plan or prepare him or her for future improvement when faced with a similar situation (S. Taylor & Schneider, 1989; Roese, 1994). Further, event simulations may help people cope with past stressors by finding meaning in the event and regaining a sense of mastery over oneself and the world (Davis & Lehman, chapter 13; S. Taylor & Schneider, 1989).

Counterfactuals can take different forms, and these forms appear to have different emotional consequences. One type of counterfactual is called an *upward comparison*, and it involves a person considering how the outcome could have been better, for example, "If only I hadn't taken a new route to the airport I wouldn't have missed my plane." This type of counterfactual consistently has been found to lead to increased feelings of regret after a negative event (e.g., Landman, 1987; Johnson, 1986).

Further, results of naturalistic studies suggest that people who imagine how a negative event could have turned out better experience greater psychological distress than those who do not engage in this type of thinking (e.g., Davis et al., 1995).

Another type of counterfactual thinking entails a person replaying the event with a worse outcome, or making a *downward comparison*. This type of counterfactual usually takes the form "At least . . . ," or "It could have been worse," and it may have more positive emotional consequences, such as feelings of relief. This type of thinking may have particularly positive consequences when a person uses it to cope with very serious events. For example, S. Taylor, Wood, and Lichtman (1983) proposed a theory of victimization which suggests that the creating of hypothetical, worse worlds in response to negative events (such as breast cancer) has a positive, self-enhancing effect (see also Roese, 1994; Roese & Olson, chapter 6).

The implicit assumption so far has been that everybody engages in counterfactual thinking to some extent, and the primary focus of research has been the identification of situational or contextual factors that determine when counterfactual thinking will occur. However, almost no attention has been given to the question of individual differences in counterfactual thinking. That is, researchers to date have generally ignored the question of whether there are some people who are more likely to engage in counterfactual thinking than others. Another way to phrase the question is, What role does personality play in the generation of counterfactuals?

In light of what is already known about counterfactual thinking, it seems likely that personality or the self would play a role in the generation of counterfactual thoughts. In particular, the functions that mental simulations might serve suggest several ways that individuals might differ in their propensity to engage in counterfactual thinking.

There are several important reasons for investigating individual differences in counterfactual thinking. First, the knowledge of what type of people are more likely to engage in counterfactual thinking can aid researchers in understanding and predicting when counterfactual thinking is most likely to occur. More important, the way in which personality characteristics are related to counterfactual thinking may provide a better understanding of the nature of counterfactual thinking, especially the functions it serves. For example, if a certain personality characteristic, such as self-esteem, is found to be related to a certain type of counterfactual, the relation may suggest the function that the counterfactual serves, in this case probably a self-enhancing function. Further, researchers have suggested that one of the major functions of mental simulations is coping with negative events. If this suggestion is true, then understanding counterfactuals better through learning about individual differences might yield a better understanding of coping processes in general. And finally, this increased understanding might help psychologists target intervention strategies for certain people, such as those with depression.

Individual differences in counterfactual thinking can take several forms, two of which we examine in this chapter. First, some people may be consistently more likely than others to mentally undo events, whether the imagined outcome is better or worse. On the other hand, some people may be consistently more likely than others to use one type of counterfactual more than another type. That is, although everybody engages in counterfactual thinking, some people may consistently generate upward counterfactuals whereas others may have a propensity to use downward counterfactuals.

EVIDENCE FOR INDIVIDUAL DIFFERENCES

Although results of several studies suggest that counterfactual thinking is a common response to negative events, results of those same studies suggest that not everybody does it. For example, Landman and Manis (1992) reported that approximately half of the respondents in three different samples said that they would do something differently in their life if they had it to do over again. These authors interpreted their results as suggesting that counterfactual thinking is common among adults. However, it is equally true that half of their respondents did *not* report engaging in counterfactual thinking, even though the interviewers explicitly asked respondents what they would do differently in their life. In this light, it appears that there are some people who just do not engage in counterfactual thinking. Because respondents were interviewed only once, it is unclear whether those who did report counterfactual thoughts were *consistently* more likely than others to engage in counterfactual thinking in their everyday life.

There is little research in which the stability of counterfactual thinking over time has been explicitly investigated. Davis (1991) did find a significant relationship between participants' reports of how often they mentally undid a negative event within a month of its occurrence and how often they currently had those thoughts. Similarly, Davis and colleagues (Davis & Lehman, chapter 13; Davis et al., 1995) found that nearly half of respondents who spontaneously reported undoing something about a motor vehicle accident in which they lost a child or spouse reported still having such thoughts from 4 to 7 years after the accident occurred. However, the limitation to both of these studies is that they employed retrospective reports of undoing following the negative event. Also, these reports were taken at the same time as current reports of counterfactuals. Thus, it is not known whether the apparent stability in counterfactuals is due to true stability or to reporting or memory bias. True stability in counterfactual thought can be tested only with a longitudinal design.

In a subsequent longitudinal study, Davis et al. (1995) suggested that there was *not* stability in counterfactual thinking over time. They based their conclusion on the finding that 18 months after the loss of a baby from Sudden Infant Death Syndrome (SIDS), parents were not undoing the same antecedents as they did 3 weeks after the loss. That is, the *content* of the counterfactual thoughts was not stable. However, Davis et al. (1995) did not test whether it was the same *individuals* who were engaging in counterfactual thoughts about the loss 18 months later, regardless of content. Thus, the question of whether there are some individuals who have a general propensity to engage in counterfactual thinking remains to be answered.

Possible Individual Differences

If indeed some people do consistently engage in more counterfactual thinking than do others, a further question is, What personality characteristics do those people possess?

Self-Esteem. S. Taylor and her colleagues (S. Taylor & Schneider, 1989; S. Taylor, Wood, & Lichtman, 1983) suggested that certain types of mental simulation in response to negative events can have a self-enhancing effect. In light of the fact that individuals with high self-esteem employ more self-enhancement strategies than do individuals with low self-esteem (Brown, Collins, & Schmidt, 1988; S. Taylor & Brown, 1988; Wheeler & Miyake, 1992), it seems likely that those with high self-esteem would engage in a pattern of mental simulation that is self-enhancing. In the first investigation of how personality characteristics might be related to counterfactual thinking, Roese and Olson (1993; see also chapter 6) tested the relation between self-esteem and counterfactual thinking. These investigators found that individuals with low self-esteem were more likely to report undoing their own actions following failure, whereas individuals with high self-esteem were more likely to undo their own actions after success. These findings are analogous to the tendency of people with high self-esteem to attribute successes to themselves and failures to external factors and are consistent with research results showing that such individuals are more motivated than those with low self-esteem to engage in self-enhancement and self-protection strategies (Brown et al., 1988; S. Taylor & Brown, 1988; Wheeler & Miyake, 1992).

Although these findings offer evidence that the self plays an important role in the generation of counterfactual thoughts, there are limitations to

Roese and Olson's (1993) study that should be addressed in future research on this topic. First, their study measured counterfactual thought
at only one point in time. Thus it cannot be concluded from their results
that some people consistently engage in more counterfactual thinking
than do others. Further, the study employed hypothetical scenarios instead of an actual event in the respondent's own life. This factor could
be important in terms of the role of personality in counterfactual thinking.

Motivational Differences. As we mentioned previously, some researchers have suggested that mental simulations may serve problem
focused functions such as future planning and preparation (Roese, 1994;
S. Taylor & Schneider, 1989), finding meaning in an event, and regaining
a sense of mastery or control after a negative event occurs (Taylor &
Schneider, 1989). If mental simulation does serve these functions, then
people who are motivated to gain control and to find meaning in events
should be more likely than others to engage in counterfactual thinking.
Desirability of control refers to individual differences in the motivation
to control events, and people who are high on this dimension have been
found to interpret a situation in a manner that satisfies the need to see
themselves in control (Burger & Cooper, 1979). In light of this fact, it
seems likely that people who strongly desire control might replay past
situations so that they feel more in control of future situations.

A similar motivation that might be relevant is the need for cognition
(Cacioppo, Petty, & Kao, 1984), which refers to an individual's propensity
to engage in and enjoy complex mental activity.[1] An individual would
likely have to enjoy thinking in order to mentally simulate several versions of an event. Further, if mental simulation serves planning, problem-solving, and meaning functions, then those who are high in need for
cognition are particularly likely to engage in counterfactual thinking.

Optimism. As we stated previously, imagining how things could have
turned out better tends to lead to negative affect, whereas imagining how
things could have turned out worse tends to lead to positive affect.

---

[1]A related construct, which was not explicitly addressed in our research, is uncertainty
orientation, which involves the amount of uncertainty surrounding the outcome of an activity
(Sorrentino & Short, 1986). Uncertainty-oriented individuals search for meaning and thus
seek out information about themselves or their environment. In contrast, certainty-oriented
individuals confine themselves to situations that do not involve uncertainty about the self
or the environment, and they will avoid diagnostic information about the self if it requires
changing what is already known and clear to them. Thus, we would expect uncertainty-
oriented individuals, like those high in need for cognition, to engage more frequently in
counterfactual thinking than certainty-oriented individuals. Another individual difference
construct that is somewhat related to need for cognition is "consideration of future
consequences"; it is discussed in depth by Gleicher et al. (chapter 10).

Consequently, people who tend to frame things in a positive light should be more likely to engage in downward counterfactuals and less likely to engage in upward counterfactuals than people who frame things negatively. Optimists may be such people. Optimism has been defined as a general expectancy for positive outcomes (Scheier & Carver, 1985). Recently, it was found that, given identical performance feedback (in terms of relative standing), optimists reported higher levels of abilities than did pessimists (McFarland & Miller, 1994, Experiment 1). Results of a second experiment suggest that these effects occurred because optimists were focusing on the positive features of the feedback and pessimists were focusing on the negative features of the feedback. If this is true, then optimists should be less likely to engage in upward counterfactuals and more likely to engage in downward counterfactuals than are pessimists.

Coping Strategies. In light of the role of mental simulation in both the problem focused and the emotion focused components of coping (Lazarus & Folkman, 1984; S. Taylor & Schneider, 1989), a person's propensity to engage in counterfactual thinking may also be related to specific coping strategies. In terms of problem focused coping, those who tend to engage in upward counterfactuals may also tend to use problem-solving coping strategies, such as active coping or planning coping (cf. Carver, Scheier, & Weintraub, 1989). In terms of emotion focused coping, then, positive, emotion focused strategies, such as positive reinterpretation or acceptance (Carver, Scheier, & Weintraub, 1989), should be differentially related to the two types of counterfactuals. Specifically, positive reinterpretation and acceptance should be negatively related to upward counterfactuals and positively related to downward counterfactuals.

Rumination. Because counterfactual thinking entails replaying past events, people who have a tendency to dwell on past events (i.e., *ruminators*) should be more likely than others to engage in counterfactual thinking. Davis' (1991) results are consistent with this hypothesis. Davis found that scores on a dispositional rumination scale were moderately related to the frequency of undoing, both in response to a hypothetical scenario and an actual life event. However, research also has shown that engaging in counterfactual thoughts is distinct from general ruminative tendencies. For example, although Davis et al. (1995) found that only people who ruminated about a past negative event imagined how it could have turned out differently, over half of the ruminators did not mention undoing the event in any way. It was also found that rumination was not related to psychological distress when counterfactuals were controlled for, but counterfactuals were related to psychological distress when rumination was controlled for (Davis et al., 1995).

Negative Affectivity. Upward counterfactuals have been linked to increased feelings of regret (e.g., Landman, 1987) and increased psychological distress (Davis et al., 1995). It has also been suggested that people who are in a bad mood are more likely than people in a good mood to engage in upward counterfactuals (Davis, 1991). Because of the link between upward counterfactuals and negative affect, people who are particularly susceptible to negative affect, such as people who score high on neuroticism, may be more likely than others to engage in upward counterfactuals. Davis' (1991) findings are consistent with this suggestion. Davis found that people who were high on neuroticism were more likely than others to imagine how a negative life event could have turned out better.

Belief in a Just World. Some people strongly believe that the world is just, that is, that people receive what they deserve in this world (Rubin & Peplau, 1975). If strong believers in a just world think that outcomes are deserved, then they should have difficulty in imagining how things could have turned out differently. In contrast, those who have a weak belief in a just world think that outcomes do not necessarily reflect the deservingness of a person, so they should more easily imagine how things could have been different. Thus, believers in a just world should engage in less counterfactual thinking than do nonbelievers.

Testing for Individual Differences

In an initial investigation of whether some people consistently engage in more counterfactual thinking than others, and what personality characteristics these people possess, Kasimatis and colleagues (Kasimatis & Sterling, 1994; Kasimatis & Wells, 1993) conducted two similar studies. In both studies, college students at a small private liberal arts college were asked to read six hypothetical scenarios, which portrayed social situations with dramatic outcomes—two with negative outcomes, two with neutral outcomes, and two with positive outcomes. For example, one neutral scenario described a situation in which the main character is registering for college courses but does not know which instructors are teaching the three sections of a course. The character is delayed in arriving at registration because of a talkative neighbor. By the time the student arrives, only two sections are open. The student flips a coin to decide which of the two remaining sections to choose and selects the section with an adequate instructor. The closed section had a terrible instructor, and the section the student did not choose had a great instructor. As they read each scenario, participants were asked to vividly imagine themselves in the situation. After having read each scenario they were asked to write down five thoughts they had in response to the scenario. Then, participants completed several personality measures. Several weeks later, participants returned. This time, they read six new scenarios which depicted different situations but which were similar to the first set in that they depicted somewhat similar events and had similar numbers of events that could be undone. The scenarios in this set were also similar in that two had negative outcomes, two had neutral outcomes, and two had positive outcomes. Participants also completed several more personality measures.

The two studies differed only in the personality measures included. In the first study, participants completed a measure of global self-esteem (Rosenberg, 1965), a measure of locus of control (Rotter, 1966), a measure of desire for control (Burger & Cooper, 1979), and a measure of optimism (Scheier & Carver, 1985). In the second study, participants completed a need for cognition scale (Cacioppo, Petty, & Kao, 1984), a belief-in-a-just-world scale (Rubin & Peplau, 1975), a rumination scale (i.e., the Rehearsal subscale of the Emotion Control Questionnaire; Rogers & Nesshover, 1987), a measure of the big five factors of personality (Costa & McCrae, 1992), and the COPE scale (Carver et al., 1989). The COPE scale is a 60-item questionnaire designed for the assessment of 13 well-defined coping strategies (and includes two experimental scales), which can be roughly categorized as problem focused (active coping, planning coping, suppression of competing activities, restraint coping, and seeking of instrumental social support) or emotion focused (seeking of emotional social support, positive reinterpretation, acceptance, denial, and turning to religion).

For both studies, participants' thoughts in response to each scenario were coded by an independent rater as reflecting an upward counterfactual regarding their own actions (e.g., "If only I had picked section A . . ."), an upward counterfactual regarding someone else's action or an external event (e.g., "If only they published the names of the instructors . . ."), a downward counterfactual regarding their own actions (e.g., "Thank goodness I talked to my neighbor for a while, or I might have ended up with the terrible instructor"), a downward counterfactual regarding someone else's actions or an external event (e.g., "If section C hadn't closed I'd be stuck with a terrible instructor"), or other type of thought (fitting into none of the other categories).

Consistency Over Time. In both studies the number and type of counterfactual responses to the scenarios varied considerably, with some participants writing no thoughts that could be coded as counterfactual and with others reporting more than 40 counterfactual thoughts across the 12 scenarios (with an average of about 16 counterfactual thoughts). Further, the results of both studies showed that this tendency was fairly consistent. Those who engaged in much counterfactual thinking in response to the first set of scenarios tended to be the same ones who reported many counterfactuals in response to the second set of scenarios ($r = .56$ and .59, for Studies 1 and 2 respectively), even though the scenarios in each measurement session were different. This pattern was true for both upward counterfactuals (r = .51 and .51, for Studies 1 and 2, respectively) and downward counterfactuals (r = .41 and .50, for Studies 1 and 2 respectively). Further, of those who did engage in a lot of counterfactual thinking, some were more likely to use upward counterfactuals, while others were more likely to use downward counterfactuals (β = −.98).

Relations With Personality Characteristics. To determine what types of individuals were likely to engage in counterfactual thinking in general and the different types of counterfactuals, Kasimatis and colleagues (Kasimatis & Sterling, 1994; Kasimatis & Wells, 1993) conducted correlation and regression analyses. Results of these analyses show that despite the evidence for temporal consistency in counterfactual thinking few significant correlations existed between the general tendency of people to engage in counterfactual thinking and their scores on personality measures. The researchers, however, did find some meaningful relationships between personality characteristics and a person's tendency to engage in specific types of counterfactual thinking. Correlations between personality measures and the different types of counterfactual thoughts are presented in Table 3.1.

One of Kasimatis and colleagues' (Kasimatis & Sterling, 1994; Kasimatis & Wells, 1993) main hypotheses was that optimists would be less likely than pessimists to engage in upward counterfactuals and more likely to engage in downward counterfactuals. The results of the first study are consistent with this prediction. The number of upward counterfactual thoughts across the scenarios was significantly and negatively related to optimism scores when variance from downward thoughts was controlled. Similarly, the number of downward counterfactual thoughts across the scenarios was significantly and positively related to optimism scores when variance from upward thoughts was controlled. In other words, people who are optimistic are less likely to imagine how events could have turned out better and more likely to imagine how events could have turned out worse.

The researchers also expected self-esteem to play a role in the generation of counterfactual thoughts. Specifically, they expected individuals with high self-esteem to engage in fewer upward counterfactuals than would individuals with low self-esteem, especially those regarding their own actions in response to negative events. The results supported this prediction. Correlations revealed a significant negative relationship between upward, self-relevant counterfactuals in response to the negative scenarios and scores on the self-esteem scale (r = −.18). This finding is consistent with Roese and Olson's (1993) findings and with the self-enhancing role of counterfactuals. Further, regression analyses showed that,

TABLE 3.1
Correlations Between Counterfactual Responses
and Personality Characteristics

Personality Characteristics	Type of Counterfactual Thought		
	Overall	Upward	Downward
Optimism	.03	[−.20]	[.21]
Self-esteem	−.05	[−.14]	[.11]
Desire for control	.02	.06	−.02
Locus of control	.08	[−.11]	[.16]
Need for cognition	−.03	.01	−.07
Rumination	.07	.03	.07
Belief in a just world	.17	.12	.18
Positive reinterpretation	−.17	−.28	−.03
Acceptance	−.05	−.19	−.04
Active coping	−.01	−.09	.05
Planning coping	.01	.01	−.01
Neuroticism	.07	.04	.10

Note. Figures in brackets represent the standardized regression coefficients for the relationship between the personality measure and one type of counterfactual, when the other type of counterfactual was controlled.

This table is adapted from "Counterfactual Thinking: Evidence for Individual Differences," by M. Kasimatis and G. L. Wells, June 1993, a poster presented at a meeting of the American Psychological Society, Chicago, and from "Further Evidence for Individual Differences in Counterfactual Thinking," by M. Kasimatis and L. Sterling, June 1994, a poster presented at a meeting of the American Psychological Society, Washington, DC. Adapted with permission.

overall, there was a negative relationship between self-esteem and upward counterfactuals, when downward counterfactuals were controlled, such that individuals with high self-esteem were consistently less likely than those with low self-esteem to imagine how things could have turned out better, regardless of whether they were undoing their own actions or the actions of others.

In light of the possible role of counterfactual thinking in gaining mastery over a negative event, the researchers expected that individuals with a high desire for control would be more likely to engage in more overall counterfactual thinking than those with a low desire for control. No support for this prediction was found. Desire for control was in no way related to a person's propensity to engage in overall, upward, or downward counterfactuals.

Although a relationship between locus of control and counterfactual thinking was not specifically predicted, the researchers thought that in light of the potential control aspect of mental simulations, locus of control might be relevant. Although results of the first study showed that there was no overall correlation between locus of control and counterfactual thinking, regression analyses did show that those with an internal locus of control were more likely to engage in downward counterfactuals, when upward counterfactuals were controlled.

Results of the second study showed few relationships between the cognitive individual differences and an individual's propensity to engage in counterfactual thinking. Specifically, no relationship was found between counterfactual thinking and need for cognition, rumination, or most of the coping strategies. The researchers further found no relation between one's propensity to engage in counterfactual thinking and neuroticism. However, results were consistent with the emotion function of counterfactual thinking in that both a positive reinterpretation coping strategy and an acceptance coping strategy were negatively related to upward counterfactuals. That is, participants who revealed a tendency to interpret stressful events in a positive manner or to simply accept negative events were less likely than others to think about how things could have turned out better. Finally, there was an unexpected positive relation between belief in a just world and downward counterfactuals; individuals who indicated a strong belief that the world is just were more likely than their counterparts to engage in downward counterfactuals in response to the scenarios. The meaning of this finding is unclear. Possibly, because the scenarios were self-referent, those individuals with a strong belief in a just world were searching for a way to *not* blame themselves for the occurrence of negative events.

In sum, results of these initial studies suggest that some people show a consistent tendency to imagine how events could have turned out differently. Some of these people are more likely to consistently imagine how things could have turned out better, and others are more likely to imagine how things could have turned out worse. Further, this tendency is meaningfully related to other personality characteristics, such as self-esteem, optimism, locus of control, and specific dispositional coping strategies.

Counterfactual Thinking and Analytical Thinking Abilities. Although the results of the first two studies were promising in terms of demonstrating individual differences in counterfactual thinking, the researchers wanted to make sure that there was not an alternative explanation for the findings. Specifically, there was the possibility that people consistently differ in their tendency to engage in counterfactual thinking because of differences in analytical thinking abilities. That is, counterfactual responses to the scenarios might merely reflect an intellectual skill rather than a personality characteristic.

We tried to rule out this possibility in a third study (Wells & Kasimatis, 1994). In the first measurement session of this study, participants read and responded to one of the sets of six scenarios that were used in the first two studies, with the same instructions. In the second measurement period, participants read and responded to a second set of scenarios, but with different instructions. Specifically, before generating thoughts in response to each scenario, participants were told what a counterfactual is and were given examples of counterfactual thoughts. Then they were asked to generate counterfactual statements in response to each of the scenarios. Participants also completed a test of analytical ability comprised of sample questions from the analytical section of the Graduate Record Examination (GRE; Brownstein & Weiner, 1985).

A cursory review of the participants' responses indicated that all participants were capable of undoing events in such a way as to change the outcome of the situation, findings suggesting that individual differences in counterfactual thinking are not due to differences in an intellectual ability. Further, results showed that there was no correlation between GRE scores and the number of counterfactuals, regardless of type of instruction, a finding suggesting that neither an individual's ability to engage counterfactual thinking nor the propensity to do so is related to analytical thinking ability. Finally, there was no correlation between the number of counterfactuals in the first measurement period and number of counterfactuals in the second measurement period (with counterfactual instructions), a finding suggesting that counterfactual thinking is something that everybody is *capable* of doing if asked but that some people naturally prefer not to do it.

Counterfactuals in Response to Life Events. Although the results of these three studies indicated that there are meaningful individual differences in counterfactual thinking, some questions remained. Specifically, the findings indicated that counterfactual thinking apparently is not correlated with the more cognitive or problem focused individual differences, such as need for cognition and rumination. It does seem possible for people to think extensively, and to enjoy thinking, without engaging in counterfactual thought, but it seems unlikely that they would engage in counterfactual thought without liking to think.

There are two potential problems with the research that might yield this finding. The first is the use of hypothetical scenarios instead of actual life events. Although participants were asked to vividly imagine themselves in situations, the artificiality of the scenarios perhaps led participants to respond in ways in which they would not naturally respond.[2] The second

---

[2]We do not believe that this is a compelling argument. If the hypothetical scenarios were too artificial for participants to relate to, then we should not have obtained the pattern of results in the first study. For example, it seems unlikely that individuals with high self-esteem would engage in self-protective strategies unless they felt that their self-esteem was threatened.

possible problem is that participants were asked to write down a certain number of thoughts in response to each scenario; that is, they were forced to think a certain amount when they might not have done so on their own. Thus, the *type* of thinking rather than *amount* of thinking was possibly being measured. In contrast, measures of need for cognition and rumination focus on an individual's propensity to engage in extensive thinking.

To address these problems, Kasimatis (1994) conducted a fourth study. To avoid the artificiality of hypothetical scenarios, Kasimatis asked college students to think about a particularly negative event that had happened to them in the past year and to describe that event. Then, to avoid the problem of forcing them to think a certain number of thoughts, participants were asked to write on a blank page the thoughts they had had about the event since it occurred. However, not all participants received the same instructions. In the past, when using a similar procedure, most counterfactual researchers explained counterfactuals to participants and then asked them how many such thoughts they had had about the event. In contrast, Kasimatis and Wells (1993) and Kasimatis and Sterling (1994) did not specifically ask for counterfactual responses because such an instruction might have affected responses. In this fourth study, Kasimatis (1994) asked half of the participants merely to record any thoughts they had had about the event since it had occurred (free-thought instructions). The other half were told that often people look back on events and think "What if . . ."; participants then were asked to list those things (if any) that they had undone in their minds to make events turn out differently, whether better or worse (counterfactual instructions). Responses in both of these instruction conditions were coded for counterfactual content. Participants also completed most of the personality measures that were included in the two studies by Kasimatis and colleagues (Kasimatis & Sterling, 1994; Kasimatis & Wells, 1993).

Results again showed a wide range of responses, with many people in both instruction conditions reporting no counterfactual thoughts and others reporting several. As the results reported in Table 3.2 indicate, participants reported significantly more counterfactuals when they were told what counterfactuals are and then asked how many they had had than when they were simply asked what they had thought about the event since its occurrence.

The implication of this finding is unclear. One possible explanation is that participants in the counterfactual-instruction condition were yielding to demand characteristics and that responses in the other condition thus represent a more valid measure of counterfactual thinking. Another possible explanation is that those in the no-counterfactual instruction condition might have been engaging in counterfactual thinking but did not record those specific thoughts because they were not requested.

TABLE 3.2
Mean Levels of Counterfactual Thoughts as a Function
of Type of Instruction

| | | Type of Instruction | |
| | | Counterfactual | Free Thought |
Dependent Variables			
Total counterfactuals	M	1.92	.47
	SD	1.51	.80
Upward counterfactuals	M	1.79	.29
	SD	1.45	.65
Downward counterfactuals	M	.14	.18
	SD	.49	.52

The most important question in this study was whether counterfactual responses to actual life events were related to personality characteristics in the same way as those to hypothetical scenarios. More specifically, Kasimatis (1994) expected to find a relation between counterfactual responses to actual life events and a need for both cognition and rumination. As the results reported in Table 3.3 indicate, the way in which personality characteristics were related to counterfactual responses to life events depended on the type of instructions participants received. For example, a positive relationship between need for cognition and upward counterfactuals was found in the counterfactual instructions condition but *not* in the free-thought condition. In contrast, there was a positive relationship between rumination and upward counterfactuals only in the free-thought instructions condition.

Further results showed that of those who received counterfactual instructions, individuals with high self-esteem were less likely than those

TABLE 3.3
Correlations Between Counterfactual Responses and
Personality Characteristics as a Function of Type of Instructions

Personality Characteristics	Counterfactual Instructions			Free-Thought Instructions		
	Overall	Upward	Downward	Overall	Upward	Downward
Desire for control	.09	.09	.02	.05	.04	.03
Locus of control	.09	.09	.01	−.07	−.15	.08
Need for cognition	.22	.20	.08	.01	−.05	.05
Rumination	.12	.09	.08	.08	.19	−.12
Belief in just world	−.08	−.23	.00	.12	−.06	.26
Positive reinterpretation	−.09	−.14	.15	−.12	−.18	.04
Religion coping	−.04	−.06	.07	−.24	−.22	−.10
Acceptance	−.03	−.10	.18	.00	−.11	.14

with low self-esteem to undo their own actions (χ^2 = 6.56). Because all participants described a negative event, these findings replicate those of Kasimatis and Wells (1993) and Roese and Olson (1993). However, no such relationship was found in the free-thought instruction condition. Similarly, when participants received counterfactual instructions the earlier finding that optimists were less likely than pessimists to engage in upward counterfactuals was again replicated (χ^2 = 3.82), but there was no such relationship in the no-counterfactual instruction condition. Finally, in the counterfactual-instruction condition, there was a positive relationship between an acceptance coping strategy and downward counterfactuals; people who tended to accept negative events were more likely to imagine how things could have been worse.

For those who received free-thought instructions, there was a positive relationship between downward counterfactuals and belief in a just world, a finding which replicates the earlier finding (Kasimatis & Sterling, 1994). These findings, along with the earlier finding, suggest that those who have a strong belief in a just world are less likely to spontaneously imagine how things could have turned out better. There was also a negative relationship between a religion coping strategy and upward counterfactuals; those who tended to turn to God or religion when faced with a stressful event were less likely than others to imagine how things could have turned out better.

Collapsing across instruction condition, Kasimatis (1994) found a negative correlation between an acceptance coping strategy and upward counterfactuals; those who tended to cope with a stressful event by accepting its occurrence were less likely than others to imagine how things could have turned out better (r = −.23). This finding is consistent with that from Kasimatis and Sterling's (1994) study. Finally, Kasimatis (1994) found no relationship between desire for control and counterfactuals, regardless of type of instruction, a finding consistent with Kasimatis and Wells' (1993) finding.

In sum, the study in which participants responded to actual life events instead of hypothetical scenarios replicated many of the earlier findings from studies that used hypothetical scenarios. However, Kasimatis (1994) also found relationships between counterfactual responses to life events and personality characteristics, relationships that were not evident in the studies with hypothetical scenarios. This difference suggests that the two tasks may not be measuring exactly the same thing. Specifically, when participants were free to write as few or as many thoughts as they wanted in response to an actual life event, upward counterfactuals were positively related to rumination and need for cognition. However, the relationships between counterfactual responses to actual life events and personality characteristics depended on the type of instructions.

CONCLUSIONS

Implications of Known Individual Differences

In light of these research results, a few important conclusions about individual differences in counterfactual thinking can be drawn. First, it is apparent that some people are consistently more likely than others to engage in counterfactual thinking. Further, this consistency is evident for both overall number of counterfactuals as well as type of counterfactual. That is, some people consistently undo events in an upward fashion ("if only . . ."), while others consistently undo events in a downward fashion ("at least . . ."). These findings represent the first prospective demonstration of stable individual differences in counterfactual thinking. They also highlight the importance of researchers taking person factors as well as situational factors into account when predicting the occurrence of counterfactual thought.

Second, the pattern of relationships between personality characteristics and an individual's propensity to engage in counterfactual thinking suggests that counterfactual thinking does serve certain functions. Specifically, the results of several studies suggest that counterfactual thinking serves an affective function. In addition to Roese's (1994) demonstration of the affective function of counterfactual thinking, the results of the studies we have discussed here indicate that optimists, individuals with high self-esteem, and those who tend to use emotion focused coping strategies (e.g., positive reinterpretation and acceptance) engage more in downward counterfactuals or less in upward counterfactuals than do those who score low on these dimensions.

In contrast, the results of the studies provide little evidence for the problem focused functions of counterfactual thinking, such as future planning and preparation or regaining mastery. Although it is likely that mental simulations have the ability to help prepare people for future events (Roese, 1994) and even to help people gain a sense of control, people apparently do not *naturally* use counterfactuals to achieve these effects. Specifically, in two studies (Kasimatis & Sterling, 1994; Kasimatis & Wells, 1993) no relation between counterfactual thinking and desire for control or between counterfactual thinking and active and planning coping strategies was found. Further, in only one study (Kasimatis, 1994) was a relation between counterfactual thinking and need for cognition found, and then only when participants were given counterfactual instructions. If people who are motivated to gain control and typically try to solve problems are not more likely than others to engage in counterfactual thinking, then that counterfactual thinking normally serves a specific preparative or planning function seems unlikely. This is not to say that counterfactual thinking cannot serve those functions. On the contrary, evidence from studies by Roese (1994) and Janoff–Bulman and colleagues (Janoff–Bulman, 1979; Janoff–Bulman & Lang–Gunn, 1988) suggests that there are specific times when a person's imagining how things could have turned out better or blaming one's own behaviors for negative outcomes can be adaptive. However, the times when upward counterfactuals serve these beneficial functions are probably limited (cf. Sherman & McConnell, chapter 7).

Finally, the pattern of findings from the studies discussed here suggests that the observed propensity for some people to engage in counterfactual thinking in response to negative events is a unique individual difference characteristic. That is, the pattern of findings is not merely reflecting individual differences in intelligence, as shown in the study by Wells and Kasimatis (1994). Nor is the apparent propensity to engage in counter-factual thinking merely a ruminative tendency. Although a moderate relation between upward counterfactuals and dispositional rumination was found in Kasimatis' (1994) study, such a relation was not found in the previous study by Kasimatis and Sterling (1994). Further, the corre-lation was not large and occurred only when participants were not given counterfactual instructions. These findings are consistent with those by Davis (1991), who found a weak but significant relation between his measure of propensity to engage in counterfactual thinking and disposi-tional rumination; and with those by Davis et al. (1995), who found that although most of their respondents reported ruminating about a car accident in which they had lost a loved one, only about half reported undoing something about the event.

Future Directions

Despite the considerable evidence for individual differences in counter-factual thinking and the interesting implications of these differences, several important questions remain. First, it is unclear how stable the propensity to engage in counterfactual thinking really is. The fact that any consistency in counterfactual responses was found is impressive because very specific responses were obtained in only two situations and in response to different scenarios. It seems likely that consistency would be more pronounced when averaged across many situations (Epstein, 1979). Future research should address this possibility.

Second, future research should explore the conditions under which people are most likely to engage in counterfactual thinking. Perhaps the role of personality in the generation of counterfactuals depends on the strength of situational determinants (Monson, Keel, Stephens, & Genung, 1982). Thus, in future research, more attention should be given to the *interaction* between person factors and situational factors in counterfactual thinking.

Third, further research on individual differences in counterfactual thinking may shed some light on the distinction between immediate counterfactual thought in response to a particular event and a dispositional tendency to engage in counterfactual thought. That there is a difference between immediate counterfactuals and counterfactuals over the long term is suggested by recent research by Gilovich and Medvec (1993, chapter 9, this volume). They found that when looking back over their lives people are more likely to regret things that they *did not* do instead of things they did do. These findings contradict Landman's (1987) assertion that people are more likely to regret actions than inactions. Gilovich and Medvec suggest that the explanation for this discrepancy is that regret follows a systematic time course. That is, actions cause more pain in the short term, but inactions are regretted more in the long term.

Fourth, future researchers should explore in more depth the relation between different types of counterfactual thinking and actual health outcomes. So far, only educated guesses can be made, based on relations with other personality characteristics. Future research should examine the daily lives of individuals to determine how the propensity to engage in counterfactual thought moderates the stress-illness relationship.

Finally, the findings that we have discussed suggest that the way in which counterfactual thinking is measured affects not only how much counterfactual thinking participants report, but also how counterfactual responses are related to other variables. Specifically, participants reported more counterfactual thoughts when instructions included an explanation of counterfactuals than when counterfactuals were not mentioned. Further, counterfactuals in response to these different instructions showed different patterns of relationships with scores on personality measures. These findings have implications for the interpreting of the counterfactual literature and for future research, although it is not clear what the implications are. One suggestion for future researchers is to examine the extent to which demand characteristics influence the results of counterfactual studies.

REFERENCES

Brown, J. D., Collins, R. L., & Schmidt, G. W. (1988). Self-esteem and direct versus indirect forms of self-enhancement. *Journal of Personality and Social Psychology, 55,* 445–453.

Brownstein, S. C., & Weiner, M. (1985). *How to prepare for the Graduate Record Examination general test* (7th Edition). Barron's Educational Series: Woodbury, NY.

Burger, J. M., & Cooper, H. M. (1979). The desirability of control. *Motivation and Emotion, 3,* 381–393.

Cacioppo, J. T., Petty, R. E., & Kao, C. F. (1984). The efficient assessment of need for cognition. *Journal of Personality Assessment, 48,* 306–307.

Carver, C. S., Scheier, M. F., & Weintraub, J. K. (1989). Assessing coping strategies: A theoretically based approach. *Journal of Personality and Social Psychology, 36*, 267–283.

Costa, P. T., & McCrae, R. R. (1992). *Revised NEO Personality Inventory (NEO–PI–R) and NEO Five Factor Inventory (NEO–FFI) professional manual.* Odessa, FL: Psychological Assessment Resources.

Davis, C. (1991). *The undoing experience: Antecedents, consequences, and individual differences.* Unpublished master's thesis, University of British Columbia, Vancouver, Canada.

Davis, C., Lehman, D., Wortman, C., Silver, R. C., & Thompson, S. (1995). Undoing of traumatic life events. *Personality and Social Psychology Bulletin, 21*, 109–124.

Epstein, S. (1979). The stability of behavior: I. On predicting most of the people much of the time. *Journal of Personality and Social Psychology, 37*, 1097–1126.

Gilovich, T., & Medvec, V. H. (1993, August). *Temporal pattern to the experience of regret.* Paper presented at a meeting of the American Psychological Association, Toronto.

Janoff–Bulman, R. (1979). Characterological versus behavioral self-blame: Inquiries into depression and rape. *Journal of Personality and Social Psychology, 37*, 1798–1809.

Janoff–Bulman, R., & Lang–Gunn, L. (1988). Coping with disease, crime, and accidents: The role of self-blame attributions. In L. Y. Abramson (Ed.), *Social cognition and clinical psychology: A synthesis* (pp. 116–147). New York: Guilford.

Johnson, J. T. (1986). The knowledge of what might have been: Affective and attributional consequences of near outcomes. *Personality and Social Psychology Bulletin, 12*, 51–62.

Kahneman, D., & Miller, D. T. (1986). Norm theory: Comparing reality to its alternatives. *Psychological Review, 93*, 136–153.

Kahneman, D., & Tversky, A. (1982). The simulation heuristic. In D. Kahneman, P. Slovic, & A. Tversky (Eds.), *Judgment under uncertainty: Heuristics and biases* (pp. 201–208). New York: Cambridge University Press.

Kasimatis, M. (1994). [Issues in the measurement of counterfactual thinking]. Unpublished raw data, Hope College, Holland, Michigan.

Kasimatis, M., & Sterling, L. (1994, June). *Further evidence for individual differences in counterfactual thinking.* Poster presented at a meeting of the American Psychological Society, Washington, DC.

Kasimatis, M., & Wells, G. L. (1993, June). *Counterfactual thinking: Evidence for individual differences.* Poster presented at a meeting of the American Psychological Society, Chicago.

Kelly, G. A. (1970). A brief introduction to personal construct theory. In D. Bannister (Ed.), *Perspectives in personal construct theory* (pp. 1–29). London: Academic Press.

Landman, J. (1987). Regret and elation following action and inaction: Affective responses to positive versus negative outcomes. *Personality and Social Psychology Bulletin, 13*, 524–536.

Landman, J., & Manis, J. D. (1992). What might have been: Counterfactual thought concerning personal decisions. *British Journal of Psychology, 83*, 473–477.

Lazarus, R. S., & Folkman, S. (1984). *Stress, appraisal, and coping.* New York: Springer.

McFarland, C., & Miller, D. T. (1994). The framing of relative performance feedback: Seeing the glass as half empty or half full. *Journal of Personality and Social Psychology, 66*, 1061–1073.

Miller, D. T., & Gunasegaram, S. (1990). Temporal order and perceived mutability of events: Implications for blame assignment. *Journal of Personality and Social Psychology, 59*, 1111–1118.

Miller, D. T., & McFarland, C. (1986). Counterfactual thinking and victim compensation: A test of norm theory. *Personality and Social Psychology Bulletin, 12*, 513–519.

Monson, T. C., Keel, R., Stephens, D., & Genung, V. (1982). Trait attributions: Relative validity, covariation with behavior, and prospect of future interaction. *Journal of Personality and Social Psychology, 42*, 1014–1024.

Roese, N. J. (1994). The functional basis of counterfactual thinking. *Journal of Personality and Social Psychology, 66*, 805–818.

Roese, N. J., & Olson, J. M. (1993). Self-esteem and counterfactual thinking. *Journal of Personality and Social Psychology, 65*, 199–206.

Rogers, D., & Nesshover, W. (1987). The construction and preliminary validation of a scale for measuring emotional control. *Personality and Individual Differences, 8*, 527–534.

Rosenberg, M. (1965). *Society and the adolescent self-image*. Princeton, NJ: Princeton University Press.

Rotter, J. (1966). Generalized expectancies for internal versus external control of reinforcement. *Psychological Monographs, 80* (1, Whole No. 609).

Rubin, Z., & Peplau, L. A. (1975). Who believes in a just world? *Journal of Social Issues, 31*(3), 65–79.

Scheier, M. F., & Carver, C. S. (1985). Optimism, coping, and health: Assessment and implications of generalized outcome expectancies. *Health Psychology, 4*, 219–247.

Sorrentino, R. M., & Short, J. C. (1986). Uncertainty orientation, motivation, and cognition. In R. M. Sorrentino & E. T. Higgins (Eds.), *Handbook of motivation and cognition: Foundations of social behavior* (Vol. 1, pp. 379–403). New York: Guilford Press.

Taylor, S. E., & Brown, J. D. (1988). Illusion and well-being: A social psychological perspective on mental health. *Psychological Bulletin, 103*, 193–210.

Taylor, S. E., & Schneider, S. K. (1989). Coping and the simulation of events. *Social Cognition, 7*, 174–194.

Taylor, S. E., Wood, J. V., & Lichtman, R. R. (1983). It could be worse: Selective evaluation as a response to victimization. *Journal of Social Issues, 39*(2), 19–40.

Wells, G. L., & Gavanski, I. (1989). Mental simulation of causality. *Journal of Personality and Social Psychology, 56*, 161–169.

Wells, G. L., & Kasimatis, M. (1994). [Counterfactual thinking and intelligence]. Unpublished raw data, Iowa State University, Ames, Iowa.

Wells, G. L., Taylor, B. R., & Turtle, J. W. (1987). The undoing of scenarios. *Journal of Personality and Social Psychology, 53*, 421–430.

Wheeler, L., & Miyake, K. (1992). Social comparison in everyday life. *Journal of Personality and Social Psychology, 62*, 760–773.

4

Comparison Processes in Counterfactual Thought

David Dunning
Cornell University

Scott F. Madey
University of Toledo

Reactions to events often not only require knowledge of what happened but also require a sense of what failed to happen. Consider Terry Malloy, the down-and-out former boxer in Elia Kazan's classic movie, *On the Waterfront*. For him, his life is not defined by the history he has experienced but rather by the history he was asked to forego. He is consumed by thoughts that he "could've been a contender . . . could've been somebody," had he not followed his brother's advice and "taken a dive" in the most important bout of his life. Or consider the two sisters in Herbert Ross's 1977 film, *The Turning Point*. One has forsaken a career in ballet to raise a family. The other chose the career and never married. The thoughts and emotions that each sibling has about her life are not so much driven by the experiences she has accumulated or the circumstances she finds herself in. Rather, they are driven by some sense of what the the life of her sister must be like, a life that reminds her of what has failed to happen in her own existence.

Researchers in counterfactual thinking have begun to investigate how people construct these "what failed to happens" or the "what might have beens" that give meaning to the events they experience (Kahneman & Miller, 1986; Miller, Turnbull, & McFarland, 1990; Wells, Taylor, & Turtle, 1987). For example, a growing body of research has focused on *when* people will spontaneously or automatically consider hypothetical alternatives without prompting (Kahneman & Miller, 1986). Another line of work has concentrated on *which* counterfactual world people will choose to employ in their assessments when there are many plausible candidates (Dunning & Hayes, 1994; Gavanski & Wells, 1989; Medvec, Madey, & Gilovich, 1994; Wells & Gavanski, 1989).

In this chapter, we propose that the work of counterfactual assessment does not end when people make their choice of counterfactual comparison worlds. There are other cognitive tasks that people must complete to render a counterfactual assessment. First, they must *simulate* that counterfactual alternative, bringing to mind specific features of that world and generating likely outcomes that the alternative would produce (Kahneman & Tversky, 1982). Second, they must *compare* that simulation to what is known or expected about present circumstances. In this chapter, we give close scrutiny to the research with regard to these final two phases of counterfactual thought.

More to the point, we propose that these last two phases of counterfactual assessment can be influenced by many psychological variables, and that the influence of these factors is revealed by *framing effects*. By framing, we refer to how the counterfactual comparison is superficially posed to or phrased by the individual. For example, there are many ways that we, the authors, could assess the effect of writing this chapter on ourselves. We could ask how writing the chapter may benefit us (e.g., "How much of a better, articulated understanding of counterfactual reasoning will we have if we write this chapter?"), or we could ask how foregoing the work would lead us to a disadvantage (e.g., "How much less of an understanding of counterfactual reasoning will we have if we decide not to write the chapter?"). We propose that people's assessments of benefits and disadvantages may vary depending on the frame of the question they adopt.

AN EXAMPLE

Consider the following example of the effect of framing on counterfactual assessment. One of us was once a teaching assistant in a social psychology class in which the instructor provided students with his own lecture notes ("socnotes"), for a nominal fee. At the end of the class, the teaching assistants decided to survey students about their opinions of these socnotes (Dunning & Parpal, 1985). How much had they improved the class experience? How much had they improved the students' performance? Toward that end, the students were asked to compare the world they inhabited (having socnotes) with a counterfactual alternative (not having the notes). Although this was a situation in which the choice of counterfactual comparison was set, it was also one in which people still had to complete the simulation and comparison phases of the assessment.

Of key interest here was the varied framing of the assessment. Some students were asked to describe the benefits of having the notes (e.g., "How much more did you get out of the class with socnotes than you would have without the notes?" "How much more prepared were you for the midterm exams with socnotes than you would have been without?"). Others were asked to characterize the disadvantages of not having the notes (e.g., "How much less would you have gotten out of the class without socnotes than you did with them?" "How much less prepared would you have been without socnotes than you were with them?").

Putatively, the questions in each condition asked for the same assessment (i.e., to compare having socnotes to not having them), and participants in each condition should generally have provided the same answers (after the scores for participants in the subtractive frame were reversed to make all participants' responses comparable). However, as the results reported in Table 4.1 indicate, participants in the having-socnotes conditions perceived much more impact than did participants in the not-having-socnotes condition. Participants in the former condition stated that the notes had made a greater difference in what they had acquired from the lectures, in their knowledge of class subject matter, in preparation for the midterm exam, and in their enjoyment of the course than the difference reported by respondents in the latter group. Overall, when students' assessments across all items were combined, participants in the having-socnotes condition perceived the notes as more impactful than did students in the not-having-socnotes condition (see Table 4.1).

CONTRAST MODEL OF JUDGMENTS
OF SIMILARITY AND DIFFERENCE

Why did these differences emerge? How did the frame of the question influence people's assessments? We argue that these framing effects can be understood from an examination of basic research on judgments of similarity and difference and more recent work on the features of the situations that people weigh when they make evaluations of this sort.

To assess the impact of socnotes on their class experience, students probably relied on some sort of *simulation heuristic* (Kahneman & Tversky, 1982). That is, they had to construct a mental model of the two worlds under consideration (having socnotes and not having socnotes) and then examine the extent to which each world suggested or precluded the outcome under consideration (e.g., knowledge of class subject matter). The student could have completed these tasks by thinking of instances that exemplied the outcome (e.g., "With socnotes, I had time to ask the instructor that question in class about a statement that confused me").

TABLE 4.1
Impact of Purchasing Prepared Lecture Notes
(Socnotes) on Class Experience

	Subject of Comparison		
Measure	Having Notes (n = 34)	Not Having Notes (n = 36)	p
How much acquired from lecture	6.9	4.5	<.005
Knowledge of subject matter	6.1	2.8	<.0001
Preparation for midterm exam	7.0	4.8	<.005
Number of questions answered/ missed on midterm exam	1.5	1.3	
Enjoyment of course	7.8	6.4	<.02
Overall[a]	.30	−.29	<.001

Note. From Dunning and Parpal (1985). All questions were answered on 19-point scales that ranged from −9 (much less) to 0 (no impact) to 9 (much more), except for the "Number of questions answered/missed," which was rated on a similar 7-point scale. In the having-notes condition, higher numbers represent that the respondent reported experiencing *more* impact on the outcome in question. All responses in the not-having-notes condition were reverse-scored, so that higher numbers indicate that the respondents reported that not having the notes would have *decreased* the degree of each outcome in question.
[a]Average of all items, after each measure standardized.

Students could have also thought of factors that promoted or reduced the consequence in question (e.g., "Because I had socnotes, I didn't have to spend time deciphering my own handwriting when studying for the class, and that allowed me to concentrate on the material"). Of key import here, students in both cases were focusing on *features*. They were considering characteristics or attributes of one world or the other that influenced whether or not they would obtain the outcome under consideration.

With this emphasis on features, the framing effect observed in the example becomes explicable. Indeed, it is directly suggested by Tversky's (1977; see also Tversky & Gati, 1978) contrast model of similarity judgment. In the model, the task of judging similarity or difference is conceived to be a feature-matching process. When given two objects to compare (as, for example, the United States and Canada), people first must generate characteristics they associate with each object. They then determine the extent to which they generate features that are shared by both objects as well as features that are unique to each. What is important in the contrast model and what drives many of the framing effects predicted by the model is that the attention paid and weight given to certain features depends on the exact wording of the similarity assessment. Specifically, in judgments of similarity or difference, one object often serves as the *subject* of the comparison, the other as the *referent*. For example, in the question "How different is Canada from the United

States?" Canada is the subject, with the United States playing the role of referent. In several experiments, Tversky demonstrated that people give more weight to the unique features of the object serving as the subject than to those of the referent.

Because of this tendency, Tversky (1977) proposed that framing effects are likely to arise when people compare a *prominent* or *familiar* object, one for which they have much information that is easily brought to mind, to a nonprominent entity. When the familiar object is made the subject of comparison, people are likely to find unique features and thus perceive much contrast. When the nonprominent object is made the subject, people are less likely to find unique attributes and thus will perceive little difference. For example, in the question "How dissimilar is Russia to Belarus?" people tend to perceive a good deal of difference between the two countries. However, when the assessment is framed as "How dissimilar is Belarus to Russia?" people tend to view the two countries as rather similar.

In the social realm, many judgmental asymmetries suggested by the contrast model have been demonstrated. For example, Holyoak and Gordon (1983; see also Read, 1987; Srull & Gaelick, 1983) asked people to compare themselves to other individuals. People perceived more contrast when the self was made the subject of comparison (e.g., "How different are you from your neighbor?") than when attention was focused on another individual (e.g., "How different is your neighbor from you?"). Holyoak and Gordon went on to show that the effect was mediated by the amount of information that people possessed about other comparison individuals. In a similar vein, Houston, Sherman, and Baker (1989) discovered that preferences between two objects (e.g., automobiles, blind dates) could be shifted by which choice was made the subject of comparison. When an object containing a set of uniquely good features was made the subject of comparison, it was preferred. When the object serving as the subject of comparison possessed uniquely negative features, it was less preferred than the referent object.

Comparing One's Present Situation to Hypothetical Alternatives

This research predicts similar framing effects in counterfactual assessment. Consider a comparison in which a person compares his or her present circumstances, such as a choice of career, to a counterfactual alternative. People can frame such comparisons in two ways. They can make their present circumstance the subject of comparison (e.g., "How different is my life in my present career from what it would be like in the career I would have otherwise pursued?"). They can also make a counterfactual alternative the subject (e.g., "How different would my life had been in my second-choice career from what it is like in my present career?"). We can predict that people will perceive more impact when their present circumstance, the "road taken," is the subject of comparison. This pattern would occur because people have vivid and prominent information about the world they inhabit, or at least much more than they have about counterfactual worlds.

We conducted two surveys to test for this proposed framing asymmetry. In the first survey, Cornell University students assessed the impact of attending Cornell as opposed to attending their second-choice college. Participants were first asked to specify the college (i.e., the other college) they would have attended had they not been accepted by Cornell. They were next asked how their college choice had affected their lives, with the comparison framed so that either their present circumstances (Cornell) or the counterfactual alternative (the other college) served as the subject of comparison. For example, participants in the Cornell focus group were asked, "How much did coming to Cornell instead of the other college affect the types of friends you have?" Participants in the other-college focus condition were asked, "How much would going to the other college instead of Cornell have affected the types of friends you have?"

In the second survey, a similar group of students assessed the impact of having chosen their specific college major over the most likely alternative. They were first asked to name the major they would have chosen if they had not selected their present major. Those in the present-major focus condition were then asked questions such as "How much has pursuing your present major instead of the other major affected your enjoyment of the classes you take?" Repondents in the other-major condition were asked, "How much has pursuing the other major instead of your present major have affected your enjoyment of the classes you take? In both investigations, participants reported the degree of influence on their lives using 20-point scales, with larger numbers indicating more difference.

The expected framing effect was observed for both surveys. As the results reported in Table 4.2 indicate, participants perceived more difference between the road taken and its alternative when they focused on Cornell as opposed to their second-choice college, stating, for example, that their coming to Cornell had had a greater impact on their study habits, the types of friends they possessed, the types of students they encountered, their academic life, and their life in general. Indeed, this pattern of responses was evident for all 13 items (although not all differences were statistically significant). Similarly, in the college-major survey, respondents perceived more difference when their chosen major as opposed to the foregone alternative was made the subject of the comparison.

TABLE 4.2
Perceived Differences Between Life at Cornell (the Road Taken)
and Second-Choice College

| | Subject of Comparison | | |
	Cornell (n = 35)	Second-Choice (n = 31)	p
Study habits	11.7	7.4	<.005
Courses	9.3	7.4	
Professors	12.7	11.7	
Career	9.0	7.7	
Groups/Organizations	10.6	9.1	
Academic life	14.0	9.5	<.001
Recreation	10.6	8.3	
Friends	12.3	7.9	<.005
Types of students	14.3	12.0	<.10
Night life	13.4	11.5	
Places to visit	15.3	13.8	
Social life	12.4	10.3	<.10
Life in general	14.3	10.9	<.005
Average of items	12.3	10.0	<.001

As the results provided in Table 4.3 indicate, when respondents were focused on their chosen major, they perceived more impact of that choice with regard to the professors they had, the level of challenge provided by their courses, and the types of students they encountered. This pattern of responses was evident for all nine items (although, again, not all differences were statistically significant).

In sum, the results of these studies demonstrate the applicability of the contrast model of difference judgments for counterfactual assessments. Respondents' assessments of the difference between two worlds, the one they experienced versus some counterfactual alternative, was largely driven by how much information they had about the world serving as the subject of the comparison. Consequently, students in our surveys reported more impact, or difference, when the road taken, or their present circumstances (a world about which they knew relatively much), was made the subject of comparison than when the counterfactual road foregone (the world about which they knew relatively little) was the subject.

Comparing the Present to the Past

If this analysis of this framing effect is accurate, similar predictions can also be made concerning the assessments people make when comparing their present circumstances to the past. Specifically, people should assign

TABLE 4.3
Perceived Differences Between Life in Present Major
Versus Second-Choice Major

	Subject of Comparison		
	Present Major (n = 25)	Second-Choice (n = 23)	p
Types of classes	15.3	12.8	
Enjoyment of classes	12.1	10.6	
Challenge in classes	11.7	8.3	<.10
Professors	14.9	11.9	<.10
Career opportunities	11.7	10.3	
Intellectual skills	12.0	9.8	
Types of students	15.5	10.8	<.005
Work habits	8.8	6.6	
Academic life	12.0	9.6	
Average of items	12.7	10.0	<.02

more impact to life changes when present circumstances as opposed to past circumstances are made the subject of the comparison. People's present circumstances are prominent. They have a rich and vivid array of information about their current day-to-day lives. In comparison, people have less information about their pasts: No one can deny that memory for events fades as time goes by. And as Ebbinghaus (1885/1964) confirmed over a century ago, this decay happens quite quickly.

We investigated this prediction by asking students to assess how much their lives had changed since coming to college. Using the same methods as those in the two surveys described previously, we surveyed Stanford University students. Some students concentrated on assessments that made their present circumstances the subject of comparison (e.g., "How much are your personal attitudes and values now at Stanford different from what they were in high school?"). Others focused on frames that rendered their past the subject of comparison (e.g., "How much different was your self-image in high school from what it's like now at Stanford?"). We expected students responding in the former frame to perceive more difference between past and present than those responding in the latter frame.

Responses by the students to the two frames differed, as is apparent from the results reported in Table 4.4. When students focused on their present circumstances, they perceived much more difference between "then and now" than when they concentrated on the past. For example, when focused on the present as opposed to the past, students perceived that coming to college had had a greater impact on their self-image, their

TABLE 4.4
Mean Perceived Difference Between Life at College
and Life at High School

| Measure | Subject of Comparison | | |
	Present (n = 26)	Past (n = 26)	p
Friends	14.4	13.2	
Types of students	15.7	14.2	
Relationship with parents	13.1	11.2	
Self-image	14.3	11.8	<.10
Eating habits	14.2	12.2	
Love life	15.5	13.2	
Groups/Organizations	12.1	12.2	
Study habits	13.2	10.7	
Recreation/Athletics	13.5	11.7	
Life goals	12.6	10.2	
Music	10.2	9.0	
Social life	13.7	13.7	
Impression on others	14.1	13.1	
Privacy	14.2	13.2	
Social skills	14.6	11.0	<.05
Attitudes and values	11.5	7.8	<.05
Hometown feelings	11.0	8.0	<.10
Responsibilities	15.3	12.7	<.10
Academic skills	12.7	11.8	
Night life	16.0	14.2	
Spending habits	12.9	12.5	
Spending free time	13.3	13.3	
Life in general	16.5	14.7	<.10
Average of all items	13.7	12.0	<.01

social skills, their attitudes and values, their feelings about their hometown, the responsibilities they possessed, and their life in general.

Focus of Comparison or Event Desirability?

Our theoretical analysis of this framing effect rests on notions of information. People have a richer, more complex, and more vivid collection of information about the road taken than they do about hypothetical alternatives. Thus, focusing respondents on their present circumstances by making that world rather than the referent the subject of comparison, should lead them to perceive greater dissimilarity between the road taken and a hypothetical alternative.

However, one could argue that the framing asymmetry might be prompted by other factors. Consider the fact that people possess a desire to see themselves as successful and happy, as people likely to experience positive outcomes. There is a long history in social psychology of people enthusiastically predicting that they will experience positive outcomes and being reticent to claim that they will confront negative ones (Dunning & Story, 1991; Weinstein, 1980). Such motivations might have produced the framing asymmetries we observed in our surveys. Perhaps the assumption can be made that the road taken is often more desirable than the road foregone (where there is a choice, presumably people would generally select the more favorable one). Thus, when the road taken is made the subject of the comparison, the attention of participants is drawn to the pleasurable side of the comparison. People may readily associate themselves with the positive outcomes contained in the road taken and, therefore, perceive much difference between the road taken and its counterfactual alternative. However, when the hypothetical alternative is made the subject, attention is drawn to less favorable possibilities. People are motivated to deny the possibility of such outcomes and so deny that taking the alternative road would lead to any change.

One final survey placed this alternative account under direct scrutiny. Participants were asked to compare the town in which they lived—Ithaca, New York—to hypothetical alternatives. Some alternative cities (e.g., Hartford, Connecticut; Atlantic City, New Jersey) were rated as less desirable than Ithaca. Some (e.g., Washington, D.C.; Chicago, Illinois) were more desirable.

Several hypotheses could be tested with this survey. If prominence of information is the driving force behind the road-taken effect, the results should reflect the phenomenon of whether or not the hypothetical alternative is more desirable than the road taken. On the other hand, if the desire to associate oneself with positive outcomes is a crucial factor, then the results should reflect an interaction between the framing manipulation and the desirability of the alternative world. When the alternative world is relatively undesirable, results should reflect the usual framing asymmetry. Focusing on the road taken, people should concentrate on positive outcomes and, hence, see much difference. Focusing on the counterfactual alternative, people should concentrate on many potential negative outcomes, wish to deny the possibility of these events, and thus report little impact. However, when the alternative world is more desirable than the road taken, the framing asymmetry should not appear, or at least be diminished. When focused on the road taken, people should generate a number of negative characteristics (ways in which Ithaca is less desirable than the alternative), wish to deny the existence of these undesirable outcomes, and thus report little disparity between the road taken and its alternative.

The survey involved students from psychology and human development courses. Students were asked to compare life in Ithaca to life in four different alternative cities. For each respondent, two of the cities were randomly selected from a larger set of cities that had been rated by a pretest sample of students to be more desirable places to live than Ithaca: Baltimore, Chicago, Denver, New York City, Philadelphia, San Francisco, Seattle, and Washington, D.C. The other two cities came from a larger set that had been rated as less desirable than Ithaca: Albany, Atlantic City, Cincinnati, Hartford, Indianapolis, Miami, Nashville, and Pittsburgh. For roughly half of the respondents, the road taken, Ithaca, was made the subject of comparison (e.g., "How much has living in Ithaca affected your social life as opposed to living in Washington, D.C.?"). For the remainder, the alternative city was made the subject (e.g., "How much would living in Washington, D.C. affect your social life as opposed to living in Ithaca?").

As the results reported in Table 4.5 indicate, respondents reported more impact when Ithaca, the road taken, was the subject of comparison than when the alternative served as the subject, whether that alternative was more or less desirable than the road taken. That is, we found no statistical interaction between the framing manipulation and the desirability of the alternative city. In short, the framing asymmetry we had observed in past studies was not prompted by a comparison between a desirable world (the road taken) and an undesirable one (the counterfactual alternative).

MENTAL ADDITION VERSUS SUBTRACTION EFFECTS

In other research, we have found another factor that influences people's counterfactual assessments: whether the judgment is framed in terms of addition or in terms of subtraction. Consider the prepared lecture notes

TABLE 4.5
Perceived Difference Between Ithaca, New York (the Road Taken)
and Hypothetical-Alternative Cities

Desirability of Alternative	Subject of Comparison		
	Road Taken ($n = 33$)	Alternative ($n = 34$)	p
High	14.7	12.9	<.05
Low	13.3	12.0	<.10
Overall	14.0	12.5	<.025

(socnotes) example, described at the beginning of the chapter, in which the exact frames were presented to participants. One of the frames can be termed *additive*. That is, respondents were asked *how much more* of an outcome they would receive because they had purchased the notes. Others confronted frames that were *subtractive* in nature. Specifically, these participants had to assess *how much less* of an outcome they would obtain if they had foregone the notes.

Dunning and Parpal (1989) discovered that the additive or subtractive nature of the counterfactual assessment had a reliable impact on the conclusions that respondents reached. Respondents tended to see an event as more impactful when they evaluated it under an additive frame than when they considered it under a subtractive one. For example, in one study (Study 1), Dunning and Parpal asked participants to consider a hypothetical scenario in which they studied a course textbook intensely for 3 hours for a hypothetical 60-question exam. They were asked how many *more* questions they would answer correctly for putting in that study session. On average, participants responded that they would answer 18.4 questions correctly because of that study session. However, when asked how many *fewer* questions they would answer correctly if they failed to study the text, they responded that their exam scores would suffer by only 14.3 points (compared to the score they would have achieved had they studied).

In another study, Dunning and Parpal (1989, Study 2) extended this phenomenon to the domain of real events. Stanford University students were asked to assess the impact of attending that university over their second-choice school. Some respondents were asked to report their assessments via additive frames (e.g., "How much more of a quality education do you receive at Stanford compared to what you would have obtained at the other college?"). Others confronted subtractive frames (e.g., "How much less of a quality education would you have received at the other college compared to what you obtain at Stanford University?"). Respondents reliably reported that attending Stanford had more impact when their counterfactual assessments were couched in additive terms than in subtractive ones. Statistically significant framing asymmetries of this sort were observed for a number of assessments: the quality of their education, their interest in their courses, the level of challenge provided by those courses, their knowledge of course subject matter, their ability to think clearly, their capacity to write well, the impression they would make on other people, their preparation for their career, the amount of pressure they were under, and the amount of time they spent studying. Under an additive frame, participants were much more likely to state that attending Stanford would increase their likelihood at obtaining their first-choice job after graduation than they were to claim that attending their second-choice college would decrease the likelihood of that success.

Results of other studies affirmed that it was the additive rather than the subtractive distinction that produced these framing asymmetries, ruling out alternative explanations. For example, in the exam-study scenario described previously, one could again propose that event desirability prompted the different assessments that respondents gave under each frame. It is pleasurable to imagine and then to report a situation in which one would receive a higher exam score. It is aversive to construct and describe a situation in which one's exam score was lower, a phenomenon that produced the more conservative estimates found under the subtractive frame.

Although plausible, this interpretation was ruled out by the findings from one additional study (Dunning & Parpal, 1989, Study 3). In this study, participants were presented with the same scenario (only this time, the exam was a 100-point test) and asked to consider how many questions they would get wrong. Some were asked under an additive frame (i.e., "Compared to studying for the test, how many more questions will you get *wrong* if you fail to look at the book for three hours?"). Others were asked the same question with a subtractive frame (i.e., "Compared to not studying for the test, how many fewer questions will you get *wrong* if you look at the book for three hours?"). Respondents tended to provide greater assessments of impact under the additive frame (mean swing in exam score was estimated to be 26.1 points) as opposed to the subtractive one (mean swing was assessed at around 20.0 points). This pattern occurred even though the additive frame in this experiment impelled respondents to consider an aversive outcome, that is, receiving a lower exam score in the class.[1]

Results of other studies have disentangled the addition-versus-subtraction effect from the road-taken phenomenon described previously in this chapter. In the Stanford University study (Dunning & Parpal, 1989) the additive and subtractive nature of the frame was confounded with the subject of comparison. Under the additive frame, the subject of comparison was an actual event that the respondents had experienced (attending Stanford). With the subtractive frame, the subject was a counterfactual alternative (the other college). As the results indicated, people perceive more contrast between an actual event and a counterfactual when the former rather than the latter is made the subject of comparison.

---

[1]Results of this study also rule out an additional alternative explanation. People plausibly could perceive more impact when the frame is posed in terms of action (e.g., what are the effects of studying?) as opposed to inaction (e.g., what are the effects of not studying?). In this study, however, participants perceived more impact after the inaction than after the action.

Results of other surveys we have conducted have shown that the mental addition–subtraction asymmetry is an effect that occurs independently of the road-taken–foregone-alternative distinction. In one such survey, we asked 228 Cornell University students to assess the impact of attending that institution over their second-choice university. The questionnaire began by asking students to name the other college that they would have attended had they not been accepted by Cornell. They were then asked to assess the impact of attending Cornell, as opposed to the other college, for three different areas of student life: how interesting (or dull) their classes were, how challenging (or easy) those classes were, and on the ease (or difficulty) of obtaining their first-choice job after graduation.[2]

Of key importance was the framing effects of the questions. Respondents answered our queries under four different frames that crossed the additive or subtractive nature of the assessment with whether the focus of comparison was on Cornell (an actual event) or on the other college (the counterfactual alternative). For some participants, the assessments they were asked to make were additive in nature and focused on Cornell (e.g., "How much more interesting are your classes at Cornell than they would have been at the other college?"). For other participants, the assessments were still additive but placed the focus on the hypothetical alternative (e.g. "How much more dull would your classes have been at the other college than they are at Cornell?"). For other participants, the assessment focused on the road taken but was subtractive (e.g., "How much less dull are your classes at Cornell than they would have been at the other college?"). For another group of respondents, the assessment focused on the alternative college and was subtractive (e.g., "How much less interesting would your classes have been at the other college than they are at Cornell?").

We predicted and found two independent framing effects (after reverse-scoring the subtractive-frame answers to make them comparable to the additive-frame responses). First, as the results reported in Table 4.6 show, respondents perceived more impact when the subject of the comparison was the event that the respondent had actually experienced,

---

[2]After answering these questions, participants were asked to compare Cornell to the other college in terms of overall academics (i.e., "How much better or worse is Cornell than the other college?"). Participants responded on 19-point scales that ranged from –9 (*Cornell much worse*) to 9 (*Cornell much better*). On the basis of their responses to these questions, the questionnaires of 13 additional participants were excluded from any data analysis. The assumption on which this research rested was that students would believe Cornell was better than their second-choice institutions and provided "more quality education" than did the others. These 13 respondents, however, named schools that they described as better than Cornell. We should note that these respondents were distributed roughly equally among the four experimental conditions and that the framing manipulations failed to influence participants' responses to these questions.

TABLE 4.6
Perceived Impact of Attending Cornell (the Road Taken)
Versus Second-Choice Under Additive and Subtractive Frames

	Subject of Comparison			
	Cornell		Other College	
Mental Operation	Addition (n = 58)	Subtraction (n = 57)	Addition (n = 55)	Subtraction (n = 58)
Interest/dullness of classes	3.0	2.5	0.6	1.9
Challenge/ease of classes	5.8	2.4	3.4	3.0
Ease/difficulty of obtaining job	3.6	2.7	2.0	0.7
Average of All Items	4.1	2.6	2.1	1.9

that is, attending Cornell. Second, participants reported more impact when the counterfactual assessment was additive as opposed to subtractive. In sum, the results of this survey demonstrate that the mental addition–subtraction asymmetry is not merely a road-taken phenomenon in disguise. Both the focus of comparison (the road taken or the one not taken) *and* the mental operation that participants were required to perform (addition versus subtraction) had independent effects on participants' perceptions of impact.

A Theoretical Model

But why should these asymmetries arise? Why should people perceive a greater difference between their world and a counterfactual one when they are asked questions under an additive frame rather than under a subtractive one?

Dunning and Parpal (1989) proposed that the mental addition-versus-subtraction effect is produced by a conjunction of two psychological phenomena. First, when comparing two objects or worlds, people tend to give relatively more weight to the features contained in the subject of the comparison than to those contained in the referent (a tendency that had also produced the road-taken phenomenon described previously). But this tendency by itself will not produce the addition-versus-subtraction asymmetry.

The second, more important tendency, has to do with what features or processes people tend to dwell on when considering some outcome, such as answering questions on an exam correctly or answering them incorrectly. According to Dunning and Parpal (1989), people tend to give weight to or to simulate factors that would *produce* the outcome over those that would *inhibit* it. Consider, for example, the outcome of answering questions correctly on an exam. How many more questions would a person answer correctly by studying the textbook? The answer is straight-forward: The textbook should contain many italicized words that are likely to appear on the examination. Knowing those words and their definitions could only increase the number of questions that a student could answer successfully. But now consider how many fewer questions a student would answer correctly if he or she failed to study. To be sure, the student would obtain a lower score, but, according to Dunning and Parpal, people are likely to consider the outcome (answering questions correctly) and still search for and simulate factors that would produce it. For example, when considering the scenario of not studying, students might emphasize factors that would help them to answer questions cor-rectly. They could recall that they have a good deal of common-sense knowledge that would allow them to weed out obviously wrong answers and help them achieve a greater number of correct answers. They might remind themselves that simple guessing often produces the desired result.

These two tendencies conspire to produce the mental addition-versus-subtraction asymmetry. When faced with an additive frame, people will focus on those features in the subject of comparison that would produce the outcome in question (e.g., knowing the words italicized in the text-book) and relatively ignore the features in the referent world (such as guessing or common sense) that would produce the outcome anyway. Hence, they perceive the "superior world" contained in the subject of the comparison as substantially different from the referent world. However, consider what people will do when faced with a subtractive frame. In this circumstance, people will give more weight to the factors in the "inferior world" (e.g., guessing) that would facilitate the outcome in question and give relatively less weight to factors in the superior world that would also produce that outcome. As a result, they perceive less of a difference between superior and inferior worlds.

There is evidence that people tend to think in terms of features or processes that would produce outcomes as opposed to those that would inhibit them. For example, in work on causal attribution, many different reseachers have remarked that people tend to attribute behaviors to factors that produce those behaviors but give little thought to potential inhibitors (Hansen, 1980; Hansen & Hall, 1985; Jones & Davis, 1965; Newtson, 1974; Nisbett & Ross, 1980; Ross, 1977; Shaver, 1981).

Results of other work, more directly focused on the process of com-parison, also reveal this tendency. Tversky (1977; see also Tversky & Gati, 1978), for example, noted a puzzling tendency when people were asked how similar two objects were as opposed to how different they were. Tversky presented respondents with two pairs of countries. One pair consisted of countries for which respondents had much information (e.g.,

West Germany and East Germany). The other pair included countries for which respondents had little information (e.g., Nepal and Ceylon). Tversky asked some respondents to select that pair that was the most similar, and a majority tended to select the pair for which they had much information (the two Germanys). Other respondents were asked to select the pair that was the most different. Contradicting the earlier group of participants, these respondents also picked the high-information pair. Tversky's explanation for this anomaly is consistent with Dunning and Parpal's (1989) explication of their framing asymmetries. When Tversky asked respondents how similar two objects were, they took *similarity* to be the outcome and gave more weight to features that the two objects shared, that is, to factors that would suggest more similarity between the objects, than to features suggesting differences. Because respondents could find more shared features in the high-information pair than in the low-information pair, respondents concluded that the former pair was the more similar one. However, when asked how different the pairs were, people began looking for features that would produce dissimilarity. Because the respondents knew of many more features that were not shared between the high-information pair than they did the low-information pair, they perceived the former pair as more different.

Shafir (1993) demonstrated a similar preoccupation with features that facilitate or produce outcome (as opposed to those that inhibit or reduce) in the realm of choice. In a series of experiments, he presented respondents with hypothetical choices. For example, they were told to imagine that they were on a jury deciding which parent should receive custody of a child in a divorce case. One parent was rather nondescript (average income, average health, average working hours). The other had a number of distinctly good qualities (e.g., above-average income) and a number of bad (extensive work-related travel). When asked to which parent they would *award* custody, a majority of the respondents said they would choose the second parent, the one with good and bad qualities. When another group of respondents was asked to which parent they would *deny* custody, a majority of participants rejected the same parent, a seeming contradiction. Shafir's analysis of this paradox was similar to Tversky's (1977) and Dunning and Parpal's (1989) explanations. The "award" frame, according to Shafir, prompted respondents to give more weight to features that would support or facilitate awarding custody (in his terms, these features were "compatible" with that outcome). Consequently, respondents gave relatively more weight to the positive features of the "some-good–some-bad" parent. However, in the "deny" frame, respondents gave relatively greater weight to features that facilitated the outcome of rejection, that is, to negative features, than to positive features. Because the some-good–some-bad parent had a greater number of undesirable features than the nondescript alternative, this parent was more likely to be rejected.

Findings from other research provide even more direct evidence that people give relatively more weight to factors that facilitate outcomes than to those that inhibit them. In recent work, Yamagishi and Miyamoto (1991) asked participants to evaluate a series of object pairs. In one study, the comparisons were between gambles involving dice. Participants could roll a die and win or lose varying amounts of money, depending on the number that came up. Some participants were asked to choose the better gamble between the pair offered. They were then asked to rate how much better that gamble was. Other participants were asked to indicate the worse gamble and then to assess how much worse that gamble was. Assessments of better versus worse depended on different features of the gambles, with people giving relatively more weight to the features that would produce the outcome (being better or worse) under consideration than to inhibitive features. When assessing the better gamble, participants gave greater weight to the potential gains that each gamble presented than they did when indicating the worse gamble. Conversely, when choosing the worse gamble, participants were more sensitive to the potential losses that each gamble presented than when they were facing the better frame. Similar tendencies were observed when participants confronted choices in other domains, such as selecting apartments and college courses. They gave greater weight to positive features when choosing the better options than when selecting the worse. They were more sensitive to undesirable features when determining which choice was worse (see Yamagishi & Miyamoto, 1993, for similar findings).

A More Direct Test

In our laboratory, we have recently completed a preliminary study that places the analysis of Dunning and Parpal (1989) under more direct scrutiny. In this study, college students thinking of pursuing graduate or professional studies were asked about their potential performance on the standardized tests required to enter those studies, such as the Graduate Record Exam (GRE) or the Law Scholastic Aptitude Test (LSAT). In particular, we asked students to consider the potential impact of taking one of the many courses offered by private companies designed to help students prepare for those exams (e.g., the Princeton Review, Kaplan). These courses offer a number of services: They provide clients practice tests, offer refresher courses in math and other topics, and suggest several test-taking strategies.

For the study, we asked students how such courses might help or hurt their performance on standardized tests. Some were asked about the potential impact of these courses under additive frames (e.g., "How much more prepared would you be if you took a test-preparatory course than you would be if you didn't take one?"). Others were asked putatively the same questions under subtractive frames (e.g., "How much less prepared would you be if you didn't take a test-prep course than you would be if you took one?"). In all, students were asked how prepared they would be to take an exam, whether they would have a competitive edge, how much time they would spend studying for an exam, how much knowledge of test-taking strategies and tactics they would have, and how confident they would be when taking the test. All of the students answered on scales that ranged from –9 (*much less*) to 9 (*much more*). As in the studies described previously, we reverse-scored the responses of students in the subtractive condition to make them comparable to those provided by respondents in the additive condition. As the results reported in Table 4.7 show, we again observed a mental addition–subtraction effect. Students saw the impact of taking a test-preparatory course to be much greater under an additive frame ($M = 4.6$) than they did under a subtractive one ($M = 3.3$).

Of key interest in this study, however, were additional measures of how respondents arrived at their assessments. For each question posed, we asked respondents to explain their response. For example, for the question on preparation, we asked respondents to "write down some reasons for your answer. In what ways would you be more or less prepared, or it wouldn't make a difference." Two coders (with no knowledge of any hypothesis) then classified these responses under four categories of reasons. The first category centered on aspects of test-prepara-

TABLE 4.7
Impact of Test-Preparatory Courses on Performance
on Graduate/Professional School Standardized Exams

	Frame		
	Additive	Subtractive	
Measure	(n = 26)	(n = 24)	p
Preparation for exams	5.3	3.6	<.08
Competitive edge	3.8	2.9	
Time spent studying	4.3	2.8	
Knowledge of test-taking strategies	5.3	3.9	
Confidence	4.7	2.9	<.09
Overall	4.6	3.3	<.04

Note. All questions were answered on 19-point scales that ranged from –9 (*much less*) to 0 (*no impact*) to 9 (*much more*). All responses in the subtractive condition were reverse-scored; high numbers indicate that the respondent reported that not taking a course would have *reduced* the degree of each outcome in question.

tory courses that would produce the outcome in question (e.g., being prepared). Examples included "Would make me more familiar with this kind of test," "I would be forced to study more," and "I'd get help, coaching from instructors." The second category consisted of test-preparatory-course features that would inhibit the relevant outcome (e.g., "I would probably think taking the practice tests they provide would be enough, and so wouldn't do anything else"). The third category focused on actions the respondents could do *on their own* to bring about the outcome in question (e.g, "I would study anyway" or "I am self-motivated to prepare"). The fourth category consisted of attributes of being on one's own that would inhibit or reduce the outcome in question, (e.g., "I would be less likely to practice" or "The fact that other people took the course would make me nervous").

We predicted that the frame, additive or subtractive, would influence the types of reasons respondents described for their assessments and that these differences would account for the addition–subtraction framing asymmetry. Toward that end, for each of the four categories, we averaged the number of reasons respondents provided on each individual item across the two coders.[3]

As the results reported in Table 4.8 show, the features that respondents cited fell within the predictions of the Dunning and Parpal (1989) analysis. Respondents in the additive frame spent more effort describing the benefits of test-preparatory courses (i.e., factors that would produce the relevant outcomes) than did participants under a subtractive frame ($p < .01$). They also cited a greater number of drawbacks inherent in test-preparatory courses (e.g., factors that would reduce the outcomes in question) than did their subtractive counterparts, albeit to a nonsignificant degree. In contrast, under a subtractive frame, respondents described a greater number of actions or events that would take place if they acted on their own than respondents in the additive frame. They described a greater number of actions they could take on their own that would produce the consequences being considered ($p < .03$) as well as a greater number of drawbacks of being on their own (i.e., aspects that would inhibit or reduce the outcome in question) than did respondents confronting an additive frame ($p < .01$).

Results of additonal analyses suggested that the framing effect observed in this study was mediated by the respondents' focus on features of either the "test-preparatory world" or "on-one's-own world." First, as the results displayed in Table 4.8 also show, the number of facilitory

---

[3]Interrater reliability between the two coders was substantial: .80 for reasons having to do with benefits of taking test-preparatory courses, .79 for the disadvantages of taking those courses, .87 for actions one could take on one's own to produce the outcomes in question, and .84 for the drawbacks of being on one's own.

TABLE 4.8
Number of Reasons Cited for Assessment of Test-Preparatory
Courses as a Function of Frame

World/Category	Frame			
	Additive (n = 26)	Subtractive (n = 24)	t	r^a
Taking Test-Preparatory Course				
Would produce outcome	1.39	1.05	2.79**	.57***
Would reduce outcome	.07	.03	1.31	−.10
Not Taking Test-Preparatory Course (i.e., Being On Own)				
Would produce outcome	.07	.18	2.29*	−.55***
Would reduce outcome	.13	.31	2.86**	.28*
Overall	1.68	1.57	.59	

Note. Table displays number of reasons listed per each individual item in the questionnaire.
[a]Correlation between number of features of this type listed and degree of impact respondent perceived (i.e, how beneficial they reported test-preparatory courses to be).
*p < .05. **p < .01. ***p < .005.

factors in the test-preparatory and on-one's-own worlds listed by respondents were significantly correlated with the amount of impact respondents thought those courses would have. When respondents listed a greater number of test preparatory course benefits, they described the courses as more impactful or beneficial ($r = .51, p < .005$). However, when they listed a greater number of actions they could take on their own to achieve the same outcomes, they assessed the courses as less beneficial ($r = −.55, p < .005$). The number of drawbacks inherent in the on-one's-own world were also correlated, albeit not as strongly, with perceptions of impact ($r = .28, p < .05$). The only type of features not correlated with perceptions of impact were those centering on drawbacks of the test-preparatory world ($r = −.10$, n.s.).

Perhaps, however, the strongest case for mediation are the results of an analysis by which we examined the impact of framing, controlled for the type and number of factors that respondents wrote about. When we conducted an analysis of covariance that controlled for the number of features that respondents cited in each of the four categories, we found that the influence of framing on perceptions of impact was nonsignificant [$t(44) = 1.38$, n.s.].

In sum, the results of this analysis suggest that the impact of framing works through the types of features that people emphasize in their counterfactual assessments. Under additive frames, people are more likely to emphasize the factors of the superior world (in this case, the test-preparatory world) than those of the inferior world that would produce the outcome in question. As a consequence, they see the superior world as very different from the inferior one. In the specific example included in this study, students were more likely to conclude that taking a test-preparatory course would help them to be more prepared and confident for the "judgment day" they would one day confront. In contrast, with a subtractive frame, respondents were more likely to consider the attributes, both facilitating and inhibiting, of the inferior world of being on one's own. For example, in the study, they were more likely to note the drawbacks of not taking a preparatory course. However, and of key importance, they were also likely to consider actions, such as studying and preparing on their own, that would facilitate success without the need for a course. With this in mind, they were less likely to see taking the test-preparatory course as different from simply being on their own. That is, they were less likely to perceive the course as impactful or beneficial.

SUMMARY AND IMPLICATIONS

In sum, through our laboratory work, we uncovered two different framing effects that occur when people compare the world they inhabit to counterfactual alternatives. These asymmetries grow out of two psychological tendencies and have to do with what features or factors people pay attention to when comparing their actual world to a counterfactual one, or two counterfactual worlds to each other.

The first tendency is people's giving relatively more weight to features contained in the subject of the comparison than they do to those of the referent. This tendency gave rise to a framing asymmetry when respondents in our surveys compared a world for which they had a rich, vivid array of information, such as their present circumstances, to one for which they had less information, such as a counterfactual alternative or the past. Making the first type of world the subject of comparison, and thus drawing attention to it, prompted respondents to perceive more impact and difference than when that world was made the referent of comparison.

The second tendency is people's giving relatively more weight to features that would produce the outcome in question than to those that would reduce it. This tendency gave rise to a mental addition–subtraction effect. People perceived more difference between two worlds when the counterfactual assessment was placed in additive terms (e.g., "How much more satisfied are you with your present career than the most likely alternative?") than when couched in subtractive ones (e.g., "How much less satisfied would you be in your most likely alternative career than you are in your present one?"). The findings from these studies carry implications for both theory and its application to counterfactual reasoning.

Theoretical Implications

In terms of theory, these findings suggest that the task of counterfactual reasoning is potentially more involved and complex than simply evoking or recruiting a counterfactual world. After a selection process, the person must construct or frame a comparison between the actual world and the counterfactual. For example, one world might be chosen as the subject of the assessment, and the other as the referent. This choice can have significant effects on the assessments that people ultimately provide. Under one frame, people may provide judgments that are noticeably different from those rendered by individuals using another frame, even though the counterfactual point of comparison is the same. In short, the act of counterfactual reasoning involves more than the single task of choosing a comparison point.

The framing asymmetries observed here and elsewhere also portray the social perceiver as a "cognitive miser" with respect to counterfactual assessment. People do not perform a complete job when comparing their circumstances to a counterfactual world; that is, they do not conduct exhaustive simulations of both subject and referent when required to make a counterfactual assessment. Instead, according to the theoretical accounts of Tversky (1977; Tversky & Gati, 1978) and our results, their attention is primarily drawn to the subject of comparison. Therefore, their assessments are predominantly driven by the information and simulations to be found in that world.

Applied Implications

This "short-circuiting" of the counterfactual assessment process has many potential, applied implications. Consider how people reach their consumer choices. Choosing one product over another is often the act of comparing two counterfactual worlds. One must construct a mental scenario of life with one product (e.g., "What would it be like to own a turbo-charged sportscar?") and compare it to life with the alternative (e.g., "What would it be like to drive the four-door coupe?"). It may be that people's preferences between two objects or prospects may be altered by the frame of comparison, with their choices primarily driven by the attributes found in the subject, not the referent, of comparison.

Such changes have already been observed. Dhar and Simonson (1991) asked participants about their preferences for business schools under two different frames. Some were asked whether they preferred Stanford Business School over Harvard Business School. When given this frame, most participants reported that they preferred Stanford. Others were asked whether they preferred Harvard over Stanford. Under this frame, most respondents asserted that they preferred Harvard. Dhar and Simonson explained this paradox by proposing that people gave weight to the many splendid and desirable features of each school but gave more weight to the features contained in the subject of the comparison than to those of the referent. Houston et al. (1989) also observed a similar subject-of-comparison bias in statements of preference. In their work, these researchers asked participants to evaluate the relative attractiveness of various objects (such as college courses, apartments, and first dates). Participants' responses depended to a great extent on those distinctive and unique features contained in the subject of comparison. When those features were mostly positive, people were more likely to prefer the subject than when those features were mostly undesirable.

Beyond the specifying of the subject of comparison, different-choice frames emphasizing the particular outcome to be concerned about may alter personal or consumer decisions. People may come to different preferences when asked which alternative is more interesting as opposed to more dull, which is desirable as opposed to undesirable, or which is better as opposed to worse. This notion was rather explicit in the work of Shafir (1993), who showed that there were circumstances in which respondents would choose one option in one frame ("Which would you choose?") but reject the same object in another ("Which would you reject?").

What is true of preferences in the personal realm may also be true of decisions concerning social policy. For example, decisions concerning abortion policy, the death penalty, and civil rights laws are based in part on people's beliefs concerning the consequences that these policies might produce. One wonders how the preferences for different social policies may differ according to how people frame the choice. For example, as a student one of this chapter's authors was once involved in a late night, undergraduate "bull" session in which he adamantly argued against the use of nuclear power, citing the dangers inherently involved in such an enterprise. In essence, his argument was framed as "How many lives are at risk because we use nuclear power?" His argument was stopped in its tracks, however, by another student who simply asked "Have you considered how many lives would be at risk if we did not have nuclear power?" The other student noted, quite accurately, that the most likely alternative to nuclear power was coal. From his boyhood days in western Pennsylvania, he knew that power from coal was inherently dangerous. Coal miners were killed in accidents. Old miners suffered from black lung. People near plants that burned coal contracted emphysema. How could one oppose nuclear power without considering the known dangers posed by the alternative?

Responses to public opinion polls also suggest, as this example does, that people do not necessarily consider alternatives when forming their opinions of social policy, alternatives that might become more salient if people adopted different frames in their assessments. For example, 70% of Americans endorse the death penalty on the typical opinion survey. However, support for the pentalty drops to 55% when the alternative of life imprisonment without parole is explicitly pointed out to them (Gallup, 1986). Future work could profitably focus on how the framing of questions, and exhortations to consider alternatives, might inform, influence, or enhance decisions about personal actions and social policy.

But perhaps the most crucial implication of this short-circuiting in counterfactual thought may lie in clinical or therapeutic settings, in which people strive to overcome personal traumas. Often, people in therapy face a consequential event and must decide between two courses of action. For example, one of the authors at one time served as a crisis-intervention counselor. In this capacity, he talked with many teenaged girls who had just discovered that they were pregnant and who had to decide whether or not to inform their parents. In this situation, most clients spent a great amount of time simulating what telling their parents would be like and came to the conclusion that they could never inform their parents of their situation. Often it was the job of the counselor to make the act of *not telling* the parents the subject of comparison (e.g., "What would it be like if you do not tell your parents?"). When forced to consider this counterfactual world explicitly, many clients came to a different understanding of their circumstances and preferred course of action.

Findings from other research show that people's understanding of the consequences of their actions depends on the frame adopted. In a recent study, Beyth–Marom, Austin, Fischhoff, Palmgren, and Jacobs–Quadrel (1993) asked adolescents and adults to consider the consequences of a number of real-world risky actions, such as drinking and driving, smoking marijuana, and having sex. The consequences that people listed were different when they considered taking the action (e.g., smoking marijuana) than when they considered *not* taking the action (e.g., refusing to smoke marijuana). When considering taking the action, both adolescent and adult respondents primarily listed bad consequences rather than good ones, at about a 4:1 ratio. When considering forgoing the action, the ratio of bad to good consequences was much different, at roughly 1 : 1. In short, the considerations that respondents articulated for doing versus not doing the action were different, depending on the frame imposed, a result suggesting that some short-circuiting had occurred as respondents completed their counterfactual assessments.

In a sense, this short-circuiting may not be surprising. The literature on clinical application often notes that clients pay too little attention to counterfactual worlds that are clearly relevant to their concerns. Therapists frequently call on their patients to engage in problem-solving, exactly by asking them to perform more complete counterfactual assessments of their situations. For example, when attempting to understand a problem, therapists often ask clients to stop focusing on circumstances that prompt a problem and to simulate a situation in which the problem does not occur. This technique involves asking the "exception question" (e.g., "What happens on those days in which your child does not throw a tantrum?") and also the "miracle question" (e.g., "Suppose your problems were magically solved. What does that world look like? How did you get there?"). In short, by specifying a relevant counterfactual world as the subject of comparison, therapists often give clients new insights about how they may address and potentially conquer the problems confronting them (for more extensive discussions, see de Shazer, 1985; Kottler, 1991; Landman, chapter 8).

Taken together, all of the research and the theory described here suggests that practitioners, whether salespeople, politicians, or therapists, may find it profitable to weigh how they frame questions to their clients. It also suggests that they should be aware that there are often multiple ways to frame comparisons and that asking clients to consider new frames may prove to be useful. But these thoughts about the applied implications of framing belie a deeper set of questions: What frames do people naturally adopt in their counterfactual assessments? Do they tend to phrase counterfactual comparisons in additive terms or in subtractive ones? Do they tend to focus on their present circumstances or on counterfactual alternatives? If such tendencies are found, is the bias a general one, or is it sensitive to situational factors? Or subject to individual differences? Such questions should be addressed so that the practical importance of the work described here can be clarified.

CONCLUDING REMARKS

Perhaps the best argument for the significance of counterfactual reasoning in everyday life comes from its prevalence in works of popular art. The reactions of characters in plays, books, and movies frequently turn on thoughts about what might have been. In addition to the movies we mentioned at the beginning of this chapter, we can cite how Scrooge's personal philosophy and behavior in the oft-filmed Dickens' classic, *A Christmas Carol*, changes after he is shown a terrible and despairing counterfactual construction of the future by the Ghost of Christmas Yet to Come. Indeed, we can also cite Frank Capra's classic, *It's a Wonderful Life*, which centers around the construction of a counterfactual. The movie's protagonist, George Bailey, Jr., poised to jump to his death from a bridge, is saved when his guardian angel reminds him of his life and compares it to a world "in which he had never been born."

Movies, however, do not necessarily mirror real life. Characters in the movies are sometimes blessed by ghosts or guardian angels who can construct the relevant counterfactual worlds for them. People in real life, in contrast, must do this work by themselves, and do so in their head. In this chapter, we have outlined some of the steps that people must take to compare a counterfactual world to the one they inhabit or to compare two potential counterfactual worlds to each other (as when happens when people must choose between two courses of action). We also outlined a few of the psychological factors that may influence people's assessments as they take these steps and have examined how the impact of those psychological factors may be revealed via framing.

This analysis about people's counterfactual assessments brings to mind a final question. If people provide different counterfactual assessments under different frames, with which frame do people provide more *accurate* appraisals? Are assessments more accurate when the road taken is made the subject of comparison? Or do people have more insight when focusing their attention on the hypothetical alternative or on the past? Presently, we have no satisfactory way to answer this question. Indeed, we wonder whether it is answerable. Suffice it to say that we take the advice that many readers will have heard before: The best decisions are made after considering all alternatives. At the very least, considering all the alternatives provides a more informed appraisal than does considering only one.

ACKNOWLEDGMENTS

We thank Mary Parpal, who assisted us in collecting some of the data reported in this chapter. Portions of this research were conducted while David Dunning was supported by National Science Foundation predoctoral fellowships. Part of the research also received financial support from National Institute of Mental Health Research Grant MH–36093, awarded to Lee Ross and Mark Lepper. We thank Andy Brothers and Meghana Karande for serving as coders in the content analysis study reported.

REFERENCES

Beyth–Marom, R., Austin, L., Fischhoff, B., Palmgren, C., & Jacobs–Quadrel, M. (1993). Perceived consequences of risky behaviors: Adults and adolescents. *Developmental Psychology, 29*, 549–563.

de Shazer, S. (1985). *Keys to solution in brief therapy.* New York: Norton.

Dhar, R., & Simonson, I. (1991). The effect of focus of comparison on consumer preferences. *Journal of Marketing Research, 29*, 430–440.

Dunning, D., & Hayes, A. F. (1994). *Evidence for egocentric comparison in social judgment.* Unpublished manuscript, Cornell University, Ithaca, NY.

Dunning, D., & Parpal, M. (1985). [Unpublished raw data].

Dunning, D., & Parpal, M. (1989). Mental addition versus subtraction in counterfactual reasoning: On assessing the impact of personal actions and life events. *Journal of Personality and Social Psychology, 57,* 5–15.

Dunning, D., & Story, A. L. (1991). Depression, realism, and the overconfidence effect: Are the sadder wiser when predicting future actions and events? *Journal of Personality and Social Psychology, 61,* 521–532.

Ebbinghaus, H. (1885/1964). *Memory.* New York: Dover.

Gallup, G., Jr. (1986). *The Gallup poll: Public opinion 1986.* Wilmington, DE: Scholarly Resources.

Gavanski, I., & Wells, G. L. (1989). Counterfactual processing of normal and exceptional events. *Journal of Experimental Social Psychology, 25,* 314–325.

Hansen, R. D. (1980). Commonsense attribution. *Journal of Personality and Social Psychology, 39,* 996–1009.

Hansen, R. D., & Hall, C. A. (1985). Discounting and augmenting facilitative and inhibitory forces: The winner takes almost all. *Journal of Personality and Social Psychology, 49,* 1482–1493.

Holyoak, K. J., & Gordon, P. C. (1983). Social reference points. *Journal of Personality and Social Psychology, 44,* 881–887.

Houston, D. A., Sherman, S. J., & Baker, S. M. (1989). The influence of unique features and direction of comparison on preferences. *Journal of Experimental Social Psychology, 25,* 121–141.

Jones, E. E., & Davis, K. E. (1965). From acts to dispositions: The attribution process in person perception. In L. Berkowitz (Ed.), *Advances in experimental social psychology* (Vol. 1, pp. 219–266). New York: Academic Press.

Kahneman, D., & Miller, D. T. (1986). Norm theory: Comparing reality to its alternatives. *Psychological Review, 93,* 136–153.

Kahneman, D., & Tversky, A. (1982). The simulation heuristic. In D. Kahneman, P. Slovic, & A. Tversky (Eds.), *Judgment under uncertainty: Heuristics and biases* (pp. 201–208). New York: Cambridge University Press.

Kottler, J. A. (1991). *The compleat therapist.* San Francisco: Jossey–Bass.

Medvec, V. H., Madey, S. F., & Gilovich, T. (in press). When less is more: Counterfactual thinking and satisfaction among Olympic medalists. *Journal of Personality and Social Psychology.*

Miller, D. T., Turnbull, W., & McFarland, C. (1990). Counterfactual thinking and social perception: Thinking about what might have been. In M. P. Zanna (Ed.), *Advances in experimental social psychology* (Vol. 23, pp. 305–331). Orlando, FL: Academic Press.

Newtson, D. (1974). Dispositional inference from effect of actions: Effects chosen and effects foregone. *Journal of Experimental Social Psychology, 10,* 489–496.

Nisbett, R. E., & Ross, L. (1980). *Human inference: Strategies and shortcomings of social judgment.* Englewood Cliffs, NJ: Prentice–Hall.

Read, S. J. (1987). Similarity and causality in the use of social analogies. *Journal of Experimental Social Psychology, 23,* 189–207.

Ross, L. (1977). The intuitive psychologist and his shortcomings: Distortions in the attribution process. In L. Berkowitz (Ed.), *Advances in experimental social psychology* (Vol. 10, pp. 147–221). New York: Academic Press.

Shafir, E. (1993). Choosing versus rejecting: Why some options are both better and worse than others. *Memory & Cognition, 21,* 546–556.

Shaver, K. (1981). Back to basics: On the role of theory in the attribution of causality. In J. H. Harvey, W. Ickes, & R. F. Kidd (Eds.), *New directions in attribution research* (Vol. 3, pp. 335–358). Hillsdale, NJ: Lawrence Erlbaum Associates.

Srull, T. K., & Gaelick, L. (1983). General principles and individual differences in the self as a habitual reference point: An examination of self–other judgments of similarity. *Social Cognition, 2,* 108–121.

Tversky, A. (1977). Features of similarity. *Psychological Review, 84,* 327–352.

Tversky, A., & Gati, I. (1978). Studies of similarity. In E. Rosch & B. B. Lloyd (Eds.), *Cognition and categorization* (pp. 42–62). Hillsdale, NJ: Lawrence Erlbaum Associates.

Weinstein, N. D. (1980). Unrealistic optimism about future life events. *Journal of Personality and Social Psychology, 39,* 806–820.

Wells, G. L., & Gavanski, I. (1989). Mental simulation of causality. *Journal of Personality and Social Psychology, 56,* 161–169.

Wells, G. L., Taylor, B. R., & Turtle, J. W. (1987). The undoing of scenarios. *Journal of Personality and Social Psychology, 53,* 421–430.

Yamagishi, K., & Miyamoto, J. M. (1991, November). *Weighting of features in judgments of superiority and inferiority.* Paper presented at the annual meeting of the Psychonomic Society, San Francisco.

Yamagishi, K., & Miyamoto, J. M. (1993, November). *Weighting of features in pleasant versus unpleasant life domains.* Paper presented at the annual meeting of the Psychonomic Society, Washington, DC.

5

Living in Neither the Best Nor Worst of All Possible Worlds: Antecedents and Consequences of Upward and Downward Counterfactual Thinking

Matthew N. McMullen
Keith D. Markman
Igor Gavanski
Indiana University

> *It was the best of times, it was the worst of times . . .*
> —Charles Dickens (1859/1980, p. 3)

As the opening line of Dickens' classic novel suggests, it is very often the case that people can imagine both better and worse alternatives to their present reality. Although Dickens was writing about events that occurred over two centuries ago, it remains just as true today that we clearly live in neither the best nor the worst of possible worlds. For instance, we can wish for the amelioration of present difficulties in the Middle East yet still take comfort in the fact that the threat of nuclear war has been greatly reduced since the end of the Cold War. On a more mundane level, it is easy for us to imagine how various aspects of our lives, such as our jobs, marriages, or physical fitness, could be both better and worse. Undoubtedly due to the pervasiveness and intrinsically fascinating qualities of this phenomenon of imagining alternatives to reality, there has been a veritable explosion of research in recent years on what have been termed mental simulation and counterfactual thinking processes.

Most of the important preliminary work in this area focused on the cognitive rules governing what events (or features of events) were more

---

Author note: Preparation of this chapter was supported by an NIMH Predoctoral Fellowship to the first author.

likely to be changed, or *counterfactualized*, often referred to as the rules of mutability (Kahneman & Tversky, 1982) or slippability (Hofstadter, 1985). Indeed, this work has told us psychologists a great deal. For instance, psychologists have learned that people are generally more likely to imagine what might have been different about exceptional (i.e., surprising or unexpected) events than about normal events (Kahneman & Miller, 1986; Kahneman & Tversky, 1982) and that the actions people take within a given situation are more readily mutated than the actions people do not take (Kahneman & Miller, 1986; Landman, 1987; but see also Gilovich & Medvec, chapter 9). Because this early work was most concerned with establishing these cognitive rules, little emphasis was placed on the delineation between different types of counterfactuals. Instead, most researchers focused on reactions to failure or negative outcomes (e.g., Landman, 1987; Wells & Gavanski, 1989) because it was assumed that these were the conditions most likely to engender counterfactual thinking.

Research focusing on reactions to failure or negative outcomes is certainly important and fascinating in its own right (e.g., see Gilovich & Medvec, chapter 9). However, we have used something this research has chosen not to focus on as a springboard for our own program of research—the fact that most outcomes that people experience in their daily lives allow imagination of both better *and* worse alternatives. Indeed, we have termed counterfactuals that improve on reality (". . . it could have been better") *upward counterfactuals* and those that worsen reality (". . . it could have been worse") *downward counterfactuals*. This perspective provides a particularly rich and exciting area of research because, as we will discuss, upward and downward counterfactuals have differential consequences for the individual. In general, we believe that a full understanding of counterfactual thinking requires a consideration of how they might serve people's motives and goal states (see also Roese & Olson, chapter 6). What are the costs and benefits of imagining what could have been?

Before discussing the consequences of counterfactual thinking, however, we first examine what leads people to differentially focus on better or worse possible worlds. We refer to these as the *antecedents* of upward and downward counterfactuals. Specifically, in this first section, we discuss how the ease of imagining different types of counterfactuals can be influenced by (1) The *controllability* of the various features of a particular event, (2) the *valence* of a particular outcome, and (3) the *repeatability* of an event. In the next section, we discuss the differential *consequences* of making counterfactuals and, in so doing, focus on upward and downward counterfactuals in addition to the more general process of undoing events. Specifically, the main focus of this section is on the effects of counterfactual thinking on *affect* and *control* and includes discussions of (1) how perceived control is acquired; (2) how the acquired perceived control in turn influences affect; and (3) how the affective response is determined by whether one is simply imagining an alternative as opposed to comparing one's present state to a counterfactual alternative. We should note that these two sections do not comprise an exhaustive review of the literature in this area but rather tend to focus on our own program of research.

ANTECEDENTS OF COUNTERFACTUAL THINKING

Ease of Imagining and the Role of Controllability

A basic tenet of Kahneman and Miller's (1986) norm theory is that it is the ease of one's imagining different outcomes that determines the counterfactual alternatives that are generated. Using a simple scenario about two tennis players, Kahneman and Miller (1986) attempted to demonstrate a person's general tendency to imagine better outcomes more often than worse outcomes. Markman, Gavanski, Sherman, and McMullen (1995) altered this scenario slightly and gave the following version to 27 Indiana University undergraduates:

> Tom and Jim both were eliminated from a tennis tournament, both on a tie-breaker. Tom lost when his opponent served an ace. Jim lost on his own unforced error. Who will feel worse about the match that night?[1]

> Tom 0%   Jim 100% (N = 27)

Kahneman and Miller's (1986) interpretation of these findings was basically that upward counterfactuals (i.e., Jim's losing on an unforced error) are cognitively easier to generate than downward counterfactuals (i.e., Tom's opponent's not having served an ace). Although this tendency may generally be the case, Markman et al. (1995) suggested that certain factors may influence the ease of imagining different outcomes. Specifically, they advanced a "controllability hypothesis" which suggests that the *controllable* features of an event should have an advantage over the *uncontrollable* features of an event in being mutable because the former are

---

[1]The original version of Kahneman and Miller's (1986) scenario asked "Who would spend more time thinking about the event?" When Markman et al. (1995) originally created the "downward" version of this scenario, however, participants were confused by this question, so it was changed to "Who would feel better about the match that night?" Thus, Markman et al. made the same change to the original Kahneman and Miller scenario for consistency.

more likely to be the *focus of attention*. In turn, as Kahneman and Miller (1986) themselves suggested, this focus of attention on particular features of an event should enhance the availability of counterfactual alternatives to these features. In terms of the tennis scenario, then, participants might have perceived that Jim, who lost on his *own* unforced error, was more in control of his own outcome than was Tom, who lost when his *opponent* aced him, and thus made more counterfactuals about Jim than about Tom.

Support for this explanation was supplied by the responses of another 27 Indiana University undergraduates to a scenario Markman et al. (1995) created in which Tom and Jim *won* a tennis match under different conditions of personal control:

> Tom and Jim both won the semifinal matches of a tennis tournament, both on a tie-breaker. Tom's winning shot hit the white line, just barely staying in. Jim won when his opponent's shot hit the top of the net and just barely bounced back over to his opponent's side. Who will feel better about the match that night?

> Tom 78%   Jim 22% (*N* = 27)

Apparently participants once again judged greater affect for the player who had control over the outcome (i.e., Tom, who barely hit the line) than for the other player. This enhanced affect suggests that this time it was easier for participants to generate downward counterfactuals for Tom, whose shot barely stayed in, than upward counterfactuals for Jim's opponent, whose shot almost made it over the net. This finding is actually inconsistent with Kahneman and Miller's (1986) notion that upward counterfactuals are generally easier to produce than downward counterfactuals.[2] In general, then, controllability may exert a good deal of influence on the ease of a person's imagining different outcomes; the focus of attention on one or another feature of a given event may determine whether an upward or a downward counterfactual is made. This hypothesis has particularly important implications because, as we describe in more detail later, the direction of the counterfactual can have affective and motivational consequences for the individual.

---

[2] One might offer a slightly different interpretation of these effects: Jim experienced relatively more negative affect for his unforced error (first scenario) because he made an *internal* attribution for his *failure*, whereas Tom experienced relatively more positive affect for hitting his shot on the line (second scenario) because he made an internal attribution for his *success* (cf. Weiner, 1985). However, it might have been perceived control over features of these events that led to the internal attributions in the first place.

The "Wheel-of-Fortune" Study. In a further test of the controllability hypothesis, Markman et al. (1995) placed participants in an experimental situation that had both controllable and uncontrollable features in order to see which were counterfactualized about more frequently. Markman et al.'s goal was not to find a main effect of controllability, per se, on direction of counterfactual generation (see Roese & Olson, 1995) but rather to find whether the controllable features of a given event were more mutable than the noncontrollable features of that event. Thus, they were interested in showing that the direction of the counterfactual could, in fact, be *either* upward *or* downward, depending on what features or aspects of the event were controllable.

Pariticipants played a computer-simulated "wheel-of-fortune" game and saw on the computer screen two wheels that spun simultaneously. They were told that the outcome of one of the wheels would determine how many lottery tickets they would win, and the other wheel would determine the number of lottery tickets won by the other participant who was present (but who was actually a confederate). The game was fixed to result in one of the two following *wheel outcomes*: In the first outcome, the participant's wheel narrowly misses hitting a jackpot of 75 lottery tickets and instead lands on the position for 10 tickets, whereas the other wheel (indicating the outcome of the other player) lands on the "bankrupt" position, that is, the *own (could have been) better–other (was) worse* outcome. In the second scenario, the participant's wheel narrowly misses landing on the bankrupt position and instead lands on the 10-ticket position, whereas the other wheel lands on the 75-ticket position, that is, the *own (could have been) worse–other (was) better* outcome. The participant's own wheel was set to narrowly miss a certain outcome in order to elicit counterfactuals of the form "I *almost* won 75 tickets" or "I *almost* went bankrupt." Kahneman and Varey (1990) termed the simulation of alternatives like these (that is, "almost happened" or had a "propensity" to happen) as *close counterfactuals*. The two wheel-outcome conditions are depicted in Figure 5.1.

Markman et al. (1995) manipulated control by giving some participants a choice of the position where their own determining wheel should start and how fast it should spin (the spin-choice condition), whereas other participants chose which wheel would be the determining wheel for them (the wheel-choice condition) and which would determine the outcome of the other player.

One main prediction was that participants would tend to *focus* on, and thus make counterfactuals about, whichever feature of the game they controlled. Thus, spin choosers would generate more within-wheel counterfactuals (focusing on what could have happened on their *own* wheel, e.g., "Had I started the wheel at a different point . . .") than would wheel choosers, whereas wheel choosers would generate more between-

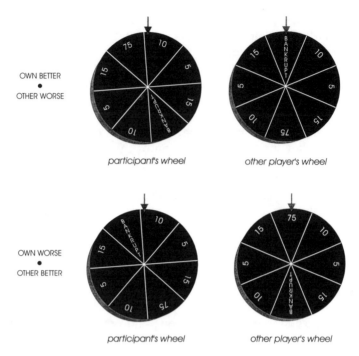

FIG. 5.1. Wheel-outcome conditions.
Note. Copyright 1995 by the Society for Personality and Social Psychology,
Inc. Adapted from Markman et al. (1995).

wheel counterfactuals (focusing on what could have happened had the
other wheel determined their outcome, e.g., "Had I played on the other
wheel . . .") than would spin choosers. In their analysis, Markman et al.
(1995) focused on the *first* counterfactual generated (see Kahneman &
Tversky, 1982); if a participant's first counterfactual was within-wheel, it
was coded as a *+1*, whereas if the first counterfactual was between-wheel,
it was coded as a *–1*. Thus, a pariicpant's tendency to make within-wheel
counterfactuals would be associated with a relatively more positive fo-
cus-of-counterfactual score, whereas a between-wheel counterfactual
would be associated with a relatively more negative focus-of-counterfac-
tual score. As the results reported in Table 5.1 indicate, there was, indeed,
a significant main effect of type of control on the focus of counterfactual
generation: Spin choosers generated far more within-wheel counterfactuals ($M = .82$), and thus far fewer between-wheel counterfactuals, than
did wheel choosers ($M = 0.18$).

A second, and perhaps more interesting prediction, was that the type
of control exerted (spin choice or wheel choice) would interact with the
wheel-outcome condition to produce the following effects for *direction* of

TABLE 5.1
Focus and Direction of the First Counterfactual Made by Participants

Wheel Outcome	Control Type	
	Spin Chooser	Wheel Chooser
Focus of First Counterfactual		
Own better/other worse	.91	.17
Own worse/other better	.73	.07
Direction of First Counterfactual		
Own better/other worse	.31	−.23
Own worse/other better	−.43	.20

Note. Positive numbers indicate relatively more within-wheel than between-wheel counterfactuals and relatively more upward than downward counterfactuals. Copyright 1995 by the Society for Personality and Social Psychology, Inc. Adapted from Markman et al. (1995).

the counterfactual: Participants whose own wheel almost hit the 75-ticket position would generate a greater proportion of upward counterfactuals (e.g., "I could have won 75 tickets . . .") if they were spin choosers than if they were wheel choosers. On the other hand, participants whose own wheel almost hit the bankrupt position would generate a greater proportion of downward counterfactuals (e.g., "I could have gone bankrupt . . .") if they were spin choosers than if they were wheel choosers. In their analysis, Markman et al. (1995) again focused on the first counterfactual generated, with upward counterfactuals receiving a +1 direction-of-counterfactual score and downward counterfactuals receiving a −1 direction-of-counterfactual score. The results of this analysis (see Table 5.1) indicate that the predicted pattern was obtained; there was a significant interaction between "Control Type" and "Wheel Outcome" on the incidence of upward and downward counterfactuals.

In sum, the specific feature of the game that a participant controlled led to a differential focus on either their own wheel or their opponent's wheel and, in turn, this differential focus seems to have had a predictable impact on the types of counterfactuals that were generated. Apparently, then, controllability is an important determinant of whether an upward or downward counterfactual is to be made. Furthermore, the fact that controllable features are more likely than others to be mutated has important affective and motivational implications for the individual (we discuss these in a later section of this chapter).

Outcome Valence

As we discussed previously, Kahneman and Miller (1986) suggested that it is harder for an individual to imagine how a favorable reality might have been worse (downward counterfactual) than to imagine how an unfavorable reality might have been better (upward counterfactual). With all things held constant, this may be the case. We suggest, however, that the *valence* of a particular outcome should also exert a powerful effect on the ease of imagining and, thus, have different and predictable effects on the generation of upward and downward counterfactuals.

Other researchers (e.g., Gavanski & Wells, 1989; Gleicher et al., 1990; Landman, 1987) have indeed examined counterfactual generation in response to both positive and negative outcomes. A drawback to this research, however, is that outcome valence was, at least partially, confounded with the ease of generating different kinds of counterfactuals. The basic problem is that only two possible outcomes were explicitly described: Either a favorable, factual outcome was paired with an unfavorable, counterfactual outcome, or an unfavorable, factual outcome was paired with a favorable, counterfactual outcome. Thus, bad outcomes were paired with better, counterfactual *default events* (cf. Wells & Gavanski, 1989), whereas good outcomes were paired with worse, counterfactual defaults. Instead, a stronger test of the effects of outcome valence on counterfactual generation should reflect what is often the true state of nature: Most outcomes that people experience in their daily lives allow the imagination of both better *and* worse alternatives.[3] For this reason, Markman, Gavanski, Sherman, and McMullen (1993) devised an experimental situation in which both types of alternatives were readily available. Additionally, they also set out to examine how outcome valence influences the *spontaneous* generation of counterfactuals; in previous work, participants had been instructed or otherwise directed to produce a specific change to a factual outcome (i.e., to make a bad outcome better or to make a good outcome worse).

Markman et al.'s (1993) predictions stemmed from the perspective that counterfactuals have motivational or functional implications (see Roese & Olson, chapter 6). Consider, for example, the unhappy owner of a "lemon" car who thinks, "If only I had bought a Honda, I wouldn't be at the service station every other week." Although the generation of such an upward counterfactual may devalue the actual outcome and make people feel worse, the simulation of routes to imagined, better realities may help people learn to improve on such outcomes in the future (S. Taylor & Schneider, 1989; Wells, B. Taylor, & Turtle, 1987). Thus, the car owner who thinks "If only I had bought a Honda . . ." may benefit from this counterfactual by learning to buy a Honda (or car of similar quality) the next time. This reasoning actually has its roots in the social-comparison research. Thus, Festinger (1954) believed that the primary purpose of social comparison is accurate self-evaluation: People compare themselves to others in

---

[3]We do admit, however, that the ease of generating each kind of counterfactual is probably somewhat correlated with the valence of the outcome.

order to evaluate their opinions and abilities. Furthermore, research findings have shown that people may compare themselves to slightly "better-off" others (i.e., engage in upward *social* comparison) in an effort to *improve* themselves (e.g., S. Taylor & Lobel, 1989; Wheeler, 1966).

On the other hand, consider the student who receives a C– on an exam and thinks, "At least I didn't fail." Such a downward counterfactual may make one feel better: In comparison to the F one could have received, a C– seems pretty good (see also Johnson & Sherman, 1990; S. Taylor, Wood, & Lichtman, 1983). Likewise, as reported in the social-comparison literature, Wills (1981) suggested that people engage in downward social comparison in order to protect and enhance their subjective well-being (e.g., "I may have gotten a C– on the exam, but I did better than Bob"). Note, however, that although downward counterfactuals may provide comfort, they might also leave one unprepared for the future; the student who simulates how a C– might have been even worse may be comforted but will fail to identify alternative strategies to improve the grade on future occasions (cf. Roese, 1994).

Given this reasoning, Markman et al. (1993) predicted that under conditions in which both better and worse alternatives were available, outcomes experienced as dissatisfying (negative) would activate a desire for something better and thus stimulate upward counterfactuals, whereas outcomes experienced as satisfying (positive) would lead to the desire to enjoy the outcome and thus would stimulate downward counterfactuals.

The "Blackjack" Study. Because Markman et al. (1993) believed that the scenario paradigms used in previous work were ill-suited for an examination of the motivational implications of counterfactual thinking, they developed a paradigm that allowed them to examine the spontaneous generation of counterfactuals by people in an actual situation involving the self. Specifically, participants played a computer-simulated blackjack game in which the objective outcome was the same in all conditions: Participants tied the dealer's hand and won $5. This allowed all participants the opportunity to make either upward ("I could have won more money") or downward ("I could have lost") counterfactuals.

Participants' perceptions of outcome valence were varied through a *framing* manipulation (see Kahneman & Tversky, 1979). The use of this kind of manipulation enabled Markman et al. (1993) to study spontaneous counterfactual generation in reaction to three differently perceived valences of an identical outcome: positive, neutral, and negative. The three conditions were framed in the following ways:

Win Condition: Participants started with no money. They were told that if their hands won (beat the dealer's hand), they would receive $20. If their hands tied (matched the dealer's hand), they would receive $5. If their hands lost (went over 21 or failed to beat or tie the dealer's), they would receive nothing.

Neutral Condition: Participants were given $5 to start. They were told that if their hands won, they would receive an additional $15. If their hands tied, they would keep their $5. If their hands lost, they would lose the $5 that they were initially given.

Lose Condition: Participants were given $20 to start. They were told that if their hands won, they would keep the $20. If their hands tied, they would *lose* $15 of the $20. If their hands lost, they would lose all $20.

In sum, the potential and actual outcomes (i.e., the net gains) were objectively the same across the win, neutral, and lose conditions. Participants in win frames were predicted to generate relatively more downward counterfactuals, whereas those in lose frames were predicted to generate relatively more upward counterfactuals. Participants' reactions to tying the dealer's hand were vocalized onto a tape recording, producing a rich set of spontaneous counterfactuals which were later coded as either upward or downward, that is, in the same way they were coded in the wheel-of-fortune study (Markman et al., 1995). As the results depicted in Figure 5.2 indicate, the predicted results were obtained (Markman et al., 1993). The main effect of "Outcome Frame" was significant, and subsequent comparisons indicated that participants in the lose frame generated more upward counterfactuals than did those in either the neutral or win frames.

From a functional perspective, then, it might be that people generate upward counterfactuals in response to negative outcomes because of a desire for future improvement, but generate downward counterfactuals in response to positive outcomes because of a desire to enjoy the present. Indeed, the participants in Markman et al.'s (1993) study did feel relatively more satisfied with their outcomes after making downward counterfactuals than after making upward counterfactuals, an effect found recently by a number of different researchers (e.g., Boninger, Gleicher, & Strathman, 1994; Markman et al., 1995; McMullen & Markman, 1994; Roese, 1994). Ironically, however, these findings suggest that upward and downward counterfactuals both hold tradeoffs for the individual: Upward counterfactuals prepare one for the future, at the expense of feeling worse, whereas downward counterfactuals help one feel better, at the expense of being ill prepared for the future.

Recently, in fact, we have been taking a "harder look" at the functionalist perspective by asking the following question: Should not people in negative affective states want to improve on their affect by making *downward* counterfactuals? This tendency would certainly be consistent with the idea that unhappy people often try to engage in *mood repair* (e.g.,

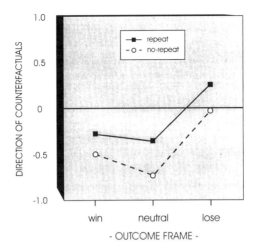

FIG. 5.2. Mean direction of counterfactuals as a function of outcome frame. Positive numbers indicate relatively more upward than downward counterfactuals; negative numbers indicate relatively more downward than upward counterfactuals.
Note. Copyright 1993 by Academic Press, Inc. Adapted from Markman et al. (1993).

Cialdini, Darby, & Vincent, 1973; Singer & Salovey, 1988). Thus far, most of the research examining the relationship between counterfactuals and negative affect has followed a similar series of steps: (1) Participants read about or experience an outcome. (2) They then generate counterfactual alternatives to that outcome. (3) The particular counterfactual generated leaves the participant feeling relatively dissatisfied. Because the measurement of affect is usually the *final* step in these experiments, however, we have no idea whether or not participants later engage in downward counterfactuals in order to try to "get out" of this state. Thus, it might be interesting for researchers to *induce* a mood state and *then* examine the counterfactuals that participants make in response to a given outcome. If a "controlled" mood-repair process were at work, one could predict that participants would generate downward counterfactuals in response to negative events. On the other hand, from the cognitive perspective that inducing a mood makes mood-congruent thought accessible (e.g., Bower, Gilligan, & Monteiro, 1981; Isen, Shalker, Clark, & Karp, 1978; Mackie & Worth, 1989) one might predict just the opposite: A negative mood would make negative thoughts about oneself more accessible, thereby accentuating the contrast between the self and more positive standards of comparison (cf. Schwarz & Bless, 1992). In our laboratory, we are currently conducting an experiment in which mood and outcome valence are orthogonally manipulated, in an attempt to tease apart these issues.

At this point, we are speculating that both cognitive *and* motivational processes might come into play in response to a negative mood or outcome. Indeed, the automatic–controlled distinction (see Shiffrin & Schneider, 1977) that has lately become popular in social psychology may be useful in describing the process whereby counterfactual alternatives are generated in response to negative outcomes or moods. The generation of upward counterfactuals may come first, driven by a quick and relatively effortless process in which the most salient causal agent in a situation is selected for mutation. Over time, however, a more controlled and thoughtful process of mood repair may take over, characterized by a greater incidence of downward counterfactuals. The following example illustrates this process: A college student who receives a C on an exam may be completely obsessed with the thought, "If only I had studied harder. . . ." As time passes, however, the student may begin to see how the outcome could have been even worse. In fact, one's peers and relatives may be some of the most influential sources of downward-counterfactual alternatives (e.g., "Don't be so hard on yourself, you could have done so much worse . . ."). An interesting test of the automatic–controlled notion would be to place participants under cognitive load (e.g., Gilbert, Pelham, & Krull, 1988) after experiencing a negative outcome (or being put in a negative mood) and to observe whether the relative incidence of downward counterfactuals decreased as a result.

As the previous discussion suggests, it is entirely possible that the tendencies of upward counterfactuals being made in response to negative outcomes and downward counterfactuals in response to positive outcomes have much less to do with functionality per se and much more to do with *context*. Thus, the effect of winning or losing, or of experiencing a positive or negative event, may be that the contrasting standard of comparison is made more salient (Schwarz & Bless, 1992), an effect that thereby leads to a focus of attention on one alternative or another (Kahneman & Miller, 1986; Markman et al., 1995). In general, we believe that the influence of various contextual or background features of a situation on the generation of counterfactuals is a fascinating avenue for future research. For instance, it may be possible to make upward or downward alternatives more salient or accessible by either explicit or implicit priming (e.g., Higgins, Rholes, & Jones, 1977; Jacoby, Kelley, Brown, & Jasechko, 1989; Srull & Wyer, 1979). An example of an explicit situational prime might be a recently viewed film. Thus, a man who is vacationing in Las Vegas and loses $200 betting the "wrong" color on the roulette wheel might be more likely to make upward counterfactuals about his performance if he had recently seen a spate of "James Bond" films wherein the protagonist always has remarkable gambling success. Viewing such films creates a prior context of success at gambling and thus renders the concept of winning more accessible. On the other hand, if the man had recently seen Eric Roberts' character in *The Pope of Greenwich Village* have his life destroyed because of an inability to pay off gambling debts, the counterfactual alternative "I could have lost a lot more . . ." may be somewhat more accessible for this individual.

Event Repeatability

A closer examination of the functionalist notion that people generate upward counterfactuals primarily to prepare for the future and downward counterfactuals primarily to comfort themselves necessitates a further delineation of the conditions under which each kind of counterfactual might be preferred. Markman et al. (1993) suggested that the potential *repeatability* of an event would provide one such important test of the functionality hypothesis. The following example illustrates this point. People who experience a particular outcome (e.g., a C– on an exam or the purchase of a "lemon" car) and who foresee the possibility of being in a similar situation in the near future (e.g., taking another exam in the course or buying another car) might be expected to generate primarily upward counterfactuals, with the goal of improving on that outcome ("I should have bought a Honda . . ."). On the other hand, for a one-time event (e.g., one's only visit to Las Vegas or one's only time in graduate school), preparation for a better "next time" is not particularly relevant. Thus, the best one can do in such a situation is to try to feel better about it by making a downward counterfactual ("It could have been worse; I could have lost more money"). In sum, Markman et al. (1993) suggested that the potential repeatability of an event is another important factor that influences the ease of imagining better or worse counterfactual alternatives.

Event repeatability was manipulated by Markman et al. (1993) in the following way: Before actually playing the blackjack game, participants in the "repeat" condition were told that the hand they were about to play would be the first in a series of four similar blackjack games that they would play. On the other hand, participants in the "no-repeat" condition were told that after playing one hand of blackjack they would go on to an unrelated task that did not involve gambling. A direction-of-counterfactual score was computed; Figure 5.2 depicts the effects of this manipulation on counterfactual generation: Participants who anticipated playing the game again (i.e., were in the repeat condition) generated relatively more upward counterfactuals than participants who did not anticipate playing the game again (i.e., were in the no-repeat condition).

These results suggest that the repeatability of an event is more likely than a nonrepeatable event to induce the goal of improving on one's outcome in the future, leading one to think about how things might have been better. On the other hand, the nonrepeatability of an event is more likely than a repeatable one to allow one to see how things could have been worse; for one-time events, preparation for a better future is largely irrelevant. Unlike in our earlier discussion of outcome valence, we are hard pressed to find an explanation for this repeatability effect except one positing that participants were focusing, at least at some level, more on the future in the repeat condition relative to those in the no-repeat condition. Markman et al. (1995) suggested, however, an important limiting condition on this effect, if upward counterfactuals are to have this preparatory function: People must have some degree of control over their actions if such events do occur in the future. Indeed, a recent paper by Roese and Olson (1995) provides support for this idea. In their study, participants made upward counterfactuals when a story character's actions were controllable, but made downward counterfactuals when these actions were uncontrollable. Thus, as with the repeatability effect, people will make upward counterfactuals if they feel that they have some control over actions they might take in the future, but will make downward counterfactuals if they lack such feelings of control.

Recent findings by Roese (1994) provide additional direct evidence for the functionality of counterfactuals. In one study, generating upward counterfactuals increased participants' intentions to perform behaviors that would facilitate achieving success, a result suggesting that upward counterfactuals can provide scripts for the future (e.g., Abelson, 1981). In another study, upward counterfactuals were shown to enhance *performance* on an anagram-solving task, relative to downward counterfactuals. On the other hand, downward counterfactuals enhanced affective reactions to task performance, relative to upward counterfactuals. We believe that the demonstration of a direct link between counterfactuals and behavior is an important step and we hope to see more of such links forged to other behavioral domains (e.g., coping, decision-making behavior) as this research area continues to grow.

There may also be some individual differences in terms of who is most likely to benefit from certain types of counterfactuals. For instance, there may be people who simply tend to focus on better or worse possible worlds, that is, people who are chronically accessible (e.g., Higgins, King, & Mavin, 1982; see also Higgins, 1987) to imagining better or worse alternatives to reality. One such distinction might be drawn between optimists and pessimists. Optimists, who tend to view things from a positive perspective, may be more inclined to make downward counterfactuals in situations in which both better and worse alternatives to reality exist (e.g., "B's aren't bad; you could be getting C's or D's"), whereas pessimists, with their more cynical view, may be more likely to make upward counterfactuals in such situations (e.g., "If only I were getting

A's; with *B*'s I'll never get into medical school"). Interestingly, the opposite prediction could also be made: Perhaps the optimism of optimists stems from the very fact that they *have* learned how to improve on the past by making upward counterfactuals! Indeed, optimists, by definition, would be more likely than pessimists to believe that they actually *can* improve in the future. Our highly speculative guess is that optimists can strategically make either upward *or* downward counterfactuals, depending on which is most functional, and, furthermore, are more likely to learn from upward counterfactuals because they believe that they can *control* what happens to them in the future. Pessimists, on the other hand, may be "stuck in a rut" of ruminative thought (e.g., Davis & Lehman, chapter 13; Martin & Tesser, 1989; Sherman & McConnell, chapter 7; Tait & Silver, 1989) predominated by upward counterfactuals about *uncontrollable* outcomes, counterfactuals that do not serve any functional value (cf. Markman et al., 1995). Thus, the findings of Roese and Olson (1995) that upward counterfactuals are made predominantly in response to controllable outcomes may be applicable only to those with a more optimistic orientation; pessimists may feel that there is little they can do to control what happens to them in the future. In general, an individual-difference approach to counterfactual thinking (see Kasimatis & Wells, chapter 3) should provide fascinating information about the antecedents of upward and downward counterfactuals.

CONSEQUENCES OF COUNTERFACTUAL THINKING

Acquisition of Perceived Control

In late 1993, then Defense Secretary Aspin offered his resignation because it was learned that he had refused a request for additional armor in Somalia, shortly before the deaths of several American soldiers there ("The Collapse of Les Aspin," 1993). Some suggested that the deaths would not have occurred if Aspin had approved the request. Others argued that "even if he had approved the armor, it probably would have arrived too late" (p. 25), and so the deaths could not have been prevented. Much of the debate focused not on the quality of or reasoning behind the decision that was made at the time but rather on the counterfactual alternatives to the decision. This example clearly demonstrates the power of counterfactual undoing in judgments of causality and responsibility, even at the expense of evaluating the facts that existed before the outcome occurred.

Indeed, findings from research on perceived control have indicated that the facts of actual control over an event are often distorted by the attributions people make (Langer, 1975; Wortman, 1976). Because counterfactuals, such as those about the Defense Secretary's decision, influence causal attributions (Wells & Gavanski, 1989), self-relevant counterfactuals should influence perceptions of personal causation or control. An individual who believes "if only I had done something differently, things would have turned out better" is implicitly accepting responsibility for the outcome through his or her consideration of counterfactual alternatives.

In three studies, McMullen and Markman (1994) investigated how counterfactual thinking influences perceived personal control and responsibility. In the first two studies, participants were instructed to recall recent events in their lives and to imagine alternatives to those events. In the first study, half of the participants recalled positive events and half recalled negative events, and all were instructed to imagine themselves engaging in whatever counterfactual behaviors or decisions seemed most natural. In the second study, all participants recalled negative events and then imagined counterfactual behaviors that resulted in a better outcome, in a worse outcome, or in the same outcome. In both studies participants coded their own counterfactuals and events for perceived control, affective evaluations, and related measures.

In the third study, participants played a computer-simulated card game, a procedure previously used with success (Markman et al., 1993, 1995). Participants played four simplified poker games; during the course of each game, participants added to their hand one of two cards. The remaining card, the one they could have but did not receive, was the "counterfactual" card. The four games each corresponded to a different counterfactual condition: In one hand, participants saw that they could have done better (upward counterfactual); in another, that they could have done worse (downward counterfactual); in a third, their hand would have been the same with either card (outcome unchanged); and in a fourth game, they were not presented with counterfactual information (no counterfactual). In addition, one third of the participants were assigned one of the two cards by the computer, one third chose their own card, and one third chose their own card by attempting to read the patterns on the backs of the cards. At the end of each hand, participants responded to open-ended questions about the hand and then completed several rating scales concerning affective evaluations and perceived control over the game. The results of these three studies are discussed in terms of five distinct theoretical issues: undoing the outcome, self-focus versus external focus, counterfactual direction, foreseeability, and scenario plausibility.

Undoing the Outcome. The primary assumption about how counterfactual thinking influences causal perceptions centers on the notion of undoing. For an event to be judged causal of an outcome, the counterfactual alternatives to the event must result in different outcomes (Wells &

Gavanski, 1989). McMullen and Markman (1994) therefore expected that increased perceived control would be related to the extent that participants' counterfactuals undid self-relevant outcomes. In the first study, results of correlational analyses indicated that the more participants' counterfactuals changed the outcomes, the more perceived control participants reported over the event. McMullen and Markman tested this question experimentally in the second study in which one group of participants was instructed to imagine engaging in different actions that did not change their outcome. Compared to this group, participants who imagined changed outcomes reported greater feelings of control. (McMullen and Markman did not find, however, that all types of counterfactuals that undo an outcome increased feelings of perceived control. We discuss these qualifications later in the sections on focus and direction.)

McMullen and Markman (1994) also wanted to examine these effects in comparison to a no-counterfactual control condition. This investigation was crucial, because they expected that control would in fact be influenced by imagining unchanged outcomes, but in the opposite direction. Self-relevant counterfactual scenarios that do not undo an outcome should lead to decreased perceptions of personal control, as in "There's nothing I could have done." To examine this issue, in the third study McMullen and Markman included a no-counterfactual control condition in addition to the outcome-undone and outcome-not-undone conditions. Results supported both hypotheses: Compared to those in the control condition, counterfactuals that undid the outcome increased perceived control, and counterfactuals that left the outcome unchanged reduced perceived control. Thus, an individual who simulates scenarios in which an outcome is undone will feel a corresponding increase in perceived control, but an individual who can simulate only scenarios in which the outcome is left unchanged will feel a corresponding reduction in perceived control. Perhaps these results will encourage researchers' greater attention to the impact not only of counterfactuals that undo outcomes but also of counterfactuals that do not undo the outcome.

Self-Focus Versus External Focus.[4] Of course, not all counterfactuals involve the self, and, therefore, not all counterfactuals lead to attributions of control to the self. In the wheel-of-fortune study (Markman et al., 1995) discussed previously, the focus of respondents' counterfactuals could have been on either external factors (e.g., "If only the computer had assigned me a different wheel"), or on decisions of the self (e.g., "If only

---

[4]We have not made distinctions among different types of external focus, such as a focus on the situation versus focus on another person, only because we have not included those distinctions in our research to date.

I had chosen a different spinning speed"). Markman et al. found that respondents focused their counterfactual mutations on those aspects of the situation over which they had more control. This pattern should be a functional strategy because attributions to the self should promote feelings of control, whereas external attributions should not. For example, someone who thinks "If only the test were easier, I would have had a better grade" is undoing the outcome, but not through some behavior of her or his own, and therefore should not have enhanced perceived control.

McMullen and Markman (1994) put this idea to experimental test in their third study. One group of participants were assigned their cards by the computer and therefore could not make "If only I had . . ." counterfactuals when they saw the counterfactual card. Rather, paralleling those in the wheel-of-fortune study (Markman et al., 1995), their counterfactuals took the form "If only the computer had assigned me a different card." As expected, there were no significant changes in perceived control due to the counterfactual manipulation in that condition. The only significant changes in perceived control occurred in the other two conditions, in which participants chose their own cards and therefore focused their counterfactuals toward their own decisions.

Whether the counterfactual focus is on the self or on external factors, however, perhaps oversimplifies the issue of personal control. There may be self-mutations that do not influence perceived control. For example, Niedenthal, Tangney, and Gavanski (1994) have made a distinction between behavioral counterfactuals, as in "If only I had . . . ," and characterological counterfactuals, as in "If only I weren't. . . ." They found that the former were related to feelings of guilt, and the latter to feelings of shame. Similarly, we would expect that to the extent participants in McMullen and Markman's (1994) card game study made counterfactuals such as "If only I were better at poker . . ." or "If only I were a lucky person . . . ," they would not acquire increased feelings of control. These characterological counterfactuals, because they merely condemn the self rather than provide insight into specific actions by which the outcome might be changed, should not enhance control (Janoff–Bulman, 1979). The influence of these, and perhaps other types of counterfactuals on perceived control, remains to be addressed in future research.

Counterfactual Direction. A unique characteristic of counterfactual thinking, independent of attribution theory, is that, when an outcome is undone, the counterfactual outcome may be either better or worse than the original outcome. A student can imagine either that studying harder would have brought about a higher grade *or* that studying even less would have brought about a lower grade. Both are examples of counterfactual undoing, and both may therefore potentially influence perceptions of causality and control. However, the functional perspective on counterfactual thinking has determined that clear asymmetries exist between upward and downward counterfactuals. From this perspective, downward counterfactuals are affectively functional and upward counterfactuals are functional for future performance (Markman et al., 1993; Roese & Olson, chapter 6). For example, Roese (1994) demonstrated that upward, not downward, counterfactuals are associated with both intentions to improve and actual improvements in performance.

In all three of their studies McMullen and Markman (1994) found that perceived control was enhanced by upward, but not downward, counterfactuals, findings consistent with this functional perspective. We find this lack of support for the role of downward counterfactuals in perceived control particularly interesting because it suggests that simple undoing is not sufficient to enhance control. Thus, personal control is more than the realization that events are contingent on one's actions; it is a belief that one could have or can bring about *better* outcomes. Perceived control may be more about potential efficacy than about personal causality: Anyone can make things worse, but it is the ability to bring about better outcomes that is truly indicative of personal control.

If downward counterfactuals have any preparative functionality, it would be to provide the individual insight into how to avoid potential pitfalls in the future. Perhaps people are generally concerned with those conditions that are sufficient to produce desirable outcomes, and upward counterfactuals best provide this information. We suspect that if people are more concerned with avoiding negative outcomes, in which case necessary conditions become important in order to know what to avoid in the future, then downward counterfactuals may play a more important role in future preparation.

Although we have argued that counterfactual direction is particularly important for understanding the acquisition of personal control in self-relevant counterfactual thinking, direction may also be a factor in causal judgments about others. Many of the studies reported in the literature on counterfactual judgments of blame incorporated negative events that were undone and that were therefore, in effect, upward counterfactuals (e.g., Kahneman & Tversky, 1982; Macrae, 1992; Miller & McFarland, 1986; Wells & Gavanski, 1989; Wells et al., 1987). Perhaps downward counterfactuals are not as influential in determining perceptions of cause, just as the studies discussed in this chapter indicate a lack of evidence for the role of downward counterfactuals in perceived personal control. This hypothesis would add counterfactual direction to several other judgmental asymmetries in causal attribution, such as additive versus subtractive frames (Dunning & Parpal, 1989) and facilitators versus inhibitors (Hansen & Hall, 1985).

Foreseeability. Another distinctive characteristic of counterfactual thinking is that by definition it occurs after the fact. The arguments to attack or to defend Defense Secretary Aspin's decision not to send additional armor to Somalia were about the actual versus the counterfactual consequences of his decision. Therefore these counterfactuals were independent of the intentionality or foreseeability of the actions that were taken at the time. Indeed, a commonly used defense by politicians, including Aspin with regard to Somalia and Attorney General Reno with regard to the deaths in Waco, is "I made the best decision possible with the information I had at the time." This is, in effect, an admission of causality but also a denial of foreseeability and, hence, a denial of personal responsibility or blame.

Several theorists have convincingly argued for making conceptual distinctions among different levels of causality based on foreseeability and intentionality (Heider, 1958; Shaver & Drown, 1986). In their third study, McMullen and Markman (1994) included two conditions based on the different types of control participants had over their choice of cards. In the first group, participants chose from two face-down cards and therefore could not possibly have foreseen the outcome due to the blind nature of their choice. A second group of participants chose from two cards with different back patterns and colors that were actually randomly determined by the computer. Participants in this second group were told, however, that the backs of the cards could help them choose the correct card. Before playing the games, participants in this condition participated in a "learning session" in which they chose cards based on the back patterns and were given false feedback about their success at choosing the cards. Thus they believed it was possible to determine the correct card. Consequently, participants in this condition had some degree of foreseeability compared to participants who simply chose their cards blindly.[5]

The results of McMullen and Markman's (1994) study showed no differences between participants who made foreseeable choices and those who made nonforeseeable choices, in terms of how the counterfactuals influenced perceived control or responsibility. Upward counterfactuals that focused on decisions of the self increased feelings of control and responsibility equally for foreseeable and nonforeseeable decisions. What is perhaps most interesting about these results is that even those partici-

---

[5]It is also true that the participants who were presented cards with differently patterned backs had more precounterfactual control than those making a blind choice. Indeed, it is difficult to imagine a situation in which increased foreseeability is not coupled with enhanced perceived control. Our point is that the nature of that increased control is foreseeability and that those participants who clearly had no foreseeability in their choices did experience enhanced control as a result of the counterfactuals with which they were presented.

pants who clearly had no foreseeability in their decisions, and therefore could easily have said "I couldn't have known any better," were still influenced by the counterfactual alternatives, just as much as participants who believed they could have known better. These results attest to the powerful, almost irrational impact of counterfactual thinking. Even lottery players who in no way could have known what numbers to pick feel a sense of self-blame when they find out how close their numbers were to the winning ones.

Scenario Plausibility. This final issue, the plausibility of the counter-factual scenarios, arose as a purely methodological problem. In their second study, McMullen and Markman (1994) instructed participants to imagine specific types of counterfactual alternatives to their recalled events according to certain directions. McMullen and Markman were concerned that some participants would simply arrive at implausible counterfactual scenarios, such as "Sure, that test was so hard I suppose I could have studied eighteen hours a day for six weeks and received a better grade." Participants were therefore asked to rate the likelihood of their having engaged in the counterfactual behavior. Results indicated that the more plausible the scenarios, as measured by these ratings, the greater their impact on changes in perceived control. McMullen and Markman noted, however, that counterfactuals did have a significant impact on perceived control even with plausibility partialled out. That is, even implausible counterfactuals may have some impact on perceived control. These results suggest that plausibility should be treated not as a necessary condition, but rather as a moderator of the counterfactual–perceived control relationship.

Conclusion. We have suggested that one of the primary consequences of a person's engaging in self-relevant counterfactual thinking is a change in perceived control. Perceived control is enhanced when an outcome can be imagined better as a result of some action or decision by the self, and control is reduced when an outcome would not have changed regardless of the self's actions. These changes in perceived control are stronger to the extent that the imagined scenarios are deemed plausible but occur regardless of whether the outcomes could have been foreseen.

The Affective-Contrast Effect: A Closer Look

The affective consequences of counterfactual thinking are perhaps the most compelling phenomena in this area. For example, in a recent "Ask Marilyn" column, in which people write to the "world's smartest person" with their questions, Mary from Virginia asked, "Last year, I missed winning the $27 million Virginia lottery by only one number. Can you say something to make me feel better?" Marilyn responded, "Mary, if I knew how to make people feel better about not having millions of dollars, we wouldn't need lotteries anymore" (Vos Savant, 1994).[6] Would psychologists studying counterfactual thinking answer Mary's question any differently? Several conceptions of the affective consequences of counterfactual thinking focus on how outcomes are undone, such that the ease of imagining how an event might not have occurred determines the affective response (e.g., Gleicher et al., 1990; Kahneman & Tversky, 1982). Others have more recently pointed to the importance of conceptualizing counterfactuals in terms of direction (Markman et al., 1993; 1995). For most events, one can imagine both better and worse possible alternatives, and the affective response is thus determined by means of a contrast effect to the imagined alternative.

All of the experiments discussed here have provided evidence for this affective-contrast effect: Participants reported feeling better or more satisfied when they made downward counterfactuals compared to participants who made upward counterfactuals and who felt worse and less satisfied. There are, however, some questions regarding the symmetry of affective responses to upward and downward counterfactuals. Roese (1994) correctly pointed out that the lack of a no-counterfactual control condition in several studies leaves doubt as to whether both directions have affective consequences or one of the two directions alone is responsible for the effect. In one of his studies that included a no-counterfactual condition, downward counterfactuals made participants feel better, but upward counterfactuals did not make participants feel worse. However, as Roese pointed out, whereas Markman et al. (1993) manipulated perceived outcome valence, Roese's study involved exclusively negative outcomes.

In fact, McMullen and Markman (1994) found the opposite pattern in their third study. Compared to those in a no-counterfactual condition, upward counterfactuals were significantly more powerful in promoting negative affect than downward counterfactuals were in promoting positive affect. However, clearly positive outcomes were used in that study: Participants were playing games and winning money. This finding is consistent with Roese's (1994) suggestion that a "floor" effect prevents upward counterfactuals from exerting their full effect on negative events and that a "ceiling" effect prevents downward counterfactuals from exerting their full effect on positive events. A single study including both a no-counterfactual condition and a manipulation of outcome valence would be very helpful in clarifying this issue.

Apart from the symmetry of the contrast effect, we have also begun to question its generality. On first inspection, it appears that Mary from

---

[6]We thank Beth Lanthier for pointing out this example.

Virginia (Vos Savant, 1994) has a clearly upward counterfactual and is inevitably faced with negative affect. Current functionalist theories of counterfactual thinking, including our own, have posited a preparative function for upward counterfactuals and an affective function for downward counterfactuals (Markman et al., 1993; Roese, 1994; for a review, see Roese & Olson, chapter 1). Indeed, we proposed a compromise between affect and future preparation such that the concern for future improvement that prompts upward counterfactuals is bound to lead to negative affect.

The affective picture may not be quite so simple, however. Findings from research in social comparison, for example, have indicated that comparison direction is not a necessary determinant of affective reactions (Buunk, Collins, S. Taylor, VanYperen, & Dakof, 1990). For example, upward comparisons indicate not only that others are better off than oneself but also that it is possible to be better off. This dual nature of comparison should be particularly true for counterfactual thinking, because it involves hypothetical scenarios involving oneself rather than comparisons to another person. The results of two lines of research based on this reasoning have suggested a positive affective role for upward counterfactuals in certain circumstances. First, can the belief that it is within her control to win the lottery mitigate some of Mary's negative affect (Vos Savant, 1994)? Second, can Mary relieve some of the pain of almost winning by avoiding comparison to the counterfactual and instead basking in the fantasy of having millions of dollars? These approaches are referred to as the *control-mediated affect* and the *comparing versus basking* approaches, respectively.

Control-Mediated Affect. In their research on how counterfactual thinking influences perceived control, McMullen and Markman (1994) had a secondary purpose: to determine the relationship between the perceived control acquired through counterfactual thinking and subsequent affect. Although both affect and perceived control are directly influenced by counterfactual thinking, they hypothesized a positive relationship between affect and control independent of the usual affective contrast effect. That is, if perceived control brings about positive affect (Dunn & Wilson, 1990; Langer, 1975), *to the extent* that people acquire feelings of personal control over an event through counterfactual thinking, they should feel somewhat better. Along the same lines, Roese (1994) suggested that an upward counterfactual "may be upsetting because it makes salient the deprived present state, yet it may also be uplifting if it gives hope for future betterment" (p. 806). When counterfactuals do lead to feelings of control, it would be useful to distinguish conceptually (and statistically) that portion of the affective response due to the contrast effect and that portion associated with perceived control. McMullen and Markman therefore used the term control-mediated affect to refer to an indirect effect of the counterfactual on affect, mediated by the perceived control acquired through counterfactual thinking.[7]

In all three of their studies on the acquisition of control through counterfactual thinking, McMullen and Markman (1994) found positive correlations between perceived control and affective evaluations of the event, with the counterfactuals' contrast effect statistically held constant. In other words, participants reported feeling better about what happened to the extent they reported greater perceived control over the event. Thus, if Mary from Virginia (Vos Savant, 1994) concludes that it was possible for her to win millions of dollars by picking the winning numbers, this perceived control over the lottery will bring about a degree of positive affect that mitigates the negative affective impact of the contrast effect. It is frustrating, yet exciting to almost win millions of dollars because that means it was *possible* to win. Someone whose numbers do not even come close to the winning numbers will not obtain that thrill of "I could have won," because they simply proved once again that winning the lottery is virtually impossible. In that case, although the contrast effect will be significantly reduced, a decreased sense of perceived control may actually bring about negative affect.

We therefore have evidence that self-relevant counterfactuals influence affect through two mediational mechanisms, the contrast effect and perceived control. What is particularly interesting about this conceptualization is that for upward counterfactuals, these mediators operate in opposite directions. The contrast effect brings about negative affect, whereas the acquired perceived control brings about positive affect. We should note that in none of the three studies did McMullen and Markman (1994) find an overall affective benefit of making upward counterfactuals, even when control was maximally enhanced. This result is likely due to the fact that the counterfactual's influence on affect via control is an *indirect* effect (i.e., mediated by control), whereas the counterfactual's influence on affect via the contrast effect is a *direct* effect. Participants making upward counterfactuals felt, at best, the same as those participants making downward counterfactuals, not better. However, participants making upward counterfactuals reported feeling significantly worse when they were not at the same time acquiring a sense of perceived control. We therefore

---

[7]McMullen and Markman (1994) prefer a mediational approach because it is consistent with their research showing that counterfactual thinking causally influences perceived control and with other research indicating that perceived control leads to positive affect (Dunn & Wilson, 1990; Langer, 1975). However, a moderator approach in which perceived control influences the relationship between counterfactuals and affect is also consistent with the data (see Baron & Kenny, 1986).

believe it is crucial to take perceived control into consideration if psychologists are to fully understand the affective implications of counterfactual thinking, particularly the functional or dysfunctional implications. For example, Davis and colleagues (Davis & Lehman, chapter 13; Davis, Lehman, Wortman, Silver, & Thompson, 1995) have found a correlation between undoing and distress among people who suffered a death in the family due to a car accident or Sudden Infant Death Syndrome. To the extent their respondents thought "If only I had done something different . . . ," they coped less effectively with the trauma as much as 4–7 years later. Is this, as Sherman and McConnell (chapter 7) suggest, an indication of the dysfunctionality of engaging in counterfactual thinking? Perhaps, but it is not clear whether participants' counterfactual ruminations were successful or unsuccessful in promoting feelings of control over the event. Findings from McMullen and Markman's (1994) research indicate that to the extent people increase their perceived control over what happened, they experience less negative affect. If, however, they make upward counterfactuals that do not enhance feelings of control, they experience the full brunt of the negative affect associated with considering how things could have been better.

In an interesting and particularly relevant set of studies, Boninger et al. (1994) argued that a focus on the future plays a key role in determining affective reactions to counterfactuals. Their argument is that the negative affect associated with upward counterfactuals should be mitigated when an individual focuses on the future. We expect that this pattern will be especially true to the extent that one gains control through the counterfactual. For example, if one imagines how the teacher could have awarded higher grades, one is unlikely to feel better by focusing on the future. If, however, one imagines how studying harder would have resulted in a better grade, a focus on the future, coupled with an enhanced sense of control, is particularly likely to minimize the negative affective consequences of the upward counterfactual.

Furthermore, consideration of control can provide a better understanding of the specific emotions experienced in response to counterfactual thinking (cf. Weiner, 1985). Several researchers have noted that in studies on counterfactuals and affect, dependent measures that included counterfactually related emotion terms, such as "disappointment," "relief," and "regret," met with relatively greater success compared to the mixed results obtained from measures with more general affect terms, such as "positive–negative," and "good–bad" (Boninger et al., 1994; Roese, 1994). In fact, emotion is often described as a discrepancy experience (Abelson, 1983; Higgins, 1987). This notion of *counterfactual emotions*, or emotions that are driven by considerations of what might have been, is particularly relevant to the research on counterfactuals, affect, and control.

The view that counterfactuals consist of both affect-provoking and causality-attributing components implies that a variety of combinations of affect and control are possible. For example, there are upward counterfactuals that result in enhanced feelings of control, and upward counterfactuals that do not enhance feelings of control. These different combinations of affect and control should result in distinct emotional reactions, beyond the simple, one-dimensional approach to affective reactions utilized in the studies on control previously discussed.

It would therefore be useful to extend some of the current theorizing to specific counterfactual emotional experiences. Niedenthal et al. (1994) have begun to do this by showing how guilt is associated with mutations of one's behavior ("If only I hadn't . . .") and how shame is associated with mutations of one's self ("If only I weren't . . ."). Tangney's (1990) findings are consistent with our contention that upward counterfactuals should lead to less negative affect when they enhance control. Tangney suggested that shame is a much more powerfully negative emotion than guilt, because guilt provides a sense that one can rectify the situation through behavior and shame does not. Although shame and guilt represent upward counterfactuals, downward counterfactuals can be analyzed in the same manner. Downward counterfactuals that focus on specific behaviors (e.g., "At least I studied hard enough") should lead to feelings of pride in one's behavior, or what Tangney (1990) termed beta pride. Downward counterfactuals that focus on qualities of the self (e.g., "At least I'm smart enough") should lead to alpha pride, or pride in the self.

In this fashion, specific emotional reactions could be predicted through consideration of counterfactual direction, focus (e.g., self vs. other), and control. For example, upward counterfactuals that focus on another's controlled actions (e.g., "If only the teacher graded easier") would provoke anger, whereas upward counterfactuals that focus on uncontrolled external factors would lead to sadness, but not anger (Weiner, 1985). Similarly, downward counterfactuals that focus on external, controllable factors would lead to feelings of gratitude (e.g., "At least the teacher gave me a good grade"), but when the external factor is not perceived to be under volitional control, a downward counterfactual would lead to feelings of luck or good fortune (e.g., "At least the grading computer accidentally gave me a better grade").

In addition, counterfactual scenarios in which the outcome is not undone should have an impact on emotional responses, because these scenarios decrease feelings of personal control. Gleicher et al. (1990) contended that affective responses would be exaggerated when counterfactual alternatives are judged probable but "blunted if alternatives are judged unlikely, so that the outcome appears inevitable" (p. 293). This pattern is certainly the case for *general* affective responses, but we would expect important *specific* emotional experiences to arise. For example, if one is unable to simulate alternative courses that the self might have taken to undo a negative outcome, a sense of helplessness might ensue. If one is unable to simulate how the situation might have been different to undo a negative outcome, frustration may result. In sum, in order to more fully understand the affective consequences of counterfactuals, researchers must consider the combination of affect and control that gives rise to a specific emotional reaction.

Comparing Versus Basking.   Our second challenge to the generality of the affective-contrast effect derives from the observation that not all counterfactual thinking must necessarily involve direct comparisons between reality and the imagined alternatives to reality that are considered. Presumably, people may imagine, fantasize, and daydream about better possible worlds simply because it makes them feel good to do so. For example, people who are instructed to relieve themselves of a negative mood frequently visualize sensual situations or happy social events (Means, Wilson, & Dlugokinski, 1987). Several mood-induction techniques incorporate what might be called a mental simulation procedure, by which respondents place themselves in imagined positive or negative affective states either by reading provided statements (e.g., Murray, H. Sujan, Hirt, & M. Sujan, 1990; Velten, 1968) or by self-directed imagery involving the recall of happy or sad events in the person's past (e.g., Bower, 1981; Salovey & Singer, 1988). This technique contrasts with the counterfactual research findings, which suggest that in order to feel better people should imagine *worse* alternatives to reality.

One resolution to this apparent inconsistency derives from the work of Tesser and colleagues in social comparison (e.g., Tesser, Millar, & Moore, 1988). They suggested that people may treat social encounters either by comparing themselves to others (as Wills, 1981, suggested) or by basking in the reflected glory ("birging") of others (as Cialdini et al., 1976, suggested). Whether comparing or birging occurs depends on the importance of the relevant dimension to one's self-concept. For example, if intelligence is very important to one's self concept and a close friend is much smarter, the comparison process would likely be invoked and one would feel bad about one's own intelligence. On the other hand, if athleticism is quite unimportant to one's self-concept, a close other who is a great athlete is likely to invoke birging, and one will feel good and attempt to become closer to that person. Thus, the self-evaluation maintenance (SEM) model assumes that social encounters may or may not be comparative in nature, and that the affective consequences will differ accordingly. Comparative processes yield, in effect, an affective-contrast effect, in that affect is displaced away from the valence of the person encountered: People feel good when comparing themselves to a worse-off other but bad when comparing themselves to a better-off other. Noncomparative, or birging, processes yield what amounts to affective assimilation: People feel good when associating with a better-off other and bad when associating with a worse-off other.

Taylor and her colleagues have also demonstrated that the affective consequences of social comparison are not as simple as the contrast effect. In a review of the social comparison literature, S. Taylor and Lobel (1989) suggested that patients with cancer often make upward comparisons to seek information and to model more successful behaviors but downward comparisons in order to evaluate one's present state. They concluded that patients "may not use their contacts with survivors and good copers for explicit self-evaluation, but rather may use them for some other purpose" (p. 572). Again, what they are suggesting is that explicit comparisons between oneself and others are not being made in those cases. Rather, the self-evaluative mode is suspended in favor of an information-gathering mode.

In a particularly relevant study, Aspinwall and S. Taylor (1993, Study 1) found that overall, mood changes were *consistent* with the direction of comparison (i.e., affective assimilation occurred). Participants listened to a student speak about either a successful or a failed academic situation. When participants were asked to indicate their mood after hearing the narrative, those who heard the positive testimonial reported increases in positive mood, and those who heard the failure testimonial reported increases in negative mood.[8] Because the experimental situation gave these participants no reason to compare their own state to that of the student they were hearing about, they were in effect basking in the success stories, a response which brought about positive affect. Likewise the failure stories brought about negative affect. Indeed, when participants were later instructed to evaluate their current situation (instructions thus invoking the comparison process), the assimilation effect disappeared, and, for participants who had experienced a recent academic setback themselves, the expected contrast effect emerged.

In a similar fashion, we suggest that mental simulation can be either comparative or noncomparative in nature and that the affective consequences will differ accordingly. Consider the individual who, dissatisfied with his or her personal reality, obtains enjoyment from fantasizing about (i.e., basking in) better realities: "If only I lived like they do on *Lifestyles of the Rich and Famous*." These counterfactual simulations of better possi-

---

[8]The only participants exhibiting the affective contrast effect for this dependent measure were persons with low self-esteem who had been put into negative moods before hearing the failure testimonial.

bilities may bring about at least temporary mood lifts. Thus, independent of a desire for control or future preparation, people may engage in upward simulations for purely affective reasons.

In one preliminary study on this issue, participants recalled recent negative events and then imagined alternatives to those events (McMullen, 1994). Half of the participants were instructed to vividly imagine better alternatives, and half were instructed to vividly imagine worse alternatives. Orthogonally, half of the participants were instructed to think about both what happened and what could have happened, instructions thus invoking comparison, and half were instructed to simulate only what could have happened, instructions thus invoking basking. Note that because all participants were imagining counterfactual alternatives to reality, the difference was only in whether they engaged in comparison to reality or not. Results of dependent measures on mood state immediately after this imagination task indicated that those participants who were basking but not comparing showed mood changes consistent with the valence of the counterfactual: Participants who simulated themselves in positive scenarios felt good; those who simulated themselves in negative scenarios felt bad. This mood-assimilation effect did not occur for participants who were comparing. However, when participants were later instructed to return to and evaluate the actual event, all displayed the usual contrast effect, without regard to whether they were earlier basking or comparing. Thus, although individuals who simulate living like the "rich and famous" may temporarily feel better by escaping their reality, in the end, when they ultimately must return to that reality, they feel even worse.

These results suggest that the affective-contrast effect is neither the only nor necessarily the most likely consequence of counterfactual thinking in all situations. Findings from research on judgments of life satisfaction similarly indicate that the affective-contrast effect is not always to be expected. The affective consequences of recalling actual happy or sad events from one's past depend on whether the recalled event is recent or long past (Strack, Schwarz, & Gschneidinger, 1985). Recent events are included in the category *my life now* and therefore yield an assimilation effect on judgments of life satisfaction, such that recalling a recent, positive event brings about positive affect. Long past events, however, are excluded from the category *my life now*, such that recalling a long past positive event is contrasted with one's current state and therefore brings about negative affect (see also Schwarz & Bless, 1992).

Our focus, however, is on *counterfactual* simulations, which cannot be included in one's current life in the same manner as recollections because they are by definition untrue. One may feel good from reminiscing about the "good old days" if indeed they did occur, but counterfactual simulations are imagined alternatives to reality and are typically assumed to be used as standards against which reality is judged. We are suggesting that in order for mental simulation to yield affective assimilation, one must suspend the type of comparative thinking in which the simulation is used as a standard of evaluation and, rather, bask in the affective tone of the simulation as one might with a fantasy. When one disengages from the simulation or uses the simulation to evaluate reality, the counterfactual information then acts as a standard against which reality is judged, and the contrast effect emerges.

Conclusion. We have argued for two specific refinements to the counterfactual affective-contrast effect. First, to the extent that people gain control from making counterfactuals, the usual negative affect associated with upward counterfactuals is mitigated. In addition, beyond a simple contrast effect, specific emotional reactions can be predicted through consideration of both the control-oriented and the affective consequences of counterfactual thinking. This dual nature of counterfactual thinking, via affective and attributional mechanisms, should be appreciated particularly when the functionality or dysfunctionality of counterfactual thinking is being considered. Second, affective reactions to counterfactuals are determined by the extent to which one is comparing alternative scenarios to one's actual state. Comparing leads to the affective-contrast effect, but basking in a simulation leads to assimilation of mood to the valence of the simulation.

SUMMARY

We have included a diagram (see Figure 5.3) summarizing the major issues addressed in the research by Markman and colleagues (Markman et al., 1993, 1995; McMullen, 1994; McMullen & Markman, 1994). We by no means suggest this as a comprehensive model of counterfactual thinking but rather as a summary of the findings from this research to date. First, the direction (upward vs. downward) and focus (i.e., what aspect of a situation is mutated) of the counterfactual that is generated is determined by factors such as whether or not one will face a similar situation in the future, what type of control one has in the situation, and the valence of the outcome. The counterfactual that is generated will then influence subsequent affective reactions to the situation, depending on the direction of the counterfactual, the extent to which the counterfactual is comparative in nature, and the degree of control that is acquired or present. Perceived control is determined by direction, whether or not the outcome is successfully undone by the counterfactual, and whether the focus is on the self or on external factors.

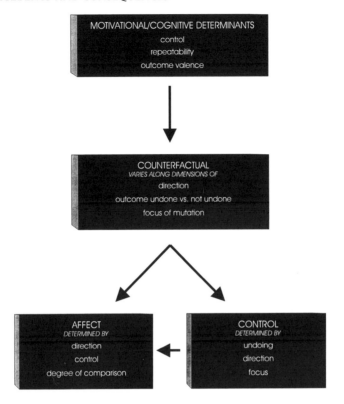

FIG. 5.3. Antecedents and consequences of counterfactual thinking.

With our review of the research, we have attempted to illuminate the antecedents and consequences of counterfactual thinking. One of the prevailing themes of this research has been the conceptualization of counterfactuals in terms of their direction: People may imagine how an event could have been better *or* could have been worse. We believe this represents an advance over most previous research that has focused solely on whether or not an outcome is undone by a counterfactual. We are hopeful that this conceptualization will foster further research that both establishes the conditions under which people imagine better or worse alternatives and provides an understanding of the resulting psychological and behavioral ramifications. A second prevailing theme in the research has been perceived control. We believe that consideration of perceived control as both a determinant and a consequence of counterfactual thinking will help to clarify such issues as the relative functionality or dysfunctionality of imagining alternatives to reality. A third theme has been an appreciation of the complexity of affective responses to counterfactual thinking. Although we believe the affective-contrast effect is a fundamental counterfactual phenomenon, we have pointed to several extensions and refinements to this effect. In sum, we hope that the research reviewed here illustrates the richness of this fascinating and rapidly growing area.

REFERENCES

Abelson, R. P. (1981). The psychological status of the script concept. *American Psychologist, 36*, 715–729.

Abelson, R. P. (1983). Whatever became of consistency theory? *Personality and Social Psychology Bulletin, 9*, 37–54.

Aspinwall, L. G., & Taylor, S. E. (1993). Effects of social comparison direction, threat, and self-esteem on affect, self-evaluation, and expected success. *Journal of Personality and Social Psychology, 64*, 708–722.

Baron, R. M., & Kenny, D. A. (1986). The moderator–mediator variable distinction in social psychological research: Conceptual, strategic, and statistical considerations. *Journal of Personality and Social Psychology, 51*, 1173–1182.

Boninger, D. S., Gleicher, F., & Strathman, A. (1994). Counterfactual thinking: From what might have been to what may be. *Journal of Personality and Social Psychology, 67*, 297–307.

Bower, G. H. (1981). Mood and memory. *American Psychologist, 36*, 129–148.

Bower, G. H., Gilligan, S. G., & Monteiro, K. P. (1981). Selectivity of learning caused by affective states. *Journal of Experimental Psychology: General, 110*, 451–473.

Buunk, B. P., Collins, R. L., Taylor, S. E., VanYperen, N. W., & Dakof, G. A. (1990). The affective consequences of social comparison: Either direction has its ups and downs. *Journal of Personality and Social Psychology, 59*, 1238–1249.

Cialdini, R. B., Borden, R. J., Thorne, A., Walker, M. R., Freeman, S., & Sloan, L. R. (1976). Basking in reflected glory: Three (football) field studies. *Journal of Personality and Social Psychology, 34*, 366–375.

Cialdini, R. B., Darby, B. L., & Vincent, J. E. (1973). Transgression and altruism: A case for hedonism. *Journal of Experimental Social Psychology, 9*, 502–516.

The collapse of Les Aspin. (1993, December 27). *Newsweek*, p. 25.

Davis, C. G., Lehman, D. R., Wortman, C. B., Silver, R. C., & Thompson, S. C. (1995). The undoing of traumatic life events. *Personality and Social Psychology Bulletin, 21*, 182–190.

Dickens, C. (1980). *A tale of two cities*. New York: Penguin. (Originally published 1859)

Dunn, D. S., & Wilson, T. D. (1990). When the stakes are high: A limit to the illusion of control effect. *Social Cognition, 8*, 305–323.

Dunning, D., & Parpal, M. (1989). Mental addition versus subtraction in counterfactual reasoning: On assessing the impact of personal actions and life events. *Journal of Personality and Social Psychology, 57*, 5–15.

Festinger, L. (1954). A theory of social comparison processes. *Human Relations, 7*, 117–140.

Gavanski, I., & Wells, G. L. (1989). Counterfactual processing of normal and exceptional events. *Journal of Experimental Social Psychology, 25*, 314–325.

Gilbert, D. T., Pelham, B. W., & Krull, D. S. (1988). On cognitive busyness: When person perceivers meet persons perceived. *Journal of Personality and Social Psychology, 54*, 733–739.

Gleicher, F., Kost, K. A., Baker, S. M., Strathman, A. J., Richman, S. A., & Sherman, S. J. (1990). The role of counterfactual thinking in judgments of affect. *Personality and Social Psychology Bulletin, 16*, 284–295.

Hansen, R. D., & Hall, C. A. (1985). Discounting and augmenting facilitative and inhibitory forces: The winner takes almost all. *Journal of Personality and Social Psychology, 49*, 1482–1493.

Heider, F. (1958). *The psychology of interpersonal relations*. New York: Wiley.

Higgins, E. T. (1987). Self-discrepancy: A theory relating self and affect. *Psychological Review, 94*, 319–340.

Higgins, E. T., King, G. A., & Mavin, G. H. (1982). Individual construct accessibility and subjective impressions and recall. *Journal of Personality and Social Psychology, 43*, 35–47.

Higgins, E. T., Rholes, W. S., & Jones, C. R. (1977). Category accessibility and impression formation. *Journal of Experimental Social Psychology, 13*, 141–154.

Hofstadter, D. R. (1985). *Metamagical themas: Questing for the essence of mind and pattern*. New York: Basic Books.

Isen, A. M., Shalker, T. E., Clark, M. S., & Karp, L. (1978). Affect, accessibility of material in memory, and behavior: A cognitive loop? *Journal of Personality and Social Psychology, 36*, 1–12.

Jacoby, L. L., Kelley, C., Brown, J., & Jasechko, J. (1989). Becoming famous overnight: Limits on the ability to avoid unconscious influences of the past. *Journal of Personality and Social Psychology, 56*, 326–338.

Janoff–Bulman, R. (1979). Characterological versus behavioral self-blame: Inquiries into depression and rape. *Journal of Personality and Social Psychology, 37*, 1798–1809.

Johnson, M. K., & Sherman, S. J. (1990). Constructing and reconstructing the past and future in the present. In E. T. Higgins & R. M. Sorrentino (Eds.), *Handbook of motivation and cognition: Foundations of social behavior* (Vol. 2, pp. 482–526). New York: Guilford.

Kahneman, D., & Miller, D. T. (1986). Norm theory: Comparing reality to its alternatives. *Psychological Review, 93*, 136–153.

Kahneman, D., & Tversky, A. (1979). Prospect theory: An analysis of decisions under risk. *Econometrica, 47*, 263–291.

Kahneman, D., & Tversky, A. (1982). The simulation heuristic. In D. Kahneman, P. Slovic, & A. Tversky (Eds.), *Judgment under uncertainty: Heuristics and biases* (pp. 201–208). New York: Cambridge University Press.

Kahneman, D., & Varey, C. A. (1990). Propensities and counterfactuals: The loser that almost won. *Journal of Personality and Social Psychology, 59*, 1101–1110.

Landman, J. (1987). Regret and elation following action and inaction: Affective responses to positive versus negative outcomes. *Personality and Social Psychology Bulletin, 13*, 524–536.

Langer, E. J. (1975). The illusion of control. *Journal of Personality and Social Psychology, 32*, 311–328.

Mackie, D. M., & Worth, L. T. (1989). Cognitive deficits and the mediation of positive affect in persuasion. *Journal of Personality and Social Psychology, 57*, 27–40.

Macrae, C. N. (1992). A tale of two curries: Counterfactual thinking and accident-related judgments. *Personality and Social Psychology Bulletin, 18*, 84–87.

Markman, K. D., Gavanski, I., Sherman, S. J., & McMullen, M. N. (1993). The mental simulation of better and worse possible worlds. *Journal of Experimental Social Psychology, 29*, 87–109.

Markman, K. D., Gavanski, I., Sherman, S. J., & McMullen, M. N. (1995). The impact of perceived control on the imagination of better and worse possible worlds. *Personality and Social Psychology Bulletin, 21*, 588–595.

Martin, L. L., & Tesser, A. (1989). Toward a motivational and structural theory of ruminative thought. In J. S. Uleman & J. A. Bargh (Eds.), *Unintended thought* (pp. 306–326). New York: Guilford.

McMullen, M. N. (1994). *Basking and comparing in counterfactual thinking*. Unpublished manuscript.

McMullen, M. N., & Markman, K. D. (1994). *Acquisition of perceived control through counterfactual thinking*. Manuscript submitted for publication.

Means, J. R., Wilson, G. L., & Dlugokinski, L. J. (1987). Self-initiated imaginal and cognitive components: Evaluation of differential effectiveness in altering unpleasant moods. *Imagination, Cognition, & Personality, 6*, 219–229.

Miller, D. T., & McFarland, C. (1986). Counterfactual thinking and victim compensation: A test of norm theory. *Personality and Social Psychology Bulletin, 12*, 513–519.

Murray, N., Sujan, H., Hirt, E. R., & Sujan, M. (1990). The influence of mood on categorization: A cognitive flexibility interpretation. *Journal of Personality and Social Psychology, 59*, 411–425.

Niedenthal, P. M., Tangney, J. P., & Gavanski, I. (1994). "If only I weren't" versus "If only I hadn't": Distinguishing shame and guilt in counterfactual thinking. *Journal of Personality and Social Psychology, 67*, 585–595.

Roese, N. J. (1994). The functional basis of counterfactual thinking. *Journal of Personality and Social Psychology, 66*, 805–818.

Roese, N. J., & Olson, J. M. (1995). Outcome controllability and counterfactual thinking. *Personality and Social Psychology Bulletin, 21*, 620–628.

Salovey, P., & Singer, J. A. (1988). Mood congruency effects in recall of childhood versus recent memories. *Journal of Social Behavior and Personality, 3*, 1–22.

Schwarz, N., & Bless, H. (1992). Constructing reality and its alternatives: An inclusion/exclusion model of assimilation and contrast effects in social judgment. In L. L. Martin & A. Tesser (Eds.), *The construction of social judgment* (pp. 217–245). Hillsdale, NJ: Lawrence Erlbaum Associates.

Shaver, K. G., & Drown, D. (1986). On causality, responsibility, and self-blame: A theoretical note. *Journal of Personality and Social Psychology, 50*, 697–702.

Shiffrin, R. M., & Schneider, W. (1977). Controlled and automatic human information-processing: II. Perceptual learning, automatic attending, and general theory. *Psychological Review, 84*, 127–190.

Singer, J. A., & Salovey, P. (1988). Mood and memory: Evaluating the network theory of affect. *Clinical Psychology Review, 8*, 221–251.

Srull, T. K., & Wyer, R. S., Jr. (1979). The role of category accessibility in the interpretation of information about persons: Some determinants and implications. *Journal of Personality and Social Psychology, 37*, 1660–1672.

Strack, F., Schwarz, N., & Gschneidinger, E. (1985). Happiness and reminiscing: The role of time perspective, mood, and mode of thinking. *Journal of Personality and Social Psychology, 49*, 1460–1469.

Tait, R., & Silver, R. C. (1989). Coming to terms with major negative life events. In J. S. Uleman & J. A. Bargh (Eds.), *Unintended thought* (pp. 351–382). New York: Guilford.

Tangney, J. P. (1990). Assessing individual differences in proneness to shame and guilt: Development of the Self-Conscious Affect and Attribution Inventory. *Journal of Personality and Social Psychology, 59*, 102–111.

Taylor, S. E., & Lobel, M. (1989). Social comparison activity under threat: Downward evaluation and upward contacts. *Psychological Review, 96*, 569–575.

Taylor, S. E., & Schneider, S. K. (1989). Coping and the simulation of events. *Social Cognition, 7*, 174–194.

Taylor, S. E., Wood, J. V., & Lichtman, R. R. (1983). It could be worse: Selective evaluation as a response to victimization. *Journal of Social Issues, 39*(2), 19–40.

Tesser, A., Millar, M. & Moore, J. (1988). Some affective consequences of social comparison and reflection processes: The pain and pleasure of being close. *Journal of Personality and Social Psychology, 54*, 49–61.

Velten, E. (1968). A laboratory task for induction of mood states. *Behavioral Research and Therapy, 6*, 473–482.

Vos Savant, M. Ask Marilyn. (1994, Feb. 20). *Parade Magazine*, p. 8.

Weiner, B. (1985). An attributional theory of achievement motivation and emotion. *Psychological Review, 92,* 548–573.

Wells, G. L., & Gavanski, I. (1989). Mental simulation of causality. *Journal of Personality and Social Psychology, 56,* 161–169.

Wells, G. L., Taylor, B. R., & Turtle, J. W. (1987). The undoing of scenarios. *Journal of Personality and Social Psychology, 53,* 421–430.

Wheeler, L. (1966). Motivation as a determinant of upward comparison. *Journal of Experimental Social Psychology, 1,* 27–31.

Wills, T. A. (1981). Downward comparison principles in social psychology. *Psychological Bulletin, 90,* 245–271.

Wortman, C. B. (1976). Causal attributions and personal control. In J. H. Harvey, W. Ickes, & R. F. Kidd (Eds.), *New directions in attribution research* (Vol. 1, pp. 23–52). Hillsdale, NJ: Lawrence Erlbaum Associates.

6

Functions of Counterfactual Thinking

Neal J. Roese
Northwestern University

James M. Olson
University of Western Ontario

What if . . . ?

With these words human beings achieve the capacity to catapult them-selves beyond the muck and malignancy of the actual into the liberating realm of the possible. What if you had invested more in mutual funds last year? What if you had learned to speak French as a child? Or, what if you had bought the winning million-dollar lottery ticket last week? Such articulations of a possible yet untrue past are called *counterfactual thoughts,* and an increasing number of researchers are recognizing the significance of their pervasive presence in people's mental lives. The above examples capture something of the range of counterfactual possi-bilities, from the mundane to the fantastic, that can easily be generated on demand.

But what essential psychological consequences emerge from people's propensity to reason counterfactually? Are such thoughts generally bene-ficial? Do they instead hamper goal-directed behavior? Or are they merely epiphenomenal and hence inconsequential? A decade of research by social psychologists has illuminated a variety of situational constraints on and affective consequences of counterfactual thinking, but less attention has been directed toward the functional value of such thoughts. For our purposes, we use the term *functional* to denote any cognitive process that may have globally beneficial consequences for the individual. As with previous functional approaches, counterfactual thoughts are examined and explained in terms of the "needs" they serve. As Katz (1960) stated,

"The functional approach is the attempt to understand the reasons people [behave] as they do. The reasons, however, are at the level of psychological motivations and not the accidents of external events and circumstances" (p. 170). Functionalism as a psychological school of thought, advanced in the late 19th century by John Dewey, William James, and others, focused on what each of many specific mental acts and behaviors "is for" (Boring, 1957, p. 555). Much of this work was informed by Darwinian evolutionary theory. Hence, behaviors were characterized in terms of their adaptive significance (e.g., fight or flight reactions that are crucial to the survival of individual organisms). The present approach shares this concern with a broadly construed survival value described nonteleologically. However, the phylogenetic origins of counterfactual thinking are at best unclear; hence, our discussion centers on the spontaneous and strategic generation of counterfactuals and the personal, psychological value of their consequences. By taking a functional approach, we hope to demonstrate consequences of counterfactual thinking that may be construed as beneficial for the individual (see McMullen, Markman, & Gavanski, chapter 5, for discussions of related ideas).

In this chapter we review research, conducted by one or both of us, that has illuminated two possible functions that counterfactual thoughts may serve: a *preparative function* (avoiding the recurrence of negative outcomes) and an *affective function* (feeling better). The present approach to elucidating these functions is to connect them to specific subtypes of counterfactual thoughts that emerge from a classification based on their semantic content and logical structure. We describe four experiments that were informed by this approach. Finally, we speculate on how a functional perspective clarifies the role of counterfactual thinking in human cognition and action.

TWO FUNCTIONS OF COUNTERFACTUAL THINKING

The research that we describe is based on the assumption of at least two conceptually distinct functions that counterfactual thoughts may serve. First, such thoughts may serve a preparative function; that is, they may illuminate means by which individuals may prepare for the future, and accordingly, improve their lot in the future. By manipulating alternatives to past actions, individuals can scrutinize and come to understand past mistakes as well as past triumphs, synthesizing them into prescriptions that may facilitate success in the future (Folger, 1984; Johnson & Sherman, 1990).

The mechanism underlying this function is based on the causal information contained in counterfactual propositions. Counterfactual conditionals are essentially causal statements (Mackie, 1974; Roese & Olson, chapter 1; Wells & Gavanski, 1989). For example, the judgment that X caused Y may directly follow from the counterfactual inference that if X had not been present, Y would not have occurred (i.e., deleting antecedent X undoes outcome Y). If Bob fails an exam, then realizes that he would have passed had he only worked through the study guide, he has identified a causally potent antecedent action. This action (working through the study guide), if performed in the future, may permit the avoidance of future failure. Thus, the mechanism underlying the preparative function is based on the counterfactual identification of a causally potent antecedent action, which in turn triggers an expectancy of the consequences of that action in the future. This realization should then heighten intentions to perform that action, which may then influence the behavioral manifestation of that action. To the extent that the original causal inference was at least partly correct, subsequent performance will be enhanced.[1] This pathway is illustrated in Fig. 6.1.

Portions of this pathway have already been demonstrated in previous research. Expectancies (in the form of explanation and imagination of future actions) may heighten intentions to perform as well as the actual performance of those actions (C. Anderson & Godfrey, 1987; Koehler, 1991; Olson, Roese, & Zanna, in press; Sherman, Skov, Hervitz, & Stock, 1981). As well, the link between intentions and behavior has been amply demonstrated (Ajzen, 1988). One goal of the research described here was the attachment of counterfactual thought processes onto the head of this causal chain.

Counterfactual thoughts may also serve an affective function; that is, they may, under some circumstances, be used to make individuals feel better. This affective function would be based on a contrast-effect mechanism (Schwarz & Bless, 1992). That is, a given outcome will be judged more favorably to the extent that a less desirable anchor is salient (Dermer, Cohen, Jacobsen, & E. Anderson, 1979), a contrast perhaps leading to feelings such as relief or joy. For example, Jennifer was bruised when she fell from her bicycle. Although in pain, she may think, "At least I didn't break anything. . . ." By generating a counterfactual that is evaluatively worse, her actual state of affairs may seem less negative by contrast.

---

[1]For present purposes, we assume that human beings are able to draw accurate causal inferences at least some of the time. Of course, a variety of evidence attests to the fallibility of human causal judgment (Nisbett & Ross, 1980) and the problems inherent in applying such inferences to future outcomes (Dawes, 1993). A central working assumption of the functionalist approach is that even if the majority of an individual's causal judgments prove inaccurate, those few judgments that are efficacious more than offset those other inaccuracies. Sherman and McConnell (chapter 7) discuss cases in which this assumption may not hold.

FIG. 6.1. Hypothesized mechanism linking counterfactuals to behavior.

Accordingly, people may strategically generate thoughts of worse alternatives in order to make themselves or others feel better.

THE DIRECTION OF COUNTERFACTUAL THOUGHTS

Although counterfactuals as a generic class of cognitions may serve these two functions, the aim of the research described here is to provide a more exact theoretical specification of the operation of these functions. With this approach counterfactuals are classified into specific subtypes which are then linked to one or the other function. Two dimensions form the basis of this classification: counterfactual *direction* (namely, counterfactuals that focus on improving versus worsening reality) and counterfactual *structure* (namely, counterfactuals that focus on adding versus subtracting antecedent events).

Direction is an evaluative dimension. Counterfactual alternatives may be described as *upward* if they represent a more desirable state of affairs than actuality, or *downward* if they refer to a relatively worse state of affairs. Upward, as opposed to downward, counterfactuals likely have greater preparative consequences. Upward alternatives may be taken as schemata for future action, making salient those scripts that are necessary to facilitate success. Consequently, "the realization of positive alternatives should make positive outcomes more likely in the future" (Johnson & Sherman, 1990, p. 512; see also Folger, 1984).

Markman, Gavanski, Sherman, and McMullen (1993; see also McMullen, Markman, & Gavanski, chapter 5) provided compelling evidence for this reasoning. In their experiment, participants played a computerized blackjack game for real money, receiving outcome feedback that, although objectively neutral, was framed either as a win, as a loss, or as neutral. Participants spontaneously generated upward counterfactuals more frequently following failure than in either of the other two conditions. Also, participants who expected to play the game again generated more upward counterfactuals than those not expecting to play again. The inference of a preparatory function was indirect: Participants who had succeeded and those with no expectation of playing again had no "need" to prepare for the future; hence the exploration of upward possibilities was of less utility. Participants who had failed and those who expected to play again, in contrast, generated more upward counterfactuals, perhaps in order to maximize their chances of winning more money in the next blackjack game.

That upward counterfactuals serve a preparative function is also indirectly supported by research reported in the social comparison literature. Researchers examining coping with negative life events have interpreted upward social comparison—that is, comparison with someone who is better off than oneself—as providing the most useful information "for potential survival and successful coping" (Taylor & Lobel, 1989, p. 573). When things are likely to improve, people are even more likely to draw preparative information from upward comparisons (Buunk, Collins, Taylor, VanYperen, & Dakof, 1990; Taylor, Buunk, & Aspinwall, 1990). Indeed, the functional nature of upward comparisons was implicit in Festinger's (1954) hypothesis of a unidirectional drive upward, which specified the motivation to become more capable than current performance levels and the resulting preference for observing more capable others. The information gleaned from such comparisons can then be employed for self-betterment. Self-focusing counterfactuals are similar to social comparisons, differing only in that the comparison is made to an alternative self rather than to some other individual. It seems likely, then, that both upward counterfactuals and upward social comparisons may serve the same preparative function.

Counterfactual thinking may also serve an affective function. People may strategically generate representations of how things could have been different in order to make themselves or others feel better. The dimension of counterfactual direction is very likely linked to this affective function as well (Johnson & Sherman, 1990). Via a contrast effect, downward counterfactuals (comparisons between a given outcome and a worse alternative) should elicit positive affect (e.g., relief), whereas upward counterfactuals (comparisons between an outcome and a better alternative) should elicit negative affect (e.g., disappointment, regret). Markman et al. (1993) provided initial evidence for this relation, showing that those manipulations that influenced counterfactual direction (i.e., outcome frame and expectancy of repeating the task) also influenced expressions of satisfaction. Thus, negative outcomes and expectations of repetition not only evoked more upward counterfactuals but greater feelings of dissatisfaction as well.

Findings from other domains are also consistent with this logic. For example, rape victims appear to draw comfort by noting that they could have been more seriously injured or even killed (Burgess & Holmstrom, 1979). People with cancer often reason that their illness could be worse or that they could already have died, resulting in more positive feelings (Taylor, Wood, & Lichtman, 1983). Downward social comparison can also result in heightened self-esteem (Reis, Gerrard, & Gibbons, 1993). Emotional regulation of this sort was hypothesized by Taylor and Schneider (1989) to underlie both counterfactual generation and social comparisons, in that a downward focus may be affectively self-enhancing and thus particularly likely under conditions of threat (Wills, 1981).

People may face a trade-off when generating either upward or downward counterfactuals (e.g., Markman et al., 1993). If they generate an upward counterfactual, they may achieve long-term benefits (i.e., preparation for the future) at the expense of immediate negative affect (i.e., realization that actuality is not as positive as it could be). If, on the other hand, people instead generate a downward counterfactual, they may sacrifice future preparation in favor of immediate affective enhancement. Markman et al. showed that people may be more likely, following negative outcomes, to resolve this dilemma in favor of upward counterfactual generation, but there may be important situational and individual-difference moderators of this effect (e.g., Boninger, Gleicher, & Strathman, 1994). We will return to this issue in our discussion of the "Susan" study.

THE STRUCTURE OF COUNTERFACTUAL THOUGHTS

We consider counterfactual structure, unlike counterfactual direction, to be essentially nonevaluative. *Additive* counterfactuals are those that add a new antecedent, one not present in reality, in order to create a counterfactual alternative. For example, Jane does not own an umbrella and got wet walking to work in the rain. She may then generate the counterfactual inference that if she did own an umbrella, then she would have stayed dry. In this case, she has added the element of umbrella ownership to her factual state of affairs in order to construct an alternative outcome. In contrast, *subtractive* counterfactuals are those that remove some factual antecedent in order to reconstruct reality. Jane might as easily think that if it had not rained, she would have remained dry. In this case, the factual element of rain was removed in order to create the alternative outcome of dryness.

In situations involving a dichotomous response option (e.g., competing vs. cooperating in a prisoner's dilemma game), additions and subtractions are logically identical: Specifying competition, for example, directly implies *not* cooperating, and specifying *not* competing implies cooperation. In such cases, the distinction between additive and subtractive counterfactuals is uninformative, at least on purely logical grounds.[2] In everyday social interaction, however, behavioral choices are rarely dichotomous. People typically select behaviors from among multiple and variegated possibilities. Here, additions and subtractions do not imply each other; each provides distinct information. As you sit down to dine at a fine restaurant, your companion may tell you to avoid the mussels, but this advice provides you with no information as to what you ought to order.

In such cases of multiple response possibilities, which likely form the backdrop for much of people's social lives, additive counterfactuals may be more likely than subtractive counterfactuals to serve a preparative function. That is, differentially generating the former instead of the latter may result in relatively more efficacious plans of action and greater resultant success. There are at least two reasons why this might be so. First, when multiple response options are available, additive counterfactuals are more specific. They focus on one response option that might have resulted in success and hence should be implemented in the future; subtractive counterfactuals merely remove one previous response option from consideration, leaving any specific prescription unstated. Second, and perhaps more important, additive counterfactuals are more creative. Whereas subtractive counterfactuals are restricted to the original set of

---

[2]Though phrasing a response in these two ways may be logically identical for a dichotomous response option, they may nevertheless be psychologically distinct (see Gilovich & Medvec, chapter 9). Findings from several programs of research have shown that the framing of propositions may have unique psychological consequences, even if the propositions are themselves logically identical. Research on the feature-positive effect (e.g., Fazio, Sherman, & Herr, 1982) and prospect theory (e.g., Kahneman & Tversky, 1979) has provided examples of such framing effects. Dunning and Madey (chapter 4) discuss framing effects in terms of their specific implications for counterfactual thinking.

response options (i.e., what actually happened), additive counterfactuals are, by definition, those that go beyond the original option set, forging novel options perhaps never considered in the past. It is this basic creativity inherent in additive counterfactuals that may be an essential feature of the improvement central to the preparative function.

THE ANDREA STUDY

One strategy of specifying the functional value of the various counterfactual subtypes is based on situational manipulations. Situations may be identified in which cognitive processes of preparative value would be most useful (i.e., personally beneficial). These processes should be more vigorous in these as opposed to other situations. In other words, people may employ that process in order to reap its benefits when those benefits are most needed. To draw a simple analogy, suppose that you have theorized that scissors serve a haircutting function. One method of demonstrating this function might be to assign workers randomly to tasks involving either long hair or long sentences. If scissors are requested more frequently in the former than in the latter condition, we may infer that scissors do indeed serve a haircutting function.

In the previously described experiment by Markman et al. (1993), they tested this logic by manipulating outcome valence and outcome repeatability. They reasoned that negative rather than positive outcomes and that repeating rather than nonrepeating outcomes represent situations in which counterfactuals that serve a preparative function would be most useful and hence most likely to occur. Upward counterfactuals were indeed more frequently generated in these than in their contrasting situations, thus providing evidence that the former carries greater preparative functionality. In other words, when situational demands created a specific need, participants generated the appropriate cognition in response to this need.

We adopted this same method in demonstrating that additive as opposed to subtractive counterfactuals better serve a preparative function (Roese & Olson, 1993b). For this experiment, participants read a paragraph depicting a student named Andrea and her preparations for a midterm examination in psychology (this scenario was adapted from one used by Gavanski & Wells, 1989).[3] In addition to her routine preparation, Andrea engaged in some additional work, but also experienced some drawbacks. This situation thereby provided a range of antecedents, both

---

[3]The participants in all of the studies described in this chapter were first-year undergraduates attending the University of Western Ontario. The studies were conducted between 1990 and 1993 while Roese was a doctoral student supervised by Olson.

facilitative and inhibitory of success, out of which participants could construct counterfactual alternatives. After reading the paragraph, participants were asked to record on paper ways that the outcome might have turned out differently.

Two variables were manipulated: outcome valence and outcome frame. First, the outcome was described as either a success (passing the exam with a good mark) or a failure (failing the exam). Second, Andrea's prior academic record was described as either good or poor. We hypothesized that additive counterfactuals would be more prominent following failure than following success, and that this pattern would be more pronounced when the outcome was framed by a history of past failure.

The counterfactual thoughts recorded by participants were classified as either additive or subtractive. Thus, counterfactual structure constituted a within-participants factor. As expected, outcome valence predicted the structure of counterfactuals, in the form of a significant two-way interaction. Additive counterfactuals were much more frequently generated following failure than following success, whereas subtractive counterfactuals were more frequently generated following success than following failure (see Table 6.1). In the failure conditions, additive counterfactuals suggested creative and novel response options that moved beyond the confines of the events described in the scenario. Further, the preponderance of additive counterfactuals was even greater when failure was framed by a history of past failure, engendering a reliable three-way interaction between outcome valence, outcome frame, and structure (see Table 6.2). In this condition, participants seemed sensitive to the fact that Andrea was in real trouble and went out of their way to provide strategically creative solutions that were not so much as hinted at in the scenario itself. This generative creativity of counterfactual thinking has not perhaps been sufficiently appreciated in previous discussions. Although certainly circumscribed by the constraints of reality and feasibility (Kahneman &

TABLE 6.1
Effect of Outcome Valence on Counterfactual Structure

		Structure	
Outcome Valence	*n*	*Additive*	*Subtractive*
Success	67	1.09$_a$	1.79$_b$
Failure	64	2.11$_a$	0.56$_b$

Note. Values indicate mean number of counterfactual thoughts of each structural type recorded by participants. Structure is a within-subjects variable. Means within rows and not sharing a common subscript differ at $p < .01$. From "The Structure of Counterfactual Thought," by N. J. Roese and J. M. Olson, 1993b, *Personality and Social Psychology Bulletin, 19*, p. 316. Copyright 1993 by the Society for Personality and Social Psychology, Inc.

TABLE 6.2
Effects of Outcome Valence and Outcome Frame
on Counterfactual Structure

Condition	n	Structure	
		Additive	Subtractive
Success Frame			
Success[a]	37	1.00	1.75[a]
Failure[b]	33	1.61	.63[b]
Failure Frame			
Success[c]	30	1.20	1.83[c]
Failure	31	2.65	.48[b]

Note. Values indicate mean number of counterfactual thoughts of each structural type recorded by participants. Structure is a within-subjects variable. From "The Structure of Counterfactual Thought," by N. J. Roese and J. M. Olson, 1993b, *Personality and Social Psychology Bulletin, 19*, p. 316. Copyright 1993 by the Society for Personality and Social Psychology, Inc.
[a]Difference between additive and subtractive, $p < .05$. [b]Difference between additive and subtractive, $p < .01$. [c]Difference between additive and subtractive, $p < .07$.

Miller, 1986; Taylor & Schneider, 1989), the results of this study nevertheless illuminate the often exuberant originality inherent in counterfactual thinking, a uniquely functional propensity that is captured in particular by additive structures.

THE LIFE EVENTS STUDY

In the previous section we described how situational manipulations may be used to provide preliminary evidence for the functional basis of counterfactual thinking. Situations were identified in which cognitive processes serving a preparative function would be likely to occur (i.e., situations in which they would be useful). Markman et al. (1993) thereby linked upward counterfactuals to a preparative function and downward counterfactuals to an affective function. Similarly, we linked additive counterfactuals to a preparative function (Roese & Olson, 1993b).

These demonstrations are necessarily indirect, however. Although it makes intuitive sense that processes that prepare one for the future should occur in situations in which they are especially useful, in the absence of direct evidence of the consequences of engaging in these processes, they could as easily represent afunctional or dysfunctional responses. The reliance of these studies on outcome manipulations is particularly troublesome, in that people may sometimes respond dysfunctionally to negative outcomes (see Davis & Lehman, chapter 13; Sherman & McConnell, chapter 7; for discussions).

A more direct approach to inferring functionality is manipulating the use versus nonuse of the target cognitive process and then observing consequences consistent with the hypothesized function. To return to our example involving the haircutting function of scissors, a cunning researcher might manipulate the availability of scissors to workers faced with a lot of long hair, then measure the amount of hair cut. Thus, to provide more direct evidence for the functional basis of counterfactual thinking, Roese (1994, Experiment 2) manipulated the generation of counterfactuals themselves and then observed consequences that could be construed as consistent with a preparative or affective function. Specifically, Roese manipulated direction and structure in a 2 × 2 design. Thus, the dependent variables of Markman et al. (1993) and of Roese and Olson (1993b) were converted into independent variables for the present research. Participants in this life events study (Roese, 1994, Experiment 2) were asked to recall a recent examination performance that they had found especially disappointing. They were then asked to consider and record on paper how this negative event could have been better or how it could have been worse (i.e., upward vs. downward counterfactuals). Participants were also asked what new elements could be added to have altered the outcome versus what elements could be removed to have altered the outcome (i.e., additive vs. subtractive counterfactuals). Table 6.3 lists two examples of each of the four counterfactual subtypes that emerged from this 2 × 2 classification (one example for each was taken from this study and one was taken from the study described next).

After completing filler tasks, participants rated their intentions to perform three success-facilitating behaviors. These behaviors were the most frequently cited by a separate sample of undergraduates asked to list means of improving their academic standing. These behaviors thus constituted the most normatively salient success-facilitating actions to our subject pool. Roese (1994) reasoned, therefore, that these should be the most likely to be evoked by any priming manipulation, including the manipulation of counterfactual generation. Recall that the causal pathway hypothesized to underlie the preparative function specified a link between counterfactuals and behavioral intentions (refer to Figure 6.1). Thus, the generation of upward and additive counterfactuals should heighten participants' intentions to perform success-facilitating behaviors.

There was indeed a main effect of direction on intentions. As predicted, consideration of upward counterfactuals led to increased intentions to perform success-facilitating behaviors (see Table 6.4). The inclusion of a control group, in which participants recalled a negative event but were not asked to generate counterfactual thoughts, permitted a closer exami-

TABLE 6.3
Examples of Counterfactual Subtypes

Counterfactual Subtype	Examples
Upward–Additive	If only I could have studied harder in the previous years of secondary school, I may not have encountered such difficulty in studying. I could have tried saying the words out loud until I recognized them.
Upward–Subtractive	If only I hadn't spent so much time on the harmonization question. I should not have assumed that a consonant would start each word.
Downward–Additive	If I had given up during the exam (even then I knew I would do poorly), it would have been worse. I could have chosen people and places as a topic and been confronted with words that were unfamiliar to me.
Downward–Subtractive	But if I didn't spend those hours studying that I did, I would have done even worse in the exam. If I hadn't skipped one of the words, I would have lost a lot more time guessing, as I was having a lot of trouble visualizing it.

Note. These four counterfactual subtypes emerge from the 2 × 2 matrix embracing direction and structure. The examples here are taken from actual participant responses. The first example of each subtype comes from the life events study (Roese, 1994, Experiment 2); the second come from the anagram study (Roese, 1994, Experiment 3).

TABLE 6.4
Effect of Counterfactual Direction on Intentions and Affect

	Counterfactual Direction		
	Upward	Downward	Control
Intention	6.35_a	5.47_b	5.11_b
Mood	3.75_a	4.37_b	3.12_a
Dis–Rel	2.49_a	3.57_b	1.93_a
n	35	35	15

Note. Values represent mean 9-point ratings. Greater values indicate greater intentions or more positive affect. "Dis–Rel" refers to the disappointed–relieved rating. Means across rows not sharing a common subscript differ at $p < .05$. From "The Functional Basis of Counterfactual Thinking," by N. J. Roese, 1994, Journal of Personality and Social Psychology, 66, p. 811. Copyright 1994 by the American Psychological Association, Inc.

nation of this effect. Upward counterfactuals were found to be largely responsible for the main effect: Participants in this condition reported significantly greater intentions than participants in the no-counterfactual control condition. The intentions of the participants generating downward counterfactuals did not differ reliably from those in the control group.

Contrary to expectations, the effects of counterfactual structure were not reliable. Roese (1994) had predicted that additive counterfactuals would result in heightened intentions relative to subtractive counterfactuals. One explanation for these null findings was evident (beyond the simplest one that structure does not serve a preparative function). Perhaps additive counterfactuals exert their preparative effect in a more highly circumscribed, domain-specific manner than do upward counterfactuals. Thus, although upward counterfactuals may induce broader (and perhaps more motivationally based) effects on a variety of intentions, the effects of additive counterfactuals might be more specific, both conceptually and temporally. If this is the case, then a retrospective self-report design, coupled with vague future possibilities, would not represent the most appropriate test of the effects of additive versus subtractive counterfactuals.

This experiment also constituted a test of the affective function. Participants rated their current mood directly following counterfactual generation. Ratings on five bipolar adjective scales (e.g., depressed–elated, unhappy–happy) were summed for this purpose. As expected, a main effect for direction on affect was significant. Downward-counterfactual generation resulted in more positive feelings than did upward-counterfactual generation (refer to Table 6.4). Inclusion of a control group again permitted a more specific description of the effect. Relative to participants in the no-counterfactual control group, participants generating downward counterfactuals reported more positive affect, but participants generating upward counterfactuals did not report more negative affect.

These affective findings are consistent with those of Markman et al. (1993), who found that manipulations that heightened upward counterfactual generation also increased satisfaction. The findings from the life events study, however, offer a more direct demonstration of the causal impact of direction on affect. The finding that the effect of direction may be largely attributable to the positive affect-enhancing effect of downward counterfactuals, and not to any affect-depressing effect of upward counterfactuals, deserves further comment. This finding may be artifactual, reflecting the focus on negative outcomes. Averaged across all conditions, affective responses were negatively polarized. A floor effect might, therefore, have limited the extent to which upward alternatives could engender even more negative affect. Yet, this state of affairs existed in other, scenario-based counterfactual studies in which an upward alternative was made salient and resulted in more negative affect (e.g., Gleicher et al.,

1990). Clearly, further research is needed before we can be confident in interpreting this effect.

THE ANAGRAM STUDY

With the results of the experiment just described, Roese (1994, Experiment 2) demonstrated the psychological consequences of an individual's considering various counterfactual subtypes and provided direct evidence for the functional basis of counterfactual thinking. In terms of the preparative function, counterfactual consequences for intentions were assumed to influence behavior in turn. The anagram study (Roese, 1994, Experiment 3) was designed to provide evidence of behavioral effects directly. Participants engaged in a computer-administered anagram task. The task involved a variety of decisions that could potentially influence performance (e.g., participants could decide on the interval between successive anagram presentations; they could select the topic area from which the anagrams were derived; they could select clues, but doing so involved a penalty to their final "score"). These and other facets of the task were intended to provide participants with a range of response options from which they could generate counterfactuals. Importantly, several of these responses could indeed have an impact on performance. Thus, to the extent that participants were able to identify counterfactually one of these as possible means of improvement, they could capitalize on that inference by implementing it in the subsequent task. Such behavior would provide a clear example of the preparative function of counterfactual thoughts.

Participants attempted to solve a set of 10 anagrams, and on completion, all received failure feedback. Participants then generated counterfactuals according to the same 2×2 design as in the previously described life events experiment, and then completed filler ratings. Only at this point did participants learn that they would attempt to solve a second set of 10 anagrams. This sequence was an important feature of the procedure in that it ensured that the counterfactuals would focus explicitly on participants' previous outcome, thereby eliminating interpretations involving expectancy effects. As well, a control group was included. Participants in this control condition performed the same tasks as those in the other four conditions, with the single exception that they were not requested to record any counterfactual thoughts.

The main dependent measure was participants' improvement in performance from the first to the second anagram set. Participants' scores on each set of 10 anagrams were a function of the total number of anagrams solved weighted by the time taken to solve them; subtracted from this value was the number of anagrams *not* solved weighted by the time spent trying to solve them. Scores did not differ on the first set as a function of the

TABLE 6.5
Effect of Counterfactual Direction on Performance

	Counterfactual Direction		
	Upward	Downward	Control
Performance	232.0_a	118.3_b	$119.3_{a,b}$
n	30	30	15

Note. Values represent score on first anagram set subtracted from score on second anagram set. Greater values indicate greater improvement in performance from the first to second set. Means not sharing a common subscript differ at $p < .05$. From "The Functional Basis of Counterfactual Thinking," by N. J. Roese, 1994, *Journal of Personality and Social Psychology, 66*, p. 813. Copyright 1994 by the American Psychological Association, Inc.

manipulated variables (the average score on this first set was 297; on the second, it was 472). Difference scores were created by the subtraction of participants' first set scores from their second set scores.

Analyses of variance (ANOVA) performed on this difference score yielded two main effects that were significant. The effects of direction and structure were both reliable (the relevant means are shown in Tables 6.5 and 6.6). As expected, the elicitation of upward counterfactuals resulted in greater improvement in performance than did downward counterfactuals. Comparisons involving the control group's scores revealed that downward counterfactuals had no negative impact on performance; rather, it was the performance-facilitating effect of upward counterfactuals that was responsible for this effect. Also, additive counterfactuals were associated with greater improvement than were subtractive counterfactuals. Again, the control group's scores clarified this effect. Subtractive counterfactuals also engendered no negative effects on performance. Hence, it was the performance-enhancing effect of additive counterfactuals that was responsible for the reliable main effect of structure.

TABLE 6.6
Effect of Counterfactual Structure on Performance

	Counterfactual Structure		
	Additive	Subtractive	Control
Performance	284.4_a	65.5_b	119.3_b
n	30	30	15

Note. Values represent score on first anagram set subtracted from score on second anagram set. Greater values indicate greater improvement in performance from the first to second set. Means not sharing a common subscript differ at $p < .05$. From "The Functional Basis of Counterfactual Thinking," by N. J. Roese, 1994, *Journal of Personality and Social Psychology, 66*, p. 813. Copyright 1994 by the American Psychological Association, Inc.

The results of this experiment provide direct support for the contention that upward as opposed to downward counterfactuals and additive as opposed to subtractive counterfactuals can in particular serve the function of preparing one for future betterment. Moreover, these findings, along with those from the life events study, support a mechanism underlying this preparative function that links together counterfactuals, expectancies, intentions, and behavior. Upward and additive counterfactuals (e.g., "If only I had done X, things would have been better") may be especially likely to be converted into scripts for future outcomes (e.g., "If I do X, things may improve in the future"). These conditional suppositions heighten intentions to perform and as well heighten the actual performance of relevant success-facilitating behaviors (e.g., C. Anderson & Godfrey, 1987; Koehler, 1991; Sherman et al., 1981). The results of the life events study are consistent with this reasoning. They showed not only that upward counterfactuals, relative to downward counterfactuals, heightened a person's intentions to perform such behaviors but also, according to control-group score comparisons, that it was largely the intention-enhancing effect of upward counterfactuals that was responsible for this effect. Results of the anagram study supplement these findings by showing that both upward and additive counterfactuals can engender improvement on a skills-based task.

The demonstration that planning specific facilitative behaviors represents one avenue by which counterfactuals lead to improvement does not preclude the operation of other mechanisms, however. An alternative mechanism might be that upward or additive counterfactuals offer individuals hope for the future (cf. Buunk et al., 1990; Taylor et al., 1990). This explanation embraces a contrast effect mechanism rather than the hypothesized causal-inference mechanism. Optimistic appraisal of a future possibility (i.e., the mere image of a better outcome) may in itself be a motivating force, causing people simply to try harder on subsequent tasks (e.g., Ruvolo & Markus, 1992). In the absence of more direct evidence, this alternative explanation remains plausible and may even operate in parallel to the mechanism emphasized in the previous discussion.

THE SUSAN STUDY

The preceding findings documented the preparative and affective consequences of generating upward and downward counterfactuals. When prompted, the consideration of upward counterfactuals causes preparative effects, whereas the consideration of downward counterfactuals causes relatively more positive affect. As we noted earlier, people may face a trade-off between preparation for the future and affective self-enhancement. Confronted by failure, individuals must choose between the long-term preparative benefits of upward-counterfactual thinking and the immediate affective benefits of downward-counterfactual thinking. If they opt for the former, they may prepare for the future at the expense of immediate negative affect, whereas if they opt for the latter, they may sacrifice future betterment for positive affect. The findings of Markman et al. (1993) showed that participants tended to resolve the dilemma in favor of the preparative function (i.e., they spontaneously considered upward counterfactuals following failure). A negative event would seem to constitute a situation in which the affective benefits of downward counterfactuals would be most useful, yet they are relatively less frequent in such cases. This begs the question of when, in fact, people do strategically construct downward alternatives that will cause them to feel better. The Susan study (Roese & Olson, 1995) addressed one possible answer.

In the Susan study (Roese & Olson, 1995), we examined whether the perceived controllability of the outcome in question might be an important moderator of individuals' consideration of upward versus downward counterfactuals. In virtually all of the counterfactual experiments testing functional interpretations, participants made decisions within achievement settings with clear goals. Participants operated with some degree of control over their own actions and over the outcomes they experienced. In these types of controllable situations, it is clearly functional to generate upward counterfactuals that may illuminate avenues by which performance can be improved in the future. However, when the outcome is perceived to be uncontrollable (e.g., random or accidental), such upward considerations are clearly of lesser utility. These thoughts may therefore be less frequent under such conditions. Following outcomes that are uncontrollable, people may be more likely to enhance their affect by considering downward alternatives. These predictions are consistent with those advanced by social comparison theorists. In particular, Wills (1981) suggested that downward social comparisons (i.e., comparing oneself to another person who is worse off) are more likely in situations in which misfortune cannot be remedied through deliberate action. In other words, when instrumental intervention is not possible (e.g., when outcomes are uncontrollable), people are more inclined to preserve or enhance self-esteem through downward comparisons.

We tested this logic using a scenario study (Roese & Olson, 1995, Experiment 1). As in the Andrea study (Roese & Olson, 1993b), several actions performed by a student (this time named Susan), preceding an important exam, were described. Outcome valence was manipulated: Susan received either a good or a poor grade. Further, the controllability of the actions preceding that outcome was also manipulated. In the controllable condition, antecedent events were the result of Susan's intentions; in the uncontrollable condition, these same events occurred by accident or by chance. For example, she experiences a poor night's sleep either because she drank too much coffee or because she had the flu. Similarly, she finds an extra 3 hours to study either because she decided to skip a class or because the class was canceled. The perceived controllability of four such antecedent events were intended to contribute to diverging perceptions of outcome controllability. After reading the paragraph, participants were asked to record on paper ways that the outcome might have turned out differently.

Participants' responses were coded as either upward or downward in their direction. Consistent with Markman et al.'s (1993) findings, a significant two-way interaction involving outcome valence and direction emerged: Upward counterfactuals were more frequently generated following failure than following success, whereas downward counterfactuals were more frequent following success than following failure. The means from this interaction are shown in Table 6.7. More important, the main predictions were confirmed in the form of a two-way interaction between outcome controllability and direction: Whereas upward counterfactuals were more frequent in the controllable than in the uncontrollable condition, downward counterfactuals were more common in the uncontrollable than in the controllable condition. The relevant means are shown in Table 6.8.

For this study (Roese & Olson, 1995), we also computed within-cell correlations between direction (number of upward counterfactuals recorded minus the number of downward counterfactuals recorded) and affect (a self-report manipulation check for the outcome-valence factor). The correlations were calculated within the success and failure conditions (a correlation between direction and affect calculated across all participants would be uninformative, given the demonstrated impact of outcome valence on both of these variables). Although direction and affect were unrelated in the success condition ($r = .14$), they were significantly correlated in the failure condition ($r = -.43$). Thus, greater proportions of

TABLE 6.7
Effect of Outcome Valence on Counterfactual Direction

Outcome Valence	n	Direction	
		Upward	Downward
Success	40	2.13$_a$	1.85$_a$
Failure	40	3.43$_b$	.33$_c$

Note. Values indicate mean number of counterfactual thoughts of each directional type recorded by participants. Direction is a within-subject variable. Means not sharing a common subscript differ at $p < .05$. From "Outcome Controllability and Counterfactual Thinking," by N. J. Roese and J. M. Olson, 1995, Personality and Social Psychology Bulletin, 21, p. 624. Copyright 1995 by the Society for Personality and Social Psychology, Inc.

TABLE 6.8
Effect of Outcome Controllability on Counterfactual Direction

		Direction	
Outcome Controllability	n	Upward	Downward
Controllable	40	3.08_a	$.73_b$
Uncontrollable	40	2.48_c	1.45_d

Note. Values indicate mean number of counterfactual thoughts of each directional type recorded by participants. Direction is a within-subject variable. Means not sharing a common subscript differ at $p < .05$. From "Outcome Controllability and Counterfactual Thinking," by N. J. Roese and J. M. Olson, 1995, Personality and Social Psychology Bulletin, 21, p. 624. Copyright 1995 by the Society for Personality and Social Psychology, Inc.

downward counterfactual thoughts were associated with more positive affect but only in the failure condition. This finding is consistent with previous evidence that counterfactual thoughts are generated spontaneously after failure but not after success (Gleicher et al., 1990; Roese & Olson, chapter 1). Thus, the counterfactuals that participants generated in the success condition might have been somewhat contrived, perhaps carrying less potent affective consequences than the more "natural" counterfactuals generated in the failure condition.

This evidence is consistent with the interpretation that when situations are construed as uncontrollable, people are more likely to generate downward counterfactual thoughts, which have the effect of engendering more positive mood states. Because the consideration of upward alternatives may illuminate avenues by which future improvement might be reached, they were more common in controllable than in uncontrollable situations. That is, in conditions in which deliberate action can "pay off," upward counterfactuals predominated. In contrast, downward counterfactual thoughts were more common in conditions perceived to be uncontrollable, presumably because there was little point to preparative action and, therefore, the affective benefits of downward thoughts predominated.

SUMMARY OF RESEARCH

We reviewed four experiments whose results illuminate the functional basis of counterfactual thinking. Focusing on two possible functions, preparative and affective, our strategy was to connect these functions to subtypes of counterfactuals emerging from a classification based on direction and structure. Results of the Andrea study (Roese & Olson, 1993b) provided preliminary evidence that additive counterfactuals may differentially serve a preparative function. Results of the life events study (Roese, 1994, Experiment 2) constituted more direct evidence that upward counterfactuals may serve a preparative function and that downward counterfactuals may serve an affective function. Findings from the anagram study (Roese, 1994, Experiment 3) provided direct evidence that both upward and additive counterfactuals may serve a preparative function, defined in terms of improvement in performance on an achievement task. Finally, findings from the Susan study (Roese & Olson, 1995) indicated one circumstance in which people may be more likely to strategically generate downward counterfactuals for their affective value, namely, outcomes perceived to be uncontrollable. We next turn to some concerns centering on the classification scheme, then conclude by considering the broader conceptual basis of this functional approach.

DIRECTION AND STRUCTURE: AN INTERACTIVE RELATION?

The relation between the two variables of counterfactual direction and structure was not explicitly examined in the present research. These two variables were conceptualized as orthogonal, permitting the specification of a 2 × 2 matrix of counterfactual subtypes. However, results of our previous research (Roese & Olson, 1993a, 1993b) suggests that the two variables may be weakly related (average $r = .24$). Thus, upward counterfactuals may co-occur with additive counterfactuals, although not strongly. This pattern would be consistent with the findings that both upward and additive counterfactuals tend to predominate after failure, though their respective patterns diverge after success. In one unpublished study by Roese and Olson (1992), which assessed the spontaneous generation of these four subtypes following success or failure, however, cell frequencies within the 2 × 2 matrix did not differ reliably.

Within the life events study (Roese, 1994, Experiment 2) and the anagram study (Roese, 1994, Experiment 3), the independence of the two variables was enforced by the nature of the manipulations (participants were instructed to record only the counterfactual subtype specified). However, it could be argued that some subtypes represent more natural, common associations between direction and structure (e.g., upward combined with additive). These subtypes should more easily come to mind, and participants might have recorded these with greater frequency when solicited relative to the solicitation of less easily conceived subtypes. However, the tests of the manipulation showed only the expected main effects and no interactions, and the correlations between direction and structure tended to be weak and nonsignificant. Although the conceptual independence of the dimensions of direction and structure is supported by such findings, the preparative impact of additive counterfactuals should, on purely logical grounds, be restricted to simulations of upward alternatives. That is, additive structures that are also downward (e.g., "If she had been really nervous, she would have failed") seem unlikely to have as strong preparative benefits, in that they specify damaging behaviors that should not be performed and, of course, that were not performed in reality. It is the additive–upward counterfactual that specifies one action that *should* have been performed; hence, it is this subtype that should be most useful. A corresponding interaction between direction and structure, such that additive counterfactuals enhance performance when they are also upward but not downward, did not emerge in any of the studies reviewed here, yet is clearly demanded if our interpretation is correct. More powerful experimental procedures may be required to detect this interaction.

OTHER FUNCTIONS?

The research reviewed here has focused on two important psychological functions that counterfactual thoughts may serve. But are there other, conceptually distinct functions also implicated in counterfactual thinking? One possibility is a *definitional* function. Counterfactual suppositions may serve to define and clarify a factual state of affairs by pointing to a contrasting yet plausible alternative state of affairs. By considering the points of divergence, one may obtain a clearer sense of the nature of actuality. Clearly, a contrast effect forms the heart of any definitional function. We have noted in this chapter that the affective function of counterfactuals may be based on a contrast effect mechanism; affective and definitional functions therefore represent two distinct consequences of making pairwise comparisons of two cognitive representations. Contrasting reality to a downward alternative may make one feel better but can also illuminate desirable features of reality that may otherwise go unappreciated. There are surely cases in which one generates a downward alternative to some plan of action without any specific intent to elicit emotional reactions; rather, the intent is to highlight the benefits of one's particular plan (e.g., "We should do it my way; otherwise we'll miss out on X, Y, and Z"). Although a definitional function of counterfactual thinking has not been subject to empirical assessment, it has formed the basis for a subgenre of literature that might appropriately be termed *counterfactual fiction*. By pinpointing some decisive event in the past and speculating on the unfolding of events had the event gone differently, writers are in a position not only to comment on but also to demonstrate vividly the merits and malignancies of the actual chain of events (e.g., Squire, 1931). To quote the back cover of a recent anthology of such stories, the authors' goal is to "alter the past in order to better see the present" (Benford & Greenberg, 1991). For example, the positive impact of 20th century American foreign intervention was cast in high relief in Moore's (1952) novel depicting a victory by the South at Gettysburg. The resultant divided and insular American states thenceforth exerted little influence on world affairs in an alternative 20th century.

An especially popular speculation focuses on the consequences of a Nazi victory in the Second World War. Such narratives typically underscore the benefits of living in a liberal-democratic rather than in an authoritarian state, thereby confirming the moral certitude of Western democratic nations (e.g., Dick, 1962; Harris, 1992). Such narratives testify to the enduring power of the Nazi experience, surely among the most grotesquely harrowing of recent history, to obsess and fascinate Western readers. The self-serving nature of such depictions is undeniable, however. By painting a compellingly *downward* counterfactual portrait of life in a contemporary Nazi state, a convenient cloak is placed over occasionally immoral consequences of American foreign intervention. Domestic debacles, such as the deficit and inner-city poverty, are also whitewashed by such downward comparisons. Unfortunately, historical alternatives predicated on an upward counterfactual comparison, which may suggest points of improvement to actuality, are rare in popular fiction (but see Winston Churchill's essay in Squire, 1931, for a curious exception).

On a more psychological level, Frank Capra's film, *It's a Wonderful Life*, is perhaps the best known counterfactual narrative. In it, hapless protagonist George Bailey envisions an alternative world in which he had never been born. As he confronts a variety of negative features of this counterfactual world, he comes to appreciate the positive features of his own reality. What was initially perceived by George to be a worthless life is, by the end of the film, regarded as a life of great value. Aside from such fictional accounts, do people strategically generate alternative versions of event sequences in order to better define and understand the events in their own lives? Although not a test of this idea, recent research suggests that people quite frequently evaluate hypotheses (and hence better define the problem at hand) by reasoning counterfactually (Farris & Revlin, 1989a, 1989b).

Another facet of this definitional function is its capacity to specify patterns by introducing counterfactual continuations or breaks to an observed sequence. Suppose a child recites a sequence of letters, "A . . . B. . . ." then abruptly stops. Another child might suggest that it is the alphabet that is being recited, defending her view with the counterfactual, "If he had continued, the next letter would have been C." Such a rhetorical counterfactual tool is extremely common in scholarly debate. In describing the American policy in the Second World War of contributing technology and raw material to the war effort while restraining troop commitment (in favor of "reliance on Soviet manpower to carry the main burden of the struggle in Europe," p. 8), historian John Gaddis (1982) deploys a counterfactual argument that continues this pattern into an alternative war outcome: "Had the atomic bomb not worked, the Russians might have been called upon to play a similar role in the Far East well after Germany's surrender" (p. 8). In this way, a pattern perhaps obscured by insufficient time or space in which to play itself out may be articulated more distinctly by its extension into a plausible counterfactual world. Similarly, an argument that an observed action *does not* represent a pattern may be supported by a counterfactual in which a progression is broken. Continuing with another World War II example: Defenders of the democratic ideals of the United States and Britain could point to the mere expediency of their alliance with Stalin's authoritarian regime. That is, staunch anticommunists of that era could argue that were it not for the far more insidious rise of Nazism, the Western democracies would never have allied themselves with the Soviet Union.[4]

It is important, though, to note the distinction between this use of counterfactuals to define reality and the common scholarly reliance on counterfactuals for causal historical analyses (e.g., Fearon, 1991; Tetlock & Belkin, 1994). For example, analyses of a counterfactual aftermath of the Cuban Missile Crisis following possible alternative decisions by Khrushchev or Kennedy (e.g., Thorson & Sylvan, 1982) are intended not to define more clearly subsequent Soviet–American relations but to defend arguments regarding the causal impact of the respective leaders' decisions. The role of counterfactuals in causal inference is perhaps not so much a function as a basic property of counterfactual propositions in general (see Mackie, 1974; Roese & Olson, chapter 1), one that may be recruited for service within other functions (e.g., the preparative function). Nevertheless, definitional effects and causal inferences may both contribute to the power of a narrative. As a result of his counterfactual revelation, George Bailey comes to appreciate both the defining features of his life (by a contrast effect) as well as the causal potency of his personal contributions.

The definitional function of counterfactual thoughts may serve as the starting point for a useful dialectic by which the individual comes to

---

[4]In furthering this stance, Churchill noted that "even if Hitler invaded Hell I would make at least a favorable reference to the Devil in the House of Commons" (Churchill, 1950, p. 370). The rhetorical impact of this counterfactual lies in its continuation (not break) of the pattern of expedient though Faustian arrangements dedicated to some nobler good.

grasp more completely his or her particular lifespace. This seems to be one of the more enduring (and endearing) lessons of George Bailey's experience. The term *dialectic* typically refers to the contrasting of incompatible arguments or ideas that may ultimately yield some higher order synthesis. The generation of alternatives to one's present life situation is the necessary first step toward this dialectical process, one which may be an important component of psychological adjustment (see Landman, 1993, for an extended discussion of this point). Theoretical speculation has only scratched the surface of this potentially significant aspect of counterfactual thinking. We look forward to further attempts to elucidate this definitional function and its many implications for psychological well-being.

CONCLUSION

The evidence accumulated under the rubric of a functional perspective paints a coherent picture of mental simulation processes, one that is grounded in the exigencies of both survival and social reality. There are perhaps three broadly conceived features of counterfactual thoughts that capture their preparative functionality, features that have emerged from a variety of empirical observations. First, counterfactuals are constrained by rules of reality and feasibility (cf. Kunda, 1990). Although with effort it is possible to construct bizarre and unlikely outcome alternatives, these tend not to be evoked spontaneously (Kahneman, chapter 14; Kahneman & Miller, 1986; Kahneman & Tversky, 1982). Rather, the inherent "reasonableness" of normatively evoked counterfactuals means that they are of greater utility in suggesting plans for the future (Folger, 1984; Taylor & Schneider, 1989). Second, counterfactual reconstructions tend to focus on mutations of personal actions. In undoing some unwanted outcome, people tend to make alterations to the decisions and actions of human beings (often themselves) rather than to the circumstances or to chance elements (Davis & Lehman, chapter 13; Davis, Lehman, Wortman, Silver, & Thompson, 1995). Third, counterfactuals also tend to focus on controllable rather than on uncontrollable actions (Girotto, Legrenzi, & Rizzo, 1991; Markman, Gavanski, Sherman, & McMullen, 1995; McMullen, Markman, & Gavanski, chapter 5). These latter two features present an obvious functional value. In everyday life, it is useful for individuals to focus on things that they can personally control and hence change. Were people to consistently mutate external or uncontrollable factors, they would be far less likely to infer avenues by which they could effect improvement. Thus, spontaneously evoked counterfactuals may be constrained by reality and center on personal, controllable actions, three features that form the basis of their preparative functional utility.

More generally, the studies described in this chapter are representative of a trend within social psychology toward more complete empirical documentation of the functional basis of various cognitive processes. Two distinct types of evidence are required to document compellingly such functionality. First, there should be strategic implementation of a given process in those situations in which it is most useful. Second, the implementation of the process should engender effects consistent with that function (i.e., it does what it is supposed to do). We have described research constituting both types of evidence for counterfactual thinking and, interestingly, these experiments were conducted in very rapid succession. Within social psychology, however, the first type of evidence has traditionally been relied on most heavily; only more recently has the second type of evidence become a common focus of research. For example, evidence for the object-appraisal function of attitudes long rested mainly on the first type of evidence, for example, that people are more likely to base a judgment on their attitudes when they are under time pressure (e.g., Kruglanski & Freund, 1983). Only very recently has evidence appeared demonstrating that holding an attitude facilitates judgments of novel stimuli (Fazio, Blascovich, & Driscoll, 1992). Similarly, a plethora of studies have shown that stereotypes are more likely to be used when processing demands become acute (e.g., Bodenhausen & Lichtenstein, 1987), but only recently has it been demonstrated that stereotypes preserve cognitive resources (Macrae, Milne, & Bodenhausen, 1994). We hope that the present research is part of a more general trend toward the equivalent reliance on both types of evidence for statements of cognitive functionality.

In closing, we emphasize that the research reviewed here does not offer an exhaustive description of the consequences of engaging in counterfactual thinking. Although we have demonstrated consequences that may be broadly construed as beneficial, there are certainly cases in which counterfactual thinking is afunctional or even dysfunctional (see Sherman & McConnell, chapter 7, for an extended discussion of this point). For example, one could muse on what life would be like if people were blimplike waterbreathers, or what would have happened had the Beatles snubbed Ringo and kept Pete Best as their drummer. Thoughts of such a fleeting, ephemeral nature likely carry little affective, cognitive, or behavioral significance: They are, in a word, afunctional. Or, one could endlessly replay past failures, reconstructing them ad infinitum with only minor alterations. This form of counterfactual rumination might promulgate depressive states. Previous examinations of ruminative coping styles have shown that individuals displaying such patterns are unlikely to take direct action to deal with their problems, are more vulnerable to chronic self-directed affect, and are at greater risk for depression (e.g., Wood, Saltzberg, Neale, Stone, & Rachmiel, 1990).

As another example of dysfunctionality, counterfactual thoughts might also be structured in such a way that precludes or retards performance enhancement. People who chronically generate counterfactuals that are self-protective (e.g., that focus on external causal antecedents of failure) or that mutate minor factors of only limited causal potency may be less likely to identify means of improving themselves in the future (cf. Roese & Olson, 1993a). Thus, in an important sense, we do not mean to assert that counterfactual effects are unceasingly beneficial for the individual. The findings described here should therefore be interpreted as one subset within a larger framework of cognitive processes ranging from the dysfunctional to the functional. Nevertheless, a functional approach has the advantage of offering a more basic foundation out of which many higher level conceptions may emerge.

ACKNOWLEDGMENTS

This chapter was written while the first author was supported by a postdoctoral fellowship, and while the second author was supported by a research grant, both from the Social Sciences and Humanities Research Council of Canada. We are grateful to Ron Deibert, Karen Grabowski, and Jim Sherman for their valuable comments on previous drafts of this chapter.

REFERENCES

Ajzen, I. (1988). *Attitudes, personality, and behavior*. Chicago: Dorsey.

Anderson, C. A., & Godfrey, S. S. (1987). Thoughts about actions: The effect of specificity and availability of imagined behavioral scripts on expectations about oneself and others. *Social Cognition, 5*, 238–258.

Benford, G., & Greenberg, M. H. (Eds.). (1991). *What might have been? Vol. 3. Alternate wars*. New York: Bantam.

Bodenhausen, G. V., & Lichtenstein, M. (1987). Social stereotypes and information processing strategies: The impact of task complexity. *Journal of Personality and Social Psychology, 52*, 871–880.

Boninger, D. S., Gleicher, F., & Strathman, A. (1994). Counterfactual thinking: From what might have been to what may be. *Journal of Personality and Social Psychology, 67*, 297–307.

Boring, E. G. (1957). *A history of experimental psychology* (2nd ed.). New York: Appleton–Century–Crofts.

Burgess, A. W., & Holmstrom, L. (1979). *Rape: Crisis and recovery*. Bowie, MD: Brady.

Buunk, B. P., Collins, R. L., Taylor, S. E., VanYperen, N. W., & Dakof, G. A. (1990). The affective consequences of social comparisons: Either direction has its ups and downs. *Journal of Personality and Social Psychology, 59*, 1238–1249.

Churchill, W. S. (1950). *The grand alliance*. Boston, MA: Houghton Mifflin.

Davis, C. G., Lehman, D. R., Wortman, C. B., Silver, R. C., & Thompson, S. C. (1995). The undoing of traumatic life events. *Personality and Social Psychology Bulletin, 21,* 109–124.

Dawes, R. M. (1993). Prediction of the future versus an understanding of the past: A basic asymmetry. *American Journal of Psychology, 106,* 1–24.

Dermer, M., Cohen, S. J., Jacobsen, E., & Anderson, E. A. (1979). Evaluative judgments of aspects of life as a function of vicarious exposure to hedonic extremes. *Journal of Personality and Social Psychology, 37,* 247–260.

Dick, P. K. (1962). *The man in the high castle.* New York: Vintage.

Farris, H., & Revlin, R. (1989a). The discovery process: A counterfactual strategy. *Social Studies of Science, 19,* 487–513.

Farris, H., & Revlin, R. (1989b). Sensible reasoning in two tasks: Rule discovery and hypothesis evaluation. *Memory and Cognition, 17,* 221–232.

Fazio, R. H., Blascovich, J., & Driscoll, D. M. (1992). On the functional value of attitudes: The influence of accessible attitudes on the ease and quality of decision making. *Personality and Social Psychology Bulletin, 18,* 388–401.

Fazio, R. H., Sherman, S. J., & Herr, P. M. (1982). The feature-positive effect in the self-perception process: Does not doing matter as much as doing? *Journal of Personality and Social Psychology, 42,* 404–411.

Fearon, J. D. (1991). Counterfactuals and hypothesis testing in political science. *World Politics, 43,* 169–195.

Festinger, L. (1954). A theory of social comparison processes. *Human Relations, 7,* 117–140.

Folger, R. (1984). Perceived injustice, referent cognitions, and the concept of comparison level. *Representative Research in Social Psychology, 14,* 88–108.

Gaddis, J. L. (1982). *Strategies of containment: A critical appraisal of postwar American national security policy.* New York: Oxford University Press.

Gavanski, I., & Wells, G. L. (1989). Counterfactual processing of normal and exceptional events. *Journal of Experimental Social Psychology, 25,* 314–325.

Girotto, V., Legrenzi, P., Rizzo, A. (1991). Event controllability in counterfactual thinking. *Acta Psychologica, 78,* 111–133.

Gleicher, F., Kost, K. A., Baker, S. M., Strathman, A. J., Richman, S. A., & Sherman, S. J. (1990). The role of counterfactual thinking in judgments of affect. *Personality and Social Psychology Bulletin, 16,* 284–295.

Harris, R. (1992). *Fatherland.* London: Arrow Books.

Johnson, M. K., & Sherman, S. J. (1990). Constructing and reconstructing the past and the future in the present. In E. T. Higgins & R. M. Sorrentino (Eds.), *Handbook of motivation and cognition: Foundations of social behavior* (Vol. 2, pp. 482–526). New York: Guilford.

Kahneman, D., & Miller, D. T. (1986). Norm theory: Comparing reality to its alternatives. *Psychological Review, 93,* 136–153.

Kahneman, D., & Tversky, A. (1979). Prospect theory: An analysis of decisions under risk. *Econometrica, 47,* 263–291.

Kahneman, D., & Tversky, A. (1982). The simulation heuristic. In D. Kahneman, P. Slovic, & A. Tversky (Eds.), *Judgment under uncertainty: Heuristics and biases* (pp. 201–208). New York: Cambridge University Press.

Katz, D. (1960). The functional approach to the study of attitudes. *Public Opinion Quarterly, 24,* 163–204.

Koehler, D. J. (1991). Explanation, imagination, and confidence in judgment. *Psychological Bulletin, 110,* 499–519.

Kruglanski, A. W., & Freund, T. (1983). The freezing and unfreezing of lay-inferences: Effects on impression primacy, ethnic stereotyping, and numerical anchoring. *Journal of Experimental Social Psychology, 19,* 448–468.

Kunda, Z. (1990). The case for motivated reasoning. *Psychological Bulletin, 108,* 480–498.

Landman, J. (1993). *Regret: The persistence of the possible.* New York: Oxford University Press.

Mackie, J. L. (1974). *Cement of the universe: A study of causation.* London: Oxford University Press.

Macrae, C. N., Milne, A. B., & Bodenhausen, G. V. (1994). Stereotypes as energy-saving devices: A peek inside the cognitive toolbox. *Journal of Personality and Social Psychology, 66,* 37–47.

Markman, K. D., Gavanski, I., Sherman, S. J., & McMullen, M. N. (1993). The mental simulation of better and worse possible worlds. *Journal of Experimental Social Psychology, 29,* 87–109.

Markman, K. D., Gavanski, I., Sherman, S. J., & McMullen, M. N. (1995). The impact of perceived control on the imagination of better and worse possible worlds. *Personality and Social Psychology Bulletin, 21,* 588–595.

Moore, W. (1952). *Bring the jubilee.* New York: Farrar, Straus, & Young.

Nisbett, R. E., & Ross, L. (1980). *Human inference: Strategies and shortcomings of social judgment.* Englewood Cliffs, NJ: Prentice–Hall.

Olson, J. M., Roese, N. J., & Zanna, M. P. (in press). Expectancies. In E. T. Higgins & A. W. Kruglanski (Eds.), *Social psychology: Handbook of basic principles.* New York: Guilford.

Reis, T. J., Gerrard, M., & Gibbons, F. X. (1993). Social comparison and the pill: Reactions to upward and downward comparison of contraceptive behavior. *Personality and Social Psychology Bulletin, 19,* 13–20.

Roese, N. J. (1994). The functional basis of counterfactual thinking. *Journal of Personality and Social Psychology, 66,* 805–818.

Roese N. J. & Olson J. M. (1992). Unpublished raw data, University of Western Ontario.

Roese, N. J., & Olson, J. M. (1993a). Self-esteem and counterfactual thinking. *Journal of Personality and Social Psychology, 65,* 199–206.

Roese, N. J., & Olson, J. M. (1993b). The structure of counterfactual thought. *Personality and Social Psychology Bulletin, 19,* 312–319.

Roese, N. J., & Olson, J. M. (1995). Outcome controllability and counterfactual thinking. *Personality and Social Psychology Bulletin, 21,* 620–628.

Ruvolo, A. P., & Markus, H. R. (1992). Possible selves and performance: The power of self-relevant imagery. *Social Cognition, 10,* 95–124.

Schwarz, N., & Bless, H. (1992). Constructing reality and its alternatives: An inclusion/exclusion model of assimilation and contrast effects in social judgment. In L. L. Martin & A. Tesser (Eds.), *The construction of social judgment* (pp. 217–245). Hillsdale, NJ: Lawrence Erlbaum Associates.

Sherman, S. J., Skov, R. B., Hervitz, E. F., & Stock, C. B. (1981). The effects of explaining hypothetical future events: From possibility to probability to actuality and beyond. *Journal of Experimental Social Psychology, 17,* 142–158.

Squire, J. C. (Ed.). (1931). *If it had happened otherwise: Lapses into imaginary history.* London: Longmans, Green, & Co.

Taylor, S. E., Buunk, B. P., & Aspinwall, L. G. (1990). Social comparison, stress, and coping. *Personality and Social Psychology Bulletin, 16,* 74–89.

Taylor, S. E., & Lobel, M. (1989). Social comparison activity under threat: Downward evaluation and upward contacts. *Psychological Review, 96,* 569–575.

Taylor, S. E., & Schneider, S. K. (1989). Coping and the simulation of events. *Social Cognition, 7,* 174–194.

Taylor, S. E., Wood, J. V., & Lichtman, R. R. (1983). It could be worse: Selective evaluation as a response to victimization. *Journal of Social Issues, 39*(2), 19–40.

Tetlock, P. E., & Belkin, A. (1994). *Counterfactual thought experiments in world politics: Logical, methodological, and psychological perspectives.* Unpublished manuscript.

Thorson, S. T., & Sylvan, D. A. (1982). Counterfactuals and the Cuban Missile Crisis. *International Studies Quarterly, 26,* 539–571.

Wells, G. L., & Gavanski, I. (1989). Mental simulation of causality. *Journal of Personality and Social Psychology, 56,* 161–169.

Wills, T. A. (1981). Downward comparison principles in social psychology. *Psychological Bulletin, 90,* 245–271.

Wood, J. V., Saltzberg, J. A., Neale, J. M., Stone, A. A., & Rachmiel, T. B. (1990). Self-focused attention, coping responses, and distressed mood in everyday life. *Journal of Personality and Social Psychology, 58,* 1027–1036.

7

Dysfunctional Implications of Counterfactual Thinking: When Alternatives to Reality Fail Us

Steven J. Sherman
Allen R. McConnell
Indiana University

Living in the here and now and focusing only on the tasks and events of the present are things that people do not do easily. Our minds wander to the past with floodings of nostalgia as we recall events, experiences, and relationships that used to be. And especially for people in the Western world, thoughts and images race to future times with feelings of hope, anticipation, or dread. This inability to stay grounded in the present or to "stop and smell the roses" was, in fact, a major theme of the counterculture of the late 1960s and early 1970s.

Related to this inability of people to keep their thoughts and feelings tied to current experiences, tasks, and issues is their inability to accept their present reality and to be satisfied with it. Instead, they have a compelling propensity to alter reality and to reflect on "what could have been," "what might have been," and "what should have been." People undo reality and find ways in which it might have been different by mutating or slipping conditions that were antecedents to the current situation. This tendency is probably no better captured than it is by Marlon Brando's lines "I could have been a contender; I could have been somebody" from *On the Waterfront*. In short, people evaluate many life events not simply by the reality of what comes to pass but also by thoughts of what might have been. This obsession with alternatives to reality, this ubiquitous imagination of other possible worlds, has been called *counterfactual thinking*, and it has become a growing area of speculation and research in psychology since the publication of a seminal paper by Kahneman and Miller in 1986.

In this research and theorizing about counterfactuals investigators have focused on several interesting and important issues. For example, in one major line of research, investigators focused on discovering which aspects of reality are most changeable or mutable (e.g., Gleicher et al., 1990; Miller & Gunasegaram, 1990). A second area of interest has involved the important affective implications of counterfactual generation (e.g., Miller, Turnbull, & McFarland, 1990; Niedenthal, Tangney, & Gavanski, 1994). Finally, there has been a good deal of work relating counterfactual thought to perceptions of causality both through specific causal constructions (Wells & Gavanski, 1989) and in more general formulations of attribution theory (Lipe, 1991).

Most recently, researchers in counterfactual thought have started to focus on the psychological functions served by a person's generating alternatives to reality. The previous chapter in this volume is, in fact, devoted to a detailed discussion of the functions of counterfactual thinking (Roese & Olson, chapter 6). The assumption is that counterfactuals must serve some very important psychological functions if they are so prevalent. The identification and understanding of these functions can help psychologists to explain why people are so compelled to imagine alternative realities.

Most theorists agree that there are three major functions served by counterfactual generation. The first of these is affect regulation. The imagination of other possible worlds can help people feel better about current reality and life's circumstances. This function is generally served by the generation of *downward counterfactuals*, that is, alternatives that are worse than what exists. Thus, after a car accident, the consequences of which were a broken leg and $5,000 damage, one might think, "If my car had swerved one more foot to the left, I would have been killed by the oncoming truck." Generating worse-world scenarios such as this makes current reality seem not so bad. That negative-affect regulation is an important function of counterfactual thought is indicated by the results of work by several researchers, who have reported a tendency for study participants to feel better following the generation of downward counterfactuals to negative experiences (Markman, Gavanski, Sherman, & McMullen, 1993; Roese, 1994).

The second important function served by counterfactual thought is preparation for the future. When life is not as good as people like or when they have not met their goals, they may focus on how to avoid these same negative outcomes or failures in the future. By generating counterfactual alternatives to reality, people can think about how outcomes could have been different, and by extension, how they might be different in the future. This preparation function is best served by generating *upward counterfactuals*, alternatives that would have led to better outcomes. Although upward counterfactuals might leave one feeling dissatisfied and blameworthy (because the negative outcome could have been avoided), they allow one to think of different courses of action, courses that should lead to happier outcomes in the future. Such counterfactual generations may be especially worthwhile when similar decisions and circumstances are likely to present themselves in the future (Markman et al., 1993) or when the outcome was perceived as controllable and, thus, changeable (Roese & Olson, 1995). Indeed, Roese (1994) found that a person's generating upward counterfactuals following failure in an anagram task led to intentions to perform success-facilitating behaviors and to actual behavioral improvement in a subsequent task.

Related to preparation for the future, a third function of counterfactual generation has recently been considered, the induction of feelings of controllability (Markman, Gavanski, Sherman, & McMullen, 1995; McMullen, Markman, & Gavanski, chapter 5). Counterfactual generation is intimately tied to perceptions of causality (Wells & Gavanski, 1989). And once a causal representation of an event is developed, the event sequence seems more sensible, predictable, and controllable. Perceiving the world as controllable and predictable is perhaps *the* major motivation in human judgment and behavior (Langer, 1975). This need can be so strong that illusions of control develop for situations in which there is clearly no objective control. In fact, the need to feel in control of one's circumstances and outcomes may lead to such illusions of control even when these perceptions carry with them terrible affective consequences.

The following is an anecdotal case. A father in Detroit had planned for his young daughter to fly to Phoenix to visit her grandparents. At the airport, the girl cried and said she didn't want to go; she was afraid to fly and to be alone on the plane. The father explained that she would be well taken care of and that the grandparents would meet her on the other end. She would have a wonderful time. The plane crashed, and the girl was killed. It was difficult for the father to believe that a random, uncontrollable event could cause his daughter's death. He blamed himself and believed that he had control over what had happened: "If only I had realized how dangerous this really was. . . ." At last report, the father was still severely depressed and unable to function normally. Similarly and more generally, rape victims and victims of serious diseases often blame themselves for what happened to them (Bulman & Wortman, 1977; Janoff–Bulman, 1979; S. Taylor, Lichtman, & Wood, 1984; Wood, Saltzberg, Neale, Stone, & Rachmiel, 1990). Despite the terrible guilt and self-directed anger that arises from such attributions, the belief that events are not arbitrary and that the actors could have done things that would have changed the outcomes ("if only . . .") is apparently worth all the grief.

This need for control implies that the events within a scenario that one had control over will be more mutable than events that were not under one's control. Markman et al. (1995) found exactly this pattern—counterfactuals to outcomes in a gambling situation were most often generated for those aspects of the setting that involved one's own decisions. Also consistent with the idea that counterfactual generation serves the function of imparting feelings of control are results reported by Roese and Olson (1993b). They found that participants used *subtractive* counterfactual changes (mutations that remove a factual feature in reconstructing reality) when they undid successful outcomes but used *additive* mutations (mutations that add new antecedents) to undo failures. These kinds of mutations are consistent with the person's need to perceive control. Such mutations imply that doing things is what leads to success and that the only reason for failure is that one did not exert control and act in a necessary way.

It is clear, then, that counterfactual thinking can and does serve positive psychological functions. Counterfactuals can repair bad feelings or prevent the onset of such feelings, they can give one hope and confidence in preparing for the future and even play a role in improving that future, and counterfactuals can allow one to feel a sense of control over life events and give one a sense that the world and its outcomes are knowable and predictable.

Interestingly, a focus on the functions of counterfactual thinking seems to have left psychologists with the feeling that counterfactuals may be the greatest thing since ESPN. They are the panacea to brighten a person's day, to give people hope, to empower them, and to improve their circumstances. Even when the downside of counterfactual generation is recognized, recent evidence seems to indicate that this downside is minimally disturbing and disruptive. For example, upward counterfactuals can lead to negative affect as one realizes that a current negative reality need not have occurred and could have been averted. Yet, findings indicate that these negative feelings may not necessarily accompany upward counterfactuals (Roese, 1994) and that such negative feelings are especially unlikely for individuals with high self-esteem (Roese & Olson, 1993a) or for people who are chronically focused on the future or who are induced to think about the future (Boninger, Gleicher, & Strathman, 1994). Thus, counterfactuals can allow people to have their cake and eat it, too—to be better prepared for the future, to feel more empowered and in control, and to feel better about their current circumstances (or at least not to feel worse).

In the remainder of this chapter, we consider the possibility that there may be a darker side to counterfactual generation, a dysfunctional side that has potentially serious negative effects on emotional states, behavior, and judgments. In general, counterfactual thinking represents a way of problem solving and a way of organizing and understanding experiences. Thus, counterfactual generation falls in the same broad category as the use of heuristic principles, the development of schemas or scripts, and the adoption of categorization techniques. The benefits of using heuristics, developing schemas, and forming categories or stereotypes are well known. They help people to simplify a complex world and to improve the efficiency and effectiveness of thought and action. But the costs of these processes and principles are also well known. They leave people subject to biases and to errors of judgment that can manifest themselves in unfortunate and self-defeating behaviors and perceptions. In the same way, psychologists should recognize that counterfactual thinking can serve some very positive functions but that it also leaves people open to thoughts and judgments that can be costly emotionally and practically. We attempt to outline and analyze some of these dysfunctions, without losing sight of the positive functions that counterfactual generation can serve.

ENDING UP WITH THE WRONG CAUSAL INFERENCE

Discussions of the functionality of counterfactuals have made clear that an important component of this functionality is the generation of a counterfactual that helps one understand the causal structure of a chain of events in an action sequence so that a changed outcome in the future is a possibility (e.g., Markman et al., 1993, 1995; Roese, 1994). Unless the causal inference based on the counterfactual generation is correct, however, this functional value of counterfactuals is questionable. And, unfortunately, the ability of people to arrive at an accurate causal analysis of an event sequence is far from perfect. The research literature is replete with examples of people displaying systematic biases in their interpretations of events and explanations of causal relations. Further, the growing evidence of mutation rules (i.e., factors that influence the mutability of events in a causal sequence) has indicated that these biases in causal analysis may inhere in the counterfactuals that such rules produce. People may mutate event features that played no role in the actual outcome and may fail to mutate features that were critical for the outcome to occur. Because of the role of counterfactual generation in causal analysis (Wells & Gavanski, 1989), the mutation of events that are not actually causal can be dysfunctional. Such counterfactuals will lead to an incorrect causal analysis and an improper understanding of the situation and may thus instigate continued poor performance in the future as well as negative affect inappropriately directed at others or even at oneself.

The results of research over the past few years have revealed a number of mutation rules that suggest when counterfactual generation is most likely to occur and which counterfactuals are the most likely to be generated. Most of these findings have been derivations and extensions of Kahneman and Miller's (1986) norm theory. In general, these rules suggest that individuals will mutate the most accessible features of a situation and not mutate features that are less accessible. More important, these mutation rules do not ensure that the features that are mutated are the actual causes of the outcome. Just as the accessibility of a feature is not an accurate indicator of that feature's frequency or probability (Tversky & Kahneman, 1973), neither is it a good indicator of causality. Yet, the counterfactual mutation of a feature implicates that feature as a primary cause of the outcome and indicates that any change in outcome in the future will best be achieved by a change in that feature.

One such bias in mutation involves the temporal sequence of events. Miller and Gunasegaram (1990) found that events that occur later in a temporal chain are more mutable than earlier events in the same sequence (but this is not true for events in a causal chain, in which the earliest items are the most mutable; Wells, B. Taylor, & Turtle, 1987). Thus, these later events are seen as more causal, and any hope of changing outcomes in the future will require that these later events be changed.

In Miller and Gunasegaram's (1990) first experiment, participants imagined themselves in the role of students in a class performing poorly on a test. They evaluated a teacher's questions critically (i.e., as being unfair) if they imagined having studied *before* the teacher wrote the questions rather than *after* the teacher wrote the questions. In other words, the teacher's poor exam (and not their own study habits) was the perceived cause of failure, due to the mutability of the late-occurring events. On the other hand, when the test was constructed prior to their studying, participants mutated their study habits and saw those as the cause of poor performance. Of course, neither analysis is rational because temporal sequence here is unrelated to cause. Yet, the counterfactual generation would have implications for future test preparation.

The temporal-sequence mutation rule can lead to unwarranted blame on the person who engages in the last action in a temporal chain. A classic example of this phenomenon is the basketball player who, with one second left on the clock, misses the winning basket. This player will be seen as the person who lost the game even if other players on the same team missed more shots and easier shots earlier in the game. Again, the ease of mutating the last event in the temporal chain in some situations leads to placing the blame on someone when others might be responsible for the ultimate outcome as much, or even more. The generation of counterfactuals also carries with it behavioral implications, such as influencing who will start in the next game.

Demonstrating another factor that affects mutation in a way that leads to an incorrect or biased causal analysis, Miller, Turnbull, and McFarland (1989) found that outcomes with an equal a priori probability of occurrence are judged to be more suspicious if there are fewer ways for the same outcome to occur. In one experiment, Miller et al. (1989) found that participants were more suspicious of the child who selected the 1 coveted chocolate-chip cookie in a jar with 19 less-desired oatmeal cookies than of the child who selected 1 chocolate-chip cookie from a jar containing 10 chocolate-chip cookies and 190 oatmeal cookies. In terms of statistical probability, selecting a chocolate-chip cookie from either jar is equally likely (5%). However, in the case of only one chocolate-chip cookie contained in the whole jar, all other alternatives result in selecting an oatmeal cookie; thus, selecting the one chocolate-chip cookie seems less likely to have occurred by chance. Consequently, the degree of suspicion (and subsequent mistrust of the child) is affected in an unwarranted way by the ease of counterfactual generation.

In addition to groundless scolding of children, Miller et al. (1990) suggest that this bias can help build and maintain stereotypes. For instance, consider two groups (a majority group of 500 members and a minority group of 50 members) that each claim to have the same small proportion of hostile members (e.g., they claim that only 2% of the members of the group are hostile). On encountering the first member of each group, you find both of them to be hostile. It is easy to imagine running into 1 of the 10 presumed hostile members of the majority group, and there is no reason to question the claim that the vast majority of this group are friendly. It is not easy to imagine running into the one and only presumed hostile member of the minority group by chance. Just as with the cookie jar scenario, fewer alternatives to the outcome make an event with fewer ways to occur (though probabilistically equivalent) seem more suspicious. Thus, a person might question the claim that only one member of the minority group is hostile and conclude that minority-group members must be more generally hostile. In this way, negative stereotypes of minority groups are more likely to be developed and maintained.

A third mutation principle involves the controllability of events. Those events over which one had control are most easily mutated and are thus most likely to be seen as causal. Of course, controllability and causality are not the same thing. Thus, people may blame themselves excessively for negative outcomes if they had control over some of the event antecedents—even if those events were in no way causal of the outcome. In a recent study involving a computer-simulated wheel-of-fortune game, Markman et al. (1995) found that participants generated more counterfactuals about the elements of the game over which they had control than about factors over which they had no control. More important, the type of counterfactual generated involved thoughts of how a change in an aspect of the game that they had controlled could have changed the outcome of the game. These counterfactuals, in turn, would have implications for decisions that participants would make in subsequent games. The irony in this study is that participants actually had no control over the situation (i.e., the outcome was rigged). In the same way, a rape victim may mutate what she wore or where she went for a walk as ways of undoing the rape, perceiving her own controllable actions as the cause.

A fourth mutation rule is that actions, relative to nonactions, produce more counterfactuals. Again, mutations lead to inferences about causal structure (actions perceived as more causal than inactions) and thus have implications for affective consequences and subsequent behavior. Although actions are more mutable than inactions, they are in no way necessarily more causal or more important to an outcome. Thus, once again, counterfactual generations and biases in mutability can lead to an inaccurate causal understanding of a situation.

Kahneman and Tversky (1982) offered the first, now classic demonstration of the greater mutability of actions as opposed to inactions. In their scenario, two people lose the same amount of money on stock investments in Company Z. Person A considered switching to another stock but decided to keep stock in Company Z, whereas Person B had stock in another company but a year before had switched to Company Z. Kahneman and Tversky found that participants expected Person B (the individual who acted) to feel worse than Person A (the person who failed to act) about losing the money. This effect was also observed by Gleicher et al. (1990). The dysfunctional implication of this phenomenon is that one who fails to act may not seek out alternatives that could have improved a negative outcome. Failing to act can be as consequential as acting in a less-than-optimal fashion, although apparently acting will evoke more useful responses (i.e., searching for alternatives to an undesired outcome) than not acting. On the other hand, psychologists should also bear in mind the implications for positive outcomes as well. An individual may see an action that occurs before a positive outcome as causal, even if the action was unrelated to the outcome. Thus, one might develop superstitious or ritualistic behaviors in order to ensure (erroneously) future successes.

A fifth mutation rule is that people tend to mutate nonnormal situations in the direction of normal occurrences. Kahneman and Miller (1986) suggested that exceptional events are more mutable than common events. In a test of this notion, Miller, B. Taylor, and Buck (1991) found that study participants typically explained deviations in gender roles by mutating the nonnormative gender's behavior to make them seem more similar to the normative gender's behavior. In a series of experiments, Miller et al.

(1991) asked participants to explain "gender gaps" for various roles (e.g., how men and women differed with respect to voting patterns). In order to establish different default gender assumptions, they conducted pretesting, providing situations in which the normative gender was male or female, respectively. Pretest results showed that participants described the typical voter as male but the typical elementary school teacher as female. In one experiment, participants were asked to explain differences in female and male voting patterns. These participants tended to explain the differences in terms of how female voters' preferences deviated from male voters' preferences. Participants also predicted that if this gender gap in voting-pattern differences were to disappear in the future, such a change would be because female voters would act more like male voters rather than vice versa.

In another experiment involving attitudes toward elementary school teachers, participants showed the same bias for the opposite gender. They explained gender differences in terms of how men acted differently from women and suggested that an elimination of the gender gap would occur if male elementary teachers acted more like female elementary teachers rather than vice versa. According to Miller et al. (1991), perception and judgment of change are based on the differential ease of generating counterfactuals (see also Hilton & Slugoski, 1986, for similar reasoning). It is easier for one to think of nonprototypic members changing their behaviors. The actions of the prototypic group are taken as givens. The implications for subsequent decisions are striking, if not alarming. For example, the nonnormative gender would be more likely than the normative gender to be blamed for any negative occurrence related to a gender gap. Of course, any attempt to "fix" the situation would be aimed at the nonnormative gender—hardly a functional outcome of counterfactual generation (see also McGill & Klein, chapter 12).

It is important to note that people sometimes do mutate mundane, normative events into exceptional ones as well. Once again, however, this differential mutability is not based on a realistic assessment of the role of an event in causing an outcome. Gavanski and Wells (1989) asked participants to consider a woman who was described either as an excellent student or as a poor student. On a particular exam, she performed either well or poorly. Thus, a good student's performing well or a poor student's performing poorly is normative, whereas a poor student's performing well or a good student's performing poorly is nonnormative. Participants were provided with both normative and nonnormative events that could be mutated to alter the outcomes. With results in contrast to the original tenets of norm theory and the findings of Miller et al. (1991), Gavanski and Wells found that participants who were provided with the normative scenarios (e.g., good student who passed the exam) mutated their alternatives *away* from normality. Only when the outcome of the scenario was nonnormative did participants mutate the exceptional events into normal events.

Whether counterfactual mutations are toward or away from normality, in their counterfactual generations and thus in their assessments of causality, people apparently tend to use a simple heuristic principle, representativeness. People believe that there must be a similarity between any effect and its underlying cause. Thus, unusual events have exceptional causes; normal outcomes have run-of-the-mill causes. Only big causes can have big outcomes. Nisbett and Ross (1980) discussed people's tendency to assume similarity between events and their causes. The important point is that this simplifying principle, which determines the ease of counterfactual mutations, can lead to a misunderstanding of the causal structure of a situation and to incorrect implications for changing an outcome.

In some respects, many of the shortcomings of these mutation rules are reminiscent of the problems associated with biased hypothesis testing. When testing a hypothesis, people often rely on a biased subset of information in that they consider only the focal hypothesis and not alternative possibilities (Klayman & Ha, 1987; Skov & Sherman, 1986; Wason, 1968). Likewise, participants in the Miller et al. (1991) gender-gaps study might not have considered an alternative possibility—perhaps something about the normative group made them different from the nonnormative group.

In addition to qualities inherent in events themselves that render them differentially salient (e.g., temporal placement), certain characteristics of the perceiver can lead to individual differences in feature accessibility and, thus, to differences in event mutability. For example, individuals with chronically accessible constructs (Higgins, King, & Mavin, 1982) should be systematically attentive to particular stimulus features and will therefore devote greater attentional resources to these dimensions, a tendency increasing the likelihood that these features will be encoded and will guide subsequent retrieval (Kahneman & Miller, 1986; Medin & Schaffer, 1978; Nosofsky, 1987; Smith & Zarate, 1992). With such effect, chronically accessible constructs should lead to mutations along these focal stimulus dimensions because they will be especially accessible to the perceiver when generating counterfactuals.

Consider a person who demonstrates chronic accessibility for the construct gender. That person will devote great attention toward encoding events and outcomes in terms of gender. That person will therefore have a predisposition to evoke gender-related counterfactuals in order to change existing situations. For instance, such a person, considering the consequences to United States Attorney General Janet Reno after the 1993 siege of the Branch Davidian compound in Waco, Texas, may form the counterfactual, "Would Janet Reno have received such sharp criticism *if* she were a man?" Consequently, counterfactuals can serve as a mechanism for the maintenance and reinforcement of chronic constructs because it should be easy for a person with a chronic expectancy to form *chronic mutations* about these well-encoded features of situations. There is one potential drawback of such a mechanism: Chronic mutations may lead a person down a biased counterfactual path, evoking many "what ifs" for features that would not have actually changed the outcome of the situation. Further, the attention devoted to a narrow range of situation features means that other dimensions that contributed more to the causal chain of events may go unnoticed, especially in situations in which one's cognitive resources are especially scant (Bargh & Thein, 1985; Bargh & Tota, 1988). Thus, perceivers may miss important causal factors in the chain of events. In the Reno case, the perceiver may focus so myopically on Reno's gender that he or she does not consider alternatives that might have led to the public criticism, for example, "Would Janet Reno have received such sharp criticism *if* the Davidians had not had innocent children inside the compound at the time the federal officials ended the standoff?"

In sum, it is clear that people will mutate event features of outcomes according to simple heuristic principles. When relying on these heuristics, they may often mutate events that played no causal role in the outcome or may fail to mutate events that were essential for the outcome to occur. Features of the events and even individual differences can contribute to this bias in generating counterfactuals. When perceivers thus arrive at faulty causal understandings based on their mutations, the counterfactuals they generate will have been dysfunctional.

Given that perceivers will frequently mutate noncausal events based on these systematic biases and will thus arrive at a misperception of the causal structure of a situation, an important question arises: How can perceivers avoid these pitfalls? A variety of strategies for eliminating biases in faulty judgments have been offered, and these strategies can be applied to counterfactual thinking as well. Lord, Lepper, and Preston (1984), for instance, found that asking participants to consider the opposite possibility was an effective strategy in the participants' avoiding biased processing of the value of a scientific study. In a similar vein, Kruglanski and Freund's (1983) theory of lay epistemology suggests that a person's entertaining a variety of alternatives helps him or her avoid the limiting aspects of cognitive processing. In many ways, lay epistemology and counterfactual generation share much in common in that *freezing* (the cessation of generating additional alternatives) leads to a person's accepting a state of affairs as irrevocable. Generating a counterfactual is dysfunctional when only highly accessible event features are mutated and a search for alternatives is thus prematurely terminated. For instance, when fans decide that the basketball player who missed the final-second shot lost the game, they fail to search for additional alternatives to this highly accessible event.

Thus, it is important for individuals to generate multiple counterfactuals, rather than being blinded by the first counterfactual that comes to mind. When people mutate the most accessible antecedent event, they may be driven more by biased processing than by sound causal inference. Also, it is important for perceivers to consider not only how mutations could have changed the outcome but also how alternative antecedent events might have led to the *same* outcome. Only then will perceivers be able to judge correctly the inevitability or the avoidability of an event and to grasp the true causal structure of the situation.

UNNECESSARY NEGATIVE AFFECT

Despite the fact that some recent findings indicate that counterfactual thinking (upward counterfactuals in particular) may not always leave people feeling bad (Boninger et al., 1994; Roese, 1994), a rather substantial amount of literature documents certain negative affective consequences of counterfactual thought. Regret is a common outcome of counterfactual generation (Landman, 1993), and it is the mutations of negative outcomes in an upward direction that generally lead to feelings of regret (Landman, 1987). Similarly, dissatisfaction with one's current situation is an often-reported consequence of upward-counterfactual generation (Markman et al., 1993). Even outcomes that are positive by any absolute standard can lead to dissatisfaction if a counterfactual world in which things are even better is entertained. For example, Medvec, Madey, and Gilovich (in press) reported that silver medal winners in Olympic competition often feel dissatisfied, presumably because of the highly accessible alternative world of winning the gold medal. Interestingly, silver medal winners are often less satisfied than bronze medal winners, whose likely counterfactual world is one with no medal at all. Thus, those who objectively achieve more end up more dissatisfied, hardly a functional outcome of counterfactual thought.

In addition to inducing feelings of regret and dissatisfaction, counterfactual generation has been implicated in the arousal of shame and guilt (Niedenthal et al., 1994). When people undo a distressing outcome by changing their personal qualities (e.g., "If only I weren't so irresponsible, I wouldn't have lost my job"), they experience shame. When they undo outcomes by mutating their own specific actions (e.g., "If only I hadn't gotten drunk that night, I wouldn't have said those nasty things"), they feel guilt. Although shame and guilt may be functional emotions in motivating beneficial changes in behavior, counterfactual generations such as those described for the father in Detroit can lead to unwarranted and debilitating feelings of guilt and shame.

Related to feelings of shame and guilt is self-blame, of which counterfactual generation is often a critical aspect. As we discussed previously, people have a strong tendency to mutate those aspects of an event sequence over which they had control. Thus, they are likely to view their own behaviors as causal of a negative outcome and to experience unwarranted blame. When one's own choices and behaviors that preceded an undesirable outcome are especially mutable, self-blame will be strong. For example, Turnbull and Mawhinney (1986, cited in Miller et al., 1990) asked participants to imagine a parking lot where they had a choice of either several parking spaces or one particular space because the rest of the lot was full. Later during the scenario, the participant's car and another car are involved in an accident when both cars pull out simultaneously and run into each other. Participants reported feeling more self-blame and said they would pay more of the other person's deductible when they had alternative parking spaces available to them than when they were forced to take the last available space in the lot. It was the ease of mutating one's own parking-space choice in the lot-not-full scenario that led these participants to view their own behavior as causal, to feel a great amount of self-blame, and to incur greater costs voluntarily.

This tendency to counterfactualize one's own behaviors that preceded negative outcomes may be especially strong for individuals with low self-esteem. Roese and Olson (1993a) asked participants to imagine that they were working with another person in various achievement domains (e.g., working with a fellow student on a joint class project, tutoring a boy in math). The outcome of the joint interaction was described as either successful or unsuccessful. After reading the scenario, participants were asked to generate counterfactuals that would change the outcome. Roese and Olson found that, following a success, participants with high self-esteem were more likely than those with low self-esteem to mutate their own actions. But following a failure, participants with low self-esteem were more likely than those with high self-esteem to mutate their own actions. These counterfactuals would of course be related to the participants' perceived locus of cause for the outcomes. Those with high self-esteem would see themselves as responsible for their successes. Those with low self-esteem would take responsibility for their failures. The nonfunctional implications of these findings are apparent. Individuals with low self-esteem may blame themselves unduly for failures, and people with high self-esteem may ignore their causal role in undesirable outcomes and not incorporate needed changes in their future behaviors. Thus, people with high self-esteem will continue to make the same mistakes, and those with low self-esteem will continually blame themselves for failures.

When the outcome with which one is trying to cope is traumatic enough or when the obsession with generating counterfactual alternatives that would have averted the event is strong enough, the self-blame that follows from these counterfactual mutations may be especially devastating. Consider again the poor father in Detroit, whose life has been destroyed not so much by the terrible tragedy involving the death of his daughter but by his inability to escape the counterfactual world in which she is still alive. Thus, counterfactuals can leave people with a double dose of bad feelings—negative affect due to the objective loss itself and further feelings of blame and regret because these losses are perceived as not having had to occur.

As we mentioned earlier, research results have shown that other kinds of traumatic events (e.g., rape, diagnosis of cancer) can lead one to ruminate and to attempt to undo outcomes that are beyond one's control (Janoff–Bulman, 1979; S. Taylor et al., 1984), with the attendant feelings of guilt and self-blame. In two field studies, Davis, Lehman, Wortman, Silver, and Thompson (1995) examined the psychological distress, ruminations, counterfactuals, and attributions of self-blame associated with adults who had lost loved ones in a variety of tragic occurrences (e.g., losing a child or spouse in a motor vehicle accident). Despite the fact that these adults played no causal role in any of the deaths, Davis et al. found that victims attempted to mutate aspects of the situation that involved their own behaviors, including trivial aspects of these behaviors that clearly had no implications for the deaths. Even when statistically controlling the analyses for general thinking about the tragedies (e.g., thinking about the accident scene), Davis et al. found a correlation between the amount counterfactual thinking and victim distress, as measured on a series of scales designed for the assessment of affect and depression.

Davis, Lehman, Silver, Wortman, and Ellard (1994) recently examined the self-directed attributions made by spinal cord injury patients. In their study, Davis et al. asked patients who had experienced spinal cord injuries in a variety of situations (e.g., motor vehicle accidents, sporting accidents) to respond to several questions: How foreseeable was the risk of injury? Do you think about ways the accident could have been avoided (general counterfactual thinking)? Do you think about how *you* could have avoided the accident (self-implicating counterfactual thinking)? How much are you to blame for the accident (personal blame)? Davis et al. found that patients' self-implicating counterfactual thoughts were directly related to their judgments of personal blame for their injuries, independently of their global causal attributions (i.e., general counterfactual thinking) and their estimates of accident foreseeability. Thus, self-blame seems to be triggered by the production of self-implicating counterfactuals even when other factors, such as foreseeability and general causal attributions, are controlled for.

The dysfunctional implications for the self of these kinds of counter-factual generations are sobering. Searching for alternative worlds following traumatic events often results in people's mutating aspects of their own behavior that would never have changed the tragic outcomes; this tendency results in heavy self-blame. Even if changing their behavior would have changed the event outcome (e.g., a rape victim's taking a *different* street home), it is clearly irrational for one to take blame for behaviors that in foresight would not have reduced the probability of the event's occurrence. It is likely that these kinds of counterfactuals do help victims in the process of coping with tragedy and in giving them a feeling of control over their lives (Janoff–Bulman, 1979; S. Taylor et al., 1984), but the despair and depression that can result from this kind of counter-factual thinking can be devastating.

If the focus on counterfactual alternatives to a current undesirable reality becomes overly obsessive, the result can be depression. When people repetitively blame themselves for failing to achieve important goals or for physical problems or personal losses, they experience a spiraling sense of loss of personal control, resulting in feeling helpless and unable to change their current circumstances (Wood et al., 1990). Martin and Tesser (1989) discussed the phenomenon of ruminative thinking as a state in which people, after facing repeated failures in achieving their goals, focus on their failure rather than on ways to overcome their obstacles. When ruminative thinkers get bogged down in their own failures, they become unable to assess the situation in order to find helpful alternatives to their actions. Although Martin and Tesser did not discuss the role of counterfactuals, per se, in their theory, it seems likely that people engaged in ruminative thought would be especially likely to ruminate about the counterfactual worlds that might have been. Such a focus on thoughts of "if only . . ." and "why me . . ." can only lead to self-pity and depression and an inability to emerge from these kinds of thoughts. Counterfactual generation of this type can lead to a cycle of unproductive thinking that feeds on itself.

We have thus discussed a variety of circumstances in which counter-factual generation of one's own behaviors can lead to negative affective experiences in the form of regret, dissatisfaction, self-blame, guilt, shame, or depression. Similarly, the ease of counterfactualizing another person's behaviors that were antecedent to a negative outcome for that person can influence the amount of affect people feel for that person or the extent to which people hold the other person blameworthy. In one case, Miller and McFarland (1986) described a victim who had been severely injured during a robbery. The robbery took place either in a store that the victim usually frequented or in a store in which he rarely shopped but decided to enter on this occasion. The victim in the unusual-store scenario was accorded more sympathy and was awarded greater compensation for his injuries than the victim in the usual-store scenario. This enhanced affect was due to the ease with which participants could generate an injury-free counterfactual world for the victim in the "unusual" store ("If only he had shopped at his regular store"). However, not all upward counterfactuals lead to enhanced sympathy for a recipient of a negative outcome. Johnson (1986) reported that participants reacted more negatively toward a woman who chose to move out of a seat and by so doing lost a large lottery that went to her original seat number than did participants who read a similar scenario in which a seat near her original position was selected in the lottery. According to Johnson, because it was easy to construct a counterfactual world in which the "seat-moving" victim had a better outcome, she was perceived as more blameworthy.

Thus, upward counterfactuals lead to enhanced affective reactions to victims of negative events. In addition, the specific affect can be quite different, depending on the circumstances surrounding the negative outcome. Two possibilities exist for explaining which type of enhanced affective reaction to victims will follow from the generation of upward counterfactuals. First, Miller et al. (1990) suggested that perceivers will try to compensate a victim in order to restore a sense of justice, but when this option is not available, they will attempt to reduce the sense of injustice by derogating the victim. In either case, compensation or derogation, the reaction will be greater when it is easy to generate a counterfactual world where the victimization did not occur. In the Miller and McFarland (1986) study, participants had the opportunity to compensate the victim. As a result, they awarded larger monetary amounts to the shopper at the unusual store, where an upward counterfactual was readily available. However, participants in the Johnson (1986) study did not have a compensation option. Thus, they attempted to restore justice by derogating the victim, moreso when an upward counterfactual was easily generated. A second explanation involves the role that the upward counterfactual plays in the attribution of culpability to the victim.[1] In the Miller and McFarland (1986) study, the upward counterfactual does not causally link the actor to the negative outcome. Because the victim's behavior is perceived as unrelated to the assault, greater sympathy is offered via the upward counterfactual in the unusual-store case because the bad outcome, having been avoidable, seems much worse. However, in the Johnson (1986) study, a causal link is possible between the actor's behavior (i.e., leaving the seat) and the negative outcome. Because perceivers make a causal link between the actor's antecedent behavior and her less-than-desirable outcome, greater blame results from this upward counterfactual.

---

[1] We thank Neal Roese for offering this explanation.

Thus, just as with the self-attributions, emotional reactions to others and behaviors toward them can be biased based on the ease of counterfactual generation and the attributional links captured in the counterfactual. The foreseeability of the outcomes or the factual bases for the decision, factors that should enter into an assessment of the quality of the decision making, may be less important than the counterfactual world that is generated. Because of this tendency, people fail to assess the rational or just levels of blame, sympathy, or compensation that a person deserves. Compensating someone with extra money just because he or she shopped at a different store is hardly an equitable decision.

Interestingly, people often react to the circumstances of others not only by counterfactualizing their behavior in the situation but by counterfactualizing their own behavior ("If we had been them"). People may blame someone who rushes to a meeting and has an accident or who follows a boss's orders to cut corners and causes the injury of a worker because they think, "If I were in that situation, I would have acted differently." Such a counterfactual comparison would be useful and functional only if the self-prediction were correct. In fact, such self-predictions are very inaccurate (Sherman, 1980). More important, they are inaccurate in a socially desirable direction. That is, people predict that they would behave far more socially desirably than they actually do. Thinking thus, people hold others to standards that they incorrectly believe they would live up to. Moreover, it is the generation of these counterfactuals about the self that leads to biases in the judgments of others. For example, people wrongly believe that they would never have shocked others if they had participated in the Milgram experiment (Sherman, 1980). (Results of analyses indicate that 67% of these participants in fact would have shocked others.) This faulty counterfactual generation leads people to perceive the typical Milgram participant as sadistic, and people would no doubt blame them and punish them for any injury caused. Once again, the easy (but perhaps inaccurate) generation of a counterfactual world can affect judgments and behaviors in a dysfunctional way.

Reacting to General Versus Specific Cases

Why can't people accept negative outcomes and circumstances as part of life and simply move on from there, thus avoiding negative affective consequences? Although psychologists have no definitive answers to this question, they can make some observations that strike us as interesting and that might point the way to answers.

We are intrigued by the fact that people seem to have no trouble at all accepting the general concept of failure or accepting a global and abstract failure rate. For example, a baseball manager would gladly accept a preseason offer of a team average of one error per three games. Prior to a season, a basketball coach would happily accept a turnover rate of seven per game. Yet, even when the specific circumstances of any game or season are well within these acceptable limits, these same managers and coaches will react quite negatively to specific errors and turnovers and will express emotion and punish players based on these errors. The players themselves will experience regret, dissatisfaction, and guilt for errors, turnovers, and missed free throws, despite their understanding that, at a general level, some number of such failures are inevitable. In other words, people may realize and accept the fact that into every life a little rain must fall, but they will still react negatively and unacceptingly to any specific storm.

This ability to rationally accept negative occurrences at a general level and yet to experience great affect and emotion about any specific negative outcome is part of a broader tendency of people to react more emotionally to specific instances than to abstract and general cases. Thus, citizens in a community will accept very well the general principle of mixing commercial centers or low-income housing with neighborhoods—just not in their backyards. People may donate nothing at all to the starving or suffering children of the world, and yet millions of dollars will be sent to a specific child who is found abandoned or who has had the misfortune of falling down a well. In the realm of interpersonal judgment, Sears (1983) demonstrated the *person-positivity bias*, a tendency to evaluate specific individuals more favorably than the general group composed of these individuals.

There are many possible reasons that people respond to specific instances more emotionally and effectually than they do to general cases. Nisbett and Ross (1980) discussed differences in responses to concrete as opposed to abstract instances. Concrete, specific events are more memorable and attention-grabbing and thus evoke more affect than do general, hypothetical events. Tulving (1972), distinguishing between episodic and semantic representations, made a similar argument. Episodic memories (likely to be involved with specific cases) are more experiential, self-referenced, contextual, and affective. In addition, specific instances may be more likely to be processed in a central manner, whereas general cases may be processed in a more peripheral way (Petty & Cacioppo, 1984). Central processing leaves deeper and more unchangeable judgments, a consequence indicating again that more affect and emotion are associated with specific instances.

Most important for purposes of this chapter, we suggest that specific instances afford postcomputed counterfactual alternatives to be used as comparison standards. Unusual or unexpected or salient features can be mutated to yield alternative possible worlds. On the other hand, general cases have no particular features that can be mutated. In this case, it is more likely that precomputed, preevent expectancies will be used as comparison standards (Kahneman & Miller, 1986). Therefore, the general case of seven turnovers per game affords no alternatives but to compare it to an expected average. Any specific turnover, on the other hand, affords many opportunities for change. As we have shown, the generation of counterfactual alternatives to reality is intimately involved in the level of emotional reaction.

In any case, an understanding of why specific instances (especially negative instances) spontaneously evoke "if onlys . . ." that lead to cringing, fist-pounding, and sadness can help psychologists to better comprehend the dysfunctional side of counterfactual generation. Moreover, perhaps those individuals who can accept some of the specific negative occurrences of life without spontaneous counterfactual generation and who do not lose sight of the general, larger picture are the best kinds of judges and decision makers. Those decision makers who can avoid the counterfactual alternatives to specific cases may be in the best position, emotionally and cognitively, to render good subsequent judgments. For example, most coaches and managers scream, grimace, and even throw chairs when errors or bad outcomes occur. A few coaches, on the other hand, seem to maintain their equanimity and composure under most circumstances. Tony LaRussa, the manager of the Oakland A's, does not cringe or scream when a relief pitcher is hammered or a defensive replacement makes an error. It would be interesting to correlate a manager or coach's reactivity to negative events, or better yet, to correlate their tendency to generate counterfactuals to their success rates.

COSTLY CHANGES IN BEHAVIORS

In addition to the emotional costs of counterfactual generation, there are important costs in terms of faulty subsequent decision making that is based on the counterfactuals. Consider again one of the major functions of counterfactual thinking—preparation for the future. Upward counterfactuals indicate how some change in a prior behavior or judgment might have led to a more successful outcome. By implication, if this change in behavior or judgment is in fact instituted in the future, better outcomes will occur. Furthermore, when an unsatisfactory outcome is experienced and one is likely to be in a similar decision-making situation again, upward counterfactuals are generated, and the aspects of the situation that are mutated are usually those that are under the control of the actor. Thus, changes in behaviors in the direction indicated by the counterfactuals can and will be made the next time.

This is all well and good, and in fact Roese (1994) showed that the generation of upward counterfactuals following unsatisfying outcomes can lead to improvements in future performance. However, such improvement and a better preparation for the future can be expected *only* if it is true that the unsatisfying outcome need not have occurred, *only* when the original judgment was faulty and could have been improved, and *only* when the actor can learn from previous mistakes. The problem is that bad judgments do not always lead to bad outcomes, and bad outcomes do not always indicate bad judgments. Unfortunately, counterfactuals seem to be generated in an almost spontaneous way whenever something negative occurs—regardless of the reasonableness of the prior behaviors or judgments. The manager who leaves the starting pitcher in for the last inning and loses the game is second-guessed: "If only he had brought in the relief pitcher, the game would have been won." The same manager who does bring in the relief pitcher and loses the game is again faced with a counterfactual world, this time a world where the starter stays in for the last inning and victory replaces defeat.

It is fine to recognize, after a bad outcome, that a different decision might have led to a different outcome in this specific case. It is quite another thing to assume that a different decision *should have been* made. Unfortunately, people assume that what need not have occurred ought not to have occurred, and what might have been is what should have been. Miller and Turnbull (1990) referred to this confusion of what might have been with what ought to be as the *counterfactual fallacy*. This fallacy, they argued, is based on the perception that highly mutable outcomes should not have occurred. It is the ability to generate counterfactual alternatives to an undesirable reality that creates the feeling that the negative outcome was avoidable. People seem to ignore the fact that mutability is quite different from what should have been done. Miller and Turnbull (1990) commented on how this tendency to view negative events that are easily counterfactualized as events that ought not to have happened can lead to mistaken judgments and decisions that violate the principles of justice and deservingness.

The counterfactual fallacy can affect both judgments of others and self-relevant judgments. In fact, many of the negative affective responses directed toward the self that were discussed earlier can be understood as consequences of the counterfactual fallacy. In addition to such affective effects, this fallacy can also lead to counterproductive behaviors. Imagine playing the following game. A card is to be drawn from a normal deck. You may choose either spades, clubs, and hearts on the one hand, or diamonds on the other. If you choose correctly, you win $100. If you choose incorrectly, you lose $100. Wisely you choose spades, clubs, and hearts, but a diamond is drawn from the deck. You lose $100. It is true that *if* you had chosen a diamond in this specific case you would have won $100. Does this mean that, given the choice again, you prepare better for the future by choosing a diamond or by refusing to play the game at all? Undoing the past need not be linked to changes in what we do in the future. But, as we saw earlier (Miller & Turnbull, 1990), the two often go hand in hand. A strategy, however poor, that would have led to an easily imagined success in the past will often be chosen over a better strategy that led to failure in the past. Thus, counterfactuals that would have changed a bad current reality to a better one are often assumed to be the best way to ensure a more satisfying future.

Such thinking and such a tendency to adopt upward counterfactuals in a prescriptive rather than in a descriptive way are tied to the fact that people are outcome-driven beings. People often judge the quality of decision making solely on the basis of the outcome. Therefore, strategies that are followed by success should be maintained. Strategies that are followed by failure should be changed, and the change should be in the direction of the most accessible upward counterfactual. In fact, we agree with Miller and Turnbull (1990) that it is likely to be the salience of the spontaneous upward counterfactual that causes the feeling that the judgment was bad and ought to be changed. This tendency to continue with strategies that are followed by success and to alter strategies that are followed by failure is, of course, exemplified by the win-then-stay–lose-then-switch strategies that people often exhibit during learning or hypothesis testing (Levine, 1959). This tendency can interfere with the ability to learn or solve problems quickly and efficiently.

Baron and Hershey (1988) demonstrated the strength and ubiquitousness of this outcome bias in decision making. In virtually every case that they tested, their participants judged the quality of thinking and the competence of the decision maker higher when the decision (the very same decision under the same antecedent conditions) was followed by a success rather than by a failure. In other words, participants confused fortune with wisdom, and misfortune with guilt. Similarly, Roese and Olson (1994) asked participants what options a decision maker in a World War I scenario should have chosen. Although participants understood that their judgments should not have been affected by the outcome, and they believed that their judgments were not so affected, their judgments were in fact very much outcome driven. That is, participants judged that decision makers should have known to make the decisions that, in hindsight, led to the successful outcome. Thus, sports managers will lose their jobs, CEOs will be fired, and prison furlough systems will be discontinued because of short-term or isolated, unsatisfactory outcomes. Furthermore, the presence of counterfactual alternatives to these unsatisfactory outcomes likely serve to motivate and to justify the decision to change. Although Baron and

Hershey (1988) did not collect counterfactual-generation data from their participants, we suspect that the ease and extent of counterfactual thinking is very much related to the extent of outcome bias.

The findings of Baron and Hershey are, of course, related to previous results by Walster (1966), who reported that participants attributed greater responsibility to an actor for the very same action when that action had more serious consequences. The same negligent act is judged more harshly when the consequences of that act are more severe. This relationship between outcome and culpability is a very important one in the United States system of jurisprudence. In many respects, this system of laws actually maintains that for many crimes culpability should be independent of consequence. In fact, framers of the Model Penal Code (American Law Institute, 1985) adopted this position in 1962, stating that culpability should ideally be based only on what an actor knew before an act or at the time of the act (although culpability is in fact often linked to outcome, as in murder cases). The same act committed under the same conditions should be punished equally regardless of the severity of the consequences. Furthermore, certain parts of the American judicial system follow this principle. Thus, recently in Bloomington, Indiana, a driver of a car that ran a red light and killed two pedestrians was punished by a fine of $65. This is the standard fine for running a red light, and the consequences of the act are immaterial, provided that there was no prior intent to kill the pedestrians. Of course the public screamed in outrage and disbelief. They wanted the punishment to fit the outcome rather than the decision to run the red light, and counterfactual generations were no doubt a major part of their arguments and their affect.

The point is that negative outcomes are not simply accepted. Rarely are such outcomes viewed as unfortunate consequences of good decisions. The counterfactual, better alternative worlds are taken not only as what could have been but also as what should have been. In this light, it is clear that upward counterfactuals can better prepare people for the future only when the initial judgment was a poor one. Given people's tendency to focus on the outcomes of decisions, however, they will sometimes change good decision rules to bad ones on the basis of the counterfactuals that they generate. In fact, changing judgment strategies based on upward-counterfactual generation ought to be most beneficial for poor decision makers, but most dysfunctional for good decision makers. It may make people feel hopeful that they can ensure success in the future simply by changing to a strategy that would have had a positive outcome for a specific instance in the past, but this thinking is far from rational decision making. Good decision making requires an analysis of the conditions under which a decision was made rather than a focus on the outcome of that decision and on the counterfactual worlds that could have emerged under different judgments for the specific instance at hand.

This discussion of the role of counterfactual generation in changing behaviors or decision-making strategies is related to three other concepts that have proved to be important in the area of human judgment and behavior: hindsight bias, foreseeability, and self-handicapping.

Hindsight Bias

Hindsight bias refers to a person's judging a prior outcome as having been more predictable and even inevitable subsequent to learning the outcome (Fischhoff, 1975; Hawkins & Hastie, 1990). In other words, in retrospect, people "knew it all along." Thus, even when a priori judgments of likelihood are wrong and when decisions based on these mistaken judgments are made, people will not learn from their errors because, after the fact, they believe that they knew it in foresight and have nothing to learn.

At first blush, it seems that hindsight bias is incompatible with counterfactual generation. If outcomes seem inevitable, then counterfactual worlds are not easily conceived or generated. However, in a recent paper, Roese and Olson (1994) pointed out that hindsight bias is not only logically compatible with counterfactual generation but also that the two may even be complementary. They discussed hindsight bias as a belief that, once an outcome is known, the causal structure of the situation is understandable. This belief does not mean, however, that the outcome was divinely predetermined. It means only that the outcome was inevitable given the known antecedent conditions. In fact, the more predetermined the outcome was under the existing conditions and choices, the more likely changes in these conditions and choices would have led to a different outcome. In other words, the more a person is certain that outcome A was predictable under condition X, the more sure the person is that a change in condition X would have led to a change in outcome. Just as the person "knows" after the fact that bringing in the relief pitcher was bound to bring up the pinch hitter who would then hit the home run, the person "knows" equally well that leaving in the starting pitcher would have led to a strikeout and a different outcome.

Thus, the generation of counterfactual alternatives to reality might be enhanced by a hindsight bias through which one sees outcomes as inevitable under the preexisting set of conditions. These two kinds of biases might then go hand in hand and lead to a change in strategy in future situations. The fact is that the hindsight assessment and the inference about the counterfactual world are both likely to be incorrect. The outcome was not as predictable from antecedent conditions as people think (hindsight bias). Nor was an alternative outcome based on the mutation of some antecedent condition as likely as people think (counterfactual-generation bias). Yet these two biases in judgment can combine, and they have the potential for turning good decisions into bad ones.

Foreseeability

The *foreseeability* of outcomes has played a role in several social-psychology theories. For example, any negative outcomes involved in a decision or a behavior are assumed not to contribute to cognitive dissonance when these negative outcomes were unforeseeable (Cooper & Fazio, 1984; Goethals, Cooper, & Naficy, 1979). Thus, finding out after the fact that a counterattitudinal essay will be used to change the attitudes of young people or will have significant negative personal ramifications should not contribute to feelings of cognitive dissonance or to attitude and behavior changes in the counterattitudinal direction.

Just as foreseeability is presumed necessary for the arousal of the aversive state of cognitive dissonance, it might likewise be proposed that the negative affective states and costly behaviors associated with counterfactual thinking will arise only if the negative outcome that is counterfactualized was foreseeable in light of antecedent conditions. Logically this relationship is true. Why should one feel blame or regret about an accident that occurred while driving home by a new route? Why should the father in Detroit suffer from so much guilt following a plane crash that was unforeseeable and of extremely low a priori likelihood? As we have shown, the affective experiences and the behaviors following counterfactual generation do not obey the dictates of logic and rationality. The accident that could have been avoided (even if unforeseeable) and the plane crash that could have been averted do indeed bring feelings of regret and guilt and self-directed anger. Apparently the arousal of these emotions and the instigation of different behaviors are sufficient to generate a counterfactual world that does not include the negative occurrence. Experiencing sadness or depression following an accident or the death of a loved one is, of course, logical. Experiencing guilt or regret or blame because the generation of a counterfactual world indicates that the negative event need not and (therefore) should not have occurred is quite another thing.

Interestingly, there may also be some question about whether foreseeability is necessary for the arousal of other aversive psychological states such as cognitive dissonance. Although the results of some studies do indicate the necessity of foreseeability (Cooper, 1971; Goethals et al., 1979), results of other research indicate that even unforeseen negative consequences can arouse dissonance. In Brehm's (1959) study, children wrote a counterattitudinal essay stating that they liked a vegetable that they actually disliked. Subsequently, some participants learned of a totally unforeseen negative consequence: Their mothers would read these essays, and perhaps a childhood full of disliked vegetables would be in store. Those children in the unforeseen-negative-consequences condition showed added cognitive dissonance and attitude change. Sherman (1970) also examined the role of unforeseen negative consequences in attitude change. Participants wrote attitude-discrepant essays. Subsequently, some participants learned that their essays would appear as signed letters in their college newspaper, an unforeseen negative consequence. Compared to the essay writers who did not experience such consequences, these participants showed increased attitude change in the counterattitudinal direction. However, such enhanced change occurred only for those who had personal choice in whether or not to write the essay, indicating that initial dissonance arousal (which is based on personal choice) is necessary for unforeseen events to have their effects.

The point is that foreseeability is a concept defined by logic and objective standards. Even when conditions and events are in fact objectively unforeseeable, people seem to believe that they should have foreseen them. As long as a different decision could have undone the negative outcome, as long as a reasonable counterfactual can be generated, people may believe that they should have known this ahead of time and that they should have done things differently so that the counterfactual world would have taken place. Once again, the dysfunctionality of counterfactual thinking is apparent. Because the generation of alternative worlds is considered a "should have" in addition to a "could have," the negative affect of failing to act accordingly is then experienced, and costly changes in behavior may be initiated.

Self-Handicapping

Yet another area in which counterfactual generation can have behavioral and judgmental consequences is that of *self-handicapping*. Self-handicapping is essentially a strategy employed in situations that threaten self-esteem and in which future performance is uncertain (Berglas & Jones, 1978; for a review, see Arkin & Baumgardner, 1985). When faced with this uncertainty, many people choose to engage in behaviors that impede their ability to be successful at these tasks but that will serve as an excuse for failure. Thus, self-handicappers actually prepare for a counterfactual *in advance*, one that can relieve them of personal responsibility and feelings of poor performance by engaging in counterproductive behaviors before the event that will evoke the counterfactual after the fact (e.g., *"If* I had studied the night before the exam instead of going out and drinking, then I would have passed").

Although there are no known experiments in which researchers have explored counterfactuals in the area of self-handicapping, the implications are clear. Engaging in behaviors ahead of time that will allow the generation of self-protective counterfactuals after the fact permits self-handicappers to maintain self-esteem in the face of uncertain conditions, even if their performance is bad. Although at first glance this use of counterfactuals seems beneficial, it is important to note that the self-handicapping activities themselves (e.g., taking drugs, not practicing, staying up too late) will probably lead to diminished performance regardless of the self-esteem benefits derived. Even if students do not feel bad or have lowered self-esteem after failing because they drank instead of studying, the fact is that their performance in all likelihood would have been better had they studied. Despite the maintenance of self-esteem that these counterfactuals provide, ultimately, engaging in the self-handicapping behavior hurts performance.

The idea that people can preconstruct counterfactual worlds to avert potential negative, undesirable states in the future is an interesting one. Consider the following situation. You are at the dog track. Before one of the races, you carefully consider all of the information available, and you decide that dog Number 3 in this race, with 5 : 1 odds, is the best bet of the day. You stand in line and are prepared to bet $100 on dog Number 3 to win. The line moves very slowly, and just before you get to the betting window the bell sounds for the race. You are shut out. You cannot make your bet. You now watch the race. Which dog do you root for? Our own experience and discussion with others make us certain that you will root for any dog but Number 3. Why? The answer has to do with your preconstructions of the counterfactual that will be generated after the outcome is known. If dog Number 3 wins, the counterfactual will be something like "If only I had gotten in line 10 seconds earlier, I would now be $500 richer." This counterfactual will bring much sadness and regret. If dog Number 3 loses, the likely counterfactual is "If I had gotten to bet, I'd now be $100 poorer—this is my lucky day." Thus, the recognition ahead of time of the counterfactuals that are to come lead you to hope for the outcome that will be associated with the mood-enhancing, downward counterfactual. Moreover, this thinking process happens despite the fact that a win by dog Number 3 would be a strong indication of your decision-making skills. Once again it is clear how judgments and feelings depend as much on the alternatives to reality as on the reality itself. This idea that anticipatory regret can enter into judgments and preferences has been discussed by decision theorists (e.g., Bell, 1982, 1985; Loomes & Sugden, 1982; see also Gleicher et al., chapter 10; Miller & B. Taylor, chapter 11).

THE COSTLY MAINTENANCE OF DYSFUNCTIONAL BEHAVIORS

According to the previous analysis, counterfactual thinking can lead to the adoption of new behaviors or to changes in judgment strategies when, in fact, such changes are not rationally warranted and are not likely to lead to better outcomes in the future. There are other cases in which self-defeating behaviors may be maintained because of the ability to generate counterfactual worlds that support these behaviors.

Consider the compulsive gambler. The objective fact is that this person is consistently losing money. This fact should indicate poor decision making and an unfavorable situation and should lead to the conclusion that the person ought to stop gambling. Gamblers, however, have an interesting way of justifying their behaviors. They look at any particular gambling loss and see in it simple ways in which they could have easily won. If only a minor change had occurred, they would have won. Thus, they maintain the illusion that they are good decision makers and gamblers, that they will learn from this outcome, and that the future will be full of winning money. It is the generation of these close counterfactual wins that keeps gamblers gambling. Gilovich (1983) demonstrated this pattern in a striking study. In a college basketball game, participants had bet either on the University of California at Los Angeles (UCLA) or on the University of Louisville. During the game, an unexpected play occurred. A UCLA player missed an easy layup at a time when UCLA could have surpassed Louisville. Louisville ultimately won. In accounting for the outcome, only the losers (UCLA bettors) generated the counterfactual world in which the layup was made (in which case they would have won the bet). Thus, both winners and losers consequently believed that they were good decision makers, and their gambling continued.

In fact, those who operate gambling establishments understand very well the importance of close counterfactuals, cases in which a losing reality was within easy grasp of a winning outcome. Losers watching a photo-finish race will see in replay and in an enlarged picture just how close they were to winning. In the game of keno, not only do the lights under the winning numbers glow, but the lights also extend a little to all surrounding numbers, a practice that makes the close counterfactuals very accessible. Therefore, through their own motivational tendencies and with a little help from the gambling establishments, gamblers who lose can see how close to winning they really were and thus maintain their habitual gambling behaviors.

Consider a hustler in pool or tennis or any other game in which money might be at stake. The goal, of course, is not only to beat the opponent but to win in a particular way. It is important that the "mark," the one duped, be left with a close counterfactual world in which winning was within grasp. A lucky drop of a ball off another ball in the final pool shot or a ball that barely clears the net in a close tennis match is sufficient to keep the mark playing again and again. Those close counterfactual worlds, which may be set up by the hustler or mentally manufactured by the mark, often keep people persisting in counterproductive behaviors.

Although one of the authors of this chapter has never been a tennis or pool hustler (although he may have been a mark), he *has* played his share of bridge. His favorite ploy is called the Grosvenor Gambit (Turner, 1980). You are declarer in a bridge contract, and you and your partner have bid to a slam that is unbeatable with simple play. Instead of simply playing the hand normally and claiming the win, you suddenly make a play that would allow the defenders to defeat the contract. However, in order to defeat the contract, they must assume that you have just made an unthinkably foolish play. They assume that you did not make such a gross error, they defend normally under the circumstances, and they hand the contract back to you. You then claim the contract, and they can then see how they could have easily defeated the contract. A normal result is achieved by an abnormal route, a situation affording the easy generation of a counterfactual world where a better outcome was achieved. This generation of a close counterfactual usually leads your opponents to scream at each other and at the same time to believe you are an idiot. You simply smile with a blank expression. They are yours for the rest of the evening.

CONCLUSION

Often automatically and sometimes inexplicably, people's minds wander to counterfactual alternatives to reality. Recent research and theorizing have been devoted to an understanding of when these counterfactual generations occur and what form and direction they will take. A key issue in this research and theorizing has been the identification of the beneficial functions served by these psychological mutations of reality (Markman et al., 1993; Roese, 1994). Moreover, several very important functions have been identified—affect regulation, preparation for the future, coping with negative life events, and bringing about perceptions of predictability and controllability for these events. Certainly these are important psychological functions.

More generally, it has been clear to social psychologists for a long time that reactions to life events, especially negative life events, depend on more than the objective reality of those events. It is the perception of the events and the interpretation of the meaning of those events that guide humans' affective, cognitive, and behavioral reactions far more than the physical reality, or true meaning, of the events. In addition, social objects and events are rarely judged on an absolute basis. People require comparison objects against which to judge events and circumstances. These comparison objects usually take the form of other people who are in similar circumstances or of similar events that have occurred in the past. The meaning and evaluation of a person's experience depend very much on the outcome of such social comparisons. In cases in which there are no readily available comparison persons or available similar past life events, people may mentally manufacture such events. Furthermore, this function may be the most general and most important function of counterfactual generation—to provide the kind of social comparison that allows people to evaluate and interpret their life experience and to give meaning to that experience. Thus, the counterfactuals that people generate play an important role in guiding their perception of events and providing a comparison framework within which they can understand those events.

We certainly do not disagree that these functions are often served well by counterfactual thinking. Nor do we disagree with the conclusion that the potential benefits of counterfactual generation are many, in terms of improved affective state, a better understanding of circumstances and their causes, and a potential for improved performance and outcomes in the future. We ask only that the potential costs of counterfactual thinking also be considered—the ways in which mutations of reality can serve to induce negative affect and emotions, lead to biased and inappropriate judgments, and instigate counterproductive and self-defeating behaviors. We have tried to point to some caveats with respect to counterfactual thinking and to speculate about ways in which the generation of counterfactuals can hamper goal-directed behavior.

As with any simplifying principle, the generation and use of counterfactuals in judging circumstances and events can introduce characteristic errors and biases into the process. More than anything, counterfactual generation is a process that results in individuals' feeling that they have a better understanding of the causal structure of life's events. Yet, as we have shown, errors and biases based on counterfactual generation can creep into this causal understanding, resulting in unwarranted and debilitating negative emotions, irrational judgments and decisions, and behavioral changes that can be counterproductive. This tendency does not imply that people should try to eliminate counterfactual thinking from their lives or to desist from the mental construction of counterfactual alternatives to reality. It means only that psychologists should be more aware of the potential dysfunctional aspects of counterfactual generation and that they should recognize some of the errors and biases that can be associated with the process. At times, no doubt, people would be better off not generating counterfactual alternatives to reality but rather simply dealing with that reality directly and accepting what comes along. Or in the words of Creedence Clearwater Revival's (1969) "Proud Mary": "And I never lost a minute of sleep, worryin' about the way things might have been."

REFERENCES

American Law Institute (1985). *Model penal code: Official draft and explanatory notes.* Philadelphia: Author.

Arkin, R. M., & Baumgardner, A. H. (1985). Self-handicapping. In J. H. Harvey & G. W. Weary (Eds.), *Attribution: Basic issues and applications* (pp. 169–202). San Diego, CA: Academic Press.

Bargh, J. A., & Thein, R. D. (1985). Individual construct accessibility, person memory, and the recall–judgment link: The case of information overload. *Journal of Personality and Social Psychology, 22,* 293–311.

Bargh, J. A., & Tota, M. E. (1988). Context-dependent automatic processing in depression: Accessibility of negative constructs with regard to self but not others. *Journal of Personality and Social Psychology, 54,* 925–939.

Baron, J., & Hershey, J. C. (1988). Outcome bias in decision evaluation. *Journal of Personality and Social Psychology, 54,* 569–579.

Bell, D. E. (1982). Regret in decision making under uncertainty. *Operations Research, 30,* 961–981.

Bell, D. E. (1985). Disappointment in decision making under uncertainty. *Operations Research, 33,* 1–27.

Berglas, S., & Jones, E. E. (1978). Drug choice as a self-handicapping strategy in response to noncontingent success. *Journal of Personality and Social Psychology, 36,* 405–417.

Boninger, D. S., Gleicher, F., & Strathman, A. (1994). Counterfactual thinking: From what might have been to what may be. *Journal of Personality and Social Psychology, 67,* 297–307.

Brehm, J. W. (1959). Increasing cognitive dissonance by a fait accompli. *Journal of Abnormal and Social Psychology, 58,* 379–382.

Bulman, J. R., & Wortman, C. B. (1977). Attributions of blame and coping in the "real world": Severe accident victims react to their lot. *Journal of Personality and Social Psychology, 35,* 351–363.

Clearwater, Creedence. (1969). Proud Mary. On *Bayou Country* [record]. Berkeley, CA: Jondora Music-BMI.

Cooper, J. (1971). Personal responsibility and dissonance: The role of foreseen consequences. *Journal of Personality and Social Psychology, 18,* 354–363.

Cooper, J., & Fazio, R. H. (1984). A new look at dissonance theory. In L. Berkowitz (Ed.), *Advances in experimental social psychology* (Vol. 17, pp. 229–266). New York: Academic Press.

Davis, C. G., Lehman, D. R., Silver, R. C., Wortman, C. B., & Ellard, J. H. (1994). *Taking more blame than is one's due: The role of counterfactual thinking.* Unpublished manuscript.

Davis, C. G., Lehman, D. R., Wortman, C. B., Silver, R. C., & Thompson, S. C. (1995). The undoing of traumatic life events. *Personality and Social Psychology Bulletin, 21,* 109–124.

Fischhoff, B. (1975). Hindsight≠foresight: The effects of outcome knowledge on judgment under uncertainty. *Journal of Experimental Psychology: Human Perception and Performance, 1,* 288–299.

Gavanski, I., & Wells, G. L. (1989). Counterfactual processing of normal and exceptional events. *Journal of Experimental Social Psychology, 25,* 314–325.

Gilovich, T. (1983). Biased evaluation and persistence in gambling. *Journal of Personality and Social Psychology, 44,* 1110–1126.

Gleicher, F., Kost, K. A., Baker, S. M., Strathman, A. J., Richman, S. A., & Sherman, S. J. (1990). The role of counterfactual thinking in judgments of affect. *Personality and Social Psychology Bulletin, 16,* 285–295.

Goethals, G. R., Cooper, J., & Naficy, A. (1979). Role of foreseen, foreseeable, and unforeseeable behavioral consequences in the arousal of cognitive dissonance. *Journal of Personality and Social Psychology, 37,* 1179–1185.

Hawkins, S. A., & Hastie, R. (1990). Hindsight: Biased judgment of past events after the outcomes are known. *Psychological Bulletin, 107,* 311–327.

Higgins, E. T., King, G. A., & Mavin, G. H. (1982). Individual construct accessibility and subjective impressions and recall. *Journal of Personality and Social Psychology, 43,* 35–47.

Hilton, D. J., & Slugoski, B. R. (1986). Knowledge-based causal attribution: The abnormal conditions focus model. *Psychological Review, 93,* 75–88.

Janoff–Bulman, R. (1979). Characterological versus behavioral self-blame: Inquiries into depression and rape. *Journal of Personality and Social Psychology, 37,* 1798–1809.

Johnson, J. T. (1986). The knowledge of what might have been: Affective and attributional consequences of near outcomes. *Personality and Social Psychology Bulletin, 12,* 51–62.

Kahneman, D., & Miller, D. T. (1986). Norm theory: Comparing reality to its alternatives. *Psychological Review, 93,* 136–153.

Kahneman, D., & Tversky, A. (1982). The simulation heuristic. In D. Kahneman, P. Slovic, & A. Tversky (Eds.), *Judgment under uncertainty: Heuristics and biases* (pp. 201–208). New York: Cambridge University Press.

Klayman, J., & Ha, Y. W. (1987). Confirmation, disconfirmation, and information in hypothesis testing. *Psychological Review, 94,* 211–228.

Kruglanski, A. W., & Freund, T. (1983). The freezing and unfreezing of lay inferences: Effects on impressional primacy, ethnic stereotyping, and numerical anchoring. *Journal of Experimental Social Psychology, 19,* 448–468.

Landman, J. (1987). Regret and elation following action and inaction: Affective responses to positive versus negative outcomes. *Personality and Social Psychology Bulletin, 13,* 524–536.

Landman, J. (1993). *Regret: The persistence of the possible.* New York: Oxford University Press.

Langer, E. J. (1975). The illusion of control. *Journal of Personality and Social Psychology, 32,* 311–328.

Levine, M. (1959). A model of hypothesis behavior in discrimination learning set. *Psychological Review, 66,* 353–366.

Lipe, M. G. (1991). Counterfactual reasoning as a framework for attribution theories. *Psychological Bulletin, 109,* 456–471.

Loomes, G., & Sugden, R. (1982). Regret theory: An alternative theory of rational choice under uncertainty. *Economic Journal, 92,* 805–824.

Lord, C. G., Lepper, M. R., & Preston, E. (1984). Considering the opposite: A corrective strategy for social judgment. *Journal of Personality and Social Psychology, 47,* 1231–1243.

Markman, K. D., Gavanski, I., Sherman, S. J., & McMullen, M. N. (1993). The mental simulation of better and worse possible worlds. *Journal of Experimental Social Psychology, 29,* 87–109.

Markman, K. D., Gavanski, I., Sherman, S. J., & McMullen, M. N. (1995). The impact of perceived control on the imagination of better and worse possible worlds. *Personality and Social Psychology Bulletin, 21,* 588–595.

Martin, L. L., & Tesser, A. (1989). Toward a motivational and structural theory of ruminative thought. In J. S. Uleman & J. A. Bargh (Eds.), *Unintended thought* (pp. 306–326). New York: Guilford.

Medin, D. L., & Schaffer, M. M. (1978). Context theory of classification learning. *Psychological Review, 85,* 207–238.

Medvec, V. H., & Gilovich, T. (in press). When less is more: Counterfactual thinking and satisfaction among Olympic medalists. *Journal of Personality and Social Psychology.*

Miller, D. T., & Gunasegaram, S. (1990). Temporal order and the perceived mutability of events: Implications for blame assignment. *Journal of Personality and Social Psychology, 59,* 1111–1118.

Miller, D. T., & McFarland, C. (1986). Counterfactual thinking and victim compensation: A test of norm theory. *Personality and Social Psychology Bulletin, 12,* 513–519.

Miller, D. T., Taylor, B., & Buck, M. L. (1991). Gender gaps: Who needs to be explained? *Journal of Personality and Social Psychology, 61,* 5–12.

Miller, D. T., & Turnbull, W. (1990). The counterfactual fallacy: Confusing what might have been with what ought to have been. *Social Justice Research, 4,* 1–19.

Miller, D. T., Turnbull, W., & McFarland, C. (1989). When a coincidence is suspicious: The role of mental simulation. *Journal of Personality and Social Psychology, 57,* 581–589.

Miller, D. T., Turnbull, W., & McFarland, C. (1990). Counterfactual thinking and social perception: Thinking about what might have been. In M. P. Zanna (Ed.), *Advances in experimental social psychology* (Vol. 23, pp. 305–331). New York: Academic Press.

Niedenthal, P. M., Tangney, J. P., & Gavanski, I. (1994). "If only I weren't" versus "If only I hadn't": Distinguishing shame and guilt in counterfactual thinking. *Journal of Personality and Social Psychology, 67,* 585–595.

Nisbett, R. E., & Ross, L. (1980). *Human inference: Strategies and shortcomings of social judgment.* Englewood Cliffs, NJ: Prentice–Hall.

Nosofsky, R. M. (1987). Attention and learning processes in the identification and categorization of integral stimuli. *Journal of Experimental Psychology: Learning, Memory, and Cognition, 13,* 87–108.

Petty, R. E., & Cacioppo, J. T. (1984). The effects of involvement on responses to argument quantity and quality: Central and peripheral routes to persuasion. *Journal of Personality and Social Psychology, 46,* 69–81.

Roese, N. J. (1994). The functional basis of counterfactual thinking. *Journal of Personality and Social Psychology, 66,* 805–818.

Roese, N. J., & Olson, J. M. (1993a). Self-esteem and counterfactual thinking. *Journal of Personality and Social Psychology, 65,* 199–206.

Roese, N. J., & Olson, J. M. (1993b). The structure of counterfactual thought. *Personality and Social Psychology Bulletin, 19,* 312–319.

Roese, N. J., & Olson, J. M. (1994). *Counterfactuals, causal attributions, and the hindsight bias: A conceptual integration.* Unpublished manuscript.

Roese, N. J., & Olson, J. M. (1995). Outcome controllability and counterfactual thinking. *Personality and Social Psychology Bulletin, 21,* 620–628.

Sears, D. O. (1983). The person–positivity bias. *Journal of Personality and Social Psychology, 44,* 233–240.

Sherman, S. J. (1970). Attitudinal effects of unforeseen consequences. *Journal of Personality and Social Psychology, 16,* 510–520.

Sherman, S. J. (1980). On the self-erasing nature of errors of prediction. *Journal of Personality and Social Psychology, 39,* 211–221.

Skov, R. B., & Sherman, S. J. (1986). Information-gathering processes: Diagnosticity, hypothesis-confirmatory strategies, and perceived hypothesis confirmation. *Journal of Experimental Social Psychology, 22,* 93–121.

Smith, E. R., & Zarate, M. A. (1992). Exemplar-based model of social judgment. *Psychological Review, 99,* 3–21.

Taylor, S. E., Lichtman, R. R., & Wood, J. V. (1984). Attributions, beliefs about control, and adjustment to breast cancer. *Journal of Personality and Social Psychology, 46,* 489–502.

Tulving, E. (1972). Episodic and semantic memory. In E. Tulving & W. Donaldson (Eds.), *Organization of memory* (pp. 381–403). New York: Academic Press.

Turnbull, W., & Mawhinney, M. (1986). *Counterfactual thinking and self-blame.* Unpublished manuscript.

Turner, F. B. (1980). The Grosvenor Gambit. In E. Kaplan & J. Rubens (Eds.), *Bridge World humor* (pp. 38–42). New York: Bridge World Magazine.

Tversky, A., & Kahneman, D. (1973). Availability: A heuristic for judging frequency and probability. *Cognitive Psychology, 5,* 207–232.

Walster, E. (1966). Assignment of responsibility for an accident. *Journal of Personality and Social Psychology, 3,* 73–79.

Wason, P. C. (1968). Reasoning about a rule. *Quarterly Journal of Experimental Psychology, 23,* 273–281.

Wells, G. L., & Gavanski, I. (1989). Mental simulation of causality. *Journal of Personality and Social Psychology, 56,* 161–169.

Wells, G. L., Taylor, B. R., & Turtle, J. W. (1987). The undoing of scenarios. *Journal of Personality and Social Psychology, 53,* 421–430.

Wood, J. V., Saltzberg, J. A., Neale, J. M., Stone, A. A., & Rachmiel, T. B. (1990). Self-focused attention, coping responses, and distressed mood in everyday life. *Journal of Personality and Social Psychology, 58,* 1027–1036.

8

Through a Glass Darkly: Worldviews, Counterfactual Thought, and Emotion

Janet Landman
University of Michigan

From February to July, 1990, I spoke on the phone several times a week with a close relative I will call Dylan. It was a time of enormous upheaval in Dylan's life. His wife was divorcing him, and she was doing it with more than the usual venom—including making serious threats to prevent him from ever again seeing his two young children, who were the lights of his life. Nearly every time we spoke, he wept. He was inconsolable, and he was medicating the condition with anti-depressants and alcohol.

I tried to help. I listened, I suggested that he talk to a therapist (which he did not do), and I tried to help him to see his situation in a different light. Looking back on it, I think that more than anything else I was trying to make a chink in his romantic and tragic stance toward life in general and his regret in particular.

To me he seemed to be under the sway of an overly romantic view of marriage, and a dangerously tragic view of divorce. According to his way of looking at marriage, there is one and only one person in the world one was meant to marry. If that marriage ends, the event is not just a mistake, it is a catastrophe. Dylan believed that in his wife he had found that one person he was meant to marry. He mourned for the loss of his children and the only woman he had ever loved. Now that the marriage was over, his life was over.

My attempts and those of others to help Dylan failed. On July 15, 1990, at age 40, he committed suicide.[1]

This version of the story of Dylan is necessarily an oversimplification. Probably any single version of the story would be. Without doubt, Dylan's worldview was not *solely* responsible for his death. Alcohol, for instance, contributed, as did his desperate financial straits. Then, too, precisely how his depression was related to his worldview I do not know. It could be argued that what I am calling his romantic/tragic sensibility was his depression talking. Or the reverse could be true—that his depression, a long-standing condition preceding the day in February when he was served with divorce papers, was an effect of his long-standing romantic/tragic sensibility. Or the causal pattern may be bidirectional, marginal, or nil. I do believe, however, that Dylan's worldview played a key role both in his depression and in his death.

In this chapter I explore counterfactual thought and emotion within the framework of the categories of romance, comedy, tragedy, and irony. I view these typically literary categories as a set of explanatory concepts that I refer to as *worldviews*, or *sensibilities*. As I see it, these worldviews operate on several levels, including the cultural, the historical, the interindividual, and the intraindividual. I indulge here in some speculation about the cultural and historical levels, but as a psychologist, I am chiefly interested in the interindividual and intraindividual levels.[2] In this chapter I define these worldviews and try to find out what testable hypotheses they might contribute to the study of the workings of counterfactual thought and emotion. Most often I focus on the emotion of regret, which has been the subject of much of my own work. Specifically, I argue that these worldviews are likely to be associated with different types of coun-

---

[1] I open with this painful personal experience with some trepidation and some hope. The reasons for my trepidation are probably fairly obvious: Using personal experiences just isn't done. Except for the brief upbeat anecdote, academic discourse in psychology situates itself firmly in the tradition that separates the personal from the analytic. The sources of my hope may be just as obvious: Personal experiences are being reported more and more—at least in other disciplines. For some time now I have been reading (and reading about) personal scholarship in literary and cultural criticism, anthropology, feminist theory, and law (e.g., Brownstein, 1982; Geertz, 1974; Kaplan, 1986; Miller, 1991; Rosaldo, 1989; Steedman, 1986; Tompkins, 1987; R. Williams, 1977). The piece that most bolstered my resolve to use this approach is the new classic, "Grief and a Headhunter's Rage." In it, anthropologist Renato Rosaldo (1989) shows how his own experience of grief at the death of his anthropologist wife, Michelle Rosaldo, aided in his understanding of how grief is expressed in a society very different from his. In my chapter, I hope to do something rather similar to what Rosaldo did, and for some of the same reasons. I relate these personal events to lend a degree of immediacy, fullness, and urgency to what I hope will prove a useful conceptual exploration relevant to the concerns of this volume.

[2] I am grateful to Neal Roese for naming the levels I had described in an early draft.

terfactual thinking and with different patterns and different intensities of emotional reaction.

FOUR WORLDVIEWS

Gleicher, Kost, Baker, Strathman, Richman, and Sherman (1990) postulated that, in response to a negative outcome or event, people engage in a four-stage psychological process:

1. They generate alternative counterfactual outcomes.
2. They generate alternative counterfactual routes to those outcomes.
3. They compare the judged probability of the actual event with that of the counterfactuals (based on the perceived probability of the possible routes).
4. They react affectively, based on these prior processes.

Gleicher et al. (1990) proposed that with positive outcomes the affective response is based only on the valence of the outcome, and the other steps of the process are skipped—unless the counterfactuals are made salient. Because the focus of this chapter is largely on negative outcomes that elicit regret and other emotions, the full four-step process—or something like it—applies. Actually, it may be premature to assume this particular *sequence*. At least three alternative sequences seem plausible: (a) affect precedes counterfactual thought (if preferences need no inferences, as Zajonc, 1980, hypothesized); (b) the relationship between affect and counterfactual thought is reciprocal and simultaneous (Markman, Gavanski, Sherman, & McMullen, 1993); (c) antecedents (as well as outcomes) may drive the generation of counterfactual thought and emotion (see Roese & Olson, chapter 1).

It is probably safe to assume that Dylan engaged in a process similar to that outlined by Gleicher et al. (1990). On being served with divorce papers (negative event), Dylan did imagine states counter to that fact—states of being a happily married husband and father. This inference is based on two of the last poems he wrote and sent me. It seems likely that he might also have imagined alternative paths that his marriage might have taken, such as having undergone successful marriage counseling or never having consented to live two doors from his in-laws. The mental process of comparing these counterfactual routes and outcome with the actual routes and outcome might have evoked in him profound regret and grief over and above that evoked by the divorce in and of itself.

But I know more about Dylan's worldview than about his counterfactual thinking. His worldview came across in many conversations we had over the years, from the poems he wrote and sent to me, and through those last long phone calls. I have termed his worldview primarily romantic and tragic in nature. These descriptors require elaboration, for the concepts of romance, comedy, tragedy, and irony have rarely figured in psychological, philosophical, or economic analysis. But their roots in the humanities are congruent with the kind of phenomenon that regret (and all emotion) is—that is, a subjective, personal experience based on a subjective and personal interpretation of reality (P. Kleinginna & A. Kleinginna, 1981; Solomon, 1993). Precisely because of the personal and subjective nature of regret and all emotion, these four categories—which I alternatively call *modes, stances, mentalities, constructions, philosophies of life, worldviews,* and *sensibilities*—seem potentially illuminative.

From this array of near-synonyms I prefer the terms *worldviews* and *sensibilities.* The term *worldview* effectively suggests the cognitive aspects involved—central attitudes and beliefs about the nature of life's obstacles and solutions, for instance. The term *sensibility* better mingles the cognitive and the emotional (and other) aspects in a nondissociated way that accurately reflects normal experience. Both words begin to connote the constellation of belief, emotion, needs, motives, and ways of relating to the world that I am concerned with.[3]

Most of what I offer here concerning these worldviews I have synthesized from the work of four scholars—two literary critics and two psychologists: Northrop Frye (1957), George Steiner (1961), Roy Schafer (1976), and Dan McAdams (1985). In his classic *Anatomy of Criticism,* Frye (1957) first classified literary plots into the four categories of comedy, romance, tragedy, and irony. Steiner's (1961) analysis of tragedy helps to distinguish between the tragic and ironic modes and to flesh out the understanding of the romantic mode. I have relied as well on Schafer's (1976) examination of how psychoanalysis reflects aspects of the comic, romantic, tragic, and ironic "visions of reality" (p. 23), that is, "ways of looking at experience and imposing meaning on it" (p. 55). Along with Schafer, I caution the reader that "there are no terse definitions of these terms on which philosophers and critics generally agree" (p. 26). Finally, McAdams (1985) has contributed to my framework certain organizing categories within each of the stances, particularly those of "central prob-

---

[3]Raymond Williams's (1977) term "structures of feeling" captures my meaning perhaps best of all: "characteristic elements of impulse, restraint, and tone; specifically affective elements of consciousness and relationships: not feeling against thought, but thought as felt and feeling as thought: practical consciousness of a present kind, in a living and interrelating continuity" (p. 132). Although the definition has much to offer, I find the phrase itself problematic because of its unfortunately reified-sounding term "structure," the dissociation of the affective from the cognitive embodied in the phrase, and its relative unfamiliarity in psychology.

lem" and "general sentiment" (p. 92). (Readers wishing a more extended treatment of these worldviews and their relationship with the experience of regret may want to consult Landman, 1993.)

This framework, however, is not a typology. It is more modest than that. Rather than types (clearly distinct, discontinuous, empirically derived categories) (Meehl, 1979; Mendelsohn, Weiss, & Feimer, 1982), I think of the worldviews as heuristic conceptual configurations that to some degree overlap—conceptually and experientially. Once these worldviews have been delineated in some detail, it should be feasible for the interested scholar to determine more precisely to what extent they represent distinctive or overlapping patterns of psychological organization. (For a model of the empirical testing of these stances with respect to intimacy and power, see McAdams, 1985.) These worldviews may prove to be useful "communications conveniences" (Mendelsohn et al., 1982, p. 1167) and explanatory categories capable of revealing deep coherence existing in surface incoherence.

In sum, I view these worldviews, or sensibilities as sets of fundamental values, beliefs, and sentiments about reality that are often tacit and taken for granted, much as the contact lenses through which individuals view the world become to them invisible and taken for granted. Though broader and more explicitly emotional, these worldviews function something like schemas (cohesive and stable cognitive structures) in their functions of directing attention; structuring experience; and guiding memory, inference, and the interpretation of events (Johnson & Sherman, 1990).

The Romantic Sensibility

From the romantic stance, life is viewed primarily as an adventure or quest involving individual struggle and ultimately heroic triumph; the romantic worldview is characterized by the following features:

- *View of Time.* Because it is based on the hope of sudden, discontinuous leaps forward, the romantic view is virtually ahistorical and atemporal.
- *Central Attitudes.* Striving against obstacles; belief in the existence of certainties, absolutes, and clear divisions between right and wrong, good and evil, hero and villain, and so forth; belief in the possibility of justice, reform, progress, perfectibility, happy endings, reconciliations, redemption, and heroic rebirth following struggle.
- *Central Problem.* How to journey onward and upward so as to emerge victorious (McAdams, 1985, p. 92).
- *Nature of Obstacles.* External, situational forces, not internal, or personal, failings; controllable forces.

- *Preferred Solution.* Action; reason and emotion; or imagination and fantasy (involving individualistic, heroic, triumphal quest).
- *Outcome.* Triumph.

The Wagnerian or Nietzschean hero is an exemplar of the floridly romantic sensibility.[4] In general, the romantic is drawn to fantasies of glory that fuel the view of life as a highly individualistic, heroic quest. The protagonist of Dostoevsky's (1864/1981) *Notes from Underground* expresses this aspect of the romantic stance toward remorse, a close cousin of regret: "I was tormented by remorse, and I would try to drive it away. . . . But I had a way out, which reconciled everything: escape into 'the lofty and the beautiful'—in my dreams, of course. I was a terrible dreamer" (p. 65).

More than any of the other worldviews, romanticism assumes the possibility of a "productive interaction between [reason and emotion], assuming optimistically that the rational would act as a check to passion, and that passion itself would be transformed, sublimated through the imagination" (Kaplan, 1986, p. 124). Dostoevsky's (1864/1981) protagonist shows this feature of romanticism, in fact going so far as to exalt the claims of desire over those of reason: "You see, gentlemen, reason is unquestionably a fine thing, but reason is no more than reason, and it gives fulfillment only to man's reasoning capacity, while desires are a manifestation of the whole of life" (p. 31).

The Comic Sensibility

The comic experience of life is an essentially optimistic one characterized by the following features:

- *View of Time.* Time is cyclic, in the sense that it is assumed that spring follows winter and the past is refurbishable.
- *Central Attitudes.* Belief in the possibility of justice, reform, progress, perfectibility, happy endings, reconciliations, redemption, and rebirth.
- *Central Problem.* "How to find happiness and stability in life . . . by minimizing interference from environmental obstacles and constraints" (McAdams, 1985, p. 92).
- *Nature of Obstacles.* Controllable, external forces.
- *Preferred Solution.* Exercise of reason; action.
- *Outcome.* Happy resolution.

---

[4]I thank Neal Roese for this idea.

The comic worldview is modern, Western, rational. It assumes that everyone is capable of summoning the resilience to get over any misfortune. It is simply a matter of reasoned action to choose to make lemonade when life gives you lemons, and to choose to find the silver lining in every cloud. (Funny how many clichés are grounded in the comic worldview, at least in this culture.)

The comic and romantic sensibilities share these features: belief in progressive, melioristic development; ascription of conflict and misery to external and controllable forces; and an emphasis on reasoned action as a primary solution to conflict and unhappiness.

The comic and romantic sensibilities differ from one another in these ways:

The romantic worldview entails a larger conception of the significance of the individual and of life.

Both are based on a progressivist assumption, but in the comic view, progress is expected to be fairly smooth in its evolution; in the romantic view, progress can take place in discontinuous leaps.

Whereas in the comic worldview, right and wrong, good and evil, hero and villain are aligned on a continuum, in the romantic view, these are drastically different polarities.

The romantic stance entails an emphasis on certainty and other absolutes not characteristic of the comic stance.

To a greater extent than the comic, the romantic sensibility prizes the articulation of heroic emotion and fantasy as precursors of the overt action it (along with the comic stance) prescribes.

The Tragic Sensibility

In the tragic vision, life is viewed through a glass darkly, as a process of decline and deterioration culminating in death. Yet decline and death are *not* in this view a good night into which the individual ought to go gently. Rather, these facts call for defiance, shaking one's fist at the gods, and, in the words of Dylan Thomas (1939), "raging against the dying of the light" (p. 128). The tragic sensibility entails the following features:

- *View of Time.* Time is linear: "Time is seen to be continuous and irreversible; choices once made are made forever; a second chance cannot be the same as the first; life is progression toward death without rebirth" (Schafer, 1976, p. 36); or time is made up of cyclic but futile phases of advance and decline.
- *Central Attitudes.* "Responsiveness to the great dilemmas, paradoxes, ambiguities, and uncertainties pervading human action and subjec-

tive experience" (Schafer, 1976, p. 35); "a sense of the inescapable
dangers, terrors, mysteries, and absurdities" of life (Schafer, 1976, p.
35); an awareness of the "loss of opportunities entailed by every
choice and by growth in any direction; . . . [and of] reversal of
fortune" (Schafer, 1976, p. 35); belief in the existence of certainties,
absolutes, and clear divisions between right and wrong, good and
evil, hero and villain, and so forth; lack of belief in the possibility of
justice, reform, progress, perfectibility, happy endings, reconciliations, redemption, and rebirth; and refusal to accept these circumstances.

- *Central Problem.* "How to avoid or minimize the danger and
  absurdities of life which threaten to overwhelm even the greatest
  human beings" (McAdams, 1985, p. 92).
- *Nature of Obstacles.* Internal failings, splits, ambivalences, polarities;
  and uncontrollable forces that "lie outside the governance of reason
  or justice" (Steiner, 1961, pp. 6–7), and "which can neither be fully
  understood nor overcome by rational prudence" (p. 8).
- *Preferred Solution.* Articulated emotion; and reflective thought
  (Schafer, 1976), with the goal of good reality testing, or seeing *the
  truth*, no matter how dark.
- *Outcome.* Irreparable disaster or catastrophe.

The lives of Oedipus and Hamlet, Martin Luther King, Jr., and John F.
Kennedy embody the tragic worldview. Although heroic in stature, they
never had a chance; they were doomed by unsympathetic forces beyond
human control. Cormac McCarthy expressed this central element of the
tragic sensibility in his 1994 novel *The Crossing*: "There is no order in the
world save that which death has put there" (cited in Hass, 1994, p. 38).

The comic and tragic sensibilities are true opposites, and not only in
their emotional valence (optimism versus pessimism) and their differential expectation of reasonable, controllable causation. They are also
opposite in the relative value each places on thought versus emotion.
Horace Walpole expressed this latter insight when he wrote, "The world
is a comedy to those that think, a tragedy to those who feel."

The tragic sensibility shares the following features with the romantic:
a large conception of the individual and the significance of life; a dualistic,
absolutistic assessment of right and wrong, good and evil, hero and
villain; the expectation that there will be obstacles in one's path; and an
emphasis on the articulation of emotion in response to life's obstacles.

The tragic sensibility differs from the romantic in that the tragic: views
obstacles as primarily internal and uncontrollable (as in the tragic flaw
of ancient and modern heroes), rather than as external and controllable;
emphasizes the articulation of reason rather than fantasy as a preferred

mode of meeting life's obstacles; eschews belief in perfection and resolution; but refuses to accept these limitations with detachment.

The Ironic Sensibility

Where the tragic vision is heavy and dark, the ironic is at once light and dark. From the ironic perspective, it is an undeniable fact that life presses on nearly everyone a mix of good and ill. But acceptance, rather than defiance, is the prescribed response to this fact. The ironic sensibility has the following features:

- *View of Time.* Time is linear: "Time is seen to be continuous and irreversible; choices once made are made forever; a second chance cannot be the same as the first; life is progression toward death without rebirth" (Schafer, 1976, p. 36); or time entails cyclic but futile phases of advance and decline.
- *Central Attitudes.* "Responsiveness to the great dilemmas, paradoxes, ambiguities, and uncertainties pervading human action and subjective experience" (Schafer, 1976, p. 35); "a sense of the inescapable dangers, terrors, mysteries, and absurdities" of life (Schafer, 1976, p. 35); an awareness of the "loss of opportunities entailed by every choice and by growth in any direction; . . . [and of] reversal of fortune" (Schafer, 1976, p. 35); rejection of certainties, absolutes, clear divisions between good and bad, right and wrong, hero and villain, and so forth; belief in and detached acceptance of the impossibility of perfection or resolution.
- *Central Problem.* "How to solve some of the mysteries of life, to gain some perspective on the chaos, ambiguities, and contradictions of human living" (McAdams, 1985, p. 93).
- *Nature of Obstacles.* Internal failings, splits, ambivalences, polarities; and uncontrollable forces that "lie outside the governance of reason or justice" (Steiner, 1961, pp. 6–7), and "which can neither be fully understood nor overcome by rational prudence" (Steiner, 1961, p. 8).
- *Preferred Solution.* Reflective thought, with the goal of good reality testing, or seeing *the truth* (Schafer, 1976); and detached acceptance.
- *Outcome.* Mixed blessings, compromises, tradeoffs.

The ironic sensibility is a modest, unemotional one with a keen appreciation of limitation, irregularity, ambiguity, subjectivity, and uncertainty. In these ways it could be called postmodern.

The ironic sensibility shares with the tragic these features: viewing time as linear and thus irreversible; viewing obstacles as primarily due to internal and uncontrollable forces; valuing good reality testing: "We see—and value seeing—that which we are most powerfully disinclined to see" (Schafer, 1976, p. 46), that is, loss, injustice, decline, destruction, death.

But the ironic differs from the tragic worldview in that the ironic has a more modest conception of the individual and of life; eschews absolutistic and dualistic views of right and wrong, good and evil, hero and villain; prescribes detached acceptance of the impossibility of perfection; expects neither unequivocally happy endings (as in the comic and the romantic visions) nor unmitigated catastrophes (as in the tragic vision), but mixed blessings, compromises, and trade-offs.

If the romantic, comic, tragic, and ironic worldviews were buildings, they would be a castle, a little red schoolhouse, a mausoleum, and a cozy housetrailer, respectively. If the romantic, comic, tragic, and ironic worldviews were movies, they would be *Casablanca* (Wallis & Curtiz, 1943), *It's a Wonderful Life* (Capra, 1946), *Apocalypse Now* (Coppola, 1979), and *Kiss of the Spider Woman* (Weisman & Babenco, 1985), respectively. If the romantic, comic, tragic, and ironic worldviews were books, they would be Dickens' *Great Expectations*, almost any mystery, Tolstoy's *Anna Karenina*, and Virginia Woolf's *Mrs. Dalloway*, respectively. In sum, these sensibilities—the romantic, comic, tragic, and ironic—represent four different (though overlapping) lenses through which people characteristically perceive, organize, remember, interpret, and emotionally experience the raw material of life.

The four worldviews have been successfully measured by McAdams (1985), though his conceptualizations and mine are not identical. McAdams's measures were based on separate interviews with 50 individuals. In tape-recorded interviews, each individual related his or her life story and philosophy of life. Each taped interview was then coded as a whole for the strength of each of the worldviews (which McAdams and Frye, 1957, called *mythic archetypes*) by two trained raters. (For more detail regarding measurement, see McAdams, 1985, chapters 2 and 3, and appendix B.)

It seems likely that the worldviews distribute themselves differentially among different times, cultures, and subcultures. The romantic and tragic worldviews give off a decided whiff of the 19th century, the modern comic worldview echoes the Enlightenment, and the ironic worldview is most postmodern.

I suspect that though there may be a few closet or defended romantics among people in the United States, the unabashed, unadulterated romantic sensibility is relatively uncommon in the culture I know best, fin de siecle America. Likewise, individuals with a long-standing, predominantly tragic worldview are also probably somewhat rare in this militantly pragmatic and optimistic culture. In this culture we tend to think of the romantic and tragic worldviews as perilously close to mental illness—especially in their uncompromising "grandiosity" and emotionality. Here the comic and ironic worldviews prevail.

Certainly Western intellectual fashion has recoiled from the romantic and tragic worldviews and embraced the comic.[5] The Enlightenment school of thought as well as its direct heir, modern science, share the central hallmarks of the comic vision, including the guiding convictions that "in reason can be found a universally applicable standard for judging validity and worth" (Shweder, 1984, p. 27); the tyranny of superstition, convention, emotion, and absolutistic dogma can and ought to be overthrown by reason; reflection is rather a waste of time unless it serves to mobilize action; and if these three propositions govern human affairs, progress will follow.

The ironic worldview seems to be competing with the comic for dominance in the late–20th-century United States. Sure signs of the ironic sensibility have materialized in science, literature, and popular culture. Ideas like quantum theory, bounded rationality, fuzzy logic, and chaos theory rely on a deeply ironic worldview in which limitation, irregularity, uncertainty, ambiguity, and complexity replace the more comic elements of epistemological certainty and precision. In the literary domain, postmodernism, deconstruction, reader-response criticism, and personal criticism insist on the indeterminacy and subjectivity of meaning. The author of a book review cleverly titled "Deride and Conquer" portrays modern culture itself as deeply ironic: "The cultural style that has emerged in the past decade or so, one that celebrates irony as a way of life, could plausibly be called postmodern. The postmodern hero is street-smart and adwise; he sees through everything; decodes everything, mostly for fun; and is always protected by his ironic detachment" (Lears, 1989, p. 59). For now, though, I am less interested in the correctness of my intuitions regarding the possible temporal and cultural constitution of these sensibilities—and more interested in exploring the possible relationships between and among these sensibilities and counterfactual thought and emotion.

To return to the events of the beginning of this chapter: I thought, as did Dylan, that the loss of his children would be a tragedy for everyone. But I knew his wife, and privately I did not think that loss tragic; so in my conversations with Dylan I focused first on that aspect. Sensing the intensity of his romanticism, I tried to assuage his hopelessness by constructing an argument that fit the romantic framework. I ventured to

---

[5]I am distinguishing here between intellectual and popular fashion. Though culture in the United States does evidence tendencies that are undeniably romantic, such as the hippie elements of the 1960s and the New Age elements of the 1990s, these are arguably intellectually more marginal than the prevailing comic and ironic worldviews.

build on his idea that there is one and only one person in the world that one was meant to marry, suggesting (tentatively, carefully, as the divorce was not final) that *if* it turns out that one married the wrong person, maybe the thing to do is set out on a quest for the right person. Until one finds the perfect person, maybe one *shouldn't* be satisfied. Because I really do not hold this view of marriage, this line of argument probably came across as inauthentic and lame.

I tried other tacks, attempting to suggest how the situation might look from within perspectives other than the romantic. I offered the more comic view that surely there is more than one person in the world one can be happy with. Within this worldview, if it turns out that one is not happy with the person he or she has married, that is sad and regrettable but not an insurmountable problem. There are plenty of other fish in the sea.

I also attempted to get Dylan to see the situation from a more ironic stance. No one is perfect; therefore, marriage always requires some accommodation, some compromise between an impossible ideal and a less-than-ideal reality. In fact, perhaps all happy marriages require both partners to be able to be happy enough with someone who is on the whole a pretty good but not perfect match. From within an ironic framework, as in the comic, there is also more than one person in the world that one can be more or less happy with. It is not particularly surprising and not at all shameful if one is not happy with the person he or she has married or vice versa. In that case, the two can decide either to make do with each other or to find someone else who also will not be perfect but (back to the comic stance) may be a better match.

My comic and ironic propositions appear to have had even less impact than the romantic on Dylan. Seemingly, once his romantic hope for a happy conclusion was dashed, the absolutism shared by the romantic and the tragic sensibilities pulled Dylan over to the tragic worldview. It was as if he were color-blind to worldviews so different from his and could not even begin to imagine a future contrary to his tragic present. If I am not mistaken, Dylan's worldview was so powerful and so impervious to other perspectives that it contributed to his death.

WORLDVIEWS, COUNTERFACTUAL THOUGHT, AND EMOTION

One of the defining features of these worldviews, then, is their significant role in emotional life. This can be further illustrated by focusing now on how a single emotion, regret, may be experienced quite differently depending on the worldview within which it is set (see Table 8.1 for a summary).

TABLE 8.1
Four Modes of Experiencing Regret

Feature	Romantic	Comic	Tragic	Ironic
View of Time	Ahistorical, atemporal: sudden, discontinuous leaps	Cyclic: second chances	Linear, irreversible	Linear, or futilely cyclic
Central Attitudes	Belief in striving against obstacles Belief in certainties and absolutes Belief in progress, perfectibility, and heroic rebirth following struggle	Belief in progress, perfectibility	Expectation of dangers, dilemmas, loss Refusal to accept these facts Belief in certainty and absolutes	Expectation of dilemma, ambiguity, uncertainty, loss Detached acceptance of these facts
Central Problem	How to venture heroically	How to maximize happiness and minimize pain	How to avoid the worst fates	How to gain some perspective
Nature of Obstacles	External, controllable	External, controllable	Internal, uncontrollable	Internal, uncontrollable
Preferred Solutions	Action Emotion Fantasy	Exercise of reason Action	Seeing the truth Feeling the truth	Seeing the truth Accepting the truth
Outcome	Triumph	Happy resolution	Irreparable loss	Compromises, trade-offs, mixed blessings

Note. From *Regret: The Persistence of the Possible* (p. 64), by J. Landman, 1993, New York: Oxford University Press. Reprinted with permission.

Regret can be briefly defined as the feeling of distress when one is sorry about something that one judges to have gone awry. It is a superordinate emotion that subsumes certain features of disappointment, sadness, remorse, and guilt but can also be distinguished from these (cf. Landman, 1993). Regret is more than a cognitive appraisal: It is an emotion. Moreover, regret is more than a neural or hormonal state of dysphoric arousal: It is also the catch at the heart and the stiffening of the muscles of the throat that Woolf described in her protagonist, Mrs. Dalloway. Regret bridges the cognitive and the emotional; the interior and the exterior; the past, present, and future; the actual and the possible.

Regret undoubtedly plays an important role in counterfactual thought, when someone compares reality with its alternatives. Whenever people wonder what might have been had they taken one job rather than another or taken up residence somewhere other than where they live, or what they would do if they won the lottery, they are engaging in counterfactual thinking—and potentially experiencing regret for a less-than-ideal status quo.

The *romantic* experience of regret is an intensely felt experience, in that the romantic sensibility is one that very much values emotional engagement and elaboration. Romantic regret arises out of the conviction that misfortune, mistakes, shortcomings, and transgressions are inevitable aspects of the heroic quest that is life. The hope is that they are obstacles that will in the end be overcome by struggle; moreover, the individual will be a better person—a hero—for having struggled against and triumphed over such obstacles. When things have gone awry, from within the romantic sensibility it is assumed to be possible to seize the opportunity to create something grand. The experience of regret within the romantic sensibility is metaphorically something like the act of building a magnificent bridge (a metaphorical Bridge of Sighs?) at last linking what is with what might yet be.

From within the *comic* worldview, it makes no sense to cry over spilled milk; for the comic experience of regret is one in which misfortune, mistakes, shortcomings, and transgressions are assumed to come out all right in the end. Negative events and their resultant regret are but brief interruptions on the way to resolution, rather like brief stops for gas or food on the way to a vacation destination. Again metaphorically, regret in the comic mode is just a temporary blip of emotion on the essentially regular and sensible screen of life. In the comic construction, one takes comfort in the assumption of the possibility of second chances to undo and redo the mistakes of the past.

From within the *tragic* perspective, regrets are as irremediable as they are unforeseeable, inevitable, and catastrophic. The tragic experience of regret is qualitatively the most painful in that it arises out of convictions that some mistakes and misfortunes are unavoidable and irremediable. Because of the dualistic thinking, priority given to "seeing the truth" rather than to seeking emotional equilibrium and the characteristic refusal to accept less than perfection, the individual with a tragic sensibility may also experience regret more frequently than others do.

From within the *ironic* worldview, regret is an inevitable but not catastrophic human experience occasioned by the facts that every human gain necessarily entails loss, every human virtue vice, and . . . every silver lining its cloud. For these reasons, along with its central feature of emotional detachment, ironic regret is likely to be significantly less intense than romantic or tragic regret. Because of the ironic expectation of mixed outcomes and its disavowal of absolutes, regret is also likely to be less frequent for the ironic sensibility.

By now it is fairly well established that counterfactual thoughts affect feelings and other forms of thought. I suggest a prior link in the chain: Worldviews may affect counterfactual thinking and therefore more specific feeling, thinking, and acting. Theorists and researchers have suggested that the relationship between counterfactual thought and affect depends on factors such as the salience and likelihood of occurrence of antecedents of an outcome, whether the antecedents take the form of action or of inaction, and the valence and extremity of the valence of the outcome. So far, these factors have been theoretically conceived as external to the individual. A number of these factors, however, can also be construed as internal to the individual, or as instantiating the manner in which the individual *relates* to the world. Perhaps most obvious, many probability judgments are clearly subjective (Dawes, 1988; Kahneman, Slovic, & Tversky, 1982). Salience, exceptionality, valence, and extremity of affective response are also, as I argue here, partly a construction of the individual. For this reason alone, worldviews are a "natural" addition to the investigation of how counterfactual thought and emotion are related. Following are a number of hypotheses based on an integration of previous work on counterfactual thought and emotion with the present framework regarding worldviews. As I was not privy to the specifics of Dylan's counterfactual thinking, other illustrations of these hypotheses are provided.

How Worldviews Shape the Nature of Counterfactual Thoughts

Recently, Geoffrey C. Ward argued in *The New York Times Book Review* (1993) that the weight of the evidence belies conspiracy-theory explanations of the murder of John F. Kennedy. In an article entitled "The Most Durable Assassination Theory: Oswald Did It Alone," Ward outlines precisely how individual madness and bad luck intersected on that November day in Dallas to bring about the murder. In the process, he provides a striking counterfactual analysis (numerals added):

> The truly frightening thing about what happened [Oswald's murder of Kennedy] . . . is not the notion that vast, murky forces somehow rule our lives, but that not even the greatest among us is safe when madness and sheer chance happen to converge.
>
> [1] Had the Cubans granted Oswald his visa, for example, he would probably have been in Havana by November, and we would not now know his name.
>
> [2] Had any one of four potential employers to whom he applied for a job when he got back to Texas decided to hire him, he would not have had the opportunity to fire upon the motorcade.
>
> [3] Had a Dallas neighbor not innocently suggested to Marina's closest friend that there might be a job for Oswald at the Texas School Book Depository; [4] had the friend not then followed up with a helpful telephone call to the man in charge; and [5] had that man—who had openings at two different locations—not happened to give Oswald the job at Dealey Plaza, he would never have gained the vantage point he needed.
>
> And, it should be emphasized, Oswald won access to that sniper's perch more than a month before he could have known that the parade route would pass beneath it, an awkward fact understandably left out of most books alleging that sinister forces conspired to put him within range. (pp. 17–18)

This passage illustrates a number of principles of counterfactual thought and emotion and their possible links with worldview.

Counterfactuals to Exceptional Versus Routine Antecedents. Previous research on counterfactual thought has established that exceptional or abnormal features of reality are generally more likely to be changed or mentally undone than routine features. In other words, when people imagine how reality might be altered, changes toward the more usual are more likely than changes toward the less usual (Kahneman & Tversky, 1982; Landman & Manis, 1992; Roese & Olson, 1993b; Wells & Gavanski, 1989; Wells, Taylor, & Turtle, 1987; but see Wells & Gavanski, 1989, and Markman, Gavanski, Sherman, & McMullen, 1993, for intriguing complications of the general pattern). This pattern first emerged in research conducted by Kahneman and Tversky (1982), who had participants read a written scenario about a hypothetical Mr. Jones who is described as having been killed in a traffic accident either after having taken an unusual route home from work or after having left work at an unusual time. Participants were asked what they would imagine occurring differently in such a scenario. Participants' counterfactual thinking more often mentally restored the scenario to a usual state than constructed an unusual state; for example, they often imagined Mr. Jones' taking his usual route home that night or leaving the office at his usual time. This pattern appears to describe most people, which is what would be expected if it is the case that most people in this culture hold a predominantly comic or ironic worldview, in which really drastic changes are not expected. Ward's (1993) analysis seems to fit this description fairly well, too. How maddeningly easy it is to mentally undo any one of the five elements he specifies, thereby converting the set of events to a less exceptional scenario than the actual scenario that placed Oswald in just the right place at just the right time to murder a young President.

Due to their penchant for expecting sudden, discontinuous, and surprising changes in circumstances, however, those with the romantic or tragic worldview may prove an exception to the rule. It is conceivable also that there may be interactions between worldview and valence of outcome. If so, individuals with predominantly comic and ironic worldviews may prefer mental alteration in the direction of the routine regardless of outcome valence. But individuals who hold a romantic worldview, with its penchant for radical changes, may prove more likely than others when something goes *wrong* to imagine exceptional changes ("If only Mr. Jones had never learned to drive" or "If only the driver of the other car had never been born," perhaps). Moreover, those with a tragic worldview may show this pattern more than anyone else even when things go *right*. This last hypothesis may appear nonsensical or irrational insofar as it seems to violate the rule of self-protective psychological functioning. The tragic worldview, however, can provide its own kind of cold comfort in preparing the individual for the worst.

Counterfactuals to Action Versus Inaction. Apparently people find it easier to imagine inaction as an alternative to action than to imagine action alternatives to inaction (Gleicher et al., 1990; Kahneman & Miller, 1986). On this dimension, Ward's (1993) passage provides a mix of anecdotal confirmation and disconfirmation. The first two counterfactuals (had the Cubans granted Oswald a visa or had one of the four potential employers to whom he applied for a job when he returned to Texas hired him) fail to support the rule in that they substitute one action for another. The last three counterfactuals, however, (had a Dallas neighbor not suggested to Marina's closest friend the possibility of a job for Oswald at the Texas School Book Depository; had the friend not followed up with a phone call to the employer; and had that man not given Oswald the job at Dealey Plaza) do appear to construct inaction as counterfactual alternatives to action and thereby follow the predicted pattern. Taken as a whole, this passage only very slightly favors the hypothesis of greater availability of inaction than of action as counterfactuals to reality.

The original norm theory explanation of this pattern entailed the idea that inaction is more "normal" than action (Kahneman & Miller, 1986). Later explanations suggest that the pattern is better accounted for by the greater salience of action than of inaction (Landman, 1987, 1993; Roese & Olson, chapter 1). The conceptual framework outlined here is compatible with either explanation; it implies that from within the romantic and comic worldviews, problem-solving action is more salient (or less abnormal) than from within the ironic and tragic worldviews. As a consequence, it is possible that the dominance of counterfactuals to action (relative to inaction) may characterize to a lesser degree or not at all those who hold a romantic or comic worldview.

Ward's (1993) passage could also be framed in terms of additive, subtractive, and substitutive counterfactual structures (Roese & Olson, 1993b). Imagining Cuba's granting Oswald a visa could be construed as an *addition*, a reconstruction of reality by adding a new element. Imagining the neighbor's not passing on word of the fatal job opening, the friend's not following up with a phone call to the employer, and the employer's not hiring Oswald are examples of *subtractive counterfactuals*, reconstructing reality by deleting existing elements. Furthermore, imagining any of the four other employers, rather than the Texas School Book Depository, hiring Oswald is a *substitutive counterfactual*, in which an addition replaces a subtraction. (Ward's passage does not by itself, however, show the previously observed pattern of more additive than subtractive counterfactuals in response to negative events [Roese & Olson, 1993b].)

Counterfactuals to Positive Versus Negative Outcomes. Although the evidence is at this time mixed, there is some support for the supposition that counterfactuals to negative outcomes are more frequently and spontaneously generated than counterfactuals to positive outcomes (Gleicher et al., 1990; Roese & Olson, 1993a; 1993b).

Conceivably the inconclusiveness of the evidence may be explained not only by methodological factors (Roese & Olson, 1993b) but also by differential distributions of worldviews in the various samples. Samples with a preponderance of individuals with ironic or tragic sensibilities may produce significantly different patterns from samples of individuals with predominantly romantic or comic sensibilities. At the extreme, it could be that regardless of actual outcome, catastrophe may be as salient to the tragic sensibility as happy endings are to the comic and romantic sensibilities and as trade-offs are to the ironic sensibility.

Upward Versus Downward Counterfactuals. Previously researchers have generally concluded that imagined improvements of reality (*upward counterfactuals*) are more spontaneously generated than imagined deteriorations of reality (*downward counterfactuals*) (Gavanski & Wells, 1989; Gleicher et al., 1990; Landman, 1987; Landman & Manis, 1992; again see Markman et al., 1993, for a complication). As Roese and Olson (1993a; 1993b) point out, although negative outcomes are likely to stimulate upward counterfactuals and positive outcomes to stimulate downward counterfactuals, the two dimensions (outcome valence and direction of counterfactual) are conceptually and experientially independent.

It seems a likely hypothesis that generating upward counterfactuals may prove most characteristic of those with a comic or romantic worldview, insofar as they spend more time than others thinking about how the world could be better. The romantic penchant for fantasy suggests that the romantic individual may even exceed the comic in generating upward counterfactuals. Perhaps those with a tragic sensibility may spontaneously generate more downward counterfactuals than anyone else. When individuals with the tragic sensibility view U.S. presidents in a crowd, they may be more haunted than the rest by mental images or forecasts of assassination. At an extreme, such individuals may actually reverse the usual pattern, more readily imagining deteriorations than improvements to reality. An ironic worldview would be expected to induce a pattern midway between the comic and tragic, one in which the individual is equally likely to think that things could be better or worse.

How Worldviews Shape the Nature and Intensity of Emotional Experience

Ward's (1993) passage also illustrates a number of ways that counterfactual thought may be related to emotion, as well as ways in which this relationship can be colored by worldview.

Counterfactual Thoughts as Amplifiers of Emotion. At the most general level, the passage illustrates the idea that emotional reactions to reality can be "blunted or exaggerated by the consideration of counterfactual alternatives to reality" (Gleicher et al., 1990, p. 293). I know the first time I read it, I found the passage absolutely appalling. The listing of explicit counterfactual alternatives to the reality of Oswald's having been at the place he was on November 22, 1963 greatly augmented my emotional reaction to that reality. It figuratively reopened the old wound of grief and regret over the assassination and poured hot oil into it.

This effect may, however, be mediated by worldview. One possibility is that the effect is limited to those whose worldviews render them more open to emotional experience, that is, those with a romantic or tragic sensibility. A less strong hypothesis is that the emotional amplification effect is just more pronounced for those with a romantic or tragic sensibility than for those with a comic or ironic sensibility.

Salience of Counterfactual Routes to Outcome. Before I read Ward's (1993) passage, the might-have-beens concerning the assassination were ghostly things hovering vaguely in my mind—"If only Oswald had not done it" or "If only he had missed." When I read Ward's passage, however, the might-have-beens took on muscular substantiality and rudely shoved their way into my imagination. This antecedent-based reaction is consistent with Roese and Olson's formulation (chapter 1). Moreover, learning that so many antecedents of the assassination could have so easily occurred differently greatly augmented the regret and sadness.

In this vein, results of previous research indicate that emotional reactions are more extreme when the contrast between the reality and what might have been is more salient. People feel much worse when positive counterfactuals to an adverse event come readily to mind and, similarly, much better when negative counterfactuals to a happy event are salient (Gleicher et al., 1990; Johnson & Sherman, 1990). Ward's (1993) passage makes forcefully salient some plausible counterfactual routes entailed in Oswald's life in late 1963. As a consequence, the emotional reaction to the outcome itself is magnified.

Again, it has not yet been tested whether this effect is entirely situational or whether one's worldview might play a role as well. It seems likely that the ironic worldview, with its blasé expectation of trade-offs, would induce relatively little in the way of salient alternatives to reality and therefore relatively little salience-based emotional amplification. Among the other three worldviews, though, the salience of alternatives to reality would depend on outcome valence and direction of counterfactuals, as discussed previously.

Probability. There is the separate matter of Ward's (1993) *interpretation*—that Kennedy's assassination is not plausibly explained by any conspiracy theory. This interpretation delivers the body blow of an inescapably tragic story. It also highlights two slightly different emphases entailed in the tragic worldview. Paradoxically, the more acceptable aspect centers in the assessment that an excruciating "loss of opportunity" and a disastrous "reversal of fortune" (Schafer, 1976, p. 35) occurred when this promising leader was murdered in his prime.

Ward's (1993) refusal to accept conspiracy theory, however, implicates a constellation of the meaning of tragedy that may prove even more troubling to many people, precisely because of their worldview. Ward tells a story in which the tragic hero is confronted with uncontrollable forces that "lie outside the governance of reason or justice" (Steiner, 1961, pp. 6–7) and that "can neither be fully understood nor overcome by rational prudence" (p. 8). Ward offers no solutions, only the bitter medicine of seeing the truth. On both counts (the disaster and the capricious route to the disaster), the story is unrelievedly tragic.

Probability judgments help shape emotional reactions to events. On this score, Gleicher et al. (1990) propose that:

> the extremity of one's affect toward an outcome will be directly proportional to the *judged likelihood of occurrence* (and judged valence) of a counterfactual outcome that has a valence that is different from reality. Thus a person should feel extremely bad if a good alternative outcome is judged as having been quite likely. Alternatively, a person should feel good if an extremely bad counterfactual alternative appears to have been highly probable. (p. 293)

This pattern begins to explain why not everyone reacts to a tragic account tragically: Reality, including the tragic account, is filtered through the lens of a particular sensibility. Probability judgments emerge from one's worldview. People who hold a tragic or ironic worldview *expect* the unpredictable more than those who hold a comic or romantic worldview do. Conceivably, then, there will be a better cognitive match between a tragic or ironic worldview and the kind of arbitrariness and unpredictability insisted on by Ward's (1993) analysis. Therefore, those with a tragic or ironic sensibility may more readily than others intellectually accept Ward's critique of the conspiracy-theory account.

Though individuals whose sensibility is primarily tragic or ironic concur in their judgments of how probable is arbitrariness in life, their characteristic emotional reactions differ enormously. The emotional reaction of the person armed with ironic detachment would by definition be less intense than that of the person with a tragic sensibility. Imagine for a moment two such persons trying to communicate with one another about their feelings in reaction to the assassination of Kennedy. The ironist might try to argue the tragedian out of his or her intense emotional reaction on the grounds that this is simply the way the world works and that the only rational thing to do is to accept it. The individual with the tragic worldview might angrily demand to know why on earth he or she should remain indifferent in the face of the tragedy.

In contrast, because people with comic and romantic sensibilities are presumably taken aback more by such an arbitrary set of events as the Kennedy assassination as explained by Ward (1993), they might actually have the most devastating emotional reactions of all. Armed neither with tragic and ironic expectations of arbitrariness nor with ironic detachment, such individuals might be expected to be highly distressed by and hence highly resistant to Ward's account. By replacing Ward's arbitrary sequence of events with a more "sensible" and predictable script (in terms of organized crime, the Central Intelligence Agency, Lyndon B. Johnson, or whatever), conspiracy theory may offer those allergic to the tragic an effective way to avoid cognitive and emotional engagement with it.

Extremity of Counterfactuals. One's sensibility may also influence how readily one generates counterfactuals extremely different in valence from an actuality. Compared to individuals with the more moderate, less dualistic and absolutistic comic or ironic sensibility, those with an intensely romantic or tragic sensibility, for instance, may tend to generate more polar opposites to reality and, therefore, to experience more intense emotional reactions to reality. Perhaps someone with a romantic sensibility, like Dylan's, for instance, when faced with an unwanted divorce, would be tortured by counterfactual thoughts of supreme marital bliss with that partner. In contrast, the counterfactual thoughts of someone with a comic or ironic sensibility might be less extremely at variance with the reality, for example, might include images of a state of wary detente with that partner.

Action Versus Inaction. A similar process may complicate the previously observed pattern of more extreme emotional reactions to outcomes attained by action than by inaction (Gleicher et al., 1990; Kahneman & Tversky, 1982; Landman, 1987). This pattern may prove most characteristic of individuals who are least given to action, that is, those with ironic or tragic worldviews. In contrast, the relative extremity of the emotional reaction to imagined counterfactuals to action may be modulated for individuals whose worldview is primarily comic or romantic. Because action is more normal, more salient, or both, for these individuals, their emotional reactions to action may prove less intense. (Alternatively, the greater emotionality of romantics may offset the modulating effect of their action orientation. Also, the dampened emotionality of ironists may offset the amplifying effect of their lack of action orientation.)

CONCLUSIONS

Ironically enough, my take on the worldviews is itself utterly postmodern in that their respective accuracy, validity, truth value, or adaptiveness are not the issue for me. Rather, I start from assumptions of indeterminacy, or at least subjectivity, on those issues. Therefore, I am inclined to devote my energies to other issues, such as exploring the ways in which one's worldview could shape the nature and intensity of counterfactual thought and emotion.

As I have conceived them, these worldviews are clearly quite broad; they presumably entail central values, emotion, needs, motives, and behavioral tendencies. Who needs such broad concepts? What do they offer psychologists?

First, this integration of the work on counterfactual thought with a worldview-based framework has produced a number of testable hypotheses capable of contributing to knowledge about the kind of thinking and feeling that is done, not in a vacuum, but in a particular psychological context.

For another thing, these worldviews may aid psychologists in understanding the persistence of and the difficulty of modifying certain patterns of counterfactual thought and their accompanying emotions. Here the thinking of Allport (1954) is helpful. Forty years ago he outlined a similar connection between specific prejudices and what I have called worldviews, or sensibilities. He posited that certain prejudices are learned *by subsidiation* rather than by direct teaching, modeling, conformity with social norms, and so forth. To the extent that specific prejudices fit into (are subsidiary to) what Allport refers to variously as the individual's "philosophy of life" (p. 318), "whole complex value-pattern[s]" (p. 317), "broad values (scheme[s one] lives by)" (p. 317), and "dominant frames of value" (p. 317), they will be especially easy to learn and difficult to unlearn. Conversely, to the extent that specific prejudices *contradict* one's dominant philosophy of life, they will prove especially difficult to learn and easy to unlearn. For example, the individual whose worldview centers on the firm belief in a just world (one in which people deserve what they get and get what they deserve) will find it easier to learn specific prejudices—for example, against the poor or others to whom the world has not been fair—because these particular prejudices are readily subsidiated to that particular worldview. Thereafter, those prejudices that are developed by subsidiation to the individual's worldview will be especially difficult to eradicate.

The principle applies as well to the interrelationships among counterfactual thought, emotion, and worldview. To the extent that specific counterfactual thoughts and emotions are subsidiary to one's worldview, they may be especially readily learned and especially difficult to modify. Conversely, to the extent that specific counterfactual thoughts and emotions fail to fit with one's worldview, they may prove particularly difficult to generate.

I believe that this was the case with Dylan. His romantic view of marriage and his correlative tragic view of divorce and of life after divorce were not merely peripheral opinions; they were central to who he was. Possibly his worldview was so central to who he was that he was unable to generate or to assimilate counterfactual thoughts or emotions that clashed with it, such as the comic thought of a happy life unmarried or a happy marriage with someone other than his first love; or the imagined ironic satisfactions of a good-enough life unmarried or a good-enough life married to someone other than his first love.

In fact, Dylan's romantic sensibility did extend beyond the domain of marriage. His formative teenage years coincided with the American "Camelot" and later with the psychedelic 1960s, and he himself lived the gentle hippie lifestyle for some years. As an adult, he spent his spare time writing (romantic) poetry and making violins. His poetry seems to have been grounded in the romantic assumption of the possibility of a productive interaction among reason and emotion and imagination (Kaplan, 1986). His violin making was a strikingly romantic activity, as well. He passionately educated himself in the details of Stradivarius's choice of woods, techniques, and varnish, with his last goal to duplicate Stradivarius's varnish. In fact, until his life was shattered by the divorce, many of our conversations focused on his latest inroads into Stradivarius's secret and on the latest news about his children. I have known only one other individual as thoroughly romantic as Dylan. On the other hand, I do know many people who seem tough-mindedly unromantic in every domain but one, the domain of love, in which they are hopeless romantics. Just how domain-specific or domain-general is one's worldview and, therefore, how extensively it shapes counterfactual thought and emotion are among the many questions on the subject still unanswered.

Also people's worldviews conceivably may vary in temporal stability, with some worldviews resisting change over time and others changing a good deal. I suspect, for instance, that some people who most adamantly hold the ironic worldview are ex-romantics who have adopted ironic detachment as a self-protective measure in reaction to disillusioning life experiences. If a worldview does change over time, though, it most likely changes to a worldview with overlapping features that are most central to that individual. For example, Dylan's primarily romantic worldview did change, but not into the self-protective ironic view as it typically does in others. It metamorphosed into the tragic view not only because of odious events but also because the elements of grand absolutism and emotional engagement shared by the romantic and tragic views were as central to Dylan's sensibility as the ironic elements of modesty of scale and emotional detachment were foreign to him.

I have become aware, now that it is finished, that the act of writing this chapter may have itself served as an act of mental undoing. At this point in the mourning process, it is curiously comforting to engage in the form of counterfactual thinking that entails imagining Dylan's reading a(nother) version of this analysis, slapping his forehead, and taking away insights that would change his life. If the chapter also serves the function of furthering scholarly attention to the vagaries of counterfactual thought and emotion, so much the better.

ACKNOWLEDGMENTS

I am grateful to Jim Olson, Penny Pierce, and Neal Roese for their very helpful readings of earlier drafts of this chapter. Portions of this chapter were adapted from *Regret: The Persistence of the Possible* (Landman, 1993) by permission of Oxford University Press.

REFERENCES

Allport, G. W. (1954). *The nature of prejudice.* Reading, MA: Addison–Wesley.
Brownstein, R. (1982). *Becoming a heroine: Reading about women in novels.* New York: Viking.
Capra, F. (Producer & Director). (1946). *It's a wonderful life* [Film]. Los Angeles, CA: The Voyager Co.
Coppola, F. (Producer & Director). (1979). *Apocalypse now* [Film]. Hollywood, CA: Paramount Home Video.
Dawes, R. M. (1988). *Rational choice in an uncertain world.* San Diego, CA: Harcourt Brace Jovanovich.
Dostoevsky, F. (1981). *Notes from underground* (M. Ginsburg, Trans.). New York: Bantam. (Original work published 1864)
Frye, N. (1957). *Anatomy of criticism: Four essays.* Princeton, NJ: Princeton University Press.
Gavanski, I., & Wells, G. L. (1989). Counterfactual processing of normal and exceptional events. *Journal of Experimental Social Psychology, 25,* 314–325.
Geertz, C. (1974). *The interpretation of cultures.* New York: Basic Books.
Gleicher, F., Kost, K. A., Baker, S. M., Strathman, A. J., Richman, S. A., & Sherman, S. J. (1990). The role of counterfactual thinking in judgments of affect. *Personality and Social Psychology Bulletin, 16,* 284–295.
Hass, R. (1994, June 12). Travels with a she-wolf. [Review of McCarthy, C. *The Crossing*]. *New York Times Book Review, 1,* 38–40.
Johnson, M. K., & Sherman, S. J. (1990). Constructing and reconstructing the past and the future in the present. In E. T. Higgins & R. M. Sorrentino (Eds.), *Handbook of motivation and cognition: Foundations of social behavior* (Vol. 2, pp. 482–526). New York: Guilford.
Kahneman, D., & Miller, D. T. (1986). Norm theory: Comparing reality to its alternatives. *Psychological Review, 93,* 136–153.
Kahneman, D., Slovic, P., & Tversky, A. (Eds.). (1982). *Judgment under uncertainty: Heuristics and biases.* New York: Cambridge University Press.
Kahneman, D., & Tversky, A. (1982). The simulation heuristic. In D. Kahneman, P. Slovic, & A. Tversky (Eds.), *Judgment under uncertainty: Heuristics and biases* (pp. 201–208). New York: Cambridge University Press.
Kaplan, C. (1986). *Sea changes: Essays on culture and feminism.* London: Verso.
Kleinginna, P. R., & Kleinginna, A. M. (1981). A categorized list of emotion definitions, with suggestions for a consensual definition. *Motivation and Emotion, 5,* 345–379.
Landman, J. (1987). Regret and elation following action and inaction. *Personality and Social Psychology Bulletin, 13,* 524–536.

Landman, J. (1993). *Regret: The persistence of the possible.* New York: Oxford University Press.

Landman, J., & Manis, J. D. (1992). What might have been: Counterfactual thought concerning personal decisions. *British Journal of Psychology, 83,* 473–477.

Lears, J. (1989, January 9–16). Deride and conquer [Review of the book *The culture of TV*]. *The Nation,* pp. 59–60.

Markman, K. D., Gavanski, I., Sherman, S. J., & McMullen, M. N. (1993). The mental simulation of better and worse possible worlds. *Journal of Experimental Social Psychology, 29,* 87–109.

McAdams, D. P. (1985). *Power, intimacy, and the life story: Personological inquiries into identity.* Homewood, IL: Dorsey.

Meehl, P. E. (1979). A funny thing happened to us on the way to the latent entities. *Journal of Personality Assessment, 43,* 564–581.

Mendelsohn, G., Weiss, D., & Feimer, N. (1982). Conceptual and empirical analysis of the typological implications of patterns of socialization and femininity. *Journal of Personality and Social Psychology, 42,* 1157–1170.

Miller, N. K. (1991). *Getting personal: Feminist occasions and other autobiographical acts.* New York: Routledge.

Roese, N. J., & Olson, J. M. (1993a). Self-esteem and counterfactual thinking. *Journal of Personality and Social Psychology, 65,* 199–206.

Roese, N. J., & Olson, J. M. (1993b). The structure of counterfactual thought. *Personality and Social Psychology Bulletin, 19,* 312–319.

Rosaldo, R. (1989). *Culture and truth: The remaking of social analysis.* Boston: Beacon.

Schafer, R. (1976). *A new language for psychoanalysis.* New Haven, CT: Yale University Press.

Shweder, R. A. (1984). Anthropology's romantic rebellion against the enlightenment, or there's more to thinking than reason and evidence. In R. A. Shweder & R. A. LeVine (Eds.), *Culture theory: Essays on mind, self, and emotion* (pp. 27–66). New York: Cambridge University Press.

Solomon, R. C. (1993). The philosophy of emotion. In M. Lewis & J. M. Haviland (Eds.), *Handbook of emotions* (pp. 3–15). New York: Guilford.

Steedman, C. K. (1986). *Landscape for a good woman: A story of two lives.* New Brunswick, NJ: Rutgers University Press.

Steiner, G. (1961). *The death of tragedy.* New York: Hill & Wang.

Thomas, D. (1939). *The collected poems of Dylan Thomas.* New York: New Directions.

Tompkins, J. (1987). Me and my shadow. *New Literary History, 19,* 169–178.

Wallis, H. B. (Producer) & Curtiz, M. (Director). (1943). *Casablanca* [Film]. Culver City, CA: MGM/UA Home Video.

Ward, G. C. (1993, November 21). The most durable assassination theory: Oswald did it alone. *New York Times Book Review,* pp. 17–18.

Weisman, D. (Producer) & Babenco, H. (Director). (1985). *Kiss of the spider woman* [Film]. Los Angeles, CA: Charter Entertainment.

Wells, G. L., & Gavanski, I. (1989). Mental simulation of causality. *Journal of Personality and Social Psychology, 56,* 161–169.

Wells, G. L., Taylor, B. R., & Turtle, J. W. (1987). The undoing of scenarios. *Journal of Personality and Social Psychology, 53,* 421–430.

Williams, R. (1977). *Marxism and literature.* New York: Oxford University Press.

Zajonc, R. B. (1980). Feeling and thinking: Preferences need no inferences. *American Psychologist, 35,* 151–175.

9

Some Counterfactual Determinants of Satisfaction and Regret

Thomas Gilovich
Victoria Husted Medvec
Cornell University

Most people are familiar with the parable of the man who was upset because he had no shoes—until he met a man with no feet. The tale is of particular interest to psychologists because it offers a fundamentally *psychological* message: A person's material conditions matter less than how those conditions are phenomenologically experienced.

Research psychologists have extended this truism by articulating some of the most common and powerful determinants of how objective outcomes are subjectively construed. One important factor is how a person's circumstances compare with those of relevant others (Crosby, 1976; Festinger, 1954; Olson, Herman, & Zanna, 1986; Suls & R. Miller, 1977; Suls & Wills, 1991; Taylor & Lobel, 1989). The same three-bedroom house can seem like a shack or a mansion depending on the housing stock on the rest of the block. Another critical determinant of the level of satisfaction with a given outcome is how it compares with expectations (Atkinson, 1964; Feather, 1967; 1969). Owning such a three-bedroom house can induce pride or shame depending on what one had in mind before meeting with a realtor.

This volume is dedicated to a third source of subjectivity—how an outcome compares to imagined counterfactual alternatives. The concern in this case is how outcomes are compared, not to preexisting expectations about what *should* have been, but with after-the-fact representations of what *might* have been (Kahneman & D. Miller, 1986). Learning that the property next door is contaminated with PCBs is upsetting, but less so if it comes with the realization that one almost bought that very same property.

Numerous studies have demonstrated that outcomes that *almost* happened can have a profound effect on a person's satisfaction with the outcomes that were in fact obtained. These studies have generally followed the strategy of holding outcome constant and varying the ease of generating different counterfactual alternatives. For example, Kahneman and Tversky (1982b) asked their participants to contemplate the reactions of two travelers who both missed their scheduled flights, one by 5 minutes and the other by 30 minutes. The outcome is the same—both must wait for the next flight—but it is easier to imagine a counterfactual world in which the first traveler arrives on time. Studies such as this have repeatedly shown that the same outcome can produce strikingly different reactions as a function of the counterfactual alternatives that are considered (Johnson, 1986; Kahneman & D. Miller, 1986; Kahneman & Tversky, 1982a, 1982b; D. Miller & McFarland, 1986; D. Miller, Turnbull, & McFarland, 1990; Turnbull, 1981; Wells & Gavanski, 1989).

The strength of these results suggests, but does not demonstrate, that the effect might be taken even further: Certain counterfactual comparisons might lead those who are objectively *worse* off to feel better than those in a superior position. Indeed, that is the implicit message of the parable with which we began. At one level, the story is about how encounters with the less fortunate can lead people to be more appreciative of their blessings than they were beforehand. At the same time, the implicit message is that those who are touched by such encounters might then derive more from life than those whose material gifts far surpass their own.

"COMING CLOSE" IN OLYMPIC COMPETITION

As an example of how doing better might nevertheless make a person feel worse, consider the mental state of silver and bronze medalists in Olympic competition. By all rights, silver medalists should be more satisfied than bronze medalists because they have performed better. But when one considers the counterfactual alternatives the athletes are likely to entertain, the situation is more complicated. To the silver medalist, the most compelling counterfactual alternative is winning the gold. By finishing just one slot away, the gold can seem well within the silver medalist's counterfactual reach. Furthermore, the intensity of such an unhappy counterfactual comparison is accentuated by the vastly different payoffs that accrue to first- and second-place finishers. In the megabusiness that sports has become, gold medalists often reap tremendous rewards in fame and fortune, whereas it is the rare silver medalist who is able to cash in on his or her accomplishments (Frank & Cook, in press). All of these considerations can lead silver medalists to focus not on what they accomplished but on what they *almost* accomplished.

For bronze medalists, the likely counterfactual comparison brings about a happier result. Bronze medalists have finished one slot away from both the second- and fourth-place finishers, but only one of these alternatives entails much of a difference in hedonic consequences. Finishing second instead of third represents little change because in both cases the person won a medal but failed to capture the coveted gold. The contrast between third and fourth places, however, is more dramatic: Third place earns a medal, whereas fourth place leaves one off the medal stand and out among the pack. Thus, for bronze medalists the consideration of what almost happened puts them in much the same position as the shoeless man who encounters someone with no feet: It induces a deep appreciation of what they have, not a disquieting focus on what they have not.

Do Bronze Medalists Have More Fun?

To examine whether bronze medalists are indeed typically happier with their performance than are silver medalists, we recently analyzed the affective reactions of Olympic medalists at two points in time—just as their performances were completed (and they learned how they had finished) and on the medal stand as they received their medals (Medvec, Madey, & Gilovich, in press). NBC's coverage of the 1992 Summer Olympic games from Barcelona, Spain, was videotaped in its entirety. From this footage, we identified all instances in which bronze and silver medalists were shown as they completed their events or as they received their medals on the medal stand. These segments were then copied onto two stimulus tapes, one of the athletes' immediate reactions as they learned how they had finished and another of the athletes as they appeared on the medal stand. These tapes were then shown to college-student judges who rated the appearance of each athlete on a 10-point "agony-to-ecstasy" scale. We averaged the judges' ratings of each athlete's appearance to create an index of how satisfied he or she appeared. To eliminate any effect of prior knowledge on the part of the raters, we only recruited judges who described themselves as having little interest in or knowledge about sports.

The results are summarized in Table 9.1. As these results show, bronze medalists appeared to be happier than silver medalists both in the im-

TABLE 9.1
Mean Satisfaction Ratings, by Condition

	Medal	
Stimulus Tape	Silver	Bronze
Immediate Reactions		
M	4.8	7.1
SD	1.9	2.0
Medal Stand		
M	4.3	5.7
SD	1.8	1.7
Mean	4.6	6.4

Note. From "When Less Is More: Counterfactual Thinking and Satisfaction Among Olympic Medalists," by V. H. Medvec, S. F. Madey, and T. Gilovich (in press).

mediate aftermath of their performance (Ms = 7.1 and 4.8, respectively) and during the awards ceremony (Ms = 5.7 and 4.3, respectively).[1] In athletics, as in other walks of life, sometimes less is more.

To investigate whether the difference in apparent satisfaction of bronze and silver medalists was due to the hypothesized asymmetry in counterfactual comparisons, we had a similar group of judges view a third videotape from the Olympic games. This tape consisted of interviews of the athletes describing their thoughts about their events and their performance. After witnessing each interview, the judges rated on a 10-point scale the extent to which the athlete in question appeared to be concerned with thoughts of "At least I . . ." versus thoughts of "I almost. . . ." As predicted, the silver medalists appeared to be more focused on what they almost accomplished (M = 5.7) than were the bronze medalists (M = 4.8). Because of this asymmetry in the direction of counterfactual comparison, coming in second place tends to produce less joy than finishing third.[2]

---

[1]It is important to note that these findings are preserved when a potential artifactual explanation is ruled out. Specifically, in certain Olympic events, the competition is structured such that bronze medalists have just won a match or a game whereas silver medalists have just lost. A bronze medalist in wrestling, for example, would have just defeated the fourth-place finisher, and the silver medalist would have just lost to the gold medal winner. One might be concerned that being in the immediate aftermath of victory or defeat could contaminate the comparison of the reactions of bronze and silver medalists. However, the findings we report remained significant when these "just won–just lost" events were deleted from the sample and only those, such as track, swimming, and gymnastics, in which the athletes simply finish first, second, and third, were included.

[2]The three sources of subjective evaluation we discussed earlier—social comparisons, expectations, and counterfactual thoughts—are of course not always independent. A person may be more likely to have counterfactual thoughts about unexpected outcomes than about those that were anticipated, and the nature of a person's counterfactual ideation may involve

What Olympians Undo

To further examine the counterfactual thoughts of Olympic athletes, we obtained permission from the United States Olympic Committee to send a questionnaire to all American silver and bronze medal winners from the Barcelona games. The response rate was surprisingly high (38 of the 54 athletes returned completed questionnaires), and those responding included the likes of Matt Biondi, Janet Evans, and Jackie Joyner-Kersee. Here we were interested in how bronze and silver medalists might counterfactually transform, or undo, the outcome; therefore, one of the questions asked was "What could have changed the outcome of . . . this event?"

How might Olympic athletes undo a performance that falls short of the gold? Do they typically erase something that hindered their performance, or do they tend to add something that would have improved it? Because of previous experiments indicating that *compelling* forces, or mental additions, are more prominent and powerful in people's mental simulations than *restraining* forces, or mental subtractions (Dunning & Parpal, 1989; Hansen & Hall, 1985; Read, 1985, cited in Kahneman & D. Miller, 1986), we expected that our respondents would tend to mentally alter their outcomes by imagining something they could have done to improve their performance. Indeed, Roese and Olson (1993a, 1993b) have shown that people tend to undo failure by adding something that would have led to success.

An examination of how the Olympic athletes chose to undo a second- or third-place finish indicates that they behaved as expected. Of the 25 responses that could be unambiguously scored on this addition–subtraction dichotomy, 20 (80%) involved adding an element that would have

comparisons with other individuals. However, as interrelated as these three processes sometimes are, it is clear that they are distinct phenomena that do not always overlap. In the present case, there are compelling reasons to believe that our Olympic results are the product of counterfactual thinking per se and are not contaminated by parallel effects of expectations or social comparison. Differential expectations cannot explain the observed difference between the reactions of bronze and silver medalists because there is no reason to believe that bronze medalists as a whole tended to exceed their expectations or that silver medalists on average tended to fall short of theirs. To be sure, the sample of silver medalists probably entered the Olympics with higher expectations on average than did the sample of bronze medalists, but they also *performed* better as well. There is no reason to believe that one group systematically over- or underperformed relative to their initial expectations. Social-comparison processes likewise do not offer a plausible alternative interpretation of the results for two reasons. First, there is nothing in social-comparison theory proper that would predict upward social comparison on the part of the silver medalists and downward social comparison on the part of the bronze medalists. Second, social-comparison processes are supposedly engaged under conditions of uncertainty, a feeling that is hardly at its peak *after* a competition with an objective outcome.

improved the athlete's performance.[3] Athletes thought the outcome would have been better, for instance, if only "I had competed in the Pan Am games the year before," "I began my comeback sooner," or "I had more scientific training." Thus, when Olympic bronze and silver medalists think of what might have been, they are more likely to focus on things they could have or should have done rather than on things they should *not* have done.

REGRETS OF OMISSION AND COMMISSION

This tendency to undo failure through additive counterfactuals implies that people may find it easy to think of things they wish they had done in their lives. This, in turn, suggests the possibility that people have more regrets over things they have *not* done in their lives than over things they *have* done. But this suggestion, however sensible it may seem at first glance, runs counter to one of the most celebrated findings in the literature on counterfactual thinking: People apparently regret negative outcomes that stem from commissions, or actions taken, more than equivalent outcomes that stem from omissions, or actions foregone (Gleicher et al., 1990; Kahneman & Tversky, 1982a; Landman, 1987). This is demonstrated most clearly in the following experiment by Kahneman and Tversky (1982a):

> Paul owns shares in Company A. During the past year he considered switching to stock in Company B, but he decided against it. He now finds that he would have been better off by $1,200 if he had switched to the stock of Company B. George owned shares in Company B. During the past year he switched to stock in Company A. He now finds that he would have been better off by $1,200 if he had kept his stock in Company B. Who feels more regret? (p. 173)

Ninety-two percent of the respondents thought that George, who traded stocks, would experience more regret than Paul, who declined to trade. The near unanimity of opinion reveals something clear-cut and important about regrets over omission and commission. People find it easy to imagine how taking an action that one need not have taken would produce tortured thoughts about what could have or should have been. Individuals are thought to "own" their actions more than their inactions, and so an action that leads to negative consequences is considered more

---

[3]An example of a response that could not be reliably scored on this dichotomy was "If only the Olympics were in the U.S."

likely to induce a disquieting sense of "This did not have to be" or "I brought this on myself."

Of course, there is no irreconcilable conflict between these data and the tendency of the Olympic medalists to focus on things they could have or should have done. Kahneman and Tversky's (1982a) data constitute a straightforward demonstration of how *much* people regret omissions and commissions; our Olympic results (and parallel findings by Roese & Olson, 1993a, 1993b) suggest a pattern as to how *many* such regrets people might have. Also, in the research on counterfactual thinking, the consequences of action and inaction are typically held constant for every participant; in our Olympic study, the athletes were left to imagine for themselves the consequences of whatever counterfactuals they generated (Medvec et al., in press).

These numerous differences notwithstanding, we nevertheless believe that these divergent findings reveal something important about regret, and together they provide the clues to a more comprehensive account of this common emotional experience. The key to this broader understanding, we believe, lies in a closer look at the aforementioned differences in method.

Recall that in Kahneman and Tversky's experiment and others like it (Gleicher et al., 1990; Landman, 1987), it is an essential methodological requirement that the consequences of action and inaction are precisely specified. George knows exactly how much his action cost him, and Paul knows the precise cost of his inaction. In cases such as this in which the consequences of action and inaction are equal—and are equally specified—the data clearly show that actions generate more regret than inactions, at least initially. But many real-life examples are not like this, of course. Obtaining a full account of the consequences of one's decisions can be difficult, particularly after a decision *not* to act. We typically see the consequences of our actions much more readily than the consequences of our inactions. When we buy a car, we drive it; when we buy a stock, we follow its performance on the financial page or in quarterly reports to shareholders. We live with the consequences of our actions. In contrast, if we decline to buy a car or pass on the purchase of a stock, we tend to maintain our old ways and, as the literature on selective exposure suggests (Frey, 1986; Sears, 1968), fail to keep up with events on the road not taken. We remain ignorant of the true implications of our inactions and are left with mere speculation about what might have been (see also Davis & Lehman, chapter 13).

As a result, the exact source of regrets of omission and commission are rather different. Regrets of commission center on those bad things that actually happened as a result of one's actions: The car is a lemon; the stock plummets. In contrast, regrets of omission involve those good things that did *not* happen, but one imagines would have happened if only one had acted.[4] The car would have been thrilling; the stock enriching. The consequences of regrets of commission are therefore finite: They are bounded by what actually happened. In contrast, the consequences of inaction are potentially infinite: They are bounded only by the imagination.

One implication of this asymmetry in the perceived consequences of action and inaction (when the consequences are not precisely specified as they typically have been in previous research) is that people may be more troubled by their regrettable inactions and less troubled by their regrettable actions than a simple rendering of previous research in the counterfactual-thinking literature would suggest. However, an even more intriguing possibility is that this asymmetry in perceived consequences may become more pronounced over time and therefore give rise to a systematic temporal pattern to the experience of regret. Because one can always add elements to the list of good things that would have happened if only one had acted, regrets of inaction may become more prominent over time. As the foregone gains accumulate, so too does the level of regret. Regrets of commission, in contrast, are likely to be more stable because of the tighter constraints imposed on the perceived consequences of action—those things that *actually happened* as a consequence of the decision to act. The net result is that in the short term people may regret their actions more than their inactions, just as the literature on counterfactual thinking suggests. Nevertheless, people may come to regret their inactions more in the long run.

What People Regret Most in Their Lives

Although the literature is silent as to whether there is a systematic temporal pattern to the experience of regret, there are suggestions that inactions loom larger in people's regrets than one might have assumed from a simple reading of the work on counterfactual thinking. For example, Kinnier and Metha (1989) asked samples of young (ages 20–29), middle-aged (35–55), and older (64 and above) respondents what they would do differently if they could live over again. The most common regret across all three samples was an inaction: They stated they would have taken

---

[4]This means, of course, that regrets of commission more often involve losses than do regrets of omission. Conversely, regrets of omission more often involve unrealized gains than do regrets of commission. Because losses have more of a hedonic impact than do foregone gains (Kahneman & Tversky, 1979, 1982b; Thaler, 1980), there is another reason, apart from the nature of one's counterfactual thoughts, that people ought to experience greater regret for their unfortunate actions—at least initially. As we discuss later, this pattern may often reverse in the long run.

their "education more seriously and worked harder on it" (p. 186). The same result was obtained in two Gallup polls conducted in 1953 and 1965 (Erskine, 1973). Inactions also predominated in the other most frequently mentioned regrets reported by Kinnier and Metha's (1989) participants— not being more assertive, not taking more risks, not spending more time with family. Interestingly, this same question was also asked of Terman's intellectually gifted respondents in 1986, when they were mostly in their 70s. Their responses revealed a similar emphasis on things they had failed to do in their lives—not finishing college or graduate school, not having been more motivated, and not aiming higher in their careers (Hattiangadi, Medvec, & Gilovich, in press).

Although the findings from these studies support the contention that people's biggest regrets involve their failures to act more than their actions, the data are limited in a number of respects. Most important, the respondents were never actually asked about their regrets. Although asking people what they would do differently if they had another chance is sure to tap into some regrets, it need not. People can look back and seize upon something they should have done differently without any sense of regret or remorse. In addition, asking people what they would *do* differently if they had the chance might have predisposed them to think of inactions: Inactions can be overturned only by doing something, whereas many actions can be undone by not doing something.

To overcome these limitations, and to ascertain more directly what people regret most in their lives, we asked people to tell us about their biggest regrets (Gilovich & Medvec, 1994). Because we were interested in obtaining the regrets of a wide range of people, we interviewed four groups of respondents. Those in three of the groups were interviewed face-to-face. One was a sample of 10 professors emeriti at Cornell University. A second was a group of 11 residents of various nursing homes in upstate New York. A third group consisted of 40 Cornell undergraduate students. The responses of participants in each of these three groups were tape-recorded and later transcribed. Finally, a group of 16 adult clerical and custodial staff members at Cornell were given questionnaires that they returned anonymously through the campus mail.

All respondents were asked (either in person or via questionnaire), "When you look back on your life to this point, what are your biggest regrets?" Those interviewed in person were asked after each response, "Is there anything else you regret?" Those filling out written questionnaires were provided with space for as many as five regrets.

Overall, the 77 respondents described 213 regrets. Each of these regrets was scored by two judges who were blind to our hypothesis. The judges determined whether each regret stemmed from an action taken, an action foregone, or some circumstance beyond the person's control (e.g., "Having polio as a child"). The judges agreed with one another on 204 of the 213 regrets. The scoring of the remaining nine was resolved by having a third judge, also blind to the hypothesis, cast a decisive vote.[5] A tabulation of the respondents' regrets indicated, as predicted, that regrets of omission predominated: Regrettable failures to act outnumbered regrettable actions by a ratio of nearly 2:1 (63% vs. 37%).

In subsidiary analyses, we examined the relationship between the age and gender of the respondents and the content of their regrets. Although we found no gender difference in the tendency to regret inactions more than actions, we did observe a slight (but not significant) tendency for regrets of omission to increase with age. In particular, 74% of the regrets listed by the two samples with the oldest respondents (the professors emeriti and the nursing-home residents) involved things they had failed to do, as compared to 61% for the two samples with the youngest participants (the students and staff members). We suspect that this latter trend would have been more pronounced had we interviewed even younger respondents. Because the future can seem limitless to the young, things undone are likely to be assigned to a less troublesome category of things yet to be done. Also, it is part of the "job" of being a child to act in ways that lead to trouble in order to determine the limits of the social and physical world. Negative outcomes that stem from their actions are therefore likely to be highly available.

We probed deeper into the precise content of the participants' regrets to determine what they reported regretting most. A categorical breakdown of the findings is presented in Table 9.2. The categorization scheme presented in Table 9.2 was designed to be balanced with respect to the action–inaction dichotomy. For example, because "did not pursue an interest in X" was a commonly mentioned regret, it appears in the inaction category alongside its complementary action, "wasted time on X."

As an examination of the results presented in Table 9.2 indicates, the most common regrets involved inactions such as missed educational opportunities, the failure to "seize the moment," and not devoting enough time and effort to personal relationships. The most common regret of action was to "rush in too soon." Another interesting feature of these data is that no one regretted spending time developing a skill or hobby,

---

[5]We were initially concerned about the difficulty of deciding whether a specific regret should be coded as an action or an inaction. After all, every action implies a corresponding inaction and vice versa. A person who says, "I regret that I joined the Navy when I was 18," may be indicating that he or she regrets the action itself or regrets not doing all the things that joining the Navy prevented him or her from doing. We decided to code each regret according to what the respondents themselves emphasized (in this case the Navy, not the lost opportunities caused by joining the Navy), and by doing so the scoring was both quite easy and, as the results indicate, highly reliable.

TABLE 9.2
Most Common Regrets

Inactions		Actions	
Regret	n	Regret	n
Missed educational opportunities	21	Bad educational choice	3
Failure to seize the moment	21	Rushed in too soon	17
Not spending enough time with friends and relatives	15	Spent time badly	4
Missed romantic opportunity	13	Unwise romantic adventure	10
Not pursuing interest in "X"	11	Wasted time on "X"	0
Missed career opportunity; insufficient effort	7	Bad career decision; wasted effort	3
Not making financial transaction	2	Unwise financial action	6
Miscellaneous inaction	38	Miscellaneous action	32
Total	128	Total	75

Note. An additional 10 regrets dealt with events outside the person's control and thus lie outside the action–inaction dichotomy. From "The Temporal Pattern to the Experience of Regret," by T. Gilovich and V. H. Medvec (1994).

even when the skill was no longer used or the hobby no longer pursued. No one reported any misgivings about time spent learning how to golf or collecting stamps, even though, as adults, they had given up golf and the stamp collection no longer held interest. This result compares to the 11 entries in the corresponding category, "Not pursuing an interest in X." This difference nicely illustrates our overall result: When people look back on their lives, it is those things that they have not done that produce the most regret.

We observed a similar emphasis on regrets of omission in additional studies based on different methodologies. For example, we conducted a telephone survey in which a random sample of adults in the Chicago metropolitan area were asked to think about their biggest regret of action and their biggest regret of inaction in their entire lives. They were then asked to specify which they regretted more. As anticipated, a large majority (70%) said that their failure to act was more regrettable (Gilovich & Medvec, 1994).

The Temporal Pattern to the Experience of Regret

These results indicate that regrets of omission loom larger in people's lives than do regrets of commission. How can this be reconciled with earlier work on counterfactual thinking that obtained the opposite result (Gleicher et al., 1990; Kahneman & D. Miller, 1986; Kahneman & Tversky,

1982a; Landman, 1987)? As mentioned earlier, we believe that both sets of findings are valid and that both reveal something important about the experience of regret. In particular, they suggest that there may be a consistent temporal pattern to the experience of regret. As the results of previous research indicate (Kahneman & Tversky, 1982a), regrets of commission generate more troublesome thoughts about what might have been and are therefore particularly intense—at least in the short term. Nevertheless, partly because of an ever-widening asymmetry in the perceived consequences of action and inaction, regrets of omission are likely to become more prominent in the long run. Over time, then, the regret "curves" may cross: Commissions may generate more regret initially, whereas omissions may be regretted more in the long run.

We conducted two studies in an effort to find evidence for such a temporal pattern. In the first study (Gilovich & Medvec, 1994), participants were presented with the following scenario:

> Dave and Jim do not know each other, but both are enrolled at the same elite East Coast university. Both are only moderately satisfied where they are and both are considering transferring to another prestigious school. Each agonizes over the decision, going back and forth between thinking he is going to stay and thinking he will leave. They ultimately make different decisions: Dave opts to stay where he is, and Jim decides to transfer. Suppose their decisions turn out badly for both of them: Dave still doesn't like it where he is and wishes he had transferred, and Jim doesn't like his new environment and wishes he had stayed. (p. 360)

The participants were then asked, in either a between-subjects or within-subjects format: 1) Who do you think would regret his decision more upon learning that it was a mistake? and/or 2) Who do you think would regret his decision more in the long run?

The results were the same for both formats: Overall, a vast majority of the respondents (76%) thought that Jim, the person who regretted doing something, would experience more regret in the short term—i.e., upon learning it was a mistake. When asked about the long term, however, the majority (63%) thought that Dave, who regretted *not* doing something, would experience more regret (Gilovich & Medvec, 1994). As anticipated, people's assessments of the experience of regret seem to vary with temporal perspective.

We also obtained evidence consistent with such a temporal pattern in a study that went beyond the scenario methodology and examined people's own real-life regrets (Gilovich & Medvec, 1994). In particular, we had a group of adult participants complete a questionnaire in which they were asked to recall (but not record) their single most regrettable action and inaction from both the past week and from their entire lives. Then, for each time period, they were asked to indicate which they regretted more, the action or the inaction. As in the previous study, the participants' responses depended on the time period under consideration. When focused on the past week, the sample was rather evenly split between those who most regretted their actions (53%) and those who most regretted their failures to act. Looking back over their entire lives to that point, however, a substantial majority of the participants (84%) reported greater regret for what they had failed to do (Gilovich & Medvec, 1994). Once again, regrettable inactions loom larger in the long run than they do in the short term.

CAUSES OF THE TEMPORAL PATTERN TO THE EXPERIENCE OF REGRET

Asymmetries in Perceived Consequences

We began our speculations about a possible temporal pattern to the experience of regret by noting the implications of an asymmetry in the perceived consequences of regrettable actions and inactions. The elements of regrets of omission (i.e., good things that would have happened if one had acted) are potentially infinite: They are limited only by the imagination. In contrast, regrets of commission are often finite: They are limited by the unfortunate things that actually happened as a result of one's actions. We collected data in support of this proposed asymmetry in perceived consequences (Gilovich & Medvec, 1995). In one study, we asked a sample of adults to think of their greatest regret of action and their greatest regret of inaction. Without describing each regret, they then rated each one on a 10-point scale indicating how different "... your life would be or would have been had you done what you regret not doing (had you not done what you regret doing)." As anticipated, the perceived consequences of inaction were greater: The average rating of how much participants thought their lives would change by undoing their regrettable inactions was significantly greater ($M = 6.8$) than the average rating of how much their lives would change by undoing their regrettable actions ($M = 4.8$).

In a second study, we likewise asked participants to think of their greatest regret of action and their greatest regret of inaction. In this study, instead of rating the perceived consequences of each regret, the participants described into a tape recorder what they thought were the damaging consequences of each regret (i.e., the underlying details or *reasons* why each decision was regrettable). The results were consistent with the postulated asymmetry in perceived consequences: Participants spent more time discussing the consequences of their most regrettable inaction ($M = 31$ sec) than those of their most regrettable action ($M = 20$ sec).

Of course, this difference between the perceived consequences of regrettable actions and those of regrettable inactions does not by itself account for the temporal pattern to the experience of regret. But one can derive this temporal pattern by noting that this difference in perceived consequences is likely to become increasingly pronounced over time. After all, one can always add elements to the list of good things that would have happened if only one had acted. As this list grows, so too does the regret over a failure to act. People tend to idealize many aspects of their distant pasts, and their lost opportunities are no exception. Regrets of commission, in contrast, are less likely to intensify with the passage of time because the perceived consequences are constrained by the bad things that actually happened as a result of the action.

Changes in Perceived Consequences

When people add to the list of benefits they think they would have obtained if only they had acted, they accentuate their regrets of omission by increasing the *number* of regrettable elements. In addition, we believe there are parallel changes in the *degree* to which these elements are regretted. Some of these changes stem from psychological processes that increase the sting of regrettable omissions with the passage of time. Others derive from processes that decrease the intensity of regrettable commissions. A complete understanding of regret requires an examination of all of these influences. We begin by discussing how regrets of action diminish with the passage of time.

Identifying Silver Linings. There are many ways that people deal with whatever negative outcomes lie at the core of their regrets (or potential regrets). Sometimes they cope by taking remedial action to negate the troublesome elements. Other times, however, there is no effective action to be taken, and so the effort to come to grips with the problem is confined to the psychological realm. People engage in "psychological work" designed to lessen the pain of the unfortunate event. We propose that people are more likely to engage in effective psychological work for their regrettable actions than for their regrettable inactions. To be sure, people also do things to come to grips with their regrettable inactions, but they tend to do this less consistently and less effectively.

The basis for this claim is easiest to see if one considers the most common means that people employ to lessen the pain of negative events—i.e., noting how much they have learned from the experience. In other words, people acknowledge that the outcome may have been regrettable, but they mentally offset the regret by identifying a silver lining that consists of how much they profited from the experience as well. Such a silver lining ("but I learned so much") is obviously much more likely to apply to regrettable actions than to regrettable inactions. A person typically learns more by doing new things than by adhering to old patterns. In fact, for most inactions the claim that "I learned so much" hardly makes sense. ("I did nothing new, but I learned so much?")

But taking stock of how much one learned from an experience is not the only way to lessen the pain of a negative outcome. There are other silver linings that serve the same purpose. "I can't stand my ex-husband, but without him I never would have had these two wonderful kids." "I know I never should have worked for that company, but that's where I met my wife."

To examine whether people are *generally* more likely to identify offsetting positive elements for their unfortunate actions than for their unfortunate failures to act, we asked a group of 60 adults to think of the single most regrettable action in their lives and the single most regrettable failure to act (Gilovich & Medvec, 1995). Once they had a specific instance of each category in mind, we asked them which regret contained the most significant silver lining. As expected, the vast majority (75%) cited their most regrettable action. The net effect of this process is that the consequences of a regrettable action will tend to be offset, and therefore diminished, with the passage of time. This is less likely to occur for a regrettable failure to act.

Differential Dissonance Reduction. Identifying a silver lining in a dark cloud can be one way of reducing the cognitive dissonance associated with a negative outcome brought on by one's freely chosen action (Aronson, 1969; Brehm & Wicklund, 1970; Cooper & Fazio, 1984; Festinger, 1957; Festinger & Walster, 1964; Wicklund & Brehm, 1976). Indeed, the statement "I learned so much" can be thought of as a generic form of reducing dissonance that can apply to almost any unfortunate course of action. As we have shown, people are more likely to employ such generic dissonance-reduction mechanisms for their regrettable actions than for their regrettable failures to act. Are people also more likely to employ other modes of dissonance reduction for their regrettable actions than for their regrettable inactions, modes more precisely tailored to the specific behavior in question?

There is reason to believe they are. As the literature on counterfactual thinking indicates, people find negative outcomes brought on by their actions initially more aversive than identical outcomes brought on by their failures to act. Also, because inaction is typically viewed as the status quo and action as a departure from the norm (Kahneman & D. Miller,

1986), people generally feel more responsible for their actions than for their inactions. Thus, precisely *because* people's unfortunate actions generate more regret initially and because they engender a greater sense of personal responsibility, they should elicit more cognitive dissonance (and dissonance reduction) than corresponding failures to act (Cooper, 1971; Cooper & Fazio, 1984; Goethals, Cooper, & Naficy, 1979; Hoyt, Henley, & Collins, 1972).

We recently documented this tendency for people to reduce dissonance more for commissions than for omissions (Gilovich, Medvec, & Chen, 1995). This was done through a laboratory analog of the "Monty Hall" problem (Engel & Venetoulias, 1991; Tierney, 1991; vos Savant, 1990a, 1990b, 1991). Participants were recruited for a study of group decision making and told that they would receive, depending on the decisions they made, either a grand prize or a modest prize for their participation. The prizes were hidden in three boxes and, as on Monty Hall's *Let's Make a Deal* television program, the participant's first task was to choose one of the boxes. Two of the boxes were said to contain modest prizes, and one was said to contain the grand prize. After selecting the initial box, the participant confronted a choice of whether to keep his or her unopened box or to trade it in for one of the remaining boxes. However, before the choice was made, the experimenter, like Monty, opened one of the two remaining boxes and revealed a modest prize. The participant's choice, then, was whether to keep his or her box or to exchange it for the remaining, unopened box.

Participants made this latter decision in consultation with another "participant" who was a partner in the group-decision task. Actually, this partner was a confederate whose job was to ensure that the participant chose in accordance with his or her randomly assigned condition—to stay with the original choice or to switch to the other box. The confederate thus influenced the participant's choice when necessary (i.e., when the participant appeared inclined toward selecting the "wrong" box) but did so in a sufficiently subtle way that the participant was unaware of any influence.[6]

---

[6]The "Monty Hall" problem was chosen for this experiment because the choice of either decision—to stay or to switch—can be made to seem compelling, and, therefore, participants could readily be influenced in the direction of their randomly assigned conditions. The correct response to the problem is to switch: By doing so, one has a 67% chance of receiving the grand prize (see below). Participants could thus be induced to switch by leading them to think along the lines of the correct solution to the underlying probability problem. However, most people's intuitions tell them that they ought to stay with their original choice. (The common view is that with only two remaining unopened boxes, there is a 50–50 chance the grand prize is in either one. With no "objective" reason to favor one over the other, most people think it best to stick with their original choice.) Thus, participants could also be induced to keep their original boxes by leading them to follow their intuitions.

The experiment was arranged so that regardless of the participant's choice, he or she received a modest prize (a Cornell bumper sticker) and missed out on the grand prize (an expensive Cornell T-shirt). The experiment was designed to ascertain whether participants who lost out on the grand prize because of an action (i.e., those who switched boxes) would experience more dissonance than those who experienced the same fate after deciding not to act (i.e., those who kept their initial boxes). As in nearly all postdecision dissonance experiments, dissonance was not measured directly; rather, it was inferred from the resulting pattern of dissonance reduction. In particular, would participants in the switch condition come to view the modest prize they received as more attractive than participants in the stay condition? To find out, participants were asked to specify the least amount of money they would accept in exchange for the bumper sticker.

The results are shown in Figure 9.1. Participants who switched boxes and received the bumper sticker demanded significantly more money in exchange than did those who received the same prize by staying with their original choice. Thus, regrettable actions seem to generate more dissonance—and more dissonance reduction—than do regrettable failures to act. The responses of both groups were also compared to those of participants in a control condition whose "decisions" were determined randomly. As dissonance theory would predict, these participants, who had no reason to feel personally responsible for their outcomes, valued the bumper sticker least of all.

One aspect of this experiment that merits further discussion concerns the relative ease of inducing participants to stay or switch. Because people believe there is a 50–50 chance that the grand prize is in either unopened box (Engel & Venetoulias, 1991; Tierney, 1991; vos Savant, 1990a; 1990b; 1991) and because they fear the prospect of giving up the winning box (see Miller & Taylor, chapter 11), most will prefer to keep the box they initially selected. Thus, inducing a participant in the stay condition to keep his or her box should have been easier than inducing a participant

---

To understand why the correct solution is to switch boxes, consider the following: A person's chance of initially selecting the box with the grand prize is obviously 33%. Because the person already knows that the "host" can only open a box containing a modest prize (uncovering the grand prize would eliminate the dilemma), nothing is really learned by revealing the contents of one of the boxes. Since nothing has changed, the chances that the person's original box contains the grand prize is still 33%, and therefore the person should switch to the other box that has a 67% chance of containing the grand prize. A more compelling account of the correct solution can be obtained by simply listing all combinations of: 1) the person's choice of initial box, 2) the host's choice of which of the two remaining boxes to open, and 3) the person's choice to stay or to switch. Such a list reveals that one wins 67% of the time when one switches and only 33% of the time when one stays (see Engel & Venetoulias, 1991; Tierney, 1991; vos Savant, 1990a, 1990b, 1991).

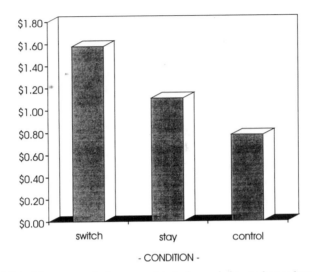

FIG. 9.1. Mean amount of money subjects demanded to exchange bumper sticker, by condition. Copyright 1995 by the Society for Personality and Social Psychology, Inc. Adapted from "Omission, Commission, and Dissonance Reduction: Overcoming Regret in the 'Monty Hall' Problem," by T. Gilovich, V. H. Medvec, and S. Chen (1995).

in the switch condition to trade it in. This raises the concern that participants in the switch condition might have experienced more dissonance, not because they engaged in commission rather than in omission, but because by acting at variance with their initial inclinations they performed a more counterattitudinal, or dissonant, act.

There are at least two reasons for rejecting this alternative interpretation, however. First, for many participants it was possible to ascertain whether they initially wanted to stay or switch, before any input from the confederate. We were thus able to compare the results from participants whose ultimate choice matched their initial inclinations with those from participants who had to be led in a particular direction. The results of this comparison did not support the alternative interpretation: Participants who initially wanted to stay but switched did not value the bumper sticker more than did those who were inclined to switch all along. Similarly, participants who initially wanted to switch but stayed did not value it more than did those who wanted to stay from the beginning. The second reason for doubting this alternative interpretation is that it is equally plausible that the difference in inducing participants to stay or to switch would produce the *opposite* pattern of results. The fact that we had to exert more effort to induce participants to switch should have made participants in the switch condition feel less responsible for the outcome than those in the stay condition. With a lessened sense of responsibility (Cooper & Fazio, 1984; Wicklund & Brehm, 1976), there should have been less dissonance, and hence less dissonance reduction, in the switch condition.

In radically condensed form, then, the results of this experiment symbolize the proposed temporal pattern to the experience of regret. Negative outcomes that stem from people's direct actions are apparently experienced as more troublesome than equivalent outcomes that stem from their inactions. However, because of the greater discord produced by regrettable actions, people mobilize more psychological repair work to come to grips with their regrets of commission. Over time, then, the consequences of regrettable actions do not seem so severe, and, therefore, it is often regrets of omission that are experienced as more troublesome.

The Relationship Between Confidence and Temporal Distance

A final source of change in the amount of regret over action and inaction stems from the tendency for confidence to vary systematically with temporal perspective: That is, people are more confident of performing well at a task the farther they are, either prospectively or retrospectively, from the "moment of truth" (Gilovich, Kerr, & Medvec, 1993). It is easy to be confident when a task is not imminent; it is harder to be so assured when the challenge is at hand. This creeping overconfidence can bolster people's regrets of omission because it robs them of their initial justification for inaction. Whatever the negative consequences of inaction might be, they are experienced as more disturbing if there is no compelling reason to have suffered them (Lecci, Okun, & Karoly, 1994).

Stated differently, many regrets of inaction stem from an inability to conquer fears or to overcome doubts when the critical time is at hand. We fail to make a career change because we are unsure of what the outcome will be. We do not ask someone for a date because we are afraid of rejection. Because these concerns—which seem so pressing when the time to act is upon us—tend to diminish with the passage of time, the reasons we had for not acting no longer have much force. And, with no compelling reason for failing to do something we wish we had done, we regret our failure to act even more. We curse ourselves by asking "Why didn't I at least try?" and torment ourselves with accusations that "I'm just too timid" or "I'm too indecisive."

This tendency for confidence to increase with temporal distance is perhaps best revealed by the results of an experiment in which Cornell students and alumni were asked to consider the impact of adding a challenging course to their workload during a typical semester (Gilovich et al., 1993). How much would the additional course affect their grade point average for the semester? The amount of sleep they got? Their extracurricular and social lives? One group of respondents consisted of Cornell alumni who had been out of college for an average of 3.5 years. Another was a group of current students who were asked how much the extra course would affect their current semester. Finally, a third group of students indicated how much it would have affected them the previous semester.

As anticipated, participants' confidence that they could cope with an increased workload was directly related to their distance from the time the extra burden was to be faced. The alumni indicated that the extra workload would take less of a toll on their academic and social lives than did either group of current students. Furthermore, those participants who were asked to make assessments for a recently completed semester expressed less concern about disruption than did those making assessments for the current semester.

It seems that the farther we are from some challenge, the less threatening it appears. From the vantage point of hindsight we might not only wish we had acted but we may fail to understand why we never acted in the first place. Our regret intensifies because our failure to act now seems inexplicable, and we torment ourselves by asking "Why didn't I . . . ?" or by imagining "If only I. . . ." A temporal shift in the source of our greatest regrets is the likely result. Regrets of action induce more thoughts of what might have been in the short term (Kahneman & D. Miller, 1986; Kahneman & Tversky, 1982a), but regrets of inaction are likely to generate more of these counterfactual thoughts in the long run. When this tendency is combined with those processes described previously that alter, over time, the perceived consequences of action and inaction, the temporal pattern we have documented is likely to be highly robust (see Gilovich & Medvec, 1995, for a discussion of additional mechanisms underlying this temporal shift—e.g., the Zeigarnik-like aspects of regrets of omission and their greater cognitive availability than regrets of commission).

CONCLUSION

We have documented two ways in which the content of people's counterfactual thoughts exert a significant influence on their happiness or well-being. Our study of Olympic medalists revealed that imagined alternatives to reality are sufficiently powerful to cause those who are objectively worse off to nonetheless feel better about their standing than those in a superior position if there are systematic differences in the direction of their counterfactual thoughts (Medvec et al., in press). Our study of regret uncovered a significant qualification of existing views on the extent to which people regret errors of omission and commission (Gilovich & Medvec, 1994). As previous research on counterfactual thinking has demonstrated (Gleicher et al., 1990; Kahneman & Tversky, 1982a; Landman, 1987), people are initially more troubled by negative outcomes brought about by their actions than by equally negative outcomes that stem from their failures to act. Over time, however, a number of psychological mechanisms collude to bolster the power of regrettable omissions and to decrease the power of regrettable commissions. The result is a temporal pattern to the experience of regret in which actions generate more regret in the short term but in which inactions are more troublesome in the long run.

Those who have studied counterfactual thinking have set their sights on one of the most complicated and elusive topics in psychology—the quality of people's affective reactions to events. As everyday experience repeatedly demonstrates, the same objective outcomes leave some people downcast and others elated. Some people experience negative events and descend into a tormented cycle of "why me's" and "if only's." Others experience the same events with a sense of good fortune brought on by thoughts of "at least I . . ." or "it's a good thing that. . . ." The determinants of which path a person takes are often mysterious, so much so that one is sometimes tempted to give up the attempt to understand and to just be thankful if one can count oneself among those who habitually put a positive spin on events.

Slowly, however, key elements of the solution to this mystery are being discovered. Earlier researchers documented the importance of how a person's experiences compare with initial expectations (Atkinson, 1964; Feather, 1967, 1969) and with the experiences of relevant others (Festinger, 1954; Suls & R. Miller, 1977; Suls & Wills, 1991; Taylor & Lobel, 1989). In more recent research, investigators have elucidated the role of adaptation phenomena (Brickman & Campbell, 1971; Brickman, Coates, & Janoff–Bulman, 1978) and of an event's contribution to "endowment" and "contrast" (Tversky & Griffin, 1991). The findings from research on counterfactual thinking brings us closer still. By examining the constraints that govern people's postcomputed thoughts of imagined alternatives to reality (Kahneman & D. Miller, 1986; Seelau, Seelau, Wells, & Windschitl, chapter 2), this research helps us to understand some of the most subtle yet powerful determinants of satisfaction and regret.

ACKNOWLEDGMENTS

Much of the research reported in this chapter was supported by Research Grants MH45531 from the National Institute of Mental Health and SBR9319558 from the National Science Foundation to Thomas Gilovich. We would like to thank Todd Bickford, Kirsten Blau, Ann Charlton, Terry Anne Buckley, Deborah Fidler, Nina Hattiangadi, Allison Himelfarb, Elena

Jeffries, Danielle Kaplan, Jennifer Lowe, Ken Savitsky, Marshall Schacht, Sarah Sirlin, and Robin Winitsky for collecting much of the data reported here.

REFERENCES

Aronson, E. (1969). The theory of cognitive dissonance: A current perspective. In L. Berkowitz (Ed.), *Advances in experimental social psychology* (Vol. 4, pp. 1–34). New York: Academic Press.

Atkinson, J. W. (1964). *An introduction to motivation*. Princeton, NJ: Van Nostrand.

Brehm, J. W., & Wicklund, R. A. (1970). Regret and dissonance reduction as a function of postdecision salience of dissonant information. *Journal of Personality and Social Psychology, 14*, 1–7.

Brickman, P., & Campbell, D. T. (1971). Hedonic relativism and planning the good society. In M. H. Appley (Ed.), *Adaptation-level theory* (pp. 287–304). New York: Academic Press.

Brickman, P., Coates, D., & Janoff-Bulman, R. J. (1978). Lottery winners and accident victims: Is happiness relative? *Journal of Personality and Social Psychology, 36*, 917–927.

Cooper, J. (1971). Personal responsibility and dissonance: The role of foreseen consequences. *Journal of Personality and Social Psychology, 18*, 354–363.

Cooper, J., & Fazio, R. H. (1984). A new look at dissonance theory. In L. Berkowitz (Ed.), *Advances in experimental social psychology* (Vol. 17, pp. 229–266). New York: Academic Press.

Crosby, F. (1976). A model of egoistical relative deprivation. *Psychological Review, 83*, 85–113.

Dunning, D., & Parpal, M. (1989). Mental addition versus subtraction in counterfactual reasoning: On assessing the impact of personal actions and life events. *Journal of Personality and Social Psychology, 57*, 5–15.

Engel, E., & Venetoulias, A. (1991). Monty Hall's probability puzzle. *Chance, 4*, 6–9.

Erskine, H. (1973). The polls: Hopes, fears, and regrets. *Public Opinion Quarterly, 37*, 132–145.

Feather, N. T. (1967). Valence of outcome and expectation of success in relation to task difficulty and perceived locus of control. *Journal of Personality and Social Psychology, 7*, 372–386.

Feather, N. T. (1969). Attribution of responsibility and valence of success and failure in relation to initial confidence and task performance. *Journal of Personality and Social Psychology, 13*, 129–144.

Festinger, L. (1954). A theory of social comparison processes. *Human Relations, 7*, 117–140.

Festinger, L. (1957). *A theory of cognitive dissonance*. Stanford, CA: Stanford University Press.

Festinger, L., & Walster, E. (1964). Post-decision regret and decision reversal. In L. Festinger (Ed.), *Conflict, decision, and dissonance* (pp. 112–127). Stanford, CA: Stanford University Press.

Frank, R. H., & Cook, P. J. (in press). *The winner-take-all society*. New York: Free Press.

Frey, D. (1986). Recent research on selective exposure to information. In L. Berkowitz (Ed.), *Advances in experimental social psychology* (Vol. 19, pp. 41–80). New York: Academic Press.

Gilovich, T., Kerr, M., & Medvec, V. H. (1993). The effect of temporal perspective on subjective confidence. *Journal of Personality and Social Psychology, 64*, 552–560.

Gilovich, T., & Medvec, V. H. (1994). The temporal pattern to the experience of regret. *Journal of Personality and Social Psychology, 67*, 357–365.

Gilovich, T., & Medvec, V. H. (1995). The experience of regret: What, when, and why. *Psychological Review, 102*, 379–395.

Gilovich, T., Medvec, V. H., & Chen, S. (1995). Omission, commission, and dissonance reduction: Coping with regret in the "Monty Hall" problem. *Personality and Social Psychology Bulletin, 21,* 182–190.

Gleicher, F., Kost, K. A., Baker, S. M., Strathman, A. J., Richman, S. A., & Sherman, S. J. (1990). The role of counterfactual thinking in judgments of affect. *Personality and Social Psychology Bulletin, 16,* 284–295.

Goethals, G. R., Cooper, J., & Naficy, A. (1979). Role of foreseen, foreseeable, and unforeseeable behavioral consequences in the arousal of cognitive dissonance. *Journal of Personality and Social Psychology, 37,* 1179–1185.

Hansen, R. D., & Hall, C. A. (1985). Discounting and augmenting facilitative and inhibitory forces: The winner takes almost all. *Journal of Personality and Social Psychology, 49,* 1482–1493.

Hattiangadi, N., Medvec, V. H., & Gilovich, T. (in press). Failing to act: Regrets of Terman's geniuses. *International Journal of Aging and Human Development.*

Hoyt, M. F., Henley, M. D., & Collins, B. E. (1972). Studies in forced compliance: Confluence of choice and consequence on attitude change. *Journal of Personality and Social Psychology, 23,* 205–210.

Johnson, J. T. (1986). The knowledge of what might have been: Affective and attributional consequences of near outcomes. *Personality and Social Psychology Bulletin, 12,* 51–62.

Kahneman, D., & Miller, D. T. (1986). Norm theory: Comparing reality to its alternatives. *Psychological Review, 93,* 136–153.

Kahneman, D., & Tversky, A. (1979). Prospect theory: An analysis of decision under risk. *Econometrica, 47,* 263–291.

Kahneman, D., & Tversky, A. (1982a). The psychology of preferences. *Scientific American, 246*(1), 160–173.

Kahneman, D., & Tversky, A. (1982b). The simulation heuristic. In D. Kahneman, P. Slovic, & A. Tversky (Eds.), *Judgment under uncertainty: Heuristics and biases* (pp. 201–208). New York: Cambridge University Press.

Kinnier, R. T., & Metha, A. T. (1989). Regrets and priorities at three stages of life. *Counseling and Values, 33,* 182–193.

Landman, J. (1987). Regret and elation following action and inaction: Affective responses to positive versus negative outcomes. *Personality and Social Psychology Bulletin, 13,* 524–536.

Lecci, L., Okun, M. A., & Karoly, P. (1994). Life regrets and current goals as predictors of psychological adjustment. *Journal of Personality and Social Psychology, 66,* 731–741.

Medvec, V. H., Madey, S. F., & Gilovich, T. (in press). When less is more: Counterfactual thinking and satisfaction among Olympic medalists. *Journal of Personality and Social Psychology.*

Miller, D. T., & McFarland, C. (1986). Counterfactual thinking and victim compensation: A test of norm theory. *Personality and Social Psychology Bulletin, 12,* 513–519.

Miller, D. T., Turnbull, W., McFarland, C. (1990). Counterfactual thinking and social perception: Thinking about what might have been. In M. P. Zanna (Ed.), *Advances in experimental social psychology,* (Vol. 22, pp. 305–331). San Diego, CA: Academic Press.

Olson, J. M., Herman, C. P., & Zanna, M. P. (Eds.). (1986). *Relative deprivation and social comparison: The Ontario Symposium* (Vol. 4). Hillsdale, NJ: Lawrence Erlbaum Associates.

Read, D. (1985). *Determinants of relative mutability.* Unpublished data, University of British Columbia, Vancouver, Canada.

Roese, N. J., & Olson, J. M. (1993a). Self-esteem and counterfactual thinking. *Journal of Personality and Social Psychology, 65,* 199–206.

Roese, N. J., & Olson, J. M. (1993b). The structure of counterfactual thought. *Personality and Social Psychology Bulletin, 19,* 312–319.

Sears, D. O. (1968). The paradox of de facto selective exposure without preferences for supportive information. In R. P. Abelson, E. Aronson, W. J. McGuire, T. M. Newcomb, M. J. Rosenberg, & P. H. Tannenbaum (Eds.), *Theories of cognitive consistency: A sourcebook* (pp. 777–787). Chicago: Rand McNally.

Suls, J. M., & Miller, R. L. (Eds.). (1977). *Social comparison processes: Theoretical and empirical perspectives.* New York: Wiley.

Suls, J. M., & Wills, T. A. (Eds.). (1991). *Social comparison: Contemporary theory and research.* Hillsdale, NJ: Lawrence Erlbaum Associates.

Taylor, S. E., & Lobel, M. (1989). Social comparison activity under threat: Downward comparison and upward contacts. *Psychological Review, 96,* 569–575.

Thaler, R. (1980). Toward a positive theory of consumer choice. *Journal of Economic Behavior and Organization, 1,* 39–60.

Tierney, J. (1991, July 21). Behind Monty Hall's doors: Puzzle, debate and answer? *The New York Times,* pp. 1, 9.

Turnbull, W. (1981). Naive conceptions of free will and the deterministic paradox. *Canadian Journal of Behavioural Science, 13,* 1–13.

Tversky, A., & Griffin, D. (1991). Endowment and contrast in judgments of well-being. In R. J. Zeckhauser (Ed.), *Strategy and choice* (pp. 297–318). Cambridge, MA: MIT Press.

vos Savant, M. (1990a, September 9). Ask Marilyn. *Parade Magazine,* 15.

vos Savant, M. (1990b, December 2). Ask Marilyn. *Parade Magazine,* 25.

vos Savant, M. (1991, February 17). Ask Marilyn. *Parade Magazine,* 12.

Wells, G. L., & Gavanski, I. (1989). Mental simulation of causality. *Journal of Personality and Social Psychology, 56,* 161–169.

Wicklund, R. A., & Brehm, J. W. (1976). *Perspectives on cognitive dissonance.* Hillsdale, NJ: Lawrence Erlbaum Associates.

10

With an Eye Toward the Future: The Impact of Counterfactual Thinking on Affect, Attitudes, and Behavior

Faith Gleicher
University of California, Santa Barbara

David S. Boninger
University of California, Los Angeles

Alan Strathman
University of Missouri

David Armor
John Hetts
University of California, Los Angeles

Mina Ahn
University of California, Santa Barbara

> *You'll conquer the present*
> *suspiciously fast,*
> *if you smell of the future*
> *—and stink of the past.*
> —Piet Hein

That counterfactuals "stink of the past" is perhaps the most well documented finding of prior research on counterfactual thinking. Thoughts about what might have been persist after an event and influence individuals' affective responses and judgments (see Roese & Olson, chapter 1). Findings from other research, including our own, however, indicate that counterfactuals can also "smell of the future" in their influence on affective responses, attitudes, and behavior. In other words, individuals' concerns and thoughts about their future prospects might shape the nature and implications of their counterfactual thoughts.

An understanding of the relationship between counterfactuals and the future requires the recognition that people regularly think about imaginary alternatives in response to real events and that such thinking has certain reliable consequences. Findings reported in the counterfactual literature suggest that counterfactual thinking reliably influences affective responses and attributional judgments about events (see Roese & Olson, chapter 1, for a more detailed review). When people can readily imagine how a negative event could have been avoided, they feel worse about that event than if they cannot imagine how it could have been avoided (Gleicher et al., 1990; Kahneman & Miller, 1986; Kahneman & Tversky, 1982; Landman, 1987; Wells & Gavanski, 1989). They also make stronger attributions of responsibility and blame for negative events that can easily be "undone" (Wells & Gavanski, 1989). Importantly, people tend not to show the same intensification of affective responses and attributions for positive events as for negative ones, probably because positive events are less likely to elicit thoughts about how they could have been different (Gleicher et al., 1990; Landman, 1987; see also Taylor, 1991, and Weiner, 1985, for theoretical perspectives consistent with these findings).

These findings suggest that counterfactual thinking is maladaptive. It presents an image of a person who berates himself or herself for "avoidable" negative events and does not credit himself or herself enough for "inevitable" positive events. In fact, research findings on the relationship between attributional style and depressive affect suggests that this pattern of thought may indeed lead to depression (e.g., Abramson, Seligman, & Teasdale, 1978; see also Sherman & McConnell, chapter 7).

Despite the consistency of these findings, we, like others interested in counterfactual thinking, were a bit too optimistic about individuals' psychological resilience to believe that counterfactual thinking was only maladaptive (see McMullen, Markman, & Gavanski, chapter 5; Roese & Olson, chapter 6). We reasoned that in order to understand more fully the consequences of counterfactual thinking, it was important to consider the time frame in which people consider and use counterfactual thoughts. In prior research investigators focused on affective responses and attributional judgments about events that had already taken place. This is a logical starting place for research on counterfactual thinking, but it is important for researchers to consider that individuals may think about imaginary alternatives to events in terms of the implications of these events for the future as well as for the past. People's immediate affective responses to these counterfactuals—as well as their attitudes, plans for the future, and behavior—may very well be determined by what the counterfactuals imply for the future as well as by what they imply for the past.

In this chapter, we review research in which both affective and behavioral consequences of a person's thinking about counterfactuals with the future in mind was explored. We first report on experiments targeting situational and dispositional determinants of future-oriented counterfactual thinking. Specifically, the purpose of these studies was the assessment of the extent to which a focus on the future ameliorated the negative affect stimulated by a person's thinking about how a negative event could have been avoided. Next, we discuss the implications of research on counterfactual thinking for understanding, more generally, how people cope with negative events. We then turn to more recent research in which the impact of counterfactual thinking on attitudes and behavior was examined. Finally, we consider these findings, and counterfactual thought more generally, in the broader context of mental simulation.

THE INTERPLAY OF DISPOSITIONAL AND SITUATIONAL FACTORS

Consider the example of a student who chooses Course Y over Course Z, then ends up hating the Course Y and receiving a bad grade for her or his trouble. This student later learns from a friend that Course Z, the rejected course, was much better than Course Y, the one taken. Findings from prior research would suggest that the student, considering the counterfactual alternative that she or he could have taken the Course Z, loved it, and received an *A*, would feel terrible. In contrast, Boninger, Gleicher, and Strathman (1994) suggested that the student would be miserable only to the extent that she or he focused on the present predicament. To the extent that the student focused on the implications of this counterfactual for future outcomes, on the other hand (i.e., that next quarter, she or he would take the good course), the student might feel less regret.

What might make an individual focus on the future implications of counterfactual thoughts? One factor is that person's dispositional tendency to think about the future as opposed to the present. The Consideration of Future Consequences Scale (CFC; Strathman, Gleicher, Boninger, & Edwards, 1994) is a measure of individual differences in the extent to which people consider the immediate versus distant implications of current behaviors and events, and so taps into a general perspective of the relevant consequences of current actions and outcomes.

People who score high in the CFC tend to consider the future implications of their behavior and to use their future goals as a guide for their present actions. They endorse such statements as "I think it is important to take warnings about negative outcomes seriously even if the negative outcome will not occur for many years" and "I consider how things might be in the future and try to influence those things with my day-to-day behavior." Individuals who score low in the CFC, in contrast, focus more on their immediate needs and concerns than on a future that they see as distant and that they expect to take care of itself. They endorse statements such as "I think that sacrificing now is usually unnecessary since future outcomes can be dealt with at a later time" and "Since my day to day work has specific outcomes, it is more important to me than behavior that has distant outcomes."

The affective responses of CFC-high-scoring and low-scoring individuals to events are likely to be influenced by their differential focus on the immediate versus distant implications of those events. Whereas the affect of low-scoring individuals might be expected to be more determined by the *immediate* implications of an event, the affect of high-scoring individuals would be more likely to be determined by the event's *future* implications. If these patterns are the case, what does that indicate about the consequences of counterfactual thinking for high-scoring and low-scoring individuals? First, given a negative event that calls to mind ways in which the event *could have been* different, individuals with high scores might also be more likely to frame the counterfactual in terms of how that event *could be* different in the future. Further, because high-scoring individuals are more concerned about their future outcomes than are low-scoring individuals, they would be more likely to be heartened in the present by thoughts of how they can improve their future outcomes.

Specifically, the prediction here is that individuals with high CFC scores would demonstrate *no difference* in reported affect as a function of whether the counterfactual would or would not undo their outcome. Boninger, Gleicher, and Strathman (1994) expected that when a counterfactual that undid the negative outcome was easily accessible, high-scoring and low-scoring individuals would think about how their negative outcome could have been avoided—exactly the type of thought that generally leads to intensified negative affect (see Roese & Olson, chapter 1, for a review). However, expected those with high CFC scores *also* to think about how they might avoid negative outcomes in the future. These thoughts, then, would *ameliorate* the intensified negative affect that is typically associated with thinking about counterfactuals that change negative outcomes.

To examine these hypotheses, Boninger, Gleicher, and Strathman (1994) asked participants with high and low CFC scores to imagine that they were the student described previously, who had just taken a horrible course after having chosen it over another course (Experiment 1). Half of the participants learned that the course not taken was just as bad as the one chosen (i.e., the counterfactual did not change their outcome), and half learned that the course not taken was much better (i.e., the counterfactual changed, or undid, their outcome). As expected, those with low CFC scores replicated findings from prior research; as the results reported in Table 10.1 show, they felt significantly worse when the counterfactual undid their negative experience than when it did not. Those with high CFC scores, on the other hand, felt no worse when the alternative course was better than when it was not. A comparison between high-scoring and low-scoring participants in the condition in which the counterfactual did not undo the outcome (i.e., the condition in which prospects for the future were dim because all known courses were terrible) revealed that those with high CFC scores reported feeling worse than those with low CFC scores. Apparently, high-scoring participants spontaneously considered the future implications of learning about the other course: When the implication was that there would be no good course, they were distressed, relative to participants with low CFC scores.

These results support the notion that the dispositional tendency to consider future consequences can moderate the impact of counterfactual thoughts on affective responses to negative events. Suspecting, however, that an important modifier of the effect of considering future consequences was the relevance of the immediate situation to the future, Boninger, Gleicher, and Strathman (1994) examined two hypotheses in a follow-up study: (1) that individuals with low CFC scores would feel worse about a negative outcome if they considered a counterfactual that undid that outcome rather than a counterfactual that did not undo the outcome, regardless of whether the situation was relevant to the present or to the future; (2) that those with high CFC scores, on the other hand, would feel worse only if the situation seemed exclusively relevant to the present. When the situation was relevant to the future, Boninger, Gleicher, and Strathman (1994) expected to replicate the effects of the prior study.

Boninger, Gleicher, and Strathman (1994) asked participants to imagine themselves as an aspiring Olympic runner. The runner sustained an injury

TABLE 10.1
Experience of Regret as a Function of CFC Score and Outcome Change

Outcome Change	CFC Score	
	High	Low
Yes	7.17$_a$	7.67$_a$
No	6.79$_a$	5.85$_b$

Note. Differences between values not sharing a common subscript differ significantly at $p < .05$, based on Newman–Keuls test. Higher numbers represent greater regret. Parallel results were found for two other measures of counterfactual affect: self-blame and wishing to go back to change the decision of which course to take. CFF = Consideration of Future Consequences Scale (Strathman, Gleicher, Boninger, & Edwards, 1994). Copyright 1994 by the American Psychological Association, Inc. From "Counterfactual Thinking: From What Might Have Been to What May Be," by D. S. Boninger, F. Gleicher, and A. Strathman, 1994.

before a race in which he or she was to compete and was given a choice of two drugs to reduce the pain of the injury. The runner chose a drug that reduced the pain during the race but that also produced nausea and fatigue that caused him or her to just barely lose the race. The runner then overheard some of the other athletes discussing their own injuries and learned that the other athletes took a drug different from the one he or she had taken.

Boninger, Gleicher, and Strathman (1994) manipulated counterfactual thinking by varying whether the counterfactual made available in the scenario (taking the other drug) undid or did not undo the actual outcome of losing the race. Participants in the condition in which the counterfactual *did not* undo the actual outcome learned that the other athletes had also suffered negative side effects, even though they took a different drug. For these participants, the counterfactual alternative to their actual outcome was "If I had taken the other drug, I would have been tired and nauseated anyway, and I probably still would have lost the race." Participants in the condition in which the counterfactual *did* undo the actual outcome, in contrast, learned that the other athletes did not experience any side effects. For these participants, the available counter-factual was "If I had taken the other drug, I would not have suffered side effects and I probably would have won the race."

The future relevance of the situation was manipulated at the close of the scenario: Participants in the "future-focus" condition read, "As you stand there listening to these other athletes, you begin thinking about the next national meet only two weeks away." In contrast, participants in the "present-focus" condition read, "As you stand there listening to these other athletes, you begin thinking about the race you just lost."[1]

The results of this experiment strongly replicated past findings with respect to the influence of counterfactual thinking on affect. Participants for whom the available counterfactual of taking the other drug undid their outcome in the race reported greater feelings of regret and self-blame. In addition, these participants were more likely to express counterfactually associated regret in response to an open-ended question.

More important, however, a three-way interaction (shown in Fig. 10.1) indicated that the combination of a tendency to consider future conse-

---

[1]Also included in this experiment was a manipulation of the salience of learning from the negative experience. Boninger, Gleicher, and Strathman included this manipulation to examine the possibility that although consideration of future consequences and a situational future focus might cause participants to think about the future, appropriate framing of the counterfactual might be necessary to lead them to think about it *optimistically*. Although there were some interesting results concerning this framing manipulation, it did not modify the interaction between consideration of future consequences, future focus, and whether or not the counterfactual undid the runner's loss in the race. For that reason, it is not considered here.

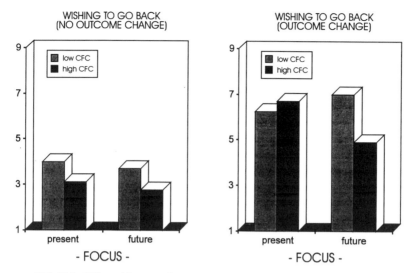

FIG. 10.1. Effect of focus and consideration of future consequences (CFC) on extent of wishing to go back when the counterfactual did not change the outcome of the race (left) and when the counterfactual changed the outcome of the race (right). Copyright 1994 by the American Psychological Association, Inc. From "Counterfactual Thinking: From What Might Have Been to What May Be," by D. S. Boninger, F. Gleicher, and A. Strathman, 1994.

quences and future focus significantly ameliorated the regret and self-blame associated with considering a counterfactual that undoes a negative event. Specifically, compared with participants with low CFC scores *or* who were focused on the present, participants with high CFC scores exhibited reduced counterfactual-related negative affect when they focused on the future. In fact, comparisons between the high-CFC–future-focus condition and conditions in which the counterfactual did *not* undo the negative outcome revealed no difference; in other words, participants with high CFC scores in the future-focus condition did not seem to exhibit the intensified negative affect typically induced by counterfactual thinking.

Together, the results of these two experiments demonstrate the moderating role of future-related thought on counterfactual affect. Results of the first experiment (Boninger, Gleicher, & Strathman, 1994) indicate that a dispositional concern about the future ameliorated the negative affect induced by thinking about how a negative event could have been different. Results of the second experiment (Boninger, Gleicher, & Strathman, 1994) suggests that the impact of this dispositional concern may be moderated by situational factors: Participants with high CFC scores experienced increased negative affect when they were focused on their present predicament but not when they were focused on the future; the negative affect of participants with low CFC scores, however, was not influenced by the manipulation of focus. In short, then, the findings from this research indicate that the perspective (future or past focus) with which people consider counterfactual alternatives to events can influence their feelings about those events.

THE ROLE OF COUNTERFACTUALS
IN THE COPING PROCESS

Considered in a broader context, these findings suggest that counterfactual thinking may have broad implications for how people cope with negative events. In investigations of the effect of counterfactual thinking on coping, the fact that coping is an activity that takes place over time is an important consideration. This process involves thoughts about past and potential future events and consists of both reactive and proactive activities. Various definitions of coping emphasize its process nature: Taylor and Schneider (1989), for instance, defined coping as a set of "regulatory activities . . . that enable people to anticipate possible stress and ward it off" (p. 174). Similarly, Lazarus and Folkman (1984) described coping as "the process of managing demands . . . that are appraised as taxing or exceeding [people's] resources" (p. 3).

When coping is considered as a process, it is clear that counterfactual thinking may influence it at many levels (see Davis & Lehman, chapter 13; Gilovich & Medvec, chapter 9; see also Taylor & Schneider, 1989, and Taylor & Pham, in press, for discussions of the effects on coping as *mental simulation*, a more general construct that includes counterfactual simulations). At first, the impact of counterfactual thinking on the individual's immediate affective reaction to the negative event may stimulate an initiation of coping efforts (e.g., the individual may begin to try to reduce the negative affect she or he is experiencing by thinking about how she or he can benefit from this experience in the future). Later, counterfactual thinking may influence the nature of both reactive and proactive coping activities and the success of these activities. Reactive activities may include attempts to manage the negative emotions induced by the negative event; proactive activities may include attempts to convince the self that similar negative events can be prevented in the future. Throughout the time course of the coping process, both the nature of counterfactuals generated (e.g., upward or downward; Markman, Gavanski, Sherman, & McMullen, 1993; Roese, 1994) and the frame in which they are considered (i.e., with respect to their immediate or more distant implications) are likely to have significant influence on coping activities. We explore these possibilities in the following discussion.

Counterfactual Thinking May Motivate Initiation of Coping Responses

In a study of participants' counterfactual thoughts following a gambling game, Markman et al. (1993) differentiated between counterfactuals that presented alternatives better than reality (i.e., *upward* counterfactuals) and those that presented alternatives worse than reality (i.e., *downward* counterfactuals). They found that when faced with a negative real outcome, individuals tended to generate upward counterfactuals. These counterfactuals, although providing them with ideas of how to prepare for the future, also made participants feel worse about their true outcomes.

Potentially, this intensified negative affect may stimulate coping responses (cf. Taylor & Schneider, 1989). It is possible, and consistent with theory regarding the relationship between affect and cognition (e.g., Lazarus, 1984; Zajonc, 1980, 1984), that individuals' initial response to their upward counterfactual thoughts is affective. This heightened affect in response to a negative event might lead them to initiate subsequent coping responses. These responses might include planning a course of action to be used in future situations or more emotion-focused responses, such as denying the upward counterfactual as unlikely or generating downward counterfactuals (Gleicher et al., 1990; Markman et al., 1993; cf. Folkman & Lazarus, 1980; Leventhal, 1982; Pearlin & Schooler, 1978).

In more traditional coping language, then, we are proposing that the counterfactual can influence both primary appraisal (of the threat posed by the negative event) and secondary appraisal (of the individual's ability to cope with the event). An upward counterfactual, for instance, influences primary appraisal by making the actual event seem even more negative and threatening to the self; a downward counterfactual has the opposite effect of minimizing the perceived threat of the event. The research findings described earlier, in which people with high CFC scores reported less distress than those with low CFC scores after a negative outcome that could have been otherwise, may be interpreted as an example of counterfactual thoughts influencing secondary appraisals. The quicker introduction of thoughts of future possibilities and ways in which to improve on future outcomes characteristic of individuals with high CFC scores may lead them to conclude that they can cope with the threat to the self posed by the negative event.

Counterfactuals May Facilitate Mastery Over Stressors

Theorists of coping distinguish between two general types of coping efforts: emotion-focused and problem-focused (Folkman & Lazarus, 1980; Leventhal, 1982; Pearlin & Schooler, 1978). Downward counterfactuals, which present an alternative worse than reality, may be especially useful in emotion-focused efforts because they provide a comparison standard that makes reality seem less bad (Roese, 1994).

On the other hand, upward counterfactuals may be more likely to lead to perceptions of control or potential for future mastery. According to Taylor (1983), regaining a sense of mastery over oneself and the world is a critical component of coping with negative events. Upward counterfactuals may be integral to the development of mastery; whenever individuals engage in "if only . . ." thinking, they may be able to regain a sense of psychological control by identifying a factor that they believe to have played a causal role in bringing about the undesired outcome (see McMullen, Markman, & Gavanski, chapter 5). Thus, the inherent structure of counterfactual simulations may yield implicit plans for future action (see also Roese, 1994; Taylor & Schneider, 1989). We return to this point later. In addition, repetition of the counterfactual simulations (and their associated plans) may make them seem more real, probable, or true (Taylor & Schneider, 1989; see also Miller & Turnbull, 1990) and therefore easier to implement in the future.

Results of several experiments have shown that the imagination of events leads to their greater perceived probability (Anderson, 1983; Carroll, 1978; Gregory, Cialdini, & Carpenter, 1982; Sherman, 1980) and sometimes their greater actual probability (Pham & Taylor, 1994; Winter & Goldy, 1993; see also Feltz & Landers, 1983, for a meta-analytic review of mental practice effects). In an interesting study, Winter and Goldy (1993) found that adolescents' mental simulation of a negotiation of the use of condoms with a sexual partner produced a higher acceptance rate of condoms than did direct experience in handling condoms. Similarly, Pham and Taylor (1994) found that students who mentally rehearsed a particular plan of action for doing well on a test (i.e., studying methods or strategies) studied more effectively and performed better than students who imagined their joy at receiving a good grade or who simply monitored their studying activity.

The evidence discussed so far suggests that the generation of counterfactuals with the future in mind leads to more effective coping: The individual perceives his or her plan for the future as likely to be effective and is more likely to carry out that plan. However, there is a potential drawback. Successful coping can quickly turn unsuccessful if the individual is confronted with a new situation that is not amenable to her or his constructed plan. Strentz and Auerbach's (1988) findings were consistent with this suggestion. In their realistic enactment of a lengthy hostage situation, participant "hostages" who had been trained in avoidant, emotion-focused coping techniques coped better than those who were trained in problem-solving techniques. This result might be explained by the fact that although participants trained in problem-solving might have had heightened expectations of success, the problem-solving strategies that they were taught to rehearse were ineffective when carried out in the context of the hostage situation. In addition, it is possible that the availability of these plans, which were generated *prior* to the event, inhibited the spontaneous generation of more adaptive plans *during* the event.

These findings suggest caution: Sometimes plans can backfire and leave people even more at a loss than they were initially. This caveat notwithstanding, the implications of theory and research on simulation effects in coping suggest an important role for counterfactual thinking.

MIDCHAPTER BREAK: BEFORE YOU GET UP

You are now halfway through this chapter. Perhaps you are considering putting it down to get something to eat, go outside for a break, or go to sleep. Before you do, think for a minute about how badly you would feel if you did not finish reading this chapter and you miss something important that later becomes central to your research. You might really wish you had read the rest of the chapter . . .

THE IMPACT OF COUNTERFACTUALS ON ATTITUDES AND BEHAVIOR

If you are still reading, perhaps the looming threat of potential regret motivated you to continue. In other words, an *anticipated* counterfactual may have influenced your behavior. Before we jump ahead to consider anticipated counterfactual thinking, however, let us step back to assess two possible ways in which counterfactual thinking can influence behavior.

Sequence 1: Counterfactuals Generated in Response to Past Events Influence Attitudes and Behavior

In the first possible sequence, counterfactuals are generated in response to events that have already occurred (in some studies, participants are asked to imagine this occurrence but are still asked to imagine it as an event that actually happens). This sequence is the one that counterfactual researchers have primarily examined. In this sequence, the individual experiences a (negative) outcome, which stimulates the generation and consideration of counterfactual thoughts. These counterfactuals subsequently influence other psychological variables of interest, such as attitudes, intentions, and behavior.

Sequence 2: Prefactuals Generated in Response to Anticipated Events Influence Attitudes and Behavior

Counterfactuals are probably most impactful when they are generated in response to an event that the individual has directly experienced (see also Fazio & Zanna, 1981). However, counterfactuals can influence behavior in a second way—when they are generated in response to *imagined* or *anticipated* events. In this second sequence, the individual imagines an anticipated (negative) outcome, along with alternatives to this imagined outcome. These alternatives lead to affective responses, which subsequently influence attitudes, intentions, and behavior. In many cases, these imagined alternatives are better termed *prefactuals* rather than counterfactuals because they are counter only to an imagined experience (Roese & Olson, 1993). Our findings indicate that these prefactuals can influence actual behavior.

People may imagine these kinds of prefactuals spontaneously. For instance, how many times have you closed the front door of your house only to wonder, "Did I turn the stove off?" You think, "I probably did." Then you falter, "Well, maybe I didn't. . . ." At this point, you invariably go through the following mental simulation: "What if I come back later to find the house on fire because I didn't turn off the stove?" You imagine yourself feeling horrible as you think, "If only I had gone back to check the stove!" These thoughts motivate you to turn around, reopen the front door, and check the stove.

In some instances, people may also be explicitly encouraged to consider simulations of this sort. Late-night television viewers are all too familiar with midnight life insurance commercials, whose sponsors surely bank on the behavioral significance of anticipated counterfactual affect. In these commercials, viewers see two small children being led by the hand toward some horrible fate (probably an orphanage). The viewers are told that the children's parents died unexpectedly, without an insurance policy to provide care for the children. Viewers are encouraged to consider how terrible they would feel if *their* children ended up in an orphanage because they failed to purchase the insurance policy that would save the children from a life of misery.

By what mechanism do counterfactuals influence attitudes, intentions, and behaviors? There seem to be two possible mechanisms: One centers on the attributional inference that arises from consideration of a counterfactual that reverses a negative outcome; the other centers on the affective response to that counterfactual. First, when a person generates a counterfactual that reverses a negative outcome, he or she is likely to make the attribution that there is an effective action that can be taken in the future. This inference can serve as the basis for behavioral decisions in the future (Roese, 1994). On the other hand, extensive findings from research indicate that this kind of counterfactual thinking leads to increased negative affect (see Roese & Olson, chapter 1). It may be that when an individual thinks about a counterfactual in advance, the motivation to avoid this negative affect influences behavioral choices. This suggestion is consistent with Weiner's (1980) model of social motivation, which points to affect as the proximal determinant of behavior. It is also consistent with models of anticipatory regret postulated by Bell (e.g., 1982) and Loomes and Sugden (1982). According to these models, individuals deciding between possible options include in their decision making the potential regret associated with each option (see Landman, 1993, for an interesting review of these models).

We suspect that the attributional and affective mechanisms can work independently or in concert. The studies described below were designed for examining the two sequences (proposed previously) by which counterfactual thinking may influence attitudes, intentions, and behaviors. In these studies, investigators did not attempt to distinguish between the attributional and affective mechanisms that may underlie both sequences, although they did actively make use of participants' naive understanding of the affective impact of counterfactuals. In the initial study, investigators examined the effects of an imagined scenario on behavioral intentions, and in two additional studies, examined the impact of prefactuals on attitudes, behavioral intentions, and actual behaviors.

Study 1: Salient Counterfactuals and Behavioral Intentions

In the first study, Boninger, Gleicher, Hetts, Armor, and Moore (1994, Experiment 1) asked participants to imagine that they had experienced the following situation, an adaptation of Kahneman and Tversky's (1982) alternate-route-home scenario (bracketed portion indicates between-subjects manipulation):

> You have two routes available by which you may commute between home and school. The first route is the one you normally take; the second is one that you take only when you want a change of scenery. Yesterday, you decided to take the normal [scenic] route home, and you got into an accident along the way. As a result, your car was seriously damaged.

Following Kahneman and Tversky's (1982) model, Boninger, Gleicher, Hetts, et al. (1994) manipulated the salience of a counterfactual by varying the normality of the route taken. It was expected that participants would be more likely to think of what could have been when they experienced the accident on the abnormal (scenic) route than when they experienced the same accident along the normal route.

After they imagined the scenario, participants responded to a series of dependent measures. Of primary interest were two measures of behavioral intentions. Participants rated, on 9-point scales, the likelihood of their taking (a) the normal route and (b) the scenic route the next time they had to commute from school.

Analysis of the responses to these measures indicated that participants who imagined that they had taken the scenic (abnormal) route the first time reported greater intention to take the normal ($M = 7.21$) rather than the scenic route ($M = 3.68$) on a subsequent occasion. However, when participants imagined taking the normal route, there was no significant difference in preference between the two routes ($Ms = 5.08$ and 5.60 for intention to take the normal and scenic routes, respectively). Thus, the results of this study suggest that when a counterfactual that would have prevented the accident was available (i.e., when participants imagined taking the scenic route), participants' future intentions were more influenced than when such a counterfactual was less available (i.e., when participants imagined taking the normal route). These results are also consistent with Meyers–Levy and Maheswaran's (1992) finding that under low-involvement conditions, variations in the temporal distance of an imaginary alternative influenced the extent to which participants were persuaded by a persuasive message.

In subsequent studies, investigators examined the impact of prefactuals, specifically the hypothesis that attitudes and behaviors may be adopted in order to prevent the occurrence of an anticipated negative event and its accompanying counterfactual regret (see also Simonson, 1992, for further evidence of the effects of anticipated regret on behavioral intentions).

Study 2: Prefactuals and Condom Use

In this experiment (Gleicher et al., 1994), participants were students enrolled in classes at a community college in Southern California. As part of AIDS Awareness Week at the college, members of the Speakers Bureau of Being Alive (a Los Angeles-based organization of individuals diagnosed as HIV-positive) were invited to preempt regularly scheduled classes in order to speak to students about HIV and AIDS. Seven of the speakers, who each spoke to two classes, served as experimenters by conducting this study at the end of their presentation.

To understand the results of this study, readers must first understand the nature of the presentations by the Being Alive speakers. According to the philosophy of the Speakers' Bureau, its members who are HIV-positive can benefit, both psychologically and physically, from speaking to others about their experiences. Therefore, the presentations vary greatly according to the preferences, needs, and experiences of the individual speakers. For instance, one speaker may emphasize prevention, whereas another may focus on the experience of having AIDS; one speaker may discuss his or her situation with ironic humor, whereas another may express intense anger. For this reason, speaker was completely crossed with experimental condition in the study. Moreover, although the speakers' credibility as experimenters increased participants' involvement in the research, the extreme variability in their presentations makes this a particularly conservative test of the simulation manipulation described later.

In each class, the speaker followed his or her presentation either with a control or with an experimental script. In the control script, which was matched in length to the experimental script, the speaker reviewed facts about the transmission of HIV and asked participants to think about these facts. In the experimental script, the speaker led participants through a detailed, scripted simulation in which the participants imagined that they engaged in unsafe sex and thereby contracted HIV, the virus that leads to AIDS. As part of this simulation, participants were also directed to think about an alternative that would have reversed their negative outcome (i.e., that they had used a condom). To specifically tap into prefactual thinking, experimenters directed participants to reflect on how much they would regret their behavior of *not* using a condom if they found afterwards that they had indeed contracted HIV.

Following this simulation (or, in the control condition, following a review of facts about HIV transmission), attitudes and behavioral intentions with respect to condoms were assessed. Participants' attitudes toward condoms were measured with three 9-point semantic-differential scales (with endpoints *useless–useful, careless–careful, healthy–unhealthy*); their intentions to use condoms were measured by questions that asked how likely they were to use a condom if they engaged in sexual activities and how important they thought it was to use a condom every time they did so.

Participants' attitudes toward condom use were significantly influenced by whether or not they had imagined contracting HIV after failing to use a condom. Those in the prefactual condition reported significantly more positive attitudes toward condoms ($M = 7.92$) than did those in the control condition ($M = 7.57$, $p < .05$).[2] Although the direction of the means

---

[2]This main effect of condition was moderated by a condition × speaker interaction. Although the overall tendency was for the counterfactual simulation condition to lead to more positive attitudes toward condoms, this tendency was not found for two of the speakers.

for participants' intentions to use condoms were in the predicted direction, this difference was not significant.

The results of this study, then, are mixed. We prefer to view them as half full rather than as half empty: Although the effect of the prefactual simulation on the measure of intention was not significant, a significant effect *was* found for attitudes toward condoms, despite the copious noise inherent in the nature of this research. To examine this hypothesis in a more controlled context, Boninger, Gleicher, Hetts, et al. (1994) simultaneously conducted a laboratory study that measured actual behavior.

Study 3: Prefactuals and Insurance

Participants in this study (Boninger, Gleicher, Hetts, et al., 1994, Experiment 2) were students in an introductory psychology course who participated in exchange for course credit. After arriving at the laboratory, participants were informed that they were to play a computer game. In this game, they would have to transfer their $10 "treasure" from a "home base" to a target destination. They were told that the available routes between the two points would appear on the computer screen and that they would navigate their way using the computer keyboard. These routes would be sprinkled with hidden pitfalls, such as avalanches, detours, washed-out bridges, and so forth. If participants encountered these pitfalls, they would have to pay an unspecified portion of the treasure in order to extract themselves. Whatever remained of the treasure at the end of the experiment, they were told, was theirs to keep.

There were two critical elements to the description of the game. First of all, participants were informed that there was an equal chance of doing well (that is, finishing with most or all of their money) versus doing poorly (that is, losing all or most of their money). Second, game participants had two insurance options available to them as well as a no-insurance option. That is, they could choose to (a) forego insurance, (b) pay a premium of $1.50 for which 25% of any treasure they lost to pitfalls would be returned to them at the end of the game, or (c) pay a premium of $3.00 for which 50% of any treasure they lost would be returned to them. The insurance options were constructed in this way to make them relatively similar in their expected payoffs.

The experimenter turned on a computer for each participant and brought up a screen that displayed "The Treasure Game." Each participant was provided with an insurance contract and was instructed to read the contract carefully and to take time to make a careful decision. This insurance contract reiterated the information about the insurance options and the likelihood of success or failure at the game and also presented the independent variable.

The independent variable consisted of the prefactual that participants were asked to consider before they made their insurance purchase decision. In all conditions, participants were reminded that the odds were 50–50 that they would fare well or poorly in the game. Participants in the antiinsurance prefactual condition were then reminded that if they spent money to buy insurance and then never used the insurance, they would end up really wishing they had never taken the insurance. Participants in the proinsurance prefactual condition, on the contrary, were asked to consider that if they chose not to take insurance and they lost all their money, they would really wish that they had taken the insurance. Two control conditions, which were later collapsed because they showed similar effects, were also included. Control participants either received no information or were asked to consider an empty, or nondirectional, prefactual (i.e., that if they did not think their decision through carefully and things did not turn out well, they would end up really wishing that they had taken more time to make their decision). Boninger, Gleicher, Hetts, et al. (1994) expected to find a trend such that participants who considered the proinsurance prefactual would be more likely to take insurance than would control participants, who would be more likely to take insurance than participants who considered the antiinsurance prefactual.[3]

Participants' decisions supported the predictions. A significant main effect of prefactual condition was found for the proportion of participants in each condition who purchased insurance. Fifty percent of participants in the antiinsurance prefactual condition took insurance, compared to 64% of those in the control condition and 72% of those in the proinsurance prefactual condition. In addition, an a priori contrast indicated a significant difference between the antiisurance prefactual and proinsurance prefactual conditions.

The results of this study, then, support the notion that behavior can be influenced by the consideration of counterfactuals in advance of a possible negative outcome (in other words, by the consideration of prefactuals). Interestingly, the two studies described here have complementary advantages and disadvantages. Whereas the insurance study provides clear and direct behavioral data, it relies on a rather simplistic gaming situation.[4] The condom study, in contrast, was an examination

---

[3]Because several participants told the experimenters during debriefing that they had trouble differentiating between the two insurance options, the dependent variable of insurance choice was collapsed into a dichotomous variable of choosing to take or not to take insurance.

[4]It also may be that subjects in the insurance study, who obviously read only one prefactual version, might have inferred the attitude of the experimenter toward insurance. If this was true, their choice to act in line with the inferred preference of the experimenter may reflect a "source effect" in addition to (or instead of) the effect of considering the prefactual alternative. This possibility will be addressed in future research.

of the effects of advance consideration of counterfactuals on attitudes and intentions in a real, complicated domain in which the final decision to use or not to use condoms is determined by many factors, only one of which is attitude toward condom use. It is perhaps the complexity of the condom-use decision, in addition to the noise of the experimental situation, that led to the mixed effects of that study. Together, however, the results of the experiments reported here provide converging evidence demonstrating the influence of counterfactual thinking on behavioral choices.

THE BROADER CONTEXT: COUNTERFACTUAL THINKING AND MENTAL SIMULATION

Throughout this chapter, we have discussed counterfactual thinking in isolation, without attempting to draw clear connections between this particular type of thought and other psychological processes. However, in order to better understand the significance of the impact of counterfactual thinking on feelings, attitudes, and behavior, it is important to place counterfactuals in the broader context of mental simulation, or imagination (see also Taylor & Pham, in press; Taylor & Schneider, 1989).

In considerations of counterfactual thought as simulation, Taylor and Pham's (in press; Pham & Taylor, 1994) analysis of the relationship between thought and action becomes particularly relevant. These authors distinguish between *outcome simulation*, in which the individual imagines a (usually desirable) outcome, and *process simulation*, in which the individual imagines the pathway by which he or she can arrive at that outcome. In their study involving introductory psychology students enrolled in an experiment on coping with examinations (Taylor & Pham, in press), the researchers manipulated whether students engaged in the outcome simulation of imagining scoring an A on their psychology midterm exam, the process simulation of studying for the midterm exam, both types of simulation, or neither type (control participants simply monitored their studying behavior). These authors found that although participants who simulated the desired outcome of receiving an A reported greater motivation to study for and do well on the test, the students who simulated the *process* actually were more confident of their ability to succeed on the test, studied longer, and performed better. According to Taylor and Pham, the process simulation led to these effects because it helped participants develop a plan for studying that they could then follow.

Taylor and Pham's (in press) distinction between outcome and process simulations is consistent with the analysis of counterfactual simulations presented in this chapter. Research on the effect of counterfactual thinking on affect is based on the assumption that individuals engage in a type of outcome simulation by using the counterfactual as a comparison standard (e.g., Johnson, 1986; Kahneman & Miller, 1986; Landman, 1987). When individuals compare an actual event to the alternative presented by the counterfactual, they feel worse when the counterfactual is better than reality, and better when the counterfactual is worse than reality (Markman et al., 1993). However, findings from other research (Boninger, Gleicher, Hetts, et al., 1994; Boninger, Gleicher, & Strathman, 1994; see also Roese, 1994) indicate that counterfactual thoughts may also constitute (and stimulate further) process simulation, which influences subsequent behavior and, thereby, subsequent outcomes.

When are counterfactual thoughts most likely to evolve into process simulations? The structure of the counterfactual generated in a situation is one likely determinant: Upward and additive counterfactuals are more likely than downward or subtractive counterfactuals to lead to plans for future behavior (Roese, 1994). Other findings indicate that an additional determinant is the extent to which the individual's focus is directed, either dispositionally or situationally, toward the future. More specifically, it seems that the individual must perceive a link between his or her behavior, the prior outcome, and potential future outcomes. This is the link that individuals who scored high on the CFC scale (Strathman et al., 1994) generally tend to perceive and the link that participants in both the condom-use and insurance studies were induced to perceive.

Also consistent with this idea is Markman, Gavanski, Sherman, and McMullen's (1995) finding that people generated more counterfactuals about aspects of a situation that they could control than about those aspects over which they had no control. It is reasonable to expect that the effective use of counterfactuals as a process simulation is limited to situations in which the individual has some hope of exerting control over his or her future outcomes (see also Markman et al., 1993; McMullen et al., chapter 5). It is precisely in these situations that counterfactual thinking serves several adaptive functions: It can ameliorate negative affect (Boninger, Gleicher, & Strathman, 1994, Experiment 1) and facilitate coping with negative events, modify attitudes (Gleicher et al., 1994), and influence behavior (Boninger, Gleicher, Hetts, et al., 1994).

There are unique characteristics and implications of counterfactual simulations that set them apart from other kinds of mental simulation (such as the simple imagination of a desired outcome). Counterfactual simulations can be differentiated from other simulations in that they are, by definition, stimulated by some real or anticipated occurrence. They are, therefore, inherently involving. Second, counterfactuals are distinguishable from other types of mental simulation in that their structure always includes an antecedent condition (e.g., "If I had done X") and a consequent condition (e.g., "Y would have occurred"). This structure provides both an outcome comparison and the suggestion of a process by which alternative outcomes could have been or could be achieved. It is perhaps this combination of outcome and process features that leads to the unique constellation of emotions induced by counterfactual simulations (e.g., a mixture of regret and self-blame). Because of the power of counterfactual simulations to stimulate emotional responses and because of their inherent process component, they may be particularly effective in spurring individuals to engage in further simulation that directly influences behavior.

CONCLUSION

This discussion points to an important feature of continuing research of the implications of counterfactual thinking: In order to draw conclusions about the effects of counterfactual thinking on behavior, it will be important for researchers to measure actual behaviors, as was begun in the program of research described here. In other words, researchers must move away from scenario studies toward the examination of counterfactual thoughts generated in real situations.

We conclude, then, with thoughts similar to those with which we began this chapter. We are too optimistic to believe that counterfactual thinking is inherently maladaptive, and the data we have presented here supports our optimistic assumptions. It seems that counterfactuals can be considered from several perspectives, only some of which lead to maladaptive effects. Our evidence suggests that to the extent that people think about imaginary alternatives with an eye toward the future, two important positive functions are served: the amelioration of counterfactually induced negative emotions and the facilitation of adaptive behavioral choices in the future. Thus, the "stink of the past" may well become the sweet smell of the future.

REFERENCES

Abramson, L. Y., Seligman, M. E. P., & Teasdale, J. D. (1978). Learned helplessness in humans: Critique & reformulation. *Journal of Abnormal Psychology, 87,* 49–74.
Anderson, C. A. (1983). Imagination and expectation: The effect of imagining behavioral scripts on personal intentions. *Journal of Personality and Social Psychology, 52,* 366–378.
Bell, D. E. (1982). Regret in decision making under uncertainty. *Operations Research, 30,* 961–981.
Boninger, D. S., Gleicher, F., Hetts, J., Armor, D., & Moore, E. (1994). *The influence of counterfactual thinking on intentions and behavior.* Unpublished raw data.
Boninger, D. S., Gleicher, F., & Strathman, A. (1994). Counterfactual thinking: From what might have been to what may be. *Journal of Personality and Social Psychology, 67,* 297–307.

Carroll, J. S. (1978). The effect of imagining an event on expectations for the event: An interpretation in terms of the availability heuristic. *Journal of Personality & Social Psychology, 36*, 1501–1511.

Fazio, R. H., & Zanna, M. P. (1981). Direct experience and attitude-behavior consistency. In L. Berkowitz (Ed.), *Advances in Experimental Social Psychology* (Vol. 14, pp. 161–202). San Diego, CA: Academic Press.

Feltz, D. L., & Landers, D. M. (1983). The effects of mental practice on motor skill learning and performance: A meta-analysis. *Journal of Sport Psychology, 5*, 25–57.

Folkman, S., & Lazarus, R. S. (1980). An analysis of coping in a middle-aged community sample. *Journal of Health & Social Behavior, 21*, 219–239.

Gleicher, F., Boninger, D. S., Neter, E., Collins, B., Dwiggins, M., Currier, R., & Thakkar, V. (1994). *The use of counterfactual simulation to change attitudes about safe sex.* Unpublished raw data.

Gleicher, F., Kost, K. A., Baker, S. M., Strathman, A., Richman, S. A., & Sherman, S. J. (1990). The role of counterfactual thinking in judgments of affect. *Personality and Social Psychology Bulletin, 16*, 284–295.

Gregory, L. W., Cialdini, R. B., & Carpenter, K. M. (1982). Self-relevant scenarios as mediators of likelihood estimates and compliance: Does imagining make it so? *Journal of Personality and Social Psychology, 43*, 89–99.

Johnson, J. T. (1986). The knowledge of what might have been: Affective and attributional consequences of near outcomes. *Personality and Social Psychology Bulletin, 12*, 51–62.

Kahneman, D., & Miller, D. T. (1986). Norm theory: Comparing reality to its alternatives. *Psychological Review, 93*, 136–153.

Kahneman, D., & Tversky, A. (1982). The simulation heuristic. In D. Kahneman, P. Slovic, & A. Tversky (Eds.), *Judgement under certainty: Heuristics and biases* (pp. 201–208). New York: Cambridge University Press.

Landman, J. (1987). Regret and elation following action and inaction. *Personality and Social Psychology Bulletin, 13*, 524–536.

Landman, J. (1993). *Regret: The persistence of the possible.* New York: Oxford University Press.

Lazarus, R. S. (1984). On the primacy of cognition. *American Psychologist, 39*, 124–129

Lazarus, R. S., & Folkman, S. (1984). *Stress, appraisal, and coping.* New York: Springer.

Leventhal, H. (1982). The integration of emotion and cognition: A view from the perceptual–motor theory of emotion. In M. S. Clark & S. T. Fiske (Eds.), *Affect and cognition* (pp. 121–156). Hillsdale, NJ: Lawrence Erlbaum Associates.

Loomes, G., & Sugden, R. (1982). Regret theory: An alternative theory of rational choice under uncertainty. *Economic Journal, 92*, 805–824.

Markman, K. D., Gavanski, I., Sherman, S. J., & McMullen, M. N. (1993). The mental simulation of better and worse possible worlds. *Journal of Experimental Social Psychology, 29*, 87–109.

Markman, K. D., Gavanski, I., Sherman, S. J., & McMullen, M. N. (1995). The impact of perceived control on the imagination of better and worse possible worlds. *Personality and Social Psychology Bulletin, 21*, 588–595.

Meyers-Levy, J., & Maheswaran, D. (1992). When timing matters: The influence of temporal distance on consumers' affective and persuasive responses. *Journal of Consumer Research, 19*, 424–433.

Miller, D. T., & Turnbull, W. (1990). The counterfactual fallacy: Confusing what might have been with what ought to have been. *Social Justice Research, 4*, 1–19.

Pearlin, L. I., & Schooler, C. (1978). The structure of coping. *Journal of Health and Social Behavior, 19*, 2–21.

Pham, L. B., & Taylor, S. E. (1994). *From thought to action: Effects of mental simulation on motivation and performance.* Manuscript submitted for publication.

Roese, N. J. (1994). The functional basis of counterfactual thinking. *Journal of Personality and Social Psychology, 66,* 805–818.

Roese, N. J., & Olson, J. M. (1993). The structure of counterfactual thought. *Personality and Social Psychology Bulletin, 19,* 312–319.

Sherman, S. J. (1980). On the self-erasing nature of errors of prediction. *Journal of Personality and Social Psychology, 39,* 211–221.

Simonson, I. (1992). The influence of anticipating regret and responsibility on purchase decisions. *Journal of Consumer Research, 19,* 105–118.

Strathman, A., Gleicher, F., Boninger, D. S., & Edwards, C. S. (1994). The consideration of future consequences: Weighing immediate and distant outcomes of behavior. *Journal of Personality and Social Psychology 66,* 742–752.

Strentz, T., & Auerbach, S. M. (1988). Adjustment to the stress of simulated captivity: Effects of emotion-focused versus problem-focused preparation on hostages differing in locus of control. *Journal of Personality and Social Psychology, 55,* 652–660.

Taylor, S. E. (1983). Adjustment to threatening events: A theory of cognitive adaptation. *American Psychologist, 38,* 1161–1173.

Taylor, S. E. (1991). Asymmetrical effects of positive and negative events: The mobilization–minimization hypothesis. *Psychological Bulletin, 110,* 67–85.

Taylor, S. E., & Pham, L. B. (in press). Mental simulation, motivation, and action. In P. M. Gollwitzer & J. A. Bargh (Eds.), *Action science: Linking cognition and motivation to behavior.* New York: Guilford.

Taylor, S. E., & Schneider, S. K. (1989). Coping and the simulation of events. *Social Cognition, 7,* 174–194.

Weiner, B. (1980). A cognitive (attribution)-emotion-action model of motivated behavior: An analysis of judgments of help-giving. *Journal of Personality and Social Psychology, 39,* 186–200.

Weiner, B. (1985). "Spontaneous" causal thinking. *Psychological Bulletin, 97,* 74–84.

Wells, G. L., & Gavanski, I. (1989). Mental simulation of causality. *Journal of Personality and Social Psychology, 56,* 161–169.

Winter, L., & Goldy, A. S. (1993). Effects of prebehavioral cognitive work on adolescents' acceptance of condoms. *Health Psychology, 12,* 308–312.

Zajonc, R. B. (1980). Feeling and thinking: Preferences need no inferences. *American Psychologist, 35,* 151–175.

Zajonc, R. B. (1984). On the primacy of affect. *American Psychologist, 39,* 117–123.

Counterfactual Thought, Regret, and Superstition: How to Avoid Kicking Yourself

Dale T. Miller
Princeton University

Brian R. Taylor
Albert Einstein College of Medicine

Some years ago a charismatic 19-year-old Spanish matador nicknamed "Yiyo" was gored to death. Yiyo's death evoked considerable public anguish and debate (Schumacher, 1985). Making his fans' reaction especially intense was the circumstance of his death: He was killed while serving as a last-minute substitute for another matador. Students of counterfactual thinking can be forgiven sly smiles and knowing nods as they read this story for it contains all the elements necessary to provide a dramatic test of the oft-cited hypothesis that events preceded by exceptional actions, such as substituting for another matador, are more easily imagined otherwise and generate more affect than events preceded by routine actions. A simple test of this hypothesis, first proposed by Kahneman and Tversky (1982b), would contrast the highly "mutable" fate of poor Yiyo with the less mutable fate of some other unfortunate "Yiyo" who had been killed by a bull he had long been scheduled to face. The two versions of the event could be presented to participants in scenario format and their reactions probed through a list of questions that might include the following: Did you have any "if only" thoughts when reading of Yiyo's death? How intense was your affective reaction to Yiyo's death? What degree of regret do you think Yiyo would have experienced if he had suffered only serious injuries rather than death? Presumably, those participants who had read the highly mutable version of Yiyo's death would report more if-only thoughts, stronger affective reactions, and greater expectations of regret.

But it was not its potential as a scenario study that intrigued us most about the account of Yiyo's death. It was what the article itself claimed made Yiyo's death so tragic: His actions had violated the widely shared belief that it is bad luck to substitute for another matador. This struck us as a curious superstition. How, we wondered, might such a belief have arisen? One possibility, of course, is that the belief is empirically grounded. There might be some reason why matadors are more likely to get injured when substituting; for example, they might be less knowledgeable about the bull. But we were drawn to another possibility, one that focused on the greater availability of counterfactual thoughts following deaths or injuries that are preceded by substitutions. In the remainder of this chapter we explore possible links between counterfactual thought and superstitions.

SUPERSTITIOUS BELIEFS AND COUNTERFACTUAL THOUGHT

We propose that there are two routes by which the counterfactual thoughts generated by a highly mutable event sequence can foster superstitious beliefs pertaining to that sequence. The first of these implicates memory distortion. The greater incidence of if only thoughts following ill-fated mutable actions might serve to make these events more available in memory and hence more subjectively probable. This hypothesis links the two processes that Tversky and Kahneman (1973) described in their original formulation of the availability heuristic: the process by which events become available in memory and the process by which events become available in imagination. We propose that event sequences that yield highly available alternative constructions tend also to be highly available in memory.

The second account for how counterfactual thoughts might affect people's decision strategies draws attention, not to people's recollection of the past, but to their contemplation of the future. People's reluctance to engage in actions easily imagined otherwise need not reflect distorted estimates of the likelihood that misfortune will follow such actions (their subjective expectancies). Such reluctance could simply reflect the regret they anticipate experiencing should misfortune occur (their subjective utilities). The force of the omen against matador substitution, for instance, might stem, not from the belief that bad things are more likely to happen when you do so, but from the belief that any bad thing that does happen will be psychologically more painful. Certainly, Yiyo's death seems to derive much of its poignancy from its circumstances. In effect, this hypothesis proposes that the *postcomputed* thoughts to which easily undoable events give rise (Kahneman & Miller, 1986) are sometimes anticipated—*precomputed*, if you will.

Separating the respective roles played by anticipatory regret and memory distortion in the development of superstitious beliefs is difficult because the two processes will so often operate in tandem. Thus, people facing the prospect of loss will tend to refrain from taking highly mutable actions both because they anticipate the aversive counterfactual thoughts that such actions could yield *and* because they better remember sequences in which similar actions led to negative outcomes. Nevertheless, we contend it is important to distinguish empirically and conceptually between these two processes, and we endeavor to do so in the present chapter. We first consider the biased-memory hypothesis.

BIASED MEMORY FOR EVENTS THAT ALMOST DID NOT HAPPEN

The hypothesis that events that almost did not happen tend to be highly available in memory might help explain a wide variety of common intuitions that have the "feel" of superstitions. As an example, consider the sense—widely shared, if our informal survey is correct—that the act of switching lines in front of busy counters virtually ensures that one's old line will speed up and one's new line will slow down. It is possible that a factual basis underlies this belief, but our analysis suggests how this belief could emerge without any empirical basis. First, we propose, following Kahneman and Tversky's (1982b) and Landman's (1987) accounts, that negative events preceded by acts of commission (e.g., being delayed after switching lines) are more likely to give rise to counterfactual, if only self-recriminations than either negative events preceded by acts of omission (e.g., being delayed after contemplating but deciding against switching lines) or positive outcomes preceded by acts of either commission or omission (e.g., being accelerated after either switching or not switching lines). Second, we propose that the greater self-recriminations that follow ill-fated acts of commission make those experiences more available in memory. Finally, we propose that the greater availability in memory of ill-fated acts of commission leads people to overestimate the commonness of these events.

The world of sports provides a rich source of beliefs that appear to derive from the tendency of some events to evoke counterfactual alternatives more strongly, and hence to be more available in memory, than others. Consider the account given by Juan Marichal, a Baseball Hall of Fame pitcher, as to why pitchers "hate" to walk batters intentionally: "It always seems that an intentionally walked batter ends up scoring." Now it is not obvious, at least to us, why intentionally walked batters would score more often than unintentionally walked batters. The holding of such a belief is understandable, however, if one assumes that the negative consequences of intentional actions (e.g., intentional walks), because they are so easily imagined otherwise, will be more available in memory. Consider another common observation from baseball authorities: The team that gets the most two-out hits generally wins the game. Why might hits that occur with two players out be any more crucial to success than hits that occur with no one out or with one player out? There may or may not be some reason this pattern is so, but even if the belief has no factual basis, our findings suggest why students of baseball might subscribe to it. The key is this: Opponents' hits that come with two players out will evoke frustrating counterfactual thoughts more readily than those that come with no one out or with one player out. Because a team's at-bat ends with its third out, hits that occur with two players out will seem closer to not having happened than those that come with no one out or with one player out (Miller & Gunasegaram, 1990; Miller & McFarland, 1986). Furthermore, two-out hits, by generating more if only self-recriminations and hindsight musings, will tend to be more available in memory. Thus, the perception that permitting two-out hits is especially costly might rest not on fact but on distorted memory. It is simply hard for people to forget what almost did not happen.

A similar process might underlie the widely held (and often ponderously repeated) belief of "experts" that third-down conversions play an especially critical role in the game of American football. Why might a team's success at gaining first downs (10-yard increments) on its (effectively) last try be any more predictive of its ultimate success than its success at gaining first downs on its first or second try? Again, whether or not an empirical relationship exists here, our account of the link between event mutability and memory availability indicates how such a belief might emerge. First, because the team in possession of the ball (i.e., offense) generally kicks the ball away if it does not gain a first down by its third try, the defense can be said to have come closer to having stopped an offense when it prevents the offense from gaining 10 yards until the offense's third down. Second, because events that almost did not happen will generate more affect and counterfactual thought, third-down conversions (from the perspective of both the offense and defense) will be more available in memory. Winners and losers alike will remember those events that almost did not happen and, consequently, accord them undue causal significance in their respective fates.[1]

---

[1]Possibly, the greater causal potency accorded two-out hits in baseball and third-down conversions in American football is due solely to their greater mutability and does not depend on their greater availability in memory. As Kahneman and Miller (1986) pointed out, events that are highly mutable tend to be more common. Still, we propose that the assumed importance of two-out hits and third-down conversions likely derives, at least partly, from the fact that participants and observers tend to overestimate the frequency with which winning teams accomplish these goals.

The erroneous beliefs produced by the amplified regret that follows ill-fated mutable actions often lead to suboptimal strategies. Consider the tendency of most tennis players to employ a second serve (placing the ball into play) that is substantially weaker than their first serve. Why should this tendency be the case? It is true, of course, that a weaker serve is generally more likely to result in the ball's landing in the service court and hence to reduce the chances of the server's double-faulting (i.e., not placing either served ball into play). But by employing a weaker serve a player also forfeits the offensive advantage that his or her first serve generally provides. The rational strategy would seem to be to calibrate the strength of one's second serve so as to optimize the odds of its landing safely and the odds of its winning the point when it does land safely. Should it be assumed that the speed of most players' second serves will reflect this calculation? Not necessarily. We suspect that the psychological pain of double-faulting wreaks calculational mischief and leads players to be too conservative with their second serve. Our logic here is as follows. The "mental kicking" that players give themselves when they double-fault (a highly mutable action) will make this type of lost point highly available in their memories and, in turn, will lead them to overestimate the frequency with which a serve of any particular strength yields a double fault—a bias that can be expected to lead them to weaker and weaker second serves. Players can also be expected to perceive double faults, along with other unforced errors, as more critical to the outcome of tennis matches than they are (e.g., "If I hadn't double-faulted so many times, I would have won"). In brief, tennis players will believe both that avoiding a double fault is more critical to success than it is and that the amount of power they need to "take off" their hardest serve to ensure the ball's landing safely is greater than it is.

Examples of biased memory for highly mutable event sequences are not restricted to the sports domain. Consider the belief, widely held by students and strongly endorsed by professors and test consultants, that with multiple-choice tests, examinees should always follow their "first instinct" and not change answers even when strongly tempted to do so. This particular piece of wisdom might or might not be grounded in empirical fact. One need not assume that it is, however, because biased-memory retrieval could be expected to be at work here as well (Miller, 1991). Recall the previously discussed finding that ill-fated acts of commission generate more counterfactual regret than do ill-fated acts of omission. If the decision to change a correct answer to an incorrect answer (an error of commission) leads to more if only self-recriminations than does the decision not to change an incorrect answer (an error of omission), instances of the former can be predicted to be more available in students' memories. This differential availability will provide them with compelling personal evidence for the wisdom of following their first instinct.

Kicking Oneself Under the Blackjack Table

We now shift the venue of our examination to the gambling casino. In a fascinating investigation of real-life decision making, Keren and Wagenaar (1985) studied experienced blackjack players in casinos throughout the Netherlands. Blackjack is a game played with an ordinary deck of playing cards, a dealer, and from one to seven players. To begin a round of blackjack, the dealer deals each player two cards facedown and deals himself or herself two cards, one facedown and one faceup. All face cards (kings, queens, jacks) are worth 10 points, other cards are worth the value of the number on the card, and an ace can be counted as either 1 or 11 points. A player may continue to ask for additional cards ("hits") until he or she wants to stop ("stand") or the total of points exceeds 21 ("bust"). The dealer must hit when his or her total hand is 16 or fewer points and stand when his or her total hand is 17 or more points. The player's object is to accumulate more points than the dealer, without busting. After all hands have been played, the dealer pays the amount bet to those players whose totals do not exceed 21 but are higher than his or her hand and collects the amount bet from those players who have busted or whose total is lower than his or her own. When a player's hand equals the dealer's, that bet is not paid.

Keren and Wagenaar (1985) compared the playing strategies of the players they observed to an optimal strategy, called *Basic*, which dictates that a player's decision to respond "hit" or "stand" should be based on not only the total of his or her hand but also on the value of the dealer's faceup card. Playing blackjack according to this strategy can reduce a player's losses to –0.4% of the expected values and is second only to card counting in effectiveness. The players observed by Keren and Wagenaar generally played optimally, with one striking exception. When a player was holding cards totaling 16 points and the dealer's upturned card ranged from a seven through an ace, Basic strategy dictates that the player take another card. (Players will lose about 65% of the time whatever they do in this situation, but the odds of winning are increased by taking another card.) However, 84% of the players observed by Keren and Wagenaar chose *not* to take another card when their card total was 16 points, a strategy contrary to the Basic prescription.

Why might players choose to stand at 16 when doing so reduces their chances of winning? Our analysis suggests one possibility. As we noted, when a blackjack player's cards total 16, the odds are that he or she will lose. But there are two ways of losing, and we propose that they will not be equally painful or equally memorable. The first type of loss involves an act of commission, the player's taking another card and busting; the second involves an act of omission, the player's standing and being outdrawn by the dealer. Losses following acts of commission, as discussed previously, can be expected both to produce greater counterfactual regret and to be more memorable. In brief, blackjack players might misjudge the odds of winning (or losing) at 16 by one strategy versus another because the differential counterfactual regret elicited by the two strategies biases players' memories.

Taylor (1991) devised a computer-simulated blackjack game to test the hypothesis that blackjack players overestimate the relative frequency of losses preceded by acts of commission. The game had two versions. In one, the taking of a card was framed as an act of commission; in the other, it was framed as an act of omission. Participants were instructed to make their decisions whether to hit or to stand as they would if they had been dealt a similar hand in a casino with $10 at stake. They were also asked to assume that the cards had been shuffled and that the deck was full before each hand was dealt. Over the course of the simulation, participants played a total of 28 hands. For 14 of these hands, the initial two cards totaled 12 points; for the remaining 14 hands, the initial two cards totaled 16 points. For every hand, the program read parameters from an internal file that determined the card values for the initial two cards and any subsequent cards requested by the participant. Half of the participants' hands at each card total (12 or 16) were designated success hands: Participants beat the dealer regardless of their decisions. The other half of their hands were designated failure hands: Participants lost to the dealer regardless of their decisions.

The omission–commission framing was induced by means of a dialogue box, which appeared on the screen 2 seconds after the cards had been dealt. In the commission–hit condition, the dialogue box contained the question "Do you want to hit?" and two option buttons, yes and no. In the commission–stand condition, the dialogue box contained the question "Do you want to stand?" and the same two option buttons. Thus, for half the participants, an act of commission (selecting the yes option) yielded another card, and for half the participants, an act of omission (selecting the no option) did so. After completing the simulation, which took approximately 20 minutes, participants were given two brief filler tasks. After completing these tasks, participants were asked to estimate, for each card total, the number of times they had won or lost by taking versus not taking another card.

We consider first the participants' memories for their experiences when holding cards totaling 16 points. Taylor (1991) hypothesized that participants in this position would overestimate the number of times that an act of commission led to a loss, irrespective of whether that act involved the taking or the refusal of a card. Responses revealed participants' tendency to overestimate the frequency of losses of both types, but the pattern of loss overestimation supported the hypothesis. In the commission–hit condition, 78% of participants overestimated their losses by commission, whereas only 33% overestimated their losses by omission. In the commission–stand condition, 89% of participants overestimated their losses by commission, whereas only 22% overestimated their losses by omission.

As expected, when the card total was 12, the framing manipulation had no effect on participants' recollections of losses. The only significant finding to emerge in this condition was participants' tendency to overestimate the number of times they had refrained from taking a card—however that was framed—and lost. Given how suboptimal such behavior is at a card count of 12—and how much regret it is likely to produce—the resultant memory distortion is not surprising.

Participants' responses to two other measures support the proposed interpretation of the memory data. The first of these measures asked participants to indicate their level of frustration at losing through each of the two routes at each of the two card totals. When their card total was 16, participants indicated that losing through an act of commission was significantly more frustrating than losing through an act of omission. This pattern was true irrespective of the content of the decision (taking or not taking another card). Consistent with their memory data, the participants' reported feelings at a card count of 12 revealed a main effect only of decision content. Irrespective of framing condition, participants indicated that they were more frustrated when they lost after refraining from taking a card (again, a very suboptimal decision) than after deciding to take a card. A final dependent measure probed participants' beliefs about the best strategy to follow at the two card totals. Here, too, when the focus was hands totaling 16, there was a strong framing effect. Participants indicated that an act of omission was the best strategy to follow at a card count of 16, regardless of whether that involved taking a card or standing. For hands with a card count of 12, there was no framing effect, but there was a main effect of decision: Participants in both framing conditions overwhelmingly endorsed the taking of a card as the best strategy.

Kicking Oneself Over the Road Taken

Taylor (1991) conducted a second test of the hypothesis that people's memories lead them to overestimate the frequency of negative outcomes for which if only thoughts are highly available. For this study Taylor manipulated the mutability of the outcome by varying its inevitability. He assumed that the amount of counterfactual thought generated by a negative fate would increase as a function of the number of fate-avoiding behavioral options originally available to the actor (Wells & Gavanski,

1989). Based on the relationship between outcome inevitability and coun-terfactual thought, the biased-memory hypothesis states that avoidable events should be more available in memory than unavoidable ones. With the assistance of a second computer simulation, Taylor (1991, Study 2) tested this hypothesis.

Participants were instructed to imagine that they were managers of a trucking company, which received weekly orders for goods and materials from another company located on an island resembling Manhattan. The trucking company's drivers could reach the customer by either of two equidistant routes—over a bridge or through a tunnel. Participants were told that their task was to "process" the order for each week and then to decide by which route they wished to ship the goods. Once they had decided on a route for a particular order, they could not change the route. The instructions indicated that both the tunnel and the bridge routes were heavily traveled and, thus, that trucks on either route could be slowed considerably by traffic jams or accidents. Participants were told that every order delivered on time resulted in a profit, whereas every late delivery resulted in a loss.

Over the course of the simulation, participants received 30 orders. For 15 of these orders, participants were informed, shortly after they had made their decision and irrespective of that decision, that they had suc-cessfully delivered the order on time. For the remaining 15 orders, they were informed, irrespective of the route they had chosen, that they had failed to deliver on time due to accidents or traffic jams on the chosen route. For the failure trials, participants were given one of two additional pieces of feedback about the delay. In the immutable-delay condition, they were told that traffic on the alternative route was also delayed and that they would not have made a profit even if they had chosen it. In the mutable-delay condition, participants were told that traffic on the other route, unlike the one they had chosen, was not delayed and that had they chosen it the order would have arrived at the destination on time. After completing the simulation, which took about 15 minutes, participants were given two brief filler tasks, followed by the dependent measures.

Participants were asked to estimate the number of times their chosen route had failed to get the order delivered on time. As predicted, partici-pants' estimation of the frequency of delays on each route depended on the inevitability of those delays. Specifically, they *overestimated* their avoidable delays by 59% but *underestimated* their unavoidable delays by 45%. Consistent with this memory bias were participants' responses to the question of which route they would advise another driver to take: A sizeable majority (73%) of participants pointed to the route on which their delays—although no less frequent—had been unavoidable. There were two additional findings of interest. First, participants described their avoidable delays as more frustrating than their unavoidable delays. Second, results of regression analysis indicated that the more frustrating participants found their avoidable delays to be the more they tended to overestimate their commonness.

Summary

The findings from Taylor's (1991) two studies strongly support the hypothesis that people's beliefs about the commonness of action–outcome sequences depend on the extent to which those sequences evoke counterfactual thought. The more if only thoughts a loss generates, the more available that loss appears to be in memory. These findings, it is important to note, do more than indicate that negative experiences are more available in memory than are positive experiences. These findings also show that some negative experiences (highly mutable ones) are more likely than others to be remembered.

ANTICIPATORY REGRET: TRYING TO AVOID A MENTAL KICKING

Biased recall of past experience can, as we have shown, lead people to misjudge the likelihood that a particular course of action will lead to a negative outcome. Biasing subjective expectancies, however, is only one of the ways that counterfactual regret can affect decision-making strategies. Counterfactual regret can also influence decision strategies through its impact on the decision maker's subjective utility function: how he or she evaluates the different possible outcomes. The more counterfactual regret an outcome is expected to generate, the more motivated the decision maker will be to avoid the outcome. This account implies that one need not look to biased experiential memory to explain superstitious behavior. People might hesitate to engage in certain "irrational" actions, not because of an unrealistic estimate of the likelihood of a negative event ensuing, but because of a (quite possibly) realistic estimate of the psychological pain that a particular action–outcome sequence might cause them. That regret can be anticipated and can guide the decisions people make has been proposed by theorists from a wide range of theoretical orientations (Bell, 1982, 1983, 1985a; Fishburn, 1983; Janis & Mann, 1977; Kahneman & Tversky, 1982a; Loomes, 1988; Loomes & Sugden, 1982, 1987a, 1987b; Simonson, 1992; Sugden, 1985; E. Walster, G. Walster, Piliavin, & Schmidt, 1973; see also Gleicher, Boninger, Strathman, Armor, Hetts, & Ahn, chapter 10).

An illustration of how anticipatory regret can guide decisions is the Spanish prohibition against matadors' switching bulls. One need not posit that matadors and their fans exaggerate the likelihood that switching bulls will lead to misfortune to account for why such behavior is pro- scribed. It is sufficient to propose that misfortunes following mutable actions are judged more aversive (see also Gilovich, Medvec, & Chen, 1995; Ritov & Baron, 1990, 1992; Spranca, Minsk, & Baron, 1991). Whether or not switching bulls is more or less likely to lead to misfortune, any misfortune that does follow a switch can be expected to generate more distress among fans and victims alike. A similar point can be made about the advice to a person to follow his or her first instinct on multiple-choice tests. Students need not think that changing answers increases the risk of a lowered score to avoid doing so. If a student anticipates being tormented by having changed a correct answer to a wrong one, he or she might reasonably ask, Why risk it? Similarly, if a blackjack player antici- pates being tormented by taking too many cards and busting, he or she might reasonably ask, Why risk it?

Because circumstances that elicit anticipatory regret will also tend to induce biased recall estimates, the assessment of the independent effects of anticipatory regret is difficult. Nevertheless, there do seem to be some instances of superstitious behavior for which a biased-memory account seems highly implausible. Consider the psychology captured by the fol- lowing sportswriter's observation: "It is a cardinal rule in basketball that when the game is on the line you don't put your opponent there. That's why coaches repeatedly impress their players that they should refrain from committing fouls under circumstances that could give game-win- ning free shots to the other team" (Goldaper, 1990). Well, why exactly is this a cardinal rule? Might it be a cardinal rule simply because a loss that results from your opponent's free shot—a shot that you in some sense caused—will provoke more haunting counterfactual thoughts than a loss that results from a shot that is less capable of being mentally undone? If so, how many basketball losses occur because players and coaches would rather lose by playing too conservatively (erring by omission) than by playing too aggressively (erring by commission)? A closer examination of how anticipatory regret can affect decision making is provided by a return to the blackjack table.

Fear of the Easily Imagined Otherwise: Back to the Blackjack Table

Recall Taylor's (1991) finding that blackjack losses following acts of com- mission were more available in memory than losses following acts of omission. We proposed that the existence of this memory bias is sufficient to account for the tendency of players—contrary to prescriptive models—to opt for inaction when their card total was 16 and the dealer's upturned card counted 10 or less. In our discussion of anticipatory regret, however, we suggested that it is not necessary to posit memory bias to account for the bias toward inaction. Players might simply prefer to lose through inaction than through action. Players, if they prefer to lose through inaction rather than through action, might be inclined to stand at 16 even if their experience has not led them to think that this is the "percentage" play.

Another computer-simulation study was conducted by Taylor (1989) to test this hypothesis. The design of this study provided participants with an experience that more closely matched a real blackjack game than did the game in the earlier study. Participants were undergraduates who were paid $5 to participate in an investigation of blackjack playing. To begin, participants were given a brief overview of the experiment along with a set of instructions both on how to play blackjack and how to interface with the computer. The program provided participants with $150 in "computer money" from which they could draw when placing their bets. Prior to each hand, participants were asked to enter a bet between $5 and $25 in multiples of $5. They were told to continue betting even if they had lost all of their money. To increase their involvement in the game, participants were told that they would receive 1 actual cent for every computer dollar they had when the game ended.

Participants were randomly assigned to play one of the two versions of the blackjack game described earlier (Taylor, 1991). The difference between the two versions occurred in the framing of the decision to take or not to take a card. In the commission–hit condition, the dialogue box that appeared after the participant was dealt his or her initial card asked "Do you want to hit?" In the commission–stand condition, it asked "Do you want to stand?" The yes and no option buttons appeared also. Both versions followed all of the rules of regular blackjack except that they did not permit betting options such as "doubling down" or "insurance" bets.

All participants played a total of 44 hands during the experimental session. For 24 of these hands, the initial two cards dealt to the participant totaled between 12 and 17 points (four hands each for the six card totals), with the dealer's upturned card ranging from a seven through an ace. In order to ensure that all participants played comparable games, as well as to keep constant the number of times their cards totaled 12 through 17, the value of the cards appearing in each hand was controlled by a program. The program also ensured that participants who played according to Basic would win on half of the four hands at each card total and lose on the other half. The remaining 20 hands consisted of various other possible card combinations. The order of presentation of the 44 hands was random.

The focus of the main analysis was on the responses of the participants when they played the four hands at each card total from 12 through 17. Participants were assigned a score ranging from 0 to 4 indicating the number of times they stood on each card total. Taylor (1989) converted these data to proportions ranging from 0 to 1 by dividing each score by 4. The mean proportion of stands on each card total for participants in both the commission–hit and commission–stand conditions are displayed in Fig. 11.1.

Results of an analysis of variance (ANOVA) performed on these data revealed a main effect for card total (12–17). Not surprisingly, participants were more likely to stand the closer the card total was to 21. No significant main effect for program (commission–hit vs. commission–stand) emerged, but the predicted interaction between program and card total did emerge. Results of simple effect analyses revealed, as predicted, that the only card total to yield a program difference was 16: In the commission–hit condition participants were more than twice as likely to stand as were participants in the commission–stand condition. The finding that participants were more likely to take a card (the normative response) at 16 when doing so was framed as an inaction than when it was framed as an action supports the anticipatory regret hypothesis. Facing a loss, participants holding 16 appeared to find it preferable to lose through inaction (saying no to the dealer's query) than through action (saying yes to the dealer's query).

As clear as these results are, they unfortunately provided no direct evidence that it was differential fear of regret that led participants in the two conditions to act differently at 16. To secure more direct evidence

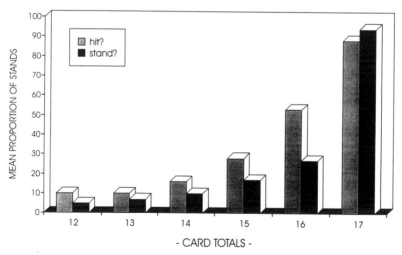

FIG. 11.1. Mean proportion of decisions to stand on each card total, by condition. From *Mental simulation and the anticipation of regret*, by B. Taylor, 1989. Unpublished master's thesis, Princeton University, Princeton, NJ.

for the mediating role of anticipatory regret, Taylor conducted a follow-up study.

Follow-up Study. In this study (Taylor, 1989), a group of participants recruited from the same population as that used for main study were instructed to play a few hands of blackjack under the two program conditions and then to rate how regretful they thought actual players would find the different decision–outcome sequences. Specifically, the instructions stated "[You will] play a few hands under a couple of different conditions and then rate [them] for how much regret you and other players might experience" (p. 27). Participants were told that they would play six hands in which the initial two cards they would be dealt would total 16. They were instructed to answer the dealer's query each time with a yes response. All participants lost on each trial; thus participants in the commission–hit condition took another card and busted on each of the six trials, and participants in the commission–stand condition stood but were outdrawn by the dealer on six trials. Participants were then asked to play another six hands, with instructions to respond to the dealer's query each time with a no response. Once again, all participants experienced losses on each trial; thus participants in the commission–hit condition stood but were outdrawn by the dealer on each trial, and participants in the commission–stand condition took a card and busted on each trial. Following the second set of six trials, participants were asked to indicate which real-game circumstance they thought would lead to more regret: responding yes and losing or responding no and losing.

The results supported the anticipatory regret interpretation of the findings from the main experiment. Participants' predictions of regret were influenced less by the form of the loss (busting vs. being outdrawn by the dealer) than by the route to the loss (pursuing an active vs. an inactive course). Thus, in both the commission–hit and commission–stand conditions, the majority of participants (70% and 85%, respectively) indicated that they would experience more regret after losing through an act of commission (responding yes) than through an act of omission (responding no).

Summary. Taken together, the findings from Taylor's (1989) main and follow-up studies offer strong support for the speculation that the normative deviation Keren and Wagenaar (1985) observed in the behavior at 16 of experienced blackjack players was due to fear of self-recrimination. The condition (commission–hit) that rendered participants most hesitant to take a card at 16, and most fearful of regret if they did, would seem to be the condition that most closely matched the actual game of blackjack—a perception confirmed by participants' ratings. As we discussed earlier, however, the greater psychological distress produced by losses through action also makes these losses more available in memory. Can one confidently conclude that anticipatory regret rather than biased memory is responsible for the normatively dubious behavior observed by Taylor (1989) and Keren and Wagenaar (1985)? Probably not, at least not without a more sophisticated design. What can be said is that Taylor's (1989) participants generally did not have much experience playing blackjack and thus did not have much opportunity to develop beliefs about the best course of actions to take at 16. Moreover, even if they had had experience, they are highly unlikely to have had experience with a version of the game in which standing was framed as an act of commission.

When We Won't Part With a Lottery Ticket

Seeking stronger support for the link between anticipatory regret and counterfactual thought, we conducted a scenario study. In the scenario two individuals were provided with the opportunity to sell a lottery ticket each had purchased. The manipulated variable was the temporal proximity to the drawing (1 hour vs. 2 weeks). Based on our anticipatory regret analysis, we predicted that people would be less willing to part with a ticket the shorter the temporal distance to the drawing. Our logic went as follows. When confronted with the situation described in the scenario, people will anticipate the regret that selling a once-held winning lottery ticket would induce in them and will factor this anticipatory regret into their decision about whether or not to sell the ticket. Further, as predicted by norm theory (Kahneman & Miller, 1986), people's anticipatory regret, along with their reluctance to sell the ticket, should increase with their ease of imagining themselves still owning the winning ticket. The more recently one sold the winning ticket, the closer will be the counterfactual world in which one was a winner and, hence, the greater will be the experienced regret. The scenario presented to and the questions asked of them were as follows.

Mr. K and Mr. T each purchased a ticket for a lottery with a multimillion dollar jackpot. Subsequently, each man was approached by a friend who offered to buy his ticket. The friend approached Mr. K two weeks before the draw and Mr. T one hour before the draw. Each man had held his ticket for about two weeks when he was approached and each had sufficient time to buy another ticket before the draw if he so wished.

Who do you think would want the highest price for his ticket?

Mr. K	19%	
Mr. T	81%	$N = 78$

Who do you think would be most reluctant to sell his ticket?

Mr. K   17%
Mr. T   83% $N = 78$

Who would have the strongest sense of having almost won the lottery if he were to sell his ticket and it won?

Mr. K   22%
Mr. T   78% $N = 78$

Who would experience the greatest amount of regret if he were to sell his ticket and it won?

Mr. K   9%
Mr. T   91% $N = 78$

Participants' responses conformed to predictions. They predicted that the anticipatory regret generated by the prospect of selling a winning ticket would be greatest when the time to the drawing was the shortest. Now, it is difficult to see how participants' predictions about Mr. K's and Mr. T's differential reluctance to sell their lottery tickets could derive from participants' biased memories of their own ticket-selling experience. This is not to say that such a belief would not develop if people were in the custom of selling tickets. The results do suggest, however, that holding such a belief is not necessary to explain the greater reluctance to do so; they also raise the possibility that the holding of similar beliefs may not be necessary to explain other behaviors that have the feel of superstitions, such as the reluctance to switch bulls.

DISCUSSION

Our focus in this chapter has been the role played by counterfactual thinking in belief formation, regret, and decision making generally. We have also sought a deeper understanding of counterfactual thinking—its origins, constraints, and consequences. We now attempt to summarize the implications of our analysis, giving special attention to conceptual problems remaining and to empirical prospects beckoning.

Implications for Decision Making

The findings from the present analysis contribute to an understanding of the link between regret and decision making in two ways. First, they reveal a previously unexplored route through which regret can affect decision making: memory-biased beliefs. The more counterfactual thought an action–outcome sequence generates the more available in memory it will be and, consequently, the more common it will seem to be. Our analysis focused on multiple-trial decisions (e.g., multiple hands of blackjack, multiple exam questions) for which it is only natural, and possibly highly adaptive, for the decision maker to form beliefs about how often particular courses of action lead to particular outcomes. What we found was that people's memories for the frequency of different sequences, and hence their beliefs about the likely consequences of different decision strategies, varied as a function of the type of loss they incurred. For example, participants' beliefs about the "smart" decision to make when holding a card total of 16 in a blackjack game were found to be biased by their systematically distorted memories of the relative frequency with which different strategies had led to blackjack losses in their experience. Specifically, participants overestimated the number of times an act of commission (taking a card or not taking a card, depending on the framing of the game) had led to a loss.

A second contribution of the present research can be found in its exploration of the determinants of anticipatory regret. Although previous regret theorists (e.g., Bell, 1982, 1985b; Sugden, 1985) noted that regret involves a comparison of what is and what might have been, the focus of the present analysis was specifically on the conditions under which thoughts of what might have been are especially salient and, hence, feelings of regret especially intense. Kahneman and Miller (1986) proposed that the intensity with which a negative outcome will evoke more positive counterfactual alternatives will follow certain rules of mutability. The blackjack example is an illustration of one such rule: Ill-fated acts of commission evoke counterfactual alternatives and, hence, regret more strongly than do ill-fated acts of omission. The Yiyo example is an illustration of another rule: Ill-fated exceptional acts (e.g., substitutions) elicit counterfactual alternatives and, hence, regret more strongly than do ill-fated routine acts. As the findings from the present analysis reveal, rules of mutability pertain not only to the degree of regret that an action–outcome sequence will evoke in an individual but also to his or her memory for the commonness of that sequence and, most relevant to decision making, to his or her willingness to undertake the action.

The factors identified by previous decision theorists as determining the magnitude of anticipatory regret differ considerably from those identified in the present analysis. The most extensive prior account of the determinants of anticipatory regret is that provided by Janis and Mann (1977). These theorists pointed to the following circumstances as the ones most likely to arouse anticipatory regret in a decision maker: (a) The most preferred choice is not necessarily superior to another alternative. (b) The negative consequences that might ensue from the decision could start to materialize almost immediately after the decision is made. (c) Significant persons in the decision maker's social network view the decision as important and will expect him or her to adhere to it. (d) New information concerning potential gains and losses can be obtained. (e) Significant persons in the decision maker's social network who are interested in this particular decision are not impatient about his or her current state of indecision and expect him or her to delay action until the alternatives have been evaluated carefully. Janis and Mann's analysis is at once broader and narrower than that proposed by Kahneman and Miller (1986). It is broader in the sense that it points to factors, such as the importance of significant others, not featured in Kahneman and Miller's analysis. It is narrower in the sense that those factors it identifies that could be predicted to feed counterfactual regret, such as the closeness of the chosen and unchosen options, are never linked explicitly to the process of counterfactual thinking.

Neither have economists' accounts of anticipatory regret provided a full analysis of the undoing process. Consider Sugden's (1985) claim that the prospect of a rejected alternative will arouse anticipatory regret in a decision maker to the extent "the individual could sensibly blame himself for not having chosen it" (p. 89). As reasonable as this statement seems, we contend that it significantly underestimates the power of the link between mental undoing and regret. According to our analysis, regret will not be restricted to circumstances in which blame is sensibly assigned to the actor. It will arise whenever the individual can easily imagine himself or herself having acted differently. It is true that deviating from routine often will violate the dictates of good sense (e.g., deciding to deviate from your custom by fighting your next duel with your rusty sword instead of with your trusty pistol), but often it will not (e.g., deciding to deviate from your custom by calling heads instead of tails in the coin toss that determines choice of weapons). We contend that the pressure felt to follow one's customary practice will be considerable even when this practice (e.g., the practice of calling tails) cannot reasonably be expected to enhance one's chances of success. Regret and self-blame do not arise only when someone has precipitated a negative outcome by engaging in an irrational or immoral action; they arise whenever a person has precipitated a negative outcome by doing something he or she can easily imagine not having done (Buck & Miller, 1994; Miller & Turnbull, 1990; Miller, Turnbull, & McFarland, 1990; see also Davis & Lehman, chapter 13).

Of course, people who experience a negative outcome after taking a highly mutable (but not suboptimal) action will often be left with the sense that what they did was "dumb." More than this, their postoutcome feeling of stupidity might foster in them the feeling that they knew at the time that their decision was stupid. In effect, the feelings of stupidity that accompany a highly mutable negative outcome will leave people feeling that they must have acted against their best judgment. This prospect suggests that counterfactual regret might enhance the well-established tendency for people to overestimate their ability to have foreseen an outcome (Fischhoff, 1975, 1982). For example, a person who experiences a negative fate after deviating from her or his custom of calling heads might reveal an especially pronounced distortion in the recollection of her or his preoutcome expectations, for example, "I knew I shouldn't have called tails." Similarly, the intense regret that attends the changing of a correct answer to an incorrect one might be accompanied by an especially pronounced form of the hindsight bias, for example, "I knew I shouldn't have changed it."

Implications for the Psychology of Counterfactual Thinking

With the present analysis we have aspired to more than the development of an understanding of the role of regret in decision making. We have also sought to develop the implications of a phenomenon Kahneman and Miller (1986) termed the emotional amplification effect: the tendency for people's affective response to an event to be enhanced when the event's causes were abnormal or mutable. Findings from the present research show that the amplified affect that is generated by a mutable negative action–outcome sequence itself has important psychological sequelae. First, the amplified affect biases people's memories for the commonness of the sequence; second, it induces anticipatory regret in people when they contemplate taking an action that might initiate the sequence.

One question pertaining to anticipatory regret that we have not yet addressed concerns its prevalence. In particular, do people anticipate regret whenever they engage in an abnormal action (deviate from routine, for example)? The answer clearly seems to be no. Not all ill-fated actions that evoke regret will, in prospect, have elicited anticipatory regret. People might experience considerable regret when they have an accident after deciding to take a different route home from work (Kahneman & Tversky, 1982b), but they are unlikely to have thought to themselves, when contemplating this decision, "If I take a different route home and have an accident, I will never forgive myself." Whether the magnitude of the anticipatory regret evoked by a prospective action–outcome sequence matches the regret the sequence actually produces will depend on the salience of the negative outcome. People do not typically worry about having an accident on the way home from work and thus will not typically experience anticipatory regret over the decision to take a different route home, however much regret that decision may subsequently evoke in them. On the other hand, if they did have such worries, they would likely experience anticipatory regret and would likely be hesitant to take the different route. We propose as a general principle that people's differential reluctance to engage in mutable as compared to immutable acts will increase as a function of their fear of a negative outcome, with that fear being a joint product of people's subjective judgment of the probability of the outcome's occurrence and their evaluation of the outcome. The more painful the negative outcome, the more regret people will anticipate and the more reluctant they will be to engage in an abnormal course of action. This principle predicts that the hesitancy to deviate from the status quo will increase with the perceived stakes. Thus, the hesitancy to change multiple-choice answers should increase with the importance of one's performance on the test.

Anticipatory regret will also increase with individuals' subjective probability estimates. Consider people's willingness to switch commercial air flights at the last minute. Findings from previous research have shown that a survivor of a plane crash is expected to experience more regret if he or she engages in the highly mutable action of switching flights shortly before takeoff (Miller et al., 1990). Should one assume from this finding that people would be reluctant to switch flights at the last minute? We propose that the reluctance will depend on their fear of crashing. People with an intense fear of flying, people who presumably think incessantly of crashing, can be expected to be very reluctant to switch flights, and possibly even to switch seats. On the other hand, those comfortable with flying might be no more hesitant to switch flights at the last minute than to take a different route home from work. In many cases, the differential hesitancy to engage in abnormal actions will reflect both the subjective probability the decision maker attaches to the occurrence of negative fate and his or her perceptions of its severity. The greater willingness of professors to switch classes than of matadors to switch bulls would seem to reflect just such a confluence of subjective probabilities and subjective utilities.

Two Processes or One?

We have claimed that people's tendency to avoid abnormal actions could reflect the regret they anticipate feeling if misfortune results and that it need not reflect their memory-distorted beliefs about the likelihood of the misfortune's occurring. Thus, we argued that the greater reluctance to sell a lottery ticket as the drawing approached did not derive from people's memories of their experiences with selling lottery tickets but from their subjective utility function: They perceived that the closer the drawing was when they parted with a winning lottery ticket the more intense their regret would be. We confess, however, that it is very difficult to rule out the presence of memory bias even in the lottery example. The difficulty arises with specifying precisely what principle it is that experience teaches. It is true people might not have previous experience with selling lottery tickets but this does not mean they have not had previous experience with similar situations, that is, situations in which they have experienced a misfortune after engaging in a highly mutable action. The lottery situation might fit the template of a more general situation and, hence, evoke a more general principle, for example, "Don't tempt fate." Perhaps the experience of having unwisely changed a multiple-choice answer at the last minute would be sufficient for people to fear that selling a lottery ticket at the last minute might be similarly ill-fated. It is left to other researchers to pursue more vigorously the possibility that subjective utility functions alone can deter people from pursuing a highly mutable course of action.

Establishing the independent role of anticipatory regret will not be easy. The most straightforward means of assessing the independent power of anticipatory regret will be to show that people will avoid an abnormal action even if they do not believe that the action is any more likely than another to lead to a negative outcome. This standard, however, may prove too strong a test for the anticipatory-regret hypothesis. The problem is this: One of the effects of anticipating that an event will make a person feel bad is that its occurrence will seem more likely (cf. Johnson & Tversky, 1983). Subjective expectancies are influenced by subjective utilities, not just by recollected experiences. Thus, as the dread of a negative outcome occurring through a particular action increases so will its subjective probability. There are at least two reasons for this pattern. First, people consider their feelings to be information (Miller & Turnbull, 1990; Schwarz, 1990) and, therefore, are disposed to overestimate the likelihood of a negative outcome based on their fear of its happening. Second, people estimate the probability of an event at least partly by the vividness with which they can imagine it (Carroll, 1978; Sherman, Cialdini, Schwartzman, & Reynolds, 1985). Thus, anticipating the counterfactual thoughts that a negative event will evoke, because it will tend to make the event more vivid, will tend to make it more subjectively likely.

Consider once again the lottery scenario involving Mr. K and Mr. T. Might the fear these men have of experiencing self-recrimination in the event they sold a winning ticket affect their estimates of the chances that a sold ticket will win? To examine this question, we provided a group of participants with the previously described lottery scenario and asked them the following three questions.

Who would be most optimistic of winning if he resisted selling his ticket?

Mr. K	12%	
Mr. T	5%	
No difference	83%	$N = 92$

Who would have the strongest expectation that his ticket would win if he were to sell it?

Mr. K	12%	
Mr. T	58%	
No difference	30%	$N = 92$

Who would have the greatest sense that he was tempting fate if he were to sell his ticket?

Mr. K	8%	
Mr. T	62%	
No difference	30%	$N = 92$

The results indicated that participants believed there would be no difference in the two men's hopes of winning were they to refuse the friend's offer. However, participants predicted that the two men would have different expectancies were they to accept the friend's offer. Mr. T (the man who sold his ticket closest to the drawing) was expected to be more optimistic that his (former) ticket would win. This result suggests that the participants' prediction that Mr. T would show greater reluctance to sell his ticket was not guided by their belief that his *retained* ticket is more likely to win. Rather, it seems guided by their belief that his *sold* ticket would be more likely to win. The decision not to sell, then, is just that—a decision not to part with the ticket, not a decision to keep the ticket. The ticket's capacity to yield satisfaction is not assumed to be enhanced by one's retaining it, even though its capacity to yield dissatisfaction is assumed to be enhanced by one's selling it.

To undertake a risky action one easily imagined otherwise (such as selling a lottery ticket close to the drawing) is to tempt fate. We contend that one tempts fate not only when one opts for one action when there exists an alternative action that makes more sense or has a better chance of a positive outcome, but also anytime one takes an action that will be easy to undo mentally. To say "It would be just my luck if I switched from this line to the other, that this line will speed up and the other will slow down" is not to commit oneself to the proposition that not switching means one's line is likely to speed up. One is just "asking for it" if one takes an action he or she knows, in retrospect, will be easy to imagine otherwise. Similarly, to insist on wearing one's lucky shoes to the final exam is not necessarily to commit oneself to the proposition that he or she will do better than others who do not own lucky shoes. Wearing the lucky shoes might not even commit the person to the proposition that he or she would do worse if he or she did not wear his or her lucky shoes. It might commit the person only to the proposition that he or she is just asking for it by not wearing them. If things turn out badly after the person chooses not to wear his or her lucky shoes, he or she will be forced to endure intense self-recriminations. In essence, having lucky shoes means one also has one or more pairs of "unlucky" shoes, the wearing of which will leave him or her fearful of impending disaster and vulnerable to relentless self-recrimination.

Reflections on Superstitions

With our present analysis we probed the psychology of superstition at a number of levels. For one thing, the analysis offers an account for why people might be hesitant to do things that they fear will lead to a bad outcome even when they cannot provide a rational account for the fear. People's hesitancies to switch lines or to throw out long-held possessions qualify as examples of this type. People often claim that although they do not know the reason that when they throw out some long-unused object they soon find themselves needing it, they know it is so and engage in the practice only against their better judgment (e.g., "You know, I have had this bat repellent for 10 years and have never used it, but—just you wait—now that I'm throwing it out, we'll be infested with bats"). The previously discussed Spanish superstition against matador substitution provides an even more dramatic example of this process.

Of course, many behaviors having the same psychological underpinnings as superstitions do not seem to be superstitions because they are assumed to be rational. The reason that blackjack players stand when they are holding 16 may have everything to do with nascent feelings of anticipatory regret but the players appear to think the strategy merely reflects playing the odds. Indeed, Meyer Lansky, the legendary crime figure and reputed gambling genius, regularly instructed blackjack players that the odds dictated that one hold at 16. The mistaken belief that the odds dictate standing at 16 might even increase with experience. Keren and Wagenaar (1985) found that experienced blackjack players frequently claimed that amateurs could be distinguished from the professional gamblers because of their tendency to take too many cards.

The fact that psychologically painful sequences (whether or not the pain is produced by self-recriminations) tend to be memorable sequences may underlie a great many superstitions. We ask the reader to consider which of the following sequences is more common in his or her experience: (1) The data from the first few research participants look good and look even better when you have run 15 per cell or (2) the data from the first few participants look good but turn to mush by the time you have run 15 per cell. Many researchers may share our intuition that the latter sequence is much more common than the former (even allowing for regression to the mean); in fact, many may even share our belief that one should not look at early data because doing so "jinxes" them. We suggest that this belief (superstition?) emerges because of the tendency for bad data following good data to be so painful. Sequences that raise, then dash, hopes will be more available in memory and hence lead to the formation of erroneous beliefs.

Is Fearing Regret Rational or Irrational?

We end with a consideration of the question of rationality. Is the behavior we have attributed to anticipatory regret more appropriately termed rational or irrational? The answer depends on what the person is trying to maximize through his or her behavior. If a person's goal is to maximize satisfaction rather than profit, then to be guided by anticipatory regret cannot be considered irrational. If changing a correct answer to a wrong answer causes a person much more pain than earning another point brings the person pleasure, then the person is hardly being irrational by refusing to change an answer that he or she thinks—but does not know for sure—is wrong. Similarly, if losing a point in tennis through double-faulting causes more pain than winning a point gives pleasure, then it is hardly irrational to have a weak second serve. Likewise people can hardly be called irrational if their custom is to arrive at airports so early that they waste much more time than an occasional missed flight would cost them. The if only thoughts that arise when one arrives a few minutes late for a flight might be so aversive that people are happy to trade hours of boredom to ensure that they are never beset by the thought "If only I had left a few minutes earlier, I would have made it." On the other hand, if people do wish to maximize profit exclusively, then the beliefs we have focused on can more appropriately be termed irrational. If a person's only goal in blackjack is to maximize profit (minimize loss) then it is irrational to refuse a card at 16.

Final Thoughts

We sought in this chapter to expand the dominion of norm theory to encompass psychological domains not previously considered to lie within its sphere of influence, in particular, people's memory for the past and their beliefs about the future. Two central claims guided our quest. The first is that the counterfactual thoughts evoked by an event sequence affect the availability of that sequence in memory. The more powerfully an event sequence evokes thoughts of what might have been, the more available in memory the sequence will be and, as a result, the more common the sequence will seem. The second central claim is that the postcomputed thoughts and images that a negative event sequence brings to mind can be precomputed. People can anticipate the self-recriminations that an ill-fated behavioral sequence will evoke in them. Moreover, it is often these feelings, the intensity of which follows from various rules of mutability, rather than people's estimates of the chances of a negative outcome that determine the actions they take. We hope that the steps taken here, as preliminary and tentative as they are, have made it at least a little easier to imagine the counterfactual world in which counterfactual thinking is well understood.

ACKNOWLEDGMENTS

The research reported in this chapter was supported by a grant to Dale Miller from the National Institute of Mental Health and a doctoral fellowship to Brian Taylor from the Social Science and Humanities Research Council of Canada. Portions of this chapter were presented at the annual meeting of the Society for Experimental Social Psychology, Columbus, Ohio, October 1991. We thank James Olson, Deborah Prentice, Neal Roese, and Jacquie Vorauer for their helpful critiques of an earlier version of this chapter.

Correspondence concerning the contents of this chapter should be addressed to Dale T. Miller, Department of Psychology, Green Hall, Princeton University, Princeton, NJ 08544–1010.

REFERENCES

Bell, D. E. (1982). Regret in decision making under uncertainty. *Operations Research, 30,* 961–981.

Bell, D. E. (1983). Risk premiums for decision regret. *Management Science, 29,* 1156–1166.

Bell, D. E. (1985a). Disappointment in decision making under uncertainty. *Operations Research, 33,* 1–27.

Bell, D. E. (1985b). Putting a premium on regret. *Management Science, 31,* 117–120.

Buck, M. L., & Miller, D. T. (1994). Reactions to incongruous negative life events. *Social Justice Research, 7,* 29–46.

Carroll, J. S. (1978). The effect of imagining an event on expectations for the event: An interpretation in terms of the availability heuristic. *Journal of Experimental Social Psychology, 14,* 88–96.

Fischhoff, B. (1975). Hindsight≠foresight: The effects of outcome knowledge on judgment under uncertainty. *Journal of Experimental Psychology: Human Perception and Performance, 1,* 288–299.

Fischhoff, B. (1982). For those condemned to study the past: Heuristics and biases in hindsight. In D. Kahneman, P. Slovic, & A. Tversky (Eds.), *Judgment under uncertainty: Heuristics and biases* (pp. 422–444). New York: Cambridge University Press.

Fishburn, P. (1983). Nontransitive measurable utility. *Journal of Mathematical Psychology, 26,* 31–67.

Gilovich, T., Medvec, V. H., & Chen, S. (1995). Omission, commission, and dissonance reduction: Coping with regret in the "Monty Hall" problem. *Personality and Social Psychology Bulletin, 21,* 182–190.

Goldaper, S. (1990, June 9). Pistons put the game on the line. *The New York Times,* p. C46.

MILLER AND TAYLOR

Janis, I. J., & Mann, L. (1977). *Decision making: A psychological analysis of conflict, choice, and commitment.* New York: Free Press.

Johnson, E. J., & Tversky, A. (1983). Affect generalization and the perception of risk. *Journal of Personality and Social Psychology, 45,* 20–31.

Kahneman, D., & Miller, D. T. (1986). Norm theory: Comparing reality to its alternatives. *Psychological Review, 93,* 136–153.

Kahneman, D., & Tversky, A. (1982a). The psychology of preferences. *Scientific American, 246*(1), 160–173.

Kahneman, D., & Tversky, A. (1982b). The simulation heuristic. In D. Kahneman, P. Slovic, & A. Tversky (Eds.), *Judgment under uncertainty: Heuristics and biases (pp. 201–208).* New York: Cambridge University Press.

Keren, G., & Wagenaar, W. A. (1985). On the psychology of playing blackjack: Normative and descriptive considerations with implications for decision theory. *Journal of Experimental Psychology: General, 114,* 133–158.

Landman, J. (1987). Regret and elation following action and inaction: Affective responses to positive versus negative outcomes. *Personality and Social Psychology Bulletin, 13,* 524–536.

Loomes, G. (1988). Further evidence of the impact of regret and disappointment in choice and uncertainty. *Economica, 55,* 47–62.

Loomes, G., & Sugden, R. (1982). Regret theory: An alternative theory of rational choice under uncertainty. *Economic Journal, 92,* 805–824.

Loomes, G., & Sugden, R. (1987a). Some implications of a more general form of regret theory. *Journal of Economic Theory, 41,* 270–287.

Loomes, G., & Sugden, R. (1987b). Testing for regret and disappointment in choice under uncertainty. *Economic Journal, 97,* 118–129.

Miller, D. T. (1991, October). *Counterfactual thinking and decision making.* Paper presented at the annual meeting of the Society for Experimental Social Psychology, Columbus, OH.

Miller, D. T., & Gunasegaram, S. (1990). Temporal order and the perceived mutability of events: Implications for blame assignment. *Journal of Personality and Social Psychology, 59,* 1111–1118.

Miller, D. T., & McFarland, C. (1986). Counterfactual thinking and victim compensation: A test of norm theory. *Personality and Social Psychology Bulletin, 12,* 513–519.

Miller, D. T., & Turnbull, W. (1990). The counterfactual fallacy: Confusing what might have been with what ought to have been. *Social Justice Research, 4,* 1–19.

Miller, D. T., Turnbull, W., & McFarland, C. (1990). Counterfactual thinking and social perception: Thinking about what might have been. In M. P. Zanna (Ed.), *Advances in experimental social psychology* (Vol. 23, pp. 305–331). New York: Academic Press.

Ritov, I., & Baron, J. (1990). Reluctance to vaccinate: Commission bias and ambiguity. *Journal of Behavioral Decision Making, 3,* 263–277.

Ritov, I., & Baron, J. (1992). Status-quo and omission biases. *Journal of Risk and Uncertainty, 5,* 49–61.

Schumacher, E. (1985, September 21). Death of "Yiyo" raises passions over bullfights. *The Globe and Mail,* p. B9.

Schwarz, N. (1990). Feelings as information: Informational and motivational functions of affective states. In E. T. Higgins & R. M. Sorrentino (Eds.), *Handbook of motivation and cognition: Foundations of social behavior* (Vol. 2, pp. 527–561). New York: Guilford.

Sherman, S. J., Cialdini, R. B., Schwartzman, D. F., & Reynolds, K. D. (1985). Imagining can heighten or lower the perceived likelihood of contracting a disease: The mediating effect of ease of imagery. *Personality and Social Psychology Bulletin, 11,* 118–127.

Simonson, I. (1992). The influence of anticipating regret and responsibility on purchase decisions. *Journal of Consumer Research, 19,* 105–118.

Spranca, M., Minsk, E., & Baron, J. (1991). Omission and commission in judgment and choice. *Journal of Experimental and Social Psychology, 27,* 76–105.

Sugden, R. (1985). Regret, recrimination and rationality. *Theory and Decision, 19,* 77–99.

Taylor, B. (1989). *Mental simulation and the anticipation of regret.* Unpublished master's thesis, Princeton University, Princeton, NJ.

Taylor, B. (1991). *The effects of counterfactual thought on affect, memory, and beliefs.* Unpublished doctoral dissertation, Princeton University, Princeton, NJ.

Tversky, A., & Kahneman, D. (1973). Availability: A heuristic for judging frequency and probability. *Cognitive Psychology, 5,* 207–232.

Walster, E., Walster, G. W., Piliavin, E., & Schmidt, L. (1973). Playing hard to get: Understanding an elusive phenomenon. *Journal of Personality and Social Psychology, 26,* 113–121.

Wells, G. L., & Gavanski, I. (1989). Mental simulation of causality. *Journal of Personality and Social Psychology, 56,* 161–169.

12

Counterfactual and Contrastive Reasoning in Explanations for Performance: Implications for Gender Bias

Ann L. McGill
Jill G. Klein
Northwestern University

Our purpose in this chapter is to examine causal explanations for performance. We focus especially on explanations for the poor performance of women as compared to men in traditionally male-oriented employment such as engineering and fire fighting. Gender-based explanations for performance, for example, "Sally did poorly because she is a woman," may have important business and social implications. These explanations may shape employment policies, judgments of job candidates, promotions, salary levels, and opportunities for further training and education. Further, these explanations may affect women's sense of themselves (e.g., "I'm just not meant to be good at such things"), their willingness to persevere through adversity (e.g., "This job is simply not suited to someone like me. Maybe I should give up and focus on having kids"), and their chance to dream (e.g., "Wanting to be a firefighter is just silly for someone like me").

In this chapter we therefore consider how people form explanations for performance and identify conditions that may bias these judgments through incomplete use of information. These biases may involve attributions to gender for which no relationship between gender and performance is indicated in the data, or attributions to gender for women's poor performance (e.g., "Mary failed because she is a woman") but attributions to individual traits for men's poor performance (e.g., "Tom failed because he is lazy"). In particular, we examine two distinct forms of reasoning in explanations for performance, counterfactual reasoning and contrastive reasoning; describe differences in the type of information considered within each type of reasoning; and identify conditions in which people are more likely to use contrastive rather than counterfactual judgment.

COUNTERFACTUAL AND CONTRASTIVE REASONING[1]

For purposes of the present chapter, we focus on a simple form of counterfactual reasoning in which an individual evaluates a possible causal candidate (X) for the event (Y) through the counterfactual question, Would the event Y have occurred if the candidate X had not? The candidate is considered a good explanation for the event if it seems unlikely that the event would have occurred were the candidate removed. For example, one might use counterfactual reasoning to evaluate whether a woman's failure was related to her gender by asking whether failure would have occurred had the company hired a man instead of a woman. If it does not appear that a man would have failed in the same position, people would be more likely to attribute the failure to the employee's being a woman.

Findings from prior research suggest two ways in which people may answer the counterfactual question. One way is through mental simulation (Wells & Gavanski, 1989). This process involves the person's removing the candidate X from her or his representation of events and imagining what might have occurred. A second way of answering the counterfactual question is to refer to existing covariation information regarding the number of instances in which the candidate factor X was absent but the event Y nevertheless occurred (Lipe, 1991). For example, in trying to determine whether being a woman caused an employee to fail, people may consider the number of men who had failed in similar positions in the same firm. If many men had failed, then the women's gender is a weaker explanation than if few men had failed.

Other researchers have examined the use of *contrastive reasoning* in causal judgments (Cheng & Novick, 1990; Hilton & Slugoski, 1986; McGill, 1989, 1990a; see also Mackie, 1974). According to these research findings, people identify causal explanations by contrasting the target episode (e.g., the employee who failed) with *background* instances in which the event did not occur (e.g., other employees who succeeded). Distinctive features between the target episode and contrasting background instances are

---

[1]Arguments presented in the following two sections of this chapter are based on ideas that were first presented in McGill and Klein (1993).

possible causal explanations. For example, if all employees who had succeeded in the past were men, the gender of the women who failed is distinctive and therefore a possible explanation for the event. By contrast, if several women had succeeded in the past, gender is a weaker explanation for the woman's poor performance.

Counterfactual and contrastive reasoning may both be described as *counterfactual* in that with each the person considers instances in which some aspect of the event has been negated (Hilton, 1990; Lipe, 1991). The two types of reasoning differ, however, in the dimension affected. Specifically, in counterfactual reasoning, one focuses on instances in which the candidate is absent (e.g., Would the employee have failed had she not been a woman?), whereas in contrastive reasoning, one considers instances in which the effect is absent (e.g., What made the difference between the employee who failed and the employees who did not fail?).[2]

Counterfactual and contrastive reasoning thus emphasize different aspects of causation and imply different weighting of covariation information (Einhorn & Hogarth, 1986). Counterfactual reasoning, by its focus on instances in which the candidate is absent, emphasizes the necessity of a factor. For example, instances in which men failed suggest that being a woman is not necessary for failure. With counterfactual reasoning, one thus emphasizes "C-cell" instances in a traditionally labeled contingency table (Lipe, 1991; Figure 12.1 displays a traditionally labeled contingency table). Alternatively, with contrastive reasoning, by its focus on instances in which the effect is absent, one emphasizes the sufficiency of a factor (Mackie, 1974). For example, instances in which other women succeeded suggest that being a woman is not a sufficient explanation for failure. Contrastive reasoning thus focuses on "B-cell" information.

Conditions for Use of Contrastive and Counterfactual Reasoning

Both counterfactual and contrastive reasoning are needed for a complete assessment of causation (Hilton, 1990). Findings from prior research suggest, however, that people use different types of reasoning under different circumstances, a tendency leading to incomplete use of covariation information (McGill & Klein, 1993). Specifically, research findings indicate that counterfactual reasoning and contrastive reasoning may correspond to different types of causal judgments, one of which involves determining whether a factor is among those that influenced an occurrence, and the

---

[2]Roese and Olson (chapter 1) refer to counterfactual reasoning as it is described in this chapter as "antecedent-contrastive" reasoning because it focuses on instances in which the candidate antecedent factor is altered, and to contrastive reasoning as "outcome-contrastive" reasoning because it focuses on instances in which the outcome is altered.

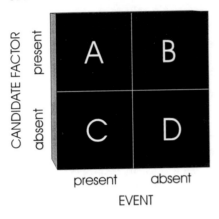

present   absent
EVENT

FIG. 12.1. Traditionally labeled
.contingency table.

other of which involves selecting factors from this larger set to create a
causal explanation for the event (Hilton, 1990; McGill, 1990b). As an
illustration of this distinction, note that most events are produced, not
by single factors, but instead by complex configurations of factors (Leddo,
Abelson, & Gross, 1984; Read, 1988). For example, the physical phenomenon fire is produced by a sparking agent, the presence of flammable
material, and the presence of oxygen. Hence, one causal judgment involves learning the factors that produce such an occurrence. For example,
one may learn that fire will not occur in the absence of oxygen. Similarly,
social outcomes, such as poor employee performance, may also result
from a configuration of factors, for example, gender of the employee,
type of supervision, company culture, technical support, and so forth. To
understand such events, one must judge whether gender should be included among the factors that caused an employee to fail.

Findings from prior research suggest that people judge such proposals
by engaging in counterfactual reasoning. That is, they judge whether a
factor is related to an occurrence by asking whether the event would
have occurred anyway were the factor in question absent (Adi, Karplus,
Lawson, & Pulos, 1978; Hilton, 1990; Wells & Gavanski, 1989). In this
sense, counterfactual reasoning is a testing mechanism by which a person
judges whether there exists a causal relationship between a proposed
factor and an event. Research findings suggest, therefore, that when
presented with an *evaluation-focused* question, which asks people to evaluate a specific causal factor (e.g., Did something about being a woman
cause the employee to fail?), people will engage in counterfactual thinking, thereby placing greater emphasis on necessity and C-cell instances.

Other research findings indicate, however, that in devising a causal
explanation for an occurrence, people typically do not report the complete
set of factors that they believe configured to produce an event. Instead
they select a subset of these factors (e.g., Einhorn & Hogarth, 1986; Hilton,

1990; Hilton & Slugoski, 1986; McGill, 1989, 1990b; see also Mackie, 1974). Rationale for this selection process is provided by past research findings indicating that people tend to initiate causal reasoning for events that are unusual or unexpected (see Weiner, 1985, for a review). In such cases, the event to be explained is not the target episode per se but the difference between the target episode and the contrasting usual or expected instances (Hastie, 1984; Hilton, 1990; Hilton & Slugoski, 1986; McGill, 1989; D. Miller, Taylor, & Buck, 1991). The purpose of the explanation is to account for the difference or deviation between the target episode and the contrasting cases (McGill, 1989). For example, if one is interested in determining why one employee failed although others in the same company succeeded, factors shared by the unsuccessful and successful employees (e.g., company culture and level of technical support) would not account for the difference in performance of the unsuccessful employee. Instead, some distinguishing factor, for example, gender of the employee or level of supervision, would explain the event. Prior research findings suggest therefore that when asked to provide an explanation for an occurrence (e.g., What caused the employee to fail?), people will first attempt to identify factors that distinguish the target episode from the contrasting background cases. Thus, in contrast to evaluation-focused questions, which ask people to evaluate a specific candidate, the more open explanation-focused questions are expected to produce contrastive thinking, with greater emphasis on sufficiency and B-cell instances.[3]

Prior Research

We recently examined the hypothesis that people may employ counterfactual and contrastive reasoning under different conditions in a pair of studies involving participants' causal attributions for poor performance (McGill & Klein, 1993). Stimuli for these experiments described a woman

---

[3]Technically speaking, use of contrastive reasoning does not involve *explicit* consideration of B-cell instances because no specific candidate factor has been identified; that is, construction of a contingency table requires prior specification of a causal candidate. Identification of factors that distinguish the target episode from the contrasting background cases in which the event did not occur involves *implicit* consideration of B-cell instances, however. For example, a factor for which there are (implicitly) many B-cell instances would not be identified as a possible causal explanation because although that factor is present in the target episode it is also present in the many cases in which the event did not occur. In contrast, a factor for which there are (implicitly) few B-cell instances may be identified as a possible causal explanation because that factor is present in the target episode and rarely associated with cases in which the event did not occur. The factor thus distinguishes the target episode from the contrasting background cases. For ease of exposition, we refer to people "using B-cell information" in contrastive reasoning to indicate the identification of factors that distinguish the target episode from cases in which the event did not occur.

who failed at a task. Participants were presented information on the prior performance by men and women on the same task and asked to indicate how likely the woman's failure was related to her gender.

We manipulated two factors in the experimental design. The first factor involved the degree of specificity of the causal question, that is, whether it preidentified gender as a possible causal explanation for the woman's failure ("Do you think something about being female caused Mary to fail at this task?") or asked participants to identify a possible explanation of their own ("What do you think caused Mary to fail?"). Following the rationale presented above regarding conditions favoring the use of counterfactual versus contrastive reasoning, we hypothesized that participants would likely engage in counterfactual reasoning when the question preidentified a specific candidate explanation and would favor contrastive reasoning when the question made no reference to a specific candidate and instead asked participants to identify a possible explanation.

We manipulated a second factor, the pattern of covariation information regarding the prior success and failure of men and women, in order to detect emphasis placed on B-cell and C-cell information. The two patterns, "men fail" and "women succeed," are shown in Table 12.1.[4] These patterns reflect the same degree of covariation between gender and performance. In both patterns, five of the seven cases support the relationship between gender and performance (specifically, one woman failed and four men succeeded), whereas two cases contradict a relationship between gender and performance. The patterns differ in whether this contradictory information is presented in the form of other women having succeeded (i.e., B-cell information) versus other men having failed (i.e., C-cell information). In the men-fail condition, there are no instances in which women had succeeded in the past (i.e., there are no B-cell instances), but one third of the men who had attempted this task had failed (i.e., there are two C-cell instances). In the women-succeed condition, there are no instances in which men had failed at this task (i.e., there are no C-cell instances), but two thirds of the women who had attempted this task had succeeded (i.e., there are two B-cell instances). Thus, greater emphasis on B-cell versus C-cell information would be indicated by different ratings of causal strength for the two covariation patterns.

Results of the experiments indicated a main effect for covariation pattern. Participants rated gender a more likely explanation in the men-fail than in the woman-succeed condition, results suggesting greater

---

[4]The men-fail and women-succeed conditions were called the "no successful females–prior unsuccessful males" and "prior successful females–no unsuccessful males" conditions, respectively, in the article in which this study was originally reported (McGill & Klein, 1993).

TABLE 12.1
Patterns of Covariation Information of Gender and Performance

Condition and Gender	Performance	
	Failure	Success
Men Fail		
Women	1	0
Men	2	4
Women Succeed		
Women	1	2
Men	0	4

Note. Copyright 1993 by the American Psychological Association, Inc. Adapted from "Contrastive and casual reasoning in counterfactual judgment," by A. L. McGill and J. G. Klein (1993).

emphasis on B-cell information and contrastive thinking than on C-cell information and counterfactual thinking. That is, participants thought gender a more likely explanation for failure when there were no instances in which women had succeeded in the past, despite evidence that men too had commonly failed at this task, than when there were two instances in which women had succeeded but no men had failed.

The main effect for covariation pattern was moderated, however, by a significant covariation pattern interaction. As predicted, participants who were not asked to evaluate a preidentified candidate but were instead asked to identify a causal explanation of their own (i.e., the causal question did not mention gender specifically) appeared to rely on contrastive thinking, placing greater emphasis on B-cell than on C-cell information. In contrast, participants who were asked to evaluate specifically whether gender was related to failure appeared to consider both B-cell and C-cell information. Additional process-tracing data indicated that participants who were asked to evaluate a preidentified candidate first engaged in contrastive thinking to ensure the factor was sufficient for the event and then engaged in counterfactual thinking to evaluate its necessity.

Implications of Findings

Results of the experiments supported the hypothesis that people may emphasize counterfactual or contrastive reasoning under different conditions. Findings also indicate the importance of contrastive reasoning in causal judgment. Across conditions, participants placed greater emphasis on B-cell information than on C-cell information in judging the strength of the causal relationship between gender and performance. That is, information about women who *can* perform a task (B-cell information) appears to decrease people's beliefs that gender is related to performance more than information about men who *cannot* perform the task (C-cell information).

The limited impact of C-cell information is evidenced in the struggle for acceptance by female firefighters. These women report that the question most commonly asked of them is whether they can carry a stricken 200-pound person from a burning building (Keegan, 1991). The women argue that although most of them cannot perform this feat (i.e., there are few B-cell instances), this question should not be used to eliminate women from consideration as firefighters because many male firefighters also cannot perform this task (i.e., there are many C-cell instances).

Arguments based on the presence of C-cell instances may be especially ineffective in the case of female firefighters: Prior beliefs about the relative strength of men and women may incline people to accept causal explanations based on gender for poor performance on physical tasks without further analysis of available data. This reliance on prior beliefs over counterfactual thinking is unfortunate, however, because people ignore the number of men who also cannot perform the feat. Such data indicate that being a woman is not necessary for failure and that another factor unrelated to gender may be a better explanation for a woman's poor performance.

To appreciate the operation of gender versus nongender-based explanations, note that individual men differ greatly in strength, likely due to a host of factors such as height, age, genetic differences in muscle mass, athletic ability, background, conditioning, and so forth. Women similarly differ in strength, again, due to a variety of individual factors. Thus, there are physically strong women and weak women, just as there are physically strong men and weak men.

True, men can lift more weight, *on average*, than can women. In a regression sense, this difference indicates that *gender explains some but not all of the variance* in strength among individuals. Thus, average differences in strength notwithstanding, many women are stronger than many men, and many tasks are easily accomplished by most men and most women, whereas other tasks are beyond the reach of most men and most women. It seems odd, therefore, to suggest that gender is *the* cause of a woman's inability to lift a weight. For example, if the task were extremely easy, such as lifting a 10-pound weight, attribution to gender would seem absurd. Women are on average physically weaker than men, but clearly a person who fails to lift such a weight is an unusually weak person, male or female, and some other explanation that is not based on gender should be considered. Similarly, if the task were extremely difficult, for example, lifting a 500-pound weight, attribution to gender for a woman's failure to do so would again seem absurd. Most people, male and female, cannot lift this weight, although there may be a few men who can do so. For one to blame gender for a woman's failing to lift an extreme weight, arguing that men and women differ in physical strength, is akin to blaming gender for not being seven feet tall, arguing that men and women differ in height.

We suggest, however, that such arguments are common and that men and women who cannot perform a task are treated differently, especially if a small number of men are able to perform the task. Specifically, we suggest that people identify gender as a possible explanation for a woman's poor performance either through contrastive reasoning or through prior expectation. Unfortunately, people do not then evaluate this explanation further by using counterfactual reasoning to determine whether a rival account that is not based on gender might better explain the event. Thus, women who cannot perform such tasks are dismissed as inappropriate by virtue of their gender.

In contrast, causal explanations for men who cannot perform the task do not involve gender but instead concern some personal and potentially correctable shortcoming compared to the men who can perform the feat. Thus, men who cannot perform the task are not dismissed as unacceptable but are instead legitimized by the few men who can perform the feat. The task is "for men" because only men can do it. Men who fail are therefore admonished to shed a few pounds, run a few miles, or spend some time in the gym but are not rejected as wholly unsuited to the task. Thus, underutilization of C-cell information enables people to adopt gender-based explanations for women's poor performance (e.g., "Myra cannot lift the weight because women lack upper body strength") and nongender-based explanations for men's poor performance (e.g., "Phil cannot lift the weight because he does not exercise enough"). Because of this reasoning, we may observe female recruits being rejected because they cannot lift the stricken victim, whereas male recruits (or veterans) who are equally incapable of lifting this weight being considered acceptable (if simply a bit out of shape).

Overview of the Experiment

We examined the hypothesis that men and women who fail at a task will be evaluated differently in the context of recruiting decisions for a fire-fighting unit. Participants in the experiment were 48 graduate students, approximately two thirds of whom were men and one third were women, at the J. L. Kellogg Graduate School of Management at Northwestern University. Participants were first presented covariation information about the prior performance of male and female trainees who attempted to carry a 200-pound test dummy. Two different patterns of information were presented. These men-fail and women-succeed patterns were the same as those employed in our earlier study and are shown in Table 12.1.

Participants were then asked five questions about the preferred composition of subsequent training classes. The first asked them to indicate the
minimum number of men to be included in a class of 50 students. We
expected that participants who were presented the men-fail pattern of
covariation information would include a greater number of men in the
program and, hence, fewer women, than participants presented the
women-succeed pattern of information. This hypothesis follows from
results of our earlier study indicating that participants perceived a stronger
causal link between gender and performance in the men-fail than in the
women-succeed condition.[5]

Participants were then informed about the performance of a specific
trainee who failed to complete the weight-lifting task. They were told
that the program required trainees to locate a 200-pound test dummy in
a smoky building and then to carry the dummy down two flights of stairs
to safety. The trainee made a good effort, locating the dummy and
carrying it down one of the two required flights of stairs. Materials
indicated that the trainee was otherwise a model recruit, intelligent and
motivated. Participants were then asked to rate on a 1–7 scale whether
the trainee should be hired, despite having failed the weight-lifting task
and, in an open-ended question, to indicate why or why not.

We expected participants' hiring decisions and subsequent rationale
to vary with gender of the recruit, which we manipulated by varying the
recruit's name, John or Mary, used in the description. Specifically, we
expected participants to be more inclined to hire the male trainee who
could not complete the carrying task than the female trainee and to offer
the rationale that the male but not the female recruit could exercise to
build strength for the weight-lifting task.

This hypothesis follows from our previous findings indicating that
people underemphasize counterfactual reasoning in questions of performance, thereby allowing different explanations for the poor performance
of women and men. Thus, participants were expected to believe that the
woman failed because of her gender and, therefore, should not be hired,
but to believe that the man failed because of a personal and potentially
correctable shortcoming and, therefore, should be hired.

Results of the Experiment

We first analyzed participants' specification of the minimum number of
men to be included in a training class of 50 students. As expected, the

---

[5]The remaining four questions about training class composition, which addressed
minimum and maximum ages of recruits and the importance of the weight-lifting task,
were included to mask the purpose of the study. There were no significant effects for these
questions by experimental condition.

minimum number of men varied with the pattern of covariation information. Those in the men-fail condition specified a greater number of men ($M = 38.82$) than did participants in the women-succeed condition ($M = 28.40$).

We then analyzed participants' ratings of their willingness to hire the trainee who had failed the weight-lifting task. Mean ratings for this measure are provided in Table 12.2. Results of the analysis indicated that participants' willingness to hire the trainee varied by gender of the trainee and pattern of covariation. Specifically, participants appeared most willing to recommend hiring when the trainee was female and prior data suggested the men-fail pattern of covariation, next most willing to hire the male trainee in the women-succeed condition, then to hire the male trainee in the men-fail condition, and least willing to hire the female trainee in the women-succeed condition.

Analysis of participants' written explanations provided additional insight into their hiring decisions. Participants' responses were coded for two factors: whether they suggested the recruit should exercise to build strength and whether they suggested that the recruit should be hired to perform tasks other than those requiring physical strength. Table 12.3 provides the number of participants in each condition who suggested that the trainee should exercise to build strength. As expected, over twice as many participants suggested that the male trainee try to build strength for the task as those who suggested the same for the female trainee. This pattern did not vary by pattern of covariation information. The table also provides the number of participants in each condition who suggested that the trainee be hired to perform tasks other than those requiring physical strength, such as crawling through small spaces or dispatching paramedic units. Findings indicated that participants thought women more suited than men to perform these tasks. This pattern also did not vary by covariation condition.

TABLE 12.2
Mean Ratings by Gender and Covariation Pattern of Willingness
to Hire the Trainee

	Covariation Pattern	
Gender of Trainee	Men Fail	Women Succeed
Male	4.31	4.93
n	15	16
Female	5.17	4.00
n	12	15

Note. Ratings were provided on a 1–7 scale with the higher numbers representing greater willingness to hire the trainees.

TABLE 12.3
Number of Participant Suggestions Contained
in Responses to Open-Ended Question

Suggestion/ Gender of Trainee	Present	Absent
Suggestion to Exercise		
Male	11	20
Female	4	23
Suggestion for Other Tasks		
Male	18	9
Female	9	22

Discussion

Results of the experiment supported the hypothesis that people will treat men and women who fail at a task differently. As was not expected, however, participants in this study exhibited greater willingness to hire the female trainee in the men-fail condition than trainees in any other condition. Given prior expectations about the relative strength of men and women, we were surprised that participants were most willing to hire the female trainee when prior data provided no evidence that women were able to accomplish the weight-lifting task. This result is more readily understood, however, when one notes that participants appeared not to want to hire this female trainee for the full range of fire-fighting duties but to perform special tasks that did not require great strength. Thus, consistent with predictions for the study, the results indicated that participants were less willing to hire the female trainee who failed than the male trainee who failed and willing instead to offer the female trainee a "special" job which they perceived as more suited to her capabilities as a woman.

Further findings consistent with the hypothesis that people rely on gender-based explanations for women but idiosyncratic explanations for men indicated that participants exhibited greater willingness to believe that the male trainee might be able to succeed with additional effort, such as exercising to build strength, compared to the female trainee. It appears therefore that people believe that men fail simply because they have not reached their full potential as men; women, on the other hand, fail because of the "uncorrectable problem" of gender.

An alternative explanation for the greater frequency with which participants suggested that the male trainee exercise to build strength compared to the female trainee is based on the assumption that participants might have held different beliefs regarding the effectiveness of weight training for men and women. That is, they might have believed that exercise was more likely to benefit the male trainee than the female trainee and so were more likely to suggest this approach for the man. Data from the experiment did not support this alternative account, however. Specifically, if participants were basing their suggestions on the probability of improved performance with exercise, then they should have been more likely to suggest that the female trainee attempt an exercise program in the women-succeed condition compared to the men-fail condition. Two of three women were able to carry the test dummy in the women-succeed condition, information indicating that the task is within women's capabilities. In contrast, no women succeeded in the men-fail condition, information suggesting that it was not possible for a woman to carry such a weight. Hence, weight training would appear to have a higher probability of ensuring success in the women-succeed than in the men-fail condition. Frequency of suggestions that the trainee exercise to build strength did not vary by covariation condition, however, results indicating that participants were not basing their judgments on expected probability of improvement.

It should be noted that participants' willingness to hire female trainees for special tasks might have been pronounced in this study because we used business students as participants. These students are exposed to substantial discussion of issues related to fairness and diversity both in and out of the classroom. Thus, students are aware that tasks are commonly accomplished in teams, that team members bring to tasks distinctive skills and knowledge, and that single, uniform screening measures such as the weight-lifting task may be discriminatory and countereffective. Despite the merit of these views, the participants in this study appeared to misapply the concepts, recognizing the importance of hiring a portfolio of skills to the team but binding these skills to gender. Thus, by offering employment in other tasks to the female but not the male trainee, participants might have solved the problem of women's employment but created other problems along the way. Specifically, participants reverse discriminated against the male trainee who failed by not offering employment in these other tasks to him; created a set of "girl jobs," which likely would not command the same pay or status as those offered to men; and suggested a hiring policy more oriented to demographic characteristics than to skills. It is disappointing that the diversity training provided to the highly intelligent and deeply motivated business students who served as participants in the study appeared to do no more than create stereotypical employment decisions, with the male recruit sent off to lift weights and the female recruits sent off to the dispatch office. We suggest that future efforts in understanding employment decisions take into account the divergence in causal explanations offered for the performance of men and women and the underemphasis on necessity and counterfactual reasoning in questions of performance—reasoning that would otherwise reveal this use of multiple causal explanations when only one may be needed.

BACKGROUND EFFECTS IN THE SELECTION
OF EXPLANATIONS FOR PERFORMANCE

In previous sections of this chapter we argued that greater use of counterfactual reasoning would limit the adoption of different causal explanations for the performance by men and women of a task. Specifically, we suggested that people who employ counterfactual reasoning would ask whether being a woman is necessary for failure and, noting the number of men who also fail, conclude that gender is not a necessary component for failure. People might then consider other explanations, not related to gender, for the performance of both men and women.

The question remains why people may initially consider gender as an explanation for a woman's but not a man's poor performance. As noted previously, prior beliefs may underlie these different explanations. Findings from other research suggest that the manner in which people apply contrastive reasoning may also guide people to different explanations for the performance of men and women. In particular, results from recent studies on the origins of the causal background indicate that different explanations for the performance of men and women may arise due to differences in the comparison cases selected for the genders (McGill, 1993).

This research derives from Kahneman and D. Miller's norm theory (1986), which describes how people construct comparison cases for events. Specifically, this theory suggests that people construct alternatives to events by holding some features, called *immutable features*, constant, but letting other features, called *mutable features*, vary. As Kahneman and Miller explained, the key ideas in the construction of comparison cases are "that the mental state of affairs can be modified in many ways, that some modifications are much more natural than others, and that some attributes are particularly resistant to change" (1986, pp. 142–143). Thus, the rules that govern mutability guide the construction of comparison cases for an event.

Although a general theory of mutability is lacking in the literature, findings from studies suggest a list of features that vary in degree of mutability. For example, findings suggest that the genders male and female differ in perceived mutability (Eagly & Kite, 1987; Gilligan, 1982; Hall, 1987; McClelland, 1975; McGill, 1993; D. Miller et al., 1991; J. Miller, 1976; Tannen, 1990). In particular, findings indicate that the gender male is generally perceived as immutable whereas the gender female is perceived as mutable (for an exception, see D. Miller et al., 1991). Differences in perceived mutability suggest that in constructing alternatives to events involving men, people hold the gender of the actor constant and allow other factors to vary. That is, male actors will typically be compared to other men. In contrast, for events involving women, gender of the actor may be allowed to vary, and female actors may be compared to men.

These hypotheses regarding differences in the comparison cases that may be adopted for men and women were recently tested in a pair of studies on participants' causal explanations for performance (McGill, 1993). In these studies, participants, told of an individual (male or female) who failed (or succeeded) at a task, were asked whether they preferred to compare this individual to men or to women who succeeded (or failed) at the same undertaking. The tasks described were rated in pretests as typically male-oriented (shooting pool, driving an obstacle course, negotiating a lower price) or typically female-oriented (typing, sewing, quieting a crying infant).

Results indicated that participants preferred to compare male actors to other men regardless of task (male-oriented, female-oriented) or outcome (success, failure), thereby identifying explanations based on individual characteristics of the actor in question. Results of comparison cases chosen for female actors varied, however, with task and outcome. Participants preferred to compare a female actor to other women when the female actor succeeded regardless of task orientation, a result suggesting explanations that address how the successful woman differs from other women; and when the female actor failed at female-oriented tasks, a result suggesting explanations that address individual shortcomings of the female actor who failed. Participants preferred, however, to compare the female actor who failed at male-oriented tasks to men, not to women, who succeeded, a result suggesting explanations in terms of gender. Thus, differences in the chosen comparison suggest different explanations for the performance of men and women.

Other factors identified in the literature as differing in perceived mutability include temporal order (D. Miller & Gunasegaram, 1990), whether the event is exceptional or routine (Kahneman & Tversky, 1982), and prominence of an actor in a story (Kahneman & D. Miller, 1986). Specifically, people appear to perceive later events in a sequence to be more mutable than earlier events, exceptional events more mutable than routine events, and focal actors in a story more mutable than background actors.

These findings regarding differences in perceived mutability and their effect on the causal background selected suggest important directions for future research. As noted previously, a general theory of mutability is needed to account for the effects of gender, temporal order, exception versus routine, and story position. Further, findings regarding the effects of gender on the causal background selected suggest other social-psychological phenomena. For example, differences in the perceived mutability of male and female actors may derive from differences in the social status of men and women (Eagly & Kite, 1987; McGill, 1993). That is, men may be perceived as the norm and women as the variants because of the greater public presence and social position of men. If this is the case, other groups that differ in social status may also differ in perceived mutability and, therefore, be subject to competing patterns of causal explanation.

This hypothesis reflects a principal mechanism specified in norm theory, specifically, that in imagining alternatives to events, people tend to return abnormal elements to their normal or default status (Kahneman & D. Miller, 1986). Changes in which people move a normal element in the direction of abnormality are rare. Thus, people may adopt different comparison cases and, hence, different causal explanations for performance depending on whether the actor is perceived to be a member of a "normal" versus an "abnormal" group. For example, Whites may be perceived as the norm and African Americans as the variant in cultures in which Whites are afforded higher social status than African Americans. This difference in perceived mutability suggests that Whites will typically be compared to other Whites and will therefore be perceived to succeed or fail based on their own merits as individuals. In contrast, African Americans may be compared to Whites or to African Americans depending on the circumstances. As with women in previous studies (McGill, 1993), African Americans may be compared to other African Americans only when they succeed, comparisons suggesting attributions that address ways in which successful African Americans differ from others in their racial group. On the other hand, African Americans who fail may be compared to Whites who succeed, comparisons suggesting attributions for failure in terms of race. Similarly, within-group comparisons may be preferred for actors in upper socioeconomic classes, comparisons suggesting attributions in terms of individual characteristics, whereas comparisons across social strata may be preferred for those of lower socioeconomic status, comparisons suggesting attributions in terms of group characteristics. Thus, differences in perceived mutability may produce causal attributions that reinforce negative perceptions of groups already struggling to achieve equal social status.

An interesting example of the role of mutability and social status in causal explanation is suggested in the pattern of explanations offered for AIDS. Given the greater social status of heterosexual men and women than of gay men and lesbians, it is likely that people would prefer within-group comparisons for heterosexual men and women but prefer to compare gay and lesbian actors to heterosexual men and women. Thus, gay men who have HIV-associated illnesses are likely to be compared to heterosexual men who are healthy. This comparison suggests sexual orientation as a possible causal explanation and the idea that the disease might have been avoided had the gay men changed or at least suppressed their sexual orientation.

One might argue that attribution for AIDS to sexual orientation has more to do with correlation than with mutability. After all, the disease is far more common among gay men than among heterosexual men. Mutability appears the stronger account, however, when one notes that AIDS is far more common among heterosexual women than among lesbians. Nonetheless, the suggestion that AIDS is caused among women by a *heterosexual orientation* and that the disease might be avoided if heterosexual women were to change or at least to suppress their hetero-sexual tendencies would likely seem to many people a strained or mis-chievous causal explanation. Instead, explanations based on charac-teristics that distinguish heterosexual women who have the disease from heterosexual women who do not, for example, choice of sexual partners (e.g., intravenous drug users) or behavior (e.g., drug use or unsafe sexual practices), would be preferred. The asymmetry of explanations for AIDS among men and women is consistent with the contention that gay and lesbian sexual orientation and heterosexual orientation differ in perceived mutability. Thus, gay men are compared to heterosexual men because gay sexual orientation is perceived as mutable whereas heterosexual women are compared to other heterosexual women because heterosexual orientation is perceived as immutable.

CONCLUSION

Findings from the research described in the preceding sections of this chapter indicate that the manner in which people apply contrastive rea-soning may incline them to identify different causal explanations for the performance of men and women or for other groups differing in social status and that counterfactual reasoning, which might detect and prevent this proliferation of causal explanations, appears underutilized in ques-tions of performance. That is, people appear not to ask the counterfactual question "Would the woman have failed had she been a man?" to evaluate whether a gender-based explanation is really necessary for the woman's performance or whether a more general explanation would account for the failure of men *and* women.

Our sense is that separate explanations for the behavior of actors in different demographic groups are quite common. For example, recent articles in the popular press have addressed explanations for teenaged pregnancy ("Radical Prophylaxis," 1992), the decline in the African American family ("Endangered Family," 1993), and the increase in crime among inner-city youth ("Growing Up Fast," 1993), implying that separate explanations should be adopted for unwanted pregnancies among adults, for the decline in the White family, and for the increase in crime among white-collar workers. We do not mean to suggest naively that social forces do not at times affect groups differently nor that there are no occasions in which separate explanations are appropriate for different groups. Our concern, however, is in understanding why counterfactual reasoning, which is so compelling in other areas of judgment as described in the chapters of this volume, may be considered less relevant when causal question involves race, gender, age, social class, or sexual orientation.

Perhaps counterfactual reasoning is underutilized is such cases because when a person tests whether or not a factor is necessary for an event, the counterfactual reasoning implicitly requires the person to determine whether separate explanations should be adopted for particular groups. For example, when one asks whether being a woman is necessary for failure, the implicit counterfactual question is whether it is sensible to separate the genders to understand the event. By social convention, however, it is commonly agreed that men and women, regardless of sexual orientation, race, and socioeconomic status, be treated and described separately. Hence, the testing role of counterfactual reasoning is obviated for questions involving social groups. Future research is needed to examine this hypothesis and, more generally, to extend the understanding of conditions favoring the use of contrastive and counterfactual reasoning in causal judgment.

REFERENCES

Adi, H., Karplus, R., Lawson, A., & Pulos, S. (1978). Intellectual development beyond elementary school. VI: Correlational reasoning. *School Science and Mathematics, 78,* 675–683.

Cheng, P. W., & Novick, L. R. (1990). Causes versus enabling conditions. *Journal of Personality and Social Psychology, 58,* 545–567.

Eagly, A. H., & Kite, M. E. (1987). Are stereotypes of nationalities applied to both men and women? *Journal of Personality and Social Psychology, 53,* 457–462.

Einhorn, H. J., & Hogarth, R. M. (1986). Judging probable cause. *Psychological Bulletin, 99,* 3–19.

Endangered family. (1993, August 30). *Newsweek, Vol. CXXII,* 17–27.

Gilligan, C. (1982). *In a different voice.* Cambridge, MA: Harvard University Press.

Growing up fast and frightened. (1993, November 22). *Newsweek, Vol. CXXII,* 52.

Hall, J. A. (1987). On explaining gender differences: The case of non-verbal communication. In P. Shaver & C. Hendrick (Eds.), *Review of personality and social psychology* (Vol. 7, pp. 177–200). Beverly Hills, CA: Sage.

Hastie, R. (1984). Causes and effects of causal attribution. *Journal of Personality and Social Psychology, 46,* 44–56.

Hilton, D. J. (1990). Conversational processes and causal explanation. *Psychological Bulletin, 107,* 65–81.

Hilton, D. J., & Slugoski, B. R. (1986). Knowledge-based causal attribution: The abnormal conditions focus model. *Psychological Review, 93,* 136–153.

Ingrassia, M. (1993, August 30). Endangered family. *Newsweek, Vol. CXXII,* 17–27.

Ingrassia, M. (1993, November 22). Growing up fast and frightened. *Newsweek, Vol. CXXII,* 52.

Kahneman, D., & Miller, D. T. (1986). Norm theory: Comparing reality to its alternatives. *Psychological Review, 93,* 136–153.

Kahneman, D., & Tversky, A. (1982). The simulation heuristic. In D. Kahneman, P. Slovic, & A. Tversky (Eds.), *Judgment under uncertainty: Heuristics and biases* (pp. 201–208). New York: Cambridge University Press.

Keegan, A. (1991, September 8). Hot seat. *Chicago Tribune Magazine,* pp. 14–16, 18, 20, 32.

Leddo, J., Abelson, R. P., & Gross, P. (1984). Conjunctive explanations: When two reasons are better than one. *Journal of Personality and Social Psychology, 47,* 933–943.

Lipe, M. G. (1991). Counterfactual reasoning as a framework for attribution theories. *Psychological Bulletin, 109,* 456–471.

Mackie, J. L. (1974). *Cement of the universe: A study of causation.* London: Oxford University Press.

McClelland, D. C. (1975). *Power: The inner experience.* New York: Irvington.

McGill, A. L. (1989). Context effects in judgments of causation. *Journal of Personality and Social Psychology, 57,* 189–200.

McGill, A. L. (1990a). Conjunctive explanations: The effect of comparison of the target episode to a contrasting background instance. *Social Cognition, 8,* 362–382.

McGill, A. L. (1990b). The effect of direction of comparison on the selection of causal explanations. *Journal of Experimental Social Psychology, 26,* 93–107.

McGill, A. L. (1993). Selection of a causal background: Role of expectation versus feature mutability. *Journal of Personality and Social Psychology, 64,* 701–707.

McGill, A. L., & Klein, J. G. (1993). Contrastive and counterfactual thinking in causal judgment. *Journal of Personality and Social Psychology, 64,* 897–905.

Miller, D. T., & Gunasegaram, S. (1990). Temporal order and the perceived mutability of events: Implications for blame assignment. *Journal of Personality and Social Psychology, 61,* 5–12.

Miller, D. T., Taylor, B., & Buck, M. L. (1991). Gender gaps: Who needs to be explained? *Journal of Personality and Social Psychology, 61,* 5–12.

Miller, J. B. (1976). *Toward a new psychology of women.* Boston, MA: Beacon Press.

Radical prophylaxis. (1992, December 14). *Times, 140,* pp .

Read, S. J. (1988). Conjunctive explanations: The effect of comparison between a chosen and nonchosen alternative. *Journal of Experimental Social Psychology, 24,* 146–162.

Tannen, D. (1990). *You just don't understand: Women and men in conversation.* New York: Morrow.

Weiner, B. (1985). "Spontaneous" causal thinking. *Psychological Bulletin, 97,* 74–84.

Wells, G. L., & Gavanski, I. (1989). Mental simulation of causality. *Journal of Personality and Social Psychology, 56,* 161–169.

Counterfactual Thinking and Coping With Traumatic Life Events

Christopher G. Davis
Darrin R. Lehman
University of British Columbia

Since Kahneman and Tversky's (1982) early observations regarding the nature of counterfactual thought (i.e., the mental simulation of alternative outcomes), considerable research has explored the properties, consequences, and roles of such cognitions. Most of this research has been on the perceiver's or observer's construal of unexpected, negative outcomes as a function of the counterfactual images these outcomes evoke.[1] The implicit assumption in much of this work is that observers (typically role-playing participants) are accurate in their perceptions of how people will feel about, or react to, a given outcome (Miller & Turnbull, 1990). For example, when observers suggest that one outcome, due to the greater mutability of its antecedents, is more traumatic than another, the implication is that such an outcome is, in fact, more traumatic and will elicit greater distress for the individual experiencing it. In this chapter, we consider this assumption in detail by reviewing existing field data. We make the point that the process of cognitive undoing for real-life victims of traumatic events seems in many ways to differ from the well-researched process that has been described for observers.

We begin by discussing the central notion of mutability, summarizing how researchers have operationalized the construct and briefly reviewing

---

[1]Although counterfactuals can follow unexpected positive events (see, e.g., Gleicher et al., 1990; Landman, 1987), in this chapter we focus exclusively on counterfactuals that follow unexpected *negative* events.

how mutability influences the perceptions and experience of negative outcomes. Next, we consider a number of consequences of counterfactual thought for those mentally undoing their own tragic outcomes. Although, understandably, the focus of laboratory-based counterfactual research has been on observers' estimations of a target person's affective reaction as a primary consequence of undoing, we suggest other effects that counterfactuals may have on the undoer. Third, we explore briefly some territory that laboratory researchers have been unable to address empirically, namely, the social context of counterfactuals. Fourth, we take up what seems to be the burning issue in the counterfactual literature right now, that is, the question of *why* people generate counterfactuals. In so doing, we discuss the role of counterfactuals from the perspective of people coping with traumatic life events.

MUTABILITY

When unexpected negative events occur, people often try to undo them mentally by simulating counterfactual alternatives. For example, if one is involved in a motor vehicle accident on the way home from work, one is apt to think, "If only I had taken a different route (or left earlier, etc.), I would've avoided the accident." Over the past decade, researchers have uncovered factors that increase or decrease the likelihood that an outcome, or a particular antecedent to that outcome, will be undone (for reviews, see Miller, Turnbull, & McFarland, 1990; Roese & Olson, chapter 1). Factors shown to affect mutability include (a) the extent to which an antecedent deviates from some intrapersonal or scripted norm (i.e., its exceptionality; e.g., Macrae, 1992; Miller & McFarland, 1986); (b) whether an antecedent was a committed, as opposed to an omitted, action (e.g., Gleicher et al., 1990; Landman, 1987); (c) the extent to which the target's own behavior is implicated in some way in the outcome (e.g., Girotto, Legrenzi, & Rizzo, 1991; Kahneman & Miller, 1986); and (d) where in the chain of events the antecedent occurs (e.g., Miller & Gunasegaram, 1990; Wells, Taylor, & Turtle, 1987). With respect to the first three factors, the research findings suggest that exceptional, committed, and personally enacted antecedents tend to be perceived as more mutable than routine, omitted, and externally determined antecedents, respectively. With respect to the fourth factor, Wells et al. (1987) suggested that when antecedents are causally related, such that one antecedent sets the stage for the next, early antecedents are perceived to be more mutable. Miller and Gunasegaram (1990), on the other hand, demonstrated that when antecedents are independent of each other, late-occurring antecedents are perceived as more mutable.

The overall findings of research on counterfactuals suggest further that the more mutable an outcome is perceived to be, the greater the affective consequences for the individual experiencing it. For example, Kahneman and Tversky (1982) presented participants with the following hypothetical scenario:

> Mr. Crane and Mr. Tees were scheduled to leave the airport on different flights, at the same time. They travelled from town in the same limousine, were caught in a traffic jam, and arrived at the airport 30 minutes after the scheduled departure time of their flights. Mr. Crane is told that his flight left on time. Mr. Tees is told that his flight was delayed, and just left five minutes ago. (p. 203)

When participants were asked subsequently who they predicted would be more upset, 96% predicted Mr. Tees, presumably because participants believed that Mr. Tees could more easily imagine the counterfactual scenario wherein he makes his flight. Thus, the highly mutable circumstances of Mr. Tees' outcome serve to heighten the intensity of his affective reaction. For negative outcomes, then, greater mutability leads to an amplification of the distress, regret, guilt, or frustration that the outcome would otherwise evoke (see also Kahneman & Miller, 1986; Landman, 1987).

Although much empirical evidence has been marshalled in support of these mutability factors, an important potential limitation is that almost all of the data have come from laboratory studies employing scenario designs (for recent exceptions, see Gilovich & Medvec, chapter 9; Markman, Gavanski, Sherman, & McMullen, 1993, 1995; Roese, 1994). Participants are presented with relatively impoverished hypothetical vignettes and asked either to make judgments about the target (e.g., blameworthiness, how much sympathy they deserve) or to estimate how the target would feel in the situation. Findings from this research have clearly indicated that observers' reactions to negative events are markedly influenced by the counterfactual images that they elicit. For instance, observers tend to be more sympathetic to the person whose victimization seems easily avoidable in retrospect, presumably because observers believe that his or her victimization will be more traumatic, induce greater distress, and be more difficult to cope with than a similar victimization that lacks highly mutable antecedents (Miller & McFarland, 1986; Miller & Turnbull, 1990).

However, what remains to be established is whether these same factors that affect observers' perceptions of mutability (and their beliefs about the consequent emotional reaction) likewise affect people *actually experiencing* the negative event. For instance, does the person with highly mutable antecedents feel worse and have greater difficulty coping with his or her real-life victimization than the person similarly afflicted but lacking the highly mutable antecedents?

This is a challenging question to address empirically. Obviously, it is not possible for researchers to randomly assign real-life victims to mutability circumstances (e.g., exceptional vs. normal antecedents). This makes it difficult to establish whether observed differences in distress (etc.) between those with and without highly mutable antecedents are due to real differences in the mutability of antecedents or due to such factors as the latter group's inability or unwillingness to search the causal chain for highly mutable counterfactual alternatives. A second problem concerns the myriad ways in which each traumatic event is unique. Even when the actual outcome is the same across all respondents (e.g., the unexpected death of an infant), each respondent's description of his or her outcome will have a different set of antecedents. Some respondents will include, in their descriptions of the events leading up to the death, a cold the child had in the week prior to the death; others will state that the child had not been sleeping well recently. The length of each respondent's causal chain of antecedent events will also differ. Some will focus on the activities of the fateful day, whereas others will recall a difficult pregnancy.

These difficulties notwithstanding, in two studies of people suddenly and unexpectedly bereaved of a loved one, Davis, Lehman, Wortman, Silver, and Thompson (1995) were unable to garner much evidence that distinctions found to be important to the undoing process in the laboratory held up in the field. In the first study, we asked respondents who had lost a spouse or a child in a motor vehicle accident 4–7 years earlier to describe any counterfactuals they had with respect to the accident and to report how frequently they had experienced these counterfactual thoughts within the past month. In the second study, parents who had lost an infant to sudden infant death syndrome (SIDS) were interviewed. In interviews approximately 3 weeks and 18 months post-loss, we asked parents to recount counterfactuals that had come to mind during the past week and to indicate the frequency with which such thoughts had occurred. An important aspect of both of these traumatic events is that in neither case was the bereaved respondent (or the deceased) legally culpable or causally implicated in the death. In the first study, accident records were screened to exclude cases in which the deceased was in a vehicle whose driver was deemed at fault. In the second study, parents had been vindicated of responsibility by the postmortem examination.

Counterfactual thoughts were indeed prevalent in the minds of these real-life victims: The majority of the bereaved in these two studies reported mentally undoing the loss of their loved one. Our next question, then, concerned whether the bereaved were focusing their counterfactuals on unusual antecedents, as might be expected from reports in the literature, or on relatively routine antecedents. We observed that, for the most part, the bereaved were mutating mundane, routine antecedents, even when they described unusual antecedents in their more general accounts of the events leading up to the death. In the motor vehicle accident study, for example, a number of respondents' loved ones had died in an accident involving an intoxicated driver. Yet not one respondent reported a counterfactual that removed the intoxicated driver from the scene even though, from an observer's perspective, one might think that this would be a highly salient and exceptional element of the situation.

Given differences in base rates in the real-world with respect to routine and exceptional antecedents, of course we did not conclude from these data that the routine are more likely to be undone than the exceptional. By definition, unusual events are rare (and hence, when they occur, are particularly salient). Moreover, as we argue later, when unusual antecedents are present in the causal chain, they are often constrained by prior circumstances that render them less mutable. In the absence of highly mutable, exceptional antecedents, many respondents might have settled for less mutable antecedents, but antecedents nevertheless over which they could have exerted some influence (for similar findings see Girotto et al., 1991; Markman et al., 1995).

We next examined whether respondents demonstrated a preference for undoing commissions rather than omissions, as the findings in the counterfactual literature indicate ought to be the case (e.g., Gleicher et al., 1990; Landman, 1987). Surprisingly, in the counterfactuals that the bereaved described, it was not at all clear that they were making distinctions in their own minds between omissions and commissions. Respondents would often report both an omission and a commission in a single counterfactual. As one parent bereaved of a SIDS baby said, "If I hadn't went to sleep; if I had stayed awake and kept my eye on him. . . ."

In other cases, the distinction between omissions and commissions was difficult insofar as the counterfactual could plausibly be interpreted both ways. For example, a parent bereaved of a child hit by an automobile while the child was playing near the roadside reported wishing that she had told her child not to play in the front yard (or near the road). This counterfactual could be interpreted as an omitted act (e.g., "I should have said, 'Don't play there' ") as easily as it could be interpreted as a commission (e.g., "I should not have let her play there").

When we could unambiguously distinguish omissions from commissions, we were again surprised to observe consistently across both bereavement samples that, counter to the suggestion in the counterfactual literature (e.g., Gleicher et al., 1990; Landman, 1987), respondents reported undoing more omitted than committed acts (for similar results, see Gilovich & Medvec, chapter 9; Roese & Olson, 1993). Although it might seem that respondents were more concerned with what they had failed to do than with what they had actually done, it should be noted that, like the base rate differential with respect to usual versus unusual events noted previously, the number of possible committed acts is limited by what actually happened whereas the possible set of omitted acts is limited only by one's imagination.

We should note that other empirical findings from these initial field studies *did* support findings from past laboratory research on counterfactual thinking. We found evidence across both bereaved samples that the more frequently people were undoing the death of their loved one, the less well they appeared to be coping. And we discovered that in describing their counterfactuals, the bereaved overwhelmingly focused on their *own* behavior (see Girotto et al., 1991; Kahneman & Miller, 1986; McMullen, Markman, & Gavanski, chapter 5). These observations suggested, first, that trying to mentally undo outcomes may add to the distress of the event and, second, that people tend to view their own behavior as more mutable than factors that are unusual but personally uncontrollable, such as the weather or another person's behavior (see also Davis, 1991). For example, as we noted earlier, respondents who were bereaved of a spouse or a child in a motor vehicle accident involving an intoxicated driver never reported counterfactuals that removed that driver from the scene. From the bereaved respondent's perspective, the presence of the intoxicated driver, like the occurrence of a freak snowstorm, represented a relatively immutable aspect of the situation; even though such an event is unusual, the respondent could not imagine how he or she, personally, could have prevented its occurrence. It is much easier to think, "If only I didn't let him go out that night, he would still be alive."

Taken together, these field data suggest that although the notion of mutability is important in the construction of counterfactual alternatives, researchers' understanding of the rules by which mutability is established is far from complete. The real-life data indicated that even when outcomes lacked what is currently understood from the laboratory research to be highly mutable antecedents, the bereaved had little difficulty producing very compelling counterfactual alternatives. In fact, the bereaved individual who did not imagine a plausible counterfactual was rare. The point here is that highly stressful life events almost never seem "inevitable."

Although those in our bereaved samples appeared to seek mutable antecedents that undid their loved one's death, they seemed to follow somewhat different rules to establish mutability. In an effort to better comprehend the process by which people generate counterfactuals to real-life traumatic life events, we went back and reviewed what our respondents had said. An interesting possibility occurred during this exercise. We noticed that the targeted antecedents in respondents' counterfactuals tended to be decision points or nodes that were not, in hindsight, appropriately or adequately thought through. For example, one father of a baby killed by SIDS was haunted by his decision not to respond to his fussing baby late one night: "I didn't get up and check the baby [when he fussed]. Quite often he'd fuss in his crib, then go back to sleep. But you don't run to the crib every time you hear a little peep. I've been told that wouldn't have done anything, but I can't help but feel that way nevertheless." Another parent who lost a baby to SIDS focused on her decision not to take her coughing baby immediately to the doctor: "Mainly I wish that I would have taken her to the doctor. I felt like I didn't want to bother him [the doctor]—like I was intruding."

From this perspective, personal actions that play a part in the negative outcome are themselves perceived as consequences of decisions. As consequences, the actions are relatively fixed and immutable, although the decisions that initiated those actions may be highly mutable (cf. Wells et al., 1987). For instance, people often do not mutate the *act* of taking a certain route home from work; rather, they mutate their *decision* to take that route.

In evaluating the mutability of a given decision, people seem to reappraise the factors that went into it. Was the decision carefully and thoughtfully made? Was an important piece of information neglected in the decision process? What reasons were considered in the decision? Were the reasons justified? If one is injured in an accident after taking an unusual route home from work, whether one mutates the "route decision" will depend on whether the decision to take that route is perceived in retrospect as ill conceived, unjustified, or foolhardy. Interestingly, and understandably, counterfactual researchers employing hypothetical scenario designs have typically been vague with respect to the reasons given for the unusual behavior enacted by targets (e.g., Gleicher et al., 1990; Kahneman & Tversky, 1982; Macrae, 1992). Landman (1987), for example, presented participants with a number of counterfactual vignettes, including instances in which a target either changed jobs, stocks, vacation spots, or sections of a biology course. In none of the instances was a reason for the change made explicit. Participants were simply told that the target acted. Given the negative outcome of the action, perhaps the implicit suggestion was that the decision to change was whimsical, foolish, or naïve. Clearly, such decisions are ripe for counterfactual thought and will no doubt elicit feelings of regret and self-denigration. If, on the other hand, participants were told that one switched vacation spots on the basis of a weather forecast or traded stocks on the basis of a trusted broker's suggestion, the decision to take the unusual or committed action, from one's own perspective, might have appeared somewhat less mutable.

Although base rates are not available, common experience suggests that more often than not, unusual or out-of-character actions follow reasoned decisions. Most people do not change jobs, trade stocks, or even alter annual vacation spots without first weighing in some detail the pros and cons of their actions. Before making important decisions (or taking bold or exceptional actions), people often mentally simulate possible outcomes (Kahneman & Tversky, 1982; Taylor & Schneider, 1989). If the potentially positive outcomes that come to mind outweigh the potentially negative outcomes (e.g., if the former are perceived as more likely), one takes the risk and acts. If the undesirable possibilities seem more likely, or too costly, one will elect not to act.

Whereas the consequences of routine actions may be just as severe as those of unusual actions, routine actions are less likely to involve thoroughly reasoned decisions each time they are enacted. Activities performed every day, such as driving to work, require little conscious decision-making effort. Many such activities are performed mindlessly (Langer, Blank, & Chanowitz, 1978). In fact, people often forget the original reason they engaged in certain routine tasks. We suggest that, as with unusual actions, when routine actions lead to unfortunate, unexpected consequences, people are likely to examine critically the reasoning behind the decision. If a valid, justifiable reason for the action is lacking, one may very likely target the decision in undoing the outcome.

People often do not recognize until well after the fact the factors that should have been considered in a given decision (Baron & Hershey, 1988). Ample social-psychological research suggests that people often base their decisions on heuristic (rather than thorough) processing (e.g., Nisbett & Ross, 1980). Thus, in hindsight, people often criticize themselves (and others) for not taking into account or not appropriately weighing factors that subsequently turn out to be critical. An example of this tendency is provided by an account of a parent whose young son died in a motor vehicle accident as he was walking home from school. Years after the event, the parent continued to think, "Maybe he'd still be alive today if I'd kept taking him to school—I stopped because he didn't want me to take him." A second example comes from an account of a father whose child was killed by an automobile as he was delivering newspapers: "Why didn't I have the alertness to think about it that night! . . . I could have driven him around the route. Why did I have to get so wrapped up in the TV?"

We are not suggesting that each antecedent act or decision is given equal attention in mental simulations. Like omitted acts (relative to committed acts; see Gleicher et al., 1990), routine acts are likely to be less salient than acts that are unusual or exceptional (Kahneman & Miller, 1986; Landman, 1987). Nevertheless, our observations suggest that unusual antecedents, when they occur, are frequently constrained by prior circumstances or by a reasoned decision that renders them relatively less mutable. Instead, people may review a decision to perform a routine task. These decisions strike them as more mutable, perhaps because less thought was put into them.

THE UNDOING PROCESS

A further observation culled from our work with actual victims of traumatic life events concerns the number of and variability in counterfactuals that respondents report (Davis, 1991; Davis et al., 1995). Given the accumulation of findings in the counterfactual literature, we had anticipated that people would tend to gravitate toward a single, highly mutable antecedent. In fact, we found that respondents would often describe several counterfactual possibilities, for example, as did one parent of a baby who died of SIDS: "I've thought about a lot of those things, like if I'd never set him down; if I'd never gone to school that morning; if I had never been going to school, leaving him in the mornings; I thought about it: checking him every 5–10 minutes instead of every 15–20 minutes. I thought about all these things I could have done but I didn't do . . ."

It is also noteworthy that counterfactuals were not, in general, maintained consistently over time. In the SIDS study, only 28% of respondents reporting counterfactuals at 18 months post-loss described a counterfactual at that time that was the same as the one they described at 3 weeks post-loss. Typically, the counterfactuals described in the later interview were completely unrelated to those reported at the earlier interview, even when the early counterfactuals were particularly compelling.

These findings have implications for researchers' understanding of the counterfactual process. Gleicher et al. (1990) proposed a four-stage model of undoing (see Roese & Olson, chapter 1 for a more detailed review of this model). Gleicher et al. suggested that initially following the outcome, the individual imagines an alternative to the outcome. For instance, a typical alternative to being injured is not being injured. In the second stage, Gleicher et al. suggested that the individual generates possible routes to the alternative outcome, frequently by mutating causal antecedents (see also Lipe, 1991; Wells & Gavanski, 1989). In the third stage, these routes, as well as the actual chain of events that led to the outcome, are judged with respect to their a priori likelihood of occurrence, ranging from a likelihood of zero (i.e., impossible) to very close to 1 (i.e., almost a sure thing). According to Gleicher et al., it is at this point that mutability factors (e.g., exceptional antecedents, committed acts) influence the process, insofar as they affect the likelihood estimate of particular alternatives. Thus, for instance, alternative scenarios that restore exceptional acts to their norms will receive higher likelihood ratings than scenarios that replace normal acts with their exceptions (cf. Gavanski & Wells, 1989).

In the final stage, Gleicher et al. (1990) posited that the intensity of the affective experience will be a function of the ratio of the likelihood of possible counterfactual alternatives relative to the a priori likelihood of the actual outcome. To the extent that the counterfactual alternatives seem more likely than the actual negative outcome, distress will be intensified.

Consistent with the theorizing of Gleicher et al. (1990), our real-life data suggest that people start with the supposition that a given outcome need not have occurred and then cognitively attempt to play out various alternative scripts that would undo the outcome. We are not convinced, however, that people generally calculate likelihood ratios for counterfactual alternatives following stressful life events. Given the intense emotional distress that individuals experience in the aftermath of traumatic events, it seems unlikely that anything more than a crude likelihood calibration would be possible. Rather, people appear to generate as many alternatives as seem plausible without reference to the likelihood of the actual outcome. The negative event simply ought not to have happened, and hence any antecedent that can plausibly be mutated will be grist for the counterfactual mill.

In generating counterfactual alternatives, as with other cognitive processes (e.g., see Hilton & Slugoski, 1986; Kahneman & Miller, 1986), our attention is naturally directed toward unusual or exceptional antecedents, if they exist. Thus, unless these highly salient antecedents are constrained by prior events or decisions, they will tend to be mentioned first as counterfactual possibilities (e.g., Kahneman & Miller, 1986; Wells et al., 1987). To the extent that the outcome is highly significant and affectively charged for the one processing it, however, he or she is also likely to seek other, nonexceptional aspects of the situation that just as plausibly could be expected to undo the outcome. The data indicate that, more often than not, mutable antecedents can be found. Stated differently, the person injured while taking his or her usual route appears just as likely to undo the accident and is just as likely to feel intense distress, regret, and frustration over not avoiding the accident as the person similarly injured while taking the unusual route (Davis et al., 1995).

CONSEQUENCES OF UNDOING

Although the focus of the counterfactual literature has been on intensity of affect as the major dependent variable of interest, we suggest that it is important to keep in mind that other consequences of counterfactual thinking are possible and deserve study (see also Roese & Olson, chapter 1).

Causality and Blame

A number of researchers have suggested that counterfactuals influence the way people assign causality and blame (e.g., Kahneman & Miller, 1986; Miller & Gunasegaram, 1990; Wells & Gavanski, 1989). For example,

Miller and Turnbull (1990) found that participants estimated that a person victimized following an out-of-character, and thus highly mutable, action would experience greater self-blame than a person similarly victimized following a routine action. Miller and Turnbull suggested that such self-blame would occur in the highly mutable case because that victim could easily imagine mutating the unusual event to its norm. The ease with which this counterfactual would come to mind would lead the victim to believe that he or she ought to have maintained the norm and thus to have contributed to his or her own victimization. In contrast, the victim with routine antecedents, because he or she did not do anything out of the ordinary, can only believe that he or she *might* have done something different. The highly mutable circumstances of the first victim's scenario presumably leads him or her to confuse what *might* have been the case with what *ought* to have been the case. Miller and Turnbull term this error the *counterfactual fallacy.*

The suggestion that the counterfactual fallacy should occur only among victims possessing highly mutable antecedents is not supported by the real-life data. In the study of SIDS parents, we found that respondents were just as likely to report feelings of guilt and responsibility when they undid routine antecedents as when they undid exceptional antecedents. Rather, it was the frequency with which people undid their loss that predicted the extent to which they experienced feelings of guilt and personal responsibility for the loss. In general, the more people were undoing (regardless of the antecedent they were undoing), the more they reported feelings of guilt and responsibility.

Wells and Gavanski (1989) suggested that counterfactuals influence blame assignment via their effect on causal ascriptions. They contended that people assign *causal* significance, in part, by considering the likelihood of the counterfactual that would undo the outcome (see also Hilton, 1990; Lipe, 1991). Wells and Gavanski (1989) demonstrated this tendency in their scenario study involving a cab driver who refused to pick up a disabled couple. Participants were told that following the cab driver's refusal, the couple decided to drive their own car and were injured when they drove off a collapsed bridge. Importantly, causality and responsibility ratings assigned to the cab driver were attenuated for other participants who were told that the cab driver also drove off the bridge. This result suggests that when the counterfactual "if only he had picked up the couple" failed to undo the outcome, the cab driver was seen as less causally significant and was blamed less, even though his behavior was the same.

Although we recognize that counterfactual thoughts may influence, or be influenced by, causal ascriptions, we suggest that distinctions can be made between the two processes. For instance, we found that although the vast majority of parents who had lost an infant to SIDS did not feel that they had caused the death, most parents nevertheless reported self-implicating counterfactual thoughts: Fully 68% of parents, when asked how they thought the death could have been avoided, reported a self-implicating counterfactual, whereas less than 20%, when asked for their hunches or theories regarding the causes of their baby's death, described a causal theory that in any way implicated their own actions or inactions. In addition, a review of the counterfactuals that parents reported made clear that, for the vast majority of cases, the events that parents were undoing were not so much causal as they were preventative (e.g., checking on the baby more frequently than was typical; see Davis et al., 1995).

Although causal statements may generally be expressed as counterfactual propositions (e.g., Lipe, 1991; see also Roese & Olson, chapter 1), we caution that not all counterfactual propositions imply a causal relation between the antecedent and the outcome. For instance, when a SIDS parent dwells on the counterfactual thought such as "If only I had been there when my baby stopped breathing . . ." the parent is not suggesting that he or she played a causal role in the death. Rather, the parent is perceiving his or her behavior as potentially sufficient to interrupt the course of events that lead to the tragic outcome. Regardless of the true causal agent of the death, it is still painfully clear to these parents that had they acted slightly differently that fateful day, their child might still be alive.

We contend that although self-implicating counterfactuals do not necessarily imply causal significance, they nevertheless have the potential to elicit feelings of guilt and self-blame. Even after removing cases in which parents reported a self-implicating causal theory for their baby's death, we found that the more frequently parents were undoing in the first few weeks following the death, the greater was their guilt and sense of personal responsibility ($rs = .40-.50$).

Because in the SIDS study causal theories were assessed in an open-ended fashion, respondents might have been discouraged from identifying less significant causal agents (e.g., their own actions). Davis, Lehman, Silver, Wortman, and Ellard (in press) examined this issue in a further study in which more than 100 respondents with spinal cord injuries (SCI) were interviewed approximately 1 week after their accident. Respondents were asked to rate on 7-point scales the extent to which they agreed or disagreed that they had caused their accident, another person or other people had caused their accident, something in the environment had caused their accident, and their accident was caused by fate or chance. Using the same 7-point scale, respondents also rated the extent to which they thought their accident was foreseeable.

Counterfactuals were assessed through a series of questions. First, respondents were asked if they ever thought their accident could have been avoided. Next, they were asked the extent to which they agreed or disagreed that they "spend a lot of time thinking about how [their] accident could have been avoided." Finally, we assessed the extent to which counterfactuals were focused on the respondent's own behavior (i.e., self-implicating counterfactuals) by asking respondents to rate on the same 7-point scale the extent to which they believed they "could have avoided the accident and therefore their spinal cord injury." The primary dependent measure was respondents' ratings of the extent to which they believed that they were to blame for their accident (again, based on the same 7-point scale).

The data indicated, as we had anticipated, that self-implicating counterfactual thoughts accounted for significant variance (7%, $p < .001$) in ratings of self-blame even after causal ratings (to all sources) *and* foreseeability estimates were controlled. That is, the more respondents agreed that they could have avoided their accident, regardless of the degree to which they believed they (themselves), others, the environment, or chance factors caused their accident, the more personal blame they assumed.

We also had trained raters estimate the extent of cause, blame, and foreseeability of the accident (using the same scales and categories given to the respondents with SCI) after reading the transcripts of each respondent's account of his or her accident. The raters were trained to follow the distinctions between cause, responsibility, and blame as outlined by Shaver (1985). Interestingly, although raters and respondents did not differ in their ratings of respondent cause and other person cause, significant differences between ratings by raters and respondents emerged on the dimensions of respondent blame and other person blame. Respondents with SCI blamed themselves more and others less, than did the trained raters. Importantly, the respondent–rater discrepancy in self-blame was significantly related to respondents' self-implicating counterfactuals, after their causal and foreseeability ratings were controlled.

These data indicate, then, that people make distinctions, first, between causal antecedents and antecedents that merely could have prevented the negative outcome and, second, between the ascription of cause and the assignment of blame (cf. Shaver, 1985; Shaver & Drown, 1986). That these *personal* actions could so easily be mutated seems to induce people to assume greater blame for their outcome than an observer would assign them.

Distress and the Persistence of Counterfactual Thoughts

A very different outcome measure with respect to counterfactuals is the duration or persistence of such thoughts. Understandably, this remains an intangible for scenario researchers. It does not make sense to ask role-playing participants to estimate *how long* they would think counter-factually or experience guilt, regret, or distress. Nor does it make sense to have participants return to the laboratory months, weeks, or even days after responding to a hypothetical vignette and to collect follow-up data from them.

The real-life data reported by Davis (1991) and Davis et al. (1995) as well as anecdotal data reported by others (e.g., Bulman & Wortman, 1977; Pynoos et al., 1993; Tait & Silver, 1989; Weiss, 1988), have indicated that people may continue to ruminate about their counterfactual thoughts for several years following the trauma. Perhaps not surprisingly, the persistence of counterfactual thoughts has been shown to be related to dispositional factors such as neuroticism and one's propensity to ruminate (Davis, 1991; see also Kasimatis & Wells, chapter 3). Yet, persistence of counterfactuals may also be a function of the distress one is experiencing. That is, dysphoria brought on by the traumatic event may promote a continuance of distressing ruminative thoughts, including undoing. Davis et al. (1995) found some evidence for this pattern, noting that the distress level of SIDS parents at 3 weeks post-loss predicted how frequently the parents would be undoing the event 18 months later, even after the undoing frequency at 3 weeks was controlled. That is, those initially most distressed by their loss were also most likely to still be ruminating about their counterfactuals 1½ years later.

Further suggestive evidence in this regard comes from studies demonstrating that negative mood hinders one's ability to dispel negative thought patterns (Pyszczynski & Greenberg, 1987). For instance, although they were not specifically concerned with counterfactual thoughts, Sutherland, Newman, and Rachman (1982) found that participants with induced dysphoria were less able to distract themselves from unwanted intrusive thoughts than were participants with induced happiness. This finding suggests that counterfactual thoughts may be part of a self-defeating cycle wherein compelling counterfactuals lead to more intense ruminations and greater distress, while the heightened distress promotes further ruminations, which may lead one to perceive the counterfactuals as more compelling.

Given that counterfactuals, in the face of traumatic life events, are generally perceived to be distressing (e.g., Davis et al., 1995; see also Kahneman & Tversky, 1982; Miller et al., 1990),[2] we need to consider the

---

[2]Although others have found for events that are less serious and emotionally distressing that people also produce *downward* counterfactuals (i.e., imagining how the outcome could have been worse; e.g., Markman et al., 1995; Roese, 1994), respondents in the studies discussed here have understandably offered only *upward* counterfactuals (i.e., imagining how the outcome could have been better). Upward counterfactuals (at least in cases where future control is not an important issue) tend to make people feel worse.

important (and to our knowledge, empirically unstudied) issue of how people attempt to put counterfactuals behind them. For example, what, if any, cognitive strategies are brought to bear to block these thoughts (Wegner & Schneider, 1989)? Do individuals tell themselves specific things to rid themselves of these mental images? Do people attempt to convince themselves that the counterfactual alternative was unlikely, unforseeable, or unreasonable? Landman (1993), reviewing literary, philosophical, and psychological contributions to the study of regret, suggested that feelings of regret following loss represent part of Freud's notion of "working-through," and are thus cathartic. In Landman's words, "normal regret can be worked through by repeated bouts of emotional engagement with reality *and* with the ghosts of what might have been. Ideally, these bouts will not occur only within the head of the individual, but interpersonally" (p. 217). Although there is no empirical evidence that directly addresses this possibility, Pennebaker's (1989) work on the disinhibition of thoughts and feelings regarding past traumatic events may provide a useful paradigm within which to pursue this issue. In any case, future research exploring how people attempt to resolve their counterfactuals would provide valuable data from a clinical point of view.

INTERPERSONAL ASPECTS OF COUNTERFACTUAL THINKING

We know of no research in which investigators have focused on the interpersonal dynamics that may significantly affect the counterfactual thought process. Yet people do not hold cognitions, such as counterfactuals, in a social vacuum. Rather, these cognitions are often shaped, or at least affected, by the thoughts and behaviors of those in their social network. It seems plausible that people in one's social network may either encourage or discourage counterfactual thought. For instance, network members may encourage counterfactual thoughts by implicitly or explicitly suggesting ways in which the person could have avoided the negative life event. Thus, a parent who loses a child to SIDS may be accused of neglectfully contributing to the death either by medical personnel or by other grieving family members who believe that more could have been done to save the child's life. On the other hand, it is also likely that some support providers might suggest to undoers that they need not be so hard on themselves; that is, that there is little use regretting actions or inactions that one could not possibly have known would lead to negative consequences (see, e.g., Gleicher et al., 1990). Findings reported in the literature on support attempts that fail (e.g., Lehman, Ellard, & Wortman, 1986; Lehman & Hemphill, 1990; Wortman & Lehman, 1985) have suggested that both of these approaches may be problematic. First, those who are led by others to believe that they could have prevented the traumatic event are likely to experience a heightened sense of guilt (and perhaps even anger directed toward the accuser). Second, although from the support provider's perspective countering another's verbalized counterfactuals may seem helpful, in fact the recipient may perceive such efforts as insensitive attempts to trivialize one's situation.

COUNTERFACTUALS IN THE NAME OF *WHAT*?

Recently, a number of researchers in the counterfactual literature have directed their attention to the question of *why* people think counterfactually. Some (e.g., Lipe, 1991; Wells & Gavanski, 1989) have suggested that counterfactuals are useful tools in understanding causality. Because attributions of causality are central to people's understanding of the social world, permitting them to predict and control events in their environment (Heider, 1958; Kelley, 1972a), counterfactuals, too, help them understand why things happen. However, it is important to recognize that people often generate counterfactuals that are inconsistent with causal explanations. We have repeatedly observed in each of our studies of people coping with real-life events (Davis et al., 1995; Davis, Lehman, Silver, Wortman, & Ellard, in press) that self-implicating counterfactuals are reported even when the cause of the event is known to reside elsewhere.

Other researchers have suggested that people engage in counterfactual thinking in an effort to gain a sense of future control (Boninger, Gleicher, & Strathman, 1994; Gleicher et al., 1990; Roese, 1994; Taylor & Schneider, 1989). Markman et al. (1993), for example, demonstrated that when participants in a computer-simulated blackjack game thought they would be playing a subsequent game (i.e., when future control was an issue), they were more likely to make (upward) counterfactuals than were participants who did not anticipate playing the game again.

Although future-control issues may encourage counterfactual thinking, we do not believe this motive accounts for all counterfactual thought. Put simply, the future-control motive cannot explain why both the bereaved and those with SCI should be so concerned with counterfactuals. Among the respondents with SCI, as with the bereaved, avoidance of a future injury does not appear to be an important psychological issue. Most of those with SCI will never again walk, much less drive a car, play football, or dive into a swimming hole; nor does it seem likely that the bereaved in the studies reported here were focusing on the possibility of behaving differently in the future to avoid the loss of another loved one.

In addition, the future-control motive cannot explain why victims' descriptions of their counterfactuals do not remain stable over time. If counterfactuals were motivated strictly by a desire for future control, presumably people would focus and maintain their attention on one or two counterfactuals that would be most likely to yield a sense that future negative outcomes could be avoided. Rather, the scant evidence on this point suggests that the counterfactual thoughts that occupy people's minds tend to change over time (Davis et al., 1995).

Nevertheless, it may be that the psychological *consequences* of counterfactual thinking may depend on whether the situation is one in which future control is an issue. For instance, when future-control opportunities exist, the negative affective consequences of counterfactual thinking (e.g., frustration, guilt, distress) may be *tempered* by the implicit suggestion in the counterfactual thoughts that similar future negative experiences may be avoided (see Boninger et al., 1994; Markman et al., 1993; Roese, 1994; Roese & Olson, 1995). This argument is analogous to Janoff–Bulman's (1979; Janoff–Bulman & Lang–Gunn, 1988) suggestion that self-blame is likely to yield positive consequences for the victim if the behavior that is blamed is, from the victim's perspective, behaviorally modifiable (or, in counterfactual terms, mutable) and lends a sense of future control. If this hypothesis is accurate, it may have significant implications for the provision of support to people coping with traumatic events, although, clearly, further research is necessary.

Markman et al. (1993) raised the interesting point that "counterfactual generation has functional value, and people tend to generate those counterfactuals that hold the greatest psychological value for them in a given situation" (p. 103). In their conceptualization (see also Roese, 1994; Roese & Olson, 1995), when future control is not a relevant psychological issue (e.g., in the case of one-time events), people will tend to produce counterfactuals that help them make the best, emotionally, of whatever outcome has occurred (i.e., they construct downward counterfactuals). They do this, Markman et al. contend, by producing counterfactuals that allow them to see "that things could have been worse and that at least those very negative outcomes did not occur" (p. 103; this overall framework borrows heavily from the progression of ideas on social comparison put forward by Shelley Taylor and her colleagues, e.g., Taylor & Lobel, 1989).

COUNTERFACTUAL THINKING
WITHIN THE CONTEXT OF COPING

But what happens when the events people are coping with are both unlikely to recur *and*, for all practical purposes, are the worst things they can imagine happening to them? When we first considered what psychological value the bereaved and the spinal cord injured respondents were deriving from their counterfactuals, we came up with the answer, "none."

Perhaps they had no implicit goal at all; that is, the inexplicable event simply compelled them to undo it. After further reflection, however, we now think it is possible that people who have experienced traumatic events such as these may, in fact, have a goal toward which their counterfactuals are working. The predominant goal may be to grapple with the philosophical question Why me? or a search for meaning in the event (Davis, Lehman, & Wortman, 1995).

We take as a starting point that people possess implicit or explicit expectations or assumptions regarding daily events in their lives as well as the general course or trajectory that their lives will take (e.g., Janoff–Bulman, 1992; Lerner, 1980; Olson, Roese, & Zanna, in press). People assume, for instance, that they are relatively invulnerable to negative events such as rape, violent crime, and serious illness (see e.g., Heine & Lehman, 1995; Weinstein, 1980). They also assume that their lives and the social world in which they live have order and purpose (e.g., Taylor, 1983; Thompson & Janigian, 1988). At a more mundane level, people expect that when they engage in specific tasks (e.g. driving to work) they will be successful, particularly when the task is performed on a regular basis.

When individuals are faced with an outcome that shatters their implicit or explicit expectations, they are likely to experience an emotional reaction, including feelings of shock and distress (e.g., Silver & Wortman, 1980), as well as a cognitive reaction, which includes appraisals of the outcome's significance (e.g., Lazarus & Folkman, 1984) and its meaning (e.g., Janoff–Bulman, 1992; Taylor, 1983). When the outcome has significant and long-term implications for the individual (e.g., a serious injury, the death of a loved one), the failed expectation will also likely threaten to shatter a deep-seated and fundamental assumption (e.g., that one is relatively invulnerable to serious injury; Janoff–Bulman, 1992). It is for this reason that people are believed to attempt to find meaning in traumatic events.

As Taylor (1983) and others (e.g., Thompson, 1991) have noted, the search for meaning generally involves more than a mere causal attribution; people often want to make sense of the event within the larger context of their lives. They try to accomplish this, in part, by philosophically reflecting on the reasons for the selective incidence of the event, that is, Why me? (see Lehman, Wortman, & Williams, 1987). The goal of this search is to restore a sense of order and purpose in their lives and thus, in large part, to preserve their threatened fundamental assumptions (Davis, Lehman, & Wortman, 1995; Janoff–Bulman, 1992; Taylor, 1989; Thompson & Janigian, 1988). Unlike causal attributions, which are determined relatively quickly (see, e.g., Downey, Silver, & Wortman, 1990), the philosophical search for meaning tends to evolve as the individual ruminates about the outcome and the circumstances surrounding it (e.g., Horowitz, 1976, 1985; Silver, Boon, & Stones, 1983; Tait & Silver, 1989). Thus we anticipate that although causal attributions will remain relatively stable over time (barring the discovery of new information), concerns about the event's meaning will ebb and flow, perhaps cued by reminders of the event.

Although, as we discussed earlier, counterfactual reasoning may be invoked to attribute causality (e.g., Lipe, 1991), the more ruminative mental exercise of undoing traumatic events, in our view, serves the important role of helping the individual make sense of his or her experience. By generating a number of plausible counterfactual possibilities, the individual is implying that the event was not random and indiscriminate in its occurrence and is thus preserving the fundamental assumption that significant events in one's life are, at minimum, *potentially* controllable, if only in retrospect. Because the psychological cost of a shattered fundamental assumption is immense (see Janoff–Bulman, 1992), people will go to great lengths to preserve them, including accepting feelings of guilt and responsibility when rationally none should be assumed (Davis et al., in press). From this vantage point, it is significant that most of the counterfactuals reported following traumatic events focused on the respondents' own decisions or behavior (e.g., Davis, 1991; Davis et al., 1995; Pynoos et al., 1993; Tait & Silver, 1989).

We should note further that undoing is by no means the only way to make sense of, or to find meaning in traumatic events. Indeed, people possessing certain belief systems that provide ready answers to the question Why me? (e.g., "It was God's Will," "It was just bad luck") may be less likely to spend a great deal of time ruminating about counterfactual alternatives. Moreover, one might expect that once meaning issues are resolved, the frequency of counterfactual thoughts would also subside. In support of this, we observed correlations ranging from .30 to .52 between contemporaneous frequencies of undoing and searching for meaning among the SIDS parents and the respondents in the motor vehicle accident study.

Although we believe the research with real-life victims reported here has added both to the counterfactual literature and stress and coping literature, clearly this work has raised many more questions than it has answered. In fact, as we have outlined in this chapter, a whole host of important questions regarding counterfactual thinking in the face of traumatic events remain unexplored. Although field research of this sort tends to be quite challenging, we suggest that the potential dividends of such empirical work far outweigh the costs.

ACKNOWLEDGMENTS

Preparation of this chapter was facilitated by a Social Sciences and Humanities Research Council (SSHRC) doctoral fellowship to Christopher G. Davis and by SSHRC Grant 410-93-1295 and an Izaak Walton Killam

Faculty Research Fellowship to Darrin R. Lehman. We thank David Mandel, Jim Olson, and Neal Roese for their helpful comments on an earlier draft of this chapter.

REFERENCES

Baron, J. & Hershey, J. C. (1988). Outcome bias in decision evaluation. *Journal of Personality and Social Psychology, 54,* 569–579.

Boninger, D. S., Gleicher, F., & Strathman, A. (1994). Counterfactual thinking: From what might have been to what may be. *Journal of Personality and Social Psychology, 67,* 297–307.

Bulman, R. J., & Wortman, C. B. (1977). Attributions of blame and coping in the "real world": Severe accident victims react to their lot. *Journal of Personality and Social Psychology, 35,* 351–363.

Davis, C. G. (1991). *The undoing experience: Antecedents, consequences, and individual differences.* Unpublished master's thesis, University of British Columbia, Vancouver, Canada.

Davis, C. G., Lehman, D. R., Silver, R. C., Wortman, C. B., & Ellard, J. H. (in press). Self-blame following a traumatic event: The role of perceived avoidability. *Personality and Social Psychology Bulletin.*

Davis, C. G., Lehman, D. R., & Wortman, C. B. (1995). *Finding meaning in traumatic life events: Making sense of the literature.* Manuscript in preparation.

Davis, C. G., Lehman, D. R., Wortman, C. B., Silver, R. C., & Thompson, S. C. (1995). The undoing of traumatic life events. *Personality and Social Psychology Bulletin, 21,* 109–124.

Downey, G., Silver, R. C., & Wortman, C. B. (1990). Reconsidering the attribution–adjustment relation following a major negative event: Coping with the loss of a child. *Journal of Personality and Social Psychology, 59,* 925–940.

Gavanski, I., & Wells, G. L. (1989). Counterfactual processing of normal and exceptional events. *Journal of Experimental Social Psychology, 25,* 314–325.

Girotto, V., Legrenzi, P., & Rizzo, A. (1991). Event controllability and counterfactual thinking. *Acta Psychologica, 78,* 111–133.

Gleicher, F., Kost, K. A., Baker, S. M., Strathman, A. J., Richman, S. A., & Sherman, S. J. (1990). The role of counterfactual thinking in judgments of affect. *Personality and Social Psychology Bulletin, 16,* 284–295.

Heider, F. (1958). *The psychology of interpersonal relations.* New York: Wiley.

Heine, S. J., & Lehman, D. R. (1995). Cultural variation in unrealistic optimism: Does the West feel more invulnerable than the East? *Journal of Personality and Social Psychology, 68,* 595–607.

Hilton, D. J. (1990). Conversational processes and causal explanation. *Psychological Bulletin, 107,* 65–81.

Hilton, D. J., & Slugoski, B. R. (1986). Knowledge-based causal attribution: The abnormal conditions focus model. *Psychological Review, 93,* 75–88.

Horowitz, M. J. (1976). *Stress response syndrome.* New York: Aronson.

Horowitz, M. J. (1985). Disasters and psychological responses to stress. *Psychiatric Annals, 15,* 161–167.

Janoff-Bulman, R. (1979). Characterological versus behavioral self-blame: Inquiries into depression and rape. *Journal of Personality and Social Psychology, 37,* 1798–1809.

Janoff-Bulman, R. (1992). *Shattered assumptions: Towards a new psychology of trauma.* New York: Free Press.

Janoff–Bulman, R., & Lang–Gunn, L. (1988). Coping with disease, crime, and accidents: The role of self-blame attributions. In L. Y. Abramson (Ed.), *Social cognition and clinical psychology: A synthesis* (pp. 116–147). New York: Guilford.

Kahneman, D., & Miller, D. T. (1986). Norm theory: Comparing reality to its alternatives. *Psychological Review, 93*, 136–153.

Kahneman, D., & Tversky, A. (1982). The simulation heuristic. In D. Kahneman, P. Slovic, & A. Tversky (Eds.), *Judgment under uncertainty: Heuristics and biases* (pp. 201–208). New York: Cambridge University Press.

Kelley, H. H. (1972a). Attribution in social interaction. In E. E. Jones, D. E. Kanouse, H. H. Kelley, R. E. Nisbett, S. Valins, & B. Weiner (Eds.), *Attribution: Perceiving the causes of behavior* (pp. 1–26). Morristown, NJ: General Learning Press.

Landman, J. (1987). Regret and elation following action and inaction: Affective responses to positive versus negative outcomes. *Personality and Social Psychology Bulletin, 13*, 524–536.

Landman, J. (1993). *Regret: The persistence of the possible.* New York: Oxford University Press.

Langer, E. J., Blank, A., & Chanowitz, B. (1978). The mindlessness of ostensibly thoughtful action. *Journal of Personality and Social Psychology, 36*, 635–642.

Lazarus, R. S., & Folkman, S. (1984). *Stress, appraisal, and coping.* New York: Springer–Verlag.

Lehman, D. R., Ellard, J. H., & Wortman, C. B. (1986). Social support for the bereaved: Recipients' and providers' perspectives on what is helpful. *Journal of Consulting and Clinical Psychology, 54*, 438–446.

Lehman, D. R., & Hemphill, K. J. (1990). Recipients' perceptions of support attempts and attributions for support attempts that fail. *Journal of Social and Personal Relationships, 7*, 563–574.

Lehman, D. R., Wortman, C. B., & Williams, A. F. (1987). Long-term effects of losing a spouse or child in a motor vehicle crash. *Journal of Personality and Social Psychology, 52*, 218–231.

Lerner, M. J. (1980). *The belief in a just world: A fundamental delusion.* New York: Plenum.

Lipe, M. G. (1991). Counterfactual reasoning as a framework for attributional theories. *Psychological Bulletin, 109*, 456–471.

Macrae, C. N. (1992). A tail of two curries: Counterfactual thinking and accident-related judgments. *Personality and Social Psychology Bulletin, 18*, 84–87.

Markman, K. D., Gavanski, I., Sherman, S. J., & McMullen, M. N. (1993). The mental simulation of better and worse possible worlds. *Journal of Experimental Social Psychology, 29*, 87–109.

Markman, K. D., Gavanski, I., Sherman, S. J., & McMullen, M. N. (1995). The impact of perceived control on the imagination of better and worse possible worlds. *Personality and Social Psychology Bulletin, 21*, 588–595.

Miller, D. T., & Gunasegaram, S. (1990). Temporal order and the perceived mutability of events: Implications for blame assignment. *Journal of Personality and Social Psychology, 59*, 1111–1118.

Miller, D. T., & McFarland, C. (1986). Counterfactual thinking and victim compensation: A test of norm theory. *Personality and Social Psychology Bulletin, 12*, 513–519.

Miller, D. T., & Turnbull, W. (1990). The counterfactual fallacy: Confusing what might have been with what ought to have been. *Social Justice Research, 4*, 1–19.

Miller, D. T., Turnbull, W., & McFarland, C. (1990). Counterfactual thinking and social perception: Thinking about what might have been. In M. P. Zanna (Ed.), *Advances in experimental social psychology* (Vol. 23, pp. 305–331). Orlando, FL: Academic Press.

Nisbett, R. E., & Ross, L. D. (1980). *Human inference: Strategies and shortcomings of social judgment.* Englewood Cliffs, NJ: Prentice–Hall.

Olson, J. M., Roese, N. J., & Zanna, M. P. (in press). Expectancies. In E. T. Higgins & A. W. Kruglanski (Eds.), *Social psychology: Handbook of basic principles.* New York: Guilford.

Pennebaker, J. W. (1989). Confession, inhibition, and disease. In L. Berkowitz (Ed.), *Advances in experimental social psychology* (Vol. 22, pp. 211–244). New York: Academic Press.

Pynoos, R. S., Goenjian, A., Tashjian, M., Karakashian, M., Manjikian, R., Manoukian, G., Steinberg, A. M., & Fairbanks, L. A. (1993). Post-traumatic stress reactions in children after the 1988 Armenian Earthquake. *British Journal of Psychiatry, 163*, 239–247.

Pyszczynski, T., & Greenberg, J. (1987). Self-regulatory perseveration and the depressive self-focusing style: A self-awareness theory of reactive depression. *Psychological Bulletin, 102*, 122–138.

Roese, N. J. (1994). The functional basis of counterfactual thinking. *Journal of Personality and Social Psychology, 66*, 805–818.

Roese, N. J., & Olson, J. M. (1993). The structure of counterfactual thought. *Personality and Social Psychology Bulletin, 19*, 312–319.

Roese, N. J., & Olson, J. M. (1995). Outcome controllability and counterfactual thinking. *Personality and Social Psychology Bulletin, 21*, 620–628.

Shaver, K. G. (1985). *The attribution of blame: Causality, responsibility, and blameworthiness.* New York: Springer–Verlag.

Shaver, K. G., & Drown, D. (1986). On causality, responsibility, and self-blame: A theoretical note. *Journal of Personality and Social Psychology, 50*, 697–702.

Silver, R. L., Boon, C., & Stones, M. H. (1983). Searching for meaning in misfortune: Making sense of incest. *Journal of Social Issues, 39*(2), 81–102.

Silver, R. L., & Wortman, C. B. (1980). Coping with undesirable life events. In J. Garber & M. E. P. Seligman (Eds.), *Human helplessness* (pp. 279–345). New York: Academic Press.

Sutherland, G., Newman, B., & Rachman, S. (1982). Experimental investigations of the relations between mood and intrusive unwanted cognitions. *British Journal of Medical Psychology, 55*, 127–138.

Tait, R., & Silver, R. C. (1989). Coming to terms with major negative life events. In J. S. Uleman & J. A. Bargh (Eds.), *Unintended thought* (pp. 351–381). New York: Guilford.

Taylor, S. E. (1983). Adjustment to threatening events: A theory of cognitive adaptation. *American Psychologist, 38*, 1161–1173.

Taylor, S. E. (1989). *Positive illusions: Creative self-deception and the healthy mind.* New York: Basic Books.

Taylor, S. E., & Lobel, M. (1989). Social comparison activity under threat: Downward evaluation and upward contacts. *Psychological Review, 96*, 569–575.

Taylor, S. E., & Schneider, S. K. (1989). Coping and the simulation of events. *Social Cognition, 7*, 174–194.

Thompson, S. C. (1991). The search for meaning following a stroke. *Basic and Applied Social Psychology, 12*, 81–96.

Thompson, S. C., & Janigian, A. J. (1988). Life schemes: A framework for understanding the search for meaning. *Journal of Social and Clinical Psychology, 7*, 260–280.

Wegner, D. M, & Schneider, D. J. (1989). Mental control: The war of the ghosts in the machine. In J. S. Uleman & J. A. Bargh (Eds.), *Unintended thought* (pp. 287–305). New York: Guilford.

Weinstein, N. J. (1980). Unrealistic optimism about future life events. *Journal of Personality and Social Psychology, 39*, 806–820.

Weiss, R. S. (1988). Loss and recovery. *Journal of Social Issues, 44*(3), 37–52.

Wells, G. L., & Gavanski, I. (1989). Mental simulation and causality. *Journal of Personality and Social Psychology, 56*, 161–169.

Wells, G. L., Taylor, B. R., & Turtle, J. W. (1987). The undoing of scenarios. *Journal of Personality and Social Psychology, 53*, 421–430.

Wortman, C. B., & Lehman, D. R. (1985). Reactions to victims of life crises: Support attempts that fail. In I. G. Sarason & B. R. Sarason (Eds.), *Social support: Theory, research and applications* (pp. 463–489). Dordrecht, Netherlands: Martinus Nijhoff.

14

Varieties of Counterfactual Thinking

Daniel Kahneman
Princeton University

The essays in this volume attest to the rapid advances achieved in a relatively short period of time in the psychological study of counterfactual thinking. Some of the advances are methodological: Research has moved far beyond vignettes to the study of real counterfactual emotions and causal intuitions in the laboratory and in the world. New topics of research have also emerged, including the preparatory function of counterfactual thinking (chapters 5, 6, and 10), and individual differences in the generation of various types of counterfactual thoughts (chapters 3 and 10). And there is more to come. In this chapter I focus on topics that may further enlarge the domain that students of counterfactual thinking call their own.

COUNTERFACTUAL THOUGHTS: AUTOMATIC AND ELABORATIVE

The notion of counterfactual thinking covers a broad range of mental activities that differ greatly in their complexity. At one extreme, the elementary response of surprise when the doorbell makes an unusual sound is associated with a counterfactual thought: The normal alternative is presumably evoked, and it is counterfactual. At the other extreme on a dimension of intentional elaboration, historians ponder an alternative world in which the South won the Civil War. The basic surprise response and the exercise in counterfactual history share an important characteristic:

Both represent the causal texture of an environment. However, we should be cautious about assuming that they generally follow the same rules.

Surprise is rooted in the orienting response, a distinct pattern of autonomic and skeletal adjustments to novel stimuli, which is found in lower animals and in human infants, and persists in adults (Lynn, 1966). The rudimentary form of counterfactual thinking that mediates the orienting response is certainly involuntary and automatic. A more complex but still automatic process is involved in the perception of causality and its associated counterfactuals. Michotte (1946) studied the conditions of temporal and spatial contiguity under which a physical event is *perceived* to have been caused by another. The temporal parameters of perceived causation are closely related to the parameters of apparent motion. Like apparent motion, the perception of causality is a backward-looking process: It is initiated by the occurrence of an event (the consequence), which triggers a search for possible causes among recent occurrences stored in memory. The process retrospectively endows the selected cause with a perceived propensity to produce the consequent event. It may also induce a rudimentary counterfactual belief that the consequence would not have occurred without the causal event. Close counterfactuals (Kahneman & Varey, 1990) are a third kind of counterfactual thought that is automatic and has perceptual character. The "fact" that a particular event almost occurred can sometimes be registered with all the immediacy of a percept.

Surprises, perceptions of causality, and close counterfactuals are explainable largely in cognitive terms. Motivational relevance and deliberate attention perhaps increase the availability and salience of these thoughts but are not necessary conditions for their occurrence. The description of motivationally relevant outcomes as the engine of counterfactual thinking (Roese & Olson, chapter 1) applies best to other modes of counterfactual thought, which involve elaboration, intent, and rumination—singly or in any combination of these factors. This argument leads to a distinction between two variants of counterfactual thought: *automatic* and *elaborative*. As in other distinctions between levels of processing (Chaiken, 1987; Petty & Cacioppo, 1986), automatic and elaborative counterfactual thoughts define a continuum rather than a typology. As in these other cases, the distinction between the primitive process and the high-level variant draws attention to two useful questions: What do the automatic and elaborative modes have in common? How do they differ? These questions define an open research problem in the domain of counterfactuals. The techniques that have proved useful in manipulating depth of processing in other domains may prove equally useful in studying possible differences between automatic and elaborative counterfactual thinking. For example, the effects of mental load on counterfactual thoughts appear to be a promising area of research.

The first wave of psychological research on counterfactuals was much concerned with negative emotions, such as frustration or regret, which were explained by the automatic activation of counterfactual thoughts about preferred alternatives to a painful reality. The landscape is now different. Roese and Olson (chapter 6) review a substantial amount of research, by themselves and by other authors (Gleicher et al., chapter 10; McMullen et al., chapter 5), which shows that the individual's needs and intentions (e.g., to learn from the experience or to defend a wounded self-image) affect both the extent of engagement in counterfactual thought and the direction this thought will take.

The focus of much recent research has been elaborative counterfactual thoughts that may have a preparatory function (Gleicher et al., chapter 10; McMullen, Markman, & Gavanski, chapter 5; Roese & Olson, chapter 6; E. Seelau, S. Seelau, Wells, & Windschitl, chapter 2; Sherman & McConnell, chapter 7). When encountering a consequence, people sometimes explore alternative choices they might have made and the likely consequences of these choices. This examination can generate behavioral intentions for the future, such as "When faced again with a choice between X and Y, choose Y—not only because X led to a bad consequence (the reality) but because Y would have led to a good one (the counterfactual)." The possibility of this form of learning raises many interesting questions. We can hope to find out about the conditions under which one learns from considering the counterfactual in addition to what one learns from the real consequence. It will also be important to find out whether people make efficient use of their knowledge in generating instructive counterfactuals and whether they make good use of counterfactual thoughts in preparing themselves for future action.

In the current functionalist perspective, aversive counterfactual emotions, such as regret and frustration, raise a question: Why would people ever generate thoughts that make them feel worse? This is a perennial puzzle, which the learning theorists of the 1950s discussed under the label of the *neurotic paradox*. What rewards reinforce the self-induced production of disabling symptoms or of painful anxiety? The question arises in the context of counterfactual emotions and also in the broader context of painful rumination about past losses: What is it that keeps these thoughts going? The search for an answer has gone in two directions. It is in the spirit of modern social psychology to explain painful rumination as a "work of mourning," a search for meaning or as an attempt to restore a belief in a just world. In a behaviorist spirit one would look for immediate rewards as an explanation of the persistence of an activity that has globally deleterious consequences. Perhaps the bereaved parents who ruminate about the counterfactuals that might have saved their child are enjoying a fantasy in which it is not yet too late?

The speculation that upward counterfactuals provide short-term rewards could eventually be tested by psychophysiological techniques.

MENTAL SIMULATION OF COMPLEX CAUSAL SYSTEMS

Counterfactual reasoning and the relation between counterfactuals and causality were topics of philosophical investigation long before they became the subject of psychological research. Philosophical analysis attempts to provide a logically coherent account of why, for example, the sentence "If Hitler had had the atom bomb, he would have won World War II" is (probably) true, whereas the sentence "If Hitler had had an extra tank he would have won World War II" is (almost certainly) false. Some philosophical investigations of the truth conditions for counterfactuals have invoked the idea of possible worlds—of which the real world is only one (Lewis, 1973).

The elaborate counterfactual constructions that philosophers have found most interesting can also be studied psychologically, but the goals of the investigation are different. The question for the psychologist is not whether a particular counterfactual assertion is true or false, but why people think that it is true or false. Another question of psychological interest is why statements such as "If Gorbachev had not been the leader of the Soviet Union in the 1980s, the Berlin Wall would still have stood at the end of the century" are often considered informative and worth debating (Greenstein, 1995; Tetlock & Belkin, 1994). A psychological analysis of both questions is likely to involve the process that has been called *mental simulation*. I now turn to a highly speculative sketch of this process, in which I go far beyond currently available evidence.

Mental simulation is a form of elaborative thinking in which one imagines the unfolding of a sequence of events, from an initial counterfactual starting point to some outcome. The outcome that is "observed" in the simulation is considered true, or at least likely to be true. Simulation can be used to evaluate conditional propositions, whether standard or counterfactual. There is no psychologically interesting difference between the counterfactual conditional "If you had loaded one more suitcase on this cart, it would have tipped over" and the conditional warning "If you load one more suitcase on this cart it will tip over." A simulation may rely on social as well as on physical knowledge. For example, simulation can be used to explore the remote branches of a social script (e.g., "What do you do in a restaurant if the waiter who served you disappears for a long time without bringing you your check?"). As in the example of the overloaded luggage cart, simulation can be applied to discover the outcomes of particular social situations. When deciding on seating arrangements for a formal dinner, the hosts may imagine Fred and Jill seated next to each other, in an attempt to figure out whether they will find anything of joint interest to talk about.

Even in these relatively simple situations, simulation is highly schematic: We do not imagine the details of the wait for the waiter or every utterance in the conversation between Jill and Fred. The simulation of historical counterfactuals is even more schematic. The possible worlds that we construct to examine conditional propositions are hardly complete. Nevertheless, I propose that the most important aspect of the phenomenology of mental simulation is that it is experienced as an act of observation, not as an act of construction. Indeed, the high confidence that is sometimes attached to the outcomes of mental simulation derives precisely from the sense that the outcome is observed, not contrived at will.

A simulation may be allowed to run freely from the initial conditions to whatever outcome it produces. Alternatively, a simulation can be constrained by a target outcome as well as by specified initial conditions. The goal of target-constrained simulations is to discover scenarios that lead to the target outcome or to assess the availability of such scenarios. The assessment of availability is used as an indication of the *propensity* of the system to produce the target outcome (Kahneman & Tversky, 1982b; Kahneman & Varey, 1990). An outcome may be judged impossible if attempts to imagine scenarios leading to it end in failure; it will be judged inevitable if all scenarios that come to mind produce it. Complexities arise in the evaluation of conditionals, both standard and counterfactual, when the condition is implausible. The statement "If the Republicans had won 80% of the seats in the House in the last election, measure X would have passed" requires a target-constrained reconstruction of the events leading to an extraordinarily lopsided result in the last election as well as a simulation of the politics of measure X, assuming this result. The entire simulation exercise is unsatisfactory if no good scenarios leading to the condition come to mind. Again, similar issues arise in the evaluation of the standard conditional "If the Republicans win 80% of the seats in the House in the next election, measure X will pass."

This analysis of mental simulation suggests an answer to the penetrating question raised by Tetlock and Belkin (1994): Why do people sometimes find their own counterfactual thoughts instructive? What new knowledge do they discover by running a mental simulation? The answer is that knowledge comes in different forms, which are accessed by different probes. A familiar example of the diversity of knowledge forms is the distinction between declarative knowledge (knowing that) and procedural knowledge (knowing how). The knowledge of causal systems that is used in mental simulation belongs in a third category. It does not involve procedures that act on the environment, nor is it stored in a format that allows direct access to verbal answers; the causal knowledge is implicit in the rules that govern the simulation.

It is the implicit nature of the knowledge used in mental simulation that makes such simulations potentially instructive, when their outcomes conflict with explicit beliefs. Thus, a believer in the inevitability of an early collapse of the Soviet Union could be surprised to discover by mental simulation that plausible alternatives to Gorbachev would have delayed the event by many years (Greenstein, 1995). The possible dissociations between explicit and implicit causal beliefs present a rich problem for future research. Under what conditions do people hold incompatible causal theories of the same system in their implicit and in their explicit beliefs? What factors control the relative accuracy of these beliefs?

Mental simulation draws on sources of knowledge that cannot be accessed otherwise, and simulation exercises can therefore be truly instructive, as Tetlock and Belkin (1994) proposed. However, it is important to remember that there is no magic in mental simulation and no guarantee that it correctly represents the causal relationships of the real world. For example, studies of naive physical intuitions have shown that these intuitions are closer to Aristotelian physics than to the truth—perhaps not surprising considering that Aristotelian physics was based in large part on thought experiments (McCloskey, 1983). In the social domain, a long history of disasters of planning and design demonstrates that the impossible sometimes happens and that the inevitable sometimes does not. Mental simulation is a form of scenario thinking, which is typically associated with more confidence than it deserves (Dawes, 1988).

A casual study of historical counterfactuals reveals that intuitions about causality and inevitability may be subject to powerful biases. Consider again the role of Gorbachev in bringing the cold war to an end. Suppose that you agree with experts who claim that his role was essential. Are you then willing to agree that the cold war came to an end in this century by chance? Probably not. Does this negative opinion survive the observation that there was a point in time at which the probability that Gorbachev would be female was approximately one half? Most people find this fact quite surprising, because it carries the clear implication that the event of Gorbachev's becoming the leader of the Soviet Union could have been undone by countless chance occurrences, of which his being born female was only one.

The surprise we experience in the realization that Gorbachev could have been born female reveals a prevalent tendency to overestimate the regularity of events and to underestimate the role of chance. Hindsight is involved, and its effects are both strong and contradictory (see also Dawes, 1993). On the one hand, hindsight leads us to exaggerate the prior probability of a scenario resembling the actual events, for example, a scenario with Gorbachev in an important role. However, hindsight also leads us to exaggerate the probability that the cold war would *not* have ended in this century if Gorbachev had not been there to do it. A simple thought experiment will justify this claim. First, form an opinion of what was a reasonable ex ante assessment—say in 1970—of the probability that the cold war would come to a peaceful end within 50 years of 1980. Next, assess how much of that probability should have been allocated to the first 20 years of this 50-year period. Obviously, the probability you assessed is higher by orders of magnitude than the aggregate ex ante probability (as of 1970) of scenarios that the world would now recognize as minor variants of the actual course of events. We are forced to the conclusion that even if Gorbachev had not done it—or not been there to do it—there was a substantial chance of the cold war ending in this century, in some quite different way. There are more possible worlds than our mind can construct, and those we do construct tend to be quite similar to the real story in which they are anchored. If you still resist this thought, consider a world in which all the members of the 1985 Politburo were girls.

Different ways of thinking about the question of whether Gorbachev made a difference appear to lead to quite different conclusions. On the one hand, it seems that the probability of the cold war ending between 1980 and 2000 (as assessed in 1970) would have been much the same if Gorbachev had been born female. On the other hand, there is a persuasive case that a quick end of the cold war was far from inevitable when Gorbachev came to power in 1985 (Greenstein, 1995). These conclusions are not contradictory, but they suggest different evaluations of Gorbachev's role. The two modes of thinking invoked in this exercise correspond to approaches that were labeled the *inside view* and the *outside view* in an analysis of intuitive forecasting (Kahneman & Lovallo, 1993; Kahneman & Tversky, 1979). Forecasting by the inside view is an attempt to divine the history of the future by building relatively specific scenarios. Forecasting by the outside view is an attempt to estimate the statistics of a relatively large category to which the case at hand belongs. In the context of counterfactual reasoning, the inside view involves the mental construction of alternative histories, whereas the outside view consists of global assignments of probability to consequences. Scenario thinking has considerable appeal in evaluating both the past and the future, and it sometimes yields knowledge that is not accessible in other ways. However, the risk of the inside view is that our confidence in the conclusions it yields ultimately derives from the limits of our imagination.

COUNTERFACTUALS AND CAUSALITY

Causality is another topic in which philosophers and psychologists share an interest. The most important philosophical sources that have affected recent psychological work on the topic are Hart and Honoré's (1959) masterful *Causation in the Law* and Mackie's (1974) *Cement of the Universe.* Here again, as in the case of counterfactuals, widely shared intuitions provide the background for both philosophical and psychological investigations. It is an empirical fact that people often agree in their causal explanations of events. This fact sets up a philosophical research agenda in which the "true" rules of causality are to be determined. The psychological agenda is again different: Intuitions about causality are data, which are to be described and explained in terms of known cognitive mechanisms. In this section I discuss perceived propensity and judged causality and the counterfactuals associated with them.

The studies by Michotte (1946) and by Heider and Simmel (1944) are among the enduring classics in the causality literature. Both studies dealt with direct, perceptual impressions of causality. Michotte investigated the spatial and temporal cues that make one event the perceived cause of another. Heider and Simmel observed the powerful impressions of intention that are induced by patterns of movement of several figures, for example, the perception that one figure "chases" the other. The moral of these studies is that causation is a distinctive perceptual quality and that causal propensity and intentionality can also be perceived directly, apparently without the mediation of any inference. Though well known and greatly admired, these studies of perceived causality have not attracted much following. The psychological study of causality has focused almost exclusively on the inferential processes of causal explanation and attribution.

Some years ago, Carol Varey and I explored a phenomenon that appears more closely related to causal perception than to causal inference: the impression that there is, or was, a propensity for an event to occur. We studied this notion of propensity by exploring the conditions under which it would be appropriate to say that an event almost happened—or almost did not happen (Kahneman & Varey, 1990). A case in point is the story of the last shot in the ball game, which would have changed the outcome. It is appropriate to say that "Team X almost won the game; they would have won if that shot had gone in." Other examples are "John almost won the race," "Sheila almost died," "Tom almost did not make it to the party." We called these cases *close counterfactuals.* In each of these examples, a strong *propensity* for the counterfactual outcome must have existed not too long before the actual outcome was determined.

A propensity implies an assessment of probability, but a high probability is not sufficient for an assignment of propensity. For example, we can be quite certain that if the world champion in chess had participated in a local amateur tournament he would have won. Now suppose the world champion sent a registration form for the tournament, but it arrived one day late. It is appropriate to say that the champion almost registered, but not that he almost won the tournament. The champion's probability of winning the tournament if he plays in it is a *disposition*, not yet a propensity. A propensity to win the tournament can be identified only by observation of the sequence of events leading most directly to that outcome. In some cases, such as a train's running on its rails, there is only a single propensity. In the case of a closely fought contest, there are propensities for several outcomes. Because the cues to propensity must be derived from the event, a runner who followed a few paces behind the leader for an entire race will not be perceived as having almost won it. In contrast, a runner who was catching up when the exhausted winner crossed the tape can be said to have almost won. All available knowledge of the causal system is brought to bear in judging propensity: The runner who almost caught up with the leader will not be said to have almost won the race if we know that a gangster was prepared to shoot her as soon as she took the lead.

Close counterfactuals reveal an important characteristic of the cognitive psychology of causality: The mind is not a determinist (see also Kvart, 1986). Even in hindsight, we can identify a system as having propensities to produce diverse outcomes. Whether or not a system is seen as deterministic is an attribution about that system; it is not necessarily a function of our knowledge of it. Thus, we have deterministic beliefs about machinery and electronic devices that we do not understand. However, "it is an important fact about causal reasoning that a sense of the necessity of consequences is often absent. In particular, there is no sense of necessity or inevitability in considering games of chance, many contests and competitions, some physical systems (e.g., weather and chance devices), or intentional actions" (Kahneman & Varey, 1990, p. 1103).

Perceived propensities have the phenomenological status of facts about the world: They are experienced as real, not as mental constructions. Indeed, propensities can be faked, as illustrated by the apparently lethal propensities seen in television wrestling. The attribution of objective reality extends both to the causes of events that do occur and to the propensities of events that do not materialize. Note that this attribution is a psychological fact, not a metaphysical claim. Readers who draw philosophical conclusions from this phenomenological observation does so at their own risk.

In a very different vein, there have been notable advances in the understanding of the conditions under which people say that "event X was the cause of event A" and of what they mean by this phrase. First, it is now generally recognized that this causal statement does not explain event A; it explains an *effect* (Kahneman & Miller, 1986), a departure of event A from a state of affairs that would be designated normal (Gavanski & Wells, 1989; Hilton, 1990; Hilton & Slugoski, 1986). The unadorned causal statement is elliptical when it fails to specify the counterfactual norm that event A violates, but the shared knowledge of speaker and listener and various conversational cues usually eliminate this ambiguity (Kahneman & Miller, 1986). Another constraint on attributions of causality is that the cause must be highly mutable, if not itself abnormal. Event X will not be considered a cause of anything unless one can readily conceive of an alternative to it. Thus, the presence of oxygen is not said to cause fires, except when oxygen is present where it was not supposed to be. Hart and Honoré (1959) observed that a cause is found by searching backward from the effect, stopping at unusual circumstances or at voluntary actions. It is clear from their treatment that the identification of a single cause by this heuristic procedure is largely conventional and is not to be taken too seriously.

The statement "X caused A" is elliptical in another way: It is generally not intended to exclude the possible role of other causal factors. Indeed, the phrase does not imply a belief in the existence of a single "true" cause of the event. The word *cause* is often used to communicate a belief about a particular counterfactual (A would not have occurred if X had not) and, at the same time, to indicate that this counterfactual is especially relevant or interesting (Hilton, 1990; Kahneman & Miller, 1986). Stating that X is the cause of A does not imply that Y is not also a cause of the same consequence. Thus, a simple causal assertion may be much more sophisticated than it appears, if the speaker and the listener both accept the background assumption that the consequence was produced by a complex causal system. In this interpretation, the causal assertion simply means "the counterfactual that A would not have occurred without X is both true and interesting."

In the analysis proposed here, a causal statement does not deny the truth of other undoing counterfactuals, although it implies a modest evaluation of their relevance. Some apparent errors of causal reasoning appear more reasonable in this charitable light. One example is the intuition that the ball game was lost because of the missed last shot. Another is the finding that two variants of a 2×2 matrix relating gender to success in a particular test in firefighter training may induce different impressions about the causal role of gender, although the correlation between gender and success is the same in both (McGill & Klein, chapter 12). Both examples can be understood in terms of the conversational relevance of the counterfactuals that they imply.

The missed last shot is not more blameworthy than any other missed shot in the game, but there is a counterfactual that is true only of the last shot: Given the score and the time remaining, the outcome of the game *could not be different* once it was missed. In other words, missing this shot was a sufficient condition for losing the game. Similarly, if every female firefighter fails a test in which a 200-pound dummy is to be carried out of danger and some male firefighters pass that test, feminine gender is a sufficient condition for failure and therefore likely to be cited as a cause (McGill & Klein, chapter 12). In terms of the conventions that regulate the use of the word *cause* in conversation, it is not an error for one to say that the missed shot caused the loss of the game or that the firefighter failed the weight-carrying test because she was a woman. The notion of a convention is important here: By convention, the definite article does not imply exclusivity in statements about "*the* cause" of an event. Sufficiency, salience, and mutability control the process in which one of the conditions surrounding an event is singled out as its cause. Of course, the causal label can have consequences: The player who missed the last shot of the game will not have a good night, and gender discrimination may be reinforced among firefighters. I suggest that these biases should be viewed as side effects of the normal operation of the conversational conventions of causal attribution, not as errors of causal reasoning.

DISTANCE AND MUTABILITY

The metaphor of *distance* between specified counterfactuals and a corresponding reality has almost irresistible appeal, and it has appeared in the work of philosophers (e.g., Lewis, 1973) as well as in psychological analyses. There is a compelling intuition that some counterfactual alternatives are "closer" to reality than others and that the close alternatives are more available and therefore more likely to evoke counterfactual emotions such as frustration or regret. The notion of distance is not restricted to the domain of counterfactuals; Lewin (1951) used psychological distance as one aspect of the *life space*. Lewinian psychological distance is affected by temporal and spatial separation and by more or less permeable boundaries that constrain access from one region of the life space to another. There are obvious parallels between the concepts of distance used in this context and in the analysis of counterfactuals.

The notion of distance is most useful in comparing counterfactual alternatives that differ from reality on the same dimension but to different degrees. An early example was the story of the two travelers who arrive to the airport on the same limousine, half an hour after the scheduled departure of their respective flights (Kahneman & Tversky, 1982b). One of the travelers finds that his plane left on time. The other traveler hears that his plane was delayed and only left 5 minutes ago. There is general agreement that the man whose plane was delayed came much closer to catching his plane and will be correspondingly much more upset. A remarkable study by Medvec, Madey, and Gilovich (in press) took the idea of distance beyond the limited world of vignettes. Using blind coding of the facial expressions of Olympic medal winners, these authors found that silver medalists looked less happy than did bronze medalists. Here again, the notion of distance is applicable because the counterfactuals can be ordered on a single dimension: The silver medalists came closer to winning the gold, and the bronze medalists came closer to winning no medal at all. This finding demonstrates that the objective quality of outcomes does not suffice to predict their psychological value; a salient and close counterfactual can cause a superior outcome to be less rewarding than an inferior one.

The concept of *mutability* draws on the same intuitions as the notion of psychological distance but in a somewhat different way. The idea is that when people consider a real episode or situation, they may be able to predict the relative availability of different counterfactual alternatives: Some aspects of reality are more mutable than others, in the sense that alternatives to them come more readily to mind. Effects of mutability can also be identified in contexts other than investigations of counterfactuals. For example, Kahneman and Miller (1986) noted that it is more natural to say of a girl that she is big for her age, not young for her size—illustrating the differential mutability of causes and effects. They also observed informally that people who were required to alter a sequence of two letters or digits typically changed the second, as expected if the last events of a sequence are most mutable. In more recent research using the same technique, Ritov and Kahneman (1995) have found that the probability of winning is a more mutable characteristic of gambles than the size of the prize. A large majority of respondents, when asked to produce an example of a gamble that is *less* attractive than the gamble "60% chance to win $30" produced a gamble in which only the probability of winning was reduced. No respondent offered a gamble in which only the prize was reduced.

Miller, Taylor, and Buck (1991) observed that social categories can sometimes be divided into a more prominent and a less prominent subsets. The prominent, or prototypical, subset is then viewed as less mutable. For example, the prototypical voter is male. A difference between the attitudes of male and female voters (e.g., the "gender gap" of the 1988 election) will then be viewed as a deviation of women from a norm. Similarly, the prototypical teacher is female, and a gender difference in that context is attributed to the peculiarities of male teachers. Most impressive, greater permanence is attributed to the features of the prominent category. Thus, the gender gap in politics was expected to be closed by female voters becoming more like male voters.

In the context of counterfactuals, the notion of mutability is invoked to predict which of several aspects of reality will most readily be altered to produce a counterfactual alternative. Mutability is also used to explain a peculiarity of the distance between possible worlds: This distance often appears to be asymmetric, so that the distance from A to B and the distance from B to A need not be the same. The set of factors that control mutability in norm theory was recently reviewed by Tetlock and Belkin (1994):

1. Exceptions are undone more readily than are routine events; the abnormal is more mutable than the normal.
2. Effects are more mutable than their causes (as illustrated by the example of a child's size and age introduced earlier).
3. According to the focus rule, the actions of an agent who is the focus of attention are most readily undone; for example, in imagining how a fatal accident could be undone people tend to make the known victim swerve away from the threat.
4. Commission is more mutable than omission.
5. The end of a series is particularly mutable; people tend to undo the last critical shot in a ball game more than any other shot.
6. Acts due to human agency are highly mutable.

As might be expected from the preceding discussion, the list of mutability factors is closely related to the list of factors that contribute to the selection of a single cause for a known event. As Hart and Honoré (1959) noted, a cause is often chosen by working backward from the consequence to the first unusual circumstance or voluntary action. Thus, Factors 1, 3, 5, and 6 affect both the availability of counterfactuals and the selection of causes. Factor 2 is related to the critical role of sufficiency in causality judgments (see also the discussion of contrastive thinking in chapters 1 and 12). A failure to mutate the effect, given the cause, is an indication of sufficiency.

Factor 4 in the list suggests that—at least in the context of human agency—the subtraction of an action is more readily imagined than the addition of an action. I return later to the issue of commission versus omission. There has been progress in the study of a closely related compatibility rule: Success is typically undone by eliminating acts (a subtractive counterfactual), but failure is undone by addition (Dunning & Madey, chapter 4; Roese & Olson, chapter 6).

The original studies of distance, mutability, and normality were conducted in a set of experimental paradigms, which shared the constraint that the outcome to be mentally undone was kept constant while other factors were varied. In an early study of undoing, for example, two scenarios leading to a fatal accident were described. The scenarios were identical except in specified details: The route taken by the victim and the time at which the victim left the office were routine in one scenario and unusual in the other (Kahneman & Tversky, 1982a). The conclusion of the study was that abnormal features of the causal chain were more mutable than normal ones. However, some results of real-life studies of counterfactual reasoning in survivors of various tragedies appear to challenge this conclusion (Davis & Lehman, chapter 13). These authors report a considerable amount of rumination about departures from routine that would have changed the outcome. The conflict is only apparent: The original claim about mutability was not that normal events will never be undone but that abnormal circumstances are more likely to be the subject of mental undoing. The real-world data do not contradict this hypothesis. They do, however, support the new conclusion that behaving normally and following standard operating procedures does not provide full protection against later regret if disaster strikes. It still appears likely that regret and rumination are likely to be worse when scenarios that undo the outcome are highly available. The issue could be settled by a comparison of the counterfactual ruminations of families in which a member has recently been the victim of an accident or of a first heart attack.

OMISSION–COMMISSION

The asymmetry between the emotional reaction to the consequences of omissions and commissions has been a major theme in the study of counterfactuals, marked by substantial advances and surprising developments. Findings from early research indicated that, with consequences controlled, commission is associated with more regret than is omission. Findings from recent research draw a far more complex picture.

The initial observation that illustrated the relation between regret and acts of commission was reported by Kahneman and Tversky (1982a). I cite it in full because it provides background for the discussion that follows.

> Mr. Paul owned shares in company A. During the past year he considered switching to stock in company B, but he decided against it. He now finds out that he would have been better off by $1,200 if he had switched to company B. Mr. George owned shares in company B. During the past year he switched to stock in company A. He now finds that he would have been better off by $1,200 if he had kept his stock in company B.
>
> Who feels greater regret? (p. 173)

A large majority of respondents (92%) believed that Mr. George is more upset. The result was explained by the assumption that inaction is the standard default (or normal) state. Because normal states are more available than abnormal ones, counterfactual inaction is more available than counterfactual action (Kahneman & Miller, 1986). The availability of the counterfactual, in turn, controls the intensity of regret.

Three features of this vignette are worth noting: The consequences of commission (switching) and omission (not switching) are precisely known and precisely matched, the regretted outcome is recent, and the emotion may be fairly intense, at least for Mr. George. This result is robust (Baron & Ritov, 1994; Gilovich & Medvec, 1994, chapter 9; Landman, 1987, 1994; Gleicher et al., 1990; Miller & Taylor, chapter 11), but it is only the beginning of the story.

One significant development is due to Baron and his collaborators, who have traced the ramifications of the differential response to adverse consequences of omission and of commission—they label it the *omission bias*—in several domains of personal decision, moral judgment, and public policy (see e.g., Baron & Ritov, 1994; Ritov & Baron, 1990, 1992; Spranca, Minsk, & Baron, 1991). A poignant example of the bias concerns the decision to vaccinate one's child when there is a finite risk of death from the disease and a smaller risk of death from the vaccination (Ritov & Baron, 1990). People treat the risk associated with the act of vaccination as if it were substantially more severe, both in the context of an individual decision and in the context of public policy, in which accountability further increases the omission bias (Tetlock & Boettger, 1994).

Gilovich, Medvec, and Chen (1995), in a brilliant experiment, took the original distinction between switching and not switching beyond the world of vignettes. They conducted a variant of the "Monty Hall" game, in which the participant initially chose one of three doors hiding prizes of different values, then had an opportunity to switch to another door after receiving additional information. A confederate subtly guided the participant either to switch or not to switch, depending on the experimental condition. The confederate was always successful. All the participants then received a consolation prize, missing the bigger prize that had been available. Gilovich et al. reasoned that the participants who switched would experience this undesirable outcome with greater dissonance. They measured dissonance reduction by the selling price that participants assigned to their consolation prize (a Cornell University bumper sticker). As predicted, participants who had switched doors set a higher selling price than those who had missed the big prize by failing to switch.

Miller and Taylor (chapter 11) have reported another elegant experimenter which generalizes the observation that switching is associated with greater regret. In a computer simulation of blackjack, the player was asked "Do you wish to hit?" or "Do you wish to stand?" The default response appeared to be no in both cases, because the yes response was associated in both conditions with more subsequent regret and also with a tendency to overestimate the frequency of bad outcomes in past experience. The same decision and the same outcome could elicit more or less regret, depending on whether the option chosen was encoded as an action or as a failure to act. The difference between omission and commission apparently derives from the basic distinction between the default case and alternatives to it (Roese & Olson, chapter 1). Miller and Taylor (chapter 11) also showed that the consequences of actions that depart from the default case are more memorable. This finding links anticipated regret to the experience of painful memories.

Gilovich and Medvec (1994, chapter 9) have obtained an important new finding: Adults looking back at their lives report more regret about failures to act than about actions. The authors offered the general hypothesis that short-term regret focuses on the consequences of actions, whereas long-term regret is mostly about failures to act. In an experimental variation of the switching design illustrated earlier, Gilovich and Medvec used a vignette about two students who are unhappy in their school. Both think of leaving. One does, the other does not, and the decision turns out bad for both of them. Respondents generally believed that the regret of discovering that one's decision had been a mistake is more intense for the student who switched schools than for the student who stayed. However, most respondents also reported the intuition that the student who had not switched would experience more regret in the long term.

Gilovich and Medvec (1994, chapter 9) offered several ideas to explain this pattern of results. A compelling observation is that the consequences of acts of commission are bounded by what actually happened, whereas the consequences of inaction "are bounded only by our imagination" (p. 266). The scope for regret is therefore greater for omission. They also noted that the greater dissonance and regret that is associated in the short term with acts of commission could cause a reversal over time: Intense dissonance induces correspondingly strong processes of dissonance reduction, which eventually reduce or eliminate the regret associated with actions. Another relevant observation is that inaction is sometimes due to last-minute fears, which appear foolish in retrospect: An obstacle that suffices to prevent one from acting is likely to appear less threatening when viewed from a distance. In this analysis, regret over inaction may intensify over time because the failure to act eventually becomes inexplicable.

I favor a somewhat different interpretation, one which considers short-term regret and long-term regret as two distinct emotions, which share the same name but are evoked by different stimuli and follow different rules. The stimuli for the two emotions are, respectively, a loss and a foregone gain, relative to different reference points. The psychological mechanism that explains the difference in the intensity of the two emotions is loss aversion (Kahneman & Tversky, 1984; Kahneman, Knetsch, & Thaler, 1991): The same difference between two states evokes a stronger reaction if it is coded as a loss than if it is coded as a foregone gain. A standard example of loss aversion is that the difference between salary offers of $50,000 and $60,000 will loom larger in the job preferences of an individual who currently earns $60,000 than in those of an individual who now earns $50,000. Acceptance of the lower paying offer involves a foregone increase of income in the latter case, an actual loss of income in the former: It is intuitively obvious that the two cases are not associated with the same intensity of pain. The story of Mr. George and Mr. Paul can be read in the same terms: Because the default state is inaction, Mr. George (who switched) is likely to code the $1,200 difference in returns as a loss, whereas the same difference will be evaluated as a foregone gain by Mr. Paul (who considered switching but did not).

Now consider what will happen with time. For many reasons, including adaptation, dissonance reduction, and the pressure of more recent events, people do not "kick themselves" indefinitely after a bad outcome. In the end, both Mr. Paul and Mr. George will make their peace with the fact that they would have been better off by $1,200 if they had made a different investment decision. There is no compelling intuition that the regret curves will cross in this example, and the research of Gilovich and Medvec (1994, chapter 9) has not provided evidence that the regret associated with the failure to act would actually increase in that case, or in any other.

What then would explain the pattern of results observed by Gilovich and Medvec? I suggest a distinction between two variants of regret: *hot regret* and *wistful regret*, which are, respectively, related to short-term and long-term evaluations of outcomes. Hot regret is the emotion to which Miller and Taylor referred in their section title "How to Avoid Kicking Yourself" (chapter 11). The wistful regret that Gilovich and Medvec (1994, chapter 9) probed is the emotion associated with pleasantly sad fantasies of what might have been. The question about life regrets that they presented to their adult respondents is naturally interpreted as follows: "How could your life have been much better than it was?" This question invites thoughts of large changes, "bounded only by imagination" (p. 266), as Gilovich and Medvec noted. The counterfactual scenarios that are evoked by the instruction to imagine large changes are more likely to involve additions than deletions, a bias which favors regrets of omission over regrets of commission (Dunning & Parpal, 1989; Dunning & Madey, chapter 4; Roese & Olson, chapter 6).

The value of the pattern of results discovered by Gilovich and Medvec (1994, chapter 11) is not diminished by this interpretation. It is true, as they said, that people contemplating their life from a standpoint to which they have adapted are likely to cite regrets about things they did not do. However, it should be remembered that there is no evidence indicating that the regret associated with anything (omission or commission) actually increases over time. In my view, Gilovich and Medvec have explored (one hesitates to say "discovered") an emotion of wistful regret, which is characteristically evoked by counterfactual thoughts of large changes in one's life—and is also characteristically less intense than the sometimes searing pain of short-term regret. Future research will surely resolve the conflict between the competing interpretations of these important results.

COUNTERFACTUAL WORLDS AND VIRTUAL KNOWLEDGE

There is a compelling intuition that the anticipation of regret is a significant factor in decision making; this intuition has led several economists to formulate regret theories of choice between gambles (Bell, 1982; Loomes & Sugden, 1982; for a review see Baron, 1994). Most generally, regret theories imply that the attractiveness of an option cannot be evaluated without reference to the context of other available options. Another apparently straightforward prediction from a regret model is that choices should be sensitive to manipulations of expectations about future states of knowledge. Because regret is a response to the counterfactual outcome of a different choice, the knowledge that the decision maker expects to have about that outcome should affect the anticipation of regret. Indeed, Ritov (1994) observed some preference reversals when she compared a condition in which only the chosen gamble would be played to a condition in which the rejected gamble would also be played and the decision maker would know its outcome.

Now consider a third variation of Ritov's (1994) experiment in which both gambles will be played but the decision maker will know only the outcome of the gamble chosen. Will the effects of regret vanish completely? The answer to this question is not yet known, but I suspect that it will be negative. An intriguing possibility is that the evaluation of options is not constrained by what the decision maker expects to know about counterfactual outcomes but by what the decision maker expects to be knowable. Thus, options may be avoided because their outcomes are likely to be regrettable even if they are not in fact likely to be regretted. Another way of formulating this hypothesis is that options are evaluated as if the decision maker, when experiencing the outcome of the decision, will be endowed with *virtual knowledge* of all other relevant outcomes.

The following thought experiment may make the notion of virtual knowledge more understandable. Imagine any decision with potentially severe consequences and in which the possibility of regret is a significant factor. Will the role of regret in preferences be much different if the threat involves a quick (regretless) death or a severe lingering injury with ample opportunity to ruminate? The hypothesis of virtual knowledge suggests that regret intuitions remain strong even when there is no living person to do the regretting. The attribution of virtual knowledge and emotion to the dead is not unique to this situation. It is certainly common for people to care about their posthumous reputation and it is also common for people to report pity for a dead person, such as a dead scientist whose major discovery turns out to have been a mistake. The hypothesis of virtual knowledge implies that outcomes are sometimes evaluated *as if* they involve an aware and suffering subject, although the awareness, the suffering, or even the subject is missing. The hypothesis does not imply that people are confused about the difference between virtual and real knowledge or experience.

Virtual knowledge may be involved in the harsh judgments that are made in hindsight. Baron and Hershey (1988) documented the widespread and pernicious tendency of people to judge decisions by their consequences even when these consequences were not foreseeable. Sherman and McConnell (chapter 7) take up a similar theme in their discussion of the intense regret that is sometimes associated with disastrous outcomes that could not have been foreseen. They write "The point is that foreseeability is a concept defined by logic and objective standards. Even when conditions and events are in fact objectively unforeseeable, people seem to believe that they should have foreseen them." Sherman and McConnell comment on the shocked response to the tale of a driver who was fined the standard $65 amount for running a red light and killing two pedestrians. We are evidently tempted to assign virtual foresight to the driver: This particular red light should have been heeded with particular care, and the punishment for failing to do so should be accordingly severe.

Miller and Gunasegaram (1990) have offered a particularly clear demonstration of virtual knowledge. They observed that the evaluation of the fairness of test questions for which students are poorly prepared depends on the order of events. The inclusion of difficult questions is perceived as unfair if the test is written at the last minute, after the students have completed their studying. On the other hand, the responsibility for the failure to know the answers appears to shift to the students if the test was written before they studied for it. These observations recall the difficulties that young children have in working out that someone watching the scene from a different vantage point may not be able to see all they see. It seems to be similarly difficult for adults, as they think about a situation, to allow for the fact that not everyone in the situation knows everything they do (Keysar, Ginzel, & Bazerman, 1994). The various

manifestations of this deficiency in perspective taking range from the
familiar hindsight effects to cases that would be classified as magical
thinking.

CONCLUDING QUESTIONS

This discussion has raised more questions than it has even attempted to
answer, and it is best summarized by a partial list of these questions. How
effective is the imaginary exploration of multiple courses of action in
improving actual decision making? Are upward counterfactuals pleasant
as well as painful, and could we use psychophysiology to tell? When are
mental simulations most likely to be accurate? When are explicit and
implicit causal beliefs most likely to conflict? How can the exaggerated
confidence in scenario thinking be controlled? When do counterfactuals
and causes have the phenomenological status of percepts? Are most
statements about causes really intended as assertions about counterfactuals? Do families who lose a member to a first heart attack or to an accident
differ significantly in their mourning? Are there two kinds of regret, and
what are their antecedents? Do people fear regret or regrettable consequences? Do they attribute virtual knowledge and virtual emotion to the
ignorant and to the dead, and what are the limits of such attributions? One
can only hope that imagining a world in which the answers to all these
questions are known may have a preparatory function.

ACKNOWLEDGMENTS

This chapter was improved by helpful comments from Dale Miller, Neal
Roese, and Ariel Rubinstein.

REFERENCES

Baron, J. (1994). *Thinking and deciding* (2nd ed.). New York: Cambridge University Press.
Baron, J., & Hershey, J. C. (1988). Outcome-bias in decision evaluation. *Journal of Personality
and Social Psychology, 54,* 569–579.
Baron, J., & Ritov, I. (1994). Reference points and omission bias. *Organizational Behavior and
Human Decision Processes, 59,* 475–498.
Bell, D. E. (1982). Regret in decision making under uncertainty. *Operations Research, 30,*
961–981.
Chaiken, S. (1987). The heuristic model of persuasion. In M. P. Zanna, J. M. Olson, & C. P.
Herman (Eds.), *Social influence: The Ontario symposium* (Vol. 5, pp. 3–39). Hillsdale, NJ:
Lawrence Erlbaum Associates.

Dawes, R. (1988). *Rational thinking in an uncertain world*. San Diego, CA: Harcourt Brace Jovanovich.

Dawes, R. (1993). Prediction of the future versus an understanding of the past: A basic asymmetry. *American Journal of Psychology, 106*, 1–24.

Dunning, D., & Parpal, M. (1989). Mental addition versus subtraction in counterfactual reasoning: On assessing the impact of personal actions and life events. *Journal of Personality and Social Psychology, 57*, 5–15.

Gavanski, I., & Wells, G. L. (1989). Counterfactual processing of normal and exceptional events. *Journal of Experimental Social Psychology, 25*, 314–325.

Gilovich, T., & Medvec, V. H. (1994). The temporal pattern to the experience of regret. *Journal of Personality and Social Psychology, 67*, 357–365.

Gilovich, T., Medvec, V. H., & Chen, S. (1995). Omission, commission and dissonance reduction: Overcoming regret in the Monty Hall problem. *Personality and Social Psychology Bulletin, 21*, 182–190.

Gleicher, F., Kost, K. A., Baker, S. M., Strathman, A. J., Richman, S. A., & Sherman, S. J. (1990). The role of counterfactual thinking in judgments of affect. *Personality and Social Psychology Bulletin, 16*, 285–295.

Greenstein, F. I. (1995). Ronald Reagan, Mikhail Gorbachev, and the end of the cold war: What difference did they make? In W. Wohlforth (Ed.), *Witnesses to the end of the cold war*. Baltimore: Johns Hopkins University Press.

Hart, H. L. A., & Honoré, A. M. (1959). *Causation in the law*. Oxford, England: Clarendon Press.

Heider, F., & Simmel, M. (1944). An experimental study of apparent behavior. *American Journal of Psychology, 57*, 243–259.

Hilton, D. J. (1990). Conversational processes and causal explanations. *Psychological Review, 97*, 65–81.

Hilton, D. J., & Slugoski, B. R. (1986). Knowledge-based causal attribution: The abnormal conditions focus model. *Psychological Review, 93*, 65–88.

Kahneman, D., Knetsch, J. L., & Thaler, R. H. (1991). The endowment effect, loss aversion, and status quo bias. *Journal of Economic Perspectives, 5*, 193–206.

Kahneman, D., & Lovallo, D. (1993). Timid choices and bold forecasts: A cognitive perspective on risk taking. *Management Science, 39*, 17–31.

Kahneman, E., & Miller, D. T. (1986). Norm theory: Comparing reality to its alternatives. *Psychological Review, 93*, 136–153.

Kahneman, D., & Tversky, A. (1979). Intuitive prediction: Biases and corrective procedures. *Management Science, 12*, 312–327.

Kahneman, D., & Tversky, A. (1982a). The simulation heuristic. In D. Kahneman, P. Slovic, & A. Tversky (Eds.), *Judgment under uncertainty: Heuristics and biases* (pp. 201–208). New York: Cambridge University Press.

Kahneman, D., & Tversky, A. (1982b). The psychology of preferences. *Scientific American, 246*(1), 160–173.

Kahneman, D., & Tversky, A. (1984). Choices, values and frames. *American Psychologist, 39*, 341–350.

Kahneman, D., & Varey, C. A. (1990). Propensities and counterfactuals: The loser that almost won. *Journal of Personality and Social Psychology, 59*, 1101–1110.

Keysar, B., Ginzel, L. E., & Bazerman, M.H. (1994). *States of affairs and states of mind: The curse of knowledge of beliefs*. Unpublished manuscript, University of Chicago.

Kvart, I. (1986). *A theory of counterfactuals*. Indianapolis, IN: Hackett.

Landman, J. (1987). Regret and elation following action and inaction: Affective responses to positive versus negative outcomes. *Personality and Social Psychology Bulletin, 13*, 524–536.

Landman, J. (1994). *Regret: The persistence of the possible*. New York: Oxford University Press.

Lewin, K. (1951). *Field theory in social science: Selected theoretical papers*. New York: Harper & Row.

Lewis, D. (1973). *Counterfactuals*. Oxford: Oxford University Press.

Loomes, G., & Sugden, R. (1982). Regret theory: An alternative theory of rational choice under uncertainty. *Economic Journal, 92*, 805–824.

Lynn, R. (1966). *Attention, arousal and the orientation reaction*. Oxford: Pergamon.

Mackie, J. L. (1974). *Cement of the universe: A study of causation*. London: Oxford University Press.

McCloskey, M. (1983). Intuitive physics. *Scientific American, 248*(4), 122–130.

Medvec, V. H., Madey, S. F., & Gilovich, T. (in press). When less is more: Counterfactual thinking and satisfaction among Olympic athletes. *Journal of Personality and Social Psychology*.

Michotte, A. E. (1946). *La perception de la causalité*. Louvain, Belgium: University of Louvain Publications.

Miller, D. T., & Gunasegaram, S. (1990). Temporal order and the perceived mutability of events: Implications for blame assignment. *Journal of Personality and Social Psychology, 59*, 1111–1118.

Miller, D. T., Taylor, B., & Buck, M. L. (1991). Gender gaps: Who needs to be explained? *Journal of Personality and Social Psychology, 61*, 5–12.

Petty, R. E., & Cacioppo, J. T. (1986). *Communication and persuasion: Central and peripheral routes to attitude change*. New York: Springer-Verlag.

Ritov, I. (1994). *Probability of regret: Anticipation of uncertainty resolution in choice*. Manuscript submitted for publication.

Ritov, I., & Baron, J. (1990). Reluctance to vaccinate: Omission bias and ambiguity. *Journal of Behavioral Decision Making, 3*, 263–277.

Ritov, I., & Baron, J. (1992). Status-quo and omission bias. *Journal of Risk and Uncertainty, 5*, 49–61.

Ritov, I., & Kahneman, D. (1995). Unpublished data.

Spranca, M., Minsk, E., & Baron, J. (1991). Omission and commission in judgment and choice. *Journal of Experimental Social Psychology, 27*, 76–105.

Tetlock, P. E., & Belkin, A. (1994). *Counterfactual thought experiments in world politics: Logical, methodological and psychological perspectives*.

Tetlock, P. E., & Boettger, R. (1994). Accountability amplifies the status quo effect when change creates victims. *Journal of Behavioral Decision Making, 7*, 1–23.

Author Index

A

Abelson, R. P., 13, 14, 24, 146, 157, 336
Abramson, L. Y., 284
Adi, H., 336
Ajzen, I., 34, 171
Akimoto, S. A., 12
Allport, G. W., 255
Anderson, C. A., 31, 171, 184, 292
Anderson, E. A., 36, 171
Arkin, R. M., 223
Armor, D., 295, 298, 299, 301
Aronson, E., 273
Aspinwall, L. G., 36, 160, 173, 184
Atkinson, J. W., 9, 21, 27, 279
Au, T. K., 5
Auerbach, S. M., 292
Austin, L., 127

B

Baker, S. M., 9, 17, 19, 20, 30, 31, 37, 58,
    61, 69, 107, 126, 140, 154, 158, 181,
    187, 200, 206, 235, 249, 250, 251,
    252, 253, 254, 264, 265, 269, 279,
    284, 291, 353, 354, 357, 359, 360,
    361, 362, 367, 368, 389

Bargh, J. A., 209
Baron, J., 61, 70, 219, 220, 360, 389, 392, 393
Baron, R. M., 156, 315, 315
Baumgardner, A. H., 223
Bazerman, M. H., 393
Belkin, A., 12, 191, 378, 379, 380, 389
Bell, D. E., 224, 295, 314, 321, 392
Benford, G., 190
Berglas, S., 223
Berlyne, D. E., 18, 19
Berscheid, E., 25
Beyth-Marom, R., 127
Biggs, A., 12
Black, M., 26
Blank, A., 360
Blascovich, J., 193
Bless, H., 19, 21, 36, 143, 144, 161, 181
Bloom, A. H., 4, 5
Bodenhausen, G. V., 193
Boettger, P., 389
Bohner, G., 19, 21
Bolles, R. C., 17
Boninger, D. S., 19, 35, 37, 38, 43, 142, 157,
    174, 202, 210, 285, 286, 287, 288,
    289, 295, 296, 298, 299, 301, 368, 369
Boon, C., 370
Borden, R. J., 159
Borgida, E., 25

Boring, E. G., 170
Bouts, P., 15, 28
Bower, G. H., 143, 159
Braine, M. D., 4
Branscombe, N. R., 12, 32, 39, 40, 46, 72
Brehm, J. W., 222, 273, 276
Brickman, P., 34, 36, 279
Brown, J. D., 22, 42, 85, 144
Brownstein, R., 234
Brownstein, S. C., 93
Buck, M. L., 13, 28, 206, 207, 208, 322, 337, 346, 347, 386
Bulman, R. J., 36, 201, 366
Burger, J. M., 86, 89
Burgess, A. W., 174
Burris, C. T., 39
Buunk, B. P., 36, 155, 173, 184

C

Cacioppo, J. T., 86, 89, 216, 376
Campbell, D. T., 279
Carpenter, K. M., 292
Carpenter, P. A., 4
Carroll, J. S., 292, 325
Carver, C. S., 87, 89
Chaiken, S., 25, 376
Chanowitz, B., 360
Chassin, B., 36
Chen, S., 37, 274, 276, 315, 389
Cheng, P. W., 334
Chisholm, R. M., 3
Churchill, W. S., 191
Cialdini, R. B., 143, 159, 292, 325
Clark, M. S., 143
Clark, R. A., 9, 21, 27
Coates, D., 279
Cohen, S. J., 36, 151
Cole, E., 18
Collins, B. E., 274, 296
Collins, R. L., 85, 155, 173, 184
Cook, P. J., 261
Cooper, H. M., 86, 89
Cooper, J., 46, 222, 273, 274, 276
Costa, P. T., 89
Crosby, F., 259
Crosby, P., 39, 40
Croyle, R., 46
Currier, R., 296

D

Dakof, G. A., 155, 173, 184
Darby, B. L., 143
Davis, C. G., 21, 29, 30, 36, 42, 45, 76, 81, 83, 84, 85, 87, 88, 98, 157, 192, 212, 356, 358, 361, 362, 364, 366, 368, 369, 370, 371
Davis, K. E., 14, 118
Dawes, R. M., 171, 247, 380
DeBono, K. G., 25
Delforge, A., 69
Dennett, D. C., 17, 21
Dermer, M., 25, 36, 171
de Shazer, S., 128
Deutsch, D., 3
Dhar, R., 125
Dick, P. K., 190
Dickens, C., 133
Dlugokinski, L. J., 159
Dostoevsky, F., 238
Downey, G., 370
Driscoll, D. M., 193
Drown, D., 152, 365
Dunn, D. S., 155, 156
Dunning, D., 15, 104, 106, 112, 114, 115, 117, 118, 119, 120, 126, 151, 263, 391
Dwiggins, M., 296

E

Eagly, A. H., 25, 346, 348
Early, D., 69
Ebbinghaus, H., 110
Edwards, C. S., 285, 287, 301
Einhorn, H. J., 12, 14, 15, 28, 335, 336
Ellard, J. H., 367
Engel, E., 274, 275
Epstein, S., 30, 31, 41, 42, 46, 98
Erskine, H., 267

F

Fairbanks, L. A., 366, 371
Farris, H., 190
Fazio, R. H., 31, 46, 175, 193, 222, 273, 274, 276, 294
Fearon, J. D., 12, 191
Feather, N. T., 259, 279
Feimer, N., 237
Feltz, D. L., 292
Festinger, L., 140, 173, 259, 273, 279

Fiedler, K., 19
Fillenbaum, S., 4
Fischhoff, B., 8, 16, 127, 221, 323
Fishburn, P., 314
Fiske, S. T., 31
Flaubert, G., 1
Folger, R., 8, 36, 170, 173, 192
Folkman, S., 82, 87, 291, 290, 370
Frank, R. H., 261
Freeman, S., 159
Freund, T., 193, 209
Frey, D., 265
Frost, D. E., 28
Frye, N., 236, 242

G

Gaborit, M., 58
Gaddis, J. L., 191
Gaelick, L., 107
Gallup, G., Jr., 127
Gastel, J., 5
Gati, I., 106, 118, 125
Gavanski, I., 4, 12, 17, 18, 19, 20, 21, 28,
    29, 32, 36, 37, 45, 58, 61, 64, 67, 72,
    82, 104, 134, 135, 137, 138, 139, 140,
    141, 142, 143, 144, 145, 146, 147,
    148, 149, 150, 151, 154, 155, 158,
    162, 171, 173, 174, 175, 176, 179,
    181, 185, 186, 192, 200, 201, 202,
    203, 205, 207, 210, 226, 235, 248,
    251, 260, 284, 290, 291, 301, 312,
    334, 336, 355, 357, 361, 362, 363,
    366, 368, 369, 383
Geertz, C., 234
Genung, V., 98
Gerrard, M., 174
Gibbons, F. X., 174
Gilbert, D. T., 144
Gilligan, C., 346
Gilligan, S. G., 143
Gilovich, T., 37, 99, 104, 210, 225, 267, 269,
    271, 273, 274, 276, 277, 278, 315,
    385, 389, 390, 391
Ginsburg, G. P., 13
Ginzel, L. E., 393
Girotto, V., 31, 32, 34, 192, 354, 357, 358
Gleicher, F., 9, 17, 19, 20, 30, 31, 35, 37, 38,
    43, 58, 61, 69, 140, 142, 154, 157,
    158, 174, 181, 187, 200, 202, 206,
    210, 235, 249, 250, 251, 252, 253,

    254, 264, 265, 269, 279, 284, 285,
    286, 287, 288, 289, 291, 295, 296,
    298, 299, 301, 353, 354, 357, 359,
    360, 361, 362, 367, 368, 369, 389
Godfrey, S. S., 31, 171, 184
Goenjian, A., 366, 371
Goethals, G. R., 222, 274
Goldpaper, S., 315
Goldy, A. S., 292
Goodman, N., 2, 3
Gordon, P. C., 107
Grabowecky, M., 47
Graziano, W., 25
Green, J., 30
Greenberg, J., 18
Greenberg, M. H., 190, 366
Greenstein, F. I., 378, 380, 381
Gregory, L. W., 292
Griffin, D., 279
Griffiths, R. J., 39
Gross, P., 336
Gschneidinger, E., 36, 161
Gunasegaram, S., 34, 69, 82, 200, 204, 308,
    347, 354, 362, 393

H

Ha, Y. W., 208
Habert, K. S., 58
Hall, C. A., 15, 30, 118, 151, 263
Hall, J. A., 346
Hansen, R. D., 15, 30, 118, 151, 263
Harkness, A. R., 25
Harris, R., 190
Hart, H. L., 12, 13, 381, 384, 387
Hass, R., 240
Hastie, R., 17, 18, 19, 221, 337
Hattiangadi, N., 267
Hawkins, S. A., 221
Hayes, A. F., 104
Hayes, J. R., 4
Heider, F., 18, 23, 24, 152, 368, 382
Heine, S. J., 370
Helson, H., 7
Hemphill, K. J., 367
Henley, M. D., 274
Herman, C. P., 259
Herr, P. M., 31, 175
Hershey, J. C., 219, 220, 360, 393
Hervitz, E. F., 44, 171, 184
Hetts, J., 295, 298, 299, 301

Higgins, E. T., 37, 42, 144, 146, 157, 208
Hilton, D. J., 12, 13, 14, 40, 45, 207, 334,
    335, 336, 337, 362, 363, 383, 384
Hirt, E. R., 159
Hoch, S. J., 1
Hofstadter, D. R., 1, 8, 24, 134
Hogarth, R. M., 12, 14, 15, 28, 335, 336
Holmstrom, L., 174
Holstein, C., 30, 31, 46
Holyoak, K. J., 107
Honoré, A. M., 12, 13, 381, 384, 387
Horowitz, M. J., 370
Houston, D. A., 107, 126
Hovland, C. I., 36
Hoyt, M. F., 274
Hsee, H. K., 24
Huh, E., 30, 31, 46

I

Ingrassia, M., 350
Isen, A. M., 19, 143

J

Jacobsen, E., 36, 171
Jacobs-Quadrel, M., 127
Jacoby, L. L., 144
Janigian, A. J., 370
Janis, I. J., 314, 321
Janoff-Bulman, 98, 150, 201, 212, 213, 279,
    369, 370, 371
Jasechko, J., 144
Jellison, J. M., 30
Johnson, E. J., 325
Johnson, J. T., 13, 19, 22, 58, 68, 69, 82,
    214, 260, 301
Johnson, M. K., 1, 43, 141, 170, 173, 174,
    237, 252
Jones, C. R., 144
Jones, E. E., 14, 118, 223

K

Kahneman, D., 4, 7, 8, 11, 16, 18, 22, 24,
    27, 28, 29, 31, 33, 36, 37, 43, 44, 45,
    58, 59, 61, 66, 67, 68, 69, 73, 81, 82,
    103, 104, 105, 134, 135, 136, 137,
    138, 139, 144, 151, 154, 175, 177,

    192, 199, 204, 206, 208, 217, 247,
    248, 249, 250, 254, 259, 260, 263,
    264, 265, 266, 269, 270, 273, 278,
    279, 284, 295, 301, 305, 306, 307,
    308, 314, 319, 321, 322, 323, 346,
    347, 348, 353, 354, 359, 360, 362,
    366, 376, 379, 381, 382, 383, 385,
    386, 388, 391
Kanazawa, S., 18, 19, 21
Kao, C. F., 86, 89
Kaplan, C., 234
Karakashian, M., 366, 371
Karoly, P., 37, 277
Karp, L., 143
Karplus, R., 336
Kasimatis, M., 88, 90, 91, 92, 94, 95, 96, 97,
    98
Katz, D., 169
Keegan, A., 340
Keel, R., 98
Kelley, C., 144
Kelley, H. H., 7, 12, 14, 18, 22, 32, 40, 368
Kelly, G. A., 81
Kenny, D. A., 156
Keren, G., 310, 318, 319, 327
Kern, D., 36
Kerr, M., 277
Keysar, B., 393
King, G. A., 146, 208
Kinnier, R. T., 267
Kirkpatrick, L. A., 41, 42, 46
Kite, M. E., 346, 348
Kitiyama, S., 5
Klayman, J., 208
Klein, J. G., 13, 14, 15, 334, 335, 338, 339
Klein, R., 37, 42
Kleinginna, A. M., 236
Kleinginna, P. R., 236
Knetsch, J. L., 391
Knight, R. T., 47
Koehler, D. J., 171, 184
Kost, K. A., 9, 17, 19, 20, 30, 31, 37, 58, 61,
    69, 140, 154, 158, 181, 187, 200, 206,
    235, 249, 250, 251, 252, 253, 254,
    264, 265, 269, 279, 284, 291, 353,
    354, 357, 359, 360, 361, 362, 367,
    368, 389
Kottler, J. A., 128
Kruglanski, A. W., 193, 209
Krull, D. S., 144
Kunda, Z., 192
Kvart, I., 3, 383

L

Lalljee, M., 13, 14
Lamb, R., 13
Landers, D. M., 292
Landman, J., 19, 20, 29, 30, 31, 37, 46, 58, 59, 61, 69, 70, 81, 82, 84, 88, 98, 134, 192, 210, 237, 245, 246, 248, 250, 251, 254, 264, 265, 270, 279, 284, 295, 301, 307, 353, 354, 357, 359, 360, 367, 389
Langer, E. J., 30, 32, 147, 155, 156, 201, 360
Lang-Gunn, L., 98, 369
Lardière, D., 5
Lawson, A., 336
Lazarus, R. S., 82, 87, 290, 291, 370
Lears, J., 243
Lecci, L., 37, 277
Leddo, J., 336
Legrenzi, P., 31, 32, 34, 192, 354, 357, 358
Lehman, D. R., 21, 29, 30, 36, 42, 45, 76, 81, 83, 84, 85, 87, 88, 98, 157, 192, 212, 356, 361, 362, 364, 366, 367, 368, 369, 370, 371
Lepper, M. R., 209
Lerner, M. J., 370
Leventhal, H., 291
Levine, M., 219
Lewin, K., 22, 23
Lewis, D., 3, 4, 378, 385
Lichtenstein, M., 193
Lichtman, R. R., 83, 85, 141, 174, 201, 212, 213
Lipe, M. G., 12, 14, 45, 200, 334, 335, 361, 363, 364, 368, 371
Lipkin, S. G., 4
Lipson, A., 30, 31, 46
Liu, L. G., 5
Lobel, M., 141, 160, 173, 279, 369
Lockwood, M., 3
Loomes, G., 224, 295, 314, 392
Lord, C. G., 209
Loux, M. J., 3
Lovallo, D., 381
Lowell, E. L., 9, 21, 27
Lundberg, C. G., 28
Lynn, R., 376

M

Mackie, D. M., 143
Mackie, J. L., 11, 12, 13, 171, 191, 334, 335, 337, 382

Macrae, C. N., 25, 26, 39, 46, 151, 193, 354, 359
Madey, S. F., 104, 385
Maheswaran, D., 23, 25, 296
Manis, J. D., 81, 84, 248, 251
Manjikian, R., 366, 371
Mann, L., 314, 321
Manoukian, G., 366, 371
Markman, K. D., 17, 19, 20, 21, 36, 42, 45, 72, 135, 136, 137, 138, 139, 140, 141, 142, 143, 144, 145, 146, 147, 148, 149, 150, 151, 152, 153, 154, 155, 156, 157, 162, 173, 174, 175, 179, 181, 185, 186, 192, 200, 201, 202, 203, 205, 210, 226, 235, 236, 248, 251, 290, 291, 301, 355, 357, 366, 368, 369
Markovits, H., 5
Markus, H. R., 5, 184
Marrs, S., 18
Martin, L. L., 147, 213
Mavin, G. H., 146, 208
McAdams, D. P., 236, 237, 238, 240, 241, 242
McClelland, D. C., 9, 21, 27, 346
McCloskey, M., 60, 380
McCrae, R. R., 89
McDonough, E. M., 58
McFarland, C., 9, 16, 22, 23, 24, 29, 31, 35, 38, 39, 40, 41, 42, 46, 82, 87, 103, 151, 200, 205, 211, 213, 214, 260, 308, 322, 324, 354, 355, 366
McGill, A. L., 7, 13, 14, 15, 21, 30, 33, 43, 334, 335, 336, 337, 338, 339, 347, 348
McMullen, M. N., 17, 19, 20, 21, 32, 36, 42, 45, 72, 135, 136, 137, 138, 139, 140, 141, 142, 143, 144, 145, 146, 147, 148, 149, 150, 151, 152, 153, 154, 155, 156, 157, 161, 162, 173, 174, 175, 179, 181, 185, 186, 192, 200, 201, 202, 203, 205, 210, 226, 235, 248, 251, 290, 291, 301, 355, 357, 361, 366, 368, 369
Means, B., 19
Means, J. R., 159
Medin, D. L., 208
Medvec, V. H., 37, 99, 104, 210, 261, 262, 265, 267, 269, 270, 271, 273, 274, 276, 278, 315, 385, 389, 390, 391
Meehl, P. E., 237
Mendelsohn, G., 237
Metha, A. T., 267

Meyers-Levy, J., 23, 25, 296
Michotte, A. E., 376, 382
Mill, J. S., 11
Millar, M. G., 18, 159
Miller, D. T., 4, 7, 13, 16, 18, 22, 24, 27, 28,
    29, 33, 34, 35, 36, 37, 38, 39, 40, 41,
    42, 43, 44, 46, 59, 61, 68, 69, 82, 87,
    103, 134, 135, 136, 139, 144, 151,
    171, 178, 192, 199, 200, 204, 205,
    206, 207, 208, 211, 213, 214, 217,
    218, 219, 249, 250, 259, 260, 263,
    269, 273, 278, 279, 284, 292, 301,
    306, 308, 309, 319, 321, 322, 323,
    324, 325, 337, 346, 347, 348, 353,
    354, 355, 358, 360, 362, 363, 366,
    383, 384, 386, 393
Miller, J. B., 346
Miller, N. K., 234
Miller, R. L., 279
Milne, A. B., 39, 193
Minsk, E., 70, 315, 389
Miyake, K., 85
Miyamoto, J. M., 120
Monson, T. C., 25, 98
Monteiro, K. P., 143
Moore, E., 295, 298, 299, 301
Moore, J., 159
Moore, W., 190
Murray, N., 159

N

Naficy, A., 222, 274
Neale, J. M., 193, 201, 213
Nesshover, W., 89
Neter, E., 296
Newman, B., 366
Newtson, D., 118
N'gbala, A., 12, 32, 72
Niedenthal, P. M., 37, 150, 158, 200, 210
Nisbett, R. E., 5, 118, 171, 208, 216, 360
Nosofsky, R. M., 208
Novick, L. R., 334
Nute, D., 3, 4, 12

O

O'Brian, D. P., 4
Ogawa, K. H., 69
Okun, M. A., 37, 277

Olson, J. M., 17, 19, 20, 21, 22, 23, 26, 27,
    30, 31, 38, 42, 43, 85, 90, 96, 137,
    146, 147, 171, 176, 177, 178, 179,
    185, 186, 187, 188, 201, 202, 211,
    218, 219, 221, 248, 250, 251, 259,
    263, 265, 294, 357, 369, 370

P

Palgrem, C., 127
Parpal, M., 15, 104, 106, 114, 115, 117, 118,
    119, 120, 122, 151, 263, 391
Pearlin, L. I., 291
Pelham, B. W., 144
Pennebaker, J. W., 367
Peplau, L. A., 88, 89
Petty, R. E., 86, 89, 216, 376
Pham, L. B., 44, 290, 292, 300
Piliavin, E., 314
Preston, E., 209
Pritchard, C. C., 58
Pulos, S., 336
Pynoos, R. S., 366, 371
Pyszcynski, T. A., 18, 366

R

Rachman, S., 366
Rachmiel, T. B., 193, 201, 213
Read, D., 263
Read, S. J., 107, 336
Reichenbach, H., 3
Reis, T. J., 174
Rescher, N., 3, 4
Revlin, R., 190
Revlis, R., 4
Reynolds, K. D., 325
Rholes, W. S., 144
Richman, S. A., 9, 17, 19, 20, 30, 31, 37, 58,
    61, 69, 140, 154, 158, 181, 187, 200,
    206, 235, 249, 250, 251, 252, 253,
    254, 264, 265, 269, 279, 284, 291,
    353, 354, 357, 359, 360, 361, 362,
    367, 368, 389
Ritov, I., 315, 386, 389, 392
Rizzo, A., 31, 32, 34, 192, 354, 357, 358
Robinson, T., 36
Roese, N. J., 17, 19, 20, 21, 22, 23, 26, 27,
    30, 31, 36, 38, 42, 43, 44, 72, 74, 82,
    83, 85, 86, 90, 96, 97, 98, 137, 141,

142, 146, 147, 151, 154, 155, 157,
171, 176, 177, 178, 179, 180, 181,
182, 183, 185, 186, 187, 188, 194,
200, 201, 202, 203, 210, 211, 218,
219, 221, 226, 248, 250, 251, 263,
265, 290, 292, 294, 295, 301, 355,
357, 366, 368, 369, 370
Rogers, D., 89
Rosaldo, R., 234
Rosenberg, M., 89
Rosenfield, D., 36
Ross, L., 5, 32, 118, 171, 208, 216, 360
Ross, M., 22
Rotter, J., 89
Rubin, Z., 88, 89
Ruvolo, A. P., 184
Ryan, K., 34
Rydell, S. M., 64

S

Salovey, P., 24, 143, 159
Saltzberg, J. A., 193, 201, 213
Sanbonmatsu, D. M., 12
Schafer, R., 236, 239, 240, 241, 242, 252
Scheier, M. F., 87, 88, 89
Schmidt, G. W., 85
Schmidt, L., 314
Schneider, D. J., 367
Schneider, S. K., 8, 82, 85, 86, 87, 140, 174,
178, 192, 290, 291, 292, 300, 360, 368
Schneider, W., 62, 144
Scholnick, E. K., 5
Schooler, C., 291
Schopenhauer, A., 19
Schumacher, E., 305
Schuring, G., 5
Schwartzman, D. F., 325
Schwarz, N., 19, 21, 36, 143, 144, 161, 171,
325
Sears, D. O., 216, 265
Seelau, E. P., 64
Seligman, M. E. P., 284
Shaffer, M. M., 208
Shafir, E., 119, 126
Shalker, T. E., 143
Shaver, K. G., 73, 118, 152, 365
Sherif, M., 36
Sherman, S. J., 1, 9, 17, 19, 20, 21, 30, 31,
32, 36, 37, 42, 43, 44, 45, 58, 61, 69,
72, 107, 126, 140, 141, 154, 158, 170,

171, 173, 174, 175, 179, 181, 184,
185, 186, 187, 192, 200, 201, 202,
203, 205, 206, 208, 210, 223, 226,
235, 237, 248, 249, 250, 251, 252,
253, 254, 264, 265, 269, 279, 284,
290, 291, 292, 301, 325, 353, 354,
355, 357, 359, 360, 361, 362, 366,
367, 368, 369, 389
Shiffrin, R. M., 62, 144
Short, J. C., 86
Shweder, R. A., 243
Silver, R. C., 21, 29, 30, 36, 42, 45, 76, 147,
157, 192, 212, 356, 361, 362, 364,
366, 368, 369, 370, 371
Simmel, M., 382
Simonson, I., 125, 296, 314
Singer, J. A., 143, 159
Skov, R. B., 44, 171, 184, 208
Sloan, L. R., 159
Slovic, P., 247
Slugoski, B. R., 12, 13, 14, 40, 45, 207, 334,
337, 362, 383
Smith, E. R., 208
Solomon, R. C., 246
Sorrentino, R. M., 86
Spears, R., 15, 28
Spranca, M., 70, 315, 389
Squire, J. C., 190
Srull, T. K., 107, 144
Staebler, C. R., 58
Steedman, C. K., 234
Steinberg, A. M., 366, 371
Steiner, G., 46, 236, 240, 241, 252
Stephens, D., 98
Sterling, L., 88, 90, 91, 94, 96, 97, 98
Stern, L. D., 18
Sternberg, R. J., 5
Stock, C. V., 44, 171, 184
Stone, A. A., 193, 201, 213
Stones, M. H., 370
Story, A. L., 112
Strack, F., 19, 21, 36, 161
Strathman, A., 9, 17, 19, 20, 30, 31, 35, 37,
38, 43, 58, 61, 69, 140, 142, 154, 157,
158, 174, 181, 187, 200, 202, 206,
210, 235, 249, 250, 251, 252, 253,
254, 264, 265, 269, 279, 284, 285,
286, 287, 288, 289, 291, 295, 301,
353, 354, 357, 359, 360, 361, 362,
367, 368, 369, 389
Strauman, T., 37, 42
Strentz, T., 292

Sugden, R., 224, 295, 314, 321, 322, 392
Sujan, H., 159
Sujan, M., 159
Suls, J. M., 279
Sutherland, G., 366
Swain, M., 12
Sylvan, D. A., 191

Tversky, A., 22, 27, 28, 29, 37, 43, 45, 58, 59, 61, 66, 67, 68, 73, 81, 104, 105, 106, 107, 118, 119, 125, 134, 138, 141, 151, 154, 175, 192, 204, 206, 248, 254, 260, 264, 265, 266, 269, 270, 273, 278, 279, 284, 295, 305, 306, 307, 323, 325, 347, 353, 355, 359, 360, 366, 379, 381, 385, 388, 391

T

V

Tait, R., 147, 366, 370, 371
Tangney, J. P., 37, 150, 158, 200, 210
Tannen, D., 346
Tashjian, M., 366, 371
Taylor, B. R., 13, 28, 34, 43, 58, 59, 64, 67, 68, 69, 82, 103, 140, 151, 204, 206, 207, 208, 311, 312, 313, 314, 315, 316, 317, 318, 319, 321, 322, 337, 346, 347, 354, 362, 386
Taylor, S. E., 8, 19, 22, 31, 36, 42, 44, 82, 83, 85, 86, 87, 140, 141, 155, 160, 173, 174, 178, 184, 192, 201, 212, 213, 248, 279, 284, 290, 291, 292, 300, 360, 368, 369
Teasdale, J. D., 284
Tesser, A., 147, 159, 213
Tetlock, P. E., 12, 191, 378, 379, 380, 389
Thakkar, V., 296
Thaler, R., 266
Thein, R. D., 209
Thibaut, J. H., 7, 22
Thomas, D., 239
Thompson, S. C., 21, 29, 30, 36, 42, 45, 76, 81, 83, 84, 85, 87, 88, 98, 157, 192, 212, 356, 361, 362, 364, 366, 368, 369, 370, 371
Thorne, A., 159
Thorson, S. T., 191
Tierney, J., 274, 275
Tolman, E. C., 9, 17, 21
Tompkins, J., 234
Tota, M. E., 209
Tulving, E., 216
Turnbull, W., 9, 16, 23, 24, 29, 31, 37, 40, 41, 42, 46, 103, 200, 205, 211, 214, 218, 219, 260, 292, 322, 324, 325, 353, 355, 363, 366
Turner, F. B., 226
Turtle, J. W., 28, 34, 43, 58, 59, 64, 67, 68, 69, 82, 103, 140, 151, 204, 248, 354, 362

Vachon, R., 5
van der Pligt, J., 15, 28
VanYperen, N. W., 155, 173, 184
Varey, C. A., 11, 22, 24, 33, 68, 137, 376, 379, 382, 383
Velton, E., 159
Venetoulias, A., 274, 275
Vincent, J. E., 143
Vinokur, A., 34
Vorster, J., 5
Vos Savant, M., 154, 156, 274, 275

W

Wagenaar, W. A., 310, 318, 319, 327
Wagner, D., 36
Walker, M. R., 159
Walster, E., 220, 273, 314
Walster, G. W., 314
Ward, G. C., 247, 249, 250, 251, 252, 253
Wason, P. C., 208
Weiner, B., 17, 19, 42, 136, 157, 158, 284, 295, 337
Weiner, M., 93
Weiner, R. L., 58
Weinstein, N. D., 21, 30, 112, 370
Weintraub, J. K., 87, 89
Weir, J. A., 39, 40, 46
Weiss, D., 237
Weiss, R. S., 366
Wells, G. L., 4, 12, 18, 19, 28, 29, 34, 43, 58, 59, 61, 64, 67, 68, 69, 82, 88, 90, 91, 92, 94, 95, 96, 97, 98, 103, 104, 134, 140, 148, 149, 151, 171, 176, 200, 201, 203, 204, 207, 248, 251, 260, 284, 312, 334, 336, 354, 361, 362, 363, 368, 383
Wegner, D. M., 367
Wheeler, L., 85, 141

White, P. A., 11, 12
Wicklund, R. A., 273, 276
Wiley, D. C., 58
Williams, A. F., 370
Williams, R., 234, 246
Wills, T. A., 38, 141, 174, 185, 279
Wilson, G. L., 159
Wilson, T. D., 155, 156
Wing, C. S., 5
Winter, L., 292
Wood, J. V., 83, 85, 141, 174, 193, 201, 212, 213
Worth, L. T., 143
Wortman, C. B., 21, 29, 30, 34, 36, 42, 45,
    76, 81, 83, 84, 85, 87, 88, 98, 147,
    157, 192, 201, 212, 356, 361, 362,
    364, 366, 367, 368, 369, 370, 371

Wyer, R. S., Jr., 144

Y

Yamagichi, K., 120

Z

Zajonc, R. B., 235, 291
Zanna, M. P., 17, 21, 23, 27, 42, 43, 46, 171,
    259, 294
Zarate, M. A., 208
Zelazny, R., 57, 58

Subject Index

A

Affect, 36–38, 153–155, 210–211, 247, 251–252, 286, 323–324, 365, 377, *see also* Regret
Attitudes, 293
Attribution, *see* Causality

B

Belief in a just world, 88, 96
Bereaved, *see* Coping
Blame, *see* Causality

C

Causality, 11–15, 71–72, 73–74, 203, 211, 362–365, 378–381, 381–385
Closeness, 22–25, 68, 137, 385–387
Consideration of future consequences, 285–286
Controllability, *see* Counterfactual, and control
Coping, 87, 290–293, 356, 369–371
  initiation of, 291
  mastery over stressors, 291–292
Counterfactual, *see also* Mental simulation
  action versus inaction, *see* Counterfactual, omission versus commission

additive versus subtractive, 21–22, 113–114, 174–175, 188, 202, 250, 387
and attitudes, 293
automatic versus elaborative, 375–376
  constraints, 59–60
  availability, 66–70
  natural-law, 64–66
  purpose, 71–75
and contrastive reasoning, 334
and control, 31–32, 72–73, 135–136, 185, 188, 201, 368
direction, *see* Counterfactual, upward versus downward
dynamic versus static, 32–34
and dysfunction, *see* Function
exceptional versus routine, 28–29, 68, 206, 248–249, 357, 362
fallacy, 218, 363
functions of, *see* Function
omission versus commission, 29–31, 69–70, 206, 249–250, 254, 264–266, 307, 310, 357, 388–392
structure, *see* Counterfactual, additive versus subtractive
persistence of, 365
upward versus downward, 21, 72, 74, 82–83, 134, 150–151, 172, 188, 200–201, 214, 250–251, 291

D

Decision making, 320–323, 359–361
Dissonance, 273–277

E

Emotion, *see* Affect
Emotional amplification, *see* Affect
Event repeatability, 145
Expectancy, 17–19, 43–44

F

Framing, 104
Foreseeability, 152, 222
Function, 21, 146, 169–171, 192–194, 200,
    225, 377
  affective, 21, 171, 181, 200
  control, 147–148, 201
  definitional, 189–192
  preparative, 21, 145–146, 170, 184, 200–201

G

Gender gap, 207

H

Hindsight bias, 221, 322–323

I

Individual differences, 84–88, 146,
    285–286, *see also* Self-esteem
Involvement, 25–26

M

Memory, biases in, 307–309
Mental simulation, 104, 105, 161, 300,
    378–381
  outcome versus process, 300
Motivation, 9, 86, *see also* Affect
Mutability, 7–8, 134, 346–347, 354–355,
    382, 385–387
Mutation, *see* Mutability

N

Norm theory, 6–8, 59, 61, 68, 348

O

Optimism, 86–87, 146
Outcome valence, 19–22, 139–140

P

Possible worlds, *see* Counterfactual
Prefactuals, 294, 296–298, *see also*
    Expectancy

R

Regret, 246, 264, 266, 308–309
  anticipatory, 224, 314–315
  confidence, 277
  hot versus wistful, 391
  temporal pattern, 269–271
  causes of, 271–278
  what people regret most, 266
Rumination, 87, 212–213

S

Self-esteem, 85–86, 95–96, 211
Self-handicapping, 223
Self-inference, 42–43, *see also* Self-esteem
Superstition, 306–307, 327
Suspicion, 40–42, 205

U

Undoing, 146–147, 288, 361–362
  consequences of, 362–367

V

Victimization, 38–40

W

Worldviews, 325
  comic, 238
  ironic, 241
  romantic, 237
  tragic, 239